Missionary Travels And Researches In South Africa

by

David Livingstone

Missionary Travels And Researches In South Africa
by David Livingstone

Copyright © 2023

All Rights reserved.

No part of this publication may be reproduced, stored in a retrieval system, or transmitted in any form or by any means, electronic, mechanical, photocopying or Otherwise, without the written permission of the publisher.
The author/editor asserts the moral right to be identified as the author/editor of this work.

ISBN: 978-93-59328-27-0

Published by

DOUBLE 9 BOOKS

2/13-B, Ansari Road
Daryaganj, New Delhi – 110002
info@double9books.com
www.double9books.com
Tel. 011-40042856

This book is under public domain

ABOUT THE AUTHOR

David Was the Husband of Mary Moffat Livingstone, A Member of the Notable Moffat Missionary Family of The 18th Century. Livingstone's Mythic Status Was Multifaceted: Protestant Missionary Martyr, Working-Class "Rags-To-Riches" Inspirational Story, Scientific Investigator and Explorer, Imperial Reformer, Anti-Slavery Crusader, And Supporter of British Commercial and Colonial Expansion. Neil Livingstone (1788-1856) and his wife Agnes (née Hunter; 1782-1865) had seven children, the second of whom was him David began working at the cotton mill of Henry Monteith & Co. in Blantyre Works when he was ten years old.

CONTENTS

Preface 7
Introduction 9
Chapter 1 16
Chapter 2 33
Chapter 3 53
Chapter 4 71
Chapter 5 88
Chapter 6 102
Chapter 7 122
Chapter 8 142
Chapter 9 160
Chapter 10 174
Chapter 11 182
Chapter 12 189
Chapter 13 203
Chapter 14 216
Chapter 15 232
Chapter 16 247
Chapter 17 264
Chapter 18 286
Chapter 19 307

Chapter 20	335
Chapter 21	352
Chapter 22	366
Chapter 23	387
Chapter 24	403
Chapter 25	424
Chapter 26	442
Chapter 27	460
Chapter 28	479
Chapter 29	502
Chapter 30	521
Chapter 31	538
Chapter 32	561

CONTENTS

Preface 7
Introduction 9
Chapter 1 16
Chapter 2 33
Chapter 3 53
Chapter 4 71
Chapter 5 88
Chapter 6 102
Chapter 7 122
Chapter 8 142
Chapter 9 160
Chapter 10 174
Chapter 11 182
Chapter 12 189
Chapter 13 203
Chapter 14 216
Chapter 15 232
Chapter 16 247
Chapter 17 264
Chapter 18 286
Chapter 19 307

Chapter 20	335
Chapter 21	352
Chapter 22	366
Chapter 23	387
Chapter 24	403
Chapter 25	424
Chapter 26	442
Chapter 27	460
Chapter 28	479
Chapter 29	502
Chapter 30	521
Chapter 31	538
Chapter 32	561

Preface

When honored with a special meeting of welcome by the Royal Geographical Society a few days after my arrival in London in December last, Sir Roderick Murchison, the President, invited me to give the world a narrative of my travels; and at a similar meeting of the Directors of the London Missionary Society I publicly stated my intention of sending a book to the press, instead of making many of those public appearances which were urged upon me. The preparation of this narrative* has taken much longer time than, from my inexperience in authorship, I had anticipated.

> Several attempts having been made to impose upon the public, as mine, spurious narratives of my travels, I beg to tender my thanks to the editors of the 'Times' and of the 'Athenaeum' for aiding to expose them, and to the booksellers of London for refusing to SUBSCRIBE for any copies.

Greater smoothness of diction and a saving of time might have been secured by the employment of a person accustomed to compilation; but my journals having been kept for my own private purposes, no one else could have made use of them, or have entered with intelligence into the circumstances in which I was placed in Africa, far from any European companion. Those who have never carried a book through the press can form no idea of the amount of toil it involves. The process has increased my respect for authors and authoresses a thousand-fold.

I can not refrain from referring, with sentiments of admiration and gratitude, to my friend Thomas Maclear, Esq., the accomplished Astronomer Royal at the Cape. I shall never cease to remember his instructions and help with real gratitude. The intercourse I had the privilege to enjoy at the Observatory enabled me to form an idea of the almost infinite variety of acquirements necessary to form a true and great astronomer, and I was led to the conviction that it will be long before the world becomes overstocked with accomplished members of that profession. Let them be always honored according to their deserts; and long may Maclear, Herschel, Airy, and others live to make known the wonders and glory of creation, and to aid in rendering the pathway of the world safe to mariners, and the dark places of the earth open to Christians!

I beg to offer my hearty thanks to my friend Sir Roderick Murchison, and also to Dr. Norton Shaw, the secretary of the Royal Geographical Society, for aiding my researches by every means in their power.

His faithful majesty Don Pedro V., having kindly sent out orders to support my late companions until my return, relieved my mind of anxiety on their account. But for this act of liberality, I should certainly have been compelled to leave England in May last; and it has afforded me the pleasure of traveling over, in imagination, every scene again, and recalling the feelings which actuated me at the time. I have much pleasure in acknowledging my deep obligations to the hospitality and kindness of the Portuguese on many occasions.

I have not entered into the early labors, trials, and successes of the missionaries who preceded me in the Bechuana country, because that has been done by the much abler pen of my father-in-law, Rev. Robert Moffat, of Kuruman, who has been an energetic and devoted actor in the scene for upward of forty years. A slight sketch only is given of my own attempts, and the chief part of the book is taken up with a detail of the efforts made to open up a new field north of the Bechuana country to the sympathies of Christendom. The prospects there disclosed are fairer than I anticipated, and the capabilities of the new region lead me to hope that by the production of the raw materials of our manufactures, African and English interests will become more closely linked than heretofore, that both countries will be eventually benefited, and that the cause of freedom throughout the world will in some measure be promoted.

Dr. Hooker, of Kew, has had the kindness to name and classify for me, as far as possible, some of the new botanical specimens which I brought over; Dr. Andrew Smith (himself an African traveler) has aided me in the zoology; and Captain Need has laid open for my use his portfolio of African sketches, for all which acts of liberality my thanks are deservedly due, as well as to my brother, who has rendered me willing aid as an amanuensis.

Although I can not profess to be a draughtsman, I brought home with me a few rough diagram-sketches, from one of which the view of the Falls of the Zambesi has been prepared by a more experienced artist.

October, 1857.

Introduction

Personal Sketch—Highland Ancestors—Family Traditions—Grandfather removes to the Lowlands—Parents—Early Labors and Efforts —Evening School—Love of Reading—Religious Impressions—Medical Education—Youthful Travels—Geology—Mental Discipline—Study in Glasgow—London Missionary Society—Native Village—Medical Diploma—Theological Studies Departure for Africa—No Claim to Literary Accomplishments.

My own inclination would lead me to say as little as possible about myself; but several friends, in whose judgment I have confidence, have suggested that, as the reader likes to know something about the author, a short account of his origin and early life would lend additional interest to this book. Such is my excuse for the following egotism; and, if an apology be necessary for giving a genealogy, I find it in the fact that it is not very long, and contains only one incident of which I have reason to be proud.

Our great-grandfather fell at the battle of Culloden, fighting for the old line of kings; and our grandfather was a small farmer in Ulva, where my father was born. It is one of that cluster of the Hebrides thus alluded to by Walter Scott:

> "And Ulva dark, and Colonsay,
> And all the group of islets gay
> That guard famed Staffa round."*

* *Lord of the Isles*, canto 4.

Our grandfather was intimately acquainted with all the traditionary legends which that great writer has since made use of in the "Tales of a Grandfather" and other works. As a boy I remember listening to him with delight, for his memory was stored with a never-ending stock of stories, many of which were wonderfully like those I have since heard while sitting by the African evening fires. Our grandmother, too, used to sing Gaelic songs, some of which, as she believed, had been composed by captive islanders languishing hopelessly among the Turks.

Grandfather could give particulars of the lives of his ancestors for six generations of the family before him; and the only point of the tradition I feel proud of is this: One of these poor hardy islanders was renowned in the district for great wisdom and prudence; and it is related that, when he was on his death-bed, he called all his children around him and said, "Now, in my lifetime, I have searched most carefully through all the traditions I could find of our family, and I never could discover that there was a dishonest man among our forefathers. If, therefore, any of you or any of your children should take to dishonest ways, it will not be because it runs in our blood: it does not belong to you. I leave this precept with you: Be honest." If, therefore, in the following pages I fall into any errors, I hope they will be dealt with as honest mistakes, and not as indicating that I have forgotten our ancient motto. This event took place at a time when the Highlanders, according to Macaulay, were much like the Cape Caffres, and any one, it was said, could escape punishment for cattle-stealing by presenting a share of the plunder to his chieftain. Our ancestors were Roman Catholics; they were made Protestants by the laird coming round with a man having a yellow staff, which would seem to have attracted more attention than his teaching, for the new religion went long afterward, perhaps it does so still, by the name of "the religion of the yellow stick".

Finding his farm in Ulva insufficient to support a numerous family, my grandfather removed to Blantyre Works, a large cotton manufactory on the beautiful Clyde, above Glasgow; and his sons, having had the best education the Hebrides afforded, were gladly received as clerks by the proprietors, Monteith and Co. He himself, highly esteemed for his unflinching honesty, was employed in the conveyance of large sums of money from Glasgow to the works, and in old age was, according to the custom of that company, pensioned off, so as to spend his declining years in ease and comfort.

Our uncles all entered his majesty's service during the last French war, either as soldiers or sailors; but my father remained at home, and, though too conscientious ever to become rich as a small tea-dealer, by his kindliness of manner and winning ways he made the heart-strings of his children twine around him as firmly as if he had possessed, and could have bestowed upon them, every worldly advantage. He reared his children in connection with the Kirk of Scotland—a religious establishment which has been an incalculable blessing to that country—but he afterward left it, and during the last twenty years of his life held the office of deacon of an independent church in Hamilton, and deserved my lasting gratitude and homage for presenting me, from my infancy, with a continuously consistent pious example, such as that ideal of which is so beautifully and truthfully portrayed in Burns's "Cottar's Saturday Night". He died in February, 1856, in peaceful hope of that mercy which we all expect through the death of our Lord and Savior. I was at the time on my way below Zumbo, expecting no greater pleasure in this country than sitting by our cottage fire and telling him my travels. I revere his memory.

The earliest recollection of my mother recalls a picture so often seen among the Scottish poor—that of the anxious housewife striving to make both ends meet. At the age of ten I was put into the factory as a "piecer", to aid by my earnings in lessening her anxiety. With a part of my first week's wages I purchased Ruddiman's "Rudiments of Latin", and pursued the study of that language for many years afterward, with unabated ardor, at an evening school, which met between the hours of eight and ten. The dictionary part of my labors was followed up till twelve o'clock, or later, if my mother did not interfere by jumping up and snatching the books out of my hands. I had to be back in the factory by six in the morning, and continue my work, with intervals for breakfast and dinner, till eight o'clock at night. I read in this way many of the classical authors, and knew Virgil and Horace better at sixteen than I do now. Our schoolmaster—happily still alive—was supported in part by the company; he was attentive and kind, and so moderate in his charges that all who wished for education might have obtained it. Many availed themselves of the privilege; and some of my schoolfellows now rank in positions far above what they appeared ever likely to come to when in the village school. If such a system were established in England, it would prove a never-ending blessing to the poor.

In reading, every thing that I could lay my hands on was devoured except novels. Scientific works and books of travels were my especial delight; though my father, believing, with many of his time who ought to have known better, that the former were inimical to religion, would have preferred to have seen me poring over the "Cloud of Witnesses", or Boston's "Fourfold State". Our difference of opinion reached the point of open rebellion on my part, and his last application of the rod was on my refusal to peruse Wilberforce's "Practical Christianity". This dislike to dry doctrinal reading, and to religious reading of every sort, continued for years afterward; but having lighted on those admirable works of Dr. Thomas Dick, "The Philosophy of Religion" and "The Philosophy of a Future State", it was gratifying to find my own ideas, that religion and science are not hostile, but friendly to each other, fully proved and enforced.

Great pains had been taken by my parents to instill the doctrines of Christianity into my mind, and I had no difficulty in understanding the theory of our free salvation by the atonement of our Savior, but it was only about this time that I really began to feel the necessity and value of a personal application of the provisions of that atonement to my own case. The change have spent the following sixteen years of my life, namely, from 1840 to 1856, in medical and missionary labors there without cost to the inhabitants.

As to those literary qualifications which are acquired by habits of writing, and which are so important to an author, my African life has not only not been favorable to the growth of such accomplishments, but quite the reverse; it has made composition irksome and laborious. I think I would rather cross the African continent again than undertake to write another book. It is far easier to travel than to write about it. I intended on going to Africa to continue my studies; but as I could not brook the idea of simply entering into other men's labors made ready to my hands, I entailed on myself, in addition to teaching, manual labor in building and other handicraft work, which made me generally as much exhausted and unfit for study in the evenings as ever I had been when a cotton-spinner. The want of time for self-improvement was the only source of regret that I experienced during my African career. The reader, remembering this, will make allowances for the mere gropings for light of a student who has the vanity to think himself "not yet too old to learn". More precise information on several subjects has necessarily been omitted in a popular work like the present; but I hope to give such details to the scientific reader through some other channel.

Chapter 1

The Bakwain Country—Study of the Language—Native Ideas regarding Comets—Mabotsa Station—A Lion Encounter—Virus of the Teeth of Lions—Names of the Bechuana Tribes—Sechele—His Ancestors—Obtains the Chieftainship—His Marriage and Government—The Kotla—First public Religious Services—Sechele's Questions—He Learns to Read—Novel mode for Converting his Tribe—Surprise at their Indifference—Polygamy—Baptism of Sechele—Opposition of the Natives—Purchase Land at Chonuane—Relations with the People—Their Intelligence—Prolonged Drought—Consequent Trials—Rain-medicine—God's Word blamed—Native Reasoning—Rain-maker—Dispute between Rain Doctor and Medical Doctor—The Hunting Hopo—Salt or animal Food a necessary of Life—Duties of a Missionary.

The general instructions I received from the Directors of the London Missionary Society led me, as soon as I reached Kuruman or Lattakoo, then, as it is now, their farthest inland station from the Cape, to turn my attention to the north. Without waiting longer at Kuruman than was necessary to recruit the oxen, which were pretty well tired by the long journey from Algoa Bay, I proceeded, in company with another missionary, to the Bakuena or Bakwain country, and found Sechele, with his tribe, located at Shokuane. We shortly after retraced our steps to Kuruman; but as the objects in view were by no means to be attained by a temporary excursion of this sort, I determined to make a fresh start into the interior as soon as possible. Accordingly, after resting three months at Kuruman, which is a kind of head station in the country, I returned to a spot about fifteen miles south of Shokuane, called Lepelole (now Litubaruba). Here, in order to obtain an accurate knowledge of the language, I cut myself off from all European society for about six months, and gained by this ordeal an insight into the habits, ways of thinking, laws, and language of that section of the Bechuanas called Bakwains, which has proved of incalculable advantage in my intercourse with them ever since.

In this second journey to Lepelole—so called from a cavern of that name—I began preparations for a settlement, by making a canal to irrigate gardens, from a stream then flowing copiously, but now quite dry. When these preparations were well advanced, I went northward to visit the Bakaa and Bamangwato, and the Makalaka, living between 22 Degrees and 23 Degrees south latitude. The Bakaa Mountains had been visited before by a trader, who, with his people, all perished from fever. In going round the northern part of these basaltic hills near Letloche I was only ten days distant from the lower part of the Zouga, which passed by the same name as Lake Ngami;* and I might then (in 1842) have discovered that lake, had discovery alone been my object. Most part of this journey beyond Shokuane was performed on foot, in consequence of the draught oxen having become sick. Some of my companions who had recently joined us, and did not know that I understood a little of their speech, were overheard by me discussing my appearance and powers: "He is not strong; he is quite slim, and only appears stout because he puts himself into those bags (trowsers); he will soon knock up." This caused my Highland blood to rise, and made me despise the fatigue of keeping them all at the top of their speed for days together, and until I heard them expressing proper opinions of my pedestrian powers.

> *Several words in the African languages begin with the ringing sound heard in the end of the word "comING". If the reader puts an 'i' to the beginning of the name of the lake, as Ingami, and then sounds the 'i' as little as possible, he will have the correct pronunciation. The Spanish n [ny] is employed to denote this sound, and Ngami is spelt nyami—naka means a tusk, nyaka a doctor. Every vowel is sounded in all native words, and the emphasis in pronunciation is put upon the penultimate.

Returning to Kuruman, in order to bring my luggage to our proposed settlement, I was followed by the news that the tribe of Bakwains, who had shown themselves so friendly toward me, had been driven from Lepelole by the Barolongs, so that my prospects for the time of forming a settlement there were at an end. One of those periodical outbreaks of war, which seem to have occurred from time immemorial, for the possession of cattle, had burst forth in the land, and had so changed the relations of the tribes to each other, that I was obliged to set out anew to look for a suitable locality for a mission station.

In going north again, a comet blazed on our sight, exciting the wonder of every tribe we visited. That of 1816 had been followed by an irruption of the Matebele, the most cruel enemies the Bechuanas ever knew, and this they thought might portend something as bad, or it might only foreshadow the death of some great chief. On this subject of comets I knew little more than they did themselves, but I had that confidence in a kind, overruling

Providence, which makes such a difference between Christians and both the ancient and modern heathen.

As some of the Bamangwato people had accompanied me to Kuruman, I was obliged to restore them and their goods to their chief Sekomi. This made a journey to the residence of that chief again necessary, and, for the first time, I performed a distance of some hundred miles on ox-back.

Returning toward Kuruman, I selected the beautiful valley of Mabotsa (lat. 25d 14' south, long. 26d 30'?) as the site of a missionary station, and thither I removed in 1843. Here an occurrence took place concerning which I have frequently been questioned in England, and which, but for the importunities of friends, I meant to have kept in store to tell my children when in my dotage. The Bakatla of the village Mabotsa were much troubled by lions, which leaped into the cattle-pens by night, and destroyed their cows. They even attacked the herds in open day. This was so unusual an occurrence that the people believed that they were bewitched—"given," as they said, "into the power of the lions by a neighboring tribe." They went once to attack the animals, but, being rather a cowardly people compared to Bechuanas in general on such occasions, they returned without killing any.

It is well known that if one of a troop of lions is killed, the others take the hint and leave that part of the country. So, the next time the herds were attacked, I went with the people, in order to encourage them to rid themselves of the annoyance by destroying one of the marauders. We found the lions on a small hill about a quarter of a mile in length, and covered with trees. A circle of men was formed round it, and they gradually closed up, ascending pretty near to each other. Being down below on the plain with a native schoolmaster, named Mebalwe, a most excellent man, I saw one of the lions sitting on a piece of rock within the now closed circle of men. Mebalwe fired at him before I could, and the ball struck the rock on which the animal was sitting. He bit at the spot struck, as a dog does at a stick or stone thrown at him; then leaping away, broke through the opening circle and escaped unhurt. The men were afraid to attack him, perhaps on account of their belief in witchcraft. When the circle was re-formed, we saw two other lions in it; but we were afraid to fire lest we should strike the men, and they allowed the beasts to burst through also. If the Bakatla had acted according to the custom of the country, they would have speared the lions in their attempt to get out. Seeing we could not get them to kill one of the lions, we bent our footsteps toward the village; in going round the end of the hill, however, I saw one of the beasts sitting on a piece of rock as before, but this time he had a little bush in front. Being about thirty yards off, I took a good aim at his body through the bush, and fired both barrels into it. The men then called out, "He is shot, he is shot!" Others cried, "He has been shot by another man too; let us go to him!" I did not see any one else shoot at him, but I saw the lion's tail erected in anger behind the bush, and, turning to the people, said, "Stop a little, till I load again." When in the act of ramming down the bullets, I heard a shout. Starting, and looking half round, I saw the lion just in the act of springing upon me. I was upon a little height; he caught my shoulder as he sprang, and we both came to the ground below together. Growling horribly close to my ear, he shook me as a terrier dog does a rat. The shock produced a stupor similar to that which seems to be felt by a mouse after the first shake of the cat. It caused a sort of dreaminess, in which there was no sense of pain nor feeling of terror, though quite conscious of all that was happening. It was like what patients partially under the influence of chloroform describe, who see all the operation, but feel not the knife. This singular condition was not the result of any mental process. The shake annihilated fear, and allowed no sense of horror in looking round at the beast. This peculiar state is probably produced in all animals killed by the carnivora; and if so, is a merciful provision by our benevolent Creator for lessening the pain of death. Turning round to relieve myself of the weight, as he had one paw on the back of my head, I saw his eyes directed to Mebalwe, who was trying to shoot him at a distance of ten or fifteen yards. His gun, a flint one, missed fire in both barrels; the lion immediately left me, and, attacking Mebalwe, bit his thigh. Another man, whose life I had saved before, after he had been tossed by a buffalo, attempted to spear the lion while he was biting Mebalwe. He left Mebalwe and caught this man by the shoulder, but at that moment the bullets he had received took effect, and he fell down dead. The whole was the work of a few moments, and must have been his paroxysms of dying rage. In order to take out the charm from him, the Bakatla on the following day made a huge bonfire over the carcass, which was declared to be that of the largest lion they had ever seen. Besides crunching the bone into splinters, he left eleven teeth wounds on the upper part of my arm.

A wound from this animal's tooth resembles a gun-shot wound; it is generally followed by a great deal of sloughing and discharge, and pains are felt in the part periodically ever afterward. I had on a tartan jacket on the occasion, and I believe that it wiped off all the virus from the teeth that pierced the flesh, for my two companions in this affray have both suffered from the peculiar pains, while I have escaped with only the inconvenience of a false joint in my limb. The man whose shoulder was wounded showed me his wound actually burst forth afresh on the same month of the following year. This curious point deserves the attention of inquirers.

The different Bechuana tribes are named after certain animals, showing probably that in former times they were addicted to animal-worship like the ancient Egyptians. The term Bakatla means "they of the monkey"; Bakuena, "they of the alligator"; Batlapi, "they of the fish": each tribe having a superstitious dread of the animal after which it is called. They also use the word "bina", to dance, in reference to the custom of thus naming themselves, so that, when you wish to ascertain what tribe they belong to, you say, "What do you dance?" It would seem as if that had been a part of the worship of old. A tribe never eats the animal which is its namesake, using the term "ila", hate or dread, in reference to killing it. We find traces of many ancient tribes in the country in individual members of those now extinct, as the Batau, "they of the lion"; the Banoga, "they of the serpent"; though no such tribes now exist. The use of the personal pronoun they, Ba-Ma, Wa, Va or Ova, Am-Ki, &c., prevails very extensively in the names of tribes in Africa. A single individual is indicated by the terms Mo or Le. Thus Mokwain is a single person of the Bakwain tribe, and Lekoa is a single white man or Englishman—Makoa being Englishmen.

I attached myself to the tribe called Bakuena or Bakwains, the chief of which, named Sechele, was then living with his people at a place called Shokuane. I was from the first struck by his intelligence, and by the marked manner in which we both felt drawn to each other. As this remarkable man has not only embraced Christianity, but expounds its doctrines to his people, I will here give a brief sketch of his career.

His great-grandfather Mochoasele was a great traveler, and the first that ever told the Bakwains of the existence of white men. In his father's lifetime two white travelers, whom I suppose to have been Dr. Cowan and Captain Donovan, passed through the country (in 1808), and, descending the River Limpopo, were, with their party, all cut off by fever. The rain-makers there, fearing lest their wagons might drive away the rain, ordered them to be thrown into the river. This is the true account of the end of that expedition, as related to me by the son of the chief at whose village they perished. He remembered, when a boy, eating part of one of the horses, and said it tasted like zebra's flesh. Thus they were not killed by the Bangwaketse, as reported, for they passed the Bakwains all well. The Bakwains were then rich in cattle; and as one of the many evidences of the desiccation of the country, streams are pointed out where thousands and thousands of cattle formerly drank, but in which water now never flows, and where a single herd could not find fluid for its support.

When Sechele was still a boy, his father, also called Mochoasele, was murdered by his own people for taking to himself the wives of his rich under-chiefs. The children being spared, their friends invited Sebituane, the chief of the Makololo, who was then in those parts, to reinstate them in the chieftainship. Sebituane surrounded the town of the Bakwains by night; and just as it began to dawn, his herald proclaimed in a loud voice that he had come to revenge the death of Mochoasele. This was followed by Sebituane's people beating loudly on their shields all round the town. The panic was tremendous, and the rush like that from a theatre on fire, while the Makololo used their javelins on the terrified Bakwains with a dexterity which they alone can employ. Sebituane had given orders to his men to spare the sons of the chief; and one of them, meeting Sechele, put him in ward by giving him such a blow on the head with a club as to render him insensible. The usurper was put to death; and Sechele, reinstated in his chieftainship, felt much attached to Sebituane. The circumstances here noticed ultimately led me, as will be seen by-and-by, into the new, well-watered country to which this same Sebituane had preceded me by many years.

Sechele married the daughters of three of his under-chiefs, who had, on account of their blood relationship, stood by him in his adversity. This is one of the modes adopted for cementing the allegiance of a tribe. The government is patriarchal, each man being, by virtue of paternity, chief of his own children. They build their huts around his, and the greater the number of children, the more his importance increases. Hence children are esteemed one of the greatest blessings, and are always treated kindly. Near the centre of each circle of huts there is a spot called a "kotla", with a fireplace; here they work, eat, or sit and gossip over the news of the day. A poor man attaches himself to the kotla of a rich one, and is considered a child of the latter. An under-chief has a number of these circles around his; and the collection of kotlas around the great one in the middle of the whole, that of the principal chief, constitutes the town. The circle of huts immediately around the kotla of the chief is composed of the huts of his wives and those of his blood relations. He attaches the under-chiefs to himself and his government by marrying, as Sechele did, their daughters, or inducing his brothers to do so. They are fond of the relationship to great families. If you meet a party of strangers, and the head man's relationship to some uncle of a certain chief is not at once proclaimed by his attendants, you may hear him whispering, "Tell him who I am." This usually involves a counting on the fingers of a part of his genealogical tree, and ends in the important announcement that the head of the party is half-cousin to some well-known ruler.

Sechele was thus seated in his chieftainship when I made his acquaintance. On the first occasion in which I ever attempted to hold a public religious service, he remarked that it was the custom of his nation, when any new subject was brought before them, to put questions on it; and he begged me to allow him to do the same in this case. On expressing my entire willingness to answer his questions, he inquired if my forefathers knew of a future judgment. I replied in the affirmative, and began to describe the scene of the "great white throne, and Him who shall sit on it, from whose face the heaven and earth shall flee away," &c. He said, "You startle me: these words make all my bones to shake; I have no more strength in me; but my forefathers were living at the same time yours were, and how is it that they did not send them word about these terrible things sooner? They all passed away into darkness without knowing whither they were going." I got out of the difficulty by explaining the geographical barriers in the North, and the gradual spread of knowledge from the South, to which we first had access by means of ships; and I expressed my belief that, as Christ had said, the whole world would yet be enlightened by the Gospel. Pointing to the great Kalahari desert, he said, "You never can cross that country to the tribes beyond; it is utterly impossible even for us black men, except in certain seasons, when more than the usual supply of rain falls, and an extraordinary growth of watermelons follows. Even we who know the country would certainly perish without them." Reasserting my belief in the words of Christ, we parted; and it will be seen farther on that Sechele himself assisted me in crossing that desert which had previously proved an insurmountable barrier to so many adventurers.

As soon as he had an opportunity of learning, he set himself to read with such close application that, from being comparatively thin, the effect of having been fond of the chase, he became quite corpulent from want of exercise. Mr. Oswell gave him his first lesson in figures, and he acquired the alphabet on the first day of my residence at Chonuane. He was by no means an ordinary specimen of the people, for I never went into the town but I was pressed to hear him read some chapters of the Bible. Isaiah was a great favorite with him; and he was wont to use the same phrase nearly which the professor of Greek at Glasgow, Sir D. K. Sandford, once used respecting the Apostle Paul, when reading his speeches in the Acts: "He was a fine fellow, that Paul!" "He was a fine man, that Isaiah; he knew how to speak." Sechele invariably offered me something to eat on every occasion of my visiting him.

Seeing me anxious that his people should believe the words of Christ, he once said, "Do you imagine these people will ever believe by your merely talking to them? I can make them do nothing except by thrashing them; and if you like, I shall call my head men, and with our litupa (whips of rhinoceros hide) we will soon make them all believe together." The idea of using entreaty and persuasion to subjects to become Christians—whose opinion on no other matter would he condescend to ask—was especially surprising to him. He considered that they ought only to be too happy to embrace Christianity at his command. During the space of two years and a half he continued to profess to his people his full conviction of the truth of Christianity; and in all discussions on the subject he took that side, acting at the same time in an upright manner in all the relations of life. He felt the difficulties of his situation long before I did, and often said, "Oh, I wish you had come to this country before I became entangled in the meshes of our customs!" In fact, he could not get rid of his superfluous wives, without appearing to be ungrateful to their parents, who had done so much for him in his adversity.

In the hope that others would be induced to join him in his attachment to Christianity, he asked me to begin family worship with him in his house. I did so; and by-and-by was surprised to hear how well he conducted the prayer in his own simple and beautiful style, for he was quite a master of his own language. At this time we were suffering from the effects of a drought, which will be described further on, and none except his family, whom he ordered to attend, came near his meeting. "In former times," said he, "when a chief was fond of hunting, all his people got dogs, and became fond of hunting too. If he was fond of dancing or music, all showed a liking to these amusements too. If the chief loved beer, they all rejoiced in strong drink. But in this case it is different. I love the Word of God, and not one of my brethren will join me." One reason why we had no volunteer hypocrites was the hunger from drought, which was associated in their minds with the presence of Christian instruction; and hypocrisy is not prone to profess a creed which seems to insure an empty stomach.

Sechele continued to make a consistent profession for about three years; and perceiving at last some of the difficulties of his case, and also feeling compassion for the poor women, who were by far the best of our scholars, I had no desire that he should be in any hurry to make a full profession by baptism, and putting away all his wives but one. His principal wife, too, was about the most unlikely subject in the tribe ever to become any thing else than an out-and-out greasy disciple of the old school. She has since become greatly altered, I hear, for the better; but again and again have I seen Sechele send her out of church to put her gown on, and away she would go with her lips shot out, the very picture of unutterable disgust at his new-fangled notions.

When he at last applied for baptism, I simply asked him how he, having the Bible in his hand, and able to read it, thought he ought to act. He went home, gave each of his superfluous wives new clothing, and all his own goods, which they had been accustomed to keep in their huts for him, and sent them to their parents with an intimation that he had no fault to find with them, but that in parting with them he wished to follow the will of God. On the day on which he and his children were baptized, great numbers came to see the ceremony. Some thought, from a stupid calumny circulated by enemies to Christianity in the south, that the converts would be made to drink an infusion of "dead men's brains", and were astonished to find that water only was used at baptism. Seeing several of the old men actually in tears during the service, I asked them afterward the cause of their weeping; they were crying to see their father, as the Scotch remark over a case of suicide, "SO FAR LEFT TO HIMSELF". They seemed to think that I had thrown the glamour over him, and that he had become mine. Here commenced an opposition which we had not previously experienced. All the friends of the divorced wives became the opponents of our religion. The attendance at school and church diminished to very few besides the chief's own family. They all treated us still with respectful kindness, but to Sechele himself they said things which, as he often remarked, had they ventured on in former times, would have cost them their lives. It was trying, after all we had done, to see our labors so little appreciated; but we had sown the good seed, and have no doubt but it will yet spring up, though we may not live to see the fruits.

Leaving this sketch of the chief, I proceed to give an equally rapid one of our dealing with his people, the Bakena, or Bakwains. A small piece of land, sufficient for a garden, was purchased when we first went to live with them, though that was scarcely necessary in a country where the idea of buying land was quite new. It was expected that a request for a suitable spot would have been made, and that we should have proceeded to occupy it as any other member of the tribe would. But we explained to them that we wished to avoid any cause of future dispute when land had become more valuable; or when a foolish chief began to reign, and we had erected large or expensive buildings, he might wish to claim the whole. These reasons were considered satisfactory. About 5 Pounds worth of goods were given for a piece of land, and an arrangement was come to that a similar piece should be allotted to any other missionary, at any other place to which the tribe might remove. The particulars of the sale sounded strangely in the ears of the tribe, but were nevertheless readily agreed to.

In our relations with this people we were simply strangers exercising no authority or control whatever. Our influence depended entirely on persuasion; and having taught them by kind conversation as well as by public instruction, I expected them to do what their own sense of right and wrong dictated. We never wished them to do right merely because it would be pleasing to us, nor thought ourselves to blame when they did wrong, although we were quite aware of the absurd idea to that effect. We saw that our teaching did good to the general mind of the people by bringing new and better motives into play. Five instances are positively known to me in which, by our influence on public opinion, war was prevented; and where, in individual cases, we failed, the people did no worse than they did before we came into the country. In general they were slow, like all the African people hereafter to be described, in coming to a decision on religious subjects; but in questions affecting their worldly affairs they were keenly alive to their own interests. They might be called stupid in matters which had not come within the sphere of their observation, but in other things they showed more intelligence than is to be met with in our own uneducated peasantry. They are remarkably accurate in their knowledge of cattle, sheep, and goats, knowing exactly the kind of pasturage suited to each; and they select with great judgment the varieties of soil best suited to different kinds of grain. They are also familiar with the habits of wild animals, and in general are well up in the maxims which embody their ideas of political wisdom.

The place where we first settled with the Bakwains is called Chonuane, and it happened to be visited, during the first year of our residence there, by one of those droughts which occur from time to time in even the most favored districts of Africa.

The belief in the gift or power of RAIN-MAKING is one of the most deeply-rooted articles of faith in this country. The chief Sechele was himself a noted rain-doctor, and believed in it implicitly. He has often assured me that he found it more difficult to give up his faith in that than in any thing else which Christianity required him to abjure. I pointed out to him that the only feasible way of watering the gardens was to select some good, never-failing river, make a canal, and irrigate the adjacent lands. This suggestion was immediately adopted, and soon the whole tribe was on the move to the Kolobeng, a stream about forty miles distant. The experiment succeeded admirably during the first year. The Bakwains made the canal and dam in exchange for my labor in assisting to build a square house for their chief. They also built their own school under my superintendence. Our house at the River Kolobeng, which gave a name to the settlement, was the third which I had reared with my own hands. A native smith taught me to weld iron; and having improved by scraps of information in that line from Mr. Moffat, and also in carpentering and gardening, I was becoming handy at almost any trade, besides doctoring and preaching; and as my wife could make candles, soap, and clothes, we came nearly up to what may be considered as indispensable in the accomplishments of a missionary family in Central Africa, namely, the husband to be a jack-of-all-trades without doors, and the wife a maid-of-all-work within. But in our second year again no rain fell. In the third the same extraordinary drought followed. Indeed, not ten inches of water fell during these two years, and the Kolobeng ran dry; so many fish were killed that the hyaenas from the whole country round collected to the feast, and were unable to finish the putrid masses. A large old alligator, which had never been known to commit any depredations, was found left high and dry in the mud among the victims. The fourth year was equally unpropitious, the fall of rain being insufficient to bring the grain to maturity. Nothing could be more trying. We dug down in the bed of the river deeper and deeper as the water receded, striving to get a little to keep the fruit-trees alive for better times, but in vain. Needles lying out of doors for months did not rust; and a mixture of sulphuric acid and water, used in a galvanic battery, parted with all its water to the air, instead of imbibing more from it, as it would have done in England. The leaves of indigenous trees were all drooping, soft, and shriveled, though not dead; and those of the mimosae were closed at midday, the same as they are at night. In the midst of this dreary drought, it was wonderful to see those tiny creatures, the ants, running about with their accustomed vivacity. I put the bulb of a thermometer three inches under the soil, in the sun, at midday, and found the mercury to stand at 132 Deg. to 134 Deg.; and if certain kinds of beetles were placed on the surface, they ran about a few seconds and expired. But this broiling heat only augmented the activity of the long-legged black ants: they never tire; their organs of motion seem endowed with the same power as is ascribed by physiologists to the muscles of the human heart, by which that part of the frame never becomes fatigued, and which may be imparted to all our bodily organs in that higher sphere to which we fondly hope to rise. Where do these ants get their moisture? Our house was built on a hard ferruginous conglomerate, in order to be out of the way of the white ant, but they came in despite the precaution; and not only were they, in this sultry weather, able individually to moisten soil to the consistency of mortar for the formation of galleries, which, in their way of working, is done by night (so that they are screened from the observation of birds by day in passing and repassing toward any vegetable matter they may wish to devour), but, when their inner chambers were laid open, these were also surprisingly humid. Yet there was no dew, and, the house being placed on a rock, they could have no subterranean passage to the bed of the river, which ran about three hundred yards below the hill. Can it be that they have the power of combining the oxygen and hydrogen of their vegetable food by vital force so as to form water?*

> *When we come to Angola, I shall describe an insect there which distills several pints of water every night.

Rain, however, would not fall. The Bakwains believed that I had bound Sechele with some magic spell, and I received deputations, in the evenings, of the old counselors, entreating me to allow him to make only a few showers: "The corn will die if you refuse, and we shall become scattered. Only let him make rain this once, and we shall all, men, women, and children, come to the school, and sing and pray as long as you please." It was in vain to protest that I wished Sechele to act just according to his own ideas of what was right, as he found the law laid down in the Bible, and it was distressing to appear hard-hearted to them. The clouds often collected promisingly over us, and rolling thunder seemed to portend refreshing showers, but next morning the sun would rise in a clear, cloudless sky; indeed, even these lowering appearances were less frequent by far than days of sunshine are in London.

The natives, finding it irksome to sit and wait helplessly until God gives them rain from heaven, entertain the more comfortable idea that they can help themselves by a variety of preparations, such as charcoal made of burned bats, inspissated renal deposit of the mountain cony— 'Hyrax capensis'—(which, by the way, is used, in the form of pills, as a good antispasmodic, under the name of "stone-sweat"*), the internal parts of different animals—as jackals' livers, baboons' and lions' hearts, and hairy calculi from the bowels of old cows—serpents' skins and vertebrae, and every kind of tuber, bulb, root, and plant to be found in the country. Although you disbelieve their efficacy in charming the clouds to pour out their refreshing treasures, yet, conscious that civility is useful every where, you kindly state that you think they are mistaken as to their power. The rain-doctor selects a particular bulbous root, pounds it, and administers a cold infusion to a sheep, which in five minutes afterward expires in convulsions. Part of the same bulb is converted into smoke, and ascends toward the sky; rain follows in a day or two. The inference is obvious. Were we as much harassed by droughts, the logic would be irresistible in England in 1857.

> * The name arises from its being always voided on one spot, in the manner practiced by others of the rhinocerontine family; and, by the action of the sun, it becomes a black, pitchy substance.

As the Bakwains believed that there must be some connection between the presence of "God's Word" in their town and these successive and distressing droughts, they looked with no good will at the church bell, but still they invariably treated us with kindness and respect. I am not aware of ever having had an enemy in the tribe. The only avowed cause of dislike was expressed by a very influential and sensible man, the uncle of Sechele. "We like you as well as if you had been born among us; you are the only white man we can become familiar with (thoaela); but we wish you to give up that everlasting preaching and praying; we can not become familiar with that at all. You see we never get rain, while those tribes who never pray as we do obtain abundance." This was a fact; and we often saw it raining on the hills ten miles off, while it would not look at us "even with one eye". If the Prince of the power of the air had no hand in scorching us up, I fear I often gave him the credit of doing so.

As for the rain-makers, they carried the sympathies of the people along with them, and not without reason. With the following arguments they were all acquainted, and in order to understand their force, we must place ourselves in their position, and believe, as they do, that all medicines act by a mysterious charm. The term for cure may be translated "charm" ('alaha').

MEDICAL DOCTOR. Hail, friend! How very many medicines you have about you this morning! Why, you have every medicine in the country here.

RAIN DOCTOR. Very true, my friend; and I ought; for the whole country needs the rain which I am making.

M. D. So you really believe that you can command the clouds? I think that can be done by God alone.

R. D. We both believe the very same thing. It is God that makes the rain, but I pray to him by means of these medicines, and, the rain coming, of course it is then mine. It was I who made it for the Bakwains for many years, when they were at Shokuane; through my wisdom, too, their women became fat and shining. Ask them; they will tell you the same as I do.

M. D. But we are distinctly told in the parting words of our Savior that we can pray to God acceptably in his name alone, and not by means of medicines.

R. D. Truly! but God told us differently. He made black men first, and did not love us as he did the white men. He made you beautiful, and gave you clothing, and guns, and gunpowder, and horses, and wagons, and many other things about which we know nothing. But toward us he had no heart. He gave us nothing except the assegai, and cattle, and rain-making; and he did not give us hearts like yours. We never love each other. Other tribes place medicines about our country to prevent the rain, so that we may be dispersed by hunger, and go to them, and augment their power. We must dissolve their charms by our medicines. God has given us one little thing, which you know nothing of. He has given us the knowledge of certain medicines by which we can make rain. WE do not despise those things which you possess, though we are ignorant of them. We don't understand your book, yet we don't despise it. YOU ought not to despise our little knowledge, though you are ignorant of it.

M. D. I don't despise what I am ignorant of; I only think you are mistaken in saying that you have medicines which can influence the rain at all.

R. D. That's just the way people speak when they talk on a subject of which they have no knowledge. When we first opened our eyes, we found our forefathers making rain, and we follow in their footsteps. You, who send to Kuruman for corn, and irrigate your garden, may do without rain; WE can not manage in that way. If we had no rain, the cattle would have no pasture, the cows give no milk, our children become lean and die, our wives run away to other tribes who do make rain and have corn, and the whole tribe become dispersed and lost; our fire would go out.

M. D. I quite agree with you as to the value of the rain; but you can not charm the clouds by medicines. You wait till you see the clouds come, then you use your medicines, and take the credit which belongs to God only.

R. D. I use my medicines, and you employ yours; we are both doctors, and doctors are not deceivers. You give a patient medicine. Sometimes God is pleased to heal him by means of your medicine; sometimes not— he dies. When he is cured, you take the credit of what God does. I do the same. Sometimes God grants us rain, sometimes not. When he does, we take the credit of the charm. When a patient dies, you don't give up trust in your medicine, neither do I when rain fails. If you wish me to leave off my medicines, why continue your own?

M. D. I give medicine to living creatures within my reach, and can see the effects, though no cure follows; you pretend to charm the clouds, which are so far above us that your medicines never reach them. The clouds usually lie in one direction, and your smoke goes in another. God alone can command the clouds. Only try and wait patiently; God will give us rain without your medicines.

R. D. Mahala-ma-kapa-a-a!! Well, I always thought white men were wise till this morning. Who ever thought of making trial of starvation? Is death pleasant, then?

M. D. Could you make it rain on one spot and not on another?

R. D. I wouldn't think of trying. I like to see the whole country green, and all the people glad; the women clapping their hands, and giving me their ornaments for thankfulness, and lullilooing for joy.

M. D. I think you deceive both them and yourself.

R. D. Well, then, there is a pair of us (meaning both are rogues).

The above is only a specimen of their way of reasoning, in which, when the language is well understood, they are perceived to be remarkably acute.

These arguments are generally known, and I never succeeded in convincing a single individual of their fallacy, though I tried to do so in every way I could think of. Their faith in medicines as charms is unbounded. The general effect of argument is to produce the impression that you are not anxious for rain at all; and it is very undesirable to allow the idea to spread that you do not take a generous interest in their welfare. An angry opponent of rain-making in a tribe would be looked upon as were some Greek merchants in England during the Russian war.

The conduct of the people during this long-continued drought was remarkably good. The women parted with most of their ornaments to purchase corn from more fortunate tribes. The children scoured the country in search of the numerous bulbs and roots which can sustain life, and the men engaged in hunting. Very great numbers of the large game, buffaloes, zebras, giraffes, tsessebes, kamas or hartebeests, kokongs or gnus, pallahs, rhinoceroses, etc., congregated at some fountains near Kolobeng, and the trap called "hopo" was constructed, in the lands adjacent, for their destruction. The hopo consists of two hedges in the form of the letter V, which are very high and thick near the angle. Instead of the hedges being joined there, they are made to form a lane of about fifty yards in length, at the extremity of which a pit is formed, six or eight feet deep, and about twelve or fifteen in breadth and length. Trunks of trees are laid across the margins of the pit, and more especially over that nearest the lane where the animals are expected to leap in, and over that farthest from the lane where it is supposed they will attempt to escape after they are in. The trees form an overlapping border, and render escape almost impossible. The whole is carefully decked with short green rushes, making the pit like a concealed pitfall. As the hedges are frequently about a mile long, and about as much apart at their extremities, a tribe making a circle three or four miles round the country adjacent to the opening, and gradually closing up, are almost sure to inclose a large body of game. Driving it up with shouts to the narrow part of the hopo, men secreted there throw their javelins into the affrighted herds, and on the animals rush to the opening presented at the converging hedges, and into the pit, till that is full of a living mass. Some escape by running over the others, as a Smithfield market-dog does over the sheep's backs. It is a frightful scene. The men, wild with excitement, spear the lovely animals with mad delight; others of the poor creatures, borne down by the weight of their dead and dying companions, every now and then make the whole mass heave in their smothering agonies.

The Bakwains often killed between sixty and seventy head of large game at the different hopos in a single week; and as every one, both rich and poor, partook of the prey, the meat counteracted the bad effects of an exclusively vegetable diet. When the poor, who had no salt, were forced to live entirely on roots, they were often troubled with indigestion. Such cases we had frequent opportunities of seeing at other times, for, the district being destitute of salt, the rich alone could afford to buy it. The native doctors, aware of the cause of the malady, usually prescribed some of that ingredient with their medicines. The doctors themselves had none, so the poor resorted to us for aid. We took the hint, and henceforth cured the disease by giving a teaspoonful of salt, minus the other remedies. Either milk or meat had the same effect, though not so rapidly as salt. Long afterward, when I was myself deprived of salt for four months, at two distinct periods, I felt no desire for that condiment, but I was plagued by very great longing for the above articles of food. This continued as long as I was confined to an exclusively vegetable diet, and when I procured a meal of flesh, though boiled in perfectly fresh rain-water, it tasted as pleasantly saltish as if slightly impregnated with the condiment. Milk or meat, obtained in however small quantities, removed entirely the excessive longing and dreaming about roasted ribs of fat oxen, and bowls of cool thick milk gurgling forth from the big-bellied calabashes; and I could then understand the thankfulness to Mrs. L. often expressed by poor Bakwain women, in the interesting condition, for a very little of either.

In addition to other adverse influences, the general uncertainty, though not absolute want of food, and the necessity of frequent absence for the purpose of either hunting game or collecting roots and fruits, proved a serious barrier to the progress of the people in knowledge. Our own education in England is carried on at the comfortable breakfast and dinner table, and by the cosy fire, as well as in the church and school. Few English people with stomachs painfully empty would be decorous at church any more than they are when these organs are overcharged. Ragged schools would have been a failure had not the teachers wisely provided food for the body as well as food for the mind; and not only must we show a friendly interest in the bodily comfort of the objects of our sympathy as a Christian duty, but we can no more hope for healthy feelings among the poor, either at home or abroad, without feeding them into them, than we can hope to see an ordinary working-bee reared into a queen-mother by the ordinary food of the hive.

Sending the Gospel to the heathen must, if this view be correct, include much more than is implied in the usual picture of a missionary, namely, a man going about with a Bible under his arm. The promotion of commerce ought to be specially attended to, as this, more speedily than any thing else, demolishes that sense of isolation which heathenism engenders, and makes the tribes feel themselves mutually dependent on, and mutually beneficial to each other. With a view to this, the missionaries at Kuruman got permission from the government for a trader to reside at the station, and a considerable trade has been the result; the trader himself has become rich enough to retire with a competence. Those laws which still prevent free commercial intercourse among the civilized nations seem to be nothing else but the remains of our own heathenism. My observations on this subject make me extremely desirous to promote the preparation of the raw materials of European manufactures in Africa, for by that means we may not only put a stop to the slave-trade, but introduce the negro family into the body corporate of nations, no one member of which can suffer without the others suffering with it. Success in this, in both Eastern and Western Africa, would lead, in the course of time, to a much larger diffusion of the blessings of civilization than efforts exclusively spiritual and educational confined to any one small tribe. These, however, it would of course be extremely desirable to carry on at the same time at large central and healthy stations, for neither civilization nor Christianity can be promoted alone. In fact, they are inseparable.

Chapter 2

The Boers—Their Treatment of the Natives—Seizure of native Children for Slaves—English Traders—Alarm of the Boers—Native Espionage—The Tale of the Cannon—The Boers threaten Sechele—In violation of Treaty, they stop English Traders and expel Missionaries—They attack the Bakwains—Their Mode of Fighting—The Natives killed and the School-children carried into Slavery—Destruction of English Property—African Housebuilding and Housekeeping—Mode of Spending the Day—Scarcity of Food—Locusts—Edible Frogs—Scavenger Beetle—Continued Hostility of the Boers—The Journey north—Preparations—Fellow-travelers—The Kalahari Desert—Vegetation—Watermelons—The Inhabitants—The Bushmen—Their nomad Mode of Life—Appearance—The Bakalahari—Their Love for Agriculture and for domestic Animals—Timid Character—Mode of obtaining Water—Female Water-suckers—The Desert—Water hidden.

Another adverse influence with which the mission had to contend was the vicinity of the Boers of the Cashan Mountains, otherwise named "Magaliesberg". These are not to be confounded with the Cape colonists, who sometimes pass by the name. The word Boer simply means "farmer", and is not synonymous with our word boor. Indeed, to the Boers generally the latter term would be quite inappropriate, for they are a sober, industrious, and most hospitable body of peasantry. Those, however, who have fled from English law on various pretexts, and have been joined by English deserters and every other variety of bad character in their distant localities, are unfortunately of a very different stamp. The great objection many of the Boers had, and still have, to English law, is that it makes no distinction between black men and white. They felt aggrieved by their supposed losses in the emancipation of their Hottentot slaves, and determined to erect themselves into a republic, in which they might pursue, without molestation, the "proper treatment of the blacks". It is almost needless to add that the "proper treatment" has always contained in it the essential element of slavery, namely, compulsory unpaid labor.

One section of this body, under the late Mr. Hendrick Potgeiter, penetrated the interior as far as the Cashan Mountains, whence a Zulu or Caffre chief, named Mosilikatze, had been expelled by the well-known Caffre

Dingaan; and a glad welcome was given them by the Bechuana tribes, who had just escaped the hard sway of that cruel chieftain. They came with the prestige of white men and deliverers; but the Bechuanas soon found, as they expressed it, "that Mosilikatze was cruel to his enemies, and kind to those he conquered; but that the Boers destroyed their enemies, and made slaves of their friends." The tribes who still retain the semblance of independence are forced to perform all the labor of the fields, such as manuring the land, weeding, reaping, building, making dams and canals, and at the same time to support themselves. I have myself been an eye-witness of Boers coming to a village, and, according to their usual custom, demanding twenty or thirty women to weed their gardens, and have seen these women proceed to the scene of unrequited toil, carrying their own food on their heads, their children on their backs, and instruments of labor on their shoulders. Nor have the Boers any wish to conceal the meanness of thus employing unpaid labor; on the contrary, every one of them, from Mr. Potgeiter and Mr. Gert Krieger, the commandants, downward, lauded his own humanity and justice in making such an equitable regulation. "We make the people work for us, in consideration of allowing them to live in our country."

I can appeal to the Commandant Krieger if the foregoing is not a fair and impartial statement of the views of himself and his people. I am sensible of no mental bias toward or against these Boers; and during the several journeys I made to the poor enslaved tribes, I never avoided the whites, but tried to cure and did administer remedies to their sick, without money and without price. It is due to them to state that I was invariably treated with respect; but it is most unfortunate that they should have been left by their own Church for so many years to deteriorate and become as degraded as the blacks, whom the stupid prejudice against color leads them to detest.

This new species of slavery which they have adopted serves to supply the lack of field-labor only. The demand for domestic servants must be met by forays on tribes which have good supplies of cattle. The Portuguese can quote instances in which blacks become so degraded by the love of strong drink as actually to sell themselves; but never in any one case, within the memory of man, has a Bechuana chief sold any of his people, or a Bechuana man his child. Hence the necessity for a foray to seize children. And those individual Boers who would not engage in it for the sake of slaves can seldom resist the two-fold plea of a well-told story of an intended uprising of the devoted tribe, and the prospect of handsome pay in the division of the captured cattle besides.

It is difficult for a person in a civilized country to conceive that any body of men possessing the common attributes of humanity (and these Boers are by no means destitute of the better feelings of our nature) should with one accord set out, after loading their own wives and children with caresses, and proceed to shoot down in cold blood men and women, of a different color, it is true, but possessed of domestic feelings and affections equal to their own. I saw and conversed with children in the houses of Boers who had, by their own and their masters' account, been captured, and in several instances I traced the parents of these unfortunates, though the plan approved by the long-headed among the burghers is to take children so young that they soon forget their parents and their native language also. It was long before I could give credit to the tales of bloodshed told by native witnesses, and had I received no other testimony but theirs I should probably have continued skeptical to this day as to the truth of the accounts; but when I found the Boers themselves, some bewailing and denouncing, others glorying in the bloody scenes in which they had been themselves the actors, I was compelled to admit the validity of the testimony, and try to account for the cruel anomaly. They are all traditionally religious, tracing their descent from some of the best men (Huguenots and Dutch) the world ever saw. Hence they claim to themselves the title of "Christians", and all the colored race are "black property" or "creatures". They being the chosen people of God, the heathen are given to them for an inheritance, and they are the rod of divine vengeance on the heathen, as were the Jews of old. Living in the midst of a native population much larger than themselves, and at fountains removed many miles from each other, they feel somewhat in the same insecure position as do the Americans in the Southern States. The first question put by them to strangers is respecting peace; and when they receive reports from disaffected or envious natives against any tribe, the case assumes all the appearance and proportions of a regular insurrection. Severe measures then appear to the most mildly disposed among them as imperatively called for, and, however bloody the massacre that follows, no qualms of conscience ensue: it is a dire necessity for the sake of peace. Indeed, the late Mr. Hendrick Potgeiter most devoutly believed himself to be the great peacemaker of the country.

But how is it that the natives, being so vastly superior in numbers to the Boers, do not rise and annihilate them? The people among whom they live are Bechuanas, not Caffres, though no one would ever learn that distinction from a Boer; and history does not contain one single instance in which the Bechuanas, even those of them who possess fire-arms, have attacked either the Boers or the English. If there is such an instance, I am certain it is not generally known, either beyond or in the Cape Colony. They have defended themselves when attacked, as in the case of Sechele, but have never engaged in offensive war with Europeans. We have a very different tale to tell of the Caffres, and the difference has always been so evident to these border

Boers that, ever since those "magnificent savages"* obtained possession of fire-arms, not one Boer has ever attempted to settle in Caffreland, or even face them as an enemy in the field. The Boers have generally manifested a marked antipathy to any thing but "long-shot" warfare, and, sidling away in their emigrations toward the more effeminate Bechuanas, have left their quarrels with the Caffres to be settled by the English, and their wars to be paid for by English gold.

* *The "United Service Journal" so styles them.*

The Bakwains at Kolobeng had the spectacle of various tribes enslaved before their eyes—the Bakatla, the Batlokua, the Bahukeng, the Bamosetla, and two other tribes of Bakwains were all groaning under the oppression of unrequited labor. This would not have been felt as so great an evil but that the young men of those tribes, anxious to obtain cattle, the only means of rising to respectability and importance among their own people, were in the habit of sallying forth, like our Irish and Highland reapers, to procure work in the Cape Colony. After laboring there three or four years, in building stone dikes and dams for the Dutch farmers, they were well content if at the end of that time they could return with as many cows. On presenting one to their chief, they ranked as respectable men in the tribe ever afterward. These volunteers were highly esteemed among the Dutch, under the name of Mantatees. They were paid at the rate of one shilling a day and a large loaf of bread between six of them. Numbers of them, who had formerly seen me about twelve hundred miles inland from the Cape, recognized me with the loud laughter of joy when I was passing them at their work in the Roggefelt and Bokkefelt, within a few days of Cape Town. I conversed with them and with elders of the Dutch Church, for whom they were working, and found that the system was thoroughly satisfactory to both parties. I do not believe that there is one Boer, in the Cashan or Magaliesberg country, who would deny that a law was made, in consequence of this labor passing to the colony, to deprive these laborers of their hardly-earned cattle, for the very cogent reason that, "if they want to work, let them work for us their masters," though boasting that in their case it would not be paid for. I can never cease to be most unfeignedly thankful that I was not born in a land of slaves. No one can understand the effect of the unutterable meanness of the slave-system on the minds of those who, but for the strange obliquity which prevents them from feeling the degradation of not being gentlemen enough to pay for services rendered, would be equal in virtue to ourselves. Fraud becomes as natural to them as "paying one's way" is to the rest of mankind.

Wherever a missionary lives, traders are sure to come; they are mutually dependent, and each aids in the work of the other; but experience shows that the two employments can not very well be combined in the same person. Such a combination would not be morally wrong, for nothing would be more fair, and apostolical too, than that the man who devotes his time to the spiritual welfare of a people should derive temporal advantage from upright commerce, which traders, who aim exclusively at their own enrichment, modestly imagine ought to be left to them. But, though it is right for missionaries to trade, the present system of missions renders it inexpedient to spend time in so doing. No missionary with whom I ever came in contact, traded; and while the traders, whom we introduced and rendered secure in the country, waxed rich, the missionaries have invariably remained poor, and have died so. The Jesuits, in Africa at least, were wiser in their generation than we; theirs were large, influential communities, proceeding on the system of turning the abilities of every brother into that channel in which he was most likely to excel; one, fond of natural history, was allowed to follow his bent; another, fond of literature, found leisure to pursue his studies; and he who was great in barter was sent in search of ivory and gold-dust; so that while in the course of performing the religious acts of his mission to distant tribes, he found the means of aiding effectually the brethren whom he had left in the central settlement.* We Protestants, with the comfortable conviction of superiority, have sent out missionaries with a bare subsistence only, and are unsparing in our laudations of some for not being worldly-minded whom our niggardliness made to live as did the prodigal son. I do not speak of myself, nor need I to do so, but for that very reason I feel at liberty to interpose a word in behalf of others. I have before my mind at this moment facts and instances which warrant my putting the case in this way: The command to "go into all the world and preach the Gospel to every creature" must be obeyed by Christians either personally or by substitute. Now it is quite possible to find men whose love for the heathen and devotion to the work will make them ready to go forth on the terms "bare subsistence", but what can be thought of the justice, to say nothing of the generosity, of Christians and churches who not only work their substitutes at the lowest terms, but regard what they give as charity! The matter is the more grave in respect to the Protestant missionary, who may have a wife and family. The fact is, there are many cases in which it is right, virtuous, and praiseworthy for a man to sacrifice every thing for a great object, but in which it would be very wrong for others, interested in the object as much as he, to suffer or accept the sacrifice, if they can prevent it.

> * *The Dutch clergy, too, are not wanting in worldly wisdom. A fountain is bought, and the lands which it can irrigate parceled out and let to villagers. As they increase in numbers, the rents rise and the church becomes rich. With 200*

Pounds per annum in addition from government, the salary amounts to 400 or 500 Pounds a year. The clergymen then preach abstinence from politics as a Christian duty. It is quite clear that, with 400 Pounds a year, but little else except pure spirituality is required.

English traders sold those articles which the Boers most dread, namely, arms and ammunition; and when the number of guns amounted to five, so much alarm was excited among our neighbors that an expedition of several hundred Boers was seriously planned to deprive the Bakwains of their guns. Knowing that the latter would rather have fled to the Kalahari Desert than deliver up their weapons and become slaves, I proceeded to the commandant, Mr. Gert Krieger, and, representing the evils of any such expedition, prevailed upon him to defer it; but that point being granted, the Boer wished to gain another, which was that I should act as a spy over the Bakwains.

I explained the impossibility of my complying with his wish, even though my principles as an Englishman had not stood in the way, by referring to an instance in which Sechele had gone with his whole force to punish an under-chief without my knowledge. This man, whose name was Kake, rebelled, and was led on in his rebellion by his father-in-law, who had been regicide in the case of Sechele's father. Several of those who remained faithful to that chief were maltreated by Kake while passing to the Desert in search of skins. We had just come to live with the Bakwains when this happened, and Sechele consulted me. I advised mild measures, but the messengers he sent to Kake were taunted with the words, "He only pretends to wish to follow the advice of the teacher: Sechele is a coward; let him come and fight if he dare." The next time the offense was repeated, Sechele told me he was going to hunt elephants; and as I knew the system of espionage which prevails among all the tribes, I never made inquiries that would convey the opinion that I distrusted them. I gave credit to his statement. He asked the loan of a black-metal pot to cook with, as theirs of pottery are brittle. I gave it and a handful of salt, and desired him to send back two tit-bits, the proboscis and fore-foot of the elephant. He set off, and I heard nothing more until we saw the Bakwains carrying home their wounded, and heard some of the women uttering the loud wail of sorrow for the dead, and others pealing forth the clear scream of victory. It was then clear that Sechele had attacked and driven away the rebel.

Mentioning this to the commandant in proof of the impossibility of granting his request, I had soon an example how quickly a story can grow among idle people. The five guns were, within one month, multiplied into a tale of five hundred, and the cooking-pot, now in a museum at Cape Town, was magnified into a cannon; "I had myself confessed to the loan." Where the five hundred guns came from, it was easy to divine; for, knowing that I used a sextant, my connection with government was a thing of course; and, as I must know all her majesty's counsels, I was questioned on the subject of the indistinct rumors which had reached them of Lord Rosse's telescope. "What right has your government to set up that large glass at the Cape to look after us behind the Cashan Mountains?"

Many of the Boers visited us afterward at Kolobeng, some for medical advice, and others to trade in those very articles which their own laws and policy forbid. When I happened to stumble upon any of them in the town, with his muskets and powder displayed, he would begin an apology, on the ground that he was a poor man, etc., which I always cut short by frankly saying that I had nothing to do with either the Boers or their laws. Many attempts were made during these visits to elicit the truth about the guns and cannon; and ignorant of the system of espionage which prevails, eager inquiries were made by them among those who could jabber a little Dutch. It is noticeable that the system of espionage is as well developed among the savage tribes as in Austria or Russia. It is a proof of barbarism. Every man in a tribe feels himself bound to tell the chief every thing that comes to his knowledge, and, when questioned by a stranger, either gives answers which exhibit the utmost stupidity, or such as he knows will be agreeable to his chief. I believe that in this way have arisen tales of their inability to count more than ten, as was asserted of the Bechuanas about the very time when Sechele's father counted out one thousand head of cattle as a beginning of the stock of his young son.

In the present case, Sechele, knowing every question put to his people, asked me how they ought to answer. My reply was, "Tell the truth." Every one then declared that no cannon existed there; and our friends, judging the answer by what they themselves would in the circumstances have said, were confirmed in the opinion that the Bakwains actually possessed artillery. This was in some degree beneficial to us, inasmuch as fear prevented any foray in our direction for eight years. During that time no winter passed without one or two tribes in the East country being plundered of both cattle and children by the Boers. The plan pursued is the following: one or two friendly tribes are forced to accompany a party of mounted Boers, and these expeditions can be got up only in the winter, when horses may be used without danger of being lost by disease. When they reach the tribe to be attacked, the friendly natives are ranged in front, to form, as they say, "a shield"; the Boers then coolly fire over their heads till the devoted people flee and leave cattle, wives, and children to the captors. This was done in nine cases during my residence in the interior, and on no occasion was a drop of Boer's blood shed. News of these deeds spread quickly among the Bakwains, and letters were repeatedly sent by the Boers to Sechele, ordering him to come and surrender himself as their vassal, and stop English traders from proceeding into the country with fire-arms for sale. But the discovery of Lake Ngami, hereafter to be described, made the traders come in five-fold greater numbers, and Sechele replied, "I was made an independent chief and placed here by God, and not by you. I was never conquered by Mosilikatze, as those tribes whom you rule over; and the English are my friends. I get every thing I wish from them. I can not hinder them from going where they like." Those who are old enough to remember the threatened invasion of our own island may understand the effect which the constant danger of a Boerish invasion had on the minds of the Bakwains; but no others can conceive how worrying were the messages and threats from the endless self-constituted authorities of the Magaliesberg Boers; and when to all this harassing annoyance was added the scarcity produced by the drought, we could not wonder at, though we felt sorry for, their indisposition to receive instruction.

The myth of the black pot assumed serious proportions. I attempted to benefit the tribes among the Boers of Magaliesberg by placing native teachers at different points. "You must teach the blacks," said Mr. Hendrick Potgeiter, the commandant in chief, "that they are not equal to us." Other Boers told me, "I might as well teach the baboons on the rocks as the Africans," but declined the test which I proposed, namely, to examine whether they or my native attendants could read best. Two of their clergymen came to baptize the children of the Boers; so, supposing these good men would assist me in overcoming the repugnance of their flock to the education of the blacks, I called on them; but my visit ended in a 'ruse' practiced by the Boerish commandant, whereby I was led, by professions of the greatest friendship, to retire to Kolobeng, while a letter passed me by another way to the other missionaries in the south, demanding my instant recall "for lending a cannon to their enemies." The colonial government was also gravely informed that the story was true, and I came to be looked upon as a most suspicious character in consequence.

These notices of the Boers are not intended to produce a sneer at their ignorance, but to excite the compassion of their friends. They are perpetually talking about their laws; but practically theirs is only the law of the strongest. The Bechuanas could never understand the changes which took place in their commandants. "Why, one can never know who is the chief among these Boers. Like the Bushmen, they have no king—they must be the Bushmen of the English." The idea that any tribe of men could be so senseless as not to have an hereditary chief was so absurd to these people, that, in order not to appear equally stupid, I was obliged to tell them that we English were so anxious to preserve the royal blood, that we had made a young lady our chief. This seemed to them a most convincing proof of our sound sense. We shall see farther on the confidence my account of our queen inspired.

The Boers, encouraged by the accession of Mr. Pretorius, determined at last to put a stop to English traders going past Kolobeng, by dispersing the tribe of Bakwains, and expelling all the missionaries. Sir George Cathcart proclaimed the independence of the Boers, the best thing that could have been done had they been between us and the Caffres. A treaty was entered into with these Boers; an article for the free passage of Englishmen to the country beyond, and also another, that no slavery should be allowed in the independent territory, were duly inserted, as expressive of the views of her majesty's government at home. "But what about the missionaries?" inquired the Boers. "YOU MAY DO AS YOU PLEASE WITH THEM," is said to have been the answer of the "Commissioner". This remark, if uttered at all, was probably made in joke: designing men, however, circulated it, and caused the general belief in its accuracy which now prevails all over the country, and doubtless led to the destruction of three mission stations immediately after. The Boers, four hundred in number, were sent by the late Mr. Pretorius to attack the Bakwains in 1852. Boasting that the English had given up all the blacks into their power, and had agreed to aid them in their subjugation by preventing all supplies of ammunition from coming into the Bechuana country, they assaulted the Bakwains, and, besides killing a considerable number of adults, carried off two hundred of our school children into slavery. The natives under Sechele defended themselves till the approach of night enabled them to flee to the mountains; and having in that defense killed a number of the enemy, the very first ever slain in this country by Bechuanas, I received the credit of having taught the tribe to kill Boers! My house, which had stood perfectly secure for years under the protection of the natives, was plundered in revenge. English gentlemen, who had come in the footsteps of Mr. Cumming to hunt in the country beyond, and had deposited large quantities of stores in the same keeping, and upward of eighty head of cattle as relays for the return journeys, were robbed of all, and, when they came back to Kolobeng, found the skeletons of the guardians strewed all over the place. The books of a good library—my solace in our solitude—were not taken away, but handfuls of the leaves were torn out and scattered over the place. My stock of medicines was smashed; and all our furniture and clothing carried off and sold at public auction to pay the expenses of the foray.

I do not mention these things by way of making a pitiful wail over my losses, nor in order to excite commiseration; for, though I do feel sorry for the loss of lexicons, dictionaries, &c., which had been the companions of my boyhood, yet, after all, the plundering only set me entirely free for my expedition to the north, and I have never since had a moment's concern for any thing I left behind. The Boers resolved to shut up the interior, and I determined to open the country, and we shall see who have been most successful in resolution, they or I.

A short sketch of African housekeeping may not prove uninteresting to the reader. The entire absence of shops led us to make every thing we needed from the raw materials. You want bricks to build a house, and must forthwith proceed to the field, cut down a tree, and saw it into planks to make the brick-moulds; the materials for doors and windows, too, are standing in the forest; and, if you want to be respected by the natives, a house of decent dimensions, costing an immense amount of manual labor, must be built. The people can not assist you much; for, though most willing to labor for wages, the Bakwains have a curious inability to make or put things square: like all Bechuanas, their dwellings are made round. In the case of three large houses, erected by myself at different times, every brick and stick had to be put square by my own right hand.

Having got the meal ground, the wife proceeds to make it into bread; an extempore oven is often constructed by scooping out a large hole in an anthill, and using a slab of stone for a door. Another plan, which might be adopted by the Australians to produce something better than their "dampers", is to make a good fire on a level piece of ground, and, when the ground is thoroughly heated, place the dough in a small, short-handled frying-pan, or simply on the hot ashes; invert any sort of metal pot over it, draw the ashes around, and then make a small fire on the top. Dough, mixed with a little leaven from a former baking, and allowed to stand an hour or two in the sun, will by this process become excellent bread.

We made our own butter, a jar serving as a churn; and our own candles by means of moulds; and soap was procured from the ashes of the plant salsola, or from wood-ashes, which in Africa contain so little alkaline matter that the boiling of successive leys has to be continued for a month or six weeks before the fat is saponified. There is not much hardship in being almost entirely dependent on ourselves; there is something of the feeling which must have animated Alexander Selkirk on seeing conveniences springing up before him from his own ingenuity; and married life is all the sweeter when so many comforts emanate directly from the thrifty striving housewife's hands.

To some it may appear quite a romantic mode of life; it is one of active benevolence, such as the good may enjoy at home. Take a single day as a sample of the whole. We rose early, because, however hot the day may have been, the evening, night, and morning at Kolobeng were deliciously refreshing; cool is not the word, where you have neither an increase of cold nor heat to desire, and where you can sit out till midnight with no fear of coughs or rheumatism. After family worship and breakfast between six and seven, we went to keep school for all who would attend—men, women, and children being all invited. School over at eleven o'clock, while the missionary's wife was occupied in domestic matters, the missionary himself had some manual labor as a smith, carpenter, or gardener, according to whatever was needed for ourselves or for the people; if for the latter, they worked for us in the garden, or at some other employment; skilled labor was thus exchanged for the unskilled. After dinner and an hour's rest, the wife attended her infant-school, which the young, who were left by their parents entirely to their own caprice, liked amazingly, and generally mustered a hundred strong; or she varied that with a sewing-school, having classes of girls to learn the art; this, too, was equally well relished. During the day every operation must be superintended, and both husband and wife must labor till the sun declines. After sunset the husband went into the town to converse with any one willing to do so, sometimes on general subjects, at other times on religion. On three nights of the week, as soon as the milking of the cows was over and it had become dark, we had a public religious service, and one of instruction on secular subjects, aided by pictures and specimens. These services were diversified by attending upon the sick and prescribing for them, giving food, and otherwise assisting the poor and wretched. We tried to gain their affections by attending to the wants of the body. The smallest acts of friendship, an obliging word and civil look, are, as St. Xavier thought, no despicable part of the missionary armor. Nor ought the good opinion of the most abject to be uncared for, when politeness may secure it. Their good word in the aggregate forms a reputation which may be well employed in procuring favor for the Gospel. Show kind attention to the reckless opponents of Christianity on the bed of sickness and pain, and they never can become your personal enemies. Here, if any where, love begets love.

When at Kolobeng, during the droughts we were entirely dependent on Kuruman for supplies of corn. Once we were reduced to living on bran, to convert which into fine meal we had to grind it three times over. We were much in want of animal food, which seems to be a greater necessary of life there than vegetarians would imagine. Being alone, we could not divide the butcher-meat of a slaughtered animal with a prospect of getting a return with regularity. Sechele had, by right of chieftainship, the breast of every animal slaughtered either at home or abroad, and he most obligingly sent us a liberal share during the whole period of our sojourn. But these supplies were necessarily so irregular that we were sometimes fain to accept a dish of locusts. These are quite a blessing in the country, so much so that the RAIN-DOCTORS sometimes promised to bring them by their incantations. The locusts are strongly vegetable in taste, the flavor varying with the plants on which they feed. There is a physiological reason why locusts and honey should be eaten together. Some are roasted and pounded into meal, which, eaten with a little salt, is palatable. It will keep thus for months. Boiled, they are disagreeable; but when they are roasted I should much prefer locusts to shrimps, though I would avoid both if possible.

In traveling we sometimes suffered considerably from scarcity of meat, though not from absolute want of food. This was felt more especially by my children; and the natives, to show their sympathy, often gave them a large kind of caterpillar, which they seemed to relish; these insects could not be unwholesome, for the natives devoured them in large quantities themselves.

Another article of which our children partook with eagerness was a very large frog, called "Matlametlo".*

> * The Pyxicephalus adspersus of Dr. Smith.
> Length of head and body, 5-1/2 inches;
> fore legs, 3 inches;
> hind legs, 6 inches.
> Width of head posteriorly, 3 inches;
> of body, 4-1/2 inches.

These enormous frogs, which, when cooked, look like chickens, are supposed by the natives to fall down from thunder-clouds, because after a heavy thunder-shower the pools, which are filled and retain water a few days, become instantly alive with this loud-croaking, pugnacious game. This phenomenon takes place in the driest parts of the desert, and in places where, to an ordinary observer, there is not a sign of life. Having been once benighted in a district of the Kalahari where there was no prospect of getting water for our cattle for a day or two, I was surprised to hear in the fine still evening the croaking of frogs. Walking out until I was certain that the musicians were between me and our fire, I found that they could be merry on nothing else but a prospect of rain. From the Bushmen I afterward learned that the matlametlo makes a hole at the root of certain bushes, and there ensconces himself during the months of drought. As he seldom emerges, a large variety of spider takes advantage of the hole, and makes its web across the orifice. He is thus furnished with a window and screen gratis;

and no one but a Bushman would think of searching beneath a spider's web for a frog. They completely eluded my search on the occasion referred to; and as they rush forth into the hollows filled by the thunder-shower when the rain is actually falling, and the Bechuanas are cowering under their skin garments, the sudden chorus struck up simultaneously from all sides seems to indicate a descent from the clouds.

The presence of these matlametlo in the desert in a time of drought was rather a disappointment, for I had been accustomed to suppose that the note was always emitted by them when they were chin-deep in water. Their music was always regarded in other spots as the most pleasant sound that met the ear after crossing portions of the thirsty desert; and I could fully appreciate the sympathy for these animals shown by Aesop, himself an African, in his fable of the "Boys and the Frogs".

It is remarkable that attempts have not been made to any extent to domesticate some of the noble and useful creatures of Africa in England. The eland, which is the most magnificent of all antelopes, would grace the parks of our nobility more than deer. This animal, from the excellence of its flesh, would be appropriate to our own country; and as there is also a splendid esculent frog nearly as large as a chicken, it would no doubt tend to perpetuate the present alliance if we made a gift of that to France.

The scavenger beetle is one of the most useful of all insects, as it effectually answers the object indicated by the name. Where they abound, as at Kuruman, the villages are sweet and clean, for no sooner are animal excretions dropped than, attracted by the scent, the scavengers are heard coming booming up the wind. They roll away the droppings of cattle at once, in round pieces often as large as billiard-balls; and when they reach a place proper by its softness for the deposit of their eggs and the safety of their young, they dig the soil out from beneath the ball till they have quite let it down and covered it: they then lay their eggs within the mass. While the larvae are growing, they devour the inside of the ball before coming above ground to begin the world for themselves. The beetles with their gigantic balls look like Atlas with the world on his back; only they go backward, and, with their heads down, push with the hind legs, as if a boy should roll a snow-ball with his legs while standing on his head. As we recommend the eland to John Bull, and the gigantic frog to France, we can confidently recommend this beetle to the dirty Italian towns and our own Sanitary Commissioners.

In trying to benefit the tribes living under the Boers of the Cashan Mountains, I twice performed a journey of about three hundred miles to the eastward of Kolobeng. Sechele had become so obnoxious to the Boers that, though anxious to accompany me in my journey, he dared not trust himself among them. This did not arise from the crime of cattle-stealing; for that crime, so common among the Caffres, was never charged against his tribe, nor, indeed, against any Bechuana tribe. It is, in fact, unknown in the country, except during actual warfare. His independence and love of the English were his only faults. In my last journey there, of about two hundred miles, on parting at the River Marikwe he gave me two servants, "to be," as he said, "his arms to serve me," and expressed regret that he could not come himself. "Suppose we went north," I said, "would you come?" He then told me the story of Sebituane having saved his life, and expatiated on the far-famed generosity of that really great man. This was the first time I had thought of crossing the Desert to Lake Ngami.

The conduct of the Boers, who, as will be remembered, had sent a letter designed to procure my removal out of the country, and their well-known settled policy which I have already described, became more fully developed on this than on any former occasion. When I spoke to Mr. Hendrick Potgeiter of the danger of hindering the Gospel of Christ among these poor savages, he became greatly excited, and called one of his followers to answer me. He threatened to attack any tribe that might receive a native teacher, yet he promised to use his influence to prevent those under him from throwing obstacles in our way. I could perceive plainly that nothing more could be done in that direction, so I commenced collecting all the information I could about the desert, with the intention of crossing it, if possible. Sekomi, the chief of the Bamangwato, was acquainted with a route which he kept carefully to himself, because the Lake country abounded in ivory, and he drew large quantities thence periodically at but small cost to himself.

Sechele, who valued highly every thing European, and was always fully alive to his own interest, was naturally anxious to get a share of that inviting field. He was most anxious to visit Sebituane too, partly, perhaps, from a wish to show off his new acquirements, but chiefly, I believe, from having very exalted ideas of the benefits he would derive from the liberality of that renowned chieftain. In age and family Sechele is the elder and superior of Sekomi; for when the original tribe broke up into Bamangwato, Bangwaketse, and Bakwains, the Bakwains retained the hereditary chieftainship; so their chief, Sechele, possesses certain advantages over Sekomi, the chief of the Bamangwato. If the two were traveling or hunting together, Sechele would take, by right, the heads of the game shot by Sekomi.

There are several vestiges, besides, of very ancient partitions and lordships of tribes. The elder brother of Sechele's father, becoming blind, gave over the chieftainship to Sechele's father. The descendants of this man pay no tribute to Sechele, though he is the actual ruler, and superior to the head of that family; and Sechele, while in every other respect supreme, calls him Kosi, or Chief. The other tribes will not begin to eat the early pumpkins of a new crop until they hear that the Bahurutse have "bitten it", and there is a public ceremony on the occasion—the son of the chief being the first to taste of the new harvest.

Sechele, by my advice, sent men to Sekomi, asking leave for me to pass along his path, accompanying the request with the present of an ox. Sekomi's mother, who possesses great influence over him, refused permission, because she had not been propitiated. This produced a fresh message; and the most honorable man in the Bakwain tribe, next to Sechele, was sent with an ox for both Sekomi and his mother. This, too, was met by refusal. It was said, "The Matebele, the mortal enemies of the Bechuanas, are in the direction of the lake, and, should they kill the white man, we shall incur great blame from all his nation."

The exact position of the Lake Ngami had, for half a century at least, been correctly pointed out by the natives, who had visited it when rains were more copious in the Desert than in more recent times, and many attempts had been made to reach it by passing through the Desert in the direction indicated; but it was found impossible, even for Griquas, who, having some Bushman blood in them, may be supposed more capable of enduring thirst than Europeans. It was clear, then, that our only chance of success was by going round, instead of through, the Desert. The best time for the attempt would have been about the end of the rainy season, in March or April, for then we should have been likely to meet with pools of rainwater, which always dry up during the rainless winter. I communicated my intention to an African traveler, Colonel Steele, then aid-de-camp to the Marquis of Tweedale at Madras, and he made it known to two other gentlemen, whose friendship we had gained during their African travel, namely, Major Vardon and Mr. Oswell. All of these gentlemen were so enamored with African hunting and African discovery that the two former must have envied the latter his good fortune in being able to leave India to undertake afresh the pleasures and pains of desert life. I believe Mr. Oswell came from his high position at a very considerable pecuniary sacrifice, and with no other end in view but to extend the boundaries of geographical knowledge. Before I knew of his coming, I had arranged that the payment for the guides furnished by Sechele should be the loan of my wagon, to bring back whatever ivory he might obtain from the chief at the lake. When, at last, Mr. Oswell came, bringing Mr. Murray with him, he undertook to defray the entire expenses of the guides, and fully executed his generous intention.

Sechele himself would have come with us, but, fearing that the much-talked-of assault of the Boers might take place during our absence, and blame be attached to me for taking him away, I dissuaded him against it by saying that he knew Mr. Oswell "would be as determined as himself to get through the Desert."

Before narrating the incidents of this journey, I may give some account of the great Kalahari Desert, in order that the reader may understand in some degree the nature of the difficulties we had to encounter.

The space from the Orange River in the south, lat. 29 Degrees, to Lake Ngami in the north, and from about 24 Degrees east long. to near the west coast, has been called a desert simply because it contains no running water, and very little water in wells. It is by no means destitute of vegetation and inhabitants, for it is covered with grass and a great variety of creeping plants; besides which there are large patches of bushes, and even trees. It is remarkably flat, but interesected in different parts by the beds of ancient rivers; and prodigious herds of certain antelopes, which require little or no water, roam over the trackless plains. The inhabitants, Bushmen and Bakalahari, prey on the game and on the countless rodentia and small species of the feline race which subsist on these. In general, the soil is light-colored soft sand, nearly pure silica. The beds of the ancient rivers contain much alluvial soil; and as that is baked hard by the burning sun, rain-water stands in pools in some of them for several months in the year.

The quantity of grass which grows on this remarkable region is astonishing, even to those who are familiar with India. It usually rises in tufts with bare spaces between, or the intervals are occupied by creeping plants, which, having their roots buried far beneath the soil, feel little the effects of the scorching sun. The number of these which have tuberous roots is very great; and their structure is intended to supply nutriment and moisture, when, during the long droughts, they can be obtained nowhere else. Here we have an example of a plant, not generally tuber-bearing, becoming so under circumstances where that appendage is necessary to act as a reservoir for preserving its life; and the same thing occurs in Angola to a species of grape-bearing vine, which is so furnished for the same purpose. The plant to which I at present refer is one of the cucurbitaceae, which bears a small, scarlet-colored, eatable cucumber. Another plant, named Leroshua, is a blessing to the inhabitants of the Desert. We see a small plant with linear leaves, and a stalk not thicker than a crow's quill; on digging down a foot or eighteen inches beneath, we come to a tuber, often as large as the head of a young child; when the rind is removed, we find it to be a mass of cellular tissue, filled with fluid much like that in a young turnip. Owing to the depth beneath the soil at which it is found, it is generally deliciously cool and refreshing. Another kind, named Mokuri, is seen in other parts of the country, where long-continued heat parches the soil. This plant is an herbaceous creeper, and deposits under ground a number of tubers, some as large as a man's head, at spots in a circle a yard or more, horizontally, from the stem. The natives strike the ground on the circumference of the circle with stones, till, by hearing a difference of sound, they know the water-bearing tuber to be beneath. They then dig down a foot or so, and find it.

But the most surprising plant of the Desert is the "Kengwe or Keme" ('Cucumis caffer'), the watermelon. In years when more than the usual quantity of rain falls, vast tracts of the country are literally covered with these melons; this was the case annually when the fall of rain was greater than it is now, and the Bakwains sent trading parties every year to the lake. It happens commonly once every ten or eleven years, and for the last three times its occurrence has coincided with an extraordinarily wet season. Then animals of every sort and name, including man, rejoice in the rich supply. The elephant, true lord of the forest, revels in this fruit, and so do the different species of rhinoceros, although naturally so diverse in their choice of pasture. The various kinds of antelopes feed on them with equal avidity, and lions, hyaenas, jackals, and mice, all seem to know and appreciate the common blessing. These melons are not, however, all of them eatable; some are sweet, and others so bitter that the whole are named by the Boers the "bitter watermelon". The natives select them by striking one melon after another with a hatchet, and applying the tongue to the gashes. They thus readily distinguish between the bitter and sweet. The bitter are deleterious, but the sweet are quite wholesome. This peculiarity of one species of plant bearing both sweet and bitter fruits occurs also in a red, eatable cucumber, often met with in the country. It is about four inches long, and about an inch and a half in diameter. It is of a bright scarlet color when ripe. Many are bitter, others quite sweet. Even melons in a garden may be made bitter by a few bitter kengwe in the vicinity. The bees convey the pollen from one to the other.

The human inhabitants of this tract of country consist of Bushmen and Bakalahari. The former are probably the aborigines of the southern portion of the continent, the latter the remnants of the first emigration of Bechuanas. The Bushmen live in the Desert from choice, the Bakalahari from compulsion, and both possess an intense love of liberty. The Bushmen are exceptions in language, race, habits, and appearance. They are the only real nomads in the country; they never cultivate the soil, nor rear any domestic animal save wretched dogs. They are so intimately acquainted with the habits of the game that they follow them in their migrations, and prey upon them from place to place, and thus prove as complete a check upon their inordinate increase as the other carnivora. The chief subsistence of the Bushmen is the flesh of game, but that is eked out by what the women collect of roots and beans, and fruits of the Desert. Those who inhabit the hot sandy plains of the Desert possess generally thin, wiry forms, capable of great exertion and of severe privations. Many are of low stature, though not dwarfish; the specimens brought to Europe have been selected, like costermongers' dogs, on account of their extreme ugliness; consequently, English ideas of the whole tribe are formed in the same way as if the ugliest specimens of the English were exhibited in Africa as characteristic of the entire British nation. That they are like baboons is in some degree true, just as these and other simiae are in some points frightfully human.

The Bakalahari are traditionally reported to be the oldest of the Bechuana tribes, and they are said to have possessed enormous herds of the large horned cattle mentioned by Bruce, until they were despoiled of them and driven into the Desert by a fresh migration of their own nation. Living ever since on the same plains with the Bushmen, subjected to the same influences of climate, enduring the same thirst, and subsisting on similar food for centuries, they seem to supply a standing proof that locality is not always sufficient of itself to account for difference in races. The Bakalahari retain in undying vigor the Bechuana love for agriculture and domestic animals. They hoe their gardens annually, though often all they can hope for is a supply of melons and pumpkins. And they carefully rear small herds of goats, though I have seen them lift water for them out of small wells with a bit of ostrich egg-shell, or by spoonfuls. They generally attach themselves to influential men in the different Bechuana tribes living adjacent to their desert home, in order to obtain supplies of spears, knives, tobacco, and dogs, in exchange for the skins of the animals they may kill. These are small carnivora of the feline species, including two species of jackal, the dark and the golden; the former, "motlose" ('Megalotis capensis' or 'Cape fennec'), has the warmest fur the country yields; the latter, "pukuye" ('Canis mesomelas' and 'C. aureus'), is very handsome when made into the skin mantle called kaross. Next in value follow the "tsipa" or small ocelot ('Felis nigripes'), the "tuane" or lynx, the wild cat, the spotted cat, and other small animals. Great numbers of 'puti' ('duiker') and 'puruhuru' ('steinbuck') skins are got too, besides those of lions, leopards, panthers, and hyaenas. During the time I was in the Bechuana country, between twenty and thirty thousand skins were made up into karosses; part of them were worn by the inhabitants, and part sold to traders: many, I believe, find their way to China. The Bakwains bought tobacco from the eastern tribes, then purchased skins with it from the Bakalahari, tanned them, and sewed them into karosses, then went south to purchase heifer-calves with them, cows being the highest form of riches known, as I have often noticed from their asking "if Queen Victoria had many cows." The compact they enter into is mutually beneficial, but injustice and wrong are often perpetrated by one tribe of Bechuanas going among the Bakalahari of another tribe, and compelling them to deliver up the skins which they may be keeping for their friends. They are a timid race, and in bodily development often resemble the aborigines of Australia. They have thin legs and arms, and large, protruding abdomens, caused by the coarse, indigestible food they eat. Their children's eyes lack lustre. I never saw them at play. A few Bechuanas may go into a village of Bakalahari, and domineer over the whole with impunity; but when these same adventurers meet the Bushmen, they are fain to change their manners to fawning sycophancy; they know that, if the request for tobacco is refused, these free sons of the Desert may settle the point as to its possession by a poisoned arrow.

The dread of visits from Bechuanas of strange tribes causes the Bakalahari to choose their residences far from water; and they not unfrequently hide their supplies by filling the pits with sand and making a fire over the spot. When they wish to draw water for use, the women come with twenty or thirty of their water-vessels in a bag or net on their backs. These water-vessels consist of ostrich egg-shells, with a hole in the end of each, such as would admit one's finger. The women tie a bunch of grass to one end of a reed about two feet long, and insert it in a hole dug as deep as the arm will reach; then ram down the wet sand firmly round it. Applying the mouth to the free end of the reed, they form a vacuum in the grass beneath, in which the water collects, and in a short time rises into the mouth. An egg-shell is placed on the ground alongside the reed, some inches below the mouth of the sucker. A straw guides the water into the hole of the vessel, as she draws mouthful after mouthful from below. The water is made to pass along the outside, not through the straw. If any one will attempt to squirt water into a bottle placed some distance below his mouth, he will soon perceive the wisdom of the Bushwoman's contrivance for giving the stream direction by means of a straw. The whole stock of water is thus passed through the woman's mouth as a pump, and, when taken home, is carefully buried. I have come into villages where, had we acted a domineering part, and rummaged every hut, we should have found nothing; but by sitting down quietly, and waiting with patience until the villagers were led to form a favorable opinion of us, a woman would bring out a shellful of the precious fluid from I know not where.

The so-called Desert, it may be observed, is by no means a useless tract of country. Besides supporting multitudes of both small and large animals, it sends something to the market of the world, and has proved a refuge to many a fugitive tribe—to the Bakalahari first, and to the other Bechuanas in turn—as their lands were overrun by the tribe of true Caffres, called Matebele. The Bakwains, the Bangwaketze, and the Bamangwato all fled thither; and the Matebele marauders, who came from the well-watered east, perished by hundreds in their attempts to follow them. One of the Bangwaketze chiefs, more wily than the rest, sent false guides to lead them on a track where, for hundreds of miles, not a drop of water could be found, and they perished in consequence. Many Bakwains perished too. Their old men, who could have told us ancient stories, perished in these flights. An intelligent Mokwain related to me how the Bushmen effectually balked a party of his tribe which lighted on their village in a state of burning thirst. Believing, as he said, that nothing human could subsist without water, they demanded some, but were coolly told by these Bushmen that they had none, and never drank any. Expecting to find them out, they resolved to watch them night and day. They persevered for some days, thinking that at last the water must come forth; but, notwithstanding their watchfulness, kept alive by most tormenting thirst, the Bakwains were compelled to exclaim, "Yak! yak! these are not men; let us go." Probably the Bushmen had been subsisting on a store hidden under ground, which had eluded the vigilance of their visitors.

Chapter 3

Departure from Kolobeng, 1st June, 1849—Companions—Our Route—Abundance of Grass—Serotli, a Fountain in the Desert—Mode of digging Wells—The Eland—Animals of the Desert—The Hyaena—The Chief Sekomi—Dangers—The wandering Guide—Cross Purposes—Slow Progress—Want of Water—Capture of a Bushwoman—The Salt-pan at Nchokotsa—The Mirage—Reach the River Zouga—The Quakers of Africa—Discovery of Lake Ngami, 1st August, 1849—Its Extent—Small Depth of Water—Position as the Reservoir of a great River System—The Bamangwato and their Chief—Desire to visit Sebituane, the Chief of the Makololo—Refusal of Lechulatebe to furnish us with Guides—Resolve to return to the Cape—The Banks of the Zouga—Pitfalls—Trees of the District—Elephants—New Species of Antelope—Fish in the Zouga.

Such was the desert which we were now preparing to cross—a region formerly of terror to the Bechuanas from the numbers of serpents which infested it and fed on the different kinds of mice, and from the intense thirst which these people often endured when their water-vessels were insufficient for the distances to be traveled over before reaching the wells.

Just before the arrival of my companions, a party of the people of the lake came to Kolobeng, stating that they were sent by Lechulatebe, the chief, to ask me to visit that country. They brought such flaming accounts of the quantities of ivory to be found there (cattle-pens made of elephants' tusks of enormous size, &c.), that the guides of the Bakwains were quite as eager to succeed in reaching the lake as any one of us could desire. This was fortunate, as we knew the way the strangers had come was impassable for wagons.

Messrs. Oswell and Murray came at the end of May, and we all made a fair start for the unknown region on the 1st of June, 1849. Proceeding northward, and passing through a range of tree-covered hills to Shokuane, formerly the residence of the Bakwains, we soon after entered on the high road to the Bamangwato, which lies generally in the bed of an ancient river or wady that must formerly have flowed N. to S. The adjacent country is perfectly flat, but covered with open forest and bush, with abundance of grass; the trees generally are a kind of acacia called "Monato", which appears a little to the south of this region, and is common as far as Angola. A large caterpillar, called "Nato", feeds by night on the leaves of these trees, and comes down by day to bury itself at the root in the sand, in order to escape the piercing rays of the sun. The people dig for it there, and are fond of it when roasted, on account of its pleasant vegetable taste. When about to pass into the chrysalis state, it buries itself in the soil, and is sometimes sought for as food even then. If left undisturbed, it comes forth as a beautiful butterfly: the transmutation was sometimes employed by me with good effect when speaking with the natives, as an illustration of our own great change and resurrection.

The soil is sandy, and there are here and there indications that at spots which now afford no water whatever there were formerly wells and cattle stations.

Boatlanama, our next station, is a lovely spot in the otherwise dry region. The wells from which we had to lift out the water for our cattle are deep, but they were well filled. A few villages of Bakalahari were found near them, and great numbers of pallahs, springbucks, Guinea-fowl, and small monkeys.

Lopepe came next. This place afforded another proof of the desiccation of the country. The first time I passed it, Lopepe was a large pool with a stream flowing out of it to the south; now it was with difficulty we could get our cattle watered by digging down in the bottom of a well.

At Mashue—where we found a never-failing supply of pure water in a sandstone rocky hollow—we left the road to the Bamangwato hills, and struck away to the north into the Desert. Having watered the cattle at a well called Lobotani, about N.W. of Bamangwato, we next proceeded to a real Kalahari fountain, called Serotli. The country around is covered with bushes and trees of a kind of leguminosae, with lilac flowers. The soil is soft white sand, very trying to the strength of the oxen, as the wheels sink into it over the felloes and drag heavily. At Serotli we found only a few hollows like those made by the buffalo and rhinoceros when they roll themselves in the mud. In a corner of one of these there appeared water, which would have been quickly lapped up by our dogs, had we not driven them away. And yet this was all the apparent supply for some eighty oxen, twenty horses, and about a score of men. Our guide, Ramotobi, who had spent his youth in the Desert, declared that, though appearances were against us, there was plenty of water at hand. We had our misgivings, for the spades were soon produced; but our guides, despising such new-fangled aid, began in good earnest to scrape out the sand with their hands. The only water we had any promise of for the next seventy miles—that is, for a journey of three days with the wagons—was to be got here. By the aid of both spades and fingers two of the holes were cleared out, so as to form pits six feet deep and about as many broad. Our guides were especially earnest in their injunctions to us not to break through the hard stratum of sand at the bottom, because they knew, if it were broken through, "the water would go away." They are quite correct, for the water seems to lie on this flooring of incipient sandstone. The value of the advice was proved in the case of an Englishman whose wits were none of the brightest, who, disregarding it, dug through the sandy stratum in the wells at Mohotluani: the water immediately flowed away downward, and the well became useless. When we came to the stratum, we found that the water flowed in on all sides close to the line where the soft sand came in contact with it. Allowing it to collect, we had enough for the horses that evening; but as there was not sufficient for the oxen, we sent them back to Lobotani, where, after thirsting four full days (ninety-six hours), they got a good supply. The horses were kept by us as necessary to procure game for the sustenance of our numerous party. Next morning we found the water had flowed in faster than at first, as it invariably does in these reservoirs, owing to the passages widening by the flow. Large quantities of the sand come into the well with the water, and in the course of a few days the supply, which may be equal to the wants of a few men only, becomes sufficient for oxen as well. In these sucking-places the Bakalahari get their supplies; and as they are generally in the hollows of ancient river-beds, they are probably the deposits from rains gravitating thither; in some cases they may be the actual fountains, which, though formerly supplying the river's flow, now no longer rise to the surface.

    Here, though the water was perfectly inaccessible to elands, large numbers of these fine animals fed around us; and, when killed, they were not only in good condition, but their stomachs actually contained considerable quantities of water.

    I examined carefully the whole alimentary canal, in order to see if there were any peculiarity which might account for the fact that this animal can subsist for months together without drinking, but found nothing. Other animals, such as the duiker ('Cephalopus mergens') or puti (of the Bechuanas), the steinbuck ('Tragulus rupestris') or puruhuru, the gemsbuck ('Oryx capensis') or kukama, and the porcupine ('Hystrix cristata'), are all able to subsist without water for many months at a time by living on bulbs and tubers containing moisture. They have sharp-pointed hoofs well adapted for digging, and there is little difficulty in comprehending their mode of subsistence. Some animals, on the other hand, are never seen but in the vicinity of water. The presence of the rhinoceros, of the buffalo and gnu ('Catoblepas gnu'), of the giraffe, the zebra, and pallah ('Antilope melampus'), is always a certain indication of water being within a distance of seven or eight miles; but one may see hundreds of elands ('Boselaphus oreas'), gemsbuck, the tolo or koodoo ('Strepsiceros capensis'), also springbucks ('Gazella euchore') and ostriches, without being warranted thereby in inferring the presence of water within thirty or forty miles. Indeed, the sleek, fat condition of the eland in such circumstances would not remove the apprehension of perishing by thirst from the mind of even a native. I believe, however, that these animals can subsist only where there is some moisture in the vegetation on which they feed; for in one year of unusual drought we saw herds of elands and flocks of ostriches crowding to the Zouga from the Desert, and very many of the latter were killed in pitfalls on the banks. As long as there is any sap in the pasturage they seldom need water. But should a traveler see the "spoor" of a rhinoceros, or buffalo, or zebra, he would at once follow it up, well assured that before he had gone many miles he would certainly reach water.

In the evening of our second day at Serotli, a hyaena, appearing suddenly among the grass, succeeded in raising a panic among our cattle. This false mode of attack is the plan which this cowardly animal always adopts. His courage resembles closely that of a turkey-cock. He will bite, if an animal is running away; but if the animal stand still, so does he. Seventeen of our draught oxen ran away, and in their flight went right into the hands of Sekomi, whom, from his being unfriendly to our success, we had no particular wish to see. Cattle-stealing, such as in the circumstances might have occurred in Caffraria, is here unknown; so Sekomi sent back our oxen, and a message strongly dissuading us against attempting the Desert. "Where are you going? You will be killed by the sun and thirst, and then all the white men will blame me for not saving you." This was backed by a private message from his mother. "Why do you pass me? I always made the people collect to hear the word that you have got. What guilt have I, that you pass without looking at me?" We replied by assuring the messengers that the white men would attribute our deaths to our own stupidity and "hard-headedness" (tlogo, e thata), "as we did not intend to allow our companions and guides to return till they had put us into our graves." We sent a handsome present to Sekomi, and a promise that, if he allowed the Bakalahari to keep the wells open for us, we would repeat the gift on our return.

After exhausting all his eloquence in fruitless attempts to persuade us to return, the under-chief, who headed the party of Sekomi's messengers, inquired, "Who is taking them?" Looking round, he exclaimed, with a face expressive of the most unfeigned disgust, "It is Ramotobi!" Our guide belonged to Sekomi's tribe, but had fled to Sechele; as fugitives in this country are always well received, and may even afterward visit the tribe from which they had escaped, Ramotobi was in no danger, though doing that which he knew to be directly opposed to the interests of his own chief and tribe.

All around Serotli the country is perfectly flat, and composed of soft white sand. There is a peculiar glare of bright sunlight from a cloudless sky over the whole scene; and one clump of trees and bushes, with open spaces between, looks so exactly like another, that if you leave the wells, and walk a quarter of a mile in any direction, it is difficult to return. Oswell and Murray went out on one occasion to get an eland, and were accompanied by one of the Bakalahari. The perfect sameness of the country caused even this son of the Desert to lose his way; a most puzzling conversation forthwith ensued between them and their guide. One of the most common phrases of the people is "Kia itumela", I thank you, or I am pleased; and the gentlemen were both quite familiar with it, and with the word "metse", water. But there is a word very similar in sound, "Kia timela", I am wandering; its perfect is "Ki timetse", I have wandered. The party had been roaming about, perfectly lost, till the sun went down; and, through their mistaking the verb "wander" for "to be pleased", and "water", the colloquy went on at intervals during the whole bitterly cold night in somewhat the following style:

"Where are the wagons?"

REAL ANSWER. "I don't know. I have wandered. I never wandered before. I am quite lost."

SUPPOSED ANSWER. "I don't know I want water. I am glad, I am quite pleased. I am thankful to you."

"Take us to the wagons, and you will get plenty of water."

REAL ANSWER (looking vacantly around). "How did I wander? Perhaps the well is there, perhaps not. I don't know. I have wandered."

SUPPOSED ANSWER. "Something about thanks; he says he is pleased, and mentions water again." The guide's vacant stare while trying to remember is thought to indicate mental imbecility, and the repeated thanks were supposed to indicate a wish to deprecate their wrath.

"Well, Livingstone HAS played us a pretty trick, giving us in charge of an idiot. Catch us trusting him again. What can this fellow mean by his thanks and talk about water? Oh, you born fool! take us to the wagons, and you will get both meat and water. Wouldn't a thrashing bring him to his senses again?" "No, no, for then he will run away, and we shall be worse off than we are now."

The hunters regained the wagons next day by their own sagacity, which becomes wonderfully quickened by a sojourn in the Desert; and we enjoyed a hearty laugh on the explanation of their midnight colloquies. Frequent mistakes of this kind occur. A man may tell his interpreter to say that he is a member of the family of the chief of the white men; "YES, YOU SPEAK LIKE A CHIEF," is the reply, meaning, as they explain it, that a chief may talk nonsense without any one daring to contradict him. They probably have ascertained, from that same interpreter, that this relative of the white chief is very poor, having scarcely any thing in his wagon.

I sometimes felt annoyed at the low estimation in which some of my hunting friends were held; for, believing that the chase is eminently conducive to the formation of a brave and noble character, and that the contest with wild beasts is well adapted for fostering that coolness in emergencies, and active presence of mind, which we all admire, I was naturally anxious that a higher estimate of my countrymen should be formed in the native mind. "Have these hunters, who come so far and work so hard, no meat at home?"—"Why, these men are rich, and could slaughter oxen every day of their lives."—"And yet they come here, and endure so much thirst for the sake of this dry meat, none of which is equal to beef?"—"Yes, it is for the sake of play besides" (the idea of sport not being in the language). This produces a laugh, as much as to say, "Ah! you know better;" or, "Your friends are fools." When they can get a man to kill large quantities of game for them, whatever HE may think of himself or of his achievements, THEY pride themselves in having adroitly turned to good account the folly of an itinerant butcher.

The water having at last flowed into the wells we had dug in sufficient quantity to allow a good drink to all our cattle, we departed from Serotli in the afternoon; but as the sun, even in winter, which it now was, is always very powerful by day, the wagons were dragged but slowly through the deep, heavy sand, and we advanced only six miles before sunset. We could only travel in the mornings and evenings, as a single day in the hot sun and heavy sand would have knocked up the oxen. Next day we passed Pepacheu (white tufa), a hollow lined with tufa, in which water sometimes stands, but it was now dry; and at night our trocheamer* showed that we had made but twenty-five miles from Serotli.

> *This is an instrument which, when fastened on the wagon-wheel, records the number of revolutions made. By multiplying this number by the circumference of the wheel, the actual distance traveled over is at once ascertained.

Ramotobi was angry at the slowness of our progress, and told us that, as the next water was three days in front, if we traveled so slowly we should never get there at all. The utmost endeavors of the servants, cracking their whips, screaming and beating, got only nineteen miles out of the poor beasts. We had thus proceeded forty-four miles from Serotli; and the oxen were more exhausted by the soft nature of the country, and the thirst, than if they had traveled double the distance over a hard road containing supplies of water: we had, as far as we could judge, still thirty miles more of the same dry work before us. At this season the grass becomes so dry as to crumble to powder in the hands; so the poor beasts stood wearily chewing, without taking a single fresh mouthful, and lowing painfully at the smell of water in our vessels in the wagons. We were all determined to succeed; so we endeavored to save the horses by sending them forward with the guide, as a means of making a desperate effort in case the oxen should fail. Murray went forward with them, while Oswell and I remained to bring the wagons on their trail as far as the cattle could drag them, intending then to send the oxen forward too.

The horses walked quickly away from us; but, on the morning of the third day, when we imagined the steeds must be near the water, we discovered them just alongside the wagons. The guide, having come across the fresh footprints of some Bushmen who had gone in an opposite direction to that which we wished to go, turned aside to follow them. An antelope had been ensnared in one of the Bushmen's pitfalls. Murray followed Ramotobi most trustingly along the Bushmen's spoor, though that led them away from the water we were in search of; witnessed the operation of slaughtering, skinning, and cutting up the antelope; and then, after a hard day's toil, found himself close upon the wagons! The knowledge still retained by Ramotobi of the trackless waste of scrub, through which we were now passing, seemed admirable. For sixty or seventy miles beyond Serotli, one clump of bushes and trees seemed exactly like another; but, as we walked together this morning, he remarked, "When we come to that hollow we shall light upon the highway of Sekomi; and beyond that again lies the River Mokoko;" which, though we passed along it, I could not perceive to be a river-bed at all.

After breakfast, some of the men, who had gone forward on a little path with some footprints of water-loving animals upon it, returned with the joyful tidings of "metse", water, exhibiting the mud on their knees in confirmation of the news being true. It does one's heart good to see the thirsty oxen rush into a pool of delicious rain-water, as this was. In they dash until the water is deep enough to be nearly level with their throat, and then they stand drawing slowly in the long, refreshing mouthfuls, until their formerly collapsed sides distend as if they would burst. So much do they imbibe, that a sudden jerk, when they come out on the bank, makes some of the water run out again from their mouths; but, as they have been days without food too, they very soon commence to graze, and of grass there is always abundance every where. This pool was called Mathuluani; and thankful we were to have obtained so welcome a supply of water.

After giving the cattle a rest at this spot, we proceeded down the dry bed of the River Mokoko. The name refers to the water-bearing stratum before alluded to; and in this ancient bed it bears enough of water to admit of permanent wells in several parts of it. We had now the assurance from Ramotobi that we should suffer no more from thirst. Twice we found rain-water in the Mokoko before we reached Mokokonyani, where the water, generally below ground elsewhere, comes to the surface in a bed of tufa. The adjacent country is all covered with low, thorny scrub, with grass, and here and there clumps of the "wait-a-bit thorn", or 'Acacia detinens'. At Lotlakani (a little reed), another spring three miles farther down, we met with the first Palmyra trees which we had seen in South Africa; they were twenty-six in number.

The ancient Mokoko must have been joined by other rivers below this, for it becomes very broad, and spreads out into a large lake, of which the lake we were now in search of formed but a very small part. We observed that, wherever an ant-eater had made his hole, shells were thrown out with the earth, identical with those now alive in the lake.

When we left the Mokoko, Ramotobi seemed, for the first time, to be at a loss as to which direction to take. He had passed only once away to the west of the Mokoko, the scenes of his boyhood. Mr. Oswell, while riding in front of the wagons, happened to spy a Bushwoman running away in a bent position, in order to escape observation. Thinking it to be a lion, he galloped up to her. She thought herself captured, and began to deliver up her poor little property, consisting of a few traps made of cords; but, when I explained that we only wanted water, and would pay her if she led us to it, she consented to conduct us to a spring. It was then late in the afternoon, but she walked briskly before our horses for eight miles, and showed us the water of Nchokotsa. After leading us to the water, she wished to go away home, if indeed she had any—she had fled from a party of her countrymen, and was now living far from all others with her husband—but as it was now dark, we wished her to remain. As she believed herself still a captive, we thought she might slip away by night; so, in order that she should not go away with the impression that we were dishonest, we gave her a piece of meat and a good large bunch of beads; at the sight of the latter she burst into a merry laugh, and remained without suspicion.

At Nchokotsa we came upon the first of a great number of salt-pans, covered with an efflorescence of lime, probably the nitrate. A thick belt of mopane-trees (a 'Bauhinia') hides this salt-pan, which is twenty miles in circumference, entirely from the view of a person coming from the southeast; and, at the time the pan burst upon our view, the setting sun was casting a beautiful blue haze over the white incrustations, making the whole look exactly like a lake. Oswell threw his hat up in the air at the sight, and shouted out a huzza which made the poor Bushwoman and the Bakwains think him mad. I was a little behind him, and was as completely deceived by it as he; but, as we had agreed to allow each other to behold the lake at the same instant, I felt a little chagrined that he had, unintentionally, got the first glance. We had no idea that the long-looked-for lake was still more than three hundred miles distant. One reason of our mistake was, that the River Zouga was often spoken of by the same name as the lake, viz., Noka ea Batletli ("River of the Batletli").

The mirage on these salinas was marvelous. It is never, I believe, seen in perfection, except over such saline incrustations. Here not a particle of imagination was necessary for realizing the exact picture of large collections of water; the waves danced along above, and the shadows of the trees were vividly reflected beneath the surface in such an admirable manner, that the loose cattle, whose thirst had not been slaked sufficiently by the very brackish water of Nchokotsa, with the horses, dogs, and even the Hottentots ran off toward the deceitful pools. A herd of zebras in the mirage looked so exactly like elephants that Oswell began to saddle a horse in order to hunt them; but a sort of break in the haze dispelled the illusion. Looking to the west and northwest from Nchokotsa, we could see columns of black smoke, exactly like those from a steam-engine, rising to the clouds, and were assured that these arose from the burning reeds of the Noka ea Batletli.

On the 4th of July we went forward on horseback toward what we supposed to be the lake, and again and again did we seem to see it; but at last we came to the veritable water of the Zouga, and found it to be a river running to the N.E. A village of Bakurutse lay on the opposite bank; these live among Batletli, a tribe having a click in their language, and who were found by Sebituane to possess large herds of the great horned cattle. They seem allied to the Hottentot family. Mr. Oswell, in trying to cross the river, got his horse bogged in the swampy bank. Two Bakwains and I managed to get over by wading beside a fishing-weir. The people were friendly, and informed us that this water came out of the Ngami. This news gladdened all our hearts, for we now felt certain of reaching our goal. We might, they said, be a moon on the way; but we had the River Zouga at our feet, and by following it we should at last reach the broad water.

Next day, when we were quite disposed to be friendly with every one, two of the Bamangwato, who had been sent on before us by Sekomi to drive away all the Bushmen and Bakalahari from our path, so that they should not assist or guide us, came and sat down by our fire. We had seen their footsteps fresh in the way, and they had watched our slow movements forward, and wondered to see how we, without any Bushmen, found our way to the waters. This was the first time they had seen Ramotobi. "You have reached the river now," said they; and we, quite disposed to laugh at having won the game, felt no ill-will to any one. They seemed to feel no enmity to us either; but, after an apparently friendly conversation, proceeded to fulfill to the last the instructions of their chief. Ascending the Zouga in our front, they circulated the report that our object was to plunder all the tribes living on the river and lake; but when they had got half way up the river, the principal man sickened of fever, turned back some distance, and died. His death had a good effect, for the villagers connected it with the injury he was attempting to do to us. They all saw through Sekomi's reasons for wishing us to fail in our attempt; and though they came to us at first armed, kind and fair treatment soon produced perfect confidence.

When we had gone up the bank of this beautiful river about ninety-six miles from the point where we first struck it, and understood that we were still a considerable distance from the Ngami, we left all the oxen and wagons, except Mr. Oswell's, which was the smallest, and one team, at Ngabisane, in the hope that they would be recruited for the home journey, while we made a push for the lake. The Bechuana chief of the Lake region, who had sent men to Sechele, now sent orders to all the people on the river to assist us, and we were received by the Bakoba, whose language clearly shows that they bear an affinity to the tribes in the north. They call themselves Bayeiye, i.e., men; but the Bechuanas call them Bakoba, which contains somewhat of the idea of slaves. They have never been known to fight, and, indeed, have a tradition that their forefathers, in their first essays at war, made their bows of the Palma Christi, and, when these broke, they gave up fighting altogether. They have invariably submitted to the rule of every horde which has overrun the countries adjacent to the rivers on which they specially love to dwell. They are thus the Quakers of the body politic in Africa.

A long time after the period of our visit, the chief of the Lake, thinking to make soldiers of them, took the trouble to furnish them with shields. "Ah! we never had these before; that is the reason we have always succumbed. Now we will fight." But a marauding party came from the Makololo, and our "Friends" at once paddled quickly, night and day, down the Zouga, never daring to look behind them till they reached the end of the river, at the point where we first saw it.

The canoes of these inland sailors are truly primitive craft: they are hollowed out of the trunks of single trees by means of iron adzes; and if the tree has a bend, so has the canoe. I liked the frank and manly bearing of these men, and, instead of sitting in the wagon, preferred a seat in one of the canoes. I found they regarded their rude vessels as the Arab does his camel. They have always fires in them, and prefer sleeping in them while on a journey to spending the night on shore. "On land you have lions," say they, "serpents, hyaenas, and your enemies; but in your canoe, behind a bank of reed, nothing can harm you." Their submissive disposition leads to their villages being frequently visited by hungry strangers. We had a pot on the fire in the canoe by the way, and when we drew near the villages devoured the contents. When fully satisfied ourselves, I found we could all look upon any intruders with perfect complacency, and show the pot in proof of having devoured the last morsel.

While ascending in this way the beautifully-wooded river, we came to a large stream flowing into it. This was the River Tamunak'le. I inquired whence it came. "Oh, from a country full of rivers—so many no one can tell their number—and full of large trees." This was the first confirmation of statements I had heard from the Bakwains who had been with Sebituane, that the country beyond was not "the large sandy plateau" of the philosophers. The prospect of a highway capable of being traversed by boats to an entirely unexplored and very populous region, grew from that time forward stronger and stronger in my mind; so much so that, when we actually came to the lake, this idea occupied such a large portion of my mental vision that the actual discovery seemed of but little importance. I find I wrote, when the emotions caused by the magnificent prospects of the new country were first awakened in my breast, that they "might subject me to the charge of enthusiasm, a charge which I wished I deserved, as nothing good or great had ever been accomplished in the world without it."*

* *Letters published by the Royal Geographical Society.*
Read 11th February and 8th April, 1850.

Twelve days after our departure from the wagons at Ngabisane we came to the northeast end of Lake Ngami; and on the 1st of August, 1849, we went down together to the broad part, and, for the first time, this fine-looking sheet of water was beheld by Europeans. The direction of the lake seemed to be N.N.E. and S.S.W. by compass. The southern portion is said to bend round to the west, and to receive the Teoughe from the north at its northwest extremity. We could detect no horizon where we stood looking S.S.W., nor could we form any idea of the extent of the lake, except from the reports of the inhabitants of the district; and, as they professed to go round it in three days, allowing twenty-five miles a day would make it seventy-five, or less than seventy geographical miles in circumference. Other guesses have been made since as to its circumference, ranging between seventy and one hundred miles. It is shallow, for I subsequently saw a native punting his canoe over seven or eight miles of the northeast end; it can never, therefore, be of much value as a commercial highway. In fact, during the months preceding the annual supply of water from the north, the lake is so shallow that it is with difficulty cattle can approach the water through the boggy, reedy banks. These are low on all sides, but on the west there is a space devoid of trees, showing that the waters have retired thence at no very ancient date. This is another of the proofs of desiccation met with so abundantly throughout the whole country. A number of dead trees lie on this space, some of them imbedded in the mud, right in the water. We were informed by the Bayeiye, who live on the lake, that when the annual inundation begins, not only trees of great size, but antelopes, as the springbuck and tsessebe ('Acronotus lunata'), are swept down by its rushing waters; the trees are gradually driven by the winds to the opposite side, and become imbedded in mud.

The water of the lake is perfectly fresh when full, but brackish when low; and that coming down the Tamunak'le we found to be so clear, cold, and soft, the higher we ascended, that the idea of melting snow was suggested to our minds. We found this region, with regard to that from which we had come, to be clearly a hollow, the lowest point being Lake Kumadau; the point of the ebullition of water, as shown by one of Newman's barometric thermometers, was only between 207-1/2 Deg. and 206 Deg., giving an elevation of not much more than two thousand feet above the level of the sea. We had descended above two thousand feet in coming to it from Kolobeng. It is the southern and lowest part of the great river system beyond, in which large tracts of country are inundated annually by tropical rains, hereafter to be described. A little of that water, which in the countries farther north produces inundation, comes as far south as 20d 20′, the latitude of the upper end of the lake, and instead of flooding the country, falls into the lake as into a reservoir. It begins to flow down the Embarrah, which divides into the rivers Tzo and Teoughe. The Tzo divides into the Tamunak'le and Mababe; the Tamunak'le discharges itself into the Zouga, and the Teoughe into the lake. The flow begins either in March or April, and the descending waters find the channels of all these rivers dried out, except in certain pools in their beds, which have long dry spaces between them. The lake itself is very low. The Zouga is but a prolongation of the Tamunak'le, and an arm of the lake reaches up to the point where the one ends and the other begins. The last is narrow and shallow, while the Zouga is broad and deep. The narrow arm of the lake, which on the map looks like a continuation of the Zouga, has never been observed to flow either way. It is as stagnant as the lake itself.

The Teoughe and Tamunak'le, being essentially the same river, and receiving their supplies from the same source (the Embarrah or Varra), can never outrun each other. If either could, or if the Teoughe could fill the lake—a thing which has never happened in modern times—then this little arm would prove a convenient escapement to prevent inundation. If the lake ever becomes lower than the bed of the Zouga, a little of the water of the Tamunak'le might flow into it instead of down the Zouga; we should then have the phenomenon of a river flowing two ways; but this has never been observed to take place here, and it is doubtful if it ever can occur in this locality. The Zouga is broad and deep when it leaves the Tamunak'le, but becomes gradually narrower as you descend about two hundred miles; there it flows into Kumadau, a small lake about three or four miles broad and twelve long. The water, which higher up begins to flow in April, does not make much progress in filling this lake till the end of June. In September the rivers cease to flow. When the supply has been more than usually abundant, a little water flows beyond Kumadau, in the bed first seen by us on the 4th of July; if the quantity were larger, it might go further in the dry rocky bed of the Zouga, since seen still further to the east. The water supply of this part of the river system, as will be more fully explained further on, takes place in channels prepared for a much more copious flow. It resembles a deserted Eastern garden, where all the embankments and canals for irrigation can be traced, but where, the main dam and sluices having been allowed to get out of repair, only a small portion can be laid under water. In the case of the Zouga the channel is perfect, but water enough to fill the whole channel never comes down; and before it finds its way much beyond Kumadau, the upper supply ceases to run and the rest becomes evaporated. The higher parts of its bed even are much broader and more capacious than the lower toward Kumadau. The water is not absorbed so much as lost in filling up an empty channel, from which it is to be removed by the air and sun. There is, I am convinced, no such thing in the country as a river running into sand and becoming lost. The phenomenon, so convenient for geographers, haunted my fancy for years; but I have failed in discovering any thing except a most insignificant approach to it.

My chief object in coming to the lake was to visit Sebituane, the great chief of the Makololo, who was reported to live some two hundred miles beyond. We had now come to a half-tribe of the Bamangwato, called Batauana. Their chief was a young man named Lechulatebe. Sebituane had conquered his father Moremi, and Lechulatebe received part of his education while a captive among the Bayeiye. His uncle, a sensible man, ransomed him; and, having collected a number of families together, abdicated the chieftainship in favor of his nephew. As Lechulatebe had just come into power, he imagined that the proper way of showing his abilities was to act directly contrary to every thing that his uncle advised. When we came, the uncle recommended him to treat us handsomely, therefore the hopeful youth presented us with a goat only. It ought to have been an ox. So I proposed to my companions to loose the animal and let him go, as a hint to his master. They, however, did not wish to insult him. I, being more of a native, and familiar with their customs, knew that this shabby present was an insult to us. We wished to purchase some goats or oxen; Lechulatebe offered us elephants' tusks. "No, we can not eat these; we want something to fill our stomachs." "Neither can I; but I hear you white men are all very fond of these bones, so I offer them; I want to put the goats into my own stomach." A trader, who accompanied us, was then purchasing ivory at the rate of ten good large tusks for a musket worth thirteen shillings. They were called "bones"; and I myself saw eight instances in which the tusks had been left to rot with the other bones where the elephant fell. The Batauana never had a chance of a market before; but, in less than two years after our discovery, not a man of them could be found who was not keenly alive to the great value of the article.

On the day after our arrival at the lake, I applied to Lechulatebe for guides to Sebituane. As he was much afraid of that chief, he objected, fearing lest other white men should go thither also, and give Sebituane guns; whereas, if the traders came to him alone, the possession of fire-arms would give him such a superiority that Sebituane would be afraid of him.

It was in vain to explain that I would inculcate peace between them—that Sebituane had been a father to him and Sechele, and was as anxious to see me as he, Lechulatebe, had been. He offered to give me as much ivory as I needed without going to that chief; but when I refused to take any, he unwillingly consented to give me guides. Next day, however, when Oswell and I were prepared to start, with the horses only, we received a senseless refusal; and like Sekomi, who had thrown obstacles in our way, he sent men to the Bayeiye with orders to refuse us a passage across the river. Trying hard to form a raft at a narrow part, I worked many hours in the water; but the dry wood was so worm-eaten it would not bear the weight of a single person. I was not then aware of the number of alligators which exist in the Zouga, and never think of my labor in the water without feeling thankful that I escaped their jaws. The season was now far advanced; and as Mr. Oswell, with his wonted generous feelings, volunteered, on the spot, to go down to the Cape and bring up a boat, we resolved to make our way south again.

Coming down the Zouga, we had now time to look at its banks. These are very beautiful, resembling closely many parts of the River Clyde above Glasgow. The formation is soft calcareous tufa, such as forms the bottom of all this basin. The banks are perpendicular on the side to which the water swings, and sloping and grassy on the other. The slopes are selected for the pitfalls designed by the Bayeiye to entrap the animals as they come to drink. These are about seven or eight feet deep, three or four feet wide at the mouth, and gradually decrease till they are only about a foot wide at the bottom. The mouth is an oblong square (the only square thing made by the Bechuanas, for every thing else is round), and the long diameter at the surface is about equal to the depth. The decreasing width toward the bottom is intended to make the animal wedge himself more firmly in by his weight and struggles. The pitfalls are usually in pairs, with a wall a foot thick left uncut between the ends of each, so that if the beast, when it feels its fore legs descending, should try to save itself from going in altogether by striding the hind legs, he would spring forward and leap into the second with a force which insures the fall of his whole body into the trap. They are covered with great care. All the excavated earth is removed to a distance, so as not to excite suspicion in the minds of the animals. Reeds and grass are laid across the top; above this the sand is thrown, and watered so as to appear exactly like the rest of the spot. Some of our party plumped into these pitfalls more than once, even when in search of them, in order to open them to prevent the loss of our cattle. If an ox sees a hole, he carefully avoids it; and old elephants have been known to precede the herd and whisk off the coverings of the pitfalls on each side all the way down to the water. We have known instances in which the old among these sagacious animals have actually lifted the young out of the trap.

The trees which adorn the banks are magnificent. Two enormous baobabs ('Adansonia digitata'), or mowanas, grow near its confluence with the lake where we took the observations for the latitude (20d 20' S.). We were unable to ascertain the longitude of the lake, as our watches were useless; it may be between 22 Deg. and 23 Deg. E. The largest of the two baobabs was 76 feet in girth. The palmyra appears here and there among trees not met with in the south. The mokuchong, or moshoma, bears an edible fruit of indifferent quality, but the tree itself would be a fine specimen of arboreal beauty in any part of the world. The trunk is often converted into canoes. The motsouri, which bears a pink plum containing a pleasant acid juice, resembles an orange-tree in its dark evergreen foliage, and a cypress in its form. It was now winter-time, and we saw nothing of the flora. The plants and bushes were dry; but wild indigo abounded, as indeed it does over large tracts of Africa. It is called mohetolo, or the "changer", by the boys, who dye their ornaments of straw with the juice. There are two kinds of cotton in the country, and the Mashona, who convert it into cloth, dye it blue with this plant.

We found the elephants in prodigious numbers on the southern bank. They come to drink by night, and after having slaked their thirst—in doing which they throw large quantities of water over themselves, and are heard, while enjoying the refreshment, screaming with delight—they evince their horror of pitfalls by setting off in a straight line to the desert, and never diverge till they are eight or ten miles off. They are smaller here than in the countries farther south. At the Limpopo, for instance, they are upward of twelve feet high; here, only eleven: farther north we shall find them nine feet only. The koodoo, or tolo, seemed smaller, too, than those we had been accustomed to see. We saw specimens of the kuabaoba, or straight-horned rhinoceros ('R. Oswellii'), which is a variety of the white ('R. simus'); and we found that, from the horn being projected downward, it did not obstruct the line of vision, so that this species is able to be much more wary than its neighbors.

We discovered an entirely new species of antelope, called leche or lechwi. It is a beautiful water-antelope of a light brownish-yellow color. Its horns—exactly like those of the 'Aigoceros ellipsiprimnus', the waterbuck, or tumogo, of the Bechuanas—rise from the head with a slight bend backward, then curve forward at the points. The chest, belly, and orbits are nearly white, the front of the legs and ankles deep brown. From the horns, along the nape to the withers, the male has a small mane of the same yellowish color with the rest of the skin, and the tail has a tuft of black hair. It is never found a mile from water; islets in marshes and rivers are its favorite haunts, and it is quite unknown except in the central humid basin of Africa. Having a good deal of curiosity, it presents a noble appearance as it stands gazing, with head erect, at the approaching stranger. When it resolves to decamp, it lowers its head, and lays its horns down to a level with the withers; it then begins with a waddling trot, which ends in its galloping and springing over bushes like the pallahs. It invariably runs to the water, and crosses it by a succession of bounds, each of which appears to be from the bottom. We thought the flesh good at first, but soon got tired of it.

Great shoals of excellent fish come down annually with the access of waters. The mullet ('Mugil Africanus') is the most abundant. They are caught in nets.

The 'Glanis siluris', a large, broad-headed fish, without scales, and barbed called by the natives "mosala"—attains an enormous size and fatness. They are caught so large that when a man carries one over his shoulder the tail reaches the ground. It is a vegetable feeder, and in many of its habits resembles the eel. Like most lophoid fishes, it has the power of retaining a large quantity of water in a part of its great head, so that it can leave the river, and even be buried in the mud of dried-up pools, without being destroyed. Another fish closely resembling this, and named 'Clarias capensis' by Dr. Smith, is widely diffused throughout the interior, and often leaves the rivers for the sake of feeding in pools. As these dry up, large numbers of them are entrapped by the people. A water-snake, yellow-spotted and dark brown, is often seen swimming along with its head above the water: it is quite harmless, and is relished as food by the Bayeiye.

They mention ten kinds of fish in their river; and, in their songs of praise to the Zouga, say, "The messenger sent in haste is always forced to spend the night on the way by the abundance of food you place before him." The Bayeiye live much on fish, which is quite an abomination to the Bechuanas of the south; and they catch them in large numbers by means of nets made of the fine, strong fibres of the hibiscus, which grows abundantly in all moist places. Their float-ropes are made of the ife, or, as it is now called, the 'Sanseviere Angolensis', a flag-looking plant, having a very strong fibre, that abounds from Kolobeng to Angola; and the floats themselves are pieces of a water-plant containing valves at each joint, which retain the air in cells about an inch long. The mode of knotting the nets is identical with our own.

They also spear the fish with javelins having a light handle, which readily floats on the surface. They show great dexterity in harpooning the hippopotamus; and, the barbed blade of the spear being attached to a rope made of the young leaves of the palmyra, the animal can not rid himself of the canoe, attached to him in whale fashion, except by smashing it, which he not unfrequently does by his teeth or by a stroke of his hind foot.

On returning to the Bakurutse, we found that their canoes for fishing were simply large bundles of reeds tied together. Such a canoe would be a ready extemporaneous pontoon for crossing any river that had reedy banks.

Chapter 4

Leave Kolobeng again for the Country of Sebituane—Reach the Zouga—The Tsetse—A Party of Englishmen—Death of Mr. Rider—Obtain Guides—Children fall sick with Fever—Relinquish the Attempt to reach Sebituane—Mr. Oswell's Elephant-hunting—Return to Kolobeng—Make a third Start thence—Reach Nchokotsa—Salt-pans—"Links", or Springs—Bushmen—Our Guide Shobo—The Banajoa—An ugly Chief—The Tsetse—Bite fatal to domestic Animals, but harmless to wild Animals and Man—Operation of the Poison—Losses caused by it—The Makololo—Our Meeting with Sebituane—Sketch of his Career—His Courage and Conquests—Manoeuvres of the Batoka—He outwits them—His Wars with the Matebele—Predictions of a native Prophet—Successes of the Makololo—Renewed Attacks of the Matebele—The Island of Loyelo—Defeat of the Matebele—Sebituane's Policy—His Kindness to Strangers and to the Poor—His sudden Illness and Death—Succeeded by his Daughter—Her Friendliness to us—Discovery, in June, 1851, of the Zambesi flowing in the Centre of the Continent—Its Size—The Mambari—The Slave-trade—Determine to send Family to England—Return to the Cape in April, 1852—Safe Transit through the Caffre Country during Hostilities—Need of a "Special Correspondent"—Kindness of the London Missionary Society—Assistance afforded by the Astronomer Royal at the Cape.

Having returned to Kolobeng, I remained there till April, 1850, and then left in company with Mrs. Livingstone, our three children, and the chief Sechele—who had now bought a wagon of his own—in order to go across the Zouga at its lower end, with the intention of proceeding up the northern bank till we gained the Tamunak'le, and of then ascending that river to visit Sebituane in the north. Sekomi had given orders to fill up the wells which we had dug with so much labor at Serotli, so we took the more eastern route through the Bamangwato town and by Letloche. That chief asked why I had avoided him in our former journeys. I replied that my reason was that I knew he did not wish me to go to the lake, and I did not want to quarrel with him. "Well," he said, "you beat me then, and I am content."

Parting with Sechele at the ford, as he was eager to visit Lechulatebe, we went along the northern woody bank of the Zouga with great labor, having to cut down very many trees to allow the wagons to pass. Our losses by oxen falling into pitfalls were very heavy. The Bayeiye kindly opened the pits when they knew of our approach; but when that was not the case, we could blame no one on finding an established custom of the country inimical to our interests. On approaching the confluence of the Tamunak'le we were informed that the fly called tsetse* abounded on its banks. This was a barrier we never expected to meet; and, as it might have brought our wagons to a complete stand-still in a wilderness, where no supplies for the children could be obtained, we were reluctantly compelled to recross the Zouga.

> * 'Glossina morsitans', the first specimens of which were brought to England in 1848 by my friend Major Vardon, from the banks of the Limpopo.

From the Bayeiye we learned that a party of Englishmen, who had come to the lake in search of ivory, were all laid low by fever, so we traveled hastily down about sixty miles to render what aid was in our power. We were grieved to find, as we came near, that Mr. Alfred Rider, an enterprising young artist who had come to make sketches of this country and of the lake immediately after its discovery, had died of fever before our arrival; but by the aid of medicines and such comforts as could be made by the only English lady who ever visited the lake, the others happily recovered. The unfinished drawing of Lake Ngami was made by Mr. Rider just before his death, and has been kindly lent for this work by his bereaved mother.

Sechele used all his powers of eloquence with Lechulatebe to induce him to furnish guides that I might be able to visit Sebituane on ox-back, while Mrs. Livingstone and the children remained at Lake Ngami. He yielded at last. I had a very superior London-made gun, the gift of Lieutenant Arkwright, on which I placed the greatest value, both on account of the donor and the impossibility of my replacing it. Lechulatebe fell violently in love with it, and offered whatever number of elephants' tusks I might ask for it. I too was enamored with Sebituane; and as he promised in addition that he would furnish Mrs. Livingstone with meat all the time of my absence, his arguments made me part with the gun. Though he had no ivory at the time to pay me, I felt the piece would be well spent on those terms, and delivered it to him. All being ready for our departure, I took Mrs. Livingstone about six miles from the town, that she might have a peep at the broad part of the lake. Next morning we had other work to do than part, for our little boy and girl were seized with fever. On the day following, all our servants were down too with the same complaint. As nothing is better in these cases than change of place, I was forced to give up the hope of seeing Sebituane that year; so, leaving my gun as part payment for guides next year, we started for the pure air of the Desert.

Some mistake had happened in the arrangement with Mr. Oswell, for we met him on the Zouga on our return, and he devoted the rest of this season to elephant-hunting, at which the natives universally declare he is the greatest adept that ever came into the country. He hunted without dogs. It is remarkable that this lordly animal is so completely harassed by the presence of a few yelping curs as to be quite incapable of attending to man. He makes awkward attempts to crush them by falling on his knees; and sometimes places his forehead against a tree ten inches in diameter; glancing on one side of the tree and then on the other, he pushes it down before him, as if he thought thereby to catch his enemies. The only danger the huntsman has to apprehend is the dogs running toward him, and thereby leading the elephant to their master. Mr. Oswell has been known to kill four large old male elephants a day. The value of the ivory in these cases would be one hundred guineas. We had reason to be proud of his success, for the inhabitants conceived from it a very high idea of English courage; and when they wished to flatter me would say, "If you were not a missionary you would just be like Oswell; you would not hunt with dogs either." When, in 1852, we came to the Cape, my black coat eleven years out of fashion, and without a penny of salary to draw, we found that Mr. Oswell had most generously ordered an outfit for the half-naked children, which cost about 200 Pounds, and presented it to us, saying he thought Mrs. Livingstone had a right to the game of her own preserves.

Foiled in this second attempt to reach Sebituane, we returned again to Kolobeng, whither we were soon followed by a number of messengers from that chief himself. When he heard of our attempts to visit him, he dispatched three detachments of his men with thirteen brown cows to Lechulatebe, thirteen white cows to Sekomi, and thirteen black cows to Sechele, with a request to each to assist the white men to reach him. Their policy, however, was to keep him out of view, and act as his agents in purchasing with his ivory the goods he wanted. This is thoroughly African; and that continent being without friths and arms of the sea, the tribes in the centre have always been debarred from European intercourse by its universal prevalence among all the people around the coasts.

Before setting out on our third journey to Sebituane, it was necessary to visit Kuruman; and Sechele, eager, for the sake of the commission thereon, to get the ivory of that chief into his own hands, allowed all the messengers to leave before our return. Sekomi, however, was more than usually gracious, and even furnished us with a guide, but no one knew the path beyond Nchokotsa which we intended to follow. When we reached that point, we found that the main spring of the gun of another of his men, who was well acquainted with the Bushmen, through whose country we should pass, had opportunely broken. I never undertook to mend a gun with greater zest than this; for, under promise of his guidance, we went to the north instead of westward. All the other guides were most liberally rewarded by Mr. Oswell.

We passed quickly over a hard country, which is perfectly flat. A little soil lying on calcareous tufa, over a tract of several hundreds of miles, supports a vegetation of fine sweet short grass, and mopane and baobab trees. On several parts of this we found large salt-pans, one of which, Ntwetwe, is fifteen miles broad and one hundred long. The latitude might have been taken on its horizon as well as upon the sea.

Although these curious spots seem perfectly level, all those in this direction have a gentle slope to the northeast: thither the rain-water, which sometimes covers them, gently gravitates. This, it may be recollected, is the direction of the Zouga. The salt dissolved in the water has by this means all been transferred to one pan in that direction, named Chuantsa; on it we see a cake of salt and lime an inch and a half thick. All the others have an efflorescence of lime and one of the nitrates only, and some are covered thickly with shells. These shells are identical with those of the mollusca of Lake Ngami and the Zouga. There are three varieties, spiral, univalve, and bivalve.

In every salt-pan in the country there is a spring of water on one side. I can remember no exception to this rule. The water of these springs is brackish, and contains the nitrate of soda. In one instance there are two springs, and one more saltish than the other. If this supply came from beds of rock salt the water would not be drinkable, as it generally is, and in some instances, where the salt contained in the pan in which these springs appear has been removed by human agency, no fresh deposit occurs. It is therefore probable that these deposits of salt are the remains of the very slightly brackish lakes of antiquity, large portions of which must have been dried out in the general desiccation. We see an instance in Lake Ngami, which, when low, becomes brackish, and this view seems supported by the fact that the largest quantities of salt have been found in the deepest hollows or lowest valleys, which have no outlet or outgoing gorge; and a fountain, about thirty miles south of the Bamangwato—the temperature of which is upward of 100 Deg.—while strongly impregnated with pure salt, being on a flat part of the country, is accompanied by no deposit.

When these deposits occur in a flat tufaceous country like the present, a large space is devoid of vegetation, on account of the nitrates dissolving the tufa, and keeping it in a state unfavorable to the growth of plants.

We found a great number of wells in this tufa. A place called Matlomagan-yana, or the "Links", is quite a chain of these never-failing springs. As they occasionally become full in seasons when no rain falls, and resemble somewhat in this respect the rivers we have already mentioned, it is probable they receive some water by percolation from the river system in the country beyond. Among these links we found many families of Bushmen; and, unlike those on the plains of the Kalahari, who are generally of short stature and light yellow color, these were tall, strapping fellows, of dark complexion. Heat alone does not produce blackness of skin, but heat with moisture seems to insure the deepest hue.

One of these Bushmen, named Shobo, consented to be our guide over the waste between these springs and the country of Sebituane. Shobo gave us no hope of water in less than a month. Providentially, however, we came sooner than we expected to some supplies of rain-water in a chain of pools. It is impossible to convey an idea of the dreary scene on which we entered after leaving this spot: the only vegetation was a low scrub in deep sand; not a bird or insect enlivened the landscape. It was, without exception, the most uninviting prospect I ever beheld; and, to make matters worse, our guide Shobo wandered on the second day. We coaxed him on at night, but he went to all points of the compass on the trails of elephants which had been here in the rainy season, and then would sit down in the path, and in his broken Sichuana say, "No water, all country only; Shobo sleeps; he breaks down; country only;" and then coolly curl himself up and go to sleep. The oxen were terribly fatigued and thirsty; and on the morning of the fourth day, Shobo, after professing ignorance of every thing, vanished altogether. We went on in the direction in which we last saw him, and about eleven o'clock began to see birds; then the trail of a rhinoceros. At this we unyoked the oxen, and they, apparently knowing the sign, rushed along to find the water in the River Mahabe, which comes from the Tamunak'le, and lay to the west of us. The supply of water in the wagons had been wasted by one of our servants, and by the afternoon only a small portion remained for the children. This was a bitterly anxious night; and next morning the less there was of water, the more thirsty the little rogues became. The idea of their perishing before our eyes was terrible. It would almost have been a relief to me to have been reproached with being the entire cause of the catastrophe; but not one syllable of upbraiding was uttered by their mother, though the tearful eye told the agony within. In the afternoon of the fifth day, to our inexpressible relief, some of the men returned with a supply of that fluid of which we had never before felt the true value.

The cattle, in rushing along to the water in the Mahabe, probably crossed a small patch of trees containing tsetse, an insect which was shortly to become a perfect pest to us. Shobo had found his way to the Bayeiye, and appeared, when we came up to the river, at the head of a party; and, as he wished to show his importance before his friends, he walked up boldly and commanded our whole cavalcade to stop, and to bring forth fire and tobacco, while he coolly sat down and smoked his pipe. It was such an inimitably natural way of showing off, that we all stopped to admire the acting, and, though he had left us previously in the lurch, we all liked Shobo, a fine specimen of that wonderful people, the Bushmen.

Next day we came to a village of Banajoa, a tribe which extends far to the eastward. They were living on the borders of a marsh in which the Mahabe terminates. They had lost their crop of corn ('Holcus sorghum'), and now subsisted almost entirely on the root called "tsitla", a kind of aroidoea, which contains a very large quantity of sweet-tasted starch. When dried, pounded into meal, and allowed to ferment, it forms a not unpleasant article of food. The women shave all the hair off their heads, and seem darker than the Bechuanas. Their huts were built on poles, and a fire is made beneath by night, in order that the smoke may drive away the mosquitoes, which abound on the Mababe and Tamunak'le more than in any other part of the country. The head man of this village, Majane, seemed a little wanting in ability, but had had wit enough to promote a younger member of the family to the office. This person, the most like the ugly negro of the tobacconists' shops I ever saw, was called Moroa Majane, or son of Majane, and proved an active guide across the River Sonta, and to the banks of the Chobe, in the country of Sebituane. We had come through another tsetse district by night, and at once passed our cattle over to the northern bank to preserve them from its ravages.

A few remarks on the Tsetse, or 'Glossina morsitans', may here be appropriate. It is not much larger than the common house-fly, and is nearly of the same brown color as the common honey-bee; the after part of the body has three or four yellow bars across it; the wings project beyond this part considerably, and it is remarkably alert, avoiding most dexterously all attempts to capture it with the hand at common temperatures; in the cool of the mornings and evenings it is less agile. Its peculiar buzz when once heard can never be forgotten by the traveler whose means of locomotion are domestic animals; for it is well known that the bite of this poisonous insect is certain death to the ox, horse, and dog. In this journey, though we were not aware of any great number having at any time lighted on our cattle, we lost forty-three fine oxen by its bite. We watched the animals carefully, and believe that not a score of flies were ever upon them.

A most remarkable feature in the bite of the tsetse is its perfect harmlessness in man and wild animals, and even calves, so long as they continue to suck the cows. We never experienced the slightest injury from them ourselves, personally, although we lived two months in their HABITAT, which was in this case as sharply defined as in many others, for the south bank of the Chobe was infested by them, and the northern bank, where our cattle were placed, only fifty yards distant, contained not a single specimen. This was the more remarkable, as we often saw natives carrying over raw meat to the opposite bank with many tsetse settled upon it.

The poison does not seem to be injected by a sting, or by ova placed beneath the skin; for, when one is allowed to feed freely on the hand, it is seen to insert the middle prong of three portions, into which the proboscis divides, somewhat deeply into the true skin; it then draws it out a little way, and it assumes a crimson color as the mandibles come into brisk operation. The previously shrunken belly swells out, and, if left undisturbed, the fly quietly departs when it is full. A slight itching irritation follows, but not more than in the bite of a mosquito. In the ox this same bite produces no more immediate effects than in man. It does not startle him as the gad-fly does; but a few days afterward the following symptoms supervene: the eye and nose begin to run, the coat stares as if the animal were cold, a swelling appears under the jaw, and sometimes at the navel; and, though the animal continues to graze, emaciation commences, accompanied with a peculiar flaccidity of the muscles, and this proceeds unchecked until, perhaps months afterward, purging comes on, and the animal, no longer able to graze, perishes in a state of extreme exhaustion. Those which are in good condition often perish soon after the bite is inflicted with staggering and blindness, as if the brain were affected by it. Sudden changes of temperature produced by falls of rain seem to hasten the progress of the complaint; but, in general, the emaciation goes on uninterruptedly for months, and, do what we will, the poor animals perish miserably.

When opened, the cellular tissue on the surface of the body beneath the skin is seen to be injected with air, as if a quantity of soap-bubbles were scattered over it, or a dishonest, awkward butcher had been trying to make it look fat. The fat is of a greenish-yellow color and of an oily consistence. All the muscles are flabby, and the heart often so soft that the fingers may be made to meet through it. The lungs and liver partake of the disease. The stomach and bowels are pale and empty, and the gall-bladder is distended with bile.

These symptoms seem to indicate what is probably the case, a poison in the blood, the germ of which enters when the proboscis is inserted to draw blood. The poison-germ, contained in a bulb at the root of the proboscis, seems capable, although very minute in quantity, of reproducing itself, for the blood after death by tsetse is very small in quantity, and scarcely stains the hands in dissection. I shall have by-and-by to mention another insect, which by the same operation produces in the human subject both vomiting and purging.

The mule, ass, and goat enjoy the same immunity from the tsetse as man and the game. Many large tribes on the Zambesi can keep no domestic animals except the goat, in consequence of the scourge existing in their country. Our children were frequently bitten, yet suffered no harm; and we saw around us numbers of zebras, buffaloes, pigs, pallahs and other antelopes, feeding quietly in the very habitat of the tsetse, yet as undisturbed by its bite as oxen are when they first receive the fatal poison. There is not so much difference in the natures of the horse and zebra, the buffalo and ox, the sheep and antelope, as to afford any satisfactory explanation of the phenomenon. Is a man not as much a domestic animal as a dog? The curious feature in the case, that dogs perish though fed on milk, whereas the calves escape so long as they continue sucking, made us imagine that the mischief might be produced by some plant in the locality, and not by tsetse; but Major Vardon, of the Madras Army, settled that point by riding a horse up to a small hill infested by the insect without allowing him time to graze, and, though he only remained long enough to take a view of the country and catch some specimens of tsetse on the animal, in ten days afterward the horse was dead.

The well-known disgust which the tsetse shows to animal excreta, as exhibited when a village is placed in its habitat, has been observed and turned to account by some of the doctors. They mix droppings of animals, human milk, and some medicines together, and smear the animals that are about to pass through a tsetse district; but this, though it proves a preventive at the time, is not permanent. There is no cure yet known for the disease. A careless herdsman allowing a large number of cattle to wander into a tsetse district loses all except the calves; and Sebituane once lost nearly the entire cattle of his tribe, very many thousands, by unwittingly coming under its influence. Inoculation does not insure immunity, as animals which have been slightly bitten in one year may perish by a greater number of bites in the next; but it is probable that with the increase of guns the game will perish, as has happened in the south, and the tsetse, deprived of food, may become extinct simultaneously with the larger animals.

The Makololo whom we met on the Chobe were delighted to see us; and as their chief Sebituane was about twenty miles down the river, Mr. Oswell and I proceeded in canoes to his temporary residence. He had come from the Barotse town of Naliele down to Sesheke as soon as he heard of white men being in search of him, and now came one hundred miles more to bid us welcome into his country. He was upon an island, with all his principal men around him, and engaged in singing when we arrived. It was more like church music than the sing-song ee ee ee, ae ae ae, of the Bechuanas of the south, and they continued the tune for some seconds after we approached. We informed him of the difficulties we had encountered, and how glad we were that they were all at an end by at last reaching his presence. He signified his own joy, and added, "Your cattle are all bitten by the tsetse, and will certainly die; but never mind, I have oxen, and will give you as many as you need." We, in our ignorance, then thought that as so few tsetse had bitten them no great mischief would follow. He then presented us with an ox and a jar of honey as food, and handed us over to the care of Mahale, who had headed the party to Kolobeng, and would now fain appropriate to himself the whole credit of our coming. Prepared skins of oxen, as soft as cloth, were given to cover us through the night; and, as nothing could be returned to this chief, Mahale became the owner of them. Long before it was day Sebituane came, and sitting down by the fire, which was lighted for our benefit behind the hedge where we lay, he narrated the difficulties he had himself experienced, when a young man, in crossing that same desert which we had mastered long afterward. As he has been most remarkable in his career, and was unquestionably the greatest man in all that country, a short sketch of his life may prove interesting to the reader.

Sebituane was about forty-five years of age; of a tall and wiry form, an olive or coffee-and-milk color, and slightly bald; in manner cool and collected, and more frank in his answers than any other chief I ever met. He was the greatest warrior ever heard of beyond the colony; for, unlike Mosilikatse, Dingaan, and others, he always led his men into battle himself. When he saw the enemy, he felt the edge of his battle-axe, and said, "Aha! it is sharp, and whoever turns his back on the enemy will feel its edge." So fleet of foot was he, that all his people knew there was no escape for the coward, as any such would be cut down without mercy. In some instances of skulking he allowed the individual to return home; then calling him, he would say, "Ah! you prefer dying at home to dying in the field, do you? You shall have your desire." This was the signal for his immediate execution.

He came from the country near the sources of the Likwa and Namagari rivers in the south, so we met him eight hundred or nine hundred miles from his birth-place. He was not the son of a chief, though related closely to the reigning family of the Basutu; and when, in an attack by Sikonyele, the tribe was driven out of one part, Sebituane was one in that immense horde of savages driven back by the Griquas from Kuruman in 1824.* He then fled to the north with an insignificant party of men and cattle. At Melita the Bangwaketse collected the Bakwains, Bakatla, and Bahurutse, to "eat them up". Placing his men in front, and the women behind the cattle, he routed the whole of his enemies at one blow. Having thus conquered Makabe, the chief of the Bangwaketse, he took immediate possession of his town and all his goods.

> * See an account of this affair in Moffat's "Missionary Enterprise in Africa".

Sebituane subsequently settled at the place called Litubaruba, where Sechele now dwells, and his people suffered severely in one of those unrecorded attacks by white men, in which murder is committed and materials laid up in the conscience for a future judgment.

A great variety of fortune followed him in the northern part of the Bechuana country; twice he lost all his cattle by the attacks of the Matabele, but always kept his people together, and retook more than he lost. He then crossed the Desert by nearly the same path that we did. He had captured a guide, and, as it was necessary to travel by night in order to reach water, the guide took advantage of this and gave him the slip. After marching till morning, and going as they thought right, they found themselves on the trail of the day before. Many of his cattle burst away from him in the phrensy of thirst, and rushed back to Serotli, then a large piece of water, and to Mashue and Lopepe, the habitations of their original owners. He stocked himself again among the Batletli, on Lake Kumadau, whose herds were of the large-horned species of cattle.* Conquering all around the lake, he heard of white men living at the west coast; and, haunted by what seems to have been the dream of his whole life, a desire to have intercourse with the white man, he passed away to the southwest, into the parts opened up lately by Messrs. Galton and Andersson. There, suffering intensely from thirst, he and his party came to a small well. He decided that the men, not the cattle, should drink it, the former being of most value, as they could fight for more should these be lost. In the morning they found the cattle had escaped to the Damaras.

> * We found the Batauana in possession of this breed when we discovered Lake Ngami. One of these horns, brought to England by Major Vardon, will hold no less than twenty-one imperial pints of water; and a pair, brought by Mr. Oswell, and now in the possession of Colonel Steele, measures from tip to tip

eight and a half feet.

Returning to the north poorer than he started, he ascended the Teoughe to the hill Sorila, and crossed over a swampy country to the eastward. Pursuing his course onward to the low-lying basin of the Leeambye, he saw that it presented no attraction to a pastoral tribe like his, so he moved down that river among the Bashubia and Batoka, who were then living in all their glory. His narrative resembled closely the "Commentaries of Caesar", and the history of the British in India. He was always forced to attack the different tribes, and to this day his men justify every step he took as perfectly just and right. The Batoka lived on large islands in the Leeambye or Zambesi, and, feeling perfectly secure in their fastnesses, often allured fugitive or wandering tribes on to uninhabited islets on pretense of ferrying them across, and there left them to perish for the sake of their goods. Sekomi, the chief of the Bamangwato, was, when a child, in danger of meeting this fate; but a man still living had compassion on him, and enabled his mother to escape with him by night. The river is so large that the sharpest eye can not tell the difference between an island and the bend of the opposite bank; but Sebituane, with his usual foresight, requested the island chief who ferried him across to take his seat in the canoe with him, and detained him by his side till all his people and cattle were safely landed. The whole Batoka country was then densely peopled, and they had a curious taste for ornamenting their villages with the skulls of strangers. When Sebituane appeared near the great falls, an immense army collected to make trophies of the Makololo skulls; but, instead of succeeding in this, they gave him a good excuse for conquering them, and capturing so many cattle that his people were quite incapable of taking any note of the sheep and goats. He overran all the high lands toward the Kafue, and settled in what is called a pastoral country, of gently undulating plains, covered with short grass and but little forest. The Makololo have never lost their love for this fine, healthy region.

But the Matebele, a Caffre or Zulu tribe, under Mosilikatse, crossed the Zambesi, and, attacking Sebituane in this choice spot, captured his cattle and women. Rallying his men, he followed and recaptured the whole. A fresh attack was also repulsed, and Sebituane thought of going farther down the Zambesi, to the country of the white men. He had an idea, whence imbibed I never could learn, that if he had a cannon he might live in peace. He had led a life of war, yet no one apparently desired peace more than he did. A prophet induced him to turn his face again to the westward. This man, by name Tlapane, was called a "senoga"—one who holds intercourse with the gods. He probably had a touch of insanity, for he was in the habit of retiring no one knew whither, but perhaps into some cave, to remain in a hypnotic or mesmeric state until the moon was full. Then, returning to the tribe quite emaciated, he excited himself, as others do who pretend to the prophetic AFFLATUS, until he was in a state of ecstasy. These pretended prophets commence their operations by violent action of the voluntary muscles. Stamping, leaping, and shouting in a peculiarly violent manner, or beating the ground with a club, they induce a kind of fit, and while in it pretend that their utterances are unknown to themselves. Tlapane, pointing eastward, said, "There, Sebituane, I behold a fire: shun it; it is a fire which may scorch thee. The gods say, go not thither." Then, turning to the west, he said, "I see a city and a nation of black men—men of the water; their cattle are red; thine own tribe, Sebituane, is perishing, and will be all consumed; thou wilt govern black men, and, when thy warriors have captured red cattle, let not the owners be killed; they are thy future tribe—they are thy city; let them be spared to cause thee to build. And thou, Ramosinii, thy village will perish utterly. If Mokari removes from that village he will perish first, and thou, Ramosinii, wilt be the last to die." Concerning himself he added, "The gods have caused other men to drink water, but to me they have given bitter water of the chukuru (rhinoceros). They call me away myself. I can not stay much longer."

This vatication, which loses much in the translation, I have given rather fully, as it shows an observant mind. The policy recommended was wise, and the deaths of the "senoga" and of the two men he had named, added to the destruction of their village, having all happened soon after, it is not wonderful that Sebituane followed implicitly the warning voice. The fire pointed to was evidently the Portuguese fire-arms, of which he must have heard. The black men referred to were the Barotse, or, as they term themselves, Baloiana; and Sebituane spared their chiefs, even though they attacked him first. He had ascended the Barotse valley, but was pursued by the Matebele, as Mosilikatse never could forgive his former defeats. They came up the river in a very large body. Sebituane placed some goats on one of the large islands of the Zambesi as a bait to the warriors, and some men in canoes to co-operate in the manoeuvre. When they were all ferried over to the island, the canoes were removed, and the Matebele found themselves completely in a trap, being perfectly unable to swim. They subsisted for some time on the roots of grass after the goats were eaten, but gradually became so emaciated that, when the Makololo landed, they had only to perform the part of executioners on the adults, and to adopt the rest into their own tribe. Afterward Mosilikatse was goaded on by his warriors to revenge this loss; so he sent an immense army, carrying canoes with them, in order that no such mishap might occur again. Sebituane had by this time incorporated the Barotse, and taught his young men to manage canoes; so he went from island to island, and watched the Matebele on the main land so closely that they could not use their canoes to cross the river any where without parting their forces. At last all the Makololo and their cattle were collected on the island of Loyelo, and lay all around, keeping watch night and day over the enemy. After some time spent in this way, Sebituane went in a canoe toward them, and, addressing them by an interpreter, asked why they wished to kill him; he had never attacked them, never harmed their chief: "Au!" he continued, "the guilt is on your side." The Matebele made no reply; but the Makololo next day saw the canoes they had carried so far lying smashed, and the owners gone. They returned toward their own country, and fever, famine, and the Batoka completed their destruction, only five men returned to Mosilikatse.

Sebituane had now not only conquered all the black tribes over an immense tract of country, but had made himself dreaded even by the terrible Mosilikatse. He never could trust this ferocious chief, however; and, as the Batoka on the islands had been guilty of ferrying his enemies across the Zambesi, he made a rapid descent upon them, and swept them all out of their island fastnesses. He thus unwittingly performed a good service to the country by completely breaking down the old system which prevented trade from penetrating into the great central valley. Of the chiefs who escaped, he said, "They love Mosilikatse, let them live with him: the Zambesi is my line of defense;" and men were placed all along it as sentinels. When he heard of our wish to visit him, he did all he could to assist our approach. Sechele, Sekomi, and Lechulatebe owed their lives to his clemency; and the latter might have paid dearly for his obstructiveness. Sebituane knew every thing that happened in the country, for he had the art of gaining the affections both of his own people and of strangers. When a party of poor men came to his town to sell their hoes or skins, no matter how ungainly they might be, he soon knew them all. A company of these indigent strangers, sitting far apart from the Makololo gentlemen around the chief, would be surprised to see him come alone to them, and, sitting down, inquire if they were hungry. He would order an attendant to bring meal, milk, and honey, and, mixing them in their sight, in order to remove any suspicion from their minds, make them feast, perhaps for the first time in their lives, on a lordly dish. Delighted beyond measure with his affability and liberality, they felt their hearts warm toward him, and gave him all the information in their power; and as he never allowed a party of strangers to go away without giving every one of them, servants and all, a present, his praises were sounded far and wide. "He has a heart! he is wise!" were the usual expressions we heard before we saw him.

He was much pleased with the proof of confidence we had shown in bringing our children, and promised to take us to see his country, so that we might choose a part in which to locate ourselves. Our plan was, that I should remain in the pursuit of my objects as a missionary, while Mr. Oswell explored the Zambesi to the east. Poor Sebituane, however, just after realizing what he had so long ardently desired, fell sick of inflammation of the lungs, which originated in and extended from an old wound got at Melita. I saw his danger, but, being a stranger, I feared to treat him medically, lest, in the event of his death, I should be blamed by his people. I mentioned this to one of his doctors, who said, "Your fear is prudent and wise; this people would blame you." He had been cured of this complaint, during the year before, by the Barotse making a large number of free incisions in the chest. The Makololo doctors, on the other hand, now scarcely cut the skin. On the Sunday afternoon in which he died, when our usual religious service was over, I visited him with my little boy Robert. "Come near," said Sebituane, "and see if I am any longer a man. I am done." He was thus sensible of the dangerous nature of his disease, so I ventured to assent, and added a single sentence regarding hope after death. "Why do you speak of death?" said one of a relay of fresh doctors; "Sebituane will never die." If I had persisted, the impression would have been produced that by speaking about it I wished him to die. After sitting with him some time, and commending him to the mercy of God, I rose to depart, when the dying chieftain, raising himself up a little from his prone position, called a servant, and said, "Take Robert to Maunku (one of his wives), and tell her to give him some milk." These were the last words of Sebituane.

We were not informed of his death until the next day. The burial of a Bechuana chief takes place in his cattle-pen, and all the cattle are driven for an hour or two around and over the grave, so that it may be quite obliterated. We went and spoke to the people, advising them to keep together and support the heir. They took this kindly; and in turn told us not to be alarmed, for they would not think of ascribing the death of their chief to us; that Sebituane had just gone the way of his fathers; and though the father had gone, he had left children, and they hoped that we would be as friendly to his children as we intended to have been to himself.

He was decidedly the best specimen of a native chief I ever met. I never felt so much grieved by the loss of a black man before; and it was impossible not to follow him in thought into the world of which he had just heard before he was called away, and to realize somewhat of the feelings of those who pray for the dead. The deep, dark question of what is to become of such as he, must, however, be left where we find it, believing that, assuredly, the "Judge of all the earth will do right."

At Sebituane's death the chieftainship devolved, as her father intended, on a daughter named Ma-mochisane. He had promised to show us his country and to select a suitable locality for our residence. We had now to look to the daughter, who was living twelve days to the north, at Naliele. We were obliged, therefore, to remain until a message came from her; and when it did, she gave us perfect liberty to visit any part of the country we chose. Mr. Oswell and I then proceeded one hundred and thirty miles to the northeast, to Sesheke; and in the end of June, 1851, we were rewarded by the discovery of the Zambesi, in the centre of the continent. This was a most important point, for that river was not previously known to exist there at all. The Portuguese maps all represent it as rising far to the east of where we now were; and if ever any thing like a chain of trading stations had existed across the country between the latitudes 12 Deg. and 18 Deg. south, this magnificent portion of the river must have been known before. We saw it at the end of the dry season, at the time when the river is about at its lowest, and yet there was a breadth of from three hundred to six hundred yards of deep flowing water. Mr. Oswell said he had never seen such a fine river, even in India. At the period of its annual inundation it rises fully twenty feet in perpendicular height, and floods fifteen or twenty miles of lands adjacent to its banks.

The country over which we had traveled from the Chobe was perfectly flat, except where there were large ant-hills, or the remains of former ones, which had left mounds a few feet high. These are generally covered with wild date-trees and palmyras, and in some parts there are forests of mimosae and mopane. Occasionally the country between the Chobe and Zambesi is flooded, and there are large patches of swamps lying near the Chobe or on its banks. The Makololo were living among these swamps for the sake of the protection the deep reedy rivers afforded them against their enemies.

Now, in reference to a suitable locality for a settlement for myself, I could not conscientiously ask them to abandon their defenses for my convenience alone. The healthy districts were defenseless, and the safe localities were so deleterious to human life, that the original Basutos had nearly all been cut off by the fever; I therefore feared to subject my family to the scourge.

As we were the very first white men the inhabitants had ever seen, we were visited by prodigious numbers. Among the first who came to see us was a gentleman who appeared in a gaudy dressing-gown of printed calico. Many of the Makololo, besides, had garments of blue, green, and red baize, and also of printed cottons; on inquiry, we learned that these had been purchased, in exchange for boys, from a tribe called Mambari, which is situated near Bihe. This tribe began the slave-trade with Sebituane only in 1850, and but for the unwillingness of Lechulatebe to allow us to pass, we should have been with Sebituane in time to have prevented it from commencing at all. The Mambari visited in ancient times the chief of the Barotse, whom Sebituane conquered, and he refused to allow any one to sell a child. They never came back again till 1850; and as they had a number of old Portuguese guns marked "Legitimo de Braga", which Sebituane thought would be excellent in any future invasion of Matebele, he offered to purchase them with cattle or ivory, but the Mambari refused every thing except boys about fourteen years of age. The Makololo declare they never heard of people being bought and sold till then, and disliked it, but the desire to possess the guns prevailed, and eight old guns were exchanged for as many boys; these were not their own children, but captives of the black races they had conquered. I have never known in Africa an instance of a parent selling his own offspring. The Makololo were afterward incited to make a foray against some tribes to the eastward; the Mambari bargaining to use their guns in the attack for the captives they might take, and the Makololo were to have all the cattle. They went off with at least two hundred slaves that year. During this foray the Makololo met some Arabs from Zanzibar, who presented them with three English muskets, and in return received about thirty of their captives.

In talking with my companions over these matters, the idea was suggested that, if the slave-market were supplied with articles of European manufacture by legitimate commerce, the trade in slaves would become impossible. It seemed more feasible to give the goods, for which the people now part with their servants, in exchange for ivory and other products of the country, and thus prevent the trade at the beginning, than to try to put a stop to it at any of the subsequent steps. This could only be effected by establishing a highway from the coast into the centre of the country.

As there was no hope of the Boers allowing the peaceable instruction of the natives at Kolobeng, I at once resolved to save my family from exposure to this unhealthy region by sending them to England, and to return alone, with a view to exploring the country in search of a healthy district that might prove a centre of civilization, and open up the interior by a path to either the east or west coast. This resolution led me down to the Cape in April, 1852, being the first time during eleven years that I had visited the scenes of civilization. Our route to Cape Town led us to pass through the centre of the colony during the twentieth month of a Caffre war; and if those who periodically pay enormous sums for these inglorious affairs wish to know how our little unprotected party could quietly travel through the heart of the colony to the capital with as little sense or sign of danger as if we had been in England, they must engage a "'Times' Special Correspondent" for the next outbreak to explain where the money goes, and who have been benefited by the blood and treasure expended.

Having placed my family on board a homeward-bound ship, and promised to rejoin them in two years, we parted, for, as it subsequently proved, nearly five years. The Directors of the London Missionary Society signified their cordial approval of my project by leaving the matter entirely to my own discretion; and I have much pleasure in acknowledging my obligations to the gentlemen composing that body for always acting in an enlightened spirit, and with as much liberality as their constitution would allow.

I have the like pleasure in confessing my thankfulness to the Astronomer Royal at the Cape, Thomas Maclear, Esq., for enabling me to recall the little astronomical knowledge which constant manual labor and the engrossing nature of missionary duties had effaced from my memory, and in adding much that I did not know before. The promise he made on parting, that he would examine and correct all my observations, had more effect in making me persevere in overcoming the difficulties of an unassisted solitary observer than any thing else; so whatever credit may be attached to the geographical positions laid down in my route must be attributed to the voluntary aid of the excellent and laborious astronomer of the Cape observatory.

Having given the reader as rapid a sketch as possible of events which attracted notice between 1840 and 1852, I now proceed to narrate the incidents of the last and longest journey of all, performed in 1852-6.

Chapter 5

Start in June, 1852, on the last and longest Journey from Cape Town— Companions—Wagon-traveling—Physical Divisions of Africa— The Eastern, Central, and Western Zones—The Kalahari Desert—Its Vegetation—Increasing Value of the Interior for Colonization— Our Route—Dutch Boers—Their Habits—Sterile Appearance of the District— Failure of Grass—Succeeded by other Plants— Vines—Animals—The Boers as Farmers—Migration of Springbucks— Wariness of Animals—The Orange River—Territory of the Griquas and Bechuanas—The Griquas—The Chief Waterboer—His wise and energetic Government—His Fidelity—Ill-considered Measures of the Colonial Government in regard to Supplies of Gunpowder—Success of the Missionaries among the Griquas and Bechuanas—Manifest Improvement of the native Character—Dress of the Natives—A full-dress Costume—A Native's Description of the Natives—Articles of Commerce in the Country of the Bechuanas—Their Unwillingness to learn, and Readiness to criticise.

Having sent my family home to England, I started in the beginning of June, 1852, on my last journey from Cape Town. This journey extended from the southern extremity of the continent to St. Paul de Loando, the capital of Angola, on the west coast, and thence across South Central Africa in an oblique direction to Kilimane (Quilimane) in Eastern Africa. I proceeded in the usual conveyance of the country, the heavy, lumbering Cape wagon drawn by ten oxen, and was accompanied by two Christian Bechuanas from Kuruman—than whom I never saw better servants any where—by two Bakwain men, and two young girls, who, having come as nurses with our children to the Cape, were returning to their home at Kolobeng. Wagon-traveling in Africa has been so often described that I need say no more than that it is a prolonged system of picnicking, excellent for the health, and agreeable to those who are not over-fastidious about trifles, and who delight in being in the open air.

Our route to the north lay near the centre of the cone-shaped mass of land which constitutes the promontory of the Cape. If we suppose this cone to be divided into three zones or longitudinal bands, we find each presenting distinct peculiarities of climate, physical appearance and population. These are more marked beyond than within the colony. At some points one district seems to be continued in and to merge into the other, but the general dissimilarity warrants the division, as an aid to memory. The eastern zone is often furnished with mountains, well wooded with evergreen succulent trees, on which neither fire nor droughts can have the smallest effect ('Strelitzia', 'Zamia horrida', 'Portulacaria afra', 'Schotia speciosa', 'Euphorbias', and 'Aloes arborescens'); and its seaboard gorges are clad with gigantic timber. It is also comparatively well watered with streams and flowing rivers. The annual supply of rain is considerable, and the inhabitants (Caffres or Zulus) are tall, muscular, and well made; they are shrewd, energetic, and brave; altogether they merit the character given them by military authorities, of being "magnificent savages". Their splendid physical development and form of skull show that, but for the black skin and woolly hair, they would take rank among the foremost Europeans.

The next division, that which embraces the centre of the continent, can scarcely be called hilly, for what hills there are are very low. It consists for the most part of extensive, slightly undulating plains. There are no lofty mountains, but few springs, and still fewer flowing streams. Rain is far from abundant, and droughts may be expected every few years. Without artificial irrigation no European grain can be raised, and the inhabitants (Bechuanas), though evidently of the same stock, originally, with those already mentioned, and closely resembling them in being an agricultural as well as a pastoral people, are a comparatively timid race, and inferior to the Caffres in physical development.

The western division is still more level than the middle one, being rugged only near the coast. It includes the great plain called the Kalahari Desert, which is remarkable for little water and very considerable vegetation.

The reason, probably, why so little rain falls on this extensive plain is that the prevailing winds of most of the interior country are easterly, with a little southing. The moisture taken up by the atmosphere from the Indian Ocean is deposited on the eastern hilly slope; and when the moving mass of air reaches its greatest elevation, it is then on the verge of the great valley, or, as in the case of the Kalahari, the great heated inland plains; there, meeting with the rarefied air of that hot, dry surface, the ascending heat gives it greater capacity for retaining all its remaining humidity, and few showers can be given to the middle and western lands in consequence of the increased hygrometric power.

This is the same phenomenon, on a gigantic scale, as that which takes place on Table Mountain, at the Cape, in what is called the spreading of the "table-cloth". The southeast wind causes a mass of air, equal to the diameter of the mountain, suddenly to ascend at least three thousand feet; the dilatation produced by altitude, with its attendant cold, causes the immediate formation of a cloud on the summit; the water in the atmosphere becomes visible; successive masses of gliding-up and passing-over air cause the continual formation of clouds, but the top of the vapory mass, or "table-cloth", is level, and seemingly motionless; on the lee side, however, the thick volumes of vapor curl over and descend, but when they reach the point below, where greater density and higher temperature impart enlarged capacity for carrying water, they entirely disappear.

Now if, instead of a hollow on the lee side of Table Mountain, we had an elevated heated plain, the clouds which curl over that side, and disappear as they do at present when a "southeaster" is blowing, might deposit some moisture on the windward ascent and top; but the heat would then impart the increased capacity the air now receives at the lower level in its descent to leeward, and, instead of an extended country with a flora of the 'Disa grandiflora', 'gladiolus', 'rushes', and 'lichens', which now appear on Table Mountain, we should have only the hardy vegetation of the Kalahari.

Why there should be so much vegetation on the Kalahari may be explained by the geological formation of the country. There is a rim or fringe of ancient rocks round a great central valley, which, dipping inward, form a basin, the bottom of which is composed of the oldest silurian rocks. This basin has been burst through and filled up in many parts by eruptive traps and breccias, which often bear in their substances angular fragments of the more ancient rocks, as shown in the fossils they contain. Now, though large areas have been so dislocated that but little trace of the original valley formation appears, it is highly probable that the basin shape prevails over large tracts of the country; and as the strata on the slopes, where most of the rain falls, dip in toward the centre, they probably guide water beneath the plains but ill supplied with moisture from the clouds. The phenomenon of stagnant fountains becoming by a new and deeper outlet never-failing streams may be confirmatory of the view that water is conveyed from the sides of the country into the bottom of the central valley; and it is not beyond the bounds of possibility that the wonderful river system in the north, which, if native information be correct, causes a considerable increase of water in the springs called Matlomagan-yana (the Links), extends its fertilizing influence beneath the plains of the Kalahari.

The peculiar formation of the country may explain why there is such a difference in the vegetation between the 20th and 30th parallels of latitude in South Africa and the same latitudes in Central Australia. The want of vegetation is as true of some parts too in the centre of South America as of Australia; and the cause of the difference holds out a probability for the success of artesian wells in extensive tracts of Africa now unpeopled solely on account of the want of surface water. We may be allowed to speculate a little at least on the fact of much greater vegetation, which, from whatever source it comes, presents for South Africa prospects of future greatness which we can not hope for in Central Australia. As the interior districts of the Cape Colony are daily becoming of higher value, offering to honest industry a fair remuneration for capital, and having a climate unequaled in salubrity for consumptive patients, I should unhesitatingly recommend any farmer at all afraid of that complaint in his family to try this colony. With the means of education already possessed, and the onward and upward movement of the Cape population, he need entertain no apprehensions of his family sinking into barbarism.

The route we at this time followed ran along the middle, or skirted the western zone before alluded to, until we reached the latitude of Lake Ngami, where a totally different country begins. While in the colony, we passed through districts inhabited by the descendants of Dutch and French refugees who had fled from religious persecution. Those living near the capital differ but little from the middle classes in English counties, and are distinguished by public spirit and general intelligence; while those situated far from the centres of civilization are less informed, but are a body of frugal, industrious, and hospitable peasantry. A most efficient system of public instruction was established in the time of Governor Sir George Napier, on a plan drawn up in a great measure by that accomplished philosopher, Sir John Herschel. The system had to contend with less sectarian rancor than elsewhere; indeed, until quite recently, that spirit, except in a mild form, was unknown.

The population here described ought not to be confounded with some Boers who fled from British rule on account of the emancipation of their Hottentot slaves, and perhaps never would have been so had not every now and then some Rip Van Winkle started forth at the Cape to justify in the public prints the deeds of blood and slave-hunting in the far interior. It is therefore not to be wondered at if the whole race is confounded and held in low estimation by those who do not know the real composition of the Cape community.

Population among the Boers increases rapidly; they marry soon, are seldom sterile, and continue to have children late. I once met a worthy matron whose husband thought it right to imitate the conduct of Abraham while Sarah was barren; she evidently agreed in the propriety of the measure, for she was pleased to hear the children by a mother of what has been thought an inferior race address her as their mother. Orphans are never allowed to remain long destitute; and instances are frequent in which a tender-hearted farmer has adopted a fatherless child, and when it came of age portioned it as his own.

Two centuries of the South African climate have not had much effect upon the physical condition of the Boers. They are a shade darker, or rather ruddier, than Europeans, and are never cadaverous-looking, as descendants of Europeans are said to be elsewhere. There is a tendency to the development of steatopyga, so characteristic of Arabs and other African tribes; and it is probable that the interior Boers in another century will become in color what the learned imagine our progenitors, Adam and Eve, to have been.

The parts of the colony through which we passed were of sterile aspect; and, as the present winter had been preceded by a severe drought, many farmers had lost two thirds of their stock. The landscape was uninviting; the hills, destitute of trees, were of a dark brown color, and the scanty vegetation on the plains made me feel that they deserved the name of Desert more than the Kalahari. When first taken possession of, these parts are said to have been covered with a coating of grass, but that has disappeared with the antelopes which fed upon it, and a crop of mesembryanthemums and crassulas occupies its place. It is curious to observe how, in nature, organizations the most dissimilar are mutually dependent on each other for their perpetuation. Here the original grasses were dependent for dissemination on the grass-feeding animals, which scattered the seeds. When, by the death of the antelopes, no fresh sowing was made, the African droughts proved too much for this form of vegetation. But even this contingency was foreseen by the Omniscient One; for, as we may now observe in the Kalahari Desert, another family of plants, the mesembryanthemums, stood ready to neutralize the aridity which must otherwise have followed. This family of plants possesses seed-vessels which remain firmly shut on their contents while the soil is hot and dry, and thus preserve the vegetative power intact during the highest heat of the torrid sun; but when rain falls, the seed-vessel opens and sheds its contents just when there is the greatest probability of their vegetating. In other plants heat and drought cause the seed-vessels to burst and shed their charge.

One of this family is edible ('Mesembryanthemum edule'); another possesses a tuberous root, which may be eaten raw; and all are furnished with thick, fleshy leaves, having pores capable of imbibing and retaining moisture from a very dry atmosphere and soil, so that, if a leaf is broken during a period of the greatest drought, it shows abundant circulating sap. The plants of this family are found much farther north, but the great abundance of the grasses prevents them from making any show. There, however, they stand ready to fill up any gap which may occur in the present prevailing vegetation; and should the grasses disappear, animal life would not necessarily be destroyed, because a reserve supply, equivalent to a fresh act of creative power, has been provided.

One of this family, 'M. turbiniforme', is so colored as to blend in well with the hue of the soil and stones around it; and a 'gryllus' of the same color feeds on it. In the case of the insect, the peculiar color is given as compensation for the deficiency of the powers of motion to enable it to elude the notice of birds. The continuation of the species is here the end in view. In the case of the plant the same device is adopted for a sort of double end, viz., perpetuation of the plant by hiding it from animals, with the view that ultimately its extensive appearance will sustain that race.

As this new vegetation is better adapted for sheep and goats in a dry country than grass, the Boers supplant the latter by imitating the process by which graminivorous antelopes have so abundantly disseminated the seed of grasses. A few wagon-loads of mesembryanthemum plants, in seed, are brought to a farm covered with a scanty crop of coarse grass, and placed on a spot to which the sheep have access in the evenings. As they eat a little every night, the seeds are dropped over the grazing grounds in this simple way, with a regularity which could not be matched except at the cost of an immense amount of labor. The place becomes in the course of a few years a sheep-farm, as these animals thrive on such herbage. As already mentioned, some plants of this family are furnished with an additional contrivance for withstanding droughts, viz., oblong tubers, which, buried deep enough beneath the soil for complete protection from the scorching sun, serve as reservoirs of sap and nutriment during those rainless periods which recur perpetually in even the most favored spots of Africa. I have adverted to this peculiarity as often seen in the vegetation of the Desert; and, though rather out of place, it may be well—while noticing a clever imitation of one process in nature by the Cape farmers—to suggest another for their consideration. The country beyond south lat. 18 Deg. abounds in three varieties of grape-bearing vines, and one of these is furnished with oblong tubers every three or four inches along the horizontal root. They resemble closely those of the asparagus. This increase of power to withstand the effects of climate might prove of value in the more arid parts of the Cape colony, grapes being well known to be an excellent restorative in the debility produced by heat: by ingrafting, or by some of those curious manipulations which we read of in books on gardening, a variety might be secured better adapted to the country than the foreign vines at present cultivated. The Americans find that some of their native vines yield wines superior to those made from the very best imported vines from France and Portugal. What a boon a vine of the sort contemplated would have been to a Rhenish missionary I met at a part in the west of the colony called Ebenezer, whose children had never seen flowers, though old enough to talk about them!

The slow pace at which we wound our way through the colony made almost any subject interesting. The attention is attracted to the names of different places, because they indicate the former existence of buffaloes, elands, and elephants, which are now to be found only hundreds of miles beyond. A few blesbucks ('Antilope pygarga'), gnus, bluebucks ('A. cerulea'), steinbucks, and the ostrich ('Struthio camelus'), continue, like the Bushmen, to maintain a precarious existence when all the rest are gone. The elephant, the most sagacious, flees the sound of fire-arms first; the gnu and ostrich, the most wary and the most stupid, last. The first emigrants found the Hottentots in possession of prodigious herds of fine cattle, but no horses, asses, or camels. The original cattle, which may still be seen in some parts of the frontier, must have been brought south from the north-northeast, for from this point the natives universally ascribe their original migration. They brought cattle, sheep, goats, and dogs; why not the horse, the delight of savage hordes? Horses thrive well in the Cape Colony when imported. Naturalists point out certain mountain ranges as limiting the habitat of certain classes of animals; but there is no Cordillera in Africa to answer that purpose, there being no visible barrier between the northeastern Arabs and the Hottentot tribes to prevent the different hordes, as they felt their way southward, from indulging their taste for the possession of this noble animal.

I am here led to notice an invisible barrier, more insurmountable than mountain ranges, but which is not opposed to the southern progress of cattle, goats, and sheep. The tsetse would prove a barrier only until its well-defined habitat was known, but the disease passing under the term of horse-sickness (peripneumonia) exists in such virulence over nearly seven degrees of latitude that no precaution would be sufficient to save these animals. The horse is so liable to this disease, that only by great care in stabling can he be kept any where between 20 Deg. and 27 Deg. S. during the time between December and April. The winter, beginning in the latter month, is the only period in which Englishmen can hunt on horseback, and they are in danger of losing all their studs some months before December. To this disease the horse is especially exposed, and it is almost always fatal. One attack, however, seems to secure immunity from a second. Cattle, too, are subject to it, but only at intervals of a few, sometimes many years; but it never makes a clean sweep of the whole cattle of a village, as it would do of a troop of fifty horses. This barrier, then, seems to explain the absence of the horse among the Hottentots, though it is not opposed to the southern migration of cattle, sheep, and goats.

When the flesh of animals that have died of this disease is eaten, it causes a malignant carbuncle, which, when it appears over any important organ, proves rapidly fatal. It is more especially dangerous over the pit of the stomach. The effects of the poison have been experienced by missionaries who had eaten properly cooked food, the flesh of sheep really but not visibly affected by the disease. The virus in the flesh of the animal is destroyed neither by boiling nor roasting. This fact, of which we have had innumerable examples, shows the superiority of experiments on a large scale to those of acute and able physiologists and chemists in the laboratory, for a well known physician of Paris, after careful investigation, considered that the virus in such cases was completely neutralized by boiling.

This disease attacks wild animals too. During our residence at Chonuan great numbers of tolos, or koodoos, were attracted to the gardens of the Bakwains, abandoned at the usual period of harvest because there was no prospect of the corn ('Holcus sorghum') bearing that year. The koodoo is remarkably fond of the green stalks of this kind of millet. Free feeding produced that state of fatness favorable for the development of this disease, and no fewer than twenty-five died on the hill opposite our house. Great numbers of gnus and zebras perished from the same cause, but the mortality produced no sensible diminution in the numbers of the game, any more than the deaths of many of the Bakwains who persisted, in spite of every remonstrance, in eating the dead meat, caused any sensible decrease in the strength of the tribe.

The farms of the Boers consist generally of a small patch of cultivated land in the midst of some miles of pasturage. They are thus less an agricultural than a pastoral people. Each farm must have its fountain; and where no such supply of water exists, the government lands are unsalable. An acre in England is thus generally more valuable than a square mile in Africa. But the country is prosperous, and capable of great improvement. The industry of the Boers augurs well for the future formation of dams and tanks, and for the greater fruitfulness that would certainly follow.

As cattle and sheep farmers the colonists are very successful. Larger and larger quantities of wool are produced annually, and the value of colonial farms increases year by year. But the system requires that with the increase of the population there should be an extension of territory. Wide as the country is, and thinly inhabited, the farmers feel it to be too limited, and they are gradually spreading to the north. This movement proves prejudicial to the country behind, for labor, which would be directed to the improvement of the colony, is withdrawn and expended in a mode of life little adapted to the exercise of industrial habits. That, however, does not much concern the rest of mankind. Nor does it seem much of an evil for men who cultivate the soil to claim a right to appropriate lands for tillage which other men only hunt over, provided some compensation for the loss of sustenance be awarded. The original idea of a title seems to have been that "subduing" or cultivating gave that right. But this rather Chartist principle must be received with limitations, for its recognition in England would lead to the seizure of all our broad ancestral acres by those who are willing to cultivate them. And, in the case under consideration, the encroachments lead at once to less land being put under the plow than is subjected to the native hoe, for it is a fact that the Basutos and Zulus, or Caffres of Natal, cultivate largely, and undersell our farmers wherever they have a fair field and no favor.

Before we came to the Orange River we saw the last portion of a migration of springbucks ('Gazella euchore', or tsepe). They come from the great Kalahari Desert, and, when first seen after crossing the colonial boundary, are said often to exceed forty thousand in number. I can not give an estimate of their numbers, for they appear spread over a vast expanse of country, and make a quivering motion as they feed, and move, and toss their graceful horns. They feed chiefly on grass; and as they come from the north about the time when the grass most abounds, it can not be want of food that prompts the movement. Nor is it want of water, for this antelope is one of the most abstemious in that respect. Their nature prompts them to seek as their favorite haunts level plains with short grass, where they may be able to watch the approach of an enemy. The Bakalahari take advantage of this feeling, and burn off large patches of grass, not only to attract the game by the new crop when it comes up, but also to form bare spots for the springbuck to range over.

It is not the springbuck alone that manifests this feeling. When oxen are taken into a country of high grass, they are much more ready to be startled; their sense of danger is increased by the increased power of concealment afforded to an enemy by such cover, and they will often start off in terror at the ill-defined outlines of each other. The springbuck, possessing this feeling in an intense degree, and being eminently gregarious, becomes uneasy as the grass of the Kalahari becomes tall. The vegetation being more sparse in the more arid south, naturally induces the different herds to turn in that direction. As they advance and increase in numbers, the pasturage becomes more scarce; it is still more so the further they go, until they are at last obliged, in order to obtain the means of subsistence, to cross the Orange River, and become the pest of the sheep-farmer in a country which contains scarcely any of their favorite grassy food. If they light on a field of wheat in their way, an army of locusts could not make a cleaner sweep of the whole than they will do. It is questionable whether they ever return, as they have never been seen as a returning body. Many perish from want of food, the country to which they have migrated being unable to support them; the rest become scattered over the colony; and in such a wide country there is no lack of room for all. It is probable that, notwithstanding the continued destruction by fire-arms, they will continue long to hold their place.

On crossing the Orange River we come into independent territory inhabited by Griquas and Bechuanas. By Griquas is meant any mixed race sprung from natives and Europeans. Those in question were of Dutch extraction, through association with Hottentot and Bushwomen. Half-castes of the first generation consider themselves superior to those of the second, and all possess in some degree the characteristics of both parents. They were governed for many years by an elected chief, named Waterboer, who, by treaty, received a small sum per annum from the colonial government for the support of schools in his country, and proved a most efficient guard of our northwest boundary. Cattle-stealing was totally unknown during the whole period of this able chief's reign; and he actually drove back, single-handed, a formidable force of marauding Mantatees that threatened to invade the colony.* But for that brave Christian man, Waterboer, there is every human probability that the northwest would have given the colonists as much trouble as the eastern frontier; for large numbers among the original Griquas had as little scruple about robbing farmers of cattle as the Caffres are reputed to have. On the election of Waterboer to the chieftainship, he distinctly declared THAT NO MARAUDING SHOULD BE ALLOWED. As the government of none of these tribes is despotic, some of his principal men, in spite of this declaration, plundered some villages of Corannas living to the south of the Orange River. He immediately seized six of the ringleaders, and, though the step put his own position in jeopardy, he summoned his council, tried, condemned, and publicly executed the whole six. This produced an insurrection, and the insurgents twice attacked his capital, Griqua Town, with the intention of deposing him; but he bravely defeated both attempts, and from that day forth, during his long reign of thirty years, not a single plundering expedition ever left his territory. Having witnessed the deleterious effects of the introduction of ardent spirits among his people, he, with characteristic energy, decreed that any Boer or Griqua bringing brandy into the country should have his property in ardent spirits confiscated and poured out on the ground. The Griqua chiefs living farther east were unable to carry this law into effect as he did, hence the greater facility with which Boers in that direction got the Griquas to part with their farms.

* For an account of this, see Moffat's "Scenes and Labors in South Africa".

Ten years after he was firmly established in power he entered into a treaty with the colonial government, and during the twenty years which followed not a single charge was ever brought against either him or his people; on the contrary, his faithful adherence to the stipulated provisions elicited numerous expressions of approbation from successive governments. A late governor, however, of whom it is impossible to speak without respect, in a paroxysm of generalship which might have been good, had it not been totally inappropriate to the case, set about conciliating a band of rebellious British subjects (Boers), who murdered the Honorable Captain Murray, by proclaiming their independence while still in open rebellion, and not only abrogated the treaty with the Griquas, but engaged to stop the long-accustomed supplies of gunpowder for the defense of the frontier, and even to prevent them from purchasing it for their own defense by lawful trade.

If it had been necessary to prevent supplies of ammunition from finding their way into the country, as it probably was, one might imagine that the exception should not have been made in favor of either Boers or Caffres, our openly-avowed enemies; but, nevertheless, the exception was made, and is still continued in favor of the Boers, while the Bechuanas and Griquas, our constant friends, are debarred from obtaining a single ounce for either defense or trade; indeed, such was the state of ignorance as to the relation of the border tribes with the English, even at Cape Town, that the magistrates, though willing to aid my researches, were sorely afraid to allow me to purchase more than ten pounds of gunpowder, lest the Bechuanas should take it from me by force. As it turned out, I actually left more than that quantity for upward of two years in an open box in my wagon at Linyanti.

The lamented Sir George Cathcart, apparently unconscious of what he was doing, entered into a treaty with the Transvaal Boers, in which articles were introduced for the free passage of English traders to the north, and for the entire prohibition of slavery in the free state. Then passed the "gunpowder ordinance", by which the Bechuanas, whom alone the Boers dare attempt to enslave, were rendered quite defenseless. The Boers never attempt to fight with Caffres, nor to settle in Caffreland. We still continue to observe the treaty. The Boers never did, and never intended to abide by its provisions; for, immediately on the proclamation of their independence, a slave-hunt was undertaken against the Bechuanas of Sechele by four hundred Boers, under Mr. Peit Scholz, and the plan was adopted which had been cherished in their hearts ever since the emancipation of the Hottentots. Thus, from unfortunate ignorance of the country he had to govern, an able and sagacious governor adopted a policy proper and wise had it been in front of our enemies, but altogether inappropriate for our friends against whom it has been applied. Such an error could not have been committed by a man of local knowledge and experience, such as that noble of colonial birth, Sir Andries Stockenstrom; and such instances of confounding friend and foe, in the innocent belief of thereby promoting colonial interests, will probably lead the Cape community, the chief part of which by no means feels its interest to lie in the degradation of the native tribes, to assert the right of choosing their own governors. This, with colonial representation in the Imperial Parliament, in addition to the local self-government already so liberally conceded, would undoubtedly secure the perpetual union of the colony to the English crown.

Many hundreds of both Griquas and Bechuanas have become Christians and partially civilized through the teaching of English missionaries. My first impressions of the progress made were that the accounts of the effects of the Gospel among them had been too highly colored. I expected a higher degree of Christian simplicity and purity than exists either among them or among ourselves. I was not anxious for a deeper insight in detecting shams than others, but I expected character, such as we imagine the primitive disciples had—and was disappointed.* When, however, I passed on to the true heathen in the countries beyond the sphere of missionary influence, and could compare the people there with the Christian natives, I came to the conclusion that, if the question were examined in the most rigidly severe or scientific way, the change effected by the missionary movement would be considered unquestionably great.

> * *The popular notion, however, of the primitive Church is perhaps not very accurate. Those societies especially which consisted of converted Gentiles—men who had been accustomed to the vices and immoralities of heathenism—were certainly any thing but pure. In spite of their conversion, some of them carried the stains and vestiges of their former state with them when they passed from the temple to the church. If the instructed and civilized Greek did not all at once rise out of his former self, and understand and realize the high ideal of his new faith, we should be careful, in judging of the work of missionaries among savage tribes, not to apply to their converts tests and standards of too great severity. If the scoffing Lucian's account of the impostor Peregrinus may be believed, we find a church probably planted by the apostles manifesting less intelligence even than modern missionary churches. Peregrinus, a notoriously wicked man, was elected to the chief place among them, while Romish priests, backed by the power of France, could not find a place at all in the*

mission churches of Tahiti and Madagascar.

We can not fairly compare these poor people with ourselves, who have an atmosphere of Christianity and enlightened public opinion, the growth of centuries, around us, to influence our deportment; but let any one from the natural and proper point of view behold the public morality of Griqua Town, Kuruman, Likatlong, and other villages, and remember what even London was a century ago, and he must confess that the Christian mode of treating aborigines is incomparably the best.

The Griquas and Bechuanas were in former times clad much like the Caffres, if such a word may be used where there is scarcely any clothing at all. A bunch of leather strings about eighteen inches long hung from the lady's waist in front, and a prepared skin of a sheep or antelope covered the shoulders, leaving the breast and abdomen bare: the men wore a patch of skin, about the size of the crown of one's hat, which barely served for the purposes of decency, and a mantle exactly like that of the women. To assist in protecting the pores of the skin from the influence of the sun by day and of the cold by night, all smeared themselves with a mixture of fat and ochre; the head was anointed with pounded blue mica schist mixed with fat; and the fine particles of shining mica, falling on the body and on strings of beads and brass rings, were considered as highly ornamental, and fit for the most fastidious dandy. Now these same people come to church in decent though poor clothing, and behave with a decorum certainly superior to what seems to have been the case in the time of Mr. Samuel Pepys in London. Sunday is well observed, and, even in localities where no missionary lives, religious meetings are regularly held, and children and adults taught to read by the more advanced of their own fellow-countrymen; and no one is allowed to make a profession of faith by baptism unless he knows how to read, and understands the nature of the Christian religion.

The Bechuana Mission has been so far successful that, when coming from the interior, we always felt, on reaching Kuruman, that we had returned to civilized life. But I would not give any one to understand by this that they are model Christians—we can not claim to be model Christians ourselves—or even in any degree superior to the members of our country churches. They are more stingy and greedy than the poor at home; but in many respects the two are exactly alike. On asking an intelligent chief what he thought of them, he replied, "You white men have no idea of how wicked we are; we know each other better than you; some feign belief to ingratiate themselves with the missionaries; some profess Christianity because they like the new system, which gives so much more importance to the poor, and desire that the old system may pass away; and the rest—a pretty large number—profess because they are really true believers." This testimony may be considered as very nearly correct.

There is not much prospect of this country ever producing much of the materials of commerce except wool. At present the chief articles of trade are karosses or mantles—the skins of which they are composed come from the Desert; next to them, ivory, the quantity of which can not now be great, inasmuch as the means of shooting elephants is sedulously debarred entrance into the country. A few skins and horns, and some cattle, make up the remainder of the exports. English goods, sugar, tea, and coffee are the articles received in exchange. All the natives of these parts soon become remarkably fond of coffee. The acme of respectability among the Bechuanas is the possession of cattle and a wagon. It is remarkable that, though these latter require frequent repairs, none of the Bechuanas have ever learned to mend them. Forges and tools have been at their service, and teachers willing to aid them, but, beyond putting together a camp-stool, no effort has ever been made to acquire a knowledge of the trades. They observe most carefully a missionary at work until they understand whether a tire is well welded or not, and then pronounce upon its merits with great emphasis, but there their ambition rests satisfied. It is the same peculiarity among ourselves which leads us in other matters, such as book-making, to attain the excellence of fault-finding without the wit to indite a page. It was in vain I tried to indoctrinate the Bechuanas with the idea that criticism did not imply any superiority over the workman, or even equality with him.

Chapter 6

Kuruman—Its fine Fountain—Vegetation of the District—Remains of ancient Forests—Vegetable Poison—The Bible translated by Mr. Moffat—Capabilities of the Language—Christianity among the Natives—The Missionaries should extend their Labors more beyond the Cape Colony—Model Christians—Disgraceful Attack of the Boers on the Bakwains—Letter from Sechele—Details of the Attack—Numbers of School-children carried away into Slavery—Destruction of House and Property at Kolobeng—The Boers vow Vengeance against me—Consequent Difficulty of getting Servants to accompany me on my Journey—Start in November, 1852—Meet Sechele on his way to England to obtain Redress from the Queen—He is unable to proceed beyond the Cape—Meet Mr. Macabe on his Return from Lake Ngami—The hot Wind of the Desert—Electric State of the Atmosphere—Flock of Swifts—Reach Litubaruba—The Cave Lepelole—Superstitions regarding it—Impoverished State of the Bakwains—Retaliation on the Boers—Slavery—Attachment of the Bechuanas to Children—Hydrophobia unknown—Diseases of the Bakwains few in number—Yearly Epidemics—Hasty Burials—Ophthalmia—Native Doctors—Knowledge of Surgery at a very low Ebb—Little Attendance given to Women at their Confinements—The "Child Medicine"—Salubrity of the Climate well adapted for Invalids suffering from pulmonary Complaints.

The permanence of the station called Kuruman depends entirely on the fine ever-flowing fountain of that name. It comes from beneath the trap-rock, of which I shall have to speak when describing the geology of the entire country; and as it usually issues at a temperature of 72 Deg. Fahr., it probably comes from the old silurian schists, which formed the bottom of the great primeval valley of the continent. I could not detect any diminution in the flow of this gushing fountain during my residence in the country; but when Mr. Moffat first attempted a settlement here, thirty-five years ago, he made a dam six or seven miles below the present one, and led out the stream for irrigation, where not a drop of the fountain-water ever now flows. Other parts, fourteen miles below the Kuruman gardens, are pointed out as having contained, within the memory of people now living, hippopotami, and pools sufficient to drown both men and cattle. This failure of water must be chiefly ascribed to the general desiccation of the country, but partly also to the amount of irrigation carried on along both banks of the stream at the mission station. This latter circumstance would have more weight were it not coincident with the failure of fountains over a wide extent of country.

Without at present entering minutely into this feature of the climate, it may be remarked that the Kuruman district presents evidence of this dry southern region having, at no very distant date, been as well watered as the country north of Lake Ngami is now. Ancient river-beds and water-courses abound, and the very eyes of fountains long since dried up may be seen, in which the flow of centuries has worn these orifices from a slit to an oval form, having on their sides the tufa so abundantly deposited from these primitive waters; and just where the splashings, made when the stream fell on the rock below, may be supposed to have reached and evaporated, the same phenomenon appears. Many of these failing fountains no longer flow, because the brink over which they ran is now too high, or because the elevation of the western side of the country lifts the land away from the water supply below; but let a cutting be made from a lower level than the brink, and through it to a part below the surface of the water, and water flows perennially. Several of these ancient fountains have been resuscitated by the Bechuanas near Kuruman, who occasionally show their feelings of self-esteem by laboring for months at deep cuttings, which, having once begun, they feel bound in honor to persevere in, though told by a missionary that they can never force water to run up hill.

It is interesting to observe the industry of many Boers in this region in making long and deep canals from lower levels up to spots destitute of the slightest indication of water existing beneath except a few rushes and a peculiar kind of coarse, reddish-colored grass growing in a hollow, which anciently must have been the eye of a fountain, but is now filled up with soft tufa. In other instances, the indication of water below consists of the rushes growing on a long, sandy ridge a foot or two in height instead of in a furrow. A deep transverse cutting made through the higher part of this is rewarded by a stream of running water. The reason why the ground covering this water is higher than the rest of the locality is that the winds carry quantities of fine dust and sand about the country, and hedges, bushes, and trees cause its deposit. The rushes in this case perform the part of the hedges, and the moisture rising as dew by night fixes the sand securely among the roots, and a height, instead of a hollow, is the result. While on this subject it may be added that there is no perennial fountain in this part of the country except those that come from beneath the quartzose trap, which constitutes the "filling up" of the ancient valley; and as the water supply seems to rest on the old silurian schists which form its bottom, it is highly probable that

Artesian wells would in several places perform the part which these deep cuttings now do.

The aspect of this part of the country during most of the year is of a light yellow color; for some months during the rainy season it is of a pleasant green mixed with yellow. Ranges of hills appear in the west, but east of them we find hundreds of miles of grass-covered plains. Large patches of these flats are covered with white calcareous tufa resting on perfectly horizontal strata of trap. There the vegetation consists of fine grass growing in tufts among low bushes of the "wait-a-bit" thorn ('Acacia detinens'), with its annoying fish-hook-like spines. Where these rocks do not appear on the surface, the soil consists of yellow sand and tall, coarse grasses, growing among berry-yielding bushes, named moretloa ('Grewia flava') and mohatla ('Tarchonanthus'), which has enough of aromatic resinous matter to burn brightly, though perfectly green. In more sheltered spots we come on clumps of the white-thorned mimosa ('Acacia horrida', also 'A. atomiphylla'), and great abundance of wild sage ('Salvia Africana'), and various leguminosae, ixias, and large-flowering bulbs: the 'Amaryllis toxicaria' and 'A. Brunsvigia multiflora' (the former a poisonous bulb) yield in the decayed lamellae a soft, silky down, a good material for stuffing mattresses.

In some few parts of the country the remains of ancient forests of wild olive-trees ('Olea similis') and of the camel-thorn ('Acacia giraffe') are still to be met with; but when these are leveled in the proximity of a Bechuana village, no young trees spring up to take their places. This is not because the wood has a growth so slow as not to be appreciable in its increase during the short period that it can be observed by man, which might be supposed from its being so excessively hard; for having measured a young tree of this species growing in the corner of Mr. Moffat's garden near the water, I found that it increased at the rate of a quarter of an inch in diameter annually during a number of years. Moreover, the larger specimens, which now find few or no successors, if they had more rain in their youth, can not be above two or three hundred years old.

It is probable that this is the tree of which the Ark of the Covenant and the Tabernacle were constructed, as it is reported to be found where the Israelites were at the time these were made. It is an imperishable wood, while that usually pointed out as the "shittim" (or 'Acacia nilotica') soon decays and wants beauty.

In association with it we always observe a curious plant, named ngotuane, which bears such a profusion of fine yellow strong-scented flowers as quite to perfume the air. This plant forms a remarkable exception to the general rule, that nearly all the plants in the dry parts of Africa are scentless, or emit only a disagreeable odor. It, moreover, contains an active poison; a French gentleman, having imbibed a mouthful or two of an infusion of its flowers as tea, found himself rendered nearly powerless. Vinegar has the peculiar property of rendering this poison perfectly inert, whether in or out of the body. When mixed with vinegar, the poison may be drunk with safety, while, if only tasted by itself, it causes a burning sensation in the throat. This gentleman described the action of the vinegar, when he was nearly deprived of power by the poison imbibed, to have been as if electricity had run along his nerves as soon as he had taken a single glassful. The cure was instantaneous and complete. I had always to regret want of opportunity for investigating this remarkable and yet controllable agent on the nervous system. Its usual proximity to camel-thorn-trees may be accounted for by the PROBABILITY that the giraffe, which feeds on this tree, MAY make use of the plant as a medicine.

During the period of my visit at Kuruman, Mr. Moffat, who has been a missionary in Africa during upward of forty years, and is well known by his interesting work, "Scenes and Labors in South Africa", was busily engaged in carrying through the press, with which his station is furnished, the Bible in the language of the Bechuanas, which is called Sichuana. This has been a work of immense labor; and as he was the first to reduce their speech to a written form, and has had his attention directed to the study for at least thirty years, he may be supposed to be better adapted for the task than any man living. Some idea of the copiousness of the language may be formed from the fact that even he never spends a week at his work without discovering new words; the phenomenon, therefore, of any man who, after a few months' or years' study of a native tongue, cackles forth a torrent of vocables, may well be wondered at, if it is meant to convey instruction. In my own case, though I have had as much intercourse with the purest idiom as most Englishmen, and have studied the language carefully, yet I can never utter an important statement without doing so very slowly, and repeating it too, lest the foreign accent, which is distinctly perceptible in all Europeans, should render the sense unintelligible. In this I follow the example of the Bechuana orators, who, on important matters, always speak slowly, deliberately, and with reiteration. The capabilities of this language may be inferred from the fact that the Pentateuch is fully expressed in Mr. Moffat's translation in fewer words than in the Greek Septuagint, and in a very considerably smaller number than in our own English version. The language is, however, so simple in its construction, that its copiousness by no means requires the explanation that the people have fallen from a former state of civilization and culture. Language seems to be an attribute of the human mind and thought; and the inflections, various as they are in the most barbarous tongues, as that of the Bushmen, are probably only proofs of the race being human, and endowed with the power of thinking; the fuller development of language taking place as the improvement of our other faculties goes on. It is fortunate that the translation of the Bible has been effected before the language became adulterated with half-uttered foreign words, and while those who have heard the eloquence of the native assemblies are still living; for the young, who are brought up in our schools, know less of the language than the missionaries; and Europeans born in the country, while possessed of the idiom perfectly, if not otherwise educated, can not be referred to for explanation of any uncommon word. A person who acted as interpreter to Sir George Cathcart actually told his excellency that the language of the Basutos was not capable of expressing the substance of a chief's diplomatic paper, while every one acquainted with Moshesh, the chief who sent it, well knows that he could in his own tongue have expressed it without study all over again in three or four different ways. The interpreter could scarcely have done as much in English.

This language both rich and poor speak correctly; there is no vulgar style; but children have a 'patois' of their own, using many words in their play which men would scorn to repeat. The Bamapela have adopted a click into their dialect, and a large infusion of the ringing "ny", which seems to have been for the purpose of preventing others from understanding them.

The fact of the complete translation of the Bible at a station seven hundred miles inland from the Cape naturally suggests the question whether it is likely to be permanently useful, and whether Christianity, as planted by modern missions, is likely to retain its vitality without constant supplies of foreign teaching? It would certainly be no cause for congratulation if the Bechuana Bible seemed at all likely to meet the fate of Elliot's Choctaw version, a specimen of which may be seen in the library of one of the American colleges—as God's word in a language which no living tongue can articulate, nor living mortal understand; but a better destiny seems in store for this, for the Sichuana language has been introduced into the new country beyond Lake Ngami. There it is the court language, and will take a stranger any where through a district larger than France. The Bechuanas, moreover, in all probability possess that imperishability which forms so remarkable a feature in the entire African race.

When converts are made from heathenism by modern missionaries, it becomes an interesting question whether their faith possesses the elements of permanence, or is only an exotic too tender for self-propagation when the fostering care of the foreign cultivators is withdrawn. If neither habits of self-reliance are cultivated, nor opportunities given for the exercise of that virtue, the most promising converts are apt to become like spoiled children. In Madagascar, a few Christians were left with nothing but the Bible in their hands; and though exposed to persecution, and even death itself, as the penalty of adherence to their profession, they increased ten-fold in numbers, and are, if possible, more decided believers now than they were when, by an edict of the queen of that island, the missionaries ceased their teaching.

In South Africa such an experiment could not be made, for such a variety of Christian sects have followed the footsteps of the London Missionary Society's successful career, that converts of one denomination, if left to their own resources, are eagerly adopted by another, and are thus more likely to become spoiled than trained to the manly Christian virtues.

Another element of weakness in this part of the missionary field is the fact of the missionary societies considering the Cape Colony itself as a proper sphere for their peculiar operations. In addition to a well-organized and efficient Dutch Reformed Established Church, and schools for secular instruction, maintained by government, in every village of any extent in the colony, we have a number of other sects, as the Wesleyans, Episcopalians, Moravians, all piously laboring at the same good work. Now it is deeply to be regretted that so much honest zeal should be so lavishly expended in a district wherein there is so little scope for success. When we hear an agent of one sect urging his friends at home to aid him quickly to occupy some unimportant nook, because, if it is not speedily laid hold of, he will "not have room for the sole of his foot," one can not help longing that both he and his friends would direct their noble aspirations to the millions of untaught heathen in the regions beyond, and no longer continue to convert the extremity of the continent into, as it were, a dam of benevolence.

I would earnestly recommend all young missionaries to go at once to the real heathen, and never to be content with what has been made ready to their hands by men of greater enterprise. The idea of making model Christians of the young need not be entertained by any one who is secretly convinced, as most men who know their own hearts are, that he is not a model Christian himself. The Israelitish slaves brought out of Egypt by Moses were not converted and elevated in one generation, though under the direct teaching of God himself. Notwithstanding the numbers of miracles he wrought, a generation had to be cut off because of unbelief. Our own elevation, also, has been the work of centuries, and, remembering this, we should not indulge in overwrought expectations as to the elevation which those who have inherited the degradation of ages may attain in our day. The principle might even be adopted by missionary societies, that one ordinary missionary's lifetime of teaching should be considered an ample supply of foreign teaching for any tribe in a thinly-peopled country, for some never will receive the Gospel at all, while in other parts, when Christianity is once planted, the work is sure to go on. A missionary is soon known to be supported by his friends at home; and though the salary is but a bare subsistence, to Africans it seems an enormous sum; and, being unable to appreciate the motives by which he is actuated, they consider themselves entitled to various services at his hands, and defrauded if these are not duly rendered. This feeling is all the stronger when a young man, instead of going boldly to the real heathen, settles down in a comfortable house and garden prepared by those into whose labors he has entered. A remedy for this evil might be found in appropriating the houses and gardens raised by the missionaries' hands to their own families. It is ridiculous to call such places as Kuruman, for instance, "Missionary Society's property". This beautiful station was made what it is, not by English money, but by the sweat and toil of fathers whose children have, notwithstanding, no place on earth which they can call a home. The Society's operations may be transferred to the north, and then the strong-built mission premises become the home of a Boer, and the stately stone church his cattle-pen. This place has been what the monasteries of Europe are said to have been when pure. The monks did not disdain to hold the plow. They introduced fruit-trees, flowers, and vegetables, in addition to teaching and emancipating the serfs. Their monasteries were mission stations, which resembled ours in being dispensaries for the sick, almshouses for the poor, and nurseries of learning. Can we learn nothing from them in their prosperity as the schools of Europe, and see naught in their history but the pollution and laziness of their decay? Can our wise men tell us why the former mission stations (primitive monasteries) were self-supporting, rich, and flourishing as pioneers of civilization and agriculture, from which we even now reap benefits, and modern mission stations are mere pauper establishments, without that permanence or ability to be self-supporting which they possessed?

Protestant missionaries of every denomination in South Africa all agree in one point, that no mere profession of Christianity is sufficient to entitle the converts to the Christian name. They are all anxious to place the Bible in the hands of the natives, and, with ability to read that, there can be little doubt as to the future. We believe Christianity to be divine, and equal to all it has to perform; then let the good seed be widely sown, and, no matter to what sect the converts may belong, the harvest will be glorious. Let nothing that I have said be interpreted as indicative of feelings inimical to any body of Christians, for I never, as a missionary, felt myself to be either Presbyterian, Episcopalian, or Independent, or called upon in any way to love one denomination less than another. My earnest desire is, that those who really have the best interests of the heathen at heart should go to them;

and assuredly, in Africa at least, self-denying labors among real heathen will not fail to be appreciated. Christians have never yet dealt fairly by the heathen and been disappointed.

When Sechele understood that we could no longer remain with him at Kolobeng, he sent his children to Mr. Moffat, at Kuruman, for instruction in all the knowledge of the white men. Mr. Moffat very liberally received at once an accession of five to his family, with their attendants.

Having been detained at Kuruman about a fortnight by the breaking of a wagon-wheel, I was thus providentially prevented from being present at the attack of the Boers on the Bakwains, news of which was brought, about the end of that time, by Masebele, the wife of Sechele. She had herself been hidden in a cleft of a rock, over which a number of Boers were firing. Her infant began to cry, and, terrified lest this should attract the attention of the men, the muzzles of whose guns appeared at every discharge over her head, she took off her armlets as playthings to quiet the child. She brought Mr. Moffat a letter, which tells its own tale. Nearly literally translated it was as follows:

"Friend of my heart's love, and of all the confidence of my heart, I am Sechele. I am undone by the Boers, who attacked me, though I had no guilt with them. They demanded that I should be in their kingdom, and I refused. They demanded that I should prevent the English and Griquas from passing (northward). I replied, These are my friends, and I can prevent no one (of them). They came on Saturday, and I besought them not to fight on Sunday, and they assented. They began on Monday morning at twilight, and fired with all their might, and burned the town with fire, and scattered us. They killed sixty of my people, and captured women, and children, and men. And the mother of Baleriling (a former wife of Sechele) they also took prisoner. They took all the cattle and all the goods of the Bakwains; and the house of Livingstone they plundered, taking away all his goods. The number of wagons they had was eighty-five, and a cannon; and after they had stolen my own wagon and that of Macabe, then the number of their wagons (counting the cannon as one) was eighty-eight. All the goods of the hunters (certain English gentlemen hunting and exploring in the north) were burned in the town; and of the Boers were killed twenty-eight. Yes, my beloved friend, now my wife goes to see the children, and Kobus Hae will convey her to you. I am, SECHELE, The Son of Mochoasele."

This statement is in exact accordance with the account given by the native teacher Mebalwe, and also that sent by some of the Boers themselves to the public colonial papers. The crime of cattle-stealing, of which we hear so much near Caffreland, was never alleged against these people, and, if a single case had occurred when I was in the country, I must have heard of it, and would at once say so. But the only crime imputed in the papers was that "Sechele was getting too saucy." The demand made for his subjection and service in preventing the English traders passing to the north was kept out of view.

Very soon after Pretorius had sent the marauding party against Kolobeng, he was called away to the tribunal of infinite justice. His policy is justified by the Boers generally from the instructions given to the Jewish warriors in Deuteronomy 20:10-14. Hence, when he died, the obituary notice ended with "Blessed are the dead who die in the Lord." I wish he had not "forbidden us to preach unto the Gentiles that they may be saved."

The report of this outrage on the Bakwains, coupled with denunciations against myself for having, as it was alleged, taught them to kill Boers, produced such a panic in the country, that I could not engage a single servant to accompany me to the north. I have already alluded to their mode of warfare, and in all previous Boerish forays the killing had all been on one side; now, however, that a tribe where an Englishman had lived had begun to shed THEIR blood as well, it was considered the strongest presumptive evidence against me. Loud vows of vengeance were uttered against my head, and threats of instant pursuit by a large party on horseback, should I dare to go into or beyond their country; and as these were coupled with the declaration that the English government had given over the whole of the native tribes to their rule, and would assist in their entire subjection by preventing fire-arms and ammunition from entering the country, except for the use of the Boers, it was not to be wondered at that I was detained for months at Kuruman from sheer inability to get wagon-drivers. The English name, from being honored and respected all over the country, had become somewhat more than suspected; and as the policy of depriving those friendly tribes of the means of defense was represented by the Boers as proof positive of the wish of the English that they should be subjugated, the conduct of a government which these tribes always thought the paragon of justice and friendship was rendered totally incomprehensible to them; they could neither defend themselves against their enemies, nor shoot the animals in the produce of which we wished them to trade.

At last I found three servants willing to risk a journey to the north; and a man of color named George Fleming, who had generously been assisted by Mr. H. E. Rutherford, a mercantile gentleman of Cape Town, to endeavor to establish a trade with the Makololo, had also managed to get a similar number; we accordingly left Kuruman on the 20th of November, and proceeded on our journey. Our servants were the worst possible specimens of those who imbibe the vices without the virtues of Europeans, but we had no choice, and were glad to get away on any terms.

When we reached Motito, forty miles off, we met Sechele on his way, as he said, "to the Queen of England." Two of his own children, and their mother, a former wife, were among the captives seized by the Boers; and being strongly imbued with the then very prevalent notion of England's justice and generosity, he thought that in consequence of the violated treaty he had a fair case to lay before her majesty. He employed all his eloquence and powers of persuasion to induce me to accompany him, but I excused myself on the ground that my arrangements were already made for exploring the north. On explaining the difficulties of the way, and endeavoring to dissuade him from the attempt, on account of the knowledge I possessed of the governor's policy, he put the pointed question, "Will the queen not listen to me, supposing I should reach her?" I replied, "I believe she would listen, but the difficulty is to get to her." "Well, I shall reach her," expressed his final determination. Others explained the difficulties more fully, but nothing could shake his resolution. When he reached Bloemfontein he found the English army just returning from a battle with the Basutos, in which both parties claimed the victory, and both were glad that a second engagement was not tried. Our officers invited Sechele to dine with them, heard his story, and collected a handsome sum of money to enable him to pursue his journey to England. The commander refrained from noticing him, as a single word in favor of the restoration of the children of Sechele would have been a virtual confession of the failure of his own policy at the very outset. Sechele proceeded as far as the Cape; but his resources being there expended, he was obliged to return to his own country, one thousand miles distant, without accomplishing the object of his journey.

On his return he adopted a mode of punishment which he had seen in the colony, namely, making criminals work on the public roads. And he has since, I am informed, made himself the missionary to his own people. He is tall, rather corpulent, and has more of the negro feature than common, but has large eyes. He is very dark, and his people swear by "Black Sechele". He has great intelligence, reads well, and is a fluent speaker. Great numbers of the tribes formerly living under the Boers have taken refuge under his sway, and he is now greater in power than he was before the attack on Kolobeng.

Having parted with Sechele, we skirted along the Kalahari Desert, and sometimes within its borders, giving the Boers a wide berth. A larger fall of rain than usual had occurred in 1852, and that was the completion of a cycle of eleven or twelve years, at which the same phenomenon is reported to have happened on three occasions. An unusually large crop of melons had appeared in consequence. We had the pleasure of meeting with Mr. J. Macabe returning from Lake Ngami, which he had succeeded in reaching by going right across the Desert from a point a little to the south of Kolobeng. The accounts of the abundance of watermelons were amply confirmed by this energetic traveler; for, having these in vast quantities, his cattle subsisted on the fluid contained in them for a period of no less than twenty-one days; and when at last they reached a supply of water, they did not seem to care much about it. Coming to the lake from the southeast, he crossed the Teoughe, and went round the northern part of it, and is the only European traveler who had actually seen it all. His estimate of the extent of the lake is higher than that given by Mr. Oswell and myself, or from about ninety to one hundred miles in circumference. Before the lake was discovered, Macabe wrote a letter in one of the Cape papers recommending a certain route as likely to lead to it. The Transvaal Boers fined him 500 dollars for writing about "ouze felt", OUR country, and imprisoned him, too, till the fine was paid. I now learned from his own lips that the public report of this is true. Mr. Macabe's companion, Mahar, was mistaken by a tribe of Barolongs for a Boer, and shot as he approached their village. When Macabe came up and explained that he was an Englishman, they expressed the utmost regret, and helped to bury him. This was the first case in recent times of an Englishman being slain by the Bechuanas. We afterward heard that there had been some fighting between these Barolongs and the Boers, and that there had been capturing of cattle on both sides. If this was true, I can only say that it was the first time that I ever heard of cattle being taken by Bechuanas. This was a Caffre war in stage the second; the third stage in the development is when both sides are equally well armed and afraid of each other; the fourth, when the English take up a quarrel not their own, and the Boers slip out of the fray.

Two other English gentlemen crossed and recrossed the Desert about the same time, and nearly in the same direction. On returning, one of them, Captain Shelley, while riding forward on horseback, lost himself, and was obliged to find his way alone to Kuruman, some hundreds of miles distant. Reaching that station shirtless, and as brown as a Griqua, he was taken for one by Mrs. Moffat, and was received by her with a salutation in Dutch, that being the language spoken by this people. His sufferings must have been far more severe than any we endured. The result of the exertions of both Shelley and Macabe is to prove that the general view of the Desert always given by the natives has been substantially correct.

Occasionally, during the very dry seasons which succeed our winter and precede our rains, a hot wind blows over the Desert from north to south. It feels somewhat as if it came from an oven, and seldom blows longer at a time than three days. It resembles in its effects the harmattan of the north of

Africa, and at the time the missionaries first settled in the country, thirty-five years ago, it came loaded with fine reddish-colored sand. Though no longer accompanied by sand, it is so devoid of moisture as to cause the wood of the best seasoned English boxes and furniture to shrink, so that every wooden article not made in the country is warped. The verls of ramrods made in England are loosened, and on returning to Europe fasten again. This wind is in such an electric state that a bunch of ostrich feathers held a few seconds against it becomes as strongly charged as if attached to a powerful electrical machine, and clasps the advancing hand with a sharp crackling sound.

When this hot wind is blowing, and even at other times, the peculiarly strong electrical state of the atmosphere causes the movement of a native in his kaross to produce therein a stream of small sparks. The first time I noticed this appearance was while a chief was traveling with me in my wagon. Seeing part of the fur of his mantle, which was exposed to slight friction by the movement of the wagon, assume quite a luminous appearance, I rubbed it smartly with the hand, and found it readily gave out bright sparks, accompanied with distinct cracks. "Don't you see this?" said I. "The white men did not show us this," he replied; "we had it long before white men came into the country, we and our forefathers of old." Unfortunately, I never inquired the name which they gave to this appearance, but I have no doubt there is one for it in the language. Otto von Guerrike is said, by Baron Humboldt, to have been the first that ever observed this effect in Europe, but the phenomenon had been familiar to the Bechuanas for ages. Nothing came of that, however, for they viewed the sight as if with the eyes of an ox. The human mind has remained here as stagnant to the present day, in reference to the physical operations of the universe, as it once did in England. No science has been developed, and few questions are ever discussed except those which have an intimate connection with the wants of the stomach.

Very large flocks of swifts ('Cypselus apus') were observed flying over the plains north of Kuruman. I counted a stream of them, which, by the time it took to pass toward the reeds of that valley, must have numbered upward of four thousand. Only a few of these birds breed at any time in this country. I have often observed them, and noticed that there was no appearance of their having paired; there was no chasing of each other, nor any playing together. There are several other birds which continue in flocks, and move about like wandering gipsies, even during the breeding season, which in this country happens in the intervals between the cold and hot seasons, cold acting somewhat in the same way here as the genial warmth of spring does in Europe. Are these the migratory birds of Europe, which return there to breed and rear their young?

On the 31st of December, 1852, we reached the town of Sechele, called, from the part of the range on which it is situated, Litubaruba. Near the village there exists a cave named Lepelole; it is an interesting evidence of the former existence of a gushing fountain. No one dared to enter the Lohaheng, or cave, for it was the common belief that it was the habitation of the Deity. As we never had a holiday from January to December, and our Sundays were the periods of our greatest exertions in teaching, I projected an excursion into the cave on a week-day to see the god of the Bakwains. The old men said that every one who went in remained there forever, adding, "If the teacher is so mad as to kill himself, let him do so alone, we shall not be to blame." The declaration of Sechele, that he would follow where I led, produced the greatest consternation. It is curious that in all their pretended dreams or visions of their god he has always a crooked leg, like the Egyptian Thau. Supposing that those who were reported to have perished in this cave had fallen over some precipice, we went well provided with lights, ladder, lines, &c.; but it turned out to be only an open cave, with an entrance about ten feet square, which contracts into two water-worn branches, ending in round orifices through which the water once flowed. The only inhabitants it seems ever to have had were baboons. I left at the end of the upper branch one of Father Mathew's leaden teetotal tickets.

I never saw the Bakwains looking so haggard and lean as at this time. Most of their cattle had been swept away by the Boers, together with about eighty fine draught oxen; and much provision left with them by two officers, Captains Codrington and Webb, to serve for their return journey south, had been carried off also. On their return these officers found the skeletons of the Bakwains where they expected to find their own goods. All the corn, clothing, and furniture of the people, too, had been consumed in the flames which the Boers had forced the subject tribes to apply to the town during the fight, so that its inhabitants were now literally starving.

Sechele had given orders to his people not to commit any act of revenge pending his visit to the Queen of England; but some of the young men ventured to go to meet a party of Boers returning from hunting, and, as the Boers became terrified and ran off, they brought their wagons to Litubaruba. This seems to have given the main body of Boers an idea that the Bakwains meant to begin a guerrilla war upon them. This "Caffre war" was, however, only in embryo, and not near that stage of development in which the natives have found out that the hide-and-seek system is the most successful.

The Boers, in alarm, sent four of their number to ask for peace! I, being present, heard the condition: "Sechele's children must be restored to him." I never saw men so completely and unconsciously in a trap as these four Boers were. Strong parties of armed Bakwains occupied every pass in the hills and gorges around; and had they not promised much more than they intended, or did perform, that day would have been their last. The commandant Scholz had appropriated the children of Sechele to be his own domestic slaves. I was present when one little boy, Khari, son of Sechele, was returned to his mother; the child had been allowed to roll into the fire, and there were three large unbound open sores on different parts of his body. His mother and the women received him with a flood of silent tears.

Slavery is said to be mild and tender-hearted in some places. The Boers assert that they are the best of masters, and that, if the English had possessed the Hottentot slaves, they would have received much worse treatment than they did: what that would have been it is difficult to imagine. I took down the names of some scores of boys and girls, many of whom I knew as our scholars; but I could not comfort the weeping mothers by any hope of their ever returning from slavery.

The Bechuanas are universally much attached to children. A little child toddling near a party of men while they are eating is sure to get a handful of the food. This love of children may arise, in a great measure, from the patriarchal system under which they dwell. Every little stranger forms an increase of property to the whole community, and is duly reported to the chief—boys being more welcome than girls. The parents take the name of the child, and often address their children as Ma (mother), or Ra (father). Our eldest boy being named Robert, Mrs. Livingstone was, after his birth, always addressed as Ma-Robert, instead of Mary, her Christian name.

I have examined several cases in which a grandmother has taken upon herself to suckle a grandchild. Masina of Kuruman had no children after the birth of her daughter Sina, and had no milk after Sina was weaned, an event which usually is deferred till the child is two or three years old. Sina married when she was seventeen or eighteen, and had twins; Masina, after at least fifteen years' interval since she had suckled a child, took possession of one of them, applied it to her breast, and milk flowed, so that she was able to nurse the child entirely. Masina was at this time at least forty years of age. I have witnessed several other cases analogous to this. A grandmother of forty, or even less, for they become withered at an early age, when left at home with a young child, applies it to her own shriveled breast, and milk soon follows. In some cases, as that of Ma-bogosing, the chief wife of Mahure, who was about thirty-five years of age, the child was not entirely dependent on the grandmother's breast, as the mother suckled it too. I had witnessed the production of milk so frequently by the simple application of the lips of the child, that I was not therefore surprised when told by the Portuguese in Eastern Africa of a native doctor who, by applying a poultice of the pounded larvae of hornets to the breast of a woman, aided by the attempts of the child, could bring back the milk. Is it not possible that the story in the "Cloud of Witnesses" of a man, during the time of persecution in Scotland, putting his child to his own breast, and finding, to the astonishment of the whole country, that milk followed the act, may have been literally true? It was regarded and is quoted as a miracle; but the feelings of the father toward the child of a murdered mother must have been as nearly as possible analogous to the maternal feeling; and, as anatomists declare the structure of both male and female breasts to be identical, there is nothing physically impossible in the alleged result. The illustrious Baron Humboldt quotes an instance of the male breast yielding milk; and, though I am not conscious of being over-credulous, the strange instances I have examined in the opposite sex make me believe that there is no error in that philosopher's statement.

The Boers know from experience that adult captives may as well be left alone, for escape is so easy in a wild country that no fugitive-slave-law can come into operation; they therefore adopt the system of seizing only the youngest children, in order that these may forget their parents and remain in perpetual bondage. I have seen mere infants in their houses repeatedly. This fact was formerly denied; and the only thing which was wanting to make the previous denial of the practice of slavery and slave-hunting by the Transvaal Boers no longer necessary was the declaration of their independence.

In conversation with some of my friends here I learned that Maleke, a chief of the Bakwains, who formerly lived on the hill Litubaruba, had been killed by the bite of a mad dog. My curiosity was strongly excited by this statement, as rabies is so rare in this country. I never heard of another case, and could not satisfy myself that even this was real hydrophobia. While I was at Mabotsa, some dogs became affected by a disease which led them to run about in an incoherent state; but I doubt whether it was any thing but an affection of the brain. No individual or animal got the complaint by inoculation from the animals' teeth; and from all that I could hear, the prevailing idea of hydrophobia not existing within the tropics seems to be quite correct.

The diseases known among the Bakwains are remarkably few. There is no consumption nor scrofula, and insanity and hydrocephalus are rare. Cancer and cholera are quite unknown. Small-pox and measles passed through the country about twenty years ago, and committed great ravages; but, though the former has since broken out on the coast repeatedly, neither disease has since traveled inland. For small-pox, the natives employed, in some parts, inoculation in the forehead with some animal deposit; in other parts, they employed the matter of the small-pox itself; and in one village they seem to have selected a virulent case for the matter used in the operation, for nearly all the village was swept off by the disease in a malignant confluent form. Where the idea came from I can not conceive. It was practiced by the Bakwains at a time when they had no intercourse, direct or indirect, with the southern missionaries. They all adopt readily the use of vaccine virus when it is brought within their reach.

A certain loathsome disease, which decimates the North American Indians, and threatens extirpation to the South Sea Islanders, dies out in the interior of Africa without the aid of medicine; and the Bangwaketse, who brought it from the west coast, lost it when they came into their own land southwest of Kolobeng. It seems incapable of permanence in any form in persons of pure African blood any where in the centre of the country. In persons of mixed blood it is otherwise; and the virulence of the secondary symptoms seemed to be, in all the cases that came under my care, in exact proportion to the greater or less amount of European blood in the patient. Among the Corannas and Griquas of mixed breed it produces the same ravages as in Europe; among half-blood Portuguese it is equally frightful in its inroads on the system; but in the pure Negro of the central parts it is quite incapable of permanence. Among the Barotse I found a disease called manassah, which closely resembles that of the 'foeda mulier' of history.

Equally unknown is stone in the bladder and gravel. I never met with a case, though the waters are often so strongly impregnated with sulphate of lime that kettles quickly become incrusted internally with the salt; and some of my patients, who were troubled with indigestion, believed that their stomachs had got into the same condition. This freedom from calculi would appear to be remarkable in the negro race, even in the United States; for seldom indeed have the most famed lithotomists there ever operated on a negro.

The diseases most prevalent are the following: pneumonia, produced by sudden changes of temperature, and other inflammations, as of the bowels, stomach, and pleura; rheumatism; disease of the heart—but these become rare as the people adopt the European dress—various forms of indigestion and ophthalmia; hooping-cough comes frequently; and every year the period preceding the rains is marked by some sort of epidemic. Sometimes it is general ophthalmia, resembling closely the Egyptian. In another year it is a kind of diarrhoea, which nothing will cure until there is a fall of rain, and any thing acts as a charm after that. One year the epidemic period was marked by a disease which looked like pneumonia, but had the peculiar symptom strongly developed of great pain in the seventh cervical process. Many persons died of it, after being in a comatose state for many hours or days before their decease. No inspection of the body being ever allowed by these people, and the place of sepulture being carefully concealed, I had to rest satisfied with conjecture. Frequently the Bakwains buried their dead in the huts where they died, for fear lest the witches (Baloi) should disinter their friends, and use some part of the body in their fiendish arts. Scarcely is the breath out of the body when the unfortunate patient is hurried away to be buried. An ant-eater's hole is often selected, in order to save the trouble of digging a grave. On two occasions while I was there this hasty burial was followed by the return home of the men, who had been buried alive, to their affrighted relatives. They had recovered, while in their graves, from prolonged swoons.

In ophthalmia the doctors cup on the temples, and apply to the eyes the pungent smoke of certain roots, the patient, at the same time, taking strong draughts of it up his nostrils. We found the solution of nitrate of silver, two or three grains to the ounce of rain-water, answer the same end so much more effectually, that every morning numbers of patients crowded round our house for the collyrium. It is a good preventive of an acute attack when poured into the eyes as soon as the pain begins, and might prove valuable for travelers. Cupping is performed with the horn of a goat or antelope, having a little hole pierced in the small end. In some cases a small piece of wax is attached, and a temporary hole made through it to the horn. When the air is well withdrawn, and kept out by touching the orifice, at every inspiration, with the point of the tongue, the wax is at last pressed together with the teeth, and the little hole in it closed up, leaving a vacuum within the horn for the blood to flow from the already scarified parts. The edges of the horn applied to the surface are wetted, and cupping is well performed, though the doctor occasionally, by separating the fibrine from the blood in a basin of water by his side, and exhibiting it, pretends that he has extracted something more than blood. He can thus explain the rationale of the cure by his own art, and the ocular demonstration given is well appreciated.

Those doctors who have inherited their profession as an heirloom from their fathers and grandfathers generally possess some valuable knowledge, the result of long and close observation; but if a man can not say that the medical art is in his family, he may be considered a quack. With the regular practitioners I always remained on the best terms, by refraining from appearing to doubt their skill in the presence of their patients. Any explanation in private was thankfully received by them, and wrong treatment changed into something more reasonable with cordial good-will, if no one but the doctor and myself were present at the conversation. English medicines were eagerly asked for and accepted by all; and we always found medical knowledge an important aid in convincing the people that we were really anxious for their welfare. We can not accuse them of ingratitude; in fact, we shall remember the kindness of the Bakwains to us as long as we live.

The surgical knowledge of the native doctors is rather at a low ebb. No one ever attempted to remove a tumor except by external applications. Those with which the natives are chiefly troubled are fatty and fibrous tumors; and as they all have the 'vis medicatrix naturae' in remarkable activity, I safely removed an immense number. In illustration of their want of surgical knowledge may be mentioned the case of a man who had a tumor as large as a child's head. This was situated on the nape of his neck, and prevented his walking straight. He applied to his chief, and he got some famous strange doctor from the East Coast to cure him. He and his assistants attempted to dissolve it by kindling on it a little fire made of a few small pieces of medicinal roots. I removed it for him, and he always walked with his head much more erect than he needed to do ever afterward. Both men and women submit to an operation without wincing, or any of that shouting which caused young students to faint in the operating theatre before the introduction of chloroform. The women pride themselves on their ability to bear pain. A mother will address her little girl, from whose foot a thorn is to be extracted, with, "Now, ma, you are a woman; a woman does not cry." A man scorns to shed tears. When we were passing one of the deep wells in the Kalahari, a boy, the son of an aged father, had been drowned in it while playing on its brink. When all hope was gone, the father uttered an exceedingly great and bitter cry. It was sorrow without hope. This was the only instance I ever met with of a man weeping in this country.

Their ideas on obstetrics are equally unscientific, and a medical man going near a woman at her confinement appeared to them more out of place than a female medical student appears to us in a dissecting-room. A case of twins, however, happening, and the ointment of all the doctors of the town proving utterly insufficient to effect the relief which a few seconds of English art afforded, the prejudice vanished at once. As it would have been out of the question for me to have entered upon this branch of the profession—as indeed it would be inexpedient for any medical man to devote himself exclusively, in a thinly-peopled country, to the practice of medicine—I thereafter reserved myself for the difficult cases only, and had the satisfaction of often conferring great benefits on poor women in their hour of sorrow. The poor creatures are often placed in a little hut built for the purpose, and are left without any assistance whatever, and the numbers of umbilical herniae which are met with in consequence is very great. The women suffer less at their confinement than is the case in civilized countries; perhaps from their treating it, not as a disease, but as an operation of nature, requiring no change of diet except a feast of meat and abundance of fresh air. The husband on these occasions is bound to slaughter for his lady an ox, or goat, or sheep, according to his means.

My knowledge in the above line procured for me great fame in a department in which I could lay no claim to merit. A woman came a distance of one hundred miles for relief in a complaint which seemed to have baffled the native doctors; a complete cure was the result. Some twelve months after she returned to her husband, she bore a son. Her husband having previously reproached her for being barren, she sent me a handsome present, and proclaimed all over the country that I possessed a medicine for the cure of sterility. The consequence was, that I was teased with applications from husbands and wives from all parts of the country. Some came upward of two hundred miles to purchase the great boon, and it was in vain for me to explain that I had only cured the disease of the other case. The more I denied, the higher their offers rose; they would give any money for the "child medicine"; and it was really heart-rending to hear the earnest entreaty, and see the tearful eye, which spoke the intense desire for offspring: "I am getting old; you see gray hairs here and there on my head, and I have no child; you know how Bechuana husbands cast their old wives away; what can I do? I have no child to bring water to me when I am sick," etc.

The whole of the country adjacent to the Desert, from Kuruman to Kolobeng, or Litubaruba, and beyond up to the latitude of Lake Ngami, is remarkable for its great salubrity of climate. Not only the natives, but Europeans whose constitutions have been impaired by an Indian climate, find the tract of country indicated both healthy and restorative. The health and longevity of the missionaries have always been fair, though mission-work is not very conducive to either elsewhere. Cases have been known in which patients have come from the coast with complaints closely resembling, if they were not actually, those of consumption; and they have recovered by the influence of the climate alone. It must always be borne in mind that the climate near the coast, from which we received such very favorable reports of the health of the British troops, is actually inferior for persons suffering from pulmonary complaints to that of any part not subjected to the influence of sea-air. I have never seen the beneficial effects of the inland climate on persons of shattered constitutions, nor heard their high praises of the benefit they have derived from traveling, without wishing that its bracing effects should become more extensively known in England. No one who has visited the region I have above mentioned fails to remember with pleasure the wild, healthful gipsy life of wagon-traveling.

A considerable proportion of animal diet seems requisite here. Independent of the want of salt, we required meat in as large quantity daily as we do in England, and no bad effects, in the way of biliousness, followed the free use of flesh, as in other hot climates. A vegetable diet causes acidity and heartburn.

Mr. Oswell thought this climate much superior to that of Peru, as far as pleasure is concerned; the want of instruments unfortunately prevented my obtaining accurate scientific data for the medical world on this subject; and were it not for the great expense of such a trip, I should have no hesitation in recommending the borders of the Kalahari Desert as admirably suited for all patients having pulmonary complaints. It is the complete antipodes to our cold, damp, English climate. The winter is perfectly dry; and as not a drop of rain falls during that period, namely, from the beginning of May to the end of August, damp and cold are never combined. However hot the day may have been at Kolobeng—and the thermometer sometimes rose, previous to a fall of rain, up to 96 Deg. in the coolest part of our house—yet the atmosphere never has that steamy feeling nor those debilitating effects so well known in India and on the coast of Africa itself. In the evenings the air becomes deliciously cool, and a pleasant refreshing night follows the hottest day. The greatest heat ever felt is not so oppressive as it is when there is much humidity in the air; and the great evaporation consequent on a fall of rain makes the rainy season the most agreeable for traveling. Nothing can exceed the balmy feeling of the evenings and mornings during the whole year. You wish for an increase neither of cold nor heat; and you can sit out of doors till midnight without ever thinking of colds or rheumatism; or you may sleep out at night, looking up to the moon till you fall asleep, without a thought or sign of moon-blindness. Indeed, during many months there is scarcely any dew.

Chapter 7

Departure from the Country of the Bakwains—Large black Ant—Land Tortoises—Diseases of wild Animals—Habits of old Lions—Cowardice of the Lion—Its Dread of a Snare—Major Vardon's Note—The Roar of the Lion resembles the Cry of the Ostrich—Seldom attacks full-grown Animals—Buffaloes and Lions—Mice—Serpents—Treading on one—Venomous and harmless Varieties—Fascination—Sekomi's Ideas of Honesty—Ceremony of the Sechu for Boys—The Boyale for young Women—Bamangwato Hills—The Unicorn's Pass—The Country beyond—Grain—Scarcity of Water—Honorable Conduct of English Gentlemen—Gordon Cumming's hunting Adventures—A Word of Advice for young Sportsmen—Bushwomen drawing Water—Ostrich—Silly Habit—Paces—Eggs—Food.

Having remained five days with the wretched Bakwains, seeing the effects of war, of which only a very inadequate idea can ever be formed by those who have not been eye-witnesses of its miseries, we prepared to depart on the 15th of January, 1853. Several dogs, in better condition by far than any of the people, had taken up their residence at the water. No one would own them; there they had remained, and, coming on the trail of the people, long after their departure from the scene of conflict, it was plain they had

"Held o'er the dead their carnival."

Hence the disgust with which they were viewed.

On our way from Khopong, along the ancient river-bed which forms the pathway to Boatlanama, I found a species of cactus, being the third I have seen in the country, namely, one in the colony with a bright red flower, one at Lake Ngami, the flower of which was liver-colored, and the present one, flower unknown. That the plant is uncommon may be inferred from the fact that the Bakwains find so much difficulty in recognizing the plant again after having once seen it, that they believe it has the power of changing its locality.

On the 21st of January we reached the wells of Boatlanama, and found them for the first time empty. Lopepe, which I had formerly seen a stream running from a large reedy pool, was also dry. The hot salt spring of

Serinane, east of Lopepe, being undrinkable, we pushed on to Mashue for its delicious waters. In traveling through this country, the olfactory nerves are frequently excited by a strong disagreeable odor. This is caused by a large jet-black ant named "Leshonya". It is nearly an inch in length, and emits a pungent smell when alarmed, in the same manner as the skunk. The scent must be as volatile as ether, for, on irritating the insect with a stick six feet long, the odor is instantly perceptible.

Occasionally we lighted upon land tortoises, which, with their unlaid eggs, make a very agreeable dish. We saw many of their trails leading to the salt fountain; they must have come great distances for this health-giving article. In lieu thereof they often devour wood-ashes. It is wonderful how this reptile holds its place in the country. When seen, it never escapes. The young are taken for the sake of their shells; these are made into boxes, which, filled with sweet-smelling roots, the women hang around their persons. When older it is used as food, and the shell converted into a rude basin to hold food or water. It owes its continuance neither to speed nor cunning. Its color, yellow and dark brown, is well adapted, by its similarity to the surrounding grass and brushwood, to render it indistinguishable; and, though it makes an awkward attempt to run on the approach of man, its trust is in its bony covering, from which even the teeth of a hyaena glance off foiled. When this long-lived creature is about to deposit her eggs, she lets herself into the ground by throwing the earth up round her shell, until only the top is visible; then covering up the eggs, she leaves them until the rains begin to fall and the fresh herbage appears; the young ones then come out, their shells still quite soft, and, unattended by their dam, begin the world for themselves. Their food is tender grass and a plant named tholona, and they frequently resort to heaps of ashes and places containing efflorescence of the nitrates for the salts these contain.

Inquiries among the Bushmen and Bakalahari, who are intimately acquainted with the habits of the game, lead to the belief that many diseases prevail among wild animals. I have seen the kokong or gnu, kama or hartebeest, the tsessebe, kukama, and the giraffe, so mangy as to be uneatable even by the natives. Reference has already been made to the peripneumonia which cuts off horses, tolos or koodoos. Great numbers also of zebras are found dead with masses of foam at the nostrils, exactly as occurs in the common "horse-sickness". The production of the malignant carbuncle called kuatsi, or selonda, by the flesh when eaten, is another proof of the disease of the tame and wild being identical. I once found a buffalo blind from ophthalmia standing by the fountain Otse; when he attempted to run he lifted up his feet in the manner peculiar to blind animals. The rhinoceros has often worms on the conjunction of his eyes; but these are not the cause of the dimness of vision which will make him charge past a man who has wounded him, if he stands perfectly still, in the belief that his enemy is a tree. It probably arises from the horn being in the line of vision, for the variety named kuabaoba, which has a straight horn directed downward away from that line, possesses acute eyesight, and is much more wary.

All the wild animals are subject to intestinal worms besides. I have observed bunches of a tape-like thread and short worms of enlarged sizes in the rhinoceros. The zebra and elephants are seldom without them, and a thread-worm may often be seen under the peritoneum of these animals. Short red larvae, which convey a stinging sensation to the hand, are seen clustering round the orifice of the windpipe (trachea) of this animal at the back of the throat; others are seen in the frontal sinus of antelopes; and curious flat, leech-like worms, with black eyes, are found in the stomachs of leches. The zebra, giraffe, eland, and kukama have been seen mere skeletons from decay of their teeth as well as from disease.

The carnivora, too, become diseased and mangy; lions become lean and perish miserably by reason of the decay of the teeth. When a lion becomes too old to catch game, he frequently takes to killing goats in the villages; a woman or child happening to go out at night falls a prey too; and as this is his only source of subsistence now, he continues it. From this circumstance has arisen the idea that the lion, when he has once tasted human flesh, loves it better than any other. A man-eater is invariably an old lion; and when he overcomes his fear of man so far as to come to villages for goats, the people remark, "His teeth are worn, he will soon kill men." They at once acknowledge the necessity of instant action, and turn out to kill him. When living far away from population, or when, as is the case in some parts, he entertains a wholesome dread of the Bushmen and Bakalahari, as soon as either disease or old age overtakes him, he begins to catch mice and other small rodents, and even to eat grass; the natives, observing undigested vegetable matter in his droppings, follow up his trail in the certainty of finding him scarcely able to move under some tree, and dispatch him without difficulty. The grass may have been eaten as medicine, as is observed in dogs.

That the fear of man often remains excessively strong in the carnivora is proved from well-authenticated cases in which the lioness, in the vicinity of towns where the large game had been unexpectedly driven away by firearms, has been known to assuage the paroxysms of hunger by devouring her own young. It must be added, that, though the effluvium which is left by the footsteps of man is in general sufficient to induce lions to avoid a village, there are exceptions; so many came about our half-deserted houses at Chonuane while we were in the act of removing to Kolobeng, that the natives who remained with Mrs. Livingstone were terrified to stir out of doors in the evenings. Bitches, also, have been known to be guilty of the horridly unnatural act of eating their own young, probably from the great desire for animal food, which is experienced by the inhabitants as well.

When a lion is met in the daytime, a circumstance by no means unfrequent to travelers in these parts, if preconceived notions do not lead them to expect something very "noble" or "majestic", they will see merely an animal somewhat larger than the biggest dog they ever saw, and partaking very strongly of the canine features; the face is not much like the usual drawings of a lion, the nose being prolonged like a dog's; not exactly such as our painters make it—though they might learn better at the Zoological Gardens—their ideas of majesty being usually shown by making their lions' faces like old women in nightcaps. When encountered in the daytime, the lion stands a second or two, gazing, then turns slowly round, and walks as slowly away for a dozen paces, looking over his shoulder; then begins to trot, and, when he thinks himself out of sight, bounds off like a greyhound. By day there is not, as a rule, the smallest danger of lions which are not molested attacking man, nor even on a clear moonlight night, except when they possess the breeding storgh* (natural affection); this makes them brave almost any danger; and if a man happens to cross to the windward of them, both lion and lioness will rush at him, in the manner of a bitch with whelps. This does not often happen, as I only became aware of two or three instances of it. In one case a man, passing where the wind blew from him to the animals, was bitten before he could climb a tree; and occasionally a man on horseback has been caught by the leg under the same circumstances. So general, however, is the sense of security on moonlight nights, that we seldom tied up our oxen, but let them lie loose by the wagons; while on a dark, rainy night, if a lion is in the neighborhood, he is almost sure to venture to kill an ox. His approach is always stealthy, except when wounded; and any appearance of a trap is enough to cause him to refrain from making the last spring. This seems characteristic of the feline species; when a goat is picketed in India for the purpose of enabling the huntsmen to shoot a tiger by night, if on a plain, he would whip off the animal so quickly by a stroke of the paw that no one could take aim; to obviate this, a small pit is dug, and the goat is picketed to a stake in the bottom; a small stone is tied in the ear of the goat, which makes him cry the whole night. When the tiger sees the appearance of a trap, he walks round and round the pit, and allows the hunter, who is lying in wait, to have a fair shot.

* *(Greek) sigma-tau-omicron-rho-gamma-eta.*

When a lion is very hungry, and lying in wait, the sight of an animal may make him commence stalking it. In one case a man, while stealthily crawling towards a rhinoceros, happened to glance behind him, and found to his horror a lion STALKING HIM; he only escaped by springing up a tree like a cat. At Lopepe a lioness sprang on the after quarter of Mr. Oswell's horse, and when we came up to him we found the marks of the claws on the horse, and a scratch on Mr. O.'s hand. The horse, on feeling the lion on him, sprang away, and the rider, caught by a wait-a-bit thorn, was brought to the ground and rendered insensible. His dogs saved him. Another English gentleman (Captain Codrington) was surprised in the same way, though not hunting the lion at the time, but turning round he shot him dead in the neck. By accident a horse belonging to Codrington ran away, but was stopped by the bridle catching a stump; there he remained a prisoner two days, and when found the whole space around was marked by the footprints of lions. They had evidently been afraid to attack the haltered horse from fear that it was a trap. Two lions came up by night to within three yards of oxen tied to a wagon, and a sheep tied to a tree, and stood roaring, but afraid to make a spring. On another occasion one of our party was lying sound asleep and unconscious of danger between two natives behind a bush at Mashue; the fire was nearly out at their feet in consequence of all being completely tired out by the fatigues of the previous day; a lion came up to within three yards of the fire, and there commenced roaring instead of making a spring: the fact of their riding-ox being tied to the bush was the only reason the lion had for not following his instinct, and making a meal of flesh. He then stood on a knoll three hundred yards distant, and roared all night, and continued his growling as the party moved off by daylight next morning.

Nothing that I ever learned of the lion would lead me to attribute to it either the ferocious or noble character ascribed to it elsewhere. It possesses none of the nobility of the Newfoundland or St. Bernard dogs. With respect to its great strength there can be no doubt. The immense masses of muscle around its jaws, shoulders, and forearms proclaim tremendous force. They would seem, however, to be inferior in power to those of the Indian tiger. Most of those feats of strength that I have seen performed by lions, such as the taking away of an ox, were not carrying, but dragging or trailing the carcass along the ground: they have sprung on some occasions on to the hind-quarters of a horse, but no one has ever seen them on the withers of a giraffe. They do not mount on the hind-quarters of an eland even, but try to tear him down with their claws. Messrs. Oswell and Vardon once saw three lions endeavoring to drag down a buffalo, and they were unable to do so for a time, though he was then mortally wounded by a two-ounce ball.*

* *This singular encounter, in the words of an eye-witness, happened as follows:*

"My South African Journal is now before me, and I have got hold of the account of the lion and buffalo affair; here it is: '15th September, 1846. Oswell and I were riding this afternoon along the banks of the Limpopo, when a waterbuck started in front of us. I dismounted, and was following it through the jungle, when three buffaloes got up, and, after going a little distance, stood still, and the nearest bull turned round and looked at me. A ball from the two-ouncer crashed into his shoulder, and they all three made off. Oswell and I followed as soon as I had reloaded, and when we were in sight of the buffalo, and gaining on him at every stride, three lions leaped on the unfortunate brute; he bellowed most lustily as he kept up a kind of running fight, but he was, of course, soon overpowered and pulled down. We had a fine view of the struggle, and saw the lions on their hind legs tearing away with teeth and claws in most ferocious style. We crept up within thirty yards, and, kneeling down, blazed away at the lions. My rifle was a single barrel, and I had no spare gun. One lion fell dead almost ON the buffalo; he had merely time to turn toward us, seize a bush with his teeth, and drop dead with the stick in his jaws. The second made off immediately; and the third raised his head, coolly looked round for a moment, then went on tearing and biting at the carcass as hard as ever. We retired a short distance to load, then again advanced and fired. The lion made off, but a ball that he received OUGHT to have stopped him, as it went clean through his shoulder-blade. He was followed up and killed, after having charged several times. Both lions were males. It is not often that one BAGS a brace of lions and a bull buffalo in about ten minutes. It was an exciting adventure, and I shall never forget it.'

"Such, my dear Livingstone, is the plain unvarnished account. The buffalo had, of course, gone close to where the lions were lying down for the day; and they, seeing him lame and bleeding, thought the opportunity too good a one to be lost.

"*Ever yours, Frank Vardon.*"

In general the lion seizes the animal he is attacking by the flank near the hind leg, or by the throat below the jaw. It is questionable whether he ever attempts to seize an animal by the withers. The flank is the most common point of attack, and that is the part he begins to feast on first. The natives and lions are very similar in their tastes in the selection of tit-bits: an eland may be seen disemboweled by a lion so completely that he scarcely seems cut up at all. The bowels and fatty parts form a full meal for even the largest lion. The jackal comes sniffing about, and sometimes suffers for his temerity by a stroke from the lion's paw laying him dead. When gorged, the lion falls fast asleep, and is then easily dispatched. Hunting a lion with dogs involves very little danger as compared with hunting the Indian tiger, because the dogs bring him out of cover and make him stand at bay, giving the hunter plenty of time for a good deliberate shot.

Where game is abundant, there you may expect lions in proportionately large numbers. They are never seen in herds, but six or eight, probably one family, occasionally hunt together. One is in much more danger of being run over when walking in the streets of London, than he is of being devoured by lions in Africa, unless engaged in hunting the animal. Indeed, nothing that I have seen or heard about lions would constitute a barrier in the way of men of ordinary courage and enterprise.

The same feeling which has induced the modern painter to caricature the lion, has led the sentimentalist to consider the lion's roar the most terrific of all earthly sounds. We hear of the "majestic roar of the king of beasts." It is, indeed, well calculated to inspire fear if you hear it in combination with the tremendously loud thunder of that country, on a night so pitchy dark that every flash of the intensely vivid lightning leaves you with the impression of stone-blindness, while the rain pours down so fast that your fire goes out, leaving you without the protection of even a tree, or the chance of your gun going off. But when you are in a comfortable house or wagon, the case is very different, and you hear the roar of the lion without any awe or alarm. The silly ostrich makes a noise as loud, yet he never was feared by man. To talk of the majestic roar of the lion is mere majestic twaddle. On my mentioning this fact some years ago, the assertion was doubted, so I have been careful ever since to inquire the opinions of Europeans, who have heard both, if they could detect any difference between the roar of a lion and that of an ostrich; the invariable answer was, that they could not when the animal was at any distance. The natives assert that they can detect a variation between the commencement of the noise of each. There is, it must be admitted, considerable difference between the singing noise of a lion when full, and his deep, gruff growl when hungry. In general the lion's voice seems to come deeper from the chest than that of the ostrich, but to this day I can distinguish between them with certainty only by knowing that the ostrich roars by day and the lion by night.

The African lion is of a tawny color, like that of some mastiffs. The mane in the male is large, and gives the idea of great power. In some lions the ends of the hair of the mane are black; these go by the name of black-maned lions, though as a whole all look of the yellow tawny color. At the time of the discovery of the lake, Messrs. Oswell and Wilson shot two specimens of another variety. One was an old lion, whose teeth were mere stumps, and his claws worn quite blunt; the other was full grown, in the prime of life, with white, perfect teeth; both were entirely destitute of mane. The lions in the country near the lake give tongue less than those further south. We scarcely ever heard them roar at all.

The lion has other checks on inordinate increase besides man. He seldom attacks full-grown animals; but frequently, when a buffalo calf is caught by him, the cow rushes to the rescue, and a toss from her often kills him. One we found was killed thus; and on the Leeambye another, which died near Sesheke, had all the appearance of having received his death-blow from a buffalo. It is questionable if a single lion ever attacks a full-grown buffalo. The amount of roaring heard at night, on occasions when a buffalo is killed, seems to indicate there are always more than one lion engaged in the onslaught.

On the plain, south of Sebituane's ford, a herd of buffaloes kept a number of lions from their young by the males turning their heads to the enemy. The young and the cows were in the rear. One toss from a bull would kill the strongest lion that ever breathed. I have been informed that in one part of India even the tame buffaloes feel their superiority to some wild animals, for they have been seen to chase a tiger up the hills, bellowing as if they enjoyed the sport. Lions never go near any elephants except the calves, which, when young, are sometimes torn by them; every living thing retires before the lordly elephant, yet a full-grown one would be an easier prey than the rhinoceros; the lion rushes off at the mere sight of this latter beast.

In the country adjacent to Mashue great numbers of different kinds of mice exist. The ground is often so undermined with their burrows that the foot sinks in at every step. Little haycocks, about two feet high, and rather more than that in breadth, are made by one variety of these little creatures. The same thing is done in regions annually covered with snow for obvious purposes, but it is difficult here to divine the reason of the haymaking in the climate of Africa.*

* *'Euryotis unisulcatus' (F. Cuvier), 'Mus pumelio' (Spar.), and 'Mus lehocla' (Smith), all possess this habit in a greater or less degree. The first-named may be seen escaping danger with its young hanging to the after-part of its body.*

Wherever mice abound, serpents may be expected, for the one preys on the other. A cat in a house is therefore a good preventive against the entrance of these noxious reptiles. Occasionally, however, notwithstanding every precaution, they do find their way in, but even the most venomous sorts bite only when put in bodily fear themselves, or when trodden upon, or when the sexes come together. I once found a coil of serpents' skins, made by a number of them twisting together in the manner described by the Druids of old. When in the country, one feels nothing of that alarm and loathing which we may experience when sitting in a comfortable English room reading about them; yet they are nasty things, and we seem to have an instinctive feeling against them. In making the door for our Mabotsa house, I happened to leave a small hole at the corner below. Early one morning a man came to call for some article I had promised. I at once went to the door, and, it being dark, trod on a serpent. The moment I felt the cold scaly skin twine round a part of my leg, my latent instinct was roused, and I jumped up higher than I ever did before or hope to do again, shaking the reptile off in the leap. I probably trod on it near the head, and so prevented it biting me, but did not stop to examine.

Some of the serpents are particularly venomous. One was killed at Kolobeng of a dark brown, nearly black color, 8 feet 3 inches long. This species (picakholu) is so copiously supplied with poison that, when a number of dogs attack it, the first bitten dies almost instantaneously, the second in about five minutes, the third in an hour or so, while the fourth may live several hours. In a cattle-pen it produces great mischief in the same way. The one we killed at Kolobeng continued to distill clear poison from the fangs for hours after its head was cut off. This was probably that which passes by the name of the "spitting serpent", which is believed to be able to eject its poison into the eyes when the wind favors its forcible expiration. They all require water, and come long distances to the Zouga, and other rivers and pools, in search of it. We have another dangerous serpent, the puff adder, and several vipers. One, named by the inhabitants "Noga-put-sane", or serpent of a kid, utters a cry by night exactly like the bleating of that animal. I heard one at a spot where no kid could possibly have been. It is supposed by the natives to lure travelers to itself by this bleating. Several varieties, when alarmed, emit a peculiar odor, by which the people become aware of their presence in a house. We have also the cobra ('Naia haje', Smith) of several colors or varieties. When annoyed, they raise their heads up about a foot from the ground, and flatten the neck in a threatening manner, darting out the tongue and retracting it with great velocity, while their fixed glassy eyes glare as if in anger. There are also various species of the genus 'Dendrophis', as the 'Bucephalus viridis', or green tree-climber. They climb trees in search of birds and eggs, and are soon discovered by all the birds in the neighborhood collecting and sounding an alarm.* Their fangs are formed not so much for injecting poison on external objects as for keeping in any animal or bird of which they have got hold. In the case of the 'Dasypeltis inornatus' (Smith), the teeth are small, and favorable for the passage of thin-shelled eggs without breaking. The egg is taken in unbroken till it is within the gullet, or about two inches behind the head. The gular teeth placed there break the shell without spilling the contents, as would be the case if the front teeth were large. The shell is then ejected. Others appear to be harmless, and even edible. Of the latter sort is the large python, metse pallah, or tari. The largest specimens of this are about 15 or 20 feet in length. They are perfectly harmless, and live on small animals, chiefly the rodentia; occasionally the steinbuck and pallah fall victims, and are sucked into its comparatively small mouth in boa-constrictor fashion. One we shot was 11 feet 10 inches long, and as thick as a man's leg. When shot through the spine, it was capable of lifting itself up about five feet high, and opened its mouth in a threatening manner, but the poor thing was more inclined to crawl away. The flesh is much relished by the Bakalahari and Bushmen. They carry away each his portion, like logs of wood, over their shoulders.

> * "As this snake, 'Bucephalus Capensis', in our opinion, is not provided with a poisonous fluid to instill into wounds which these fangs may inflict, they must consequently be intended for a purpose different to those which exist in poisonous reptiles. Their use seems to be to offer obstacles to the retrogression of animals, such as birds, etc., while they are only partially within the mouth; and from the circumstance of these fangs being directed backward, and not admitting of being raised so as to form an angle with the edge of the jaw, they are well fitted to act as powerful holders when once they penetrate the skin and soft parts of the prey which their possessors may be in the act of swallowing. Without such fangs escapes would be common; with such they are rare.
>
> "The natives of South Africa regard the 'Bucephalus Capensis' as poisonous; but in their opinion we can not concur, as we

have not been able to discover the existence of any glands manifestly organized for the secretion of poison. The fangs are inclosed in a soft, pulpy sheath, the inner surface of which is commonly coated with a thin glairy secretion. This secretion possibly may have something acrid and irritating in its qualities, which may, when it enters a wound, cause pain and even swelling, but nothing of greater importance.

"The 'Bucephalus Capensis' is generally found on trees, to which it resorts for the purpose of catching birds, upon which it delights to feed. The presence of a specimen in a tree is generally soon discovered by the birds of the neighborhood, who collect around it and fly to and fro, uttering the most piercing cries, until some one, more terror-struck than the rest, actually scans its lips, and, almost without resistance, becomes a meal for its enemy. During such a proceeding the snake is generally observed with its head raised about ten or twelve inches above the branch round which its body and tail are entwined, with its mouth open and its neck inflated, as if anxiously endeavoring to increase the terror which it would almost appear it was aware would sooner or later bring within its grasp some one of the feathered group.

"Whatever may be said in ridicule of fascination, it is nevertheless true that birds, and even quadrupeds, are, under certain circumstances, unable to retire from the presence of certain of their enemies; and, what is even more extraordinary, unable to resist the propensity to advance from a situation of actual safety into one of the most imminent danger. This I have often seen exemplified in the case of birds and snakes; and I have heard of instances equally curious, in which antelopes and other quadrupeds have been so bewildered by the sudden appearance of crocodiles, and by the grimaces and contortions they practiced, as to be unable to fly or even move from the spot toward which they were approaching to seize them."—Dr. Andrew Smith's "Reptilia".

In addition to these interesting statements of the most able *naturalist from whom I have taken this note, it may be added that fire exercises a fascinating effect on some kinds of toads. They may be seen rushing into it in the evenings without ever starting back on feeling pain. Contact with the hot embers rather increases the energy with which they strive to gain the hottest parts, and they never cease their struggles for the centre even when their juices are coagulating and their limbs stiffening in the roasting heat. Various insects, also, are thus fascinated; but the scorpions may be seen coming away from the fire in fierce disgust, and they are so irritated as to inflict at that time their most painful stings.*

Some of the Bayeiye we met at Sebituane's Ford pretended to be unaffected by the bite of serpents, and showed the feat of lacerating their arms with the teeth of such as are unfurnished with the poison-fangs. They also swallow the poison, by way of gaining notoriety; but Dr. Andrew Smith put the sincerity of such persons to the test by offering them the fangs of a really poisonous variety, and found they shrank from the experiment.

When we reached the Bamangwato, the chief, Sekomi, was particularly friendly, collected all his people to the religious services we held, and explained his reasons for compelling some Englishmen to pay him a horse. "They would not sell him any powder, though they had plenty; so he compelled them to give it and the horse for nothing. He would not deny the extortion to me; that would be 'boherehere' (swindling)." He thus thought extortion better than swindling. I could not detect any difference in the morality of the two transactions, but Sekomi's ideas of honesty are the lowest I have met with in any Bechuana chief, and this instance is mentioned as the only approach to demanding payment for leave to pass that I have met with in the south. In all other cases the difficulty has been to get a chief to give us men to show the way, and the payment has only been for guides. Englishmen have always very properly avoided giving that idea to the native mind which we shall hereafter find prove troublesome, that payment ought to be made for passage through a country.

All the Bechuana and Caffre tribes south of the Zambesi practice circumcision ('boguera'), but the rites observed are carefully concealed. The initiated alone can approach, but in this town I was once a spectator of the second part of the ceremony of the circumcision, called "sechu". Just at the dawn of day, a row of boys of nearly fourteen years of age stood naked in the kotla, each having a pair of sandals as a shield on his hands. Facing them stood the men of the town in a similar state of nudity, all armed with long thin wands, of a tough, strong, supple bush called moretloa ('Grewia flava'), and engaged in a dance named "koha", in which questions are put to the boys, as "Will you guard the chief well?" "Will you herd the cattle well?" and, while the latter give an affirmative response, the men rush forward to them, and each aims a full-weight blow at the back of one of the boys. Shielding himself with the sandals above his head, he causes the supple wand to descend and bend into his back, and every stroke inflicted thus makes the blood squirt out of a wound a foot or eighteen inches long. At the end of the dance, the boys' backs are seamed with wounds and weals, the scars of which remain through life. This is intended to harden the young soldiers, and prepare them for the rank of men. After this ceremony, and after killing a rhinoceros, they may marry a wife.

In the "koha" the same respect is shown to age as in many other of their customs. A younger man, rushing from the ranks to exercise his wand on the backs of the youths, may be himself the object of chastisement by the older, and, on the occasion referred to, Sekomi received a severe cut on the leg from one of his gray-haired people. On my joking with some of the young men on their want of courage, notwithstanding all the beatings of which they bore marks, and hinting that our soldiers were brave without suffering so much, one rose up and said, "Ask him if, when he and I were compelled by a lion to stop and make a fire, I did not lie down and sleep as well as himself." In other parts a challenge to try a race would have been given, and you may frequently see grown men adopting that means of testing superiority, like so many children.

The sechu is practiced by three tribes only. Boguera is observed by all the Bechuanas and Caffres, but not by the negro tribes beyond 20 Deg. south. The "boguera" is a civil rather than a religious rite. All the boys of an age between ten and fourteen or fifteen are selected to be the companions for life of one of the sons of the chief. They are taken out to some retired spot in the forest, and huts are erected for their accommodation; the old men go out and teach them to dance, initiating them, at the same time, into all the mysteries of African politics and government. Each one is expected to compose an oration in praise of himself, called a "leina" or name, and to be able to repeat it with sufficient fluency. A good deal of beating is required to bring them up to the required excellency in different matters, so that, when they return from the close seclusion in which they are kept, they have generally a number of scars to show on their backs. These bands or regiments, named mepato in the plural and mopato in the singular, receive particular appellations; as, the Matsatsi—the suns; the Mabusa—the rulers; equivalent to our Coldstreams or Enniskillens; and, though living in different parts of the town, they turn out at the call, and act under the chief's son as their commander. They recognize a sort of equality and partial communism ever afterward, and address each other by the title of molekane or comrade. In cases of offence against their rules, as eating alone when any of their comrades are within call, or in cases of cowardice or dereliction of duty, they may strike one another, or any member of a younger mopato, but never any one of an older band; and when three or four companies have been made, the oldest no longer takes the field in time of war, but remains as a guard over the women and children. When a fugitive comes to a tribe, he is directed to the mopato analogous to that to which in his own tribe he belongs, and does duty as a member. No one of the natives knows how old he is. If asked his age, he answers by putting another question, "Does a man remember when he was born?" Age is reckoned by the number of mepato they have seen pass through the formulae of admission. When they see four or five mepato younger than themselves, they are no longer obliged to bear arms. The oldest individual I ever met boasted he had seen eleven sets of boys submit to the boguera. Supposing him to have been fifteen when he saw his own, and fresh bands were added every six or seven years, he must have been about forty when he saw the fifth, and may have attained seventy-five or eighty years, which is no great age; but it seemed so to them, for he had now doubled the age for superannuation among them. It is an ingenious plan for attaching the members of the tribe to the chief's family, and for imparting a discipline which renders the tribe easy of command. On their return to the town from attendance on the ceremonies of initiation, a prize is given to the lad who can run fastest, the article being placed where all may see the winner run up to snatch it. They are then considered men (banona, viri), and can sit among the elders in the kotla. Formerly they were only boys (basimane, pueri). The first missionaries set their faces against the boguera, on account of its connection with heathenism, and the fact that the youths learned much evil, and became disobedient to their parents. From the general success of these men, it is perhaps better that younger missionaries should tread in their footsteps; for so much evil may result from breaking down the authority on which, to those who can not read, the whole system of our influence appears to rest, that innovators ought to be made to propose their new measures as the Locrians did new laws—with ropes around their necks.

Probably the "boguera" was only a sanitary and political measure; and there being no continuous chain of tribes practicing the rite between the Arabs and the Bechuanas, or Caffres, and as it is not a religious ceremony, it can scarcely be traced, as is often done, to a Mohammedan source.

A somewhat analogous ceremony (boyale) takes place for young women, and the protegees appear abroad drilled under the surveillance of an old lady to the carrying of water. They are clad during the whole time in a dress composed of ropes made of alternate pumpkin-seeds and bits of reed strung together, and wound round the body in a figure-of-eight fashion. They are inured in this way to bear fatigue, and carry large pots of water under the guidance of the stern old hag. They have often scars from bits of burning charcoal having been applied to the forearm, which must have been done to test their power of bearing pain.

The Bamangwato hills are part of the range called Bakaa. The Bakaa tribe, however, removed to Kolobeng, and is now joined to that of Sechele. The range stands about 700 or 800 feet above the plains, and is composed of great masses of black basalt. It is probably part of the latest series of volcanic rocks in South Africa. At the eastern end these hills have curious fungoid or cup-shaped hollows, of a size which suggests the idea of craters. Within these are masses of the rock crystallized in the columnar form of this formation. The tops of the columns are quite distinct, of the hexagonal form, like the bottom of the cells of a honeycomb, but they are not parted from each other as in the Cave of Fingal. In many parts the lava-streams may be recognized, for there the rock is rent and split in every direction, but no soil is yet found in the interstices. When we were sitting in the evening, after a hot day, it was quite common to hear these masses of basalt split and fall among each other with the peculiar ringing sound which makes people believe that this rock contains much iron. Several large masses, in splitting thus by the cold acting suddenly on parts expanded by the heat of the day, have slipped down the sides of the hills, and, impinging against each other, have formed cavities in which the Bakaa took refuge against their enemies. The numerous chinks and crannies left by these huge fragments made it quite impossible for their enemies to smoke them out, as was done by the Boers to the people of Mankopane.

This mass of basalt, about six miles long, has tilted up the rocks on both the east and west; these upheaved rocks are the ancient silurian schists which formed the bottom of the great primaeval valley, and, like all the recent volcanic rocks of this country, have a hot fountain in their vicinity, namely, that of Serinane.

In passing through these hills on our way north we enter a pass named Manakalongwe, or Unicorn's Pass. The unicorn here is a large edible caterpillar, with an erect, horn-like tail. The pass was also called Porapora (or gurgling of water), from a stream having run through it. The scene must have been very different in former times from what it is now. This is part of the River Mahalapi, which so-called river scarcely merits the name, any more than the meadows of Edinburgh deserve the title of North Loch. These hills are the last we shall see for months. The country beyond consisted of large patches of trap-covered tufa, having little soil or vegetation except tufts of grass and wait-a-bit thorns, in the midst of extensive sandy, grass-covered plains. These yellow-colored, grassy plains, with moretloa and mahatla bushes, form quite a characteristic feature of the country. The yellow or dun-color prevails during a great part of the year. The Bakwain hills are an exception to the usual flat surface, for they are covered with green trees to their tops, and the valleys are often of the most lovely green. The trees are larger too, and even the plains of the Bakwain country contain trees instead of bushes. If you look north from the hills we are now leaving, the country partakes of this latter character. It appears as if it were a flat covered with a forest of ordinary sized trees from 20 to 30 feet high, but when you travel over it they are not so closely planted but that a wagon with care may be guided among them. The grass grows in tufts of the size of one's hat, with bare soft sand between. Nowhere here have we an approach to English lawns, or the pleasing appearance of English greensward.

In no part of this country could European grain be cultivated without irrigation. The natives all cultivate the dourrha or holcus sorghum, maize, pumpkins, melons, cucumbers, and different kinds of beans; and they are entirely dependent for the growth of these on rains. Their instrument of culture is the hoe, and the chief labor falls on the female portion of the community. In this respect the Bechuanas closely resemble the Caffres. The men engage in hunting, milk the cows, and have the entire control of the cattle; they prepare the skins, make the clothing, and in many respects may be considered a nation of tailors.

When at Sekomi's we generally have heard his praises sounded by a man who rises at break of day, and utters at the top of his voice the oration which that ruler is said to have composed at his boguera. This repetition of his "leina", or oration, is so pleasing to a chief, that he generally sends a handsome present to the man who does it.

JANUARY 28TH. Passing on to Letloche, about twenty miles beyond the Bamangwato, we found a fine supply of water. This is a point of so much interest in that country that the first question we ask of passers by is, "Have you had water?" the first inquiry a native puts to a fellow-countryman is, "Where is the rain?" and, though they are by no means an untruthful nation, the answer generally is, "I don't know—there is none—we are killed with hunger and by the sun." If news is asked for, they commence with, "There is no news: I heard some lies only," and then tell all they know.

This spot was Mr. Gordon Cumming's furthest station north. Our house at Kolobeng having been quite in the hunting-country, rhinoceros and buffaloes several times rushed past, and I was able to shoot the latter twice from our own door. We were favored by visits from this famous hunter during each of the five years of his warfare with wild animals. Many English gentlemen following the same pursuits paid their guides and assistants so punctually that in making arrangements for them we had to be careful that four did not go where two only were wanted: they knew so well that an Englishman would pay that they depended implicitly on his word of honor, and not only would they go and hunt for five or six months in the north, enduring all the hardships of that trying mode of life, with little else but meat of game to subsist on, but they willingly went seven hundred or eight hundred miles to Graham's Town, receiving for wages only a musket worth fifteen shillings.

No one ever deceived them except one man; and as I believed that he was afflicted with a slight degree of the insanity of greediness, I upheld the honor of the English name by paying his debts. As the guides of Mr. Cumming were furnished through my influence, and usually got some strict charges as to their behavior before parting, looking upon me in the light of a father, they always came to give me an account of their service, and told most of those hunting adventures which have since been given to the world, before we had the pleasure of hearing our friend relate them himself by our own fireside. I had thus a tolerably good opportunity of testing their accuracy, and I have no hesitation in saying that for those who love that sort of thing Mr. Cumming's book conveys a truthful idea of South African hunting. Some things in it require explanation, but the numbers of animals said to have been met with and killed are by no means improbable, considering the amount of large game then in the country. Two other gentlemen hunting in the same region destroyed in one season no fewer than seventy-eight rhinoceroses alone. Sportsmen, however, would not now find an equal number, for as guns are introduced among the tribes all these fine animals melt away like snow in spring. In the more remote districts, where fire-arms have not yet been introduced, with the single exception of the rhinoceros, the game is to be found in numbers much greater than Mr. Cumming ever saw. The tsetse is, however, an insuperable barrier to hunting with horses there, and Europeans can do nothing on foot. The step of the elephant when charging the hunter, though apparently not quick, is so long that the pace equals the speed of a good horse at a canter. A young sportsman, no matter how great among pheasants, foxes, and hounds, would do well to pause before resolving to brave fever for the excitement of risking such a terrific charge; the scream or trumpeting of this enormous brute when infuriated is more like what the shriek of a French steam-whistle would be to a man standing on the dangerous part of a rail-road than any other earthly sound: a horse unused to it will sometimes stand shivering instead of taking his rider out of danger. It has happened often that the poor animal's legs do their duty so badly that he falls and causes his rider to be trodden into a mummy; or, losing his presence of mind, the rider may allow the horse to dash under a tree and crack his cranium against a branch. As one charge from an elephant has made embryo Nimrods bid a final adieu to the chase, incipient Gordon Cummings might try their nerves by standing on railways till the engines were within a few yards of them. Hunting elephants on foot would be not less dangerous,* unless the Ceylon mode of killing them by one shot could be followed: it has never been tried in Africa.

> * Since writing the above statement, it has received confirmation in the reported death of Mr. Wahlberg while hunting elephants on foot at Lake Ngami.

Advancing to some wells beyond Letloche, at a spot named Kanne, we found them carefully hedged round by the people of a Bakalahari village situated near the spot. We had then sixty miles of country in front without water, and very distressing for the oxen, as it is generally deep soft sand. There is one sucking-place, around which were congregated great numbers of Bushwomen with their egg-shells and reeds. Mathuluane now contained no water, and Motlatsa only a small supply, so we sent the oxen across the country to the deep well Nkauane, and half were lost on the way. When found at last they had been five whole days without water. Very large numbers of elands were met with as usual, though they seldom can get a sip of drink. Many of the plains here have large expanses of grass without trees, but you seldom see a treeless horizon. The ostrich is generally seen quietly feeding on some spot where no one can approach him without being detected by his wary eye. As the wagon moves along far to the windward he thinks it is intending to circumvent him, so he rushes up a mile or so from the leeward, and so near to the front oxen that one sometimes gets a shot at the silly bird. When he begins to run all the game in sight follow his example. I have seen this folly taken advantage of when he was feeding quietly in a valley open at both ends. A number of men would commence running, as if to cut off his retreat from the end through which the wind came; and although he had the whole country hundreds of miles before him by going to the other end, on he madly rushed to get past the men, and so was speared. He never swerves from the course he once adopts, but only increases his speed.

When the ostrich is feeding his pace is from twenty to twenty-two inches; when walking, but not feeding, it is twenty-six inches; and when terrified, as in the case noticed, it is from eleven and a half to thirteen and even fourteen feet in length. Only in one case was I at all satisfied of being able to count the rate of speed by a stop-watch, and, if I am not mistaken, there were thirty in ten seconds; generally one's eye can no more follow the legs than it can the spokes of a carriage-wheel in rapid motion. If we take the above number, and twelve feet stride as the average pace, we have a speed of twenty-six miles an hour. It can not be very much above that, and is therefore slower than a railway locomotive. They are sometimes shot by the horseman making a cross cut to their undeviating course, but few Englishmen ever succeed in killing them.

The ostrich begins to lay her eggs before she has fixed on a spot for a nest, which is only a hollow a few inches deep in the sand, and about a yard in diameter. Solitary eggs, named by the Bechuanas "lesetla", are thus found lying forsaken all over the country, and become a prey to the jackal. She seems averse to risking a spot for a nest, and often lays her eggs in that of another ostrich, so that as many as forty-five have been found in one nest. Some eggs contain small concretions of the matter which forms the shell, as occurs also in the egg of the common fowl: this has given rise to the idea of stones in the eggs. Both male and female assist in the incubations; but the numbers of females being always greatest, it is probable that cases occur in which the females have the entire charge. Several eggs lie out of the nest, and are thought to be intended as food for the first of the newly-hatched brood till the rest come out and enable the whole to start in quest of food. I have several times seen newly-hatched young in charge of the cock, who made a very good attempt at appearing lame in the plover fashion, in order to draw off the attention of pursuers. The young squat down and remain immovable when too small to run far, but attain a wonderful degree of speed when about the size of common fowls. It can not be asserted that ostriches are polygamous, though they often appear to be so. When caught they are easily tamed, but are of no use in their domesticated state.

The egg is possessed of very great vital power. One kept in a room during more than three months, in a temperature about 60 Deg., when broken was found to have a partially-developed live chick in it. The Bushmen carefully avoid touching the eggs, or leaving marks of human feet near them, when they find a nest. They go up the wind to the spot, and with a long stick remove some of them occasionally, and, by preventing any suspicion, keep the hen laying on for months, as we do with fowls. The eggs have a strong, disagreeable flavor, which only the keen appetite of the Desert can reconcile one to. The Hottentots use their trowsers to carry home the twenty or twenty-five eggs usually found in a nest; and it has happened that an Englishman, intending to imitate this knowing dodge, comes to the wagons with blistered legs, and, after great toil, finds all the eggs uneatable, from having been some time sat upon. Our countrymen invariably do best when they continue to think, speak, and act in their own proper character.

The food of the ostrich consists of pods and seeds of different kinds of leguminous plants, with leaves of various plants; and, as these are often hard and dry, he picks up a great quantity of pebbles, many of which are as large as marbles. He picks up also some small bulbs, and occasionally a wild melon to afford moisture, for one was found with a melon which had choked him by sticking in his throat. It requires the utmost address of the Bushmen, crawling for miles on their stomachs, to stalk them successfully; yet the quantity of feathers collected annually shows that the numbers slain must be considerable, as each bird has only a few in the wings and tail. The male bird is of a jet black glossy color, with the single exception of the white feathers, which are objects of trade. Nothing can be finer than the adaptation of those flossy feathers for the climate of the Kalahari, where these birds abound; for they afford a perfect shade to the body, with free ventilation beneath them. The hen ostrich is of a dark brownish-gray color, and so are the half-grown cocks.

The organs of vision in this bird are placed so high that he can detect an enemy at a great distance, but the lion sometimes kills him. The flesh is white and coarse, though, when in good condition, it resembles in some degree that of a tough turkey. It seeks safety in flight; but when pursued by dogs it may be seen to turn upon them and inflict a kick, which is vigorously applied, and sometimes breaks the dog's back.

Chapter 8

Effects of Missionary Efforts—Belief in the Deity—Ideas of the Bakwains on Religion—Departure from their Country—Salt-pans—Sour Curd—Nchokotsa—Bitter Waters—Thirst suffered by the wild Animals—Wanton Cruelty in Hunting—Ntwetwe—Mowana-trees—Their extraordinary Vitality—The Mopane-tree—The Morala—The Bushmen—Their Superstitions—Elephant-hunting—Superiority of civilized over barbarous Sportsmen—The Chief Kaisa—His Fear of Responsibility—Beauty of the Country at Unku—The Mohonono Bush—Severe Labor in cutting our Way—Party seized with Fever—Escape of our Cattle—Bakwain Mode of recapturing them—Vagaries of sick Servants— Discovery of grape-bearing Vines—An Ant-eater—Difficulty of passing through the Forest—Sickness of my Companion—The Bushmen—Their Mode of destroying Lions—Poisons—The solitary Hill—A picturesque Valley—Beauty of the Country—Arrive at the Sanshureh River—The flooded Prairies—A pontooning Expedition—A night Bivouac—The Chobe— Arrive at the Village of Moremi—Surprise of the Makololo at our sudden Appearance—Cross the Chobe on our way to Linyanti.

The Bakalahari, who live at Motlatsa wells, have always been very friendly to us, and listen attentively to instruction conveyed to them in their own tongue. It is, however, difficult to give an idea to a European of the little effect teaching produces, because no one can realize the degradation to which their minds have been sunk by centuries of barbarism and hard struggling for the necessaries of life: like most others, they listen with respect and attention, but, when we kneel down and address an unseen Being, the position and the act often appear to them so ridiculous that they can not refrain from bursting into uncontrollable laughter. After a few services they get over this tendency. I was once present when a missionary attempted to sing among a wild heathen tribe of Bechuanas, who had no music in their composition; the effect on the risible faculties of the audience was such that the tears actually ran down their cheeks. Nearly all their thoughts are directed to the supply of their bodily wants, and this has been the case with the race for ages. If asked, then, what effect the preaching of the Gospel has at the commencement on such individuals, I am unable to tell, except that some have confessed long afterward that they then first began to pray in secret. Of the effects of a long-continued course of instruction there can be no reasonable doubt, as mere nominal belief has never been considered sufficient proof of conversion by any body of missionaries; and, after the change which has been brought about by this agency, we have good reason to hope well for the future—those I have myself witnessed behaving in the manner described, when kindly treated in sickness often utter imploring words to Jesus, and I believe sometimes really do pray to him in their afflictions. As that great Redeemer of the guilty seeks to save all he can, we may hope that they find mercy through His blood, though little able to appreciate the sacrifice He made. The indirect and scarcely appreciable blessings of Christian missionaries going about doing good are thus probably not so despicable as some might imagine; there is no necessity for beginning to tell even the most degraded of these people of the existence of a God or of a future state, the facts being universally admitted. Every thing that can not be accounted for by common causes is ascribed to the Deity, as creation, sudden death, etc. "How curiously God made these things!" is a common expression; as is also, "He was not killed by disease, he was killed by God." And, when speaking of the departed—though there is naught in the physical appearance of the dead to justify the expression—they say, "He has gone to the gods," the phrase being identical with "abiit ad plures".

On questioning intelligent men among the Bakwains as to their former knowledge of good and evil, of God and the future state, they have scouted the idea of any of them ever having been without a tolerably clear conception on all these subjects. Respecting their sense of right and wrong, they profess that nothing we indicate as sin ever appeared to them as otherwise, except the statement that it was wrong to have more wives than one; and they declare that they spoke in the same way of the direct influence exercised by God in giving rain in answer to prayers of the rain-makers, and in granting deliverances in times of danger, as they do now, before they ever heard of white men. The want, however, of any form of public worship, or of idols, or of formal prayers or sacrifice, make both Caffres and Bechuanas appear as among the most godless races of mortals known any where. But, though they all possess a distinct knowledge of a deity and of a future state, they show so little reverence, and feel so little connection with either, that it is not surprising that some have supposed them entirely ignorant on the subject. At Lotlakani we met an old Bushman who at first seemed to have no conception of morality whatever; when his heart was warmed by our presents of meat, he sat by the fire relating his early adventures: among these was killing five other Bushmen. "Two," said he, counting on his fingers, "were females, one a male, and the other two calves." "What a villain you are, to boast of killing women and children of your own nation!

what will God say when you appear before him?" "He will say," replied he, "that I was a very clever fellow." This man now appeared to me as without any conscience, and, of course, responsibility; but, on trying to enlighten him by further conversation, I discovered that, though he was employing the word that is used among the Bakwains when speaking of the Deity, he had only the idea of a chief, and was all the while referring to Sekomi, while his victims were a party of rebel Bushmen against whom he had been sent. If I had known the name of God in the Bushman tongue the mistake could scarcely have occurred. It must, however, be recollected, while reflecting on the degradation of the natives of South Africa, that the farther north, the more distinct do the native ideas on religious subjects become, and I have not had any intercourse with either Caffres or Bushmen in their own tongues.

Leaving Motlatsa on the 8th of February, 1853, we passed down the Mokoko, which, in the memory of persons now living, was a flowing stream. We ourselves once saw a heavy thunder-shower make it assume its ancient appearance of running to the north. Between Lotlakani and Nchokotsa we passed the small well named Orapa; and another called Thutsa lay a little to our right—its water is salt and purgative; the salt-pan Chuantsa, having a cake of salt one inch and a half in thickness, is about ten miles to the northeast of Orapa. This deposit contains a bitter salt in addition, probably the nitrate of lime; the natives, in order to render it palatable and wholesome, mix the salt with the juice of a gummy plant, then place it in the sand and bake it by making a fire over it; the lime then becomes insoluble and tasteless.

The Bamangwato keep large flocks of sheep and goats at various spots on this side of the Desert. They thrive wonderfully well wherever salt and bushes are to be found. The milk of goats does not coagulate with facility, like that of cows, on account of its richness; but the natives have discovered that the infusion of the fruit of a solanaceous plant, Toluane, quickly produces the effect. The Bechuanas put their milk into sacks made of untanned hide, with the hair taken off. Hung in the sun, it soon coagulates; the whey is then drawn off by a plug at the bottom, and fresh milk added, until the sack is full of a thick, sour curd, which, when one becomes used to it, is delicious. The rich mix this in the porridge into which they convert their meal, and, as it is thus rendered nutritious and strength-giving, an expression of scorn is sometimes heard respecting the poor or weak, to the effect that "they are water-porridge men." It occupies the place of our roast beef.

At Nchokotsa, the rainy season having this year been delayed beyond the usual time, we found during the day the thermometer stand at 96 Deg. in the coolest possible shade. This height at Kolobeng always portended rain at hand. At Kuruman, when it rises above 84 Deg., the same phenomenon may be considered near; while farther north it rises above 100 Deg. before the cooling influence of the evaporation from rain may be expected. Here the bulb of the thermometer, placed two inches beneath the soil, stood at 128 Deg. All around Nchokotsa the country looked parched, and the glare from the white efflorescence which covers the extensive pans on all sides was most distressing to the eyes. The water of Nchokotsa was bitter, and presented indications not to be mistaken of having passed through animal systems before. All these waters contain nitrates, which stimulate the kidneys and increase the thirst. The fresh additions of water required in cooking meat, each imparting its own portion of salt, make one grumble at the cook for putting too much seasoning in, while in fact he has put in none at all, except that contained in the water. Of bitter, bad, disgusting waters I have drunk not a few nauseous draughts; you may try alum, vitriol, boiling, etc., etc., to convince yourself that you are not more stupid than travelers you will meet at home, but the ammonia and other salts are there still; and the only remedy is to get away as quickly as possible to the north.

We dug out several wells; and as we had on each occasion to wait till the water flowed in again, and then allow our cattle to feed a day or two and slake their thirst thoroughly, as far as that could be done, before starting, our progress was but slow. At Koobe there was such a mass of mud in the pond, worked up by the wallowing rhinoceros to the consistency of mortar, that only by great labor could we get a space cleared at one side for the water to ooze through and collect in for the oxen. Should the rhinoceros come back, a single roll in the great mass we had thrown on one side would have rendered all our labor vain. It was therefore necessary for us to guard the spot at night. On these great flats all around we saw in the white sultry glare herds of zebras, gnus, and occasionally buffaloes, standing for days, looking wistfully toward the wells for a share of the nasty water. It is mere wanton cruelty to take advantage of the necessities of these poor animals, and shoot them down one after another, without intending to make the smallest use of either the flesh, skins, or horns. In shooting by night, animals are more frequently wounded than killed; the flowing life-stream increases the thirst, so that in desperation they come slowly up to drink in spite of the danger, "I must drink, though I die." The ostrich, even when not wounded, can not, with all his wariness, resist the excessive desire to slake his burning thirst. It is Bushman-like practice to take advantage of its piteous necessities, for most of the feathers they obtain are procured in this way; but they eat the flesh, and are so far justifiable.

I could not order my men to do what I would not do myself, but, though I tried to justify myself on the plea of necessity, I could not adopt this mode of hunting. If your object is to secure the best specimens for a museum, it may be allowable, and even deserving of commendation, as evincing a desire to kill only those really wanted; but if, as has been practiced by some Griquas and others who came into the country after Mr. Cumming, and fired away indiscriminately, great numbers of animals are wounded and allowed to perish miserably, or are killed on the spot and left to be preyed on by vultures and hyenas, and all for the sole purpose of making a "bag", then I take it to be evident that such sportsmen are pretty far gone in the hunting form of insanity.

My men shot a black rhinoceros in this way, and I felt glad to get away from the only place in which I ever had any share in night-hunting. We passed over the immense pan Ntwetwe, on which the latitude could be taken as at sea. Great tracts of this part of the country are of calcareous tufa, with only a thin coating of soil; numbers of "baobab" and "mopane" trees abound all over this hard, smooth surface. About two miles beyond the northern bank of the pan we unyoked under a fine specimen of the baobab, here called, in the language of Bechuanas, Mowana; it consisted of six branches united into one trunk. At three feet from the ground it was eighty-five feet in circumference.

These mowana-trees are the most wonderful examples of vitality in the country; it was therefore with surprise that we came upon a dead one at Tlomtla, a few miles beyond this spot. It is the same as those which Adamson and others believed, from specimens seen in Western Africa, to have been alive before the flood. Arguing with a peculiar mental idiosyncracy resembling color-blindness, common among the French of the time, these savans came to the conclusion that "therefore there never was any flood at all." I would back a true mowana against a dozen floods, provided you do not boil it in hot sea-water; but I can not believe that any of those now alive had a chance of being subjected to the experiment of even the Noachian deluge. The natives make a strong cord from the fibres contained in the pounded bark. The whole of the trunk, as high as they can reach, is consequently often quite denuded of its covering, which in the case of almost any other tree would cause its death, but this has no effect on the mowana except to make it throw out a new bark, which is done in the way of granulation. This stripping of the bark is repeated frequently, so that it is common to see the lower five or six feet an inch or two less in diameter than the parts above; even portions of the bark which have broken in the process of being taken off, but remain separated from the parts below, though still connected with the tree above, continue to grow, and resemble closely marks made in the necks of the cattle of the island of Mull and of Caffre oxen, where a piece of skin is detached and allowed to hang down. No external injury, not even a fire, can destroy this tree from without; nor can any injury be done from within, as it is quite common to find it hollow; and I have seen one in which twenty or thirty men could lie down and sleep as in a hut. Nor does cutting down exterminate it, for I saw instances in Angola in which it continued to grow in length after it was lying on the ground. Those trees called exogenous grow by means of successive layers on the outside. The inside may be dead, or even removed altogether, without affecting the life of the tree. This is the case with most of the trees of our climate. The other class is called endogenous, and increases by layers applied to the inside; and when the hollow there is full, the growth is stopped—the tree must die. Any injury is felt most severely by the first class on the bark; by the second on the inside; while the inside of the exogenous may be removed, and the outside of the endogenous may be cut, without stopping the growth in the least. The mowana possesses the powers of both. The reason is that each of the laminae possesses its own independent vitality; in fact, the baobab is rather a gigantic bulb run up to seed than a tree. Each of eighty-four concentric rings had, in the case mentioned, grown an inch after the tree had been blown over. The roots, which may often be observed extending along the surface of the ground forty or fifty yards from the trunk, also retain their vitality after the tree is laid low; and the Portuguese now know that the best way to treat them is to let them alone, for they occupy much more room when cut down than when growing.

    The wood is so spongy and soft that an axe can be struck in so far with a good blow that there is great difficulty in pulling it out again. In the dead mowana mentioned the concentric rings were well seen. The average for a foot at three different places was eighty-one and a half of these rings. Each of the laminae can be seen to be composed of two, three, or four layers of ligneous tubes; but supposing each ring the growth of one year, and the semidiameter of a mowana of one hundred feet in circumference about seventeen feet, if the central point were in the centre of the tree, then its age would lack some centuries of being as old as the Christian era (1400). Though it possesses amazing vitality, it is difficult to believe that this great baby-looking bulb or tree is as old as the Pyramids.

    The mopane-tree ('bauhinia') is remarkable for the little shade its leaves afford. They fold together and stand nearly perpendicular during the heat of the day, so that only the shadow of their edges comes to the ground. On these leaves the small larvae of a winged insect appear covered over with a sweet, gummy substance. The people collect this in great quantities, and use it as food;* and the lopane—large caterpillars three inches long, which feed on the leaves, and are seen strung together—share the same fate.

    * *I am favored with Mr. Westwood's remarks on this insect as follows:*

"Taylor Institution, Oxford, July 9, 1857.

"The insect (and its secretion) on the leaves of the bauhinia, and which is eaten by the Africans, proves to be a species of Psylla, a genus of small, very active Homoptera, of which we have one very common species in the box; but our species, Psylla buxi, emits its secretion in the shape of very long, white, cotton-like filaments. But there is a species in New Holland, found on the leaves of the Eucalyptus, which emits a secretion very similar to that of Dr. Livingstone's species. This Australian secretion (and its insect originator) is known by the name of wo-me-la, and, like Dr. Livingstone's, it is scraped off the leaves and eaten by the aborigines as a saccharine dainty. The insects found beneath the secretion, brought home by Dr. Livingstone, are in the pupa state, being flattened, with large scales at the sides of the body, inclosing the future wings of the insect. The body is pale yellowish-colored, with dark-brown spots. It will be impossible to describe the species technically until we receive the perfect insect. The secretion itself is flat and circular, apparently deposited in concentric rings, gradually increasing in size till the patches are about a quarter or a third of an inch in diameter.

Jno. O. Westwood."

In passing along we see every where the power of vegetation in breaking up the outer crust of tufa. A mopane-tree, growing in a small chink, as it increases in size rends and lifts up large fragments of the rock all around it, subjecting them to the disintegrating influence of the atmosphere. The wood is hard, and of a fine red color, and is named iron-wood by the Portuguese. The inhabitants, observing that the mopane is more frequently struck by lightning than other trees, caution travelers never to seek its shade when a thunder-storm is near—"Lightning hates it;" while another tree, the "Morala", which has three spines opposite each other on the branches, and has never been known to be touched by lightning, is esteemed, even as far as Angola, a protection against the electric fluid. Branches of it may be seen placed on the houses of the Portuguese for the same purpose. The natives, moreover, believe that a man is thoroughly protected from an enraged elephant if he can get into the shade of this tree. There may not be much in this, but there is frequently some foundation of truth in their observations.

At Rapesh we came among our old friends the Bushmen, under Horoye. This man, Horoye, a good specimen of that tribe, and his son Mokantsa and others, were at least six feet high, and of a darker color than the Bushmen of the south. They have always plenty of food and water; and as they frequent the Zouga as often as the game in company with which they live, their life is very different from that of the inhabitants of the thirsty plains of the Kalahari. The animal they refrain from eating is the goat, which fact, taken in connection with the superstitious dread which exists in every tribe toward a particular animal, is significant of their feelings to the only animals they could have domesticated in their desert home. They are a merry laughing set, and do not tell lies wantonly. They have in their superstitious rites more appearance of worship than the Bechuanas; and at a Bushman's grave we once came to on the Zouga, the observances showed distinctly that they regarded the dead as still in another state of being; for they addressed him, and requested him not to be offended even though they wished still to remain a little while longer in this world.

Those among whom we now were kill many elephants, and when the moon is full choose that time for the chase, on account of its coolness. Hunting this animal is the best test of courage this country affords. The Bushmen choose the moment succeeding a charge, when the elephant is out of breath, to run in and give him a stab with their long-bladed spears. In this case the uncivilized have the advantage over us, but I believe that with half their training Englishmen would beat the Bushmen. Our present form of civilization does not necessarily produce effeminacy, though it unquestionably increases the beauty, courage, and physical powers of the race. When at Kolobeng I took notes of the different numbers of elephants killed in the course of the season by the various parties which went past our dwelling, in order to form an idea of the probable annual destruction of this noble animal. There were parties of Griquas, Bechuanas, Boers, and Englishmen. All were eager to distinguish themselves, and success depended mainly on the courage which leads the huntsman to go close to the animal, and not waste the force of his shot on the air. It was noticeable that the average for the natives was under one per man, for the Griquas one per man, for the Boers two, and for the English officers twenty each. This was the more remarkable, as the Griquas, Boers, and Bechuanas employed both dogs and natives to assist them, while the English hunters generally had no assistance from either. They approached to within thirty yards of the animal, while the others stood at a distance of a hundred yards, or even more, and of course spent all the force of their bullets on the air. One elephant was found by Mr. Oswell with quite a crowd of bullets in his side, all evidently fired in this style, and they had not gone near the vital parts.

It would thus appear that our more barbarous neighbors do not possess half the courage of the civilized sportsman. And it is probable that in this respect, as well as in physical development, we are superior to our ancestors. The coats of mail and greaves of the Knights of Malta, and the armor from the Tower exhibited at the Eglinton tournament, may be considered decisive as to the greater size attained by modern civilized men.

At Maila we spent a Sunday with Kaisa, the head man of a village of Mashona, who had fled from the iron sway of Mosilikatse, whose country lies east of this. I wished him to take charge of a packet of letters for England, to be forwarded when, as is the custom of the Bamangwato, the Bechuanas come hither in search of skins and food among the Bushmen; but he could not be made to comprehend that there was no danger in the consignment. He feared the responsibility and guilt if any thing should happen to them; so I had to bid adieu to all hope of letting my family hear of my welfare till I should reach the west coast.

At Unku we came into a tract of country which had been visited by refreshing showers long before, and every spot was covered with grass run up to seed, and the flowers of the forest were in full bloom. Instead of the dreary prospect around Koobe and Nchokotsa, we had here a delightful scene, all the ponds full of water, and the birds twittering joyfully. As the game can now obtain water every where, they become very shy, and can not be found in their accustomed haunts.

1ST MARCH. The thermometer in the shade generally stood at 98 Degrees from 1 to 3 P.M., but it sank as low as 65 Deg. by night, so that the heat was by no means exhausting. At the surface of the ground, in the sun, the thermometer marked 125 Deg., and three inches below it 138 Deg. The hand can not be held on the ground, and even the horny soles of the feet of the natives must be protected by sandals of hide; yet the ants were busy working on it. The water in the ponds was as high as 100 Deg.; but as water does not conduct heat readily downward, deliciously cool water may be obtained by any one walking into the middle and lifting up the water from the bottom to the surface with his hands.

Proceeding to the north, from Kama-kama, we entered into dense Mohonono bush, which required the constant application of the axe by three of our party for two days. This bush has fine silvery leaves, and the bark has a sweet taste. The elephant, with his usual delicacy of taste, feeds much on it. On emerging into the plains beyond, we found a number of Bushmen, who afterward proved very serviceable. The rains had been copious, but now great numbers of pools were drying up. Lotus-plants abounded in them, and a low, sweet-scented plant covered their banks. Breezes came occasionally to us from these drying-up pools, but the pleasant odor they carried caused sneezing in both myself and people; and on the 10th of March (when in lat. 19d 16' 11" S., long. 24d 24' E.) we were brought to a stand by four of the party being seized with fever. I had seen this disease before, but did not at once recognize it as the African fever; I imagined it was only a bilious attack, arising from full feeding on flesh, for, the large game having been very abundant, we always had a good supply; but instead of the first sufferers recovering soon, every man of our party was in a few days laid low, except a Bakwain and myself. He managed the oxen, while I attended to the wants of the patients, and went out occasionally with the Bushmen to get a zebra or buffalo, so as to induce them to remain with us.

Here for the first time I had leisure to follow the instructions of my kind teacher, Mr. Maclear, and calculated several longitudes from lunar distances. The hearty manner in which that eminent astronomer and frank, friendly man had promised to aid me in calculating and verifying my work, conduced more than any thing else to inspire me with perseverance in making astronomical observations throughout the journey.

The grass here was so tall that the oxen became uneasy, and one night the sight of a hyaena made them rush away into the forest to the east of us. On rising on the morning of the 19th, I found that my Bakwain lad had run away with them. This I have often seen with persons of this tribe, even when the cattle are startled by a lion. Away go the young men in company with them, and dash through bush and brake for miles, till they think the panic is a little subsided; they then commence whistling to the cattle in the manner they do when milking the cows: having calmed them, they remain as a guard till the morning. The men generally return with their shins well peeled by the thorns. Each comrade of the Mopato would expect his fellow to act thus, without looking for any other reward than the brief praise of the chief. Our lad, Kibopechoe, had gone after the oxen, but had lost them in the rush through the flat, trackless forest. He remained on their trail all the next day and all the next night. On Sunday morning, as I was setting off in search of him, I found him near the wagon. He had found the oxen late in the afternoon of Saturday, and had been obliged to stand by them all night. It was wonderful how he managed without a compass, and in such a country, to find his way home at all, bringing about forty oxen with him.

The Bechuanas will keep on the sick-list as long as they feel any weakness; so I at last began to be anxious that they should make a little exertion to get forward on our way. One of them, however, happening to move a hundred yards from the wagon, fell down, and, being unobserved, remained the whole night in the pouring rain totally insensible; another was subjected to frequent swooning; but, making beds in the wagons for these our worst cases, with the help of the Bakwain and the Bushmen, we moved slowly on. We had to nurse the sick like children; and, like children recovering from illness, the better they became the more impudent they grew. This was seen in the peremptory orders they would give with their now piping voices. Nothing that we did pleased them; and the laughter with which I received their ebullitions, though it was only the real expression of gladness at their recovery, and amusement at the ridiculous part they acted, only increased their chagrin. The want of power in the man who guided the two front oxen, or, as he was called, the "leader", caused us to be entangled with trees, both standing and fallen, and the labor of cutting them down was even more severe than ordinary; but, notwithstanding an immense amount of toil, my health continued good.

We wished to avoid the tsetse of our former path, so kept a course on the magnetic meridian from Lurilopepe. The necessity of making a new path much increased our toil. We were, however, rewarded in lat. 18 Degrees with a sight we had not enjoyed the year before, namely, large patches of grape-bearing vines. There they stood before my eyes; but the sight was so entirely unexpected that I stood some time gazing at the clusters of grapes with which they were loaded, with no more thought of plucking than if I had been beholding them in a dream. The Bushmen know and eat them; but they are not well flavored on account of the great astringency of the seeds, which are in shape and size like split peas. The elephants are fond of the fruit, plant, and root alike. I here found an insect which preys on ants; it is about an inch and a quarter long, as thick as a crow-quill, and covered with black hair. It puts its head into a little hole in the ground, and quivers its tail rapidly; the ants come near to see it, and it snaps up each as he comes within the range of the forceps on its tail. As its head is beneath the ground, it becomes a question how it can guide its tail to the ants. It is probably a new species of ant-lion ('Myrmeleon formicaleo'), great numbers of which, both in the larvae and complete state, are met with. The ground under every tree is dotted over with their ingenious pitfalls, and the perfect insect, the form of which most persons are familiar with in the dragon-fly, may be seen using its tail in the same active manner as this insect did. Two may be often seen joined in their flight, the one holding on by the tail-forceps to the neck of the other. On first observing this imperfect insect, I imagined the forceps were on its head; but when the insect moved, their true position was seen.

The forest, through which we were slowly toiling, daily became more dense, and we were kept almost constantly at work with the axe; there was much more leafiness in the trees here than farther south. The leaves are chiefly of the pinnate and bi-pinnate forms, and are exceedingly beautiful when seen against the sky; a great variety of the papilionaceous family grow in this part of the country.

Fleming had until this time always assisted to drive his own wagon, but about the end of March he knocked up, as well as his people. As I could not drive two wagons, I shared with him the remaining water, half a caskful, and went on, with the intention of coming back for him as soon as we should reach the next pool. Heavy rain now commenced; I was employed the whole day in cutting down trees, and every stroke of the axe brought down a thick shower on my back, which in the hard work was very refreshing, as the water found its way down into my shoes. In the evening we met some Bushmen, who volunteered to show us a pool; and having unyoked, I walked some miles in search of it. As it became dark they showed their politeness—a quality which is by no means confined entirely to the civilized—by walking in front, breaking the branches which hung across the path, and pointing out the fallen trees. On returning to the wagon, we found that being left alone had brought out some of Fleming's energy, for he had managed to come up.

As the water in this pond dried up, we were soon obliged to move again. One of the Bushmen took out his dice, and, after throwing them, said that God told him to go home. He threw again in order to show me the command, but the opposite result followed; so he remained and was useful, for we lost the oxen again by a lion driving them off to a very great distance. The lions here are not often heard. They seem to have a wholesome dread of the Bushmen, who, when they observe evidence of a lion's having made a full meal, follow up his spoor so quietly that his slumbers are not disturbed. One discharges a poisoned arrow from a distance of only a few feet, while his companion simultaneously throws his skin cloak on the beast's head. The sudden surprise makes the lion lose his presence of mind, and he bounds away in the greatest confusion and terror. Our friends here showed me the poison which they use on these occasions. It is the entrails of a caterpillar called N'gwa, half an inch long. They squeeze out these, and place them all around the bottom of the barb, and allow the poison to dry in the sun. They are very careful in cleaning their nails after working with it, as a small portion introduced into a scratch acts like morbid matter in dissection wounds. The agony is so great that the person cuts himself, calls for his mother's breast as if he were returned in idea to his childhood again, or flies from human habitations a raging maniac. The effects on the lion are equally terrible. He is heard moaning in distress, and becomes furious, biting the trees and ground in rage.

As the Bushmen have the reputation of curing the wounds of this poison, I asked how this was effected. They said that they administer the caterpillar itself in combination with fat; they also rub fat into the wound, saying that "the N'gwa wants fat, and, when it does not find it in the body, kills the man: we give it what it wants, and it is content:" a reason which will commend itself to the enlightened among ourselves.

The poison more generally employed is the milky juice of the tree Euphorbia ('E. arborescens'). This is particularly obnoxious to the equine race. When a quantity is mixed with the water of a pond a whole herd of zebras will fall dead from the effects of the poison before they have moved away two miles. It does not, however, kill oxen or men. On them it acts as a drastic purgative only. This substance is used all over the country, though in some places the venom of serpents and a certain bulb, 'Amaryllis toxicaria', are added, in order to increase the virulence.

Father Pedro, a Jesuit, who lived at Zumbo, made a balsam, containing a number of plants and CASTOR OIL, as a remedy for poisoned arrow-wounds. It is probable that he derived his knowledge from the natives as I did, and that the reputed efficacy of the balsam is owing to its fatty constituent.

In cases of the bites of serpents a small key ought to be pressed down firmly on the wound, the orifice of the key being applied to the puncture, until a cupping-glass can be got from one of the natives. A watch-key pressed firmly on the point stung by a scorpion extracts the poison, and a mixture of fat or oil and ipecacuanha relieves the pain.

The Bushmen of these districts are generally fine, well-made men, and are nearly independent of every one. We observed them to be fond of a root somewhat like a kidney potato, and the kernel of a nut, which Fleming thought was a kind of betel; the tree is a fine, large-spreading one, and the leaves palmate. From the quantities of berries and the abundance of game in these parts, the Bushmen can scarcely ever be badly off for food. As I could, without much difficulty, keep them well supplied with meat, and wished them to remain, I proposed that they should bring their wives to get a share, but they remarked that the women could always take care of themselves.

None of the men of our party had died, but two seemed unlikely to recover; and Kibopechoe, my willing Mokwain, at last became troubled with boils, and then got all the symptoms of fever. As he lay down, the others began to move about, and complained of weakness only. Believing that frequent change of place was conducive to their recovery, we moved along as much as we could, and came to the hill N'gwa (lat. 18d 27' 20" S., long. 24d 13' 36" E.). This being the only hill we had seen since leaving

Bamangwato, we felt inclined to take off our hats to it. It is three or four hundred feet high, and covered with trees. Its geographical position is pretty accurately laid down from occultation and other observations. I may mention that the valley on its northern side, named Kandehy or Kandehai, is as picturesque a spot as is to be seen in this part of Africa. The open glade, surrounded by forest trees of various hues, had a little stream meandering in the centre. A herd of reddish-colored antelopes (pallahs) stood on one side, near a large baobab, looking at us, and ready to run up the hill; while gnus, tsessebes, and zebras gazed in astonishment at the intruders. Some fed carelessly, and others put on the peculiar air of displeasure which these animals sometimes assume before they resolve on flight. A large white rhinoceros came along the bottom of the valley with his slow sauntering gait without noticing us; he looked as if he meant to indulge in a mud bath. Several buffaloes, with their dark visages, stood under the trees on the side opposite to the pallahs. It being Sunday, all was peace, and, from the circumstances in which our party was placed, we could not but reflect on that second stage of our existence which we hope will lead us into scenes of perfect beauty. If pardoned in that free way the Bible promises, death will be a glorious thing; but to be consigned to wait for the Judgment-day, with nothing else to ponder on but sins we would rather forget, is a cheerless prospect.

Our Bushmen wished to leave us, and, as there was no use in trying to thwart these independent gentlemen, I paid them, and allowed them to go. The payment, however, acted as a charm on some strangers who happened to be present, and induced them to volunteer their aid.

The game hereabouts is very tame. Koodoos and giraffes stood gazing at me as a strange apparition when I went out with the Bushmen. On one occasion a lion came at daybreak, and went round and round the oxen. I could only get a glimpse of him occasionally from the wagon-box; but, though barely thirty yards off, I could not get a shot. He then began to roar at the top of his voice; but the oxen continuing to stand still, he was so disgusted that he went off, and continued to use his voice for a long time in the distance. I could not see that he had a mane; if he had not, then even the maneless variety can use their tongues. We heard others also roar; and, when they found they could not frighten the oxen, they became equally angry. This we could observe in their tones.

As we went north the country became very lovely; many new trees appeared; the grass was green, and often higher than the wagons; the vines festooned the trees, among which appeared the real banian ('Ficus Indica'), with its drop-shoots, and the wild date and palmyra, and several other trees which were new to me; the hollows contained large patches of water. Next came water-courses, now resembling small rivers, twenty yards broad and four feet deep. The further we went, the broader and deeper these became; their bottoms contained great numbers of deep holes, made by elephants wading in them; in these the oxen floundered desperately, so that our wagon-pole broke, compelling us to work up to the breast in water for three hours and a half; yet I suffered no harm.

We at last came to the Sanshureh, which presented an impassable barrier, so we drew up under a magnificent baobab-tree, (lat. 18d 4' 27" S., long. 24d 6' 20" E.), and resolved to explore the river for a ford. The great quantity of water we had passed through was part of the annual inundation of the Chobe; and this, which appeared a large, deep river, filled in many parts with reeds, and having hippopotami in it, is only one of the branches by which it sends its superabundant water to the southeast. From the hill N'gwa a ridge of higher land runs to the northeast, and bounds its course in that direction. We, being ignorant of this, were in the valley, and the only gap in the whole country destitute of tsetse. In company with the Bushmen I explored all the banks of the Sanshureh to the west till we came into tsetse on that side. We waded a long way among the reeds in water breast deep, but always found a broad, deep space free from vegetation and unfordable. A peculiar kind of lichen, which grows on the surface of the soil, becomes detached and floats on the water, giving out a very disagreeable odor, like sulphureted hydrogen, in some of these stagnant waters.

We made so many attempts to get over the Sanshureh, both to the west and east of the wagon, in the hope of reaching some of the Makololo on the Chobe, that my Bushmen friends became quite tired of the work. By means of presents I got them to remain some days; but at last they slipped away by night, and I was fain to take one of the strongest of my still weak companions and cross the river in a pontoon, the gift of Captains Codrington and Webb. We each carried some provisions and a blanket, and penetrated about twenty miles to the westward, in the hope of striking the Chobe. It was much nearer to us in a northerly direction, but this we did not then know. The plain, over which we splashed the whole of the first day, was covered with water ankle deep, and thick grass which reached above the knees. In the evening we came to an immense wall of reeds, six or eight feet high, without any opening admitting of a passage. When we tried to enter, the water always became so deep that we were fain to desist. We concluded that we had come to the banks of the river we were in search of, so we directed our course to some trees which appeared in the south, in order to get a bed and a view of the adjacent locality. Having shot a leche, and made a glorious fire, we got a good cup of tea and had a comfortable night. While collecting wood that evening, I found a bird's nest consisting of live leaves sewn together with threads of the spider's web. Nothing could exceed the airiness of this pretty contrivance; the threads had been pushed through small punctures and thickened to resemble a knot. I unfortunately lost it. This was the second nest I had seen resembling that of the tailor-bird of India.

Next morning, by climbing the highest trees, we could see a fine large sheet of water, but surrounded on all sides by the same impenetrable belt of reeds. This is the broad part of the River Chobe, and is called Zabesa. Two tree-covered islands seemed to be much nearer to the water than the shore on which we were, so we made an attempt to get to them first. It was not the reeds alone we had to pass through; a peculiar serrated grass, which at certain angles cut the hands like a razor, was mingled with the reed, and the climbing convolvulus, with stalks which felt as strong as whipcord, bound the mass together. We felt like pigmies in it, and often the only way we could get on was by both of us leaning against a part and bending it down till we could stand upon it. The perspiration streamed off our bodies, and as the sun rose high, there being no ventilation among the reeds, the heat was stifling, and the water, which was up to the knees, felt agreeably refreshing. After some hours' toil we reached one of the islands. Here we met an old friend, the bramble-bush. My strong moleskins were quite worn through at the knees, and the leather trowsers of my companion were torn and his legs bleeding. Tearing my handkerchief in two, I tied the pieces round my knees, and then encountered another difficulty. We were still forty or fifty yards from the clear water, but now we were opposed by great masses of papyrus, which are like palms in miniature, eight or ten feet high, and an inch and a half in diameter. These were laced together by twining convolvulus, so strongly that the weight of both of us could not make way into the clear water. At last we fortunately found a passage prepared by a hippopotamus. Eager as soon as we reached the island to look along the vista to clear water, I stepped in and found it took me at once up to the neck.

Returning nearly worn out, we proceeded up the bank of the Chobe till we came to the point of departure of the branch Sanshureh; we then went in the opposite direction, or down the Chobe, though from the highest trees we could see nothing but one vast expanse of reed, with here and there a tree on the islands. This was a hard day's work; and when we came to a deserted Bayeiye hut on an ant-hill, not a bit of wood or any thing else could be got for a fire except the grass and sticks of the dwelling itself. I dreaded the "Tampans", so common in all old huts; but outside of it we had thousands of mosquitoes, and cold dew began to be deposited, so we were fain to crawl beneath its shelter.

We were close to the reeds, and could listen to the strange sounds which are often heard there. By day I had seen water-snakes putting up their heads and swimming about. There were great numbers of otters ('Lutra inunguis', F. Cuvier), which have made little spoors all over the plains in search of the fishes, among the tall grass of these flooded prairies; curious birds, too, jerked and wriggled among these reedy masses, and we heard human-like voices and unearthly sounds, with splash, guggle, jupp, as if rare fun were going on in their uncouth haunts. At one time something came near us, making a splashing like that of a canoe or hippopotamus; thinking it to be the Makololo, we got up, listened, and shouted; then discharged a gun several times; but the noise continued without intermission for an hour. After a damp, cold night we set to, early in the morning, at our work of exploring again, but left the pontoon in order to lighten our labor. The ant-hills are here very high, some thirty feet, and of a base so broad that trees grow on them; while the lands, annually flooded, bear nothing but grass. From one of these ant-hills we discovered an inlet to the Chobe; and, having gone back for the pontoon, we launched ourselves on a deep river, here from eighty to one hundred yards wide. I gave my companion strict injunctions to stick by the pontoon in case a hippopotamus should look at us; nor was this caution unnecessary, for one came up at our side and made a desperate plunge off. We had passed over him. The wave he made caused the pontoon to glide quickly away from him.

We paddled on from midday till sunset. There was nothing but a wall of reed on each bank, and we saw every prospect of spending a supperless night in our float; but just as the short twilight of these parts was commencing, we perceived on the north bank the village of Moremi, one of the Makololo, whose acquaintance I had made on our former visit, and who was now located on the island Mahonta (lat. 17d 58' S., long. 24d 6' E.). The villagers looked as we may suppose people do who see a ghost, and in their figurative way of speaking said, "He has dropped among us from the clouds, yet came riding on the back of a hippopotamus! We Makololo thought no one could cross the Chobe without our knowledge, but here he drops among us like a bird."

Next day we returned in canoes across the flooded lands, and found that, in our absence, the men had allowed the cattle to wander into a very small patch of wood to the west containing the tsetse; this carelessness cost me ten fine large oxen. After remaining a few days, some of the head men of the Makololo came down from Linyanti, with a large party of Barotse, to take us across the river. This they did in fine style, swimming and diving among the oxen more like alligators than men, and taking the wagons to pieces and carrying them across on a number of canoes lashed together. We were now among friends; so going about thirty miles to the north, in order to avoid the still flooded lands on the north of the Chobe, we turned westward toward Linyanti (lat. 18d 17′ 20″ S., long. 23d 50′ 9″ E.), where we arrived on the 23d of May, 1853. This is the capital town of the Makololo, and only a short distance from our wagon-stand of 1851 (lat. 18d 20′ S., long. 23d 50′ E.).

Chapter 9

Reception at Linyanti—The court Herald—Sekeletu obtains the Chieftainship from his Sister—Mpepe's Plot—Slave-trading Mambari — Their sudden Flight—Sekeletu narrowly escapes Assassination— Execution of Mpepe—The Courts of Law—Mode of trying Offenses— Sekeletu's Reason for not learning to read the Bible—The Disposition made of the Wives of a deceased Chief—Makololo Women—They work but little—Employ Serfs—Their Drink, Dress, and Ornaments—Public Religious Services in the Kotla—Unfavorable Associations of the place—Native Doctors—Proposals to teach the Makololo to read—Sekeletu's Present—Reason for accepting it—Trading in Ivory—Accidental Fire—Presents for Sekeletu—Two Breeds of native Cattle—Ornamenting the Cattle—The Women and the Looking-glass—Mode of preparing the Skins of Oxen for Mantles and for Shields—Throwing the Spear.

The whole population of Linyanti, numbering between six and seven thousand souls, turned out en masse to see the wagons in motion. They had never witnessed the phenomenon before, we having on the former occasion departed by night. Sekeletu, now in power, received us in what is considered royal style, setting before us a great number of pots of boyaloa, the beer of the country. These were brought by women, and each bearer takes a good draught of the beer when she sets it down, by way of "tasting", to show that there is no poison.

The court herald, an old man who occupied the post also in Sebituane's time, stood up, and after some antics, such as leaping, and shouting at the top of his voice, roared out some adulatory sentences, as, "Don't I see the white man? Don't I see the comrade of Sebituane? Don't I see the father of Sekeletu?"—"We want sleep."—"Give your son sleep, my lord," etc., etc. The perquisites of this man are the heads of all the cattle slaughtered by the chief, and he even takes a share of the tribute before it is distributed and taken out of the kotla. He is expected to utter all the proclamations, call assemblies, keep the kotla clean, and the fire burning every evening, and when a person is executed in public he drags away the body.

I found Sekeletu a young man of eighteen years of age, of that dark yellow or coffee-and-milk color, of which the Makololo are so proud, because it distinguishes them considerably from the black tribes on the rivers. He is about five feet seven in height, and neither so good looking nor of so much ability as his father was, but is equally friendly to the English. Sebituane installed his daughter Mamochisane into the chieftainship long before his death, but, with all his acuteness, the idea of her having a husband who should not be her lord did not seem to enter his mind. He wished to make her his successor, probably in imitation of some of the negro tribes with whom he had come into contact; but, being of the Bechuana race, he could not look upon the husband except as the woman's lord; so he told her all the men were hers—she might take any one, but ought to keep none. In fact, he thought she might do with the men what he could do with the women; but these men had other wives; and, according to a saying in the country, "the tongues of women can not be governed," they made her miserable by their remarks. One man whom she chose was even called her wife, and her son the child of Mamochisane's wife; but the arrangement was so distasteful to Mamochisane herself that, as soon as Sebituane died, she said she never would consent to govern the Makololo so long as she had a brother living. Sekeletu, being afraid of another member of the family, Mpepe, who had pretensions to the chieftainship, urged his sister strongly to remain as she had always been, and allow him to support her authority by leading the Makololo when they went forth to war. Three days were spent in public discussion on the point. Mpepe insinuated that Sekeletu was not the lawful son of Sebituane, on account of his mother having been the wife of another chief before her marriage with Sebituane; Mamochisane, however, upheld Sekeletu's claims, and at last stood up in the assembly and addressed him with a womanly gush of tears: "I have been a chief only because my father wished it. I always would have preferred to be married and have a family like other women. You, Sekeletu, must be chief, and build up your father's house." This was a death-blow to the hopes of Mpepe.

As it will enable the reader to understand the social and political relations of these people, I will add a few more particulars respecting Mpepe. Sebituane, having no son to take the leadership of the "Mopato" of the age of his daughter, chose him, as the nearest male relative, to occupy that post; and presuming from Mpepe's connection with his family that he would attend to his interests and relieve him from care, he handed his cattle over to his custody. Mpepe removed to the chief town, "Naliele", and took such effectual charge of all the cattle that Sebituane saw he could only set matters on their former footing by the severe measure of Mpepe's execution. Being unwilling to do this, and fearing the enchantments which, by means of a number of Barotse doctors, Mpepe now used in a hut built for the purpose, and longing for peaceful retirement after thirty years' fighting, he heard with pleasure of our arrival at the lake, and came down as far as Sesheke to meet us. He had an idea, picked up from some of the numerous strangers who visited him, that white men had a "pot (a cannon) in their towns which would burn up any attacking party;" and he thought if he could only get this he would be able to "sleep" the remainder of his days in peace. This he hoped to obtain from the white men. Hence the cry of the herald, "Give us sleep." It is remarkable how anxious for peace those who have been fighting all their lives appear to be.

When Sekeletu was installed in the chieftainship, he felt his position rather insecure, for it was believed that the incantations of Mpepe had an intimate connection with Sebituane's death. Indeed, the latter had said to his son, "That hut of incantation will prove fatal to either you or me."

When the Mambari, in 1850, took home a favorable report of this new market to the west, a number of half-caste Portuguese slave-traders were induced to come in 1853; and one, who resembled closely a real Portuguese, came to Linyanti while I was there. This man had no merchandise, and pretended to have come in order to inquire "what sort of goods were necessary for the market." He seemed much disconcerted by my presence there. Sekeletu presented him with an elephant's tusk and an ox; and when he had departed about fifty miles to the westward, he carried off an entire village of the Bakalahari belonging to the Makololo. He had a number of armed slaves with him; and as all the villagers—men, women, and children—were removed, and the fact was unknown until a considerable time afterward, it is not certain whether his object was obtained by violence or by fair promises. In either case, slavery must have been the portion of these poor people. He was carried in a hammock, slung between two poles, which appearing to be a bag, the Makololo named him "Father of the Bag".

Mpepe favored these slave-traders, and they, as is usual with them, founded all their hopes of influence on his successful rebellion. My arrival on the scene was felt to be so much weight in the scale against their interests. A large party of Mambari had come to Linyanti when I was floundering on the prairies south of the Chobe. As the news of my being in the neighborhood reached them their countenances fell; and when some Makololo, who had assisted us to cross the river, returned with hats which I had given them, the Mambari betook themselves to precipitate flight. It is usual for visitors to ask formal permission before attempting to leave a chief, but the sight of the hats made the Mambari pack up at once. The Makololo inquired the cause of the hurry, and were told that, if I found them there, I should take all their slaves and goods from them; and, though assured by Sekeletu that I was not a robber, but a man of peace, they fled by night, while I was still sixty miles off. They went to the north, where, under the protection of Mpepe, they had erected a stockade of considerable size. There, several half-caste slave-traders, under the leadership of a native Portuguese, carried on their traffic, without reference to the chief into whose country they had unceremoniously introduced themselves; while Mpepe, feeding them with the cattle of Sekeletu, formed a plan of raising himself, by means of their fire-arms, to be the head of the Makololo. The usual course which the slave-traders adopt is to take a part in the political affairs of each tribe, and, siding with the strongest, get well paid by captures made from the weaker party. Long secret conferences were held by the slave-traders and Mpepe, and it was deemed advisable for him to strike the first blow; so he provided himself with a small battle-axe, with the intention of cutting Sekeletu down the first time they met.

My object being first of all to examine the country for a healthy locality, before attempting to make a path to either the East or West Coast, I proposed to Sekeletu the plan of ascending the great river which we had discovered in 1851. He volunteered to accompany me, and, when we got about sixty miles away, on the road to Sesheke, we encountered Mpepe. The Makololo, though possessing abundance of cattle, had never attempted to ride oxen until I advised it in 1851. The Bechuanas generally were in the same condition, until Europeans came among them and imparted the idea of riding. All their journeys previously were performed on foot. Sekeletu and his companions were mounted on oxen, though, having neither saddle nor bridle, they were perpetually falling off. Mpepe, armed with his little axe, came along a path parallel to, but a quarter of a mile distant from, that of our party, and, when he saw Sekeletu, he ran with all his might toward us; but Sekeletu, being on his guard, galloped off to an adjacent village. He then withdrew somewhere till all our party came up. Mpepe had given his own party to understand that he would cut down Sekeletu, either on their first meeting, or at the breaking up of their first conference. The former intention having been thus frustrated, he then determined to effect his purpose after their first interview. I happened to sit down between the two in the hut where they met. Being tired with riding all day in the sun, I soon asked Sekeletu where I should sleep, and he replied, "Come, I will show you." As we rose together, I unconsciously covered Sekeletu's body with mine, and saved him from the blow of the assassin. I knew nothing of the plot, but remarked that all Mpepe's men kept hold of their arms, even after we had sat down—a thing quite unusual in the presence of a chief; and when Sekeletu showed me the hut in which I was to spend the night, he said to me, "That man wishes to kill me." I afterward learned that some of Mpepe's attendants had divulged the secret; and, bearing in mind his father's instructions, Sekeletu put Mpepe to death that night. It was managed so quietly, that, although I was sleeping within a few yards of the scene, I knew nothing of it till the next day. Nokuane went to the fire, at which Mpepe sat, with a handful of snuff, as if he were about to sit down and regale himself therewith. Mpepe said to him, "Nsepisa" (cause me to take a pinch); and, as he held out his hand, Nokuane caught hold of it, while another man seized the other hand, and, leading him out a mile, speared him. This is the common mode of executing criminals. They are not allowed to speak; though on one occasion a man, feeling his wrist held too tightly, said, "Hold me gently, can't you? you will soon be led out in the same way yourselves." Mpepe's men fled to the Barotse, and, it being unadvisable for us to go thither during the commotion which followed on Mpepe's death, we returned to Linyanti.

The foregoing may be considered as a characteristic specimen of their mode of dealing with grave political offenses. In common cases there is a greater show of deliberation. The complainant asks the man against whom he means to lodge his complaint to come with him to the chief. This is never refused. When both are in the kotla, the complainant stands up and states the whole case before the chief and the people usually assembled there. He stands a few seconds after he has done this, to recollect if he has forgotten any thing. The witnesses to whom he has referred then rise up and tell all they themselves have seen or heard, but not any thing that they have heard from others. The defendant, after allowing some minutes to elapse so that he may not interrupt any of the opposite party, slowly rises, folds his cloak around him, and, in the most quiet, deliberate way he can assume—yawning, blowing his nose, etc.—begins to explain the affair, denying the charge, or admitting it, as the case may be. Sometimes, when galled by his remarks, the complainant utters a sentence of dissent; the accused turns quietly to him, and says, "Be silent: I sat still while you were speaking; can't you do the same? Do you want to have it all to yourself?" And as the audience acquiesce in this bantering, and enforce silence, he goes on till he has finished all he wishes to say in his defense. If he has any witnesses to the truth of the facts of his defense, they give their evidence. No oath is administered; but occasionally, when a statement is questioned, a man will say, "By my father," or "By the chief, it is so." Their truthfulness among each other is quite remarkable; but their system of government is such that Europeans are not in a position to realize it readily. A poor man will say, in his defense against a rich one, "I am astonished to hear a man so great as he make a false accusation;" as if the offense of falsehood were felt to be one against the society which the individual referred to had the greatest interest in upholding.

If the case is one of no importance, the chief decides it at once; if frivolous, he may give the complainant a scolding, and put a stop to the case in the middle of the complaint, or he may allow it to go on without paying any attention to it whatever. Family quarrels are often treated in this way, and then a man may be seen stating his case with great fluency, and not a soul listening to him. But if it is a case between influential men, or brought on by under-chiefs, then the greatest decorum prevails. If the chief does not see his way clearly to a decision, he remains silent; the elders then rise one by one and give their opinions, often in the way of advice rather than as decisions; and when the chief finds the general sentiment agreeing in one view, he delivers his judgment accordingly. He alone speaks sitting; all others stand.

No one refuses to acquiesce in the decision of the chief, as he has the power of life and death in his hands, and can enforce the law to that extent if he chooses; but grumbling is allowed, and, when marked favoritism is shown to any relative of the chief, the people generally are not so astonished at the partiality as we would be in England.

This system was found as well developed among the Makololo as among the Bakwains, or even better, and is no foreign importation. When at Cassange, my men had a slight quarrel among themselves, and came to me, as to their chief, for judgment. This had occurred several times before, so without a thought I went out of the Portuguese merchant's house in which I was a guest, sat down, and heard the complaint and defense in the usual way. When I had given my decision in the common admonitory form, they went off apparently satisfied. Several Portuguese, who had been viewing the proceedings with great interest, complimented me on the success of my teaching them how to act in litigation; but I could not take any credit to myself for the system which I had found ready-made to my hands.

Soon after our arrival at Linyanti, Sekeletu took me aside, and pressed me to mention those things I liked best and hoped to get from him. Any thing, either in or out of his town, should be freely given if I would only mention it. I explained to him that my object was to elevate him and his people to be Christians; but he replied he did not wish to learn to read the Book, for he was afraid "it might change his heart, and make him content with only one wife, like Sechele." It was of little use to urge that the change of heart implied a contentment with one wife equal to his present complacency in polygamy. Such a preference after the change of mind could not now be understood by him any more than the real, unmistakable pleasure of religious services can by those who have not experienced what is known by the term the "new heart". I assured him that nothing was expected but by his own voluntary decision. "No, no; he wanted always to have five wives at least." I liked the frankness of Sekeletu, for nothing is so wearying to the spirit as talking to those who agree with every thing advanced.

Sekeletu, according to the system of the Bechuanas, became possessor of his father's wives, and adopted two of them; the children by these women are, however, in these cases, termed brothers. When an elder brother dies, the same thing occurs in respect of his wives; the brother next in age takes them, as among the Jews, and the children that may be born of those women he calls brothers also. He thus raises up seed to his departed relative. An uncle of Sekeletu, being a younger brother of Sebituane, got that chieftain's head-wife or queen: there is always one who enjoys this title. Her hut is called the great house, and her children inherit the chieftainship. If she dies, a new wife is selected for the same position, and enjoys the same privileges, though she may happen to be a much younger woman than the rest.

The majority of the wives of Sebituane were given to influential under-chiefs; and, in reference to their early casting off the widow's weeds, a song was sung, the tenor of which was that the men alone felt the loss of their father Sebituane, the women were so soon supplied with new husbands that their hearts had not time to become sore with grief.

The women complain because the proportions between the sexes are so changed now that they are not valued as they deserve. The majority of the real Makololo have been cut off by fever. Those who remain are a mere fragment of the people who came to the north with Sebituane. Migrating from a very healthy climate in the south, they were more subject to the febrile diseases of the valley in which we found them than the black tribes they conquered. In comparison with the Barotse, Batoka, and Banyeti, the Makololo have a sickly hue. They are of a light brownish-yellow color, while the tribes referred to are very dark, with a slight tinge of olive. The whole of the colored tribes consider that beauty and fairness are associated, and women long for children of light color so much, that they sometimes chew the bark of a certain tree in hopes of producing that effect. To my eye the dark color is much more agreeable than the tawny hue of the half-caste, which that of the Makololo ladies closely resembles. The women generally escaped the fever, but they are less fruitful than formerly, and, to their complaint of being undervalued on account of the disproportion of the sexes, they now add their regrets at the want of children, of whom they are all excessively fond.

The Makololo women work but little. Indeed, the families of that nation are spread over the country, one or two only in each village, as the lords of the land. They all have lordship over great numbers of subjected tribes, who pass by the general name Makalaka, and who are forced to render certain services, and to aid in tilling the soil; but each has his own land under cultivation, and otherwise lives nearly independent. They are proud to be called Makololo, but the other term is often used in reproach, as betokening inferiority. This species of servitude may be termed serfdom, as it has to be rendered in consequence of subjection by force of arms, but it is necessarily very mild. It is so easy for any one who is unkindly treated to make his escape to other tribes, that the Makololo are compelled to treat them, to a great extent, rather as children than slaves. Some masters, who fail from defect of temper or disposition to secure the affections of the conquered people, frequently find themselves left without a single servant, in consequence of the absence and impossibility of enforcing a fugitive-slave law, and the readiness with which those who are themselves subjected assist the fugitives across the rivers in canoes. The Makololo ladies are liberal in their presents of milk and other food, and seldom require to labor, except in the way of beautifying their own huts and court-yards. They drink large quantities of boyaloa or o-alo, the buza of the Arabs, which, being made of the grain called holcus sorghum or "durasaifi", in a minute state of subdivision, is very nutritious, and gives that plumpness of form which is considered beautiful. They dislike being seen at their potations by persons of the opposite sex. They cut their woolly hair quite short, and delight in having the whole person shining with butter. Their dress is a kilt reaching to the knees; its material is ox-hide, made as soft as cloth. It is not ungraceful. A soft skin mantle is thrown across the shoulders when the lady is unemployed, but when engaged in any sort of labor she throws this aside, and works in the kilt alone. The ornaments most coveted are large brass anklets as thick as the little finger, and armlets of both brass and ivory, the latter often an inch broad. The rings are so heavy that the ankles are often blistered by the weight pressing down; but it is the fashion, and is borne as magnanimously as tight lacing and tight shoes among ourselves. Strings of beads are hung around the neck, and the fashionable colors being light green and pink, a trader could get almost any thing he chose for beads of these colors.

At our public religious services in the kotla, the Makololo women always behaved with decorum from the first, except at the conclusion of the prayer. When all knelt down, many of those who had children, in following the example of the rest, bent over their little ones; the children, in terror of being crushed to death, set up a simultaneous yell, which so tickled the whole assembly there was often a subdued titter, to be turned into a hearty laugh as soon as they heard Amen. This was not so difficult to overcome in them as similar peccadilloes were in the case of the women farther south. Long after we had settled at Mabotsa, when preaching on the most solemn subjects, a woman might be observed to look round, and, seeing a neighbor seated on her dress, give her a hunch with the elbow to make her move off; the other would return it with interest, and perhaps the remark, "Take the nasty thing away, will you?" Then three or four would begin to hustle the first offenders, and the men to swear at them all, by way of enforcing silence.

Great numbers of little trifling things like these occur, and would not be worth the mention but that one can not form a correct idea of missionary work except by examination of the minutiae. At the risk of appearing frivolous to some, I shall continue to descend to mere trifles.

The numbers who attended at the summons of the herald, who acted as beadle, were often from five to seven hundred. The service consisted of reading a small portion of the Bible and giving an explanatory address, usually short enough to prevent weariness or want of attention. So long as we continue to hold services in the kotla, the associations of the place are unfavorable to solemnity; hence it is always desirable to have a place of worship as soon as possible; and it is of importance, too, to treat such place with reverence, as an aid to secure that serious attention which religious subjects demand. This will appear more evident when it is recollected that, in the very spot where we had been engaged in acts of devotion, half an hour after a dance would be got up; and these habits can not be at first opposed without the appearance of assuming too much authority over them. It is always unwise to hurt their feelings of independence. Much greater influence will be gained by studying how you may induce them to act aright, with the impression that they are doing it of their own free will. Our services having necessarily been all in the open air, where it is most difficult to address large bodies of people, prevented my recovering so entirely from the effects of clergyman's sore throat as I expected, when my uvula was excised at the Cape.

To give an idea of the routine followed for months together, on other days as well as on Sundays, I may advert to my habit of treating the sick for complaints which seemed to surmount the skill of their own doctors. I refrained from going to any one unless his own doctor wished it, or had given up the case. This led to my having a selection of the severer cases only, and prevented the doctors being offended at my taking their practice out of their hands. When attacked by fever myself, and wishing to ascertain what their practices were, I could safely intrust myself in their hands on account of their well-known friendly feelings.

The plan of showing kindness to the natives in their bodily ailments secures their friendship; this is not the case to the same degree in old missions, where the people have learned to look upon relief as a right—a state of things which sometimes happens among ourselves at home. Medical aid is therefore most valuable in young missions, though at all stages it is an extremely valuable adjunct to other operations.

I proposed to teach the Makololo to read, but, for the reasons mentioned, Sekeletu at first declined; after some weeks, however, Motibe, his father-in-law, and some others, determined to brave the mysterious book. To all who have not acquired it, the knowledge of letters is quite unfathomable; there is naught like it within the compass of their observation; and we have no comparison with any thing except pictures, to aid them in comprehending the idea of signs of words. It seems to them supernatural that we see in a book things taking place, or having occurred at a distance. No amount of explanation conveys the idea unless they learn to read. Machinery is equally inexplicable, and money nearly as much so until they see it in actual use. They are familiar with barter alone; and in the centre of the country, where gold is totally unknown, if a button and sovereign were left to their choice, they would prefer the former on account of its having an eye.

In beginning to learn, Motibe seemed to himself in the position of the doctor, who was obliged to drink his potion before the patient, to show that it contained nothing detrimental; after he had mastered the alphabet, and reported the thing so far safe, Sekeletu and his young companions came forward to try for themselves. He must have resolved to watch the effects of the book against his views on polygamy, and abstain whenever he perceived any tendency, in reading it, toward enforcing him to put his wives away. A number of men learned the alphabet in a short time and were set to teach others, but before much progress could be made I was on my way to Loanda.

As I had declined to name any thing as a present from Sekeletu, except a canoe to take me up the river, he brought ten fine elephants' tusks and laid them down beside my wagon. He would take no denial, though I told him I should prefer to see him trading with Fleming, a man of color from the West Indies, who had come for the purpose. I had, during the eleven years of my previous course, invariably abstained from taking presents of ivory, from an idea that a religious instructor degraded himself by accepting gifts from those whose spiritual welfare he professed to seek. My precedence of all traders in the line of discovery put me often in the way of very handsome offers, but I always advised the donors to sell their ivory to traders, who would be sure to follow, and when at some future time they had become rich by barter, they might remember me or my children. When Lake Ngami was discovered I might have refused permission to a trader who accompanied us; but when he applied for leave to form part of our company, knowing that Mr. Oswell would no more trade than myself, and that the people of the lake would be disappointed if they could not dispose of their ivory, I willingly granted a sanction, without which his people would not at that time have ventured so far. This was surely preferring the interest of another to my own. The return I got for this was a notice in one of the Cape papers that this "man was the true discoverer of the lake!"

The conclusion I had come to was, that it is quite lawful, though perhaps not expedient, for missionaries to trade; but barter is the only means by which a missionary in the interior can pay his way, as money has no value. In all the journeys I had previously undertaken for wider diffusion of the Gospel, the extra expenses were defrayed from my salary of 100 Pounds per annum. This sum is sufficient to enable a missionary to live in the interior of South Africa, supposing he has a garden capable of yielding corn and vegetables; but should he not, and still consider that six or eight months can not lawfully be spent simply in getting goods at a lower price than they can be had from itinerant traders, the sum mentioned is barely sufficient for the poorest fare and plainest apparel. As we never felt ourselves justified in making journeys to the colony for the sake of securing bargains, the most frugal living was necessary to enable us to be a little charitable to others; but when to this were added extra traveling expenses, the wants of an increasing family, and liberal gifts to chiefs, it was difficult to make both ends meet. The pleasure of missionary labor would be enhanced if one could devote his life to the heathen, without drawing a salary from a society at all. The luxury of doing good from one's own private resources, without appearing to either natives or Europeans to be making a gain of it, is far preferable, and an object worthy the ambition of the rich. But few men of fortune, however, now devote themselves to Christian missions, as of old. Presents were always given to the chiefs whom we visited, and nothing accepted in return; but when Sebituane (in 1851) offered some ivory, I took it, and was able by its sale to present his son with a number of really useful articles of a higher value than I had ever been able to give before to any chief. In doing this, of course, I appeared to trade, but, feeling I had a right to do so, I felt perfectly easy in my mind; and, as I still held the view of the inexpediency of combining the two professions, I was glad of the proposal of one of the most honorable merchants of Cape Town, Mr. H. E. Rutherford, that he should risk a sum of money in Fleming's hands for the purpose of attempting to develop a trade with the Makololo. It was to this man I suggested Sekeletu should sell the tusks which he had presented for my acceptance, but the chief refused to take them back from me. The goods which Fleming had brought were ill adapted for the use of the natives, but he got a pretty good load of ivory in exchange; and though it was his first attempt at trading, and the distance traveled over made the expenses enormous, he was not a loser by the trip. Other traders followed, who demanded 90 lbs. of ivory for a musket. The Makololo, knowing nothing of steelyards, but supposing that they were meant to cheat them, declined to trade except by exchanging one bull and one cow elephant's tusk for each gun. This would average 70 lbs. of ivory, which sells at the Cape for 5s. per pound, for a second-hand musket worth 10s. I, being sixty miles distant, did not witness this attempt at barter, but, anxious to enable my countrymen to drive a brisk trade, told the Makololo to sell my ten tusks on their own account for whatever they would bring. Seventy tusks were for sale, but, the parties not understanding each other's talk, no trade was established; and when I passed the spot some time afterward, I found that the whole of that ivory had been destroyed by an accidental fire, which broke out in the village when all the people were absent. Success in trade is as much dependent on knowledge of the language as success in traveling.

I had brought with me as presents an improved breed of goats, fowls, and a pair of cats. A superior bull was bought, also as a gift to Sekeletu, but I was compelled to leave it on account of its having become foot-sore. As the Makololo are very fond of improving the breed of their domestic animals, they were much pleased with my selection. I endeavored to bring the bull, in performance of a promise made to Sebituane before he died. Admiring a calf which we had with us, he proposed to give me a cow for it, which in the native estimation was offering three times its value. I presented it to him at once, and promised to bring him another and a better one. Sekeletu was much gratified by my attempt to keep my word given to his father.

They have two breeds of cattle among them. One, called the Batoka, because captured from that tribe, is of diminutive size, but very beautiful, and closely resembles the short-horns of our own country. The little pair presented by the King of Portugal to H.R.H. the prince consort, is of this breed. They are very tame, and remarkably playful; they may be seen lying on their sides by the fires in the evening; and, when the herd goes out, the herdsman often precedes them, and has only to commence capering to set them all a gamboling. The meat is superior to that of the large animal. The other, or Barotse ox, is much larger, and comes from the fertile Barotse Valley. They stand high on their legs, often nearly six feet at the withers;

and they have large horns. Those of one of a similar breed that we brought from the lake measured from tip to tip eight and a half feet.

The Makololo are in the habit of shaving off a little from one side of the horns of these animals when still growing, in order to make them curve in that direction and assume fantastic shapes. The stranger the curvature, the more handsome the ox is considered to be, and the longer this ornament of the cattle-pen is spared to beautify the herd. This is a very ancient custom in Africa, for the tributary tribes of Ethiopia are seen, on some of the most ancient Egyptian monuments, bringing contorted-horned cattle into Egypt.

All are remarkably fond of their cattle, and spend much time in ornamenting and adorning them. Some are branded all over with a hot knife, so as to cause a permanent discoloration of the hair, in lines like the bands on the hide of a zebra. Pieces of skin two or three inches long and broad are detached, and allowed to heal in a dependent position around the head—a strange style of ornament; indeed, it is difficult to conceive in what their notion of beauty consists. The women have somewhat the same ideas with ourselves of what constitutes comeliness. They came frequently and asked for the looking-glass; and the remarks they made—while I was engaged in reading, and apparently not attending to them—on first seeing themselves therein, were amusingly ridiculous. "Is that me?" "What a big mouth I have!" "My ears are as big as pumpkin-leaves." "I have no chin at all." Or, "I would have been pretty, but am spoiled by these high cheek-bones." "See how my head shoots up in the middle!" laughing vociferously all the time at their own jokes. They readily perceive any defect in each other, and give nicknames accordingly. One man came alone to have a quiet gaze at his own features once, when he thought I was asleep; after twisting his mouth about in various directions, he remarked to himself, "People say I am ugly, and how very ugly I am indeed!"

The Makololo use all the skins of their oxen for making either mantles or shields. For the former, the hide is stretched out by means of pegs, and dried. Ten or a dozen men then collect round it with small adzes, which, when sharpened with an iron bodkin, are capable of shaving off the substance of the skin on the fleshy side until it is quite thin; when sufficiently thin, a quantity of brain is smeared over it, and some thick milk. Then an instrument made of a number of iron spikes tied round a piece of wood, so that the points only project beyond it, is applied to it in a carding fashion, until the fibres of the bulk of it are quite loose. Milk or butter is applied to it again, and it forms a garment nearly as soft as cloth.

The shields are made of hides partially dried in the sun, and then beaten with hammers until they are stiff and dry. Two broad belts of a differently-colored skin are sewed into them longitudinally, and sticks inserted to make them rigid and not liable to bend easily. The shield is a great protection in their way of fighting with spears, but they also trust largely to their agility in springing aside from the coming javelin. The shield assists when so many spears are thrown that it is impossible not to receive some of them. Their spears are light javelins; and, judging from what I have seen them do in elephant-hunting, I believe, when they have room to make a run and discharge them with the aid of the jerk of stopping, they can throw them between forty and fifty yards. They give them an upward direction in the discharge, so that they come down on the object with accelerated force. I saw a man who in battle had received one in the shin; the excitement of the moment prevented his feeling any pain; but, when the battle was over, the blade was found to have split the bone, and become so impacted in the cleft that no force could extract it. It was necessary to take an axe and press the split bone asunder before the weapon could be taken out.

Chapter 10

The Fever—Its Symptoms—Remedies of the native Doctors—Hospitality of Sekeletu and his People—One of their Reasons for Polygamy—They cultivate largely—The Makalaka or subject Tribes—Sebituane's Policy respecting them—Their Affection for him—Products of the Soil—Instrument of Culture—The Tribute—Distributed by the Chief—A warlike Demonstration—Lechulatebe's Provocations—The Makololo determine to punish him—The Bechuanas—Meaning of the Term—Three Divisions of the great Family of South Africans.

On the 30th of May I was seized with fever for the first time. We reached the town of Linyanti on the 23d; and as my habits were suddenly changed from great exertion to comparative inactivity, at the commencement of the cold season I suffered from a severe attack of stoppage of the secretions, closely resembling a common cold. Warm baths and drinks relieved me, and I had no idea but that I was now recovering from the effects of a chill, got by leaving the warm wagon in the evening in order to conduct family worship at my people's fire. But on the 2d of June a relapse showed to the Makololo, who knew the complaint, that my indisposition was no other than the fever, with which I have since made a more intimate acquaintance. Cold east winds prevail at this time; and as they come over the extensive flats inundated by the Chobe, as well as many other districts where pools of rain-water are now drying up, they may be supposed to be loaded with malaria and watery vapor, and many cases of fever follow. The usual symptoms of stopped secretion are manifested—shivering and a feeling of coldness, though the skin is quite hot to the touch of another. The heat in the axilla, over the heart and region of the stomach, was in my case 100 Deg.; but along the spine and at the nape of the neck 103 Deg. The internal processes were all, with the exception of the kidneys and liver, stopped; the latter, in its efforts to free the blood of noxious particles, often secretes enormous quantities of bile. There were pains along the spine, and frontal headache. Anxious to ascertain whether the natives possessed the knowledge of any remedy of which we were ignorant, I requested the assistance of one of Sekeletu's doctors. He put some roots into a pot with water, and, when it was boiling, placed it on a spot beneath a blanket thrown around both me and it. This produced no immediate effect; he then got a small bundle of different kinds of medicinal woods, and, burning them in a potsherd nearly to ashes, used the smoke and hot vapor arising from them as an auxiliary to the other in causing diaphoresis. I fondly hoped that they had a more potent remedy than our own medicines afford; but after being stewed in their vapor-baths, smoked like a red herring over green twigs, and charmed 'secundem artem', I concluded that I could cure the fever more quickly than they can. If we employ a wet sheet and a mild aperient in combination with quinine, in addition to the native remedies, they are an important aid in curing the fever, as they seem to have the same stimulating effects on the alimentary canal as these means have on the external surface. Purgatives, general bleedings, or indeed any violent remedies, are injurious; and the appearance of a herpetic eruption near the mouth is regarded as an evidence that no internal organ is in danger. There is a good deal in not "giving in" to this disease. He who is low-spirited, and apt to despond at every attack, will die sooner than the man who is not of such a melancholic nature.

The Makololo had made a garden and planted maize for me, that, as they remarked when I was parting with them to proceed to the Cape, I might have food to eat when I returned, as well as other people. The maize was now pounded by the women into fine meal. This they do in large wooden mortars, the counterpart of which may be seen depicted on the Egyptian monuments.* Sekeletu added to this good supply of meal ten or twelve jars of honey, each of which contained about two gallons. Liberal supplies of ground-nuts ('Arachis hypogoea') were also furnished every time the tributary tribes brought their dues to Linyanti, and an ox was given for slaughter every week or two. Sekeletu also appropriated two cows to be milked for us every morning and evening. This was in accordance with the acknowledged rule throughout this country, that the chief should feed all strangers who come on any special business to him and take up their abode in his kotla. A present is usually given in return for the hospitality, but, except in cases where their aboriginal customs have been modified, nothing would be asked. Europeans spoil the feeling that hospitality is the sacred duty of the chiefs by what in other circumstances is laudable conduct. No sooner do they arrive than they offer to purchase food, and, instead of waiting till a meal is prepared for them in the evening, cook for themselves, and then often decline even to partake of that which has been made ready for their use. A present is also given, and before long the natives come to expect a gift without having offered any equivalent.

Unfortunately, the illustration shown with this paragraph cannot be shown in this ASCII file. It has the following caption: 'Egyptian Pestle and Mortar, Sieves, Corn Vessels, and Kilt, identical with those in use by the Makololo and Makalaka. — From Sir G. Wilkinson's "Ancient Egyptians".' — A. L., 1997.

Strangers frequently have acquaintances among the under-chiefs, to whose establishments they turn aside, and are treated on the same principle that others are when they are the guests of the chief. So generally is the duty admitted, that one of the most cogent arguments for polygamy is that a respectable man with only one wife could not entertain strangers as he ought. This reason has especial weight where the women are the chief cultivators of the soil, and have the control over the corn, as at Kolobeng. The poor, however, who have no friends, often suffer much hunger, and the very kind attention Sebituane lavished on all such was one of the reasons of his great popularity in the country.

The Makololo cultivate a large extent of land around their villages. Those of them who are real Basutos still retain the habits of that tribe, and may be seen going out with their wives with their hoes in hand — a state of things never witnessed at Kolobeng, or among any other Bechuana or Caffre tribe. The great chief Moshesh affords an example to his people annually by not only taking the hoe in hand, but working hard with it on certain public occasions. His Basutos are of the same family with the Makololo to whom I refer. The younger Makololo, who have been accustomed from their infancy to lord it over the conquered Makalaka, have unfortunately no desire to imitate the agricultural tastes of their fathers, and expect their subjects to perform all the manual labor. They are the aristocracy of the country, and once possessed almost unlimited power over their vassals. Their privileges were, however, much abridged by Sebituane himself.

I have already mentioned that the tribes which Sebituane subjected in this great country pass by the general name of Makalaka. The Makololo were composed of a great number of other tribes, as well as of these central negroes. The nucleus of the whole were Basuto, who came with Sebituane from a comparatively cold and hilly region in the south. When he conquered various tribes of the Bechuanas, as Bakwains, Bangwaketze, Bamangwato, Batauana, etc., he incorporated the young of these tribes into his own. Great mortality by fever having taken place in the original stock, he wisely adopted the same plan of absorption on a large scale with the Makalaka. So we found him with even the sons of the chiefs of the Barotse closely attached to his person; and they say to this day, if any thing else but natural death had assailed their father, every one of them would have laid down his life in his defense. One reason for their strong affection was their emancipation by the decree of Sebituane, "all are children of the chief."

The Makalaka cultivate the 'Holcus sorghum', or dura, as the principal grain, with maize, two kinds of beans, ground-nuts ('Arachis hypogoea'), pumpkins, watermelons, and cucumbers. They depend for success entirely upon rain. Those who live in the Barotse valley cultivate in addition the sugar-cane, sweet potato, and manioc ('Jatropha manihot'). The climate there, however, is warmer than at Linyanti, and the Makalaka increase the fertility of their gardens by rude attempts at artificial irrigation.

The instrument of culture over all this region is a hoe, the iron of which the Batoka and Banyeti obtain from the ore by smelting. The amount of iron which they produce annually may be understood when it is known that most of the hoes in use at Linyanti are the tribute imposed on the smiths of those subject tribes.

Sekeletu receives tribute from a great number of tribes in corn or dura, ground-nuts, hoes, spears, honey, canoes, paddles, wooden vessels, tobacco, mutokuane ('Cannabis sativa'), various wild fruits (dried), prepared skins, and ivory. When these articles are brought into the kotla, Sekeletu has the honor of dividing them among the loungers who usually congregate there. A small portion only is reserved for himself. The ivory belongs nominally to him too, but this is simply a way of making a fair distribution of the profits. The chief sells it only with the approbation of his counselors, and the proceeds are distributed in open day among the people as before. He has the choice of every thing; but if he is not more liberal to others than to himself, he loses in popularity. I have known instances in this and other tribes in which individuals aggrieved, because they had been overlooked, fled to other chiefs. One discontented person, having fled to Lechulatebe, was encouraged to go to a village of the Bapalleng, on the River Cho or Tso, and abstracted the tribute of ivory thence which ought to have come to Sekeletu. This theft enraged the whole of the Makololo, because they all felt it to be a personal loss. Some of Lechulatebe's people having come on a visit to Linyanti, a demonstration was made, in which about five hundred Makololo, armed, went through a mimic fight; the principal warriors pointed their spears toward the lake where Lechulatebe lives, and every thrust in that direction was answered by all with the shout, "Ho-o!" while every stab on the ground drew out a simultaneous "Huzz!" On these occasions all capable of bearing arms, even the old, must turn out at the call. In the time of Sebituane, any one remaining in his house was searched for and killed without mercy.

This offense of Lechulatebe was aggravated by repetition, and by a song sung in his town accompanying the dances, which manifested joy at the death of Sebituane. He had enjoined his people to live in peace with those at the lake, and Sekeletu felt disposed to follow his advice; but Lechulatebe had now got possession of fire-arms, and considered himself more than a match for the Makololo. His father had been dispossessed of many cattle by Sebituane, and, as forgiveness is not considered among the virtues by the heathen, Lechulatebe thought he had a right to recover what he could. As I had a good deal of influence with the Makololo, I persuaded them that, before they could have peace, they must resolve to give the same blessing to others, and they never could do that without forgiving and forgetting ancient feuds. It is hard to make them feel that shedding of human blood is a great crime; they must be conscious that it is wrong, but, having been accustomed to bloodshed from infancy, they are remarkably callous to the enormity of the crime of destroying human life.

I sent a message at the same time to Lechulatebe advising him to give up the course he had adopted, and especially the song; because, though Sebituane was dead, the arms with which he had fought were still alive and strong.

Sekeletu, in order to follow up his father's instructions and promote peace, sent ten cows to Lechulatebe to be exchanged for sheep; these animals thrive well in a bushy country like that around the lake, but will scarcely live in the flat prairies between the net-work of waters north of the Chobe. The men who took the cows carried a number of hoes to purchase goats besides. Lechulatebe took the cows and sent back an equal number of sheep. Now, according to the relative value of sheep and cows in these parts, he ought to have sent sixty or seventy.

One of the men who had hoes was trying to purchase in a village without formal leave from Lechulatebe; this chief punished him by making him sit some hours on the broiling hot sand (at least 130 Deg.). This farther offense put a stop to amicable relations between the two tribes altogether. It was a case in which a very small tribe, commanded by a weak and foolish chief, had got possession of fire-arms, and felt conscious of ability to cope with a numerous and warlike race. Such cases are the only ones in which the possession of fire-arms does evil. The universal effect of the diffusion of the more potent instruments of warfare in Africa is the same as among ourselves. Fire-arms render wars less frequent and less bloody. It is indeed exceedingly rare to hear of two tribes having guns going to war with each other; and, as nearly all the feuds, in the south at least, have been about cattle, the risk which must be incurred from long shots generally proves a preventive to the foray.

The Makololo were prevailed upon to keep the peace during my residence with them, but it was easy to perceive that public opinion was against sparing a tribe of Bechuanas for whom the Makololo entertained the most sovereign contempt. The young men would remark, "Lechulatebe is herding our cows for us; let us only go, we shall 'lift' the price of them in sheep," etc.

As the Makololo are the most northerly of the Bechuanas, we may glance back at this family of Africans before entering on the branch of the negro family which the Makololo distinguish by the term Makalaka. The name Bechuana seems derived from the word Chuana—alike, or equal with the personal pronoun Ba (they) prefixed, and therefore means fellows or equals. Some have supposed the name to have arisen from a mistake of some traveler, who, on asking individuals of this nation concerning the tribes living beyond them, received the answer, Bachuana, "they (are) alike"; meaning, "They are the same as we are"; and that this nameless traveler, who never wrote a word about them, managed to ingraft his mistake as a generic term on a nation extending from the Orange River to 18 Deg. south latitude.*

> * The Makololo have conquered the country as far as 14 Deg. south, but it is still peopled chiefly by the black tribes named Makalaka.

As the name was found in use among those who had no intercourse with Europeans, before we can receive the above explanation we must believe that the unknown traveler knew the language sufficiently well to ask a question, but not to understand the answer. We may add, that the way in which they still continue to use the word seems to require no fanciful interpretation. When addressed with any degree of scorn, they reply, "We are Bachuana, or equals—we are not inferior to any of our nation," in exactly the same sense as Irishmen or Scotchmen, in the same circumstances, would reply, "We are Britons," or "We are Englishmen." Most other tribes are known by the terms applied to them by strangers only, as the Caffres, Hottentots, and Bushmen. The Bechuanas alone use the term to themselves as a generic one for the whole nation. They have managed, also, to give a comprehensive name to the whites, viz., Makoa, though they can not explain the derivation of it any more than of their own. It seems to mean "handsome", from the manner in which they use it to indicate beauty; but there is a word so very like it meaning "infirm", or "weak", that Burchell's conjecture is probably the right one. "The different Hottentot tribes were known by names terminating in 'kua', which means 'man', and the Bechuanas simply added the prefix Ma, denoting a nation." They themselves were first known as Briquas, or "goat-men". The language of the Bechuanas is termed Sichuana; that of the whites (or Makoa) is called Sekoa.

The Makololo, or Basuto, have carried their powers of generalization still farther, and arranged the other parts of the same great family of South Africans into three divisions: 1st. The Matebele, or Makonkobi—the Caffre family living on the eastern side of the country; 2d. The Bakoni, or Basuto; and, 3d. The Bakalahari, or Bechuanas, living in the central parts, which includes all those tribes living in or adjacent to the great Kalahari Desert.

1st. The Caffres are divided by themselves into various subdivisions, as Amakosa, Amapanda, and other well-known titles. They consider the name Caffre as an insulting epithet.

The Zulus of Natal belong to the same family, and they are as famed for their honesty as their brethren who live adjacent to our colonial frontier are renowned for cattle-lifting. The Recorder of Natal declared of them that history does not present another instance in which so much security for life and property has been enjoyed, as has been experienced, during the whole period of English occupation, by ten thousand colonists, in the midst of one hundred thousand Zulus.

The Matebele of Mosilikatse, living a short distance south of the Zambesi, and other tribes living a little south of Tete and Senna, are members of this same family. They are not known beyond the Zambesi River. This was the limit of the Bechuana progress north too, until Sebituane pushed his conquests farther.

2d. The Bakoni and Basuto division contains, in the south, all those tribes which acknowledge Moshesh as their paramount chief. Among them we find the Batau, the Baputi, Makolokue, etc., and some mountaineers on the range Maluti, who are believed, by those who have carefully sifted the evidence, to have been at one time guilty of cannibalism. This has been doubted, but their songs admit the fact to this day, and they ascribe their having left off the odious practice of entrapping human prey to Moshesh having given them cattle. They are called Marimo and Mayabathu, men-eaters, by the rest of the Basuto, who have various subdivisions, as Makatla, Bamakakana, Matlapatlapa, etc.

The Bakoni farther north than the Basuto are the Batlou, Baperi, Bapo, and another tribe of Bakuena, Bamosetla, Bamapela or Balaka, Babiriri, Bapiri, Bahukeng, Batlokua, Baakhahela, etc., etc.; the whole of which tribes are favored with abundance of rain, and, being much attached to agriculture, raise very large quantities of grain. It is on their industry that the more distant Boers revel in slothful abundance, and follow their slave-hunting and cattle-stealing propensities quite beyond the range of English influence and law. The Basuto under Moshesh are equally fond of cultivating the soil. The chief labor of hoeing, driving away birds, reaping, and winnowing, falls to the willing arms of the hard-working women; but as the men, as well as their wives, as already stated, always work, many have followed the advice of the missionaries, and now use plows and oxen instead of the hoe.

3d. The Bakalahari, or western branch of the Bechuana family, consists of Barolong, Bahurutse, Bakuena, Bangwaketse, Bakaa, Bamangwato, Bakurutse, Batauana, Bamatlaro, and Batlapi. Among the last the success of missionaries has been greatest. They were an insignificant and filthy people when first discovered; but, being nearest to the colony, they have had opportunities of trading; and the long-continued peace they have enjoyed, through the influence of religious teaching, has enabled them to amass great numbers of cattle. The young, however, who do not realize their former degradation, often consider their present superiority over the less-favored tribes in the interior to be entirely owing to their own greater wisdom and more intellectual development.

Chapter 11

Departure from Linyanti for Sesheke—Level Country—Ant-hills—Wild Date-trees—Appearance of our Attendants on the March—The Chief's Guard—They attempt to ride on Ox-back—Vast Herds of the new Antelopes, Leches, and Nakongs—The native way of hunting them—Reception at the Villages—Presents of Beer and Milk—Eating with the Hand—The Chief provides the Oxen for Slaughter—Social Mode of Eating—The Sugar-cane—Sekeletu's novel Test of Character— Cleanliness of Makololo Huts—Their Construction and Appearance—The Beds—Cross the Leeambye—Aspect of this part of the Country—The small Antelope Tianyane unknown in the South—Hunting on foot—An Eland.

Having waited a month at Linyanti (lat. 18d 17' 20" S., long. 23d 50' 9" E.), we again departed, for the purpose of ascending the river from Sesheke (lat. 17d 31' 38" S., long. 25d 13' E.). To the Barotse country, the capital of which is Nariele or Naliele (lat. 15d 24' 17" S., long. 23d 5' 54" E.), I went in company with Sekeletu and about one hundred and sixty attendants. We had most of the young men with us, and many of the under-chiefs besides. The country between Linyanti and Sesheke is perfectly flat, except patches elevated only a few feet above the surrounding level. There are also many mounds where the gigantic ant-hills of the country have been situated or still appear: these mounds are evidently the work of the termites. No one who has not seen their gigantic structures can fancy the industry of these little laborers; they seem to impart fertility to the soil which has once passed through their mouths, for the Makololo find the sides of ant-hills the choice spots for rearing early maize, tobacco, or any thing on which they wish to bestow especial care. In the parts through which we passed the mounds are generally covered with masses of wild date-trees; the fruit is small, and no tree is allowed to stand long, for, having abundance of food, the Makololo have no inclination to preserve wild fruit-trees; accordingly, when a date shoots up to seed, as soon as the fruit is ripe they cut down the tree rather than be at the trouble of climbing it. The other parts of the more elevated land have the camel-thorn ('Acacia giraffae'), white-thorned mimosa ('Acacia horrida'), and baobabs. In sandy spots there are palmyras somewhat similar to the Indian, but with a smaller seed. The soil on all the flat parts is a rich, dark, tenacious loam, known as the "cotton-ground" in

India; it is covered with a dense matting of coarse grass, common on all damp spots in this country. We had the Chobe on our right, with its scores of miles of reed occupying the horizon there. It was pleasant to look back on the long-extended line of our attendants, as it twisted and bent according to the curves of the footpath, or in and out behind the mounds, the ostrich feathers of the men waving in the wind. Some had the white ends of ox-tails on their heads, Hussar fashion, and others great bunches of black ostrich feathers, or caps made of lions' manes. Some wore red tunics, or various-colored prints which the chief had bought from Fleming; the common men carried burdens; the gentlemen walked with a small club of rhinoceros-horn in their hands, and had servants to carry their shields; while the "Machaka", battle-axe men, carried their own, and were liable at any time to be sent off a hundred miles on an errand, and expected to run all the way.

Sekeletu is always accompanied by his own Mopato, a number of young men of his own age. When he sits down they crowd around him; those who are nearest eat out of the same dish, for the Makololo chiefs pride themselves on eating with their people. He eats a little, then beckons his neighbors to partake. When they have done so, he perhaps beckons to some one at a distance to take a share; that person starts forward, seizes the pot, and removes it to his own companions. The comrades of Sekeletu, wishing to imitate him in riding on my old horse, leaped on the backs of a number of half-broken Batoka oxen as they ran, but, having neither saddle nor bridle, the number of tumbles they met with was a source of much amusement to the rest. Troops of leches, or, as they are here called, "lechwes", appeared feeding quite heedlessly all over the flats; they exist here in prodigious herds, although the numbers of them and of the "nakong" that are killed annually must be enormous. Both are water antelopes, and, when the lands we now tread upon are flooded, they betake themselves to the mounds I have alluded to. The Makalaka, who are most expert in the management of their small, thin, light canoes, come gently toward them; the men stand upright in the canoe, though it is not more than fifteen or eighteen inches wide and about fifteen feet long; their paddles, ten feet in height, are of a kind of wood called molompi, very light, yet as elastic as ash. With these they either punt or paddle, according to the shallowness or depth of the water. When they perceive the antelopes beginning to move they increase their speed, and pursue them with great velocity. They make the water dash away from the gunwale, and, though the leche goes off by a succession of prodigious bounds, its feet appearing to touch the bottom at each spring, they manage to spear great numbers of them.

The nakong often shares a similar fate. This is a new species, rather smaller than the leche, and in shape has more of paunchiness than any antelope I ever saw. Its gait closely resembles the gallop of a dog when tired. The hair is long and rather sparse, so that it is never sleek-looking. It is of a grayish-brown color, and has horns twisted in the manner of a koodoo, but much smaller, and with a double ridge winding round each of them.

Its habitat is the marsh and the muddy bogs; the great length of its foot between the point of the toe and supplemental hoofs enables it to make a print about a foot in length; it feeds by night, and lies hid among the reeds and rushes by day; when pursued, it dashes into sedgy places containing water, and immerses the whole body, leaving only the point of the nose and ends of the horns exposed. The hunters burn large patches of reed in order to drive the nakong out of his lair; occasionally the ends of the horns project above the water; but when it sees itself surrounded by enemies in canoes, it will rather allow its horns to be scorched in the burning reed than come forth from its hiding-place.

When we arrived at any village the women all turned out to lulliloo their chief. Their shrill voices, to which they give a tremulous sound by a quick motion of the tongue, peal forth, "Great lion!" "Great chief!" "Sleep, my lord!" etc. The men utter similar salutations; and Sekeletu receives all with becoming indifference. After a few minutes' conversation and telling the news, the head man of the village, who is almost always a Makololo, rises, and brings forth a number of large pots of beer. Calabashes, being used as drinking-cups, are handed round, and as many as can partake of the beverage do so, grasping the vessels so eagerly that they are in danger of being broken.

They bring forth also large pots and bowls of thick milk; some contain six or eight gallons; and each of these, as well as of the beer, is given to a particular person, who has the power to divide it with whom he pleases. The head man of any section of the tribe is generally selected for this office. Spoons not being generally in fashion, the milk is conveyed to the mouth with the hand. I often presented my friends with iron spoons, and it was curious to observe how their habit of hand-eating prevailed, though they were delighted with the spoons. They lifted out a little with the utensil, then put it on the left hand, and ate it out of that.

As the Makololo have great abundance of cattle, and the chief is expected to feed all who accompany him, he either selects an ox or two of his own from the numerous cattle stations that he possesses at different spots all over the country, or is presented by the head men of the villages he visits with as many as he needs by way of tribute. The animals are killed by a thrust from a small javelin in the region of the heart, the wound being purposely small in order to avoid any loss of blood, which, with the internal parts, are the perquisites of the men who perform the work of the butcher; hence all are eager to render service in that line. Each tribe has its own way of cutting up and distributing an animal. Among the Makololo the hump and ribs belong to the chief; among the Bakwains the breast is his perquisite. After the oxen are cut up, the different joints are placed before Sekeletu, and he apportions them among the gentlemen of the party. The whole is rapidly divided by their attendants, cut into long strips, and so many of these are thrown into the fires at once that they are nearly put out. Half broiled and burning hot, the meat is quickly handed round; every one gets a mouthful, but no one except the chief has time to masticate. It is not the enjoyment of eating they aim at, but to get as much of the food into the stomach as possible during the short time the others are cramming as well as themselves, for no one can eat more than a mouthful after the others have finished. They are eminently gregarious in their eating; and, as they despise any one who eats alone, I always poured out two cups of coffee at my own meals, so that the chief, or some one of the principal men, might partake along with me. They all soon become very fond of coffee; and, indeed, some of the tribes attribute greater fecundity to the daily use of this beverage. They were all well acquainted with the sugar-cane, as they cultivate it in the Barotse country, but knew nothing of the method of extracting the sugar from it. They use the cane only for chewing. Sekeletu, relishing the sweet coffee and biscuits, of which I then had a store, said "he knew my heart loved him by finding his own heart warming to my food." He had been visited during my absence at the Cape by some traders and Griquas, and "their coffee did not taste half so nice as mine, because they loved his ivory and not himself." This was certainly an original mode of discerning character.

    Sekeletu and I had each a little gipsy-tent in which to sleep. The Makololo huts are generally clean, while those of the Makalaka are infested with vermin. The cleanliness of the former is owing to the habit of frequently smearing the floors with a plaster composed of cowdung and earth. If we slept in the tent in some villages, the mice ran over our faces and disturbed our sleep, or hungry prowling dogs would eat our shoes and leave only the soles. When they were guilty of this and other misdemeanors, we got the loan of a hut. The best sort of Makololo huts consist of three circular walls, with small holes as doors, each similar to that in a dog-house; and it is necessary to bend down the body to get in, even when on all-fours. The roof is formed of reeds or straight sticks, in shape like a Chinaman's hat, bound firmly together with circular bands, which are lashed with the strong inner bark of the mimosa-tree. When all prepared except the thatch, it is lifted on to the circular wall, the rim resting on a circle of poles, between each of which the third wall is built. The roof is thatched with fine grass, and sewed with the same material as the lashings; and, as it projects far beyond the walls, and reaches within four feet of the ground, the shade is the best to be found in the country. These huts are very cool in the hottest day, but are close and deficient in ventilation by night.

The bed is a mat made of rushes sewn together with twine; the hip-bone soon becomes sore on the hard flat surface, as we are not allowed to make a hole in the floor to receive the prominent part called trochanter by anatomists, as we do when sleeping on grass or sand.

Our course at this time led us to a part above Sesheke, called Katonga, where there is a village belonging to a Bashubia man named Sekhosi—latitude 17d 29' 13", longitude 24d 33'. The river here is somewhat broader than at Sesheke, and certainly not less than six hundred yards. It flows somewhat slowly in the first part of its eastern course. When the canoes came from Sekhosi to take us over, one of the comrades of Sebituane rose, and, looking to Sekeletu, called out, "The elders of a host always take the lead in an attack." This was understood at once; and Sekeletu, with all the young men, were obliged to give the elders the precedence, and remain on the southern bank and see that all went orderly into the canoes. It took a considerable time to ferry over the whole of our large party, as, even with quick paddling, from six to eight minutes were spent in the mere passage from bank to bank.

Several days were spent in collecting canoes from different villages on the river, which we now learned is called by the whole of the Barotse the Liambai or Leeambye. This we could not ascertain on our first visit, and, consequently, called the river after the town "Sesheke". This term Sesheke means "white sand-banks", many of which exist at this part. There is another village in the valley of the Barotse likewise called Sesheke, and for the same reason; but the term Leeambye means "the large river", or the river PAR EXCELLENCE. Luambeji, Luambesi, Ambezi, Ojimbesi, and Zambesi, etc., are names applied to it at different parts of its course, according to the dialect spoken, and all possess a similar signification, and express the native idea of this magnificent stream being the main drain of the country.

In order to assist in the support of our large party, and at the same time to see the adjacent country, I went several times, during our stay, to the north of the village for game. The country is covered with clumps of beautiful trees, among which fine open glades stretch away in every direction; when the river is in flood these are inundated, but the tree-covered elevated spots are much more numerous here than in the country between the Chobe and the Leeambye. The soil is dark loam, as it is every where on spots reached by the inundation, while among the trees it is sandy, and not covered so densely with grass as elsewhere. A sandy ridge covered with trees, running parallel to, and about eight miles from the river, is the limit of the inundation on the north; there are large tracts of this sandy forest in that direction, till you come to other districts of alluvial soil and fewer trees. The latter soil is always found in the vicinity of rivers which either now overflow their banks annually, or formerly did so. The people enjoy rain in sufficient quantity to raise very large supplies of grain and ground-nuts.

This district contains great numbers of a small antelope named Tianyane, unknown in the south. It stands about eighteen inches high, is very graceful in its movements, and utters a cry of alarm not unlike that of the domestic fowl; it is of a brownish-red color on the sides and back, with the belly and lower part of the tail white; it is very timid, but the maternal affection that the little thing bears to its young will often induce it to offer battle even to a man approaching it. When the young one is too tender to run about with the dam, she puts one foot on the prominence about the seventh cervical vertebra, or withers; the instinct of the young enables it to understand that it is now required to kneel down, and to remain quite still till it hears the bleating of its dam. If you see an otherwise gregarious she-antelope separated from the herd, and going alone any where, you may be sure she has laid her little one to sleep in some cozy spot. The color of the hair in the young is better adapted for assimilating it with the ground than that of the older animals, which do not need to be screened from the observation of birds of prey. I observed the Arabs at Aden, when making their camels kneel down, press the thumb on the withers in exactly the same way the antelopes do with their young; probably they have been led to the custom by seeing this plan adopted by the gazelle of the Desert.

Great numbers of buffaloes, zebras, tsessebes, tahaetsi, and eland, or pohu, grazed undisturbed on these plains, so that very little exertion was required to secure a fair supply of meat for the party during the necessary delay. Hunting on foot, as all those who have engaged in it in this country will at once admit, is very hard work indeed. The heat of the sun by day is so great, even in winter, as it now was, that, had there been any one on whom I could have thrown the task, he would have been most welcome to all the sport the toil is supposed to impart. But the Makololo shot so badly, that, in order to save my powder, I was obliged to go myself.

We shot a beautiful cow-eland, standing in the shade of a fine tree. It was evident that she had lately had her calf killed by a lion, for there were five long deep scratches on both sides of her hind-quarters, as if she had run to the rescue of her calf, and the lion, leaving it, had attacked herself, but was unable to pull her down. When lying on the ground, the milk flowing from the large udder showed that she must have been seeking the shade, from the distress its non-removal in the natural manner caused. She was a beautiful creature, and Lebeole, a Makololo gentleman who accompanied me, speaking in reference to its size and beauty, said, "Jesus ought to have given us these instead of cattle." It was a new, undescribed variety of this splendid antelope. It was marked with narrow white bands across the body, exactly like those of the koodoo, and had a black patch of more than a handbreadth on the outer side of the fore-arm.

Chapter 12

Procure Canoes and ascend the Leeambye—Beautiful Islands—Winter Landscape—Industry and Skill of the Banyeti—Rapids—Falls of Gonye—Tradition—Annual Inundations—Fertility of the great Barotse Valley—Execution of two Conspirators—The Slave-dealer's Stockade—Naliele, the Capital, built on an artificial Mound—Santuru, a great Hunter—The Barotse Method of commemorating any remarkable Event—Better Treatment of Women—More religious Feeling—Belief in a future State, and in the Existence of spiritual Beings—Gardens—Fish, Fruit, and Game—Proceed to the Limits of the Barotse Country— Sekeletu provides Rowers and a Herald—The River and Vicinity— Hippopotamus-hunters—No healthy Location—Determine to go to Loanda— Buffaloes, Elands, and Lions above Libonta—Interview with the Mambari— Two Arabs from Zanzibar—Their Opinion of the Portuguese and the English —Reach the Town of Ma-Sekeletu—Joy of the People at the first Visit of their Chief—Return to Sesheke—Heathenism.

Having at last procured a sufficient number of canoes, we began to ascend the river. I had the choice of the whole fleet, and selected the best, though not the largest; it was thirty-four feet long by twenty inches wide. I had six paddlers, and the larger canoe of Sekeletu had ten. They stand upright, and keep the stroke with great precision, though they change from side to side as the course demands. The men at the head and stern are selected from the strongest and most expert of the whole. The canoes, being flat bottomed, can go into very shallow water; and whenever the men can feel the bottom they use the paddles, which are about eight feet long, as poles to punt with. Our fleet consisted of thirty-three canoes, and about one hundred and sixty men. It was beautiful to see them skimming along so quickly, and keeping the time so well. On land the Makalaka fear the Makololo; on water the Makololo fear them, and can not prevent them from racing with each other, dashing along at the top of their speed, and placing their masters' lives in danger. In the event of a capsize, many of the Makololo would sink like stones. A case of this kind happened on the first day of our voyage up. The wind, blowing generally from the east, raises very large waves on the Leeambye. An old doctor of the Makololo had his canoe filled by one of these waves, and, being unable to swim, was lost. The

Barotse who were in the canoe with him saved themselves by swimming, and were afraid of being punished with death in the evening for not saving the doctor as well. Had he been a man of more influence, they certainly would have suffered death.

We proceeded rapidly up the river, and I felt the pleasure of looking on lands which had never been seen by a European before. The river is, indeed, a magnificent one, often more than a mile broad, and adorned with many islands of from three to five miles in length. Both islands and banks are covered with forest, and most of the trees on the brink of the water send down roots from their branches like the banian, or 'Ficus Indica'. The islands at a little distance seem great rounded masses of sylvan vegetation reclining on the bosom of the glorious stream. The beauty of the scenery of some of the islands is greatly increased by the date-palm, with its gracefully curved fronds and refreshing light green color, near the bottom of the picture, and the lofty palmyra towering far above, and casting its feathery foliage against a cloudless sky. It being winter, we had the strange coloring on the banks which many parts of African landscape assume. The country adjacent to the river is rocky and undulating, abounding in elephants and all other large game, except leches and nakongs, which seem generally to avoid stony ground. The soil is of a reddish color, and very fertile, as is attested by the great quantity of grain raised annually by the Banyeti. A great many villages of this poor and very industrious people are situated on both banks of the river: they are expert hunters of the hippopotami and other animals, and very proficient in the manufacture of articles of wood and iron. The whole of this part of the country being infested with the tsetse, they are unable to rear domestic animals. This may have led to their skill in handicraft works. Some make large wooden vessels with very neat lids, and wooden bowls of all sizes; and since the idea of sitting on stools has entered the Makololo mind, they have shown great taste in the different forms given to the legs of these pieces of furniture.

Other Banyeti, or Manyeti, as they are called, make neat and strong baskets of the split roots of a certain tree, while others excel in pottery and iron. I can not find that they have ever been warlike. Indeed, the wars in the centre of the country, where no slave-trade existed, have seldom been about any thing else but cattle. So well known is this, that several tribes refuse to keep cattle because they tempt their enemies to come and steal. Nevertheless, they have no objection to eat them when offered, and their country admits of being well stocked. I have heard of but one war having occurred from another cause. Three brothers, Barolongs, fought for the possession of a woman who was considered worth a battle, and the tribe has remained permanently divided ever since.

From the bend up to the north, called Katima-molelo (I quenched fire), the bed of the river is rocky, and the stream runs fast, forming a succession of rapids and cataracts, which prevent continuous navigation when the water is low. The rapids are not visible when the river is full, but the cataracts of Nambwe, Bombwe, and Kale must always be dangerous. The fall at each of these is between four and six feet. But the falls of Gonye present a much more serious obstacle. There we were obliged to take the canoes out of the water, and carry them more than a mile by land. The fall is about thirty feet. The main body of water, which comes over the ledge of rock when the river is low, is collected into a space seventy or eighty yards wide before it takes the leap, and, a mass of rock being thrust forward against the roaring torrent, a loud sound is produced. Tradition reports the destruction in this place of two hippopotamus-hunters, who, over-eager in the pursuit of a wounded animal, were, with their intended prey, drawn down into the frightful gulf. There is also a tradition of a man, evidently of a superior mind, who left his own countrymen, the Barotse, and came down the river, took advantage of the falls, and led out a portion of the water there for irrigation. Such minds must have arisen from time to time in these regions, as well as in our own country, but, ignorant of the use of letters, they have left no memorial behind them. We dug out some of an inferior kind of potato ('Sisinyane') from his garden, for when once planted it never dies out. This root is bitter and waxy, though it is cultivated. It was not in flower, so I can not say whether it is a solanaceous plant or not. One never expects to find a grave nor a stone of remembrance set up in Africa; the very rocks are illiterate, they contain so few fossils. Those here are of reddish variegated, hardened sandstone, with madrepore holes in it. This, and broad horizontal strata of trap, sometimes a hundred miles in extent, and each layer having an inch or so of black silicious matter on it, as if it had floated there while in a state of fusion, form a great part of the bottom of the central valley. These rocks, in the southern part of the country especially, are often covered with twelve or fifteen feet of soft calcareous tufa. At Bombwe we have the same trap, with radiated zeolite, probably mesotype, and it again appears at the confluence of the Chobe, farther down.

As we passed up the river, the different villages of Banyeti turned out to present Sekeletu with food and skins, as their tribute. One large village is placed at Gonye, the inhabitants of which are required to assist the Makololo to carry their canoes past the falls. The tsetse here lighted on us even in the middle of the stream. This we crossed repeatedly, in order to make short cuts at bends of the river. The course is, however, remarkably straight among the rocks; and here the river is shallow, on account of the great breadth of surface which it covers. When we came to about 16d 16' S. latitude, the high wooded banks seemed to leave the river, and no more tsetse appeared. Viewed from the flat, reedy basin in which the river then flowed, the banks seemed prolonged into ridges, of the same wooded character, two or three hundred feet high, and stretched away to the N.N.E. and N.N.W. until they were twenty or thirty miles apart. The intervening space, nearly one hundred miles in length, with the Leeambye winding gently near the middle, is the true Barotse valley. It bears a close resemblance to the valley of the Nile, and is inundated annually, not by rains, but by the Leeambye, exactly as Lower Egypt is flooded by the Nile. The villages of the Barotse are built on mounds, some of which are said to have been raised artificially by Santuru, a former chief of the Barotse, and during the inundation the whole valley assumes the appearance of a large lake, with the villages on the mounds like islands, just as occurs in Egypt with the villages of the Egyptians. Some portion of the waters of inundation comes from the northwest, where great floodings also occur, but more comes from the north and northeast, descending the bed of the Leeambye itself. There are but few trees in this valley: those which stand on the mounds were nearly all transplanted by Santuru for shade. The soil is extremely fertile, and the people are never in want of grain, for, by taking advantage of the moisture of the inundation, they can take two crops a year. The Barotse are strongly attached to this fertile valley; they say, "Here hunger is not known." There are so many things besides corn which a man can find in it for food, that it is no wonder they desert from Linyanti to return to this place.

The great valley is not put to a tithe of the use it might be. It is covered with coarse succulent grasses, which afford ample pasturage for large herds of cattle; these thrive wonderfully, and give milk copiously to their owners. When the valley is flooded, the cattle are compelled to leave it and go to the higher lands, where they fall off in condition; their return is a time of joy.

It is impossible to say whether this valley, which contains so much moisture, would raise wheat as the valley of the Nile does. It is probably too rich, and would make corn run entirely to straw, for one species of grass was observed twelve feet high, with a stem as thick as a man's thumb. At present the pasturage is never eaten off, though the Makololo possess immense herds of cattle.

There are no large towns, the mounds on which the towns and villages are built being all small, and the people require to live apart on account of their cattle.

This visit was the first Sekeletu had made to these parts since he attained the chieftainship. Those who had taken part with Mpepe were consequently in great terror. When we came to the town of Mpepe's father, as he and another man had counseled Mamochisane to put Sekeletu to death and marry Mpepe, the two were led forth and tossed into the river. Nokuane was again one of the executioners. When I remonstrated against human blood being shed in the offhand way in which they were proceeding, the counselors justified their acts by the evidence given by Mamochisane, and calmly added, "You see we are still Boers; we are not yet taught."

Mpepe had given full permission to the Mambari slave-dealers to trade in all the Batoka and Bashukulompo villages to the east of this. He had given them cattle, ivory, and children, and had received in return a large blunderbuss to be mounted as a cannon. When the slight circumstance of my having covered the body of the chief with my own deranged the whole conspiracy, the Mambari, in their stockade, were placed in very awkward circumstances. It was proposed to attack them and drive them out of the country at once; but, dreading a commencement of hostilities, I urged the difficulties of that course, and showed that a stockade defended by perhaps forty muskets would be a very serious affair. "Hunger is strong enough for that," said an under-chief; "a very great fellow is he." They thought of attacking them by starvation. As the chief sufferers in case of such an attack would have been the poor slaves chained in gangs, I interceded for them, and the result of an intercession of which they were ignorant was that they were allowed to depart in peace.

Naliele, the capital of the Barotse, is built on a mound which was constructed artificially by Santuru, and was his store-house for grain. His own capital stood about five hundred yards to the south of that, in what is now the bed of the river. All that remains of the largest mound in the valley are a few cubic yards of earth, to erect which cost the whole of the people of Santuru the labor of many years. The same thing has happened to another ancient site of a town, Linangelo, also on the left bank. It would seem, therefore, that the river in this part of the valley must be wearing eastward. No great rise of the river is required to submerge the whole valley; a rise of ten feet above the present low-water mark would reach the highest point it ever attains, as seen in the markings of the bank on which stood Santuru's ancient capital, and two or three feet more would deluge all the villages. This never happens, though the water sometimes comes so near the foundations of the huts that the people can not move outside the walls of reeds which encircle their villages. When the river is compressed among the high rocky banks near Gonye, it rises sixty feet.

The influence of the partial obstruction it meets with there is seen in the more winding course of the river north of 16 Deg.; and when the swell gets past Katima-molelo, it spreads out on the lands on both banks toward Sesheke.

Santuru, at whose ancient granary we are staying, was a great hunter, and very fond of taming wild animals. His people, aware of his taste, brought to him every young antelope they could catch, and, among other things, two young hippopotami. These animals gamboled in the river by day, but never failed to remember to come up to Naliele for their suppers of milk and meal. They were the wonder of the country, till a stranger, happening to come to visit Santuru, saw them reclining in the sun, and speared one of them on the supposition that it was wild. The same unlucky accident happened to one of the cats I had brought to Sekeletu. A stranger, seeing an animal he had never viewed before, killed it, and brought the trophy to the chief, thinking that he had made a very remarkable discovery; we thereby lost the breed of cats, of which, from the swarms of mice, we stood in great need.

On making inquiries to ascertain whether Santuru, the Moloiana, had ever been visited by white men, I could find no vestige of any such visit;* there is no evidence of any of Santuru's people having ever seen a white man before the arrival of Mr. Oswell and myself in 1851. The people have, it is true, no written records; but any remarkable event here is commemorated in names, as was observed by Park to be the case in the countries he traversed. The year of our arrival is dignified by the name of the year when the white men came, or of Sebituane's death; but they prefer the former, as they avoid, if possible, any direct reference to the departed. After my wife's first visit, great numbers of children were named Ma-Robert, or mother of Robert, her eldest child; others were named Gun, Horse, Wagon, Monare, Jesus, etc.; but though our names, and those of the native Portuguese who came in 1853, were adopted, there is not a trace of any thing of the sort having happened previously among the Barotse: the visit of a white man is such a remarkable event, that, had any taken place during the last three hundred years, there must have remained some tradition of it.

The Barotse call themselves the Baloiana or little Baloi, as if they had been an offset from Loi, or Lui, as it is often spelt. As Lui had been visited by Portuguese, but its position not well ascertained, my inquiries referred to the identity of Naliele with Lui. On asking the head man of the Mambari party, named Porto, whether he had ever heard of Naliele being visited previously, he replied in the negative, and stated that he "had himself attempted to come from Bihe three times, but had always been prevented by the tribe called Ganguellas." He nearly succeeded in 1852, but was driven back. He now (in 1853) attempted to go eastward from Naliele, but came back to the Barotse on being unable to go beyond Kainko's village, which is situated on the Bashukulompo River, and eight days distant. The whole party was anxious to secure a reward believed to be promised by the Portuguese government. Their want of success confirmed my impression that I ought to go westward. Porto kindly offered to aid me, if I would go with him to Bihe; but when I declined, he preceded me to Loanda, and was publishing his Journal when I arrived at that city. Ben Habib told me that Porto had sent letters to Mozambique by the Arab, Ben Chombo, whom I knew; and he has since asserted, in Portugal, that he himself went to Mozambique as well as his letters!

But Santuru was once visited by the Mambari, and a distinct recollection of that visit is retained. They came to purchase slaves, and both Santuru and his head men refused them permission to buy any of the people. The Makololo quoted this precedent when speaking of the Mambari, and said that they, as the present masters of the country, had as good a right to expel them as Santuru. The Mambari reside near Bihe, under an Ambonda chief named Kangombe. They profess to use the slaves for domestic purposes alone.

Some of these Mambari visited us while at Naliele. They are of the Ambonda family, which inhabits the country southeast of Angola, and speak the Bunda dialect, which is of the same family of languages with the Barotse, Bayeiye, etc., or those black tribes comprehended under the general term Makalaka. They plait their hair in three-fold cords, and lay them carefully down around the sides of the head. They are quite as dark as the Barotse, but have among them a number of half-castes, with their peculiar yellow sickly hue. On inquiring why they had fled on my approach to Linyanti, they let me know that they had a vivid idea of the customs of English cruisers on the coast. They showed also their habits in their own country by digging up and eating, even here where large game abounds, the mice and moles which infest the country. The half-castes, or native Portuguese, could all read and write, and the head of the party, if not a real Portuguese, had European hair, and, influenced probably by the letter of recommendation which I held from the Chevalier Duprat, his most faithful majesty's Arbitrator in the British and Portuguese Mixed Commission at Cape Town, was evidently anxious to show me all the kindness in his power. These persons I feel assured were the first individuals of Portuguese blood who ever saw the Zambesi in the centre of the country, and they had reached it two years after our discovery in 1851.

The town or mound of Santuru's mother was shown to me; this was the first symptom of an altered state of feeling with regard to the female sex that I had observed. There are few or no cases of women being elevated to the headships of towns further south. The Barotse also showed some relics of their chief, which evinced a greater amount of the religious feeling than I had ever known displayed among Bechuanas. His more recent capital, Lilonda, built, too, on an artificial mound, is covered with different kinds of trees, transplanted when young by himself. They form a grove on the end of the mound, in which are to be seen various instruments of iron just in the state he left them. One looks like the guard of a basket-hilted sword; another has an upright stem of the metal, on which are placed branches worked at the ends into miniature axes, hoes, and spears; on these he was accustomed to present offerings, according as he desired favors to be conferred in undertaking hewing, agriculture, or fighting. The people still living there, in charge of these articles, were supported by presents from the chief; and the Makololo sometimes follow the example. This was the nearest approach to a priesthood I met. When I asked them to part with one of these relics, they replied, "Oh no, he refuses." "Who refuses?" "Santuru," was their reply, showing their belief in a future state of existence. After explaining to them, as I always did when opportunity offered, the nature of true worship, and praying with them in the simple form which needs no offering from the worshiper except that of the heart, and planting some fruit-tree seeds in the grove, we departed.

Another incident, which occurred at the confluence of the Leeba and Leeambye, may be mentioned here, as showing a more vivid perception of the existence of spiritual beings, and greater proneness to worship than among the Bechuanas. Having taken lunar observations in the morning, I was waiting for a meridian altitude of the sun for the latitude; my chief boatman was sitting by, in order to pack up the instruments as soon as I had finished; there was a large halo, about 20 Deg. in diameter, round the sun; thinking that the humidity of the atmosphere, which this indicated, might betoken rain, I asked him if his experience did not lead him to the same view. "Oh no," replied he; "it is the Barimo (gods or departed spirits), who have called a picho; don't you see they have the Lord (sun) in the centre?"

While still at Naliele I walked out to Katongo (lat. 15d 16' 33"), on the ridge which bounds the valley of the Barotse in that direction, and found it covered with trees. It is only the commencement of the lands which are never inundated; their gentle rise from the dead level of the valley much resembles the edge of the Desert in the valley of the Nile. But here the Banyeti have fine gardens, and raise great quantities of maize, millet, and native corn ('Holcus sorghum'), of large grain and beautifully white. They grow, also, yams, sugar-cane, the Egyptian arum, sweet potato ('Convululus batata'), two kinds of manioc or cassava ('Jatropha manihot' and 'J. utilissima', a variety containing scarcely any poison), besides pumpkins, melons, beans, and ground-nuts. These, with plenty of fish in the river, its branches and lagoons, wild fruits and water-fowl, always make the people refer to the Barotse as the land of plenty. The scene from the ridge, on looking back, was beautiful. One can not see the western side of the valley in a cloudy day, such as that was when we visited the stockade, but we could see the great river glancing out at different points, and fine large herds of cattle quietly grazing on the green succulent herbage, among numbers of cattle-stations and villages which are dotted over the landscape. Leches in hundreds fed securely beside them, for they have learned only to keep out of bow-shot, or two hundred yards. When guns come into a country the animals soon learn their longer range, and begin to run at a distance of five hundred yards.

I imagined the slight elevation (Katongo) might be healthy, but was informed that no part of this region is exempt from fever. When the waters begin to retire from this valley, such masses of decayed vegetation and mud are exposed to the torrid sun that even the natives suffer severely from attacks of fever. The grass is so rank in its growth that one can not see the black alluvial soil of the bottom of this periodical lake. Even when the grass falls down in winter, or is "laid" by its own weight, one is obliged to lift the feet so high, to avoid being tripped up by it, as to make walking excessively fatiguing. Young leches are hidden beneath it by their dams; and the Makololo youth complain of being unable to run in the Barotse land on this account. There was evidently no healthy spot in this quarter; and the current of the river being about four and a half miles per hour (one hundred yards in sixty seconds), I imagined we might find what we needed in the higher lands, from which the river seemed to come. I resolved, therefore, to go to the utmost limits of the Barotse country before coming to a final conclusion. Katongo was the best place we had seen; but, in order to accomplish a complete examination, I left Sekeletu at Naliele, and ascended the river. He furnished me with men, besides my rowers, and among the rest a herald, that I might enter his villages in what is considered a dignified manner. This, it was supposed, would be effected by the herald shouting out at the top of his voice, "Here comes the lord; the great lion;" the latter phrase being "tau e tona", which, in his imperfect way of pronunciation, became "Sau e tona", and so like "the great sow" that I could not receive the honor with becoming gravity, and had to entreat him, much to the annoyance of my party, to be silent.

In our ascent we visited a number of Makololo villages, and were always received with a hearty welcome, as messengers to them of peace, which they term "sleep". They behave well in public meetings, even on the first occasion of attendance, probably from the habit of commanding the Makalaka, crowds of whom swarm in every village, and whom the Makololo women seem to consider as especially under their charge.

The river presents the same appearance of low banks without trees as we have remarked it had after we came to 16d 16', until we arrive at Libonta (14d 59' S. lat.). Twenty miles beyond that, we find forest down to the water's edge, and tsetse. Here I might have turned back, as no locality can be inhabited by Europeans where that scourge exists; but hearing that we were not far from the confluence of the River of Londa or Lunda, named Leeba or Loiba, and the chiefs of that country being reported to be friendly to strangers, and therefore likely to be of use to me on my return from the west coast, I still pushed on to latitude 14d 11' 3" S. There the Leeambye assumes the name Kabompo, and seems to be coming from the east. It is a fine large river, about three hundred yards wide, and the Leeba two hundred and fifty. The Loeti, a branch of which is called Langebongo, comes from W.N.W., through a level grassy plain named Mango; it is about one hundred yards wide, and enters the Leeambye from the west; the waters of the Loeti are of a light color, and those of the Leeba of a dark mossy hue. After the Loeti joins the Leeambye the different colored waters flow side by side for some distance unmixed.

Before reaching the Loeti we came to a number of people from the Lobale region, hunting hippopotami. They fled precipitately as soon as they saw the Makololo, leaving their canoes and all their utensils and clothing. My own Makalaka, who were accustomed to plunder wherever they went, rushed after them like furies, totally regardless of my shouting. As this proceeding would have destroyed my character entirely at Lobale, I took my stand on a commanding position as they returned, and forced them to lay down all the plunder on a sand-bank, and leave it there for its lawful owners.

It was now quite evident that no healthy location could be obtained in which the Makololo would be allowed to live in peace. I had thus a fair excuse, if I had chosen to avail myself of it, of coming home and saying that the "door was shut", because the Lord's time had not yet come. But believing that it was my duty to devote some portion of my life to these (to me at least) very confiding and affectionate Makololo, I resolved to follow out the second part of my plan, though I had failed in accomplishing the first. The Leeba seemed to come from the N. and by W., or N.N.W.; so, having an old Portuguese map, which pointed out the Coanza as rising from the middle of the continent in 9 Deg. S. lat., I thought it probable that, when we had ascended the Leeba (from 14d 11') two or three degrees, we should then be within one hundred and twenty miles of the Coanza, and find no difficulty in following it down to the coast near Loanda. This was the logical deduction; but, as is the case with many a plausible theory, one of the premises was decidedly defective. The Coanza, as we afterward found, does not come from any where near the centre of the country.

The numbers of large game above Libonta are prodigious, and they proved remarkably tame. Eighty-one buffaloes defiled in slow procession before our fire one evening, within gunshot; and herds of splendid elands stood by day, without fear, at two hundred yards distance. They were all of the striped variety, and with their forearm markings, large dewlaps, and sleek skins, were a beautiful sight to see. The lions here roar much more than in the country near the lake, Zouga, and Chobe. One evening we had a good opportunity of hearing the utmost exertions the animal can make in that line. We had made our beds on a large sand-bank, and could be easily seen from all sides. A lion on the opposite shore amused himself for hours by roaring as loudly as he could, putting, as is usual in such cases, his mouth near the ground, to make the sound reverberate. The river was too broad for a ball to reach him, so we let him enjoy himself, certain that he durst not have been guilty of the impertinence in the Bushman country. Wherever the game abounds, these animals exist in proportionate numbers. Here they were very frequently seen, and two of the largest I ever saw seemed about as tall as common donkeys; but the mane made their bodies appear rather larger.

A party of Arabs from Zanzibar were in the country at this time. Sekeletu had gone from Naliele to the town of his mother before we arrived from the north, but left an ox for our use, and instructions for us to follow him thither. We came down a branch of the Leeambye called Marile, which departs from the main river in latitude 15d 15′ 43″ S., and is a fine deep stream about sixty yards wide. It makes the whole of the country around Naliele an island. When sleeping at a village in the same latitude as Naliele town, two of the Arabs mentioned made their appearance. They were quite as dark as the Makololo, but, having their heads shaved, I could not compare their hair with that of the inhabitants of the country. When we were about to leave they came to bid adieu, but I asked them to stay and help us to eat our ox. As they had scruples about eating an animal not blooded in their own way, I gained their good-will by saying I was quite of their opinion as to getting quit of the blood, and gave them two legs of an animal slaughtered by themselves. They professed the greatest detestation of the Portuguese, "because they eat pigs;" and disliked the English, "because they thrash them for selling slaves." I was silent about pork; though, had they seen me at a hippopotamus two days afterward, they would have set me down as being as much a heretic as any of that nation; but I ventured to tell them that I agreed with the English, that it was better to let the children grow up and comfort their mothers when they became old, than to carry them away and sell them across the sea. This they never attempt to justify; "they want them only to cultivate the land, and take care of them as their children." It is the same old story, justifying a monstrous wrong on pretense of taking care of those degraded portions of humanity which can not take care of themselves; doing evil that good may come.

These Arabs, or Moors, could read and write their own language readily; and, when speaking about our Savior, I admired the boldness with which they informed me "that Christ was a very good prophet, but Mohammed was far greater." And with respect to their loathing of pork, it may have some foundation in their nature; for I have known Bechuanas, who had no prejudice against the wild animal, and ate the tame without scruple, yet, unconscious of any cause of disgust, vomit it again. The Bechuanas south of the lake have a prejudice against eating fish, and allege a disgust to eating any thing like a serpent. This may arise from the remnants of serpent-worship floating in their minds, as, in addition to this horror of eating such animals, they sometimes render a sort of obeisance to living serpents by clapping their hands to them, and refusing to destroy the reptiles; but in the case of the hog they are conscious of no superstitious feeling.

Having parted with our Arab friends, we proceeded down the Marile till we re-entered the Leeambye, and went to the town of Ma-Sekeletu (mother of Sekeletu), opposite the island of Loyela. Sekeletu had always supplied me most liberally with food, and, as soon as I arrived, presented me with a pot of boiled meat, while his mother handed me a large jar of butter, of which they make great quantities for the purpose of anointing their bodies. He had himself sometimes felt the benefit of my way of putting aside a quantity of the meat after a meal, and had now followed my example by ordering some to be kept for me. According to their habits, every particle of an ox is devoured at one meal; and as the chief can not, without a deviation from their customs, eat alone, he is often compelled to suffer severely from hunger before another meal is ready. We henceforth always worked into each other's hands by saving a little for each other; and when some of the sticklers for use and custom grumbled, I advised them to eat like men, and not like vultures.

As this was the first visit which Sekeletu had paid to this part of his dominions, it was to many a season of great joy. The head men of each village presented oxen, milk, and beer, more than the horde which accompanied him could devour, though their abilities in that line are something wonderful. The people usually show their joy and work off their excitement in dances and songs. The dance consists of the men standing nearly naked in a circle, with clubs or small battle-axes in their hands, and each roaring at the loudest pitch of his voice, while they simultaneously lift one leg, stamp heavily twice with it, then lift the other and give one stamp with that; this is the only movement in common. The arms and head are often thrown about also in every direction; and all this time the roaring is kept up with the utmost possible vigor; the continued stamping makes a cloud of dust ascend, and they leave a deep ring in the ground where they stood. If the scene were witnessed in a lunatic asylum it would be nothing out of the way, and quite appropriate even, as a means of letting off the excessive excitement of the brain; but here gray-headed men joined in the performance with as much zest as others whose youth might be an excuse for making the perspiration stream off their bodies with the exertion. Motibe asked what I thought of the Makololo dance. I replied, "It is very hard work, and brings but small profit." "It is," replied he, "but it is very nice, and Sekeletu will give us an ox for dancing for him." He usually does slaughter an ox for the dancers when the work is over.

The women stand by, clapping their hands, and occasionally one advances into the circle, composed of a hundred men, makes a few movements, and then retires. As I never tried it, and am unable to enter into the spirit of the thing, I can not recommend the Makololo polka to the dancing world, but I have the authority of no less a person than Motibe, Sekeletu's father-in-law, for saying "it is very nice." They often asked if white people ever danced. I thought of the disease called St. Vitus's dance, but could not say that all our dancers were affected by it, and gave an answer which, I ought to be ashamed to own, did not raise some of our young countrywomen in the estimation of the Makololo.

As Sekeletu had been waiting for me at his mother's, we left the town as soon as I arrived, and proceeded down the river. Our speed with the stream was very great, for in one day we went from Litofe to Gonye, a distance of forty-four miles of latitude; and if we add to this the windings of the river, in longitude the distance will not be much less than sixty geographical miles. At this rate we soon reached Sesheke, and then the town of Linyanti.

I had been, during a nine weeks' tour, in closer contact with heathenism than I had ever been before; and though all, including the chief, were as kind and attentive to me as possible, and there was no want of food (oxen being slaughtered daily, sometimes ten at a time, more than sufficient for the wants of all), yet to endure the dancing, roaring, and singing, the jesting, anecdotes, grumbling, quarreling, and murdering of these children of nature, seemed more like a severe penance than any thing I had before met with in the course of my missionary duties. I took thence a more intense disgust at heathenism than I had before, and formed a greatly elevated opinion of the latent effects of missions in the south, among tribes which are reported to have been as savage as the Makololo. The indirect benefits which, to a casual observer, lie beneath the surface and are inappreciable, in reference to the probable wide diffusion of Christianity at some future time, are worth all the money and labor that have been expended to produce them.

Chapter 13

Preliminary Arrangements for the Journey—A Picho—Twenty-seven Men appointed to accompany me to the West—Eagerness of the Makololo for direct Trade with the Coast—Effects of Fever—A Makololo Question—The lost Journal—Reflections—The Outfit for the Journey—11th November, 1853, leave Linyanti, and embark on the Chobe—Dangerous Hippopotami—Banks of Chobe—Trees—The Course of the River—The Island Mparia at the Confluence of the Chobe and the Leeambye— Anecdote—Ascend the Leeambye—A Makalaka Mother defies the Authority of the Makololo Head Man at Sesheke—Punishment of Thieves—Observance of the new Moon—Public Addresses at Sesheke—Attention of the People—Results—Proceed up the River—The Fruit which yields 'Nux vomica'—Other Fruits—The Rapids—Birds—Fish—Hippopotami and their Young.

Linyanti, SEPTEMBER, 1853. The object proposed to the Makololo seemed so desirable that it was resolved to proceed with it as soon as the cooling influence of the rains should be felt in November. The longitude and latitude of Linyanti (lat. 18d 17′ 20″ S., long. 23d 50′ 9″ E.) showed that St. Philip de Benguela was much nearer to us than Loanda; and I might have easily made arrangements with the Mambari to allow me to accompany them as far as Bihe, which is on the road to that port; but it is so undesirable to travel in a path once trodden by slave-traders that I preferred to find out another line of march.

Accordingly, men were sent at my suggestion to examine all the country to the west, to see if any belt of country free from tsetse could be found to afford us an outlet. The search was fruitless. The town and district of Linyanti are surrounded by forests infested by this poisonous insect, except at a few points, as that by which we entered at Sanshureh and another at Sesheke. But the lands both east and west of the Barotse valley are free from this insect plague. There, however, the slave-trade had defiled the path, and no one ought to follow in its wake unless well armed. The Mambari had informed me that many English lived at Loanda, so I prepared to go thither. The prospect of meeting with countrymen seemed to overbalance the toils of the longer march.

A "picho" was called to deliberate on the steps proposed. In these assemblies great freedom of speech is allowed; and on this occasion one of the old diviners said, "Where is he taking you to? This white man is throwing you away. Your garments already smell of blood." It is curious to observe how much identity of character appears all over the world. This man was a noted croaker. He always dreamed something dreadful in every expedition, and was certain that an eclipse or comet betokened the propriety of flight. But Sebituane formerly set his visions down to cowardice, and Sekeletu only laughed at him now. The general voice was in my favor; so a band of twenty-seven were appointed to accompany me to the west. These men were not hired, but sent to enable me to accomplish an object as much desired by the chief and most of his people as by me. They were eager to obtain free and profitable trade with white men. The prices which the Cape merchants could give, after defraying the great expenses of a long journey hither, being very small, made it scarce worth while for the natives to collect produce for that market; and the Mambari, giving only a few bits of print and baize for elephants' tusks worth more pounds than they gave yards of cloth, had produced the belief that trade with them was throwing ivory away. The desire of the Makololo for direct trade with the sea-coast coincided exactly with my own conviction that no permanent elevation of a people can be effected without commerce. Neither could there be a permanent mission here, unless the missionaries should descend to the level of the Makololo, for even at Kolobeng we found that traders demanded three or four times the price of the articles we needed, and expected us to be grateful to them besides for letting us have them at all.

The three men whom I had brought from Kuruman had frequent relapses of the fever; so, finding that instead of serving me I had to wait on them, I decided that they should return to the south with Fleming as soon as he had finished his trading. I was then entirely dependent on my twenty-seven men, whom I might name Zambesians, for there were two Makololo only, while the rest consisted of Barotse, Batoka, Bashubia, and two of the Ambonda.

The fever had caused considerable weakness in my own frame, and a strange giddiness when I looked up suddenly to any celestial object, for every thing seemed to rush to the left, and if I did not catch hold of some object, I fell heavily on the ground: something resembling a gush of bile along the duct from the liver caused the same fit to occur at night, whenever I turned suddenly round.

The Makololo now put the question, "In the event of your death, will not the white people blame us for having allowed you to go away into an unhealthy, unknown country of enemies?" I replied that none of my friends would blame them, because I would leave a book with Sekeletu, to be sent to Mr. Moffat in case I did not return, which would explain to him all that had happened until the time of my departure. The book was a volume of my Journal; and, as I was detained longer than I expected at Loanda, this book, with a letter, was delivered by Sekeletu to a trader, and I have been unable to trace it. I regret this now, as it contained valuable notes on the habits of wild animals, and the request was made in the letter to convey the volume to my family. The prospect of passing away from this fair and beautiful world thus came before me in a pretty plain, matter-of-fact form, and it did seem a serious thing to leave wife and children—to break up all connection with earth, and enter on an untried state of existence; and I find myself in my journal pondering over that fearful migration which lands us in eternity, wondering whether an angel will soothe the fluttering soul, sadly flurried as it must be on entering the spirit world, and hoping that Jesus might speak but one word of peace, for that would establish in the bosom an everlasting calm. But as I had always believed that, if we serve God at all, it ought to be done in a manly way, I wrote to my brother, commending our little girl to his care, as I was determined to "succeed or perish" in the attempt to open up this part of Africa. The Boers, by taking possession of all my goods, had saved me the trouble of making a will; and, considering the light heart now left in my bosom, and some faint efforts to perform the duty of Christian forgiveness, I felt that it was better to be the plundered party than one of the plunderers.

When I committed the wagon and remaining goods to the care of the Makololo, they took all the articles except one box into their huts; and two warriors, Ponuane and Mahale, brought forward each a fine heifer calf. After performing a number of warlike evolutions, they asked the chief to witness the agreement made between them, that whoever of the two should kill a Matebele warrior first, in defense of the wagon, should possess both the calves.

I had three muskets for my people, a rifle and double-barreled smoothbore for myself; and, having seen such great abundance of game in my visit to the Leeba, I imagined that I could easily supply the wants of my party. Wishing also to avoid the discouragement which would naturally be felt on meeting any obstacles if my companions were obliged to carry heavy loads, I took only a few biscuits, a few pounds of tea and sugar, and about twenty of coffee, which, as the Arabs find, though used without either milk or sugar, is a most refreshing beverage after fatigue or exposure to the sun. We carried one small tin canister, about fifteen inches square, filled with spare shirting, trowsers, and shoes, to be used when we reached civilized life, and others in a bag, which were expected to wear out on the way;

another of the same size for medicines; and a third for books, my stock being a Nautical Almanac, Thomson's Logarithm Tables, and a Bible; a fourth box contained a magic lantern, which we found of much use. The sextant and artificial horizon, thermometer, and compasses were carried apart. My ammunition was distributed in portions through the whole luggage, so that, if an accident should befall one part, we could still have others to fall back upon. Our chief hopes for food were upon that; but in case of failure, I took about 20 lbs. of beads, worth 40s., which still remained of the stock I brought from Cape Town, a small gipsy tent, just sufficient to sleep in, a sheep-skin mantle as a blanket, and a horse-rug as a bed. As I had always found that the art of successful travel consisted in taking as few "impedimenta" as possible, and not forgetting to carry my wits about me, the outfit was rather spare, and intended to be still more so when we should come to leave the canoes. Some would consider it injudicious to adopt this plan, but I had a secret conviction that if I did not succeed, it would not be for want of the "knick-knacks" advertised as indispensable for travelers, but from want of "pluck", or because a large array of baggage excited the cupidity of the tribes through whose country we wished to pass.

The instruments I carried, though few, were the best of their kind. A sextant, by the famed makers Troughton and Sims, of Fleet Street; a chronometer watch, with a stop to the seconds hand—an admirable contrivance for enabling a person to take the exact time of observations: it was constructed by Dent, of the Strand (61), for the Royal Geographical Society, and selected for the service by the President, Admiral Smythe, to whose judgment and kindness I am in this and other matters deeply indebted. It was pronounced by Mr. Maclear to equal most chronometers in performance. For these excellent instruments I have much pleasure in recording my obligations to my good friend Colonel Steele, and at the same time to Mr. Maclear for much of my ability to use them. Besides these, I had a thermometer by Dollond; a compass from the Cape Observatory, and a small pocket one in addition; a good small telescope with a stand capable of being screwed into a tree.

11TH OF NOVEMBER, 1853. Left the town of Linyanti, accompanied by Sekeletu and his principal men, to embark on the Chobe. The chief came to the river in order to see that all was right at parting. We crossed five branches of the Chobe before reaching the main stream: this ramification must be the reason why it appeared so small to Mr. Oswell and myself in 1851. When all the departing branches re-enter, it is a large, deep river. The spot of embarkation was the identical island where we met Sebituane, first known as the island of Maunku, one of his wives. The chief lent me his own canoe, and, as it was broader than usual, I could turn about in it with ease.

The Chobe is much infested by hippopotami, and, as certain elderly males are expelled the herd, they become soured in their temper, and so misanthropic as to attack every canoe that passes near them. The herd is never dangerous, except when a canoe passes into the midst of it when all are asleep, and some of them may strike the canoe in terror. To avoid this, it is generally recommended to travel by day near the bank, and by night in the middle of the stream. As a rule, these animals flee the approach of man. The "solitaires", however, frequent certain localities well known to the inhabitants on the banks, and, like the rogue elephants, are extremely dangerous. We came, at this time, to a canoe which had been smashed to pieces by a blow from the hind foot of one of them. I was informed by my men that, in the event of a similar assault being made upon ours, the proper way was to dive to the bottom of the river, and hold on there for a few seconds, because the hippopotamus, after breaking a canoe, always looks for the people on the surface, and, if he sees none, he soon moves off. I have seen some frightful gashes made on the legs of the people who have had the misfortune to be attacked, and were unable to dive. This animal uses his teeth as an offensive weapon, though he is quite a herbivorous feeder. One of these "bachelors", living near the confluence, actually came out of his lair, and, putting his head down, ran after some of our men who were passing with very considerable speed.

The part of the river called Zabesa, or Zabenza, is spread out like a little lake, surrounded on all sides by dense masses of tall reeds. The river below that is always one hundred or one hundred and twenty yards broad, deep, and never dries up so much as to become fordable. At certain parts, where the partial absence of reeds affords a view of the opposite banks, the Makololo have placed villages of observation against their enemies the Matebele. We visited all these in succession, and found here, as every where in the Makololo country, orders had preceded us, "that Nake (nyake means doctor) must not be allowed to become hungry."

The banks of the Chobe, like those of the Zouga, are of soft calcareous tufa, and the river has cut out for itself a deep, perpendicular-sided bed. Where the banks are high, as at the spot where the wagons stood in 1851, they are covered with magnificent trees, the habitat of tsetse, and the retreat of various antelopes, wild hogs, zebras, buffaloes, and elephants.

Among the trees may be observed some species of the 'Ficus Indica', light-green colored acacias, the splendid motsintsela, and evergreen cypress-shaped motsouri. The fruit of the last-named was ripe, and the villagers presented many dishes of its beautiful pink-colored plums; they are used chiefly to form a pleasant acid drink. The motsintsela is a very lofty tree, yielding a wood of which good canoes are made; the fruit is nutritious and good, but, like many wild fruits of this country, the fleshy parts require to be enlarged by cultivation: it is nearly all stone.

The course of the river we found to be extremely tortuous; so much so, indeed, as to carry us to all points of the compass every dozen miles. Some of us walked from a bend at the village of Moremi to another nearly due east of that point, in six hours, while the canoes, going at more than double our speed, took twelve to accomplish the voyage between the same two places. And though the river is from thirteen to fifteen feet in depth at its lowest ebb, and broad enough to allow a steamer to ply upon it, the suddenness of the bendings would prevent navigation; but, should the country ever become civilized, the Chobe would be a convenient natural canal. We spent forty-two and a half hours, paddling at the rate of five miles an hour, in coming from Linyanti to the confluence; there we found a dike of amygdaloid lying across the Leeambye.

This amygdaloid with analami and mesotype contains crystals, which the water gradually dissolves, leaving the rock with a worm-eaten appearance. It is curious to observe that the water flowing over certain rocks, as in this instance, imbibes an appreciable, though necessarily most minute, portion of the minerals they contain. The water of the Chobe up to this point is of a dark mossy hue, but here it suddenly assumes a lighter tint; and wherever this light color shows a greater amount of mineral, there are not mosquitoes enough to cause serious annoyance to any except persons of very irritable temperaments.

The large island called Mparia stands at the confluence. This is composed of trap (zeolite, probably mesotype) of a younger age than the deep stratum of tufa in which the Chobe has formed its bed, for, at the point where they come together, the tufa has been transformed into saccharoid limestone.

The actual point of confluence of these two rivers, the Chobe and the Leeambye, is ill defined, on account of each dividing into several branches as they inosculate; but when the whole body of water collects into one bed, it is a goodly sight for one who has spent many years in the thirsty south. Standing on one bank, even the keen eye of the natives can not detect whether two large islands, a few miles east of the junction, are main land or not. During a flight in former years, when the present chief Sekomi was a child in his mother's arms, the Bamangwato men were separated from their women, and inveigled on to one of these islands by the Makalaka chief of Mparia, on pretense of ferrying them across the Leeambye. They were left to perish after seeing their wives taken prisoners by these cruel lords of the Leeambye, and Sekomi owed his life to the compassion of one of the

Bayeiye, who, pitying the young chieftain, enabled his mother to make her escape by night.

After spending one night at the Makololo village on Mparia, we left the Chobe, and, turning round, began to ascend the Leeambye; on the 19th of November we again reached the town of Sesheke. It stands on the north bank of the river, and contains a large population of Makalaka, under Moriantsane, brother-in-law of Sebituane. There are parties of various tribes here, assembled under their respective head men, but a few Makololo rule over all. Their sway, though essentially despotic, is considerably modified by certain customs and laws. One of the Makalaka had speared an ox belonging to one of the Makololo, and, being unable to extract the spear, was thereby discovered to be the perpetrator of the deed. His object had been to get a share of the meat, as Moriantsane is known to be liberal with any food that comes into his hands. The culprit was bound hand and foot, and placed in the sun to force him to pay a fine, but he continued to deny his guilt. His mother, believing in the innocence of her son, now came forward, with her hoe in hand, and, threatening to cut down any one who should dare to interfere, untied the cords with which he had been bound and took him home. This open defiance of authority was not resented by Moriantsane, but referred to Sekeletu at Linyanti.

The following circumstance, which happened here when I was present with Sekeletu, shows that the simple mode of punishment, by forcing a criminal to work out a fine, did not strike the Makololo mind until now.

A stranger having visited Sesheke for the purpose of barter, was robbed by one of the Makalaka of most of his goods. The thief, when caught, confessed the theft, and that he had given the articles to a person who had removed to a distance. The Makololo were much enraged at the idea of their good name being compromised by this treatment of a stranger. Their customary mode of punishing a crime which causes much indignation is to throw the criminal into the river; but, as this would not restore the lost property, they were sorely puzzled how to act. The case was referred to me, and I solved the difficulty by paying for the loss myself, and sentencing the thief to work out an equivalent with his hoe in a garden. This system was immediately introduced, and thieves are now sentenced to raise an amount of corn proportioned to their offenses. Among the Bakwains, a woman who had stolen from the garden of another was obliged to part with her own entirely: it became the property of her whose field was injured by the crime.

There is no stated day of rest in any part of this country, except the day after the appearance of the new moon, and the people then refrain only from going to their gardens. A curious custom, not to be found among the

Bechuanas, prevails among the black tribes beyond them. They watch most eagerly for the first glimpse of the new moon, and, when they perceive the faint outline after the sun has set deep in the west, they utter a loud shout of "Kua!" and vociferate prayers to it. My men, for instance, called out, "Let our journey with the white man be prosperous! Let our enemies perish, and the children of Nake become rich! May he have plenty of meat on this journey!" etc., etc.

I gave many public addresses to the people of Sesheke under the outspreading camel-thorn-tree, which serves as a shade to the kotla on the high bank of the river. It was pleasant to see the long lines of men, women, and children winding along from different quarters of the town, each party following behind their respective head men. They often amounted to between five and six hundred souls, and required an exertion of voice which brought back the complaint for which I had got the uvula excised at the Cape. They were always very attentive; and Moriantsane, in order, as he thought, to please me, on one occasion rose up in the middle of the discourse, and hurled his staff at the heads of some young fellows whom he saw working with a skin instead of listening. My hearers sometimes put very sensible questions on the subjects brought before them; at other times they introduced the most frivolous nonsense immediately after hearing the most solemn truths. Some begin to pray to Jesus in secret as soon as they hear of the white man's God, with but little idea of what they are about; and no doubt are heard by Him who, like a father, pitieth his children. Others, waking by night, recollect what has been said about the future world so clearly that they tell next day what a fright they got by it, and resolve not to listen to the teaching again; and not a few keep to the determination not to believe, as certain villagers in the south, who put all their cocks to death because they crowed the words, "Tlang lo rapeleng"—"Come along to prayers".

On recovering partially from a severe attack of fever which remained upon me ever since our passing the village of Moremi on the Chobe, we made ready for our departure up the river by sending messages before us to the villages to prepare food. We took four elephants' tusks, belonging to Sekeletu, with us, as a means of testing the difference of prices between the Portuguese, whom we expected to reach, and the white traders from the south. Moriantsane supplied us well with honey, milk, and meal. The rains were just commencing in this district; but, though showers sufficient to lay the dust had fallen, they had no influence whatever on the amount of water in the river, yet never was there less in any part than three hundred yards of a deep flowing stream.

Our progress up the river was rather slow; this was caused by waiting opposite different villages for supplies of food. We might have done with much less than we got; but my Makololo man, Pitsane, knew of the generous orders of Sekeletu, and was not at all disposed to allow them to remain a dead letter. The villages of the Banyeti contributed large quantities of mosibe, a bright red bean yielded by a large tree. The pulp inclosing the seed is not much thicker than a red wafer, and is the portion used. It requires the addition of honey to render it at all palatable.

To these were added great numbers of the fruit which yields a variety of the nux vomica, from which we derive that virulent poison strychnia. The pulp between the nuts is the part eaten, and it is of a pleasant juicy nature, having a sweet acidulous taste. The fruit itself resembles a large yellow orange, but the rind is hard, and, with the pips and bark, contains much of the deadly poison. They evince their noxious qualities by an intensely bitter taste. The nuts, swallowed inadvertently, cause considerable pain, but not death; and to avoid this inconvenience, the people dry the pulp before the fire, in order to be able the more easily to get rid of the noxious seeds.

A much better fruit, called mobola, was also presented to us. This bears, around a pretty large stone, as much of the fleshy part as the common date, and it is stripped off the seeds and preserved in bags in a similar manner to that fruit. Besides sweetness, the mobola has the flavor of strawberries, with a touch of nauseousness. We carried some of them, dried as provisions, more than a hundred miles from this spot.

The next fruit, named mamosho (mother of morning), is the most delicious of all. It is about the size of a walnut, and, unlike most of the other uncultivated fruits, has a seed no larger than that of a date. The fleshy part is juicy, and somewhat like the cashew-apple, with a pleasant acidity added. Fruits similar to those which are here found on trees are found on the plains of the Kalahari, growing on mere herbaceous plants. There are several other examples of a similar nature. Shrubs, well known as such in the south, assume the rank of trees as we go to the north; and the change is quite gradual as our latitude decreases, the gradations being herbaceous plants, shrubs, bushes, small, then large trees. But it is questionable if, in the cases of mamosho, mobola, and mawa, the tree and shrub are identical, though the fruits so closely resemble each other; for I found both the dwarf and tree in the same latitude. There is also a difference in the leaves, and they bear at different seasons.

The banks of the river were at this time appearing to greater advantage than before. Many trees were putting on their fresh green leaves, though they had got no rain, their lighter green contrasting beautifully with the dark motsouri, or moyela, now covered with pink plums as large as cherries. The rapids, having comparatively little water in them, rendered our passage difficult. The canoes must never be allowed to come broadside on to the stream, for, being flat-bottomed, they would, in that case, be at once capsized, and every thing in them be lost. The men work admirably, and are always in good humor; they leap into the water without the least hesitation, to save the canoe from being caught by eddies or dashed against the rocks. Many parts were now quite shallow, and it required great address and power in balancing themselves to keep the vessel free from rocks, which lay just beneath the surface. We might have got deeper water in the middle, but the boatmen always keep near the banks, on account of danger from the hippopotami. But, though we might have had deeper water farther out, I believe that no part of the rapids is very deep. The river is spread out more than a mile, and the water flows rapidly over the rocky bottom. The portions only three hundred yards wide are very deep, and contain large volumes of flowing water in narrow compass, which, when spread over the much larger surface at the rapids, must be shallow. Still, remembering that this was the end of the dry season, when such rivers as the Orange do not even contain a fifth part of the water of the Chobe, the difference between the rivers of the north and south must be sufficiently obvious.

The rapids are caused by rocks of dark brown trap, or of hardened sandstone, stretching across the stream. In some places they form miles of flat rocky bottom, with islets covered with trees. At the cataracts noted in the map, the fall is from four to six feet, and, in guiding up the canoe, the stem goes under the water, and takes in a quantity before it can attain the higher level. We lost many of our biscuits in the ascent through this.

These rocks are covered with a small, hard aquatic plant, which, when the surface is exposed, becomes dry and crisp, crackling under the foot as if it contained much stony matter in its tissue. It probably assists in disintegrating the rocks; for, in parts so high as not to be much exposed to the action of the water or the influence of the plant, the rocks are covered with a thin black glaze.

In passing along under the overhanging trees of the banks, we often saw the pretty turtle-doves sitting peacefully on their nests above the roaring torrent. An ibis* had perched her home on the end of a stump. Her loud, harsh scream of "Wa-wa-wa", and the piping of the fish-hawk, are sounds which can never be forgotten by any one who has sailed on the rivers north of 20 Deg. south. If we step on shore, the 'Charadrius caruncula', a species of plover, a most plaguy sort of "public-spirited individual", follows you, flying overhead, and is most persevering in its attempts to give fair warning to all the animals within hearing to flee from the approaching danger.

The alarm-note, "tinc-tinc-tinc", of another variety of the same family ('Pluvianus armatus' of Burchell) has so much of a metallic ring, that this bird is called "setula-tsipi", or hammering-iron. It is furnished with a sharp spur on its shoulder, much like that on the heel of a cock, but scarcely half an inch in length. Conscious of power, it may be seen chasing the white-necked raven with great fury, and making even that comparatively large bird call out from fear. It is this bird which is famed for its friendship with the crocodile of the Nile by the name 'siksak', and which Mr. St. John actually saw performing the part of toothpicker to the ugly reptile. They are frequently seen on the sand-banks with the alligator, and, to one passing by, often appear as if on that reptile's back; but I never had the good fortune to witness the operation described not only by St. John and Geoffrey St. Hilaire, but also by Herodotus. However, that which none of these authors knew my head boatman, Mashauana, stopped the canoe to tell us, namely, that a water-turtle which, in trying to ascend a steep bank to lay her eggs, had toppled on her back, thus enabling us to capture her, was an infallible omen of good luck for our journey.

* The 'Hagidash', Latham; or 'Tantalus capensis' of Lich.

Among the forest-trees which line the banks of the rocky parts of the Leeambye several new birds were observed. Some are musical, and the songs are pleasant in contrast with the harsh voice of the little green, yellow-shouldered parrots of the country. There are also great numbers of jet-black weavers, with yellowish-brown band on the shoulders.

Here we saw, for the first time, a pretty little bird, colored dark blue, except the wings and tail, which were of a chocolate hue. From the tail two feathers are prolonged beyond the rest six inches. Also, little birds colored white and black, of great vivacity, and always in companies of six or eight together, and various others. From want of books of reference, I could not decide whether they were actually new to science.

Francolins and Guinea-fowl abound along the banks; and on every dead tree and piece of rock may be seen one or two species of the web-footed 'Plotus', darter, or snake-bird. They sit most of the day sunning themselves over the stream, sometimes standing erect with their wings outstretched; occasionally they may be seen engaged in fishing by diving, and, as they swim about, their bodies are so much submerged that hardly any thing appears above the water but their necks. The chief time of feeding is by night, and, as the sun declines, they may be seen in flocks flying from their roosting-places to the fishing-grounds. This is a most difficult bird to catch when disabled. It is thoroughly expert in diving—goes down so adroitly and comes up again in the most unlikely places, that the people, though most skillful in the management of the canoes, can rarely secure them. The rump of the darter is remarkably prolonged, and capable of being bent, so as to act both as a rudder in swimming, and as a lever to lift the bird high enough out of the water to give free scope to its wings. It can rise at will from the water by means of this appendage.

The fine fish-hawk, with white head and neck, and reddish-chocolate colored body, may also frequently be seen perched on the trees, and fish are often found dead which have fallen victims to its talons. One most frequently seen in this condition is itself a destroyer of fish. It is a stout-bodied fish, about fifteen or eighteen inches long, of a light yellow color, and gayly ornamented with stripes and spots. It has a most imposing array of sharp, conical teeth outside the lips—objects of dread to the fisherman, for it can use them effectually. One which we picked up dead had killed itself by swallowing another fish, which, though too large for its stomach and throat, could not be disgorged.

This fish-hawk generally kills more prey than it can devour. It eats a portion of the back of the fish, and leaves the rest for the Barotse, who often had a race across the river when they saw an abandoned morsel lying on the opposite sand-banks. The hawk is, however, not always so generous, for, as I myself was a witness on the Zouga, it sometimes plunders the purse of the pelican. Soaring overhead, and seeing this large, stupid bird fishing beneath, it watches till a fine fish is safe in the pelican's pouch; then descending, not very quickly, but with considerable noise of wing, the pelican looks up to see what is the matter, and, as the hawk comes near, he supposes that he is about to be killed, and roars out "Murder!" The opening of his mouth enables the hawk to whisk the fish out of the pouch, upon which the pelican does not fly away, but commences fishing again, the fright having probably made him forget he had any thing in his purse.

A fish called mosheba, about the size of a minnow, often skims along the surface for several yards, in order to get out of the way of the canoe. It uses the pectoral fins, as the flying-fish do, but never makes a clean flight. It is rather a succession of hops along the surface, made by the aid of the side fins. It never becomes large.

Numbers of iguanos (mpulu) sit sunning themselves on overhanging branches of the trees, and splash into the water as we approach. They are highly esteemed as an article of food, the flesh being tender and gelatinous. The chief boatman, who occupies the stem, has in consequence a light javelin always at hand to spear them if they are not quickly out of sight. These, and large alligators gliding in from the banks with a heavy plunge as we come round a sudden bend of the stream, were the occurrences of every hour as we sped up the river.

The rapids in the part of the river between Katima-molelo and Nameta are relieved by several reaches of still, deep water, fifteen or twenty miles long. In these very large herds of hippopotami are seen, and the deep furrows they make, in ascending the banks to graze during the nights, are every where apparent. They are guided back to the water by the scent, but a long continued pouring rain makes it impossible for them to perceive, by that means, in which direction the river lies, and they are found bewildered on the land. The hunters take advantage of their helplessness on these occasions to kill them.

It is impossible to judge of the numbers in a herd, for they are almost always hidden beneath the waters; but as they require to come up every few minutes to breathe, when there is a constant succession of heads thrown up, then the herd is supposed to be large. They love a still reach of the stream, as in the more rapid parts of the channel they are floated down so quickly that much exertion is necessary to regain the distance lost by frequently swimming up again: such constant exertion disturbs them in their nap. They prefer to remain by day in a drowsy, yawning state, and, though their eyes are open, they take little notice of things at a distance. The males utter a loud succession of snorting grunts, which may be heard a mile off. The canoe in which I was, in passing over a wounded one, elicited a distinct grunting, though the animal lay entirely under water.

The young, when very little, take their stand on the neck of the dam, and the small head, rising above the large, comes soonest to the surface. The dam, knowing the more urgent need of her calf, comes more frequently to the surface when it is in her care. But in the rivers of Londa, where they are much in danger of being shot, even the hippopotamus gains wit by experience; for, while those in the Zambesi put up their heads openly to blow, those referred to keep their noses among water-plants, and breathe so quietly that one would not dream of their existence in the river except by footprints on the banks.

Chapter 14

Increasing Beauty of the Country—Mode of spending the Day—The People and the Falls of Gonye—A Makololo Foray—A second prevented, and Captives delivered up—Politeness and Liberality of the People—The Rains—Present of Oxen—The fugitive Barotse—Sekobinyane's Misgovernment—Bee-eaters and other Birds—Fresh-water Sponges—Current—Death from a Lion's Bite at Libonta—Continued Kindness—Arrangements for spending the Night during the Journey—Cooking and Washing—Abundance of animal Life—Different Species of Birds—Water-fowl—Egyptian Geese—Alligators—Narrow Escape of one of my Men—Superstitious Feelings respecting the Alligator—Large Game—The most vulnerable Spot—Gun Medicine—A Sunday—Birds of Song—Depravity; its Treatment—Wild Fruits—Green Pigeons—Shoals of Fish—Hippopotami.

30TH OF NOVEMBER, 1853. At Gonye Falls. No rain has fallen here, so it is excessively hot. The trees have put on their gayest dress, and many flowers adorn the landscape, yet the heat makes all the leaves droop at midday and look languid for want of rain. If the country increases as much in beauty in front as it has done within the last four degrees of latitude, it will be indeed a lovely land.

We all felt great lassitude in traveling. The atmosphere is oppressive both in cloud and sunshine. The evaporation from the river must be excessively great, and I feel as if the fluids of the system joined in the general motion of watery vapor upward, as enormous quantities of water must be drunk to supply its place.

When under way our usual procedure is this: We get up a little before five in the morning; it is then beginning to dawn. While I am dressing, coffee is made; and, having filled my pannikin, the remainder is handed to my companions, who eagerly partake of the refreshing beverage. The servants are busy loading the canoes, while the principal men are sipping the coffee, and, that being soon over, we embark. The next two hours are the most pleasant part of the day's sail. The men paddle away most vigorously; the Barotse, being a tribe of boatmen, have large, deeply-developed chests and shoulders, with indifferent lower extremities. They often engage in loud scolding of each other in order to relieve the tedium of their work.

About eleven we land, and eat any meat which may have remained from the previous evening meal, or a biscuit with honey, and drink water.

After an hour's rest we again embark and cower under an umbrella. The heat is oppressive, and, being weak from the last attack of fever, I can not land and keep the camp supplied with flesh. The men, being quite uncovered in the sun, perspire profusely, and in the afternoon begin to stop, as if waiting for the canoes which have been left behind. Sometimes we reach a sleeping-place two hours before sunset, and, all being troubled with languor, we gladly remain for the night. Coffee again, and a biscuit, or a piece of coarse bread made of maize meal, or that of the native corn, make up the bill of fare for the evening, unless we have been fortunate enough to kill something, when we boil a potful of flesh. This is done by cutting it up into long strips and pouring in water till it is covered. When that is boiled dry, the meat is considered ready.

The people at Gonye carry the canoes over the space requisite to avoid the falls by slinging them on poles tied on diagonally. They place these on their shoulders, and, setting about the work with good humor, soon accomplish the task. They are a merry set of mortals; a feeble joke sets them off in a fit of laughter. Here, as elsewhere, all petitioned for the magic lantern, and, as it is a good means of conveying instruction, I willingly complied.

The falls of Gonye have not been made by wearing back, like those of Niagara, but are of a fissure form. For many miles below, the river is confined in a narrow space of not more than one hundred yards wide. The water goes boiling along, and gives the idea of great masses of it rolling over and over, so that even the most expert swimmer would find it difficult to keep on the surface. Here it is that the river, when in flood, rises fifty or sixty feet in perpendicular height. The islands above the falls are covered with foliage as beautiful as can be seen any where. Viewed from the mass of rock which overhangs the fall, the scenery was the loveliest I had seen.

Nothing worthy of note occurred on our way up to Nameta. There we heard that a party of the Makololo, headed by Lerimo, had made a foray to the north and up the Leeba, in the very direction in which we were about to proceed. Mpololo, the uncle of Sekeletu, is considered the head man of the Barotse valley; and the perpetrators had his full sanction, because Masiko, a son of Santuru, the former chief of the Barotse, had fled high up the Leeambye, and, establishing himself there, had sent men down to the vicinity of Naliele to draw away the remaining Barotse from their allegiance. Lerimo's party had taken some of this Masiko's subjects prisoners, and destroyed several villages of the Balonda, to whom we were going. This was in direct opposition to the policy of Sekeletu, who wished to be at peace with these northern tribes; and Pitsane, my head man, was the bearer of orders to Mpololo to furnish us with presents for the very chiefs they had attacked. Thus we were to get large pots of clarified butter and bunches of beads, in confirmation of the message of peace we were to deliver.

When we reached Litofe, we heard that a fresh foray was in contemplation, but I sent forward orders to disband the party immediately. At Ma-Sekeletu's town we found the head offender, Mpololo himself, and I gave him a bit of my mind, to the effect that, as I was going with the full sanction of Sekeletu, if any harm happened to me in consequence of his ill-advised expedition, the guilt would rest with him. Ma-Sekeletu, who was present, heartily approved all I said, and suggested that all the captives taken by Lerimo should be returned by my hand, to show Masiko that the guilt of the foray lay not with the superior persons of the Makololo, but with a mere servant. Her good sense appeared in other respects besides, and, as this was exactly what my own party had previously resolved to suggest, we were pleased to hear Mpololo agree to do what he was advised. He asked me to lay the matter before the under-chiefs of Naliele, and when we reached that place, on the 9th of December, I did so in a picho, called expressly for the purpose. Lerimo was present, and felt rather crestfallen when his exploit was described by Mohorisi, one of my companions, as one of extreme cowardice, he having made an attack upon the defenseless villagers of Londa, while, as we had found on our former visit, a lion had actually killed eight people of Naliele without his daring to encounter it. The Makololo are cowardly in respect to animals, but brave against men. Mpololo took all the guilt upon himself before the people, and delivered up a captive child whom his wife had in her possession; others followed his example, till we procured the release of five of the prisoners. Some thought, as Masiko had tried to take their children by stratagem, they ought to take his by force, as the two modes suited the genius of each people— the Makalaka delight in cunning, and the Makololo in fighting; and others thought, if Sekeletu meant them to be at peace with Masiko, he ought to have told them so.

It is rather dangerous to tread in the footsteps of a marauding party with men of the same tribe as the aggressors, but my people were in good spirits, and several volunteers even offered to join our ranks. We, however, adhered strictly to the orders of Sekeletu as to our companions, and refused all others.

The people of every village treated us most liberally, presenting, besides oxen, butter, milk, and meal, more than we could stow away in our canoes. The cows in this valley are now yielding, as they frequently do, more milk than the people can use, and both men and women present butter in such quantity that I shall be able to refresh my men as we move along. Anointing the skin prevents the excessive evaporation of the fluids of the body, and acts as clothing in both sun and shade. They always made their presents gracefully. When an ox was given, the owner would say, "Here is a little bit of bread for you." This was pleasing, for I had been accustomed to the Bechuanas presenting a miserable goat, with the pompous exclamation, "Behold an ox!" The women persisted in giving me copious supplies of shrill praises, or "lullilooing"; but, though I frequently told them to modify their "great lords" and "great lions" to more humble expressions, they so evidently intended to do me honor that I could not help being pleased with the poor creatures' wishes for our success.

The rains began while we were at Naliele; this is much later than usual; but, though the Barotse valley has been in need of rain, the people never lack abundance of food. The showers are refreshing, but the air feels hot and close; the thermometer, however, in a cool hut, stands only at 84 Deg. The access of the external air to any spot at once raises its temperature above 90 Deg. A new attack of fever here caused excessive languor; but, as I am already getting tired of quoting my fevers, and never liked to read travels myself where much was said about the illnesses of the traveler, I shall henceforth endeavor to say little about them.

We here sent back the canoe of Sekeletu, and got the loan of others from Mpololo. Eight riding oxen, and seven for slaughter, were, according to the orders of that chief, also furnished; some were intended for our own use, and others as presents to the chiefs of the Balonda. Mpololo was particularly liberal in giving all that Sekeletu ordered, though, as he feeds on the cattle he has in charge, he might have felt it so much abstracted from his own perquisites. Mpololo now acts the great man, and is followed every where by a crowd of toadies, who sing songs in disparagement of Mpepe, of whom he always lived in fear. While Mpepe was alive, he too was regaled with the same fulsome adulation, and now they curse him. They are very foul-tongued; equals, on meeting, often greet each other with a profusion of oaths, and end the volley with a laugh.

In coming up the river to Naliele we met a party of fugitive Barotse returning to their homes, and, as the circumstance illustrates the social status of these subjects of the Makololo, I introduce it here. The villagers in question were the children, or serfs, if we may use the term, of a young man of the same age and tribe as Sekeletu, who, being of an irritable temper, went by the nickname of Sekobinyane—a little slavish thing. His treatment of his servants was so bad that most of them had fled; and when the Mambari came, and, contrary to the orders of Sekeletu, purchased slaves, Sekobinyane sold one or two of the Barotse children of his village. The rest fled immediately to Masiko, and were gladly received by that Barotse chief as his subjects.

When Sekeletu and I first ascended the Leeambye, we met Sekobinyane coming down, on his way to Linyanti. On being asked the news, he remained silent about the loss of his village, it being considered a crime among the Makololo for any one to treat his people so ill as to cause them to run away from him. He then passed us, and, dreading the vengeance of Sekeletu for his crime, secretly made his escape from Linyanti to Lake Ngami. He was sent for, however, and the chief at the lake delivered him up, on Sekeletu declaring that he had no intention of punishing him otherwise than by scolding. He did not even do that, as Sekobinyane was evidently terrified enough, and also became ill through fear.

The fugitive villagers remained only a few weeks with their new master Masiko, and then fled back again, and were received as if they had done nothing wrong. All united in abusing the conduct of Sekobinyane, and no one condemned the fugitives; and the cattle, the use of which they had previously enjoyed, never having been removed from their village, they re-established themselves with apparent gladness.

This incident may give some idea of the serfdom of the subject tribes, and, except that they are sometimes punished for running away and other offenses, I can add nothing more by way of showing the true nature of this form of servitude.

Leaving Naliele, amid abundance of good wishes for the success of our expedition, and hopes that we might return accompanied with white traders, we began again our ascent of the river. It was now beginning to rise, though the rains had but just commenced in the valley. The banks are low, but cleanly cut, and seldom sloping. At low water they are from four to eight feet high, and make the river always assume very much the aspect of a canal. They are in some parts of whitish, tenacious clay, with strata of black clay intermixed, and black loam in sand, or pure sand stratified. As the river rises it is always wearing to one side or the other, and is known to have cut across from one bend to another, and to form new channels. As we coast along the shore, pieces which are undermined often fall in with a splash like that caused by the plunge of an alligator, and endanger the canoe.

These perpendicular banks afford building-places to a pretty bee-eater,[*] which loves to breed in society. The face of the sand-bank is perforated with hundreds of holes leading to their nests, each of which is about a foot apart from the other; and as we pass they pour out of their hiding-places, and float overhead.

* 'Merops apiaster' and 'M. bullockoides' (Smith).

A speckled kingfisher is seen nearly every hundred yards, which builds in similar spots, and attracts the attention of herd-boys, who dig out its nest for the sake of the young. This, and a most lovely little blue and orange kingfisher, are seen every where along the banks, dashing down like a shot into the water for their prey. A third, seen more rarely, is as large as a pigeon, and is of a slaty color.

Another inhabitant of the banks is the sand-martin, which also likes company in the work of raising a family. They never leave this part of the country. One may see them preening themselves in the very depth of winter, while the swallows, of which we shall yet speak, take winter trips. I saw sand-martins at the Orange River during a period of winter frost; it is, therefore, probable that they do not migrate even from thence.

Around the reeds, which in some parts line the banks, we see fresh-water sponges. They usually encircle the stalk, and are hard and brittle, presenting numbers of small round grains near their circumference.

The river was running at the rate of five miles an hour, and carried bunches of reed and decaying vegetable matter on its surface; yet the water was not discolored. It had, however, a slightly yellowish-green tinge, somewhat deeper than its natural color. This arose from the quantity of sand carried by the rising flood from sand-banks, which are annually shifted from one spot to another, and from the pieces falling in as the banks are worn; for when the water is allowed to stand in a glass, a few seconds suffice for its deposit at the bottom. This is considered an unhealthy period. When waiting, on one occasion, for the other canoes to come up, I felt no inclination to leave the one I was in; but my head boatman, Mashauana, told me never to remain on board while so much vegetable matter was floating down the stream.

17TH DECEMBER. At Libonta. We were detained for days together collecting contributions of fat and butter, according to the orders of Sekeletu, as presents to the Balonda chiefs. Much fever prevailed, and ophthalmia was rife, as is generally the case before the rains begin. Some of my own men required my assistance, as well as the people of Libonta. A lion had done a good deal of mischief here, and when the people went to attack it two men were badly wounded; one of them had his thigh-bone quite broken, showing the prodigious power of this animal's jaws. The inflammation produced by the teeth-wounds proved fatal to one of them.

Here we demanded the remainder of the captives, and got our number increased to nineteen. They consisted of women and children, and one young man of twenty. One of the boys was smuggled away in the crowd as we embarked. The Makololo under-chiefs often act in direct opposition to the will of the head chief, trusting to circumstances and brazenfacedness to screen themselves from his open displeasure; and as he does not always find it convenient to notice faults, they often go to considerable lengths in wrong-doing.

Libonta is the last town of the Makololo; so, when we parted from it, we had only a few cattle-stations and outlying hamlets in front, and then an uninhabited border country till we came to Londa or Lunda. Libonta is situated on a mound like the rest of the villages in the Barotse valley, but here the tree-covered sides of the valley begin to approach nearer the river. The village itself belongs to two of the chief wives of Sebituane, who furnished us with an ox and abundance of other food. The same kindness was manifested by all who could afford to give any thing; and as I glance over their deeds of generosity recorded in my journal, my heart glows with gratitude to them, and I hope and pray that God may spare me to make them some return.

Before leaving the villages entirely, we may glance at our way of spending the nights. As soon as we land, some of the men cut a little grass for my bed, while Mashauana plants the poles of the little tent. These are used by day for carrying burdens, for the Barotse fashion is exactly like that of the natives of India, only the burden is fastened near the ends of the pole, and not suspended by long cords. The bed is made, and boxes ranged on each side of it, and then the tent pitched over all. Four or five feet in front of my tent is placed the principal or kotla fire, the wood for which must be collected by the man who occupies the post of herald, and takes as his perquisite the heads of all the oxen slaughtered, and of all the game too. Each person knows the station he is to occupy, in reference to the post of honor at the fire in front of the door of the tent. The two Makololo occupy my right and left, both in eating and sleeping, as long as the journey lasts. But Mashauana, my head boatman, makes his bed at the door of the tent as soon as I retire. The rest, divided into small companies according to their tribes, make sheds all round the fire, leaving a horseshoe-shaped space in front sufficient for the cattle to stand in. The fire gives confidence to the oxen, so the men are always careful to keep them in sight of it. The sheds are formed by planting two stout forked poles in an inclined direction, and placing another over these in a horizontal position. A number of branches are then stuck in the ground in the direction to which the poles are inclined, the twigs drawn down to the horizontal pole and tied with strips of bark. Long grass is then laid over the branches in sufficient quantity to draw off the rain, and we have sheds open to the fire in front, but secure from beasts behind. In less than an hour we were usually all under cover. We never lacked abundance of grass during the whole journey. It is a picturesque sight at night, when the clear bright moon of these climates glances on the sleeping forms around, to look out upon the attitudes of profound repose both men and beasts assume. There being no danger from wild animals in such a night, the fires are allowed almost to go out; and as there is no fear of hungry dogs coming over sleepers and devouring the food, or quietly eating up the poor fellows' blankets, which at best were but greasy skins, which sometimes happened in the villages, the picture was one of perfect peace.

The cooking is usually done in the natives' own style, and, as they carefully wash the dishes, pots, and the hands before handling food, it is by no means despicable. Sometimes alterations are made at my suggestion, and then they believe that they can cook in thorough white man's fashion. The cook always comes in for something left in the pot, so all are eager to obtain the office.

I taught several of them to wash my shirts, and they did it well, though their teacher had never been taught that work himself. Frequent changes of linen and sunning of my blanket kept me more comfortable than might have been anticipated, and I feel certain that the lessons of cleanliness rigidly instilled by my mother in childhood helped to maintain that respect which these people entertain for European ways. It is questionable if a descent to barbarous ways ever elevates a man in the eyes of savages.

When quite beyond the inhabited parts, we found the country abounding in animal life of every form. There are upward of thirty species of birds on the river itself. Hundreds of the 'Ibis religiosa' come down the Leeambye with the rising water, as they do on the Nile; then large white pelicans, in flocks of three hundred at a time, following each other in long extending line, rising and falling as they fly so regularly all along as to look like an extended coil of birds; clouds of a black shell-eating bird, called linongolo ('Anastomus lamelligerus'); also plovers, snipes, curlews, and herons without number.

There are, besides the more common, some strange varieties. The pretty white 'ardetta' is seen in flocks, settling on the backs of large herds of buffaloes, and following them on the wing when they run; while the kala ('Textor erythrorhynchus') is a better horseman, for it sits on the withers when the animal is at full speed.

Then those strange birds, the scissor-bills, with snow-white breast, jet-black coat, and red beak, sitting by day on the sand-banks, the very picture of comfort and repose. Their nests are only little hollows made on these same sand-banks, without any attempt of concealment; they watch them closely, and frighten away the marabou and crows from their eggs by feigned attacks at their heads. When man approaches their nests, they change their tactics, and, like the lapwing and ostrich, let one wing drop and make one leg limp, as if lame. The upper mandible being so much shorter than the lower, the young are more helpless than the stork in the fable with the flat dishes, and must have every thing conveyed into the mouth by the parents till they are able to provide for themselves. The lower mandible, as thin as a paper-knife, is put into the water while the bird skims along the surface, and scoops up any little insects it meets. It has great length of wing, and can continue its flight with perfect ease, the wings acting, though kept above the level of the body. The wonder is, how this plowing of the surface of the water can be so well performed as to yield a meal, for it is usually done in the dark. Like most aquatic feeders, they work by night, when insects and fishes rise to the surface. They have great affection for their young, its amount being increased in proportion to the helplessness of the offspring.

There are also numbers of spoonbills, nearly white in plumage; the beautiful, stately flamingo; the Numidian crane, or demoiselle, some of which, tamed at Government House, Cape Town, struck every one as most graceful ornaments to a noble mansion, as they perched on its pillars. There are two cranes besides—one light blue, the other also light blue, but with a white neck; and gulls ('Procellaria') of different sizes abound.

One pretty little wader, an avoset, appears as if standing on stilts, its legs are so long; and its bill seems bent the wrong way, or upward. It is constantly seen wading in the shallows, digging up little slippery insects, the peculiar form of the bill enabling it to work them easily out of the sand. When feeding, it puts its head under the water to seize the insect at the bottom, then lifts it up quickly, making a rapid gobbling, as if swallowing a wriggling worm.

The 'Parra Africana' runs about on the surface, as if walking on water, catching insects. It too has long, thin legs, and extremely long toes, for the purpose of enabling it to stand on the floating lotus-leaves and other aquatic plants. When it stands on a lotus-leaf five inches in diameter, the spread of the toes, acting on the principle of snow-shoes, occupies all the surface, and it never sinks, though it obtains a livelihood, not by swimming or flying, but by walking on the water.

Water-birds, whose prey or food requires a certain aim or action in one direction, have bills quite straight in form, as the heron and snipe; while those which are intended to come in contact with hard substances, as breaking shells, have the bills gently curved, in order that the shock may not be communicated to the brain.

The Barotse valley contains great numbers of large black geese.* They may be seen every where walking slowly about, feeding. They have a strong black spur on the shoulder, like the armed plover, and as strong as that on the heel of a cock, but are never seen to use them, except in defense of their young. They choose ant-hills for their nests, and in the time of laying the Barotse consume vast quantities of their eggs. There are also two varieties of geese, of somewhat smaller size, but better eating. One of these, the Egyptian goose, or Vulpanser, can not rise from the water, and during the floods of the river great numbers are killed by being pursued in canoes. The third is furnished with a peculiar knob on the beak. These, with myriads of ducks of three varieties, abound every where on the Leeambye. On one occasion the canoe neared a bank on which a large flock was sitting. Two shots furnished our whole party with a supper, for we picked up seventeen ducks and a goose. No wonder the Barotse always look back to this fruitful valley as the Israelites did to the flesh-pots of Egypt. The poorest persons are so well supplied with food from their gardens, fruits from the forest trees, and fish from the river, that their children, when taken into the service of the Makololo, where they have only one large meal a day, become quite emaciated, and pine for a return to their parents.

* 'Anser leucagaster' and 'melanogaster'.

Part of our company marched along the banks with the oxen, and part went in the canoes, but our pace was regulated by the speed of the men on shore. Their course was rather difficult, on account of the numbers of departing and re-entering branches of the Leeambye, which they had to avoid or wait at till we ferried them over. The number of alligators is prodigious, and in this river they are more savage than in some others Many children are carried off annually at Sesheke and other towns; for, notwithstanding the danger, when they go down for water they almost always must play a while. This reptile is said by the natives to strike the victim with its tail, then drag him in and drown him. When lying in the water watching for prey, the body never appears. Many calves are lost also, and it is seldom that a number of cows can swim over at Sesheke without some loss. I never could avoid shuddering on seeing my men swimming across these branches, after one of them had been caught by the thigh and taken below. He, however, retained, as nearly all of them in the most trying circumstances do, his full presence of mind, and, having a small, square, ragged-edged javelin with him, when dragged to the bottom gave the alligator a stab behind the shoulder. The alligator, writhing in pain, left him, and he came out with the deep marks of the reptile's teeth on his thigh. Here the people have no antipathy to persons who have met with such an adventure, but, in the Bamangwato and Bakwain tribes, if a man is either bitten or even has had water splashed over him by the reptile's tail, he is expelled his tribe. When on the Zouga we saw one of the Bamangwato living among the Bayeiye, who had the misfortune to have been bitten and driven out of his tribe in consequence. Fearing that I would regard him with the same disgust which his countrymen profess to feel, he would not tell me the cause of his exile, but the Bayeiye informed me of it, and the scars of the teeth were visible on his thigh. If the Bakwains happened to go near an alligator they would spit on the ground, and indicate its presence by saying "Boleo ki bo"—"There is sin". They imagine the mere sight of it would give inflammation of the eyes; and though they eat the zebra without hesitation, yet if one bites a man he is expelled the tribe, and obliged to take his wife and family away to the Kalahari. These curious relics of the animal-worship of former times scarcely exist among the Makololo. Sebituane acted on the principle, "Whatever is food for men is food for me;" so no man is here considered unclean. The Barotse appear inclined to pray to alligators and eat them too, for when I wounded a water-antelope, called mochose, it took to the water; when near the other side of the river an alligator appeared at its tail, and then both sank together. Mashauana, who was nearer to it than I, told me that, "though he had called to it to let his meat alone, it refused to listen." One day we passed some Barotse lads who had speared an alligator, and were waiting in expectation of its floating soon after. The meat has a strong musky odor, not at all inviting for any one except the very hungry.

When we had gone thirty or forty miles above Libonta we sent eleven of our captives to the west, to the chief called Makoma, with an explanatory message. This caused some delay; but as we were loaded with presents of food from the Makololo, and the wild animals were in enormous herds, we fared sumptuously. It was grievous, however, to shoot the lovely creatures, they were so tame. With but little skill in stalking, one could easily get within fifty or sixty yards of them. There I lay, looking at the graceful forms and motions of beautiful pokus,* leches, and other antelopes, often till my men, wondering what was the matter, came up to see, and frightened them away. If we had been starving, I could have slaughtered them with as little hesitation as I should cut off a patient's leg; but I felt a doubt, and the antelopes got the benefit of it. Have they a guardian spirit over them? I have repeatedly observed, when I approached a herd lying beyond an ant-hill with a tree on it, and viewed them with the greatest caution, they very soon showed symptoms of uneasiness. They did not sniff danger in the wind, for I was to leeward of them; but the almost invariable apprehension of danger which arose, while unconscious of the direction in which it lay, made me wonder whether each had what the ancient physicians thought we all possessed, an archon, or presiding spirit.

* I propose to name this new species 'Antilope Vardonii', after the African traveler, Major Vardon.

If we could ascertain the most fatal spot in an animal, we could dispatch it with the least possible amount of suffering; but as that is probably the part to which the greatest amount of nervous influence is directed at the moment of receiving the shot, if we can not be sure of the heart or brain, we are never certain of speedy death. Antelopes, formed for a partially amphibious existence, and other animals of that class, are much more tenacious of life than those which are purely terrestrial. Most antelopes, when in distress or pursued, make for the water. If hunted, they always do. A leche shot right through the body, and no limb-bone broken, is almost sure to get away, while a zebra, with a wound of no greater severity, will probably drop down dead. I have seen a rhinoceros, while standing apparently chewing the cud, drop down dead from a shot in the stomach, while others shot through one lung and the stomach go off as if little hurt. But if one should crawl up silently to within twenty yards either of the white or black rhinoceros, throwing up a pinch of dust every now and then, to find out that the anxiety to keep the body concealed by the bushes has not led him to the windward side, then sit down, rest the elbow on the knees, and aim, slanting a little upward, at a dark spot behind the shoulders, it falls stone dead.

To show that a shock on the part of the system to which much nervous force is at the time directed will destroy life, it may be mentioned that an eland, when hunted, can be dispatched by a wound which does little more than injure the muscular system; its whole nervous force is then imbuing the organs of motion; and a giraffe, when pressed hard by a good horse only two or three hundred yards, has been known to drop down dead, without any wound being inflicted at all. A full gallop by an eland or giraffe quite dissipates its power, and the hunters, aware of this, always try to press them at once to it, knowing that they have but a short space to run before the animals are in their power. In doing this, the old sportsmen are careful not to go too close to the giraffe's tail, for this animal can swing his hind foot round in a way which would leave little to choose between a kick with it and a clap from the arm of a windmill.

When the nervous force is entire, terrible wounds may be inflicted without killing; a tsessebe having been shot through the neck while quietly feeding, we went to him, and one of the men cut his throat deep enough to bleed him largely. He started up after this and ran more than a mile, and would have got clear off had not a dog brought him to bay under a tree, where we found him standing.

My men, having never had fire-arms in their hands before, found it so difficult to hold the musket steady at the flash of fire in the pan, that they naturally expected me to furnish them with "gun medicine", without which, it is almost universally believed, no one can shoot straight. Great expectations had been formed when I arrived among the Makololo on this subject; but, having invariably declined to deceive them, as some for their own profit have done, my men now supposed that I would at last consent, and thereby relieve myself from the hard work of hunting by employing them after due medication. This I was most willing to do, if I could have done it honestly; for, having but little of the hunting 'furore' in my composition, I always preferred eating the game to killing it. Sulphur is the remedy most admired, and I remember Sechele giving a large price for a very small bit. He also gave some elephants' tusks, worth 30 Pounds, for another medicine which was to make him invulnerable to musket balls. As I uniformly recommended that these things should be tested by experiment, a calf was anointed with the charm and tied to a tree. It proved decisive, and Sechele remarked it was "pleasanter to be deceived than undeceived." I offered sulphur for the same purpose, but that was declined, even though a person came to the town afterward and rubbed his hands with a little before a successful trial of shooting at a mark.

I explained to my men the nature of a gun, and tried to teach them, but they would soon have expended all the ammunition in my possession. I was thus obliged to do all the shooting myself ever afterward. Their inability was rather a misfortune; for, in consequence of working too soon after having been bitten by the lion, the bone of my left arm had not united well. Continual hard manual labor, and some falls from ox-back, lengthened the ligament by which the ends of the bones were united, and a false joint was the consequence. The limb has never been painful, as those of my companions on the day of the rencounter with the lion have been, but, there being a joint too many, I could not steady the rifle, and was always obliged to shoot with the piece resting on the left shoulder. I wanted steadiness of aim, and it generally happened that the more hungry the party became, the more frequently I missed the animals.

We spent a Sunday on our way up to the confluence of the Leeba and Leeambye. Rains had fallen here before we came, and the woods had put on their gayest hue. Flowers of great beauty and curious forms grow every where; they are unlike those in the south, and so are the trees. Many of the forest-tree leaves are palmated and largely developed; the trunks are covered with lichens, and the abundance of ferns which appear in the woods shows we are now in a more humid climate than any to the south of the Barotse valley. The ground begins to swarm with insect life; and in the cool, pleasant mornings the welkin rings with the singing of birds, which is not so delightful as the notes of birds at home, because I have not been familiar with them from infancy. The notes here, however, strike the mind by their loudness and variety, as the wellings forth from joyous hearts of praise to Him who fills them with overflowing gladness. All of us rise early to enjoy the luscious balmy air of the morning. We then have worship; but, amid all the beauty and loveliness with which we are surrounded, there is still a feeling of want in the soul in viewing one's poor companions, and hearing bitter, impure words jarring on the ear in the perfection of the scenes of Nature, and a longing that both their hearts and ours might be brought into harmony with the Great Father of Spirits. I pointed out, in, as usual, the simplest words I could employ, the remedy which God has presented to us, in the inexpressibly precious gift of His own Son, on whom the Lord "laid the iniquity of us all." The great difficulty in dealing with these people is to make the subject plain. The minds of the auditors can not be understood by one who has not mingled much with them. They readily pray for the forgiveness of sins, and then sin again; confess the evil of it, and there the matter ends.

I shall not often advert to their depravity. My practice has always been to apply the remedy with all possible earnestness, but never allow my own mind to dwell on the dark shades of men's characters. I have never been able to draw pictures of guilt, as if that could awaken Christian sympathy. The evil is there. But all around in this fair creation are scenes of beauty, and to turn from these to ponder on deeds of sin can not promote a healthy state of the faculties. I attribute much of the bodily health I enjoy to following the plan adopted by most physicians, who, while engaged in active, laborious efforts to assist the needy, at the same time follow the delightful studies of some department of natural history. The human misery and sin we endeavor to alleviate and cure may be likened to the sickness and impurity of some of the back slums of great cities. One contents himself by ministering to the sick and trying to remove the causes, without remaining longer in the filth than is necessary for his work; another, equally anxious for the public good, stirs up every cesspool, that he may describe its reeking vapors, and, by long contact with impurities, becomes himself infected, sickens, and dies.

The men went about during the day, and brought back wild fruits of several varieties, which I had not hitherto seen. One, called mogametsa, is a bean with a little pulp round it, which tastes like sponge-cake; another, named mawa, grows abundantly on a low bush. There are many berries and edible bulbs almost every where. The mamosho or moshomosho, and milo (a medlar), were to be found near our encampment. These are both good, if indeed one can be a fair judge who felt quite disposed to pass a favorable verdict on every fruit which had the property of being eatable at all. Many kinds are better than our crab-apple or sloe, and, had they the care and culture these have enjoyed, might take high rank among the fruits of the world. All that the Africans have thought of has been present gratification; and now, as I sometimes deposit date-seeds in the soil, and tell them I have no hope whatever of seeing the fruit, it seems to them as the act of the South Sea Islanders appears to us, when they planted in their gardens iron nails received from Captain Cook.

There are many fruits and berries in the forests, the uses of which are unknown to my companions. Great numbers of a kind of palm I have never met with before were seen growing at and below the confluence of the Loeti and Leeambye; the seed probably came down the former river. It is nearly as tall as the palmyra. The fruit is larger than of that species; it is about four inches long, and has a soft yellow pulp round the kernel or seed; when ripe, it is fluid and stringy, like the wild mango, and not very pleasant to eat.

Before we came to the junction of the Leeba and Leeambye we found the banks twenty feet high, and composed of marly sandstone. They are covered with trees, and the left bank has the tsetse and elephants. I suspect the fly has some connection with this animal, and the Portuguese in the district of Tete must think so too, for they call it the 'Musca da elephant' (the elephant fly).

The water of inundation covers even these lofty banks, but does not stand long upon them; hence the crop of trees. Where it remains for any length of time, trees can not live. On the right bank, or that in which the Loeti flows, there is an extensive flat country called Manga, which, though covered with grass, is destitute in a great measure of trees.

Flocks of green pigeons rose from the trees as we passed along the banks, and the notes of many birds told that we were now among strangers of the feathered tribe. The beautiful trogon, with bright scarlet breast and black back, uttered a most peculiar note, similar to that we read of as having once been emitted by Memnon, and likened to the tuning of a lyre. The boatmen answered it by calling "Nama, nama!"—meat, meat—as if they thought that a repetition of the note would be a good omen for our success in hunting. Many more interesting birds were met; but I could make no collection, as I was proceeding on the plan of having as little luggage as possible, so as not to excite the cupidity of those through whose country we intended to pass.

Vast shoals of fish come down the Leeambye with the rising waters, as we observed they also do in the Zouga. They are probably induced to make this migration by the increased rapidity of the current dislodging them from their old pasture-grounds higher up the river. Insects constitute but a small portion of the food of many fish. Fine vegetable matter, like slender mosses, growing on the bottom, is devoured greedily; and as the fishes are dislodged from the main stream by the force of the current, and find abundant pasture on the flooded plains, the whole community becomes disturbed and wanders.

The mosala ('Clarias Capensis' and 'Glanis siluris'), the mullet ('Mugil Africanus'), and other fishes, spread over the Barotse valley in such numbers that when the waters retire all the people are employed in cutting them up and drying them in the sun. The supply exceeds the demand, and the land in numerous places is said to emit a most offensive smell. Wherever you see the Zambesi in the centre of the country, it is remarkable for the abundance of animal life in and upon its waters, and on the adjacent banks.

We passed great numbers of hippopotami. They are very numerous in the parts of the river where they are never hunted. The males appear of a dark color, the females of yellowish brown. There is not such a complete separation of the sexes among them as among elephants. They spend most of their time in the water, lolling about in a listless, dreamy manner. When they come out of the river by night, they crop off the soft succulent grasses very neatly. When they blow, they puff up the water about three feet high.

Chapter 15

Message to Masiko, the Barotse Chief, regarding the Captives—Navigation of the Leeambye—Capabilities of this District—The Leeba—Flowers and Bees—Buffalo-hunt—Field for a Botanist—Young Alligators; their savage Nature—Suspicion of the Balonda—Sekelenke's Present—A Man and his two Wives—Hunters—Message from Manenko, a female Chief—Mambari Traders—A Dream—Sheakondo and his People—Teeth-filing—Desire for Butter—Interview with Nyamoana, another female Chief—Court Etiquette—Hair versus Wool—Increase of Superstition—Arrival of Manenko; her Appearance and Husband—Mode of Salutation—Anklets—Embassy, with a Present from Masiko—Roast Beef—Manioc—Magic Lantern—Manenko an accomplished Scold: compels us to wait—Unsuccessful Zebra-hunt.

On the 27th of December we were at the confluence of the Leeba and Leeambye (lat. 14d 10′ 52″ S., long. 23d 35′ 40″ E.). Masiko, the Barotse chief, for whom we had some captives, lived nearly due east of this point. They were two little boys, a little girl, a young man, and two middle-aged women. One of these was a member of a Babimpe tribe, who knock out both upper and lower front teeth as a distinction. As we had been informed by the captives on the previous Sunday that Masiko was in the habit of seizing all orphans, and those who have no powerful friend in the tribe whose protection they can claim, and selling them for clothing to the Mambari, we thought the objection of the women to go first to his town before seeing their friends quite reasonable, and resolved to send a party of our own people to see them safely among their relatives. I told the captive young man to inform Masiko that he was very unlike his father Santuru, who had refused to sell his people to Mambari. He will probably be afraid to deliver such a message himself, but it is meant for his people, and they will circulate it pretty widely, and Masiko may yet feel a little pressure from without. We sent Mosantu, a Batoka man, and his companions, with the captives. The Barotse whom we had were unwilling to go to Masiko, since they owe him allegiance as the son of Santuru, and while they continue with the Makololo are considered rebels. The message by Mosantu was, that "I was sorry to find that Santuru had not borne a wiser son. Santuru loved to govern men, but Masiko wanted to govern wild beasts only, as he sold his people to the Mambari;" adding an explanation of the return of the captives, and an injunction to him to live in peace, and prevent his people kidnapping the children and canoes of the Makololo, as a continuance in these deeds would lead to war, which I wished to prevent. He was also instructed to say, if Masiko wanted fuller explanation of my views, he must send a sensible man to talk with me at the first town of the Balonda, to which I was about to proceed.

We ferried Mosantu over to the left bank of the Leeba. The journey required five days, but it could not have been at a quicker rate than ten or twelve miles per day; the children were between seven and eight years of age, and unable to walk fast in a hot sun.

Leaving Mosantu to pursue his course, we shall take but one glance down the river, which we are now about to leave, for it comes at this point from the eastward, and our course is to be directed to the northwest, as we mean to go to Loanda in Angola. From the confluence, where we now are, down to Mosioatunya, there are many long reaches, where a vessel equal to the Thames steamers plying between the bridges could run as freely as they do on the Thames. It is often, even here, as broad as that river at London Bridge, but, without accurate measurement of the depth, one could not say which contained most water. There are, however, many and serious obstacles to a continued navigation for hundreds of miles at a stretch. About ten miles below the confluence of the Loeti, for instance, there are many large sand-banks in the stream; then you have a hundred miles to the River Simah, where a Thames steamer could ply at all times of the year; but, again, the space between Simah and Katima-molelo has five or six rapids with cataracts, one of which, Gonye, could not be passed at any time without portage. Between these rapids there are reaches of still, deep water, of several miles in length. Beyond Katima-molelo to the confluence of the Chobe you have nearly a hundred miles again, of a river capable of being navigated in the same way as in the Barotse valley.

Now I do not say that this part of the river presents a very inviting prospect for extemporaneous European enterprise; but when we have a pathway which requires only the formation of portages to make it equal to our canals for hundreds of miles, where the philosophers supposed there was naught but an extensive sandy desert, we must confess that the future partakes at least of the elements of hope. My deliberate conviction was and is that the part of the country indicated is as capable of supporting millions of inhabitants as it is of its thousands. The grass of the Barotse valley, for instance, is such a densely-matted mass that, when "laid", the stalks bear each other up, so that one feels as if walking on the sheaves of a hay-stack, and the leches nestle under it to bring forth their young. The soil which produces this, if placed under the plow, instead of being mere pasturage, would yield grain sufficient to feed vast multitudes.

We now began to ascend the Leeba. The water is black in color as compared with the main stream, which here assumes the name of Kabompo. The Leeba flows placidly, and, unlike the parent river, receives numbers of little rivulets from both sides. It winds slowly through the most charming meadows, each of which has either a soft, sedgy centre, large pond, or trickling rill down the middle. The trees are now covered with a profusion of the freshest foliage, and seem planted in groups of such pleasant, graceful outline that art could give no additional charm. The grass, which had been burned off and was growing again after the rains, was short and green, and all the scenery so like that of a carefully-tended gentleman's park, that one is scarcely reminded that the surrounding region is in the hands of simple nature alone. I suspect that the level meadows are inundated annually, for the spots on which the trees stand are elevated three or four feet above them, and these elevations, being of different shapes, give the strange variety of outline of the park-like woods. Numbers of a fresh-water shell are scattered all over these valleys. The elevations, as I have observed elsewhere, are of a soft, sandy soil, and the meadows of black, rich alluvial loam. There are many beautiful flowers, and many bees to sip their nectar. We found plenty of honey in the woods, and saw the stages on which the Balonda dry their meat, when they come down to hunt and gather the produce of the wild hives. In one part we came upon groups of lofty trees as straight as masts, with festoons of orchilla-weed hanging from the branches. This, which is used as a dye-stuff, is found nowhere in the dry country to the south. It prefers the humid climate near the west coast.

A large buffalo was wounded, and ran into the thickest part of the forest, bleeding profusely. The young men went on his trail; and, though the vegetation was so dense that no one could have run more than a few yards, most of them went along quite carelessly, picking and eating a fruit of the melon family called Mponko. When the animal heard them approach he always fled, shifting his stand and doubling on his course in the most cunning manner. In other cases I have known them to turn back to a point a few yards from their own trail, and then lie down in a hollow waiting for the hunter to come up. Though a heavy, lumbering-looking animal, his charge is then rapid and terrific. More accidents happen by the buffalo and the black rhinoceros than by the lion. Though all are aware of the mischievous nature of the buffalo when wounded, our young men went after him quite carelessly. They never lose their presence of mind, but, as a buffalo charges back in a forest, dart dexterously out of his way behind a tree, and, wheeling round, stab him as he passes.

A tree in flower brought the pleasant fragrance of hawthorn hedges back to memory; its leaves, flowers, perfumes, and fruit resembled those of the hawthorn, only the flowers were as large as dog-roses, and the "haws" like boys' marbles. Here the flowers smell sweetly, while few in the south emit any scent at all, or only a nauseous odor. A botanist would find a rich harvest on the banks of the Leeba. This would be his best season, for the flowers all run rapidly to seed, and then insects of every shape spring into existence to devour them. The climbing plants display great vigor of growth, being not only thick in the trunk, but also at the very point, in the manner of quickly-growing asparagus. The maroro or malolo now appears, and is abundant in many parts between this and Angola. It is a small bush with a yellow fruit, and in its appearance a dwarf "anona". The taste is sweet, and the fruit is wholesome: it is full of seeds, like the custard-apple.

On the 28th we slept at a spot on the right bank from which had just emerged two broods of alligators. We had seen many young ones as we came up, so this seems to be their time of coming forth from the nests, for we saw them sunning themselves on sand-banks in company with the old ones. We made our fire in one of the deserted nests, which were strewed all over with the broken shells. At the Zouga we saw sixty eggs taken out of one such nest alone. They are about the size of those of a goose, only the eggs of the alligator are of the same diameter at both ends, and the white shell is partially elastic, from having a strong internal membrane and but little lime in its composition. The distance from the water was about ten feet, and there were evidences of the same place having been used for a similar purpose in former years. A broad path led up from the water to the nest, and the dam, it was said by my companions, after depositing the eggs, covers them up, and returns afterward to assist the young out of the place of confinement and out of the egg. She leads them to the edge of the water, and then leaves them to catch small fish for themselves. Assistance to come forth seems necessary, for here, besides the tough membrane of the shell, they had four inches of earth upon them; but they do not require immediate aid for food, because they all retain a portion of yolk, equal to that of a hen's egg, in a membrane in the abdomen, as a stock of nutriment, while only beginning independent existence by catching fish. Fish is the principal food of both small and large, and they are much assisted in catching them by their broad, scaly tails. Sometimes an alligator, viewing a man in the water from the opposite bank, rushes across the stream with wonderful agility, as is seen by the high ripple he makes on the surface caused by his rapid motion at the bottom; but in general they act by stealth, sinking underneath as soon as they see man. They seldom leave the water to catch prey, but often come out by day to enjoy the pleasure of basking in the sun. In walking along the bank of the Zouga once, a small one, about three feet long, made a dash at my feet, and caused me to rush quickly in another direction; but this is unusual, for I never heard of a similar case. A wounded leche, chased into any of the lagoons in the Barotse valley, or a man or dog going in for the purpose of bringing out a dead one, is almost sure to be seized, though the alligators may not appear on the surface. When employed in looking for food they keep out of sight; they fish chiefly by night. When eating, they make a loud, champing noise, which when once heard is never forgotten.

The young, which had come out of the nests where we spent the night, did not appear wary; they were about ten inches long, with yellow eyes, and pupil merely a perpendicular slit. They were all marked with transverse slips of pale green and brown, half an inch broad. When speared, they bit the weapon savagely, though their teeth were but partially developed, uttering at the same time a sharp bark like that of a whelp when it first begins to use its voice. I could not ascertain whether the dam devours them, as reported, or whether the ichneumon has the same reputation here as in Egypt. Probably the Barotse and Bayeiye would not look upon it as a benefactor; they prefer to eat the eggs themselves, and be their own ichneumons. The white of the egg does not coagulate, but the yolk does, and this is the only part eaten.

As the population increases, the alligators will decrease, for their nests will be oftener found; the principal check on their inordinate multiplication seems to be man. They are more savage and commit more mischief in the Leeambye than in any other river. After dancing long in the moonlight nights, young men run down to the water to wash off the dust and cool themselves before going to bed, and are thus often carried away. One wonders they are not afraid; but the fact is, they have as little sense of danger impending over them as the hare has when not actually pursued by the hound, and in many rencounters, in which they escape, they had not time to be afraid, and only laugh at the circumstance afterward: there is a want of calm reflection. In many cases, not referred to in this book, I feel more horror now in thinking on dangers I have run than I did at the time of their occurrence.

When we reached the part of the river opposite to the village of Manenko, the first female chief whom we encountered, two of the people called Balunda, or Balonda, came to us in their little canoe. From them we learned that Kolimbota, one of our party, who had been in the habit of visiting these parts, was believed by the Balonda to have acted as a guide to the marauders under Lerimo, whose captives we were now returning. They very naturally suspected this, from the facility with which their villages had been found, and, as they had since removed them to some distance from the river, they were unwilling to lead us to their places of concealment. We were in bad repute, but, having a captive boy and girl to show in evidence of Sekeletu and ourselves not being partakers in the guilt of inferior men, I could freely express my desire that all should live in peace. They evidently felt that I ought to have taught the Makololo first, before coming to them, for they remarked that what I advanced was very good, but guilt lay at the door of the Makololo for disturbing the previously existing peace. They then went away to report us to Manenko.

When the strangers visited us again in the evening, they were accompanied by a number of the people of an Ambonda chief named Sekelenke. The Ambonda live far to the N.W.; their language, the Bonda, is the common dialect in Angola. Sekelenke had fled, and was now living with his village as a vassal of Masiko. As notices of such men will perhaps convey the best idea of the state of the inhabitants to the reader, I shall hereafter allude to the conduct of Sekelenke, whom I at present only introduce. Sekelenke had gone with his villagers to hunt elephants on the right bank of the Leeba, and was now on his way back to Masiko. He sent me a dish of boiled zebra's flesh, and a request that I should lend him a canoe to ferry his wives and family across the river to the bank on which we were encamped. Many of Sekelenke's people came to salute the first white man they ever had an opportunity of seeing; but Sekelenke himself did not come near. We heard he was offended with some of his people for letting me know he was among the company. He said that I should be displeased with him for not coming and making some present. This was the only instance in which I was shunned in this quarter.

As it would have been impolitic to pass Manenko, or any chief, without at least showing so much respect as to call and explain the objects of our passing through the country, we waited two entire days for the return of the messengers to Manenko; and as I could not hurry matters, I went into the adjacent country to search for meat for the camp.

The country is furnished largely with forest, having occasionally open lawns covered with grass, not in tufts as in the south, but so closely planted that one can not see the soil. We came upon a man and his two wives and children, burning coarse rushes and the stalks of tsitla, growing in a brackish marsh, in order to extract a kind of salt from the ashes. They make a funnel of branches of trees, and line it with grass rope, twisted round until it is, as it were, a beehive-roof inverted. The ashes are put into water, in a calabash, and then it is allowed to percolate through the small hole in the bottom and through the grass. When this water is evaporated in the sun, it yields sufficient salt to form a relish with food. The women and children fled with precipitation, but we sat down at a distance, and allowed the man time to gain courage enough to speak. He, however, trembled excessively at the apparition before him; but when we explained that our object was to hunt game, and not men, he became calm, and called back his wives. We soon afterward came to another party on the same errand with ourselves. The man had a bow about six feet long, and iron-headed arrows about thirty inches in length; he had also wooden arrows neatly barbed, to shoot in cases where he might not be quite certain of recovering them again. We soon afterward got a zebra, and gave our hunting acquaintances such a liberal share that we soon became friends. All whom we saw that day then came with us to the encampment to beg a little meat; and as they have so little salt, I have no doubt they felt grateful for what we gave.

Sekelenke and his people, twenty-four in number, defiled past our camp carrying large bundles of dried elephants' meat. Most of them came to say good-by, and Sekelenke himself sent to say that he had gone to visit a wife living in the village of Manenko. It was a mere African manoeuvre to gain information, and not commit himself to either one line of action or another with respect to our visit. As he was probably in the party before us, I replied that it was all right, and when my people came up from Masiko I would go to my wife too. Another zebra came to our camp, and, as we had friends near, it was shot. It was the 'Equus montanus', though the country is perfectly flat, and was finely marked down to the feet, as all the zebras are in these parts.

To our first message, offering a visit of explanation to Manenko, we got an answer, with a basket of manioc roots, that we must remain where we were till she should visit us. Having waited two days already for her, other messengers arrived with orders for me to come to her. After four days of rains and negotiation, I declined going at all, and proceeded up the river to the small stream Makondo (lat. 13d 23' 12" S.), which enters the Leeba from the east, and is between twenty and thirty yards broad.

JANUARY 1ST, 1854. We had heavy rains almost every day; indeed, the rainy season had fairly set in. Baskets of the purple fruit called mawa were frequently brought to us by the villagers; not for sale, but from a belief that their chiefs would be pleased to hear that they had treated us well; we gave them pieces of meat in return.

When crossing at the confluence of the Leeba and Makondo, one of my men picked up a bit of a steel watch-chain of English manufacture, and we were informed that this was the spot where the Mambari cross in coming to Masiko. Their visits explain why Sekelenke kept his tusks so carefully. These Mambari are very enterprising merchants: when they mean to trade with a town, they deliberately begin the affair by building huts, as if they knew that little business could be transacted without a liberal allowance of time for palaver. They bring Manchester goods into the heart of Africa;

these cotton prints look so wonderful that the Makololo could not believe them to be the work of mortal hands. On questioning the Mambari they were answered that English manufactures came out of the sea, and beads were gathered on its shore. To Africans our cotton mills are fairy dreams. "How can the irons spin, weave, and print so beautifully?" Our country is like what Taprobane was to our ancestors—a strange realm of light, whence came the diamond, muslin, and peacocks; an attempt at explanation of our manufactures usually elicits the expression, "Truly ye are gods!"

When about to leave the Makondo, one of my men had dreamed that Mosantu was shut up a prisoner in a stockade: this dream depressed the spirits of the whole party, and when I came out of my little tent in the morning, they were sitting the pictures of abject sorrow. I asked if we were to be guided by dreams, or by the authority I derived from Sekeletu, and ordered them to load the boats at once; they seemed ashamed to confess their fears; the Makololo picked up courage and upbraided the others for having such superstitious views, and said this was always their way; if even a certain bird called to them, they would turn back from an enterprise, saying it was unlucky. They entered the canoes at last, and were the better of a little scolding for being inclined to put dreams before authority. It rained all the morning, but about eleven we reached the village of Sheakondo, on a small stream named Lonkonye. We sent a message to the head man, who soon appeared with two wives, bearing handsome presents of manioc: Sheakondo could speak the language of the Barotse well, and seemed awestruck when told some of the "words of God". He manifested no fear, always spoke frankly, and when he made an asseveration, did so by simply pointing up to the sky above him. The Balonda cultivate the manioc or cassava extensively; also dura, ground-nuts, beans, maize, sweet potatoes, and yams, here called "lekoto", but as yet we see only the outlying villages.

The people who came with Sheakondo to our bivouac had their teeth filed to a point by way of beautifying them, though those which were left untouched were always the whitest; they are generally tattooed in various parts, but chiefly on the abdomen: the skin is raised in small elevated cicatrices, each nearly half an inch long and a quarter of an inch in diameter, so that a number of them may constitute a star, or other device. The dark color of the skin prevents any coloring matter being deposited in these figures, but they love much to have the whole surface of their bodies anointed with a comfortable varnish of oil. In their unassisted state they depend on supplies of oil from the Palma Christi, or castor-oil plant, or from various other oliferous seeds, but they are all excessively fond of clarified butter or ox fat. Sheakondo's old wife presented some manioc roots, and then politely requested to be anointed with butter: as I had been bountifully supplied by the Makololo, I gave her as much as would suffice, and as they have little clothing, I can readily believe that she felt her comfort greatly enhanced thereby.

The favorite wife, who was also present, was equally anxious for butter. She had a profusion of iron rings on her ankles, to which were attached little pieces of sheet iron, to enable her to make a tinkling as she walked in her mincing African style; the same thing is thought pretty by our own dragoons in walking jauntingly.

We had so much rain and cloud that I could not get a single observation for either longitude or latitude for a fortnight. Yet the Leeba does not show any great rise, nor is the water in the least discolored. It is slightly black, from the number of mossy rills which fall into it. It has remarkably few birds and fish, while the Leeambye swarms with both. It is noticeable that alligators here possess more of the fear of man than in the Leeambye. The Balonda have taught them, by their poisoned arrows, to keep out of sight. We did not see one basking in the sun. The Balonda set so many little traps for birds that few appear. I observed, however, many (to me) new small birds of song on its banks. More rain has been falling in the east than here, for the Leeambye was rising fast and working against the sandy banks so vigorously that a slight yellow tinge was perceptible in it.

One of our men was bitten by a non-venomous serpent, and of course felt no harm. The Barotse concluded that this was owing to many of them being present and seeing it, as if the sight of human eyes could dissolve the poison and act as a charm.

On the 6th of January we reached the village of another female chief, named Nyamoana, who is said to be the mother of Manenko, and sister of Shinte or Kabompo, the greatest Balonda chief in this part of the country. Her people had but recently come to the present locality, and had erected only twenty huts. Her husband, Samoana, was clothed in a kilt of green and red baize, and was armed with a spear and a broadsword of antique form, about eighteen inches long and three broad. The chief and her husband were sitting on skins placed in the middle of a circle thirty paces in diameter, a little raised above the ordinary level of the ground, and having a trench round it. Outside the trench sat about a hundred persons of all ages and both sexes. The men were well armed with bows, arrows, spears, and broadswords. Beside the husband sat a rather aged woman, having a bad outward squint in the left eye. We put down our arms about forty yards off, and I walked up to the centre of the circular bench, and saluted him in the usual way by clapping the hands together in their fashion. He pointed to his wife, as much as to say, the honor belongs to her. I saluted her in the same way, and a mat having been brought, I squatted down in front of them.

The talker was then called, and I was asked who was my spokesman. Having pointed to Kolimbota, who knew their dialect best, the palaver began in due form. I explained the real objects I had in view, without any attempt to mystify or appear in any other character than my own, for I have always been satisfied that, even though there were no other considerations, the truthful way of dealing with the uncivilized is unquestionably the best. Kolimbota repeated to Nyamoana's talker what I had said to him. He delivered it all verbatim to her husband, who repeated it again to her. It was thus all rehearsed four times over, in a tone loud enough to be heard by the whole party of auditors. The response came back by the same roundabout route, beginning at the lady to her husband, etc.

After explanations and re-explanations, I perceived that our new friends were mixing up my message of peace and friendship with Makololo affairs, and stated that it was not delivered on the authority of any one less than that of their Creator, and that if the Makololo did again break His laws and attack the Balonda, the guilt would rest with the Makololo and not with me. The palaver then came to a close.

By way of gaining their confidence, I showed them my hair, which is considered a curiosity in all this region. They said, "Is that hair? It is the mane of a lion, and not hair at all." Some thought that I had made a wig of lion's mane, as they sometimes do with fibres of the "ife", and dye it black, and twist it so as to resemble a mass of their own wool. I could not return the joke by telling them that theirs was not hair, but the wool of sheep, for they have none of these in the country; and even though they had, as Herodotus remarked, "the African sheep are clothed with hair, and men's heads with wool." So I had to be content with asserting that mine was the real original hair, such as theirs would have been had it not been scorched and frizzled by the sun. In proof of what the sun could do, I compared my own bronzed face and hands, then about the same in complexion as the lighter-colored Makololo, with the white skin of my chest. They readily believed that, as they go nearly naked and fully exposed to that influence, we might be of common origin after all. Here, as every where, when heat and moisture are combined, the people are very dark, but not quite black. There is always a shade of brown in the most deeply colored. I showed my watch and pocket compass, which are considered great curiosities; but, though the lady was called on by her husband to look, she would not be persuaded to approach near enough.

These people are more superstitious than any we had yet encountered; though still only building their village, they had found time to erect two little sheds at the chief dwelling in it, in which were placed two pots having charms in them. When asked what medicine they contained, they replied, "Medicine for the Barimo;" but when I rose and looked into them, they said they were medicine for the game. Here we saw the first evidence of the existence of idolatry in the remains of an old idol at a deserted village. It was simply a human head carved on a block of wood. Certain charms mixed with red ochre and white pipe-clay are dotted over them when they are in use; and a crooked stick is used in the same way for an idol when they have no professional carver.

As the Leeba seemed still to come from the direction in which we wished to go, I was desirous of proceeding farther up with the canoes; but Nyamoana was anxious that we should allow her people to conduct us to her brother Shinte; and when I explained the advantage of water-carriage, she represented that her brother did not live near the river, and, moreover, there was a cataract in front, over which it would be difficult to convey the canoes. She was afraid, too, that the Balobale, whose country lies to the west of the river, not knowing the objects for which we had come, would kill us. To my reply that I had been so often threatened with death if I visited a new tribe that I was now more afraid of killing any one than of being killed, she rejoined that the Balobale would not kill me, but the Makololo would all be sacrificed as their enemies. This produced considerable effect on my companions, and inclined them to the plan of Nyamoana, of going to the town of her brother rather than ascending the Leeba. The arrival of Manenko herself on the scene threw so much weight into the scale on their side that I was forced to yield the point.

Manenko was a tall, strapping woman about twenty, distinguished by a profusion of ornaments and medicines hung round her person; the latter are supposed to act as charms. Her body was smeared all over with a mixture of fat and red ochre, as a protection against the weather; a necessary precaution, for, like most of the Balonda ladies, she was otherwise in a state of frightful nudity. This was not from want of clothing, for, being a chief, she might have been as well clad as any of her subjects, but from her peculiar ideas of elegance in dress. When she arrived with her husband, Sambanza, they listened for some time to the statements I was making to the people of Nyamoana, after which the husband, acting as spokesman, commenced an oration, stating the reasons for their coming, and, during every two or three seconds of the delivery, he picked up a little sand, and rubbed it on the upper part of his arms and chest. This is a common mode of salutation in Londa; and when they wish to be excessively polite, they bring a quantity of ashes or pipe-clay in a piece of skin, and, taking up handfuls, rub it on the chest and upper front part of each arm; others, in saluting, drum their ribs with their elbows; while others still touch the ground with one cheek after the other, and clap their hands. The chiefs go through the manoeuvre of rubbing the sand on the arms, but only make a feint at picking up some. When Sambanza had finished his oration, he rose up, and showed his ankles ornamented with a bundle of copper rings; had they been very heavy, they would have made him adopt a straggling walk. Some chiefs have really so many as to be forced, by the weight and size, to keep one foot apart from the other, the weight being a serious inconvenience in walking. The gentlemen like Sambanza, who wish to imitate their betters, do so in their walk; so you see men, with only a few ounces of ornament on their legs, strutting along as if they had double the number of pounds. When I smiled at Sambanza's walk, the people remarked, "That is the way in which they show off their lordship in these parts."

Manenko was quite decided in the adoption of the policy of friendship with the Makololo which we recommended; and, by way of cementing the bond, she and her counselors proposed that Kolimbota should take a wife among them. By this expedient she hoped to secure his friendship, and also accurate information as to the future intentions of the Makololo. She thought that he would visit the Balonda more frequently afterward, having the good excuse of going to see his wife; and the Makololo would never, of course, kill the villagers among whom so near a relative of one of their own children dwells. Kolimbota, I found, thought favorably of the proposition, and it afterward led to his desertion from us.

On the evening of the day in which Manenko arrived, we were delighted by the appearance of Mosantu and an imposing embassy from Masiko. It consisted of all his under-chiefs, and they brought a fine elephant's tusk, two calabashes of honey, and a large piece of blue baize, as a present. The last was intended perhaps to show me that he was a truly great chief, who had such stores of white men's goods at hand that he could afford to give presents of them; it might also be intended for Mosantu, for chiefs usually remember the servants; I gave it to him. Masiko expressed delight, by his principal men, at the return of the captives, and at the proposal of peace and alliance with the Makololo. He stated that he never sold any of his own people to the Mambari, but only captives whom his people kidnapped from small neighboring tribes. When the question was put whether his people had been in the habit of molesting the Makololo by kidnapping their servants and stealing canoes, it was admitted that two of his men, when hunting, had gone to the Makololo gardens, to see if any of their relatives were there.

As the great object in all native disputes is to get both parties to turn over a new leaf, I explained the desirableness of forgetting past feuds, accepting the present Makololo professions as genuine, and avoiding in future to give them any cause for marauding. I presented Masiko with an ox, furnished by Sekeletu as provision for ourselves. All these people are excessively fond of beef and butter, from having been accustomed to them in their youth, before the Makololo deprived them of cattle. They have abundance of game, but I am quite of their opinion that, after all, there is naught in the world equal to roast beef, and that in their love for it the English show both good taste and sound sense. The ox was intended for Masiko, but his men were very anxious to get my sanction for slaughtering it on the spot. I replied that when it went out of my hands I had no more to do with it. They, however, wished the responsibility of slaughtering it to rest with me; if I had said they might kill it, not many ounces would have remained in the morning. I would have given permission, but had nothing else to offer in return for Masiko's generosity.

We were now without any provisions except a small dole of manioc roots each evening from Nyamoana, which, when eaten raw, produce poisonous effects. A small loaf, made from nearly the last morsel of maize-meal from Libonta, was my stock, and our friends from Masiko were still more destitute; yet we all rejoiced so much at their arrival that we resolved to spend a day with them. The Barotse of our party, meeting with relatives and friends among the Barotse of Masiko, had many old tales to tell; and, after pleasant hungry converse by day, we regaled our friends with the magic lantern by night, and, in order to make the thing of use to all, we removed our camp up to the village of Nyamoana. This is a good means of arresting the attention, and conveying important facts to the minds of these people.

When erecting our sheds at the village, Manenko fell upon our friends from Masiko in a way that left no doubt on our minds but that she is a most accomplished scold. Masiko had, on a former occasion, sent to Samoana for a cloth, a common way of keeping up intercourse, and, after receiving it, sent it back, because it had the appearance of having had "witchcraft medicine" on it; this was a grave offense, and now Manenko had a good excuse for venting her spleen, the embassadors having called at her village, and slept in one of the huts without leave. If her family was to be suspected of dealing in evil charms, why were Masiko's people not to be thought guilty of leaving the same in her hut? She advanced and receded in true oratorical style, belaboring her own servants as well for allowing the offense, and, as usual in more civilized feminine lectures, she leaned over the objects of her ire, and screamed forth all their faults and failings ever since they were born, and her despair of ever seeing them become better, until they were all "killed by alligators". Masiko's people followed the plan of receiving this torrent of abuse in silence, and, as neither we nor they had any thing to eat, we parted next morning. In reference to Masiko selling slaves to the Mambari, they promised to explain the relationship which exists between even the most abject of his people and our common Father; and that no more kidnapping ought to be allowed, as he ought to give that peace and security to the smaller tribes on his eastern borders which he so much desired to obtain himself from the Makololo. We promised to return through his town when we came back from the sea-coast.

Manenko gave us some manioc roots in the morning, and had determined to carry our baggage to her uncle's, Kabompo or Shinte. We had heard a sample of what she could do with her tongue; and as neither my men nor myself had much inclination to encounter a scolding from this black Mrs. Caudle, we made ready the packages; but she came and said the men whom she had ordered for the service had not yet come; they would arrive to-morrow. Being on low and disagreeable diet, I felt annoyed at this further delay, and ordered the packages to be put into the canoes to proceed up the river without her servants; but Manenko was not to be circumvented in this way; she came forward with her people, and said her uncle would be angry if she did not carry forward the tusks and goods of Sekeletu, seized the luggage, and declared that she would carry it in spite of me. My men succumbed sooner to this petticoat government than I felt inclined to do, and left me no power; and, being unwilling to encounter her tongue, I was moving off to the canoes, when she gave me a kind explanation, and, with her hand on my shoulder, put on a motherly look, saying, "Now, my little man, just do as the rest have done." My feelings of annoyance of course vanished, and I went out to try and get some meat.

The only game to be found in these parts are the ZEBRA, the KUALATA or tahetsi ('Aigoceros equina'), kama ('Bubalus caama'), buffaloes, and the small antelope hakitenwe ('Philantomba').

The animals can be seen here only by following on their trail for many miles. Urged on by hunger, we followed that of some zebras during the greater part of the day: when within fifty yards of them, in a dense thicket, I made sure of one, but, to my infinite disgust, the gun missed fire, and off they bounded. The climate is so very damp, from daily heavy rains, that every thing becomes loaded with moisture, and the powder in the gun-nipples can not be kept dry. It is curious to mark the intelligence of the game; in districts where they are much annoyed by fire-arms, they keep out on the most open spots of country they can find, in order to have a widely-extended range of vision, and a man armed is carefully shunned. From the frequency with which I have been allowed to approach nearer without than with a gun, I believe they know the difference between safety and danger in the two cases. But here, where they are killed by the arrows of the Balonda, they select for safety the densest forest, where the arrow can not be easily shot. The variation in the selection of standing-spots during the day may, however, be owing partly to the greater heat of the sun, for here it is particularly sharp and penetrating. However accounted for, the wild animals here do select the forests by day, while those farther south generally shun these covers, and, on several occasions, I have observed there was no sunshine to cause them to seek for shade.

Chapter 16

Nyamoana's Present—Charms—Manenko's pedestrian Powers—An Idol— Balonda Arms—Rain—Hunger—Palisades—Dense Forests—Artificial Beehives—Mushrooms—Villagers lend the Roofs of their Houses—Divination and Idols—Manenko's Whims—A night Alarm—Shinte's Messengers and Present—The proper Way to approach a Village—A Merman—Enter Shinte's Town: its Appearance—Meet two half-caste Slave-traders—The Makololo scorn them—The Balonda real Negroes—Grand Reception from Shinte—His Kotla—Ceremony of Introduction—The Orators—Women—Musicians and Musical Instruments—A disagreeable Request—Private Interviews with Shinte—Give him an Ox—Fertility of Soil—Manenko's new Hut—Conversation with Shinte—Kolimbota's Proposal—Balonda's Punctiliousness—Selling Children—Kidnapping—Shinte's Offer of a Slave—Magic Lantern—Alarm of Women— Delay—Sambanza returns intoxicated—The last and greatest Proof of Shinte's Friendship.

11TH OF JANUARY, 1854. On starting this morning, Samoana (or rather Nyamoana, for the ladies are the chiefs here) presented a string of beads, and a shell highly valued among them, as an atonement for having assisted Manenko, as they thought, to vex me the day before. They seemed anxious to avert any evil which might arise from my displeasure; but having replied that I never kept my anger up all night, they were much pleased to see me satisfied. We had to cross, in a canoe, a stream which flows past the village of Nyamoana. Manenko's doctor waved some charms over her, and she took some in her hand and on her body before she ventured upon the water. One of my men spoke rather loudly when near the doctor's basket of medicines. The doctor reproved him, and always spoke in a whisper himself, glancing back to the basket as if afraid of being heard by something therein. So much superstition is quite unknown in the south, and is mentioned here to show the difference in the feelings of this new people, and the comparative want of reverence on these points among Caffres and Bechuanas.

Manenko was accompanied by her husband and her drummer; the latter continued to thump most vigorously until a heavy, drizzling mist set in and compelled him to desist. Her husband used various incantations and vociferations to drive away the rain, but down it poured incessantly, and on our Amazon went, in the very lightest marching order, and at a pace that few of the men could keep up with. Being on ox-back, I kept pretty close to our leader, and asked her why she did not clothe herself during the rain, and learned that it is not considered proper for a chief to appear effeminate. He or she must always wear the appearance of robust youth, and bear vicissitudes without wincing. My men, in admiration of her pedestrian powers, every now and then remarked, "Manenko is a soldier;" and thoroughly wet and cold, we were all glad when she proposed a halt to prepare our night's lodging on the banks of a stream.

The country through which we were passing was the same succession of forest and open lawns as formerly mentioned: the trees were nearly all evergreens, and of good, though not very gigantic size. The lawns were covered with grass, which, in thickness of crop, looked like ordinary English hay. We passed two small hamlets surrounded by gardens of maize and manioc, and near each of these I observed, for the first time, an ugly idol common in Londa—the figure of an animal, resembling an alligator, made of clay. It is formed of grass, plastered over with soft clay; two cowrie-shells are inserted as eyes, and numbers of the bristles from the tail of an elephant are stuck in about the neck. It is called a lion, though, if one were not told so, he would conclude it to be an alligator. It stood in a shed, and the Balonda pray and beat drums before it all night in cases of sickness.

Some of the men of Manenko's train had shields made of reeds, neatly woven into a square shape, about five feet long and three broad. With these, and short broadswords and sheaves of iron-headed arrows, they appeared rather ferocious. But the constant habit of wearing arms is probably only a substitute for the courage they do not possess. We always deposited our fire-arms and spears outside a village before entering it, while the Balonda, on visiting us at our encampment, always came fully armed, until we ordered them either to lay down their weapons or be off. Next day we passed through a piece of forest so dense that no one could have penetrated it without an axe. It was flooded, not by the river, but by the heavy rains which poured down every day, and kept those who had clothing constantly wet. I observed, in this piece of forest, a very strong smell of sulphureted hydrogen. This I had observed repeatedly in other parts before. I had attacks of fever of the intermittent type again and again, in consequence of repeated drenchings in these unhealthy spots.

On the 11th and 12th we were detained by incessant rains, and so heavy I never saw the like in the south. I had a little tapioca and a small quantity of Libonta meal, which I still reserved for worse times. The patience of my men under hunger was admirable; the actual want of the present is never so painful as the thought of getting nothing in the future. We thought the people of some large hamlets very niggardly and very independent of their chiefs, for they gave us and Manenko nothing, though they had large fields of maize in an eatable state around them. When she went and kindly begged some for me, they gave her five ears only. They were subjects of her uncle; and, had they been Makololo, would have been lavish in their gifts to the niece of their chief. I suspected that they were dependents of some of Shinte's principal men, and had no power to part with the maize of their masters.

Each house of these hamlets has a palisade of thick stakes around it, and the door is made to resemble the rest of the stockade; the door is never seen open; when the owner wishes to enter, he removes a stake or two, squeezes his body in, then plants them again in their places, so that an enemy coming in the night would find it difficult to discover the entrance. These palisades seem to indicate a sense of insecurity in regard to their fellow-men, for there are no wild beasts to disturb them; the bows and arrows have been nearly as efficacious in clearing the country here as guns have in the country farther south. This was a disappointment to us, for we expected a continuance of the abundance of game in the north which we found when we first came up to the confluence of the Leeba and Leeambye.

A species of the silver-tree of the Cape ('Leucodendron argenteum') is found in abundance in the parts through which we have traveled since leaving Samoana's. As it grows at a height of between two and three thousand feet above the level of the sea, on the Cape Table Mountain, and again on the northern slope of the Cashan Mountains, and here at considerably greater heights (four thousand feet), the difference of climate prevents the botanical range being considered as affording a good approximation to the altitude. The rapid flow of the Leeambye, which once seemed to me evidence of much elevation of the country from which it comes, I now found, by the boiling point of water, was fallacious.*

> * On examining this subject when I returned to Linyanti, I found that, according to Dr. Arnott, a declivity of three inches per mile gives a velocity in a smooth, straight channel of three miles an hour. The general velocity of the Zambesi is three miles and three quarters per hour, though in the rocky parts it is sometimes as much as four and a half. If, however, we make allowances for roughness of bottom, bendings of channel, and sudden descents at cataracts, and say the declivity is even seven inches per mile, those 800 miles between the east coast and the great falls would require less

than 500 feet to give the observed velocity, and the additional distance to this point would require but 150 feet of altitude more. If my observation of this altitude may be depended on, we have a steeper declivity for the Zambesi than for some other great rivers. The Ganges, for instance, is said to be at 1800 miles from its mouth only 800 feet above the level of the sea, and water requires a month to come that distance. But there are so many modifying circumstances, it is difficult to draw any reliable conclusion from the currents. The Chobe is sometimes heard of as flooded, about 40 miles above Linyanti, a fortnight before the inundation reaches that point, but it is very tortuous. The great river Magdalena falls only 500 feet in a thousand miles; other rivers much more.

The forests became more dense as we went north. We traveled much more in the deep gloom of the forest than in open sunlight. No passage existed on either side of the narrow path made by the axe. Large climbing plants entwined themselves around the trunks and branches of gigantic trees like boa constrictors, and they often do constrict the trees by which they rise, and, killing them, stand erect themselves. The bark of a fine tree found in abundance here, and called "motuia", is used by the Barotse for making fish-lines and nets, and the "molompi", so well adapted for paddles by its lightness and flexibility, was abundant. There were other trees quite new to my companions; many of them ran up to a height of fifty feet of one thickness, and without branches.

In these forests we first encountered the artificial beehives so commonly met with all the way from this to Angola. They consist of about five feet of the bark of a tree fifteen or eighteen inches in diameter. Two incisions are made right round the tree at points five feet apart, then one longitudinal slit from one of these to the other; the workman next lifts up the bark on each side of this slit, and detaches it from the trunk, taking care not to break it, until the whole comes from the tree. The elasticity of the bark makes it assume the form it had before; the slit is sewed or pegged up with wooden pins, and ends made of coiled grass-rope are inserted, one of which has a hole for the ingress of the bees in the centre, and the hive is complete. These hives are placed in a horizontal position on high trees in different parts of the forest, and in this way all the wax exported from Benguela and Loanda is collected. It is all the produce of free labor. A "piece of medicine" is tied round the trunk of the tree, and proves sufficient protection against thieves. The natives seldom rob each other, for all believe that certain medicines can inflict disease and death; and though they consider that these are only known to a few, they act on the principle that it is best to let them all alone. The gloom of these forests strengthens the superstitious feelings of the people. In other quarters, where they are not subjected to this influence, I have heard the chiefs issue proclamations to the effect that real witchcraft medicines had been placed at certain gardens from which produce had been stolen, the thieves having risked the power of the ordinary charms previously placed there.

This being the rainy season, great quantities of mushrooms were met with, and were eagerly devoured by my companions: the edible variety is always found growing out of ant-hills, and attains the diameter of the crown of a hat; they are quite white, and very good, even when eaten raw; they occupy an extensive region of the interior; some, not edible, are of a brilliant red, and others are of the same light blue as the paper used by apothecaries to put up their medicines.

There was a considerable pleasure, in spite of rain and fever, in this new scenery. The deep gloom contrasted strongly with the shadeless glare of the Kalahari, which had left an indelible impression on my memory. Though drenched day by day at this time, and for months afterward, it was long before I could believe that we were getting too much of a good thing. Nor could I look at water being thrown away without a slight, quick impression flitting across the mind that we were guilty of wasting it. Every now and then we emerged from the deep gloom into a pretty little valley, having a damp portion in the middle; which, though now filled with water, at other times contains moisture enough for wells only. These wells have shades put over them in the form of little huts.

We crossed, in canoes, a little never-failing stream, which passes by the name of Lefuje, or "the rapid". It comes from a goodly high mountain, called Monakadzi (the woman), which gladdened our eyes as it rose to our sight about twenty or thirty miles to the east of our course. It is of an oblong shape, and seemed at least eight hundred feet above the plains. The Lefuje probably derives its name from the rapid descent of the short course it has to flow from Monakadzi to the Leeba.

The number of little villages seemed about equal to the number of valleys. At some we stopped and rested, the people becoming more liberal as we advanced. Others we found deserted, a sudden panic having seized the inhabitants, though the drum of Manenko was kept beaten pretty constantly, in order to give notice of the approach of great people. When we had decided to remain for the night at any village, the inhabitants lent us the roofs of their huts, which in form resemble those of the Makololo, or a

Chinaman's hat, and can be taken off the walls at pleasure. They lifted them off, and brought them to the spot we had selected as our lodging, and, when my men had propped them up with stakes, they were then safely housed for the night. Every one who comes to salute either Manenko or ourselves rubs the upper parts of the arms and chest with ashes; those who wish to show profounder reverence put some also on the face.

We found that every village had its idols near it. This is the case all through the country of the Balonda, so that, when we came to an idol in the woods, we always knew that we were within a quarter of an hour of human habitations. One very ugly idol we passed rested on a horizontal beam placed on two upright posts. This beam was furnished with two loops of cord, as of a chain, to suspend offerings before it. On remarking to my companions that these idols had ears, but that they heard not, etc., I learned that the Balonda, and even the Barotse, believe that divination may be performed by means of these blocks of wood and clay; and though the wood itself could not hear, the owners had medicines by which it could be made to hear and give responses, so that if an enemy were approaching they would have full information. Manenko having brought us to a stand on account of slight indisposition and a desire to send forward notice of our approach to her uncle, I asked why it was necessary to send forward information of our movements, if Shinte had idols who could tell him every thing. "She did it only,"* was the reply. It is seldom of much use to show one who worships idols the folly of idolatry without giving something else as an object of adoration instead. They do not love them. They fear them, and betake themselves to their idols only when in perplexity and danger.

* *This is a curious African idiom, by which a person implies he had no particular reason for his act.*

While delayed, by Manenko's management, among the Balonda villages, a little to the south of the town of Shinte, we were well supplied by the villagers with sweet potatoes and green maize; Sambanza went to his mother's village for supplies of other food. I was laboring under fever, and did not find it very difficult to exercise patience with her whims; but it being Saturday, I thought we might as well go to the town for Sunday (15th). "No; her messenger must return from her uncle first." Being sure that the answer of the uncle would be favorable, I thought we might go on at once, and not lose two days in the same spot. "No, it is our custom;" and every thing else I could urge was answered in the genuine pertinacious lady style. She ground some meal for me with her own hands, and when she brought it told me she had actually gone to a village and begged corn for the purpose. She said this with an air as if the inference must be drawn by even a stupid white man: "I know how to manage, don't I?" It was refreshing to get food which could be eaten without producing the unpleasantness described by the Rev. John Newton, of St. Mary's, Woolnoth, London, when obliged to eat the same roots while a slave in the West Indies. The day (January 14th), for a wonder, was fair, and the sun shone, so as to allow us to dry our clothing and other goods, many of which were mouldy and rotten from the long-continued damp. The guns rusted, in spite of being oiled every evening.

During the night we were all awakened by a terrific shriek from one of Manenko's ladies. She piped out so loud and long that we all imagined she had been seized by a lion, and my men snatched up their arms, which they always place so as to be ready at a moment's notice, and ran to the rescue; but we found the alarm had been caused by one of the oxen thrusting his head into her hut and smelling her: she had put her hand on his cold, wet nose, and thought it was all over with her.

On Sunday afternoon messengers arrived from Shinte, expressing his approbation of the objects we had in view in our journey through the country, and that he was glad of the prospect of a way being opened by which white men might visit him, and allow him to purchase ornaments at pleasure. Manenko now threatened in sport to go on, and I soon afterward perceived that what now seemed to me the dilly-dallying way of this lady was the proper mode of making acquaintance with the Balonda; and much of the favor with which I was received in different places was owing to my sending forward messengers to state the object of our coming before entering each town and village. When we came in sight of a village we sat down under the shade of a tree and sent forward a man to give notice who we were and what were our objects. The head man of the village then sent out his principal men, as Shinte now did, to bid us welcome and show us a tree under which we might sleep. Before I had profited by the rather tedious teaching of Manenko, I sometimes entered a village and created unintentional alarm. The villagers would continue to look upon us with suspicion as long as we remained. Shinte sent us two large baskets of manioc and six dried fishes. His men had the skin of a monkey, called in their tongue "poluma" ('Colobus guereza'), of a jet black color, except the long mane, which is pure white: it is said to be found in the north, in the country of Matiamvo, the paramount chief of all the Balonda. We learned from them that they are in the habit of praying to their idols when unsuccessful in killing game or in any other enterprise. They behaved with reverence at our religious services. This will appear important if the reader remembers the almost total want of prayer and reverence we encountered in the south.

Our friends informed us that Shinte would be highly honored by the presence of three white men in his town at once. Two others had sent forward notice of their approach from another quarter (the west); could it be Barth or Krapf? How pleasant to meet with Europeans in such an out-of-the-way region! The rush of thoughts made me almost forget my fever. Are they of the same color as I am? "Yes; exactly so." And have the same hair? "Is that hair? we thought it was a wig; we never saw the like before; this white man must be of the sort that lives in the sea." Henceforth my men took the hint, and always sounded my praises as a true specimen of the variety of white men who live in the sea. "Only look at his hair; it is made quite straight by the sea-water!"

I explained to them again and again that, when it was said we came out of the sea, it did not mean that we came from beneath the water; but the fiction has been widely spread in the interior by the Mambari that the real white men live in the sea, and the myth was too good not to be taken advantage of by my companions; so, notwithstanding my injunctions, I believe that, when I was out of hearing, my men always represented themselves as led by a genuine merman: "Just see his hair!" If I returned from walking to a little distance, they would remark of some to whom they had been holding forth, "These people want to see your hair."

As the strangers had woolly hair like themselves, I had to give up the idea of meeting any thing more European than two half-caste Portuguese, engaged in trading for slaves, ivory, and bees'-wax.

16TH. After a short march we came to a most lovely valley about a mile and a half wide, and stretching away eastward up to a low prolongation of Monakadzi. A small stream meanders down the centre of this pleasant green glen; and on a little rill, which flows into it from the western side, stands the town of Kabompo, or, as he likes best to be called, Shinte. (Lat. 12d 37' 35" S., long. 22d 47' E.) When Manenko thought the sun was high enough for us to make a lucky entrance, we found the town embowered in banana and other tropical trees having great expansion of leaf; the streets are straight, and present a complete contrast to those of the Bechuanas, which are all very tortuous. Here, too, we first saw native huts with square walls and round roofs. The fences or walls of the courts which surround the huts are wonderfully straight, and made of upright poles a few inches apart, with strong grass or leafy bushes neatly woven between. In the courts were small plantations of tobacco, and a little solanaceous plant which the Balonda use as a relish; also sugar-cane and bananas. Many of the poles have grown again, and trees of the 'Ficus Indica' family have been planted around, in order to give to the inhabitants a grateful shade: they regard this tree with some sort of veneration as a medicine or charm. Goats were browsing about, and, when we made our appearance, a crowd of negroes, all fully armed, ran toward us as if they would eat us up; some had guns, but the manner in which they were held showed that the owners were more accustomed to bows and arrows than to white men's weapons. After surrounding and staring at us for an hour, they began to disperse.

The two native Portuguese traders of whom we had heard had erected a little encampment opposite the place where ours was about to be made. One of them, whose spine had been injured in youth—a rare sight in this country—came and visited us. I returned the visit next morning. His tall companion had that sickly yellow hue which made him look fairer than myself, but his head was covered with a crop of unmistakable wool. They had a gang of young female slaves in a chain, hoeing the ground in front of their encampment to clear it of weeds and grass; these were purchased recently in Lobale, whence the traders had now come. There were many Mambari with them, and the establishment was conducted with that military order which pervades all the arrangements of the Portuguese colonists. A drum was beaten and trumpet sounded at certain hours, quite in military fashion. It was the first time most of my men had seen slaves in chains. "They are not men," they exclaimed (meaning they are beasts), "who treat their children so."

The Balonda are real negroes, having much more wool on their heads and bodies than any of the Bechuana or Caffre tribes. They are generally very dark in color, but several are to be seen of a lighter hue; many of the slaves who have been exported to Brazil have gone from this region; but while they have a general similarity to the typical negro, I never could, from my own observation, think that our ideal negro, as seen in tobacconists' shops, is the true type. A large proportion of the Balonda, indeed, have heads somewhat elongated backward and upward, thick lips, flat noses, elongated 'ossa calces', etc., etc.; but there are also many good-looking, well-shaped heads and persons among them.

17TH, TUESDAY. We were honored with a grand reception by Shinte about eleven o'clock. Sambanza claimed the honor of presenting us, Manenko being slightly indisposed. The native Portuguese and Mambari went fully armed with guns, in order to give Shinte a salute; their drummer and trumpeter making all the noise that very old instruments would produce. The kotla, or place of audience, was about a hundred yards square, and two graceful specimens of a species of banian stood near one end; under one of these sat Shinte, on a sort of throne covered with a leopard's skin. He had on a checked jacket, and a kilt of scarlet baize edged with green; many strings of large beads hung from his neck, and his limbs were covered with iron and copper armlets and bracelets; on his head he wore a helmet made of beads woven neatly together, and crowned with a great bunch of goose-feathers. Close to him sat three lads with large sheaves of arrows over their shoulders.

When we entered the kotla, the whole of Manenko's party saluted Shinte by clapping their hands, and Sambanza did obeisance by rubbing his chest and arms with ashes. One of the trees being unoccupied, I retreated to it for the sake of the shade, and my whole party did the same. We were now about forty yards from the chief, and could see the whole ceremony. The different sections of the tribe came forward in the same way that we did, the head man of each making obeisance with ashes which he carried with him for the purpose; then came the soldiers, all armed to the teeth, running and shouting toward us, with their swords drawn, and their faces screwed up so as to appear as savage as possible, for the purpose, I thought, of trying whether they could not make us take to our heels. As we did not, they turned round toward Shinte and saluted him, then retired. When all had come and were seated, then began the curious capering usually seen in pichos. A man starts up, and imitates the most approved attitudes observed in actual fight, as throwing one javelin, receiving another on the shield, springing to one side to avoid a third, running backward or forward, leaping, etc. This over, Sambanza and the spokesman of Nyamoana stalked backward and forward in front of Shinte, and gave forth, in a loud voice, all they had been able to learn, either from myself or people, of my past history and connection with the Makololo; the return of the captives; the wish to open the country to trade; the Bible as a word from heaven; the white man's desire for the tribes to live in peace: he ought to have taught the Makololo that first, for the Balonda never attacked them, yet they had assailed the Balonda: perhaps he is fibbing, perhaps not; they rather thought he was; but as the Balonda had good hearts, and Shinte had never done harm to any one, he had better receive the white man well, and send him on his way. Sambanza was gayly attired, and, besides a profusion of beads, had a cloth so long that a boy carried it after him as a train.

Behind Shinte sat about a hundred women, clothed in their best, which happened to be a profusion of red baize. The chief wife of Shinte, one of the Matebele or Zulus, sat in front with a curious red cap on her head. During the intervals between the speeches, these ladies burst forth into a sort of plaintive ditty; but it was impossible for any of us to catch whether it was in praise of the speaker, of Shinte, or of themselves. This was the first time I had ever seen females present in a public assembly. In the south the women are not permitted to enter the kotla; and even when invited to come to a religious service there, would not enter until ordered to do so by the chief; but here they expressed approbation by clapping their hands, and laughing to different speakers; and Shinte frequently turned round and spoke to them.

A party of musicians, consisting of three drummers and four performers on the piano, went round the kotla several times, regaling us with their music. Their drums are neatly carved from the trunk of a tree, and have a small hole in the side covered with a bit of spider's web: the ends are covered with the skin of an antelope pegged on; and when they wish to tighten it, they hold it to the fire to make it contract: the instruments are beaten with the hands.

The piano, named "marimba", consists of two bars of wood placed side by side, here quite straight, but, farther north, bent round so as to resemble half the tire of a carriage-wheel; across these are placed about fifteen wooden keys, each of which is two or three inches broad, and fifteen or eighteen inches long; their thickness is regulated according to the deepness of the note required: each of the keys has a calabash beneath it; from the upper part of each a portion is cut off to enable them to embrace the bars, and form hollow sounding-boards to the keys, which also are of different sizes, according to the note required; and little drumsticks elicit the music. Rapidity of execution seems much admired among them, and the music is pleasant to the ear. In Angola the Portuguese use the marimba in their dances.

When nine speakers had concluded their orations, Shinte stood up, and so did all the people. He had maintained true African dignity of manner all the while, but my people remarked that he scarcely ever took his eyes off me for a moment. About a thousand people were present, according to my calculation, and three hundred soldiers. The sun had now become hot; and the scene ended by the Mambari discharging their guns.

18TH. We were awakened during the night by a message from Shinte, requesting a visit at a very unseasonable hour. As I was just in the sweating stage of an intermittent, and the path to the town lay through a wet valley, I declined going. Kolimbota, who knows their customs best, urged me to go; but, independent of sickness, I hated words of the night and deeds of darkness. "I was neither a hyaena nor a witch." Kolimbota thought that we ought to conform to their wishes in every thing: I thought we ought to have some choice in the matter as well, which put him into high dudgeon. However, at ten next morning we went, and were led into the courts of Shinte, the walls of which were woven rods, all very neat and high. Many trees stood within the inclosure and afforded a grateful shade. These had been planted, for we saw some recently put in, with grass wound round the trunk to protect them from the sun. The otherwise waste corners of the streets were planted with sugar-cane and bananas, which spread their large light leaves over the walls.

The Ficus Indica tree, under which we now sat, had very large leaves, but showed its relationship to the Indian banian by sending down shoots toward the ground. Shinte soon came, and appeared a man of upward of fifty-five years of age, of frank and open countenance, and about the middle height. He seemed in good humor, and said he had expected yesterday "that a man who came from the gods would have approached and talked to him." That had been my own intention in going to the reception; but when we came and saw the formidable preparations, and all his own men keeping at least forty yards off from him, I yielded to the solicitations of my men, and remained by the tree opposite to that under which he sat. His remark confirmed my previous belief that a frank, open, fearless manner is the most winning with all these Africans. I stated the object of my journey and mission, and to all I advanced the old gentleman clapped his hands in approbation. He replied through a spokesman; then all the company joined in the response by clapping of hands too.

After the more serious business was over, I asked if he had ever seen a white man before. He replied, "Never; you are the very first I have seen with a white skin and straight hair; your clothing, too, is different from any we have ever seen." They had been visited by native Portuguese and Mambari only.

On learning from some of the people that "Shinte's mouth was bitter for want of tasting ox-flesh," I presented him with an ox, to his great delight; and, as his country is so well adapted for cattle, I advised him to begin a trade in cows with the Makololo. He was pleased with the idea, and when we returned from Loanda, we found that he had profited by the hint, for he had got three, and one of them justified my opinion of the country, for it was more like a prize heifer for fatness than any we had seen in Africa. He soon afterward sent us a basket of green maize boiled, another of manioc-meal, and a small fowl. The maize shows by its size the fertility of the black soil of all the valleys here, and so does the manioc, though no manure is ever applied. We saw manioc attain a height of six feet and upward, and this is a plant which requires the very best soil.

During this time Manenko had been extremely busy with all her people in getting up a very pretty hut and court-yard, to be, as she said, her residence always when white men were brought by her along the same path. When she heard that we had given an ox to her uncle, she came forward to us with the air of one wronged, and explained that "this white man belonged to her; she had brought him here, and therefore the ox was hers, not Shinte's." She ordered her men to bring it, got it slaughtered by them, and presented her uncle with a leg only. Shinte did not seem at all annoyed at the occurrence.

19TH. I was awakened at an early hour by a messenger from Shinte; but the thirst of a raging fever being just assuaged by the bursting forth of a copious perspiration, I declined going for a few hours. Violent action of the heart all the way to the town did not predispose me to be patient with the delay which then occurred, probably on account of the divination being unfavorable: "They could not find Shinte." When I returned to bed, another message was received, "Shinte wished to say all he had to tell me at once." This was too tempting an offer, so we went, and he had a fowl ready in his hand to present, also a basket of manioc-meal, and a calabash of mead. Referring to the constantly-recurring attacks of fever, he remarked that it was the only thing which would prevent a successful issue to my journey, for he had men to guide me who knew all the paths which led to the white men. He had himself traveled far when a young man. On asking what he would recommend for the fever, "Drink plenty of the mead, and as it gets in, it will drive the fever out." It was rather strong, and I suspect he liked the remedy pretty well, even though he had no fever. He had always been a friend to Sebituane, and, now that his son Sekeletu was in his place, Shinte was not merely a friend, but a father to him; and if a son asks a favor, the father must give it. He was highly pleased with the large calabashes of clarified butter and fat which Sekeletu had sent him, and wished to detain Kolimbota, that he might send a present back to Sekeletu by his hands. This proposition we afterward discovered was Kolimbota's own, as he had heard so much about the ferocity of the tribes through which we were to pass that he wished to save his skin. It will be seen farther on that he was the only one of our party who returned with a wound.

We were particularly struck, in passing through the village, with the punctiliousness of manners shown by the Balonda. The inferiors, on meeting their superiors in the street, at once drop on their knees and rub dust on their arms and chest; they continue the salutation of clapping the hands until the great ones have passed. Sambanza knelt down in this manner till the son of Shinte had passed him.

We several times saw the woman who occupies the office of drawer of water for Shinte; she rings a bell as she passes along to give warning to all to keep out of her way; it would be a grave offense for any one to come near her, and exercise an evil influence by his presence on the drink of the chief. I suspect that offenses of the slightest character among the poor are made the pretext for selling them or their children to the Mambari. A young man of Lobale had fled into the country of Shinte, and located himself without showing himself to the chief. This was considered an offense sufficient to warrant his being seized and offered for sale while we were there. He had not reported himself, so they did not know the reason of his running away from his own chief, and that chief might accuse them of receiving a criminal. It was curious to notice the effect of the slave-trade in blunting the moral susceptibility: no chief in the south would treat a fugitive in this way. My men were horrified at the act, even though old Shinte and his council had some show of reason on their side; and both the Barotse and the Makololo declared that, if the Balonda only knew of the policy pursued by them to fugitives, but few of the discontented would remain long with Shinte. My men excited the wonder of his people by stating that every one of them had one cow at least in his possession.

Another incident, which occurred while we were here, may be mentioned, as of a character totally unknown in the south. Two children, of seven and eight years old, went out to collect firewood a short distance from their parents' home, which was a quarter of a mile from the village, and were kidnapped; the distracted parents could not find a trace of them. This happened so close to the town, where there are no beasts of prey, that we suspect some of the high men of Shinte's court were the guilty parties: they can sell them by night. The Mambari erect large huts of a square shape to stow these stolen ones in; they are well fed, but aired by night only. The frequent kidnapping from outlying hamlets explains the stockades we saw around them; the parents have no redress, for even Shinte himself seems fond of working in the dark. One night he sent for me, though I always stated I liked all my dealings to be aboveboard. When I came he presented me with a slave girl about ten years old; he said he had always been in the habit of presenting his visitors with a child. On my thanking him, and saying that I thought it wrong to take away children from their parents, that I wished him to give up this system altogether, and trade in cattle, ivory, and bees'-wax, he urged that she was "to be a child" to bring me water, and that a great man ought to have a child for the purpose, yet I had none. As I replied that I had four children, and should be very sorry if my chief were to take my little girl and give her away, and that I would prefer this child to remain and carry water for her own mother, he thought I was dissatisfied with her size, and sent for one a head taller; after many explanations of our abhorrence of slavery, and how displeasing it must be to God to see his children selling one another, and giving each other so much grief as this child's mother must feel, I declined her also. If I could have taken her into my family for the purpose of instruction, and then returned her as a free woman, according to a promise I should have made to the parents, I might have done so; but to take her away, and probably never be able to secure her return, would have produced no good effect on the minds of the Balonda; they would not then have seen evidence of our hatred to slavery, and the kind attentions of my friends would, as it almost always does in similar cases, have turned the poor thing's head. The difference in position between them and us is as great as between the lowest and highest in England, and we know the effects of sudden elevation on wiser heads than hers, whose owners had not been born to it.

Shinte was most anxious to see the pictures of the magic lantern; but fever had so weakening an effect, and I had such violent action of the heart, with buzzing in the ears, that I could not go for several days; when I did go for the purpose, he had his principal men and the same crowd of court beauties near him as at the reception. The first picture exhibited was Abraham about to slaughter his son Isaac; it was shown as large as life, and the uplifted knife was in the act of striking the lad; the Balonda men remarked that the picture was much more like a god than the things of wood or clay they worshiped. I explained that this man was the first of a race to whom God had given the Bible we now held, and that among his children our Savior appeared. The ladies listened with silent awe; but, when I moved the slide, the uplifted dagger moving toward them, they thought it was to be sheathed in their bodies instead of Isaac's. "Mother! mother!" all shouted at once, and off they rushed helter-skelter, tumbling pell-mell over each other, and over the little idol-huts and tobacco-bushes: we could not get one of them back again. Shinte, however, sat bravely through the whole, and afterward examined the instrument with interest. An explanation was always added after each time of showing its powers, so that no one should imagine there was aught supernatural in it; and had Mr. Murray, who kindly brought it from England, seen its popularity among both Makololo and Balonda, he would have been gratified with the direction his generosity then took. It was the only mode of instruction I was ever pressed to repeat. The people came long distances for the express purpose of seeing the objects and hearing the explanations.

One can not get away quickly from these chiefs; they like to have the honor of strangers residing in their villages. Here we had an additional cause of delay in frequent rains; twenty-four hours never elapsed without heavy showers; every thing is affected by the dampness; surgical instruments become all rusty, clothing mildewed, and shoes mouldy; my little tent was now so rotten and so full of small holes that every smart shower caused a fine mist to descend on my blanket, and made me fain to cover the head with it. Heavy dews lay on every thing in the morning, even inside the tent;

there is only a short time of sunshine in the afternoon, and even that is so interrupted by thunder-showers that we can not dry our bedding.

The winds coming from the north always bring heavy clouds and rain; in the south, the only heavy rains noticed are those which come from the northeast or east. The thermometer falls as low as 72 Degrees when there is no sunshine, though, when the weather is fair, the protected thermometer generally rises as high as 82 Degrees, even in the mornings and evenings.

24TH. We expected to have started to-day, but Sambanza, who had been sent off early in the morning for guides, returned at midday without them, and drunk. This was the first case of real babbling intoxication we had seen in this region. The boyaloa, or beer of the country, has more of a stupefying than exciting nature; hence the beer-bibbers are great sleepers; they may frequently be seen lying on their faces sound asleep. This peculiarity of posture was ascribed, by no less an authority than Aristotle, to wine, while those who were sent asleep by beer were believed "to lie upon their backs."

Sambanza had got into a state of inebriation from indulging in mead, similar to that which Shinte presented to us, which is much more powerful than boyaloa. As far as we could collect from his incoherent sentences, Shinte had said the rain was too heavy for our departure, and the guides still required time for preparation. Shinte himself was busy getting some meal ready for my use in the journey. As it rained nearly all day, it was no sacrifice to submit to his advice and remain. Sambanza staggered to Manenko's hut; she, however, who had never promised "to love, honor, and obey him," had not been "nursing her wrath to keep it warm," so she coolly bundled him into the hut, and put him to bed.

As the last proof of friendship, Shinte came into my tent, though it could scarcely contain more than one person, looked at all the curiosities, the quicksilver, the looking-glass, books, hair-brushes, comb, watch, etc., etc., with the greatest interest; then closing the tent, so that none of his own people might see the extravagance of which he was about to be guilty, he drew out from his clothing a string of beads, and the end of a conical shell, which is considered, in regions far from the sea, of as great value as the Lord Mayor's badge is in London. He hung it round my neck, and said, "There, now you HAVE a proof of my friendship."

My men informed me that these shells are so highly valued in this quarter, as evidences of distinction, that for two of them a slave might be bought, and five would be considered a handsome price for an elephant's tusk worth ten pounds. At our last interview old Shinte pointed out our principal guide, Intemese, a man about fifty, who was, he said, ordered to remain by us till we should reach the sea; that I had now left Sekeletu far behind, and must henceforth look to Shinte alone for aid, and that it would always be most cheerfully rendered. This was only a polite way of expressing his wishes for my success. It was the good words only of the guides which were to aid me from the next chief, Katema, on to the sea; they were to turn back on reaching him; but he gave a good supply of food for the journey before us, and, after mentioning as a reason for letting us go even now that no one could say we had been driven away from the town, since we had been several days with him, he gave a most hearty salutation, and we parted with the wish that God might bless him.

Chapter 17

Leave Shinte—Manioc Gardens—Mode of preparing the poisonous kind—Its general Use—Presents of Food—Punctiliousness of the Balonda— Their Idols and Superstition—Dress of the Balonda—Villages beyond Lonaje—Cazembe—Our Guides and the Makololo—Night Rains—Inquiries for English cotton Goods—Intemese's Fiction—Visit from an old Man—Theft—Industry of our Guide—Loss of Pontoon—Plains covered with Water—Affection of the Balonda for their Mothers—A Night on an Island—The Grass on the Plains—Source of the Rivers—Loan of the Roofs of Huts—A Halt—Fertility of the Country through which the Lokalueje flows—Omnivorous Fish—Natives' Mode of catching them— The Village of a Half-brother of Katema, his Speech and Present—Our Guide's Perversity—Mozenkwa's pleasant Home and Family—Clear Water of the flooded Rivers—A Messenger from Katema—Quendende's Village: his Kindness—Crop of Wool—Meet People from the Town of Matiamvo—Fireside Talk—Matiamvo's Character and Conduct—Presentation at Katema's Court: his Present, good Sense, and Appearance—Interview on the following Day—Cattle—A Feast and a Makololo Dance—Arrest of a Fugitive— Dignified old Courtier—Katema's lax Government—Cold Wind from the North—Canaries and other singing Birds—Spiders, their Nests and Webs—Lake Dilolo—Tradition—Sagacity of Ants.

26TH. Leaving Shinte, with eight of his men to aid in carrying our luggage, we passed, in a northerly direction, down the lovely valley on which the town stands, then went a little to the west through pretty open forest, and slept at a village of Balonda. In the morning we had a fine range of green hills, called Saloisho, on our right, and were informed that they were rather thickly inhabited by the people of Shinte, who worked in iron, the ore of which abounds in these hills.

The country through which we passed possessed the same general character of flatness and forest that we noticed before. The soil is dark, with a tinge of red—in some places it might be called red—and appeared very fertile. Every valley contained villages of twenty or thirty huts, with gardens of manioc, which here is looked upon as the staff of life. Very little labor is required for its cultivation. The earth is drawn up into oblong beds, about three feet broad and one in height, and in these are planted pieces of the manioc stalk, at four feet apart. A crop of beans or ground-nuts is sown between them, and when these are reaped the land around the manioc is cleared of weeds. In from ten to eighteen months after planting, according to the quality of the soil, the roots are fit for food. There is no necessity for reaping soon, as the roots do not become bitter and dry until after three years. When a woman takes up the roots, she thrusts a piece or two of the upper stalks into the hole she has made, draws back the soil, and a new crop is thereby begun. The plant grows to a height of six feet, and every part of it is useful: the leaves may be cooked as a vegetable. The roots are from three to four inches in diameter, and from twelve to eighteen inches long.

There are two varieties of the manioc or cassava—one sweet and wholesome, the other bitter and containing poison, but much more speedy in its growth than the former. This last property causes its perpetuation. When we reached the village of Kapende, on the banks of the rivulet Lonaje, we were presented with so much of the poisonous kind that we were obliged to leave it. To get rid of the poison, the people place it four days in a pool of water. It then becomes partially decomposed, and is taken out, stripped of its skin, and exposed to the sun. When dried, it is easily pounded into a fine white meal, closely resembling starch, which has either a little of the peculiar taste arising from decomposition, or no more flavor than starch. When intended to be used as food, this meal is stirred into boiling water: they put in as much as can be moistened, one man holding the vessel and the other stirring the porridge with all his might. This is the common mess of the country. Though hungry, we could just manage to swallow it with the aid of a little honey, which I shared with my men as long as it lasted. It is very unsavory (Scottice: wersh); and no matter how much one may eat, two hours afterward he is as hungry as ever. When less meal is employed, the mess is exactly like a basin of starch in the hands of a laundress; and if the starch were made from diseased potatoes, some idea might be formed of the Balonda porridge, which hunger alone forced us to eat. Santuru forbade his nobles to eat it, as it caused coughing and expectoration.

Our chief guide, Intemese, sent orders to all the villages around our route that Shinte's friends must have abundance of provisions. Our progress was impeded by the time requisite for communicating the chief's desire and consequent preparation of meal. We received far more food from Shinte's people than from himself. Kapende, for instance, presented two large baskets of meal, three of manioc roots steeped and dried in the sun and ready to be converted into flour, three fowls, and seven eggs, with three smoke-dried fishes; and others gave with similar liberality. I gave to the head men small bunches of my stock of beads, with an apology that we were now on our way to the market for these goods. The present was always politely received.

We had an opportunity of observing that our guides had much more etiquette than any of the tribes farther south. They gave us food, but would not partake of it when we had cooked it, nor would they eat their own food in our presence. When it was cooked they retired into a thicket and ate their porridge; then all stood up, and clapped their hands, and praised Intemese for it. The Makololo, who are accustomed to the most free and easy manners, held out handfuls of what they had cooked to any of the Balonda near, but they refused to taste. They are very punctilious in their manners to each other. Each hut has its own fire, and when it goes out they make it afresh for themselves rather than take it from a neighbor. I believe much of this arises from superstitious fears. In the deep, dark forests near each village, as already mentioned, you see idols intended to represent the human head or a lion, or a crooked stick smeared with medicine, or simply a small pot of medicine in a little shed, or miniature huts with little mounds of earth in them. But in the darker recesses we meet with human faces cut in the bark of trees, the outlines of which, with the beards, closely resemble those seen on Egyptian monuments. Frequent cuts are made on the trees along all the paths, and offerings of small pieces of manioc roots or ears of maize are placed on branches. There are also to be seen every few miles heaps of sticks, which are treated in cairn fashion, by every one throwing a small branch to the heap in passing; or a few sticks are placed on the path, and each passer-by turns from his course, and forms a sudden bend in the road to one side. It seems as if their minds were ever in doubt and dread in these gloomy recesses of the forest, and that they were striving to propitiate, by their offerings, some superior beings residing there.

The dress of the Balonda men consists of the softened skins of small animals, as the jackal or wild cat, hung before and behind from a girdle round the loins. The dress of the women is of a nondescript character; but they were not immodest. They stood before us as perfectly unconscious of any indecorum as we could be with our clothes on. But, while ignorant of their own deficiency, they could not maintain their gravity at the sight of the nudity of my men behind. Much to the annoyance of my companions, the young girls laughed outright whenever their backs were turned to them.

After crossing the Lonaje, we came to some pretty villages, embowered, as the negro villages usually are, in bananas, shrubs, and manioc, and near the banks of the Leeba we formed our encampment in a nest of serpents, one of which bit one of our men, but the wound was harmless. The people of the surrounding villages presented us with large quantities of food, in obedience to the mandate of Shinte, without expecting any equivalent. One village had lately been transferred hither from the country of Matiamvo. They, of course, continue to acknowledge him as paramount chief; but the frequent instances which occur of people changing from one part of the country to another, show that the great chiefs possess only a limited power. The only peculiarity we observed in these people is the habit of plaiting the beard into a three-fold cord.

The town of the Balonda chief Cazembe was pointed out to us as lying to the N.E. and by E. from the town of Shinte, and great numbers of people in this quarter have gone thither for the purpose of purchasing copper anklets, made at Cazembe's, and report the distance to be about five days' journey. I made inquiries of some of the oldest inhabitants of the villages at which we were staying respecting the visit of Pereira and Lacerda to that town. An old gray-headed man replied that they had often heard of white men before, but never had seen one, and added that one had come to Cazembe when our informant was young, and returned again without entering this part of the country. The people of Cazembe are Balonda or Baloi, and his country has been termed Londa, Lunda, or Lui, by the Portuguese.

It was always difficult to get our guides to move away from a place. With the authority of the chief, they felt as comfortable as king's messengers could, and were not disposed to forego the pleasure of living at free quarters. My Makololo friends were but ill drilled as yet; and since they had never left their own country before, except for purposes of plunder, they did not take readily to the peaceful system we now meant to follow. They either spoke too imperiously to strangers, or, when reproved for that, were disposed to follow the dictation of every one we met. When Intemese, our guide, refused to stir toward the Leeba on the 31st of January, they would make no effort to induce him to go; but, having ordered them to get ready, Intemese saw the preparations, and soon followed the example. It took us about four hours to cross the Leeba, which is considerably smaller here than where we left it—indeed, only about a hundred yards wide. It has the same dark mossy hue. The villagers lent us canoes to effect our passage; and, having gone to a village about two miles beyond the river, I had the satisfaction of getting observations for both longitude and latitude—for the former, the distance between Saturn and the Moon, and for the latter a meridian altitude of Canopus. Long. 22d 57' E., lat. 12d 6' 6" S.

These were the only opportunities I had of ascertaining my whereabouts in this part of Londa. Again and again did I take out the instruments, and, just as all was right, the stars would be suddenly obscured by clouds. I had never observed so great an amount of cloudiness in any part of the south country; and as for the rains, I believe that years at Kolobeng would not have made my little tent so rotten and thin as one month had done in Londa.

I never observed in the south the heavy night and early morning rains we had in this country. They often continued all night, then became heavier about an hour before dawn. Or if fair during the night, as day drew nigh, an extremely heavy, still, pouring rain set in without warning. Five out of every six days we had this pouring rain, at or near break of day, for months together; and it soon beat my tent so thin, that a mist fell through on my face and made every thing damp. The rains were occasionally, but not always, accompanied with very loud thunder.

FEBRUARY 1ST. This day we had a fine view of two hills called Piri (Peeri), meaning "two", on the side of the river we had left. The country there is named Mokwankwa. And there Intemese informed us one of Shinte's children was born, when he was in his progress southward from the country of Matiamvo. This part of the country would thus seem not to have been inhabited by the people of Shinte at any very remote period. He told me himself that he had come into his present country by command of Matiamvo.

Here we were surprised to hear English cotton cloth much more eagerly inquired after than beads and ornaments. They are more in need of clothing than the Bechuana tribes living adjacent to the Kalahari Desert, who have plenty of skins for the purpose. Animals of all kinds are rare here, and a very small piece of calico is of great value.

In the midst of the heavy rain, which continued all the morning, Intemese sent to say he was laid up with pains in the stomach, and must not be disturbed; but when it cleared up, about eleven, I saw our friend walking off to the village, and talking with a very loud voice. On reproaching him for telling an untruth, he turned it off with a laugh by saying he really had a complaint in his stomach, which I might cure by slaughtering one of the oxen and allowing him to eat beef. He was evidently reveling in the abundance of good food the chief's orders brought us; and he did not feel the shame I did when I gave a few beads only in return for large baskets of meal.

A very old man visited us here with a present of maize: like the others, he had never before seen a white man, and, when conversing with him, some of the young men remarked that they were the true ancients, for they had now seen more wonderful things than their forefathers.

One of Intemese's men stole a fowl given me by a lady of the village. When charged with the theft, every one of Intemese's party vociferated his innocence and indignation at being suspected, continuing their loud asseverations and gesticulations for some minutes. One of my men, Loyanke, went off to the village, brought the lady who had presented the fowl to identify it, and then pointed to the hut in which it was hidden. The

Balonda collected round him, evincing great wrath; but Loyanke seized his battle-axe in the proper manner for striking, and, placing himself on a little hillock, soon made them moderate their tones. Intemese then called on me to send one of my people to search the huts if I suspected his people. The man sent soon found it, and brought it out, to the confusion of Intemese and the laughter of our party. This incident is mentioned to show that the greater superstition which exists here does not lead to the practice of the virtues. We never met an instance like this of theft from a white man among the Makololo, though they complain of the Makalaka as addicted to pilfering. The honesty of the Bakwains has been already noticed. Probably the estimation in which I was held as a public benefactor, in which character I was not yet known to the Balonda, may account for the sacredness with which my property was always treated before. But other incidents which happened subsequently showed, as well as this, that idolaters are not so virtuous as those who have no idols.

As the people on the banks of the Leeba were the last of Shinte's tribe over which Intemese had power, he was naturally anxious to remain as long as possible. He was not idle, but made a large wooden mortar and pestle for his wife during our journey. He also carved many wooden spoons and a bowl; then commenced a basket; but as what he considered good living was any thing but agreeable to us, who had been accustomed to milk and maize, we went forward on the 2d without him. He soon followed, but left our pontoon, saying it would be brought by the head man of the village. This was a great loss, as we afterward found; it remained at this village more than a year, and when we returned a mouse had eaten a hole in it.

We entered on an extensive plain beyond the Leeba, at least twenty miles broad, and covered with water, ankle deep in the shallowest parts. We deviated somewhat from our N.W. course by the direction of Intemese, and kept the hills Piri nearly on our right during a great part of the first day, in order to avoid the still more deeply flooded plains of Lobale (Luval?) on the west. These, according to Intemese, are at present impassable on account of being thigh deep. The plains are so perfectly level that rain-water, which this was, stands upon them for months together. They were not flooded by the Leeba, for that was still far within its banks. Here and there, dotted over the surface, are little islands, on which grow stunted date-bushes and scraggy trees. The plains themselves are covered with a thick sward of grass, which conceals the water, and makes the flats appear like great pale yellow-colored prairie-lands, with a clear horizon, except where interrupted here and there by trees. The clear rain-water must have stood some time among the grass, for great numbers of lotus-flowers were seen in full blow; and the runs of water tortoises and crabs were observed; other animals also, which prey on the fish that find their way to the plains.

The continual splashing of the oxen keeps the feet of the rider constantly wet, and my men complain of the perpetual moisture of the paths by which we have traveled in Londa as softening their horny soles. The only information we can glean is from Intemese, who points out the different localities as we pass along, and among the rest "Mokala a Mama", his "mamma's home". It was interesting to hear this tall gray-headed man recall the memories of boyhood. All the Makalaka children cleave to the mother in cases of separation, or removal from one part of the country to another. This love for mothers does not argue superior morality in other respects, or else Intemese has forgotten any injunctions his mamma may have given him not to tell lies. The respect, however, with which he spoke of her was quite characteristic of his race. The Bechuanas, on the contrary, care nothing for their mothers, but cling to their fathers, especially if they have any expectation of becoming heirs to their cattle. Our Bakwain guide to the lake, Rachosi, told me that his mother lived in the country of Sebituane, but, though a good specimen of the Bechuanas, he laughed at the idea of going so far as from the Lake Ngami to the Chobe merely for the purpose of seeing her. Had he been one of the Makalaka, he never would have parted from her.

We made our beds on one of the islands, and were wretchedly supplied with firewood. The booths constructed by the men were but sorry shelter, for the rain poured down without intermission till midday. There is no drainage for the prodigious masses of water on these plains, except slow percolation into the different feeders of the Leeba, and into that river itself. The quantity of vegetation has prevented the country from becoming furrowed by many rivulets or "nullahs". Were it not so remarkably flat, the drainage must have been effected by torrents, even in spite of the matted vegetation.

That these extensive plains are covered with grasses only, and the little islands with but scraggy trees, may be accounted for by the fact, observable every where in this country, that, where water stands for any length of time, trees can not live. The want of speedy drainage destroys them, and injures the growth of those that are planted on the islands, for they have no depth of earth not subjected to the souring influence of the stagnant water. The plains of Lobale, to the west of these, are said to be much more extensive than any we saw, and their vegetation possesses similar peculiarities. When the stagnant rain-water has all soaked in, as must happen during the months in which there is no rain, travelers are even put to straits for want of water. This is stated on native testimony; but I can very well believe that level plains, in which neither wells nor gullies are met with, may, after the dry season, present the opposite extreme to what we witnessed. Water, however, could always be got by digging, a proof of which we had on our return when brought to a stand on this very plain by severe fever: about twelve miles from the Kasai my men dug down a few feet, and found an abundant supply; and we saw on one of the islands the garden of a man who, in the dry season, had drunk water from a well in like manner. Plains like these can not be inhabited while the present system of cultivation lasts. The population is not yet so very large as to need them. They find garden-ground enough on the gentle slopes at the sides of the rivulets, and possess no cattle to eat off the millions of acres of fine hay we were now wading through. Any one who has visited the Cape Colony will understand me when I say that these immense crops resemble sown grasses more than the tufty vegetation of the south.

I would here request the particular attention of the reader to the phenomena these periodically deluged plains present, because they have a most important bearing on the physical geography of a very large portion of this country. The plains of Lobale, to the west of this, give rise to a great many streams, which unite, and form the deep, never-failing Chobe. Similar extensive flats give birth to the Loeti and Kasai, and, as we shall see further on, all the rivers of an extensive region owe their origin to oozing bogs, and not to fountains.

When released from our island by the rain ceasing, we marched on till we came to a ridge of dry inhabited land in the N.W. The inhabitants, according to custom, lent us the roofs of some huts to save the men the trouble of booth-making. I suspect that the story in Park's "Travels", of the men lifting up the hut to place it on the lion, referred to the roof only. We leave them for the villagers to replace at their leisure. No payment is expected for the use of them. By night it rained so copiously that all our beds were flooded from below; and from this time forth we always made a furrow round each booth, and used the earth to raise our sleeping-places. My men turned out to work in the wet most willingly; indeed, they always did. I could not but contrast their conduct with that of Intemese. He was thoroughly imbued with the slave spirit, and lied on all occasions without compunction. Untruthfulness is a sort of refuge for the weak and oppressed. We expected to move on the 4th, but he declared that we were so near Katema's, if we did not send forward to apprise that chief of our approach, he would certainly impose a fine. It rained the whole day, so we were reconciled to the delay; but on Sunday, the 5th, he let us know that we were still two days distant from Katema. We unfortunately could not manage without him, for the country was so deluged, we should have been brought to a halt before we went many miles by some deep valley, every one of which was full of water.

Intemese continued to plait his basket with all his might, and would not come to our religious service. He seemed to be afraid of our incantations, but was always merry and jocular.

6TH. Soon after starting we crossed a branch of the Lokalueje by means of a canoe, and in the afternoon passed over the main stream by a like conveyance. The former, as is the case with all branches of rivers in this country, is called nyuana Kalueje (child of the Kalueje). Hippopotami exist in the Lokalueje, so it may be inferred to be perennial, as the inhabitants asserted. We can not judge of the size of the stream from what we now saw. It had about forty yards of deep, fast-flowing water, but probably not more than half that amount in the dry season. Besides these, we crossed numerous feeders in our N.N.W. course, and, there being no canoes, got frequently wet in the course of the day. The oxen in some places had their heads only above water, and the stream, flowing over their backs, wetted our blankets, which we used as saddles. The arm-pit was the only safe spot for carrying the watch, for there it was preserved from rains above and waters below. The men on foot crossed these gullies holding up their burdens at arms' length.

The Lokalueje winds from northeast to southwest into the Leeba. The country adjacent to its banks is extremely fine and fertile, with here and there patches of forest or clumps of magnificent trees. The villagers through whose gardens we passed continue to sow and reap all the year round. The grains, as maize, lotsa ('Pennisetum typhoideum'), lokesh or millet, are to be seen at all stages of their growth—some just ripe, while at this time the Makololo crops are not half grown. My companions, who have a good idea of the different qualities of soils, expressed the greatest admiration of the agricultural capabilities of the whole of Londa, and here they were loud in their praises of the pasturage. They have an accurate idea of the varieties of grasses best adapted for different kinds of stock, and lament because here there are no cows to feed off the rich green crop, which at this time imparts special beauty to the landscape.

Great numbers of the omnivorous feeding fish, 'Glanis siluris', or mosala, spread themselves over the flooded plains, and, as the waters retire, try to find their way back again to the rivers. The Balonda make earthen dikes and hedges across the outlets of the retreating waters, leaving only small spaces through which the chief part of the water flows. In these open spaces they plant creels, similar in shape to our own, into which the fish can enter, but can not return. They secure large quantities of fish in this way, which, when smoke-dried, make a good relish for their otherwise insipid food. They use also a weir of mats made of reeds sewed together, with but half an inch between each. Open spaces are left for the insertion of the creels as before.

In still water, a fish-trap is employed of the same shape and plan as the common round wire mouse-trap, which has an opening surrounded with wires pointing inward. This is made of reeds and supple wands, and food is placed inside to attract the fish.

Besides these means of catching fish, they use a hook of iron without a barb; the point is bent inward instead, so as not to allow the fish to escape. Nets are not so common as in the Zouga and Leeambye, but they kill large quantities of fishes by means of the bruised leaves of a shrub, which may be seen planted beside every village in the country.

On the 7th we came to the village of Soana Molopo, a half-brother of Katema, a few miles beyond the Lokalueje. When we went to visit him, we found him sitting with about one hundred men. He called on Intemese to give some account of us, though no doubt it had been done in private before. He then pronounced the following sentences: "The journey of the white man is very proper, but Shinte has disturbed us by showing the path to the Makololo who accompany him. He ought to have taken them through the country without showing them the towns. We are afraid of the Makololo." He then gave us a handsome present of food, and seemed perplexed by my sitting down familiarly, and giving him a few of our ideas. When we left, Intemese continued busily imparting an account of all we had given to Shinte and Masiko, and instilling the hope that Soana Molopo might obtain as much as they had received. Accordingly, when we expected to move on the morning of the 8th, we got some hints about the ox which Soana Molopo expected to eat, but we recommended him to get the breed of cattle for himself, seeing his country was so well adapted for rearing stock. Intemese also refused to move; he, moreover, tried to frighten us into parting with an ox by saying that Soana Molopo would send forward a message that we were a marauding party; but we packed up and went on without him. We did not absolutely need him, but he was useful in preventing the inhabitants of secluded villages from betaking themselves to flight. We wished to be on good terms with all, and therefore put up with our guide's peccadilloes. His good word respecting us had considerable influence, and he was always asked if we had behaved ourselves like men on the way. The Makololo are viewed as great savages, but Intemese could not justly look with scorn on them, for he has the mark of a large gash on his arm, got in fighting; and he would never tell the cause of battle, but boasted of his powers as the Makololo do, till asked about a scar on his back, betokening any thing but bravery.

Intemese was useful in cases like that of Monday, when we came upon a whole village in a forest enjoying their noonday nap. Our sudden appearance in their midst so terrified them that one woman nearly went into convulsions from fear. When they saw and heard Intemese, their terror subsided.

As usual, we were caught by rains after leaving Soana Molopo's, and made our booths at the house of Mozinkwa, a most intelligent and friendly man belonging to Katema. He had a fine large garden in cultivation, and well hedged round. He had made the walls of his compound, or court-yard, of branches of the banian, which, taking root, had grown to be a live hedge of that tree. Mozinkwa's wife had cotton growing all round her premises, and several plants used as relishes to the insipid porridge of the country. She cultivated also the common castor-oil plant, and a larger shrub ('Jatropha curcas'), which also yields a purgative oil. Here, however, the oil is used for anointing the heads and bodies alone. We saw in her garden likewise the Indian bringalls, yams, and sweet potatoes. Several trees were planted in the middle of the yard, and in the deep shade they gave stood the huts of his fine family. His children, all by one mother, very black, but comely to view, were the finest negro family I ever saw. We were much pleased with the frank friendship and liberality of this man and his wife. She asked me to bring her a cloth from the white man's country; but, when we returned, poor Mozinkwa's wife was in her grave, and he, as is the custom, had abandoned trees, garden, and huts to ruin. They can not live on a spot where a favorite wife has died, probably because unable to bear the remembrance of the happy times they have spent there, or afraid to remain in a spot where death has once visited the establishment. If ever the place is revisited, it is to pray to her, or make some offering. This feeling renders any permanent village in the country impossible.

We learned from Mozinkwa that Soana Molopo was the elder brother of Katema, but that he was wanting in wisdom; and Katema, by purchasing cattle and receiving in a kind manner all the fugitives who came to him, had secured the birthright to himself, so far as influence in the country is concerned. Soana's first address to us did not savor much of African wisdom.

FRIDAY, 10TH. On leaving Mozinkwa's hospitable mansion we crossed another stream, about forty yards wide, in canoes. While this tedious process was going on, I was informed that it is called the Mona-Kalueje, or brother of Kalueje, as it flows into that river; that both the Kalueje and Livoa flow into the Leeba; and that the Chifumadze, swollen by the Lotembwa, is a feeder of that river also, below the point where we lately crossed it. It may be remarked here that these rivers were now in flood, and that the water was all perfectly clear. The vegetation on the banks is so thickly planted that the surface of the earth is not abraded by the torrents. The grass is laid flat, and forms a protection to the banks, which are generally a stiff black loam. The fact of canoes being upon them shows that, though not large, they are not like the southern rivulets, which dry up during most of the year, and render canoes unnecessary.

As we were crossing the river we were joined by a messenger from Katema, called Shakatwala. This person was a sort of steward or factotum to his chief. Every chief has one attached to his person, and, though generally poor, they are invariably men of great shrewdness and ability. They act the part of messengers on all important occasions, and possess considerable authority in the chief's household. Shakatwala informed us that Katema had not received precise information about us, but if we were peaceably disposed, as he loved strangers, we were to come to his town. We proceeded forthwith, but were turned aside, by the strategy of our friend Intemese, to the village of Quendende, the father-in-law of Katema. This fine old man was so very polite that we did not regret being obliged to spend Sunday at his village. He expressed his pleasure at having a share in the honor of a visit as well as Katema, though it seemed to me that the conferring that pleasure required something like a pretty good stock of impudence, in leading twenty-seven men through the country without the means of purchasing food. My men did a little business for themselves in the begging line; they generally commenced every interview with new villagers by saying "I have come from afar; give me something to eat." I forbade this at first, believing that, as the Makololo had a bad name, the villagers gave food from fear. But, after some time, it was evident that in many cases maize and manioc were given from pure generosity. The first time I came to this conclusion was at the house of Mozinkwa; scarcely any one of my men returned from it without something in his hand; and as they protested they had not begged, I asked himself, and found that it was the case, and that he had given spontaneously. In other parts the chiefs attended to my wants, and the common people gave liberally to my men. I presented some of my razors and iron spoons to different head men, but my men had nothing to give; yet every one tried to appropriate an individual in each village as "Molekane", or comrade, and the villagers often assented; so, if the reader remembers the molekane system of the Mopato, he may perceive that those who presented food freely would expect the Makololo to treat them in like manner, should they ever be placed in similar circumstances. Their country is so fertile that they are in no want of food themselves; however, their generosity was remarkable; only one woman refused to give some of my men food, but her husband calling out to her to be more liberal, she obeyed, scolding all the while.

In this part of the country, buffaloes, elands, koodoos, and various antelopes are to be found, but we did not get any, as they are exceedingly wary from being much hunted. We had the same woodland and meadow as before, with here and there pleasant negro villages; and being all in good health, could enjoy the fine green scenery.

Quendende's head was a good specimen of the greater crop of wool with which the negroes of Londa are furnished. The front was parted in the middle, and plaited into two thick rolls, which, falling down behind the ears, reached the shoulders; the rest was collected into a large knot, which lay on the nape of the neck. As he was an intelligent man, we had much conversation together: he had just come from attending the funeral of one of his people, and I found that the great amount of drum-beating which takes place on these occasions was with the idea that the Barimo, or spirits, could be drummed to sleep. There is a drum in every village, and we often hear it going from sunset to sunrise. They seem to look upon the departed as vindictive beings, and, I suspect, are more influenced by fear than by love. In beginning to speak on religious subjects with those who have never heard of Christianity, the great fact of the Son of God having come down from heaven to die for us is the prominent theme. No fact more striking can be mentioned. "He actually came to men. He himself told us about his Father, and the dwelling-place whither he has gone. We have his words in this book, and he really endured punishment in our stead from pure love," etc. If this fails to interest them, nothing else will succeed.

We here met with some people just arrived from the town of Matiamvo (Muata yanvo), who had been sent to announce the death of the late chieftain of that name. Matiamvo is the hereditary title, muata meaning lord or chief. The late Matiamvo seems, from the report of these men, to have become insane, for he is said to have sometimes indulged the whim of running a muck in the town and beheading whomsoever he met, until he had quite a heap of human heads. Matiamvo explained this conduct by saying that his people were too many, and he wanted to diminish them. He had absolute power of life and death. On inquiring whether human sacrifices were still made, as in the time of Pereira, at Cazembe's, we were informed that these had never been so common as was represented to Pereira, but that it occasionally happened, when certain charms were needed by the chief, that a man was slaughtered for the sake of some part of his body. He added that he hoped the present chief would not act like his (mad) predecessor, but kill only those who were guilty of witchcraft or theft. These men were very much astonished at the liberty enjoyed by the Makololo; and when they found that all my people held cattle, we were told that Matiamvo alone had a herd. One very intelligent man among them asked, "If he should make a canoe, and take it down the river to the Makololo, would he get a cow for it?" This question, which my men answered in the affirmative, was important, as showing the knowledge of a water communication from the country of Matiamvo to the Makololo; and the river runs through a fertile country abounding in large timber. If the tribes have intercourse with each other, it exerts a good influence on their chiefs to hear what other tribes think of their deeds. The Makololo have such a bad name, on account of their perpetual forays, that they have not been known in Londa except as ruthless destroyers. The people in Matiamvo's country submit to much wrong from their chiefs, and no voice can be raised against cruelty, because they are afraid to flee elsewhere.

We left Quendende's village in company with Quendende himself, and the principal man of the embassadors of Matiamvo, and after two or three miles' march to the N.W., came to the ford of the Lotembwa, which flows southward. A canoe was waiting to ferry us over, but it was very tedious work; for, though the river itself was only eighty yards wide, the whole valley was flooded, and we were obliged to paddle more than half a mile to get free of the water. A fire was lit to warm old Quendende, and enable him to dry his tobacco-leaves. The leaves are taken from the plant, and spread close to the fire until they are quite dry and crisp; they are then put into a snuff-box, which, with a little pestle, serves the purpose of a mill to grind them into powder; it is then used as snuff. As we sat by the fire, the embassadors communicated their thoughts freely respecting the customs of their race. When a chief dies, a number of servants are slaughtered with him to form his company in the other world. The Barotse followed the same custom, and this and other usages show them to be genuine negroes, though neither they nor the Balonda resemble closely the typical form of that people. Quendende said if he were present on these occasions he would hide his people, so that they might not be slaughtered. As we go north, the people become more bloodily superstitious.

We were assured that if the late Matiamvo took a fancy to any thing, such, for instance, as my watch-chain, which was of silver wire, and was a great curiosity, as they had never seen metal plaited before, he would order a whole village to be brought up to buy it from a stranger. When a slave-trader visited him, he took possession of all his goods; then, after ten days or a fortnight, he would send out a party of men to pounce upon some considerable village, and, having killed the head man, would pay for all the goods by selling the inhabitants. This has frequently been the case, and nearly all the visitants he ever had were men of color. On asking if Matiamvo did not know he was a man, and would be judged, in company with those he destroyed, by a Lord who is no respector of persons? the embassador replied, "We do not go up to God, as you do; we are put into the ground." I could not ascertain that even those who have such a distinct perception of the continued existence of departed spirits had any notion of heaven; they appear to imagine the souls to be always near the place of sepulture.

After crossing the River Lotembwa we traveled about eight miles, and came to Katema's straggling town (lat. 11d 35′ 49″ S., long. 22d 27′ E.). It is more a collection of villages than a town. We were led out about half a mile from the houses, that we might make for ourselves the best lodging we could of the trees and grass, while Intemese was taken to Katema to undergo the usual process of pumping as to our past conduct and professions. Katema soon afterward sent a handsome present of food.

Next morning we had a formal presentation, and found Katema seated on a sort of throne, with about three hundred men on the ground around, and thirty women, who were said to be his wives, close behind him. The main body of the people were seated in a semicircle, at a distance of fifty yards. Each party had its own head man stationed at a little distance in front, and, when beckoned by the chief, came near him as councilors. Intemese gave our history, and Katema placed sixteen large baskets of meal before us, half a dozen fowls, and a dozen eggs, and expressed regret that we had slept hungry: he did not like any stranger to suffer want in his town; and added, "Go home, and cook and eat, and you will then be in a fit state to speak to me at an audience I will give you to-morrow." He was busily engaged in hearing the statements of a large body of fine young men who had fled from Kangenke, chief of Lobale, on account of his selling their relatives to the native Portuguese who frequent his country. Katema is a tall man, about forty years of age, and his head was ornamented with a helmet of beads and feathers. He had on a snuff-brown coat, with a broad band of tinsel down the arms, and carried in his hand a large tail made of the caudal extremities of a number of gnus. This has charms attached to it, and he continued waving it in front of himself all the time we were there. He seemed in good spirits, laughing heartily several times. This is a good sign, for a man who shakes his sides with mirth is seldom difficult to deal with. When we rose to take leave, all rose with us, as at Shinte's.

Returning next morning, Katema addressed me thus: "I am the great Moene (lord) Katema, the fellow of Matiamvo. There is no one in the country equal to Matiamvo and me. I have always lived here, and my forefathers too. There is the house in which my father lived. You found no human skulls near the place where you are encamped. I never killed any of the traders; they all come to me. I am the great Moene Katema, of whom you have heard." He looked as if he had fallen asleep tipsy, and dreamed of his greatness. On explaining my objects to him, he promptly pointed out three men who would be our guides, and explained that the northwest path was the most direct, and that by which all traders came, but that the water at present standing on the plains would reach up to the loins; he would therefore send us by a more northerly route, which no trader had yet traversed. This was more suited to our wishes, for we never found a path safe that had been trodden by slave-traders.

We presented a few articles, which pleased him highly: a small shawl, a razor, three bunches of beads, some buttons, and a powder-horn. Apologizing for the insignificance of the gift, I wished to know what I could bring him from Loanda, saying, not a large thing, but something small. He laughed heartily at the limitation, and replied, "Every thing of the white people would be acceptable, and he would receive any thing thankfully; but the coat he then had on was old, and he would like another." I introduced the subject of the Bible, but one of the old councilors broke in, told all he had picked up from the Mambari, and glided off into several other subjects. It is a misery to speak through an interpreter, as I was now forced to do. With a body of men like mine, composed as they were of six different tribes, and all speaking the language of the Bechuanas, there was no difficulty in communicating on common subjects with any tribe we came to; but doling out a story in which they felt no interest, and which I understood only sufficiently well to perceive that a mere abridgment was given, was uncommonly slow work. Neither could Katema's attention be arrested, except by compliments, of which they have always plenty to bestow as well as receive. We were strangers, and knew that, as Makololo, we had not the best of characters, yet his treatment of us was wonderfully good and liberal.

I complimented him on the possession of cattle, and pleased him by telling him how he might milk the cows. He has a herd of about thirty, really splendid animals, all reared from two which he bought from the Balobale when he was young. They are generally of a white color, and are quite wild, running off with graceful ease like a herd of elands on the approach of a stranger. They excited the unbounded admiration of the Makololo, and clearly proved that the country was well adapted for them. When Katema wishes to slaughter one, he is obliged to shoot it as if it were a buffalo. Matiamvo is said to possess a herd of cattle in a similar state. I never could feel certain as to the reason why they do not all possess cattle in a country containing such splendid pasturage.

As Katema did not offer an ox, as would have been done by a Makololo or Caffre chief, we slaughtered one of our own, and all of us were delighted to get a meal of meat, after subsisting so long on the light porridge and green maize of Londa. On occasions of slaughtering an animal, some pieces of it are in the fire before the skin is all removed from the body. A frying-pan full of these pieces having been got quickly ready, my men crowded about their father, and I handed some all round. It was a strange sight to the Balonda, who were looking on, wondering. I offered portions to them too, but these were declined, though they are excessively fond of a little animal food to eat with their vegetable diet. They would not eat with us, but they would take the meat and cook it in their own way, and then use it. I thought at one time that they had imported something from the Mohammedans, and the more especially as an exclamation of surprise, "Allah", sounds like the Illah of the Arabs; but we found, a little farther on, another form of salutation, of Christian (?) origin, "Ave-rie" (Ave Marie). The salutations probably travel farther than the faith. My people, when satisfied with a meal like that which they enjoy so often at home, amused themselves by an uproarious dance. Katema sent to ask what I had given them to produce so much excitement. Intemese replied it was their custom, and they meant no harm. The companion of the ox we slaughtered refused food for two days, and went lowing about for him continually. He seemed inconsolable for his loss, and tried again and again to escape back to the Makololo country. My men remarked, "He thinks they will kill me as well as my friend." Katema thought it the result of art, and had fears of my skill in medicine, and of course witchcraft. He refused to see the magic lantern.

One of the affairs which had been intrusted by Shinte to Intemese was the rescue of a wife who had eloped with a young man belonging to Katema. As this was the only case I have met with in the interior in which a fugitive was sent back to a chief against his own will, I am anxious to mention it. On Intemese claiming her as his master's wife, she protested loudly against it, saying "she knew she was not going back to be a wife again; she was going back to be sold to the Mambari." My men formed many friendships with the people of Katema, and some of the poorer classes said in confidence, "We wish our children could go back with you to the Makololo country; here we are all in danger of being sold." My men were of opinion that it was only the want of knowledge of the southern country which prevented an exodus of all the lower portions of Londa population thither.

It is remarkable how little people living in a flat forest country like this know of distant tribes. An old man, who said he had been born about the same time as the late Matiamvo, and had been his constant companion through life, visited us; and as I was sitting on some grass in front of the little gipsy tent mending my camp stool, I invited him to take a seat on the grass beside me. This was peremptorily refused: "he had never sat on the ground during the late chief's reign, and he was not going to degrade himself now." One of my men handed him a log of wood taken from the fire, and helped him out of the difficulty. When I offered him some cooked meat on a plate, he would not touch that either, but would take it home. So I humored him by sending a servant to bear a few ounces of meat to the town behind him. He mentioned the Lolo (Lulua) as the branch of the Leeambye which flows southward or S.S.E.; but the people of Matiamvo had never gone far down it, as their chief had always been afraid of encountering a tribe whom, from the description given, I could recognize as the Makololo. He described five rivers as falling into the Lolo, viz., the Lishish, Liss or Lise, Kalileme, Ishidish, and Molong. None of these are large, but when they are united in the Lolo they form a considerable stream. The country through which the Lolo flows is said to be flat, fertile, well peopled, and there are large patches of forest. In this report he agreed perfectly with the people of Matiamvo, whom we had met at Quendende's village. But we never could get him, or any one in this quarter, to draw a map on the ground, as people may readily be got to do in the south.

Katema promised us the aid of some of his people as carriers, but his rule is not very stringent or efficient, for they refused to turn out for the work. They were Balobale; and he remarked on their disobedience that, though he received them as fugitives, they did not feel grateful enough to obey, and if they continued rebellious he must drive them back whence they came; but there is little fear of that, as all the chiefs are excessively anxious to collect men in great numbers around them. These Balobale would not go, though our guide Shakatwala ran after some of them with a drawn sword. This degree of liberty to rebel was very striking to us, as it occurred in a country where people may be sold, and often are so disposed of when guilty of any crime; and we well knew that open disobedience like this among the Makololo would be punished with death without much ceremony.

On Sunday, the 19th, both I and several of our party were seized with fever, and I could do nothing but toss about in my little tent, with the thermometer above 90 Deg., though this was the beginning of winter, and my men made as much shade as possible by planting branches of trees all round and over it. We have, for the first time in my experience in Africa, had a cold wind from the north. All the winds from that quarter are hot, and those from the south are cold, but they seldom blow from either direction.

20TH. We were glad to get away, though not on account of any scarcity of food; for my men, by giving small presents of meat as an earnest of their sincerity, formed many friendships with the people of Katema. We went about four or five miles in a N.N.W. direction, then two in a westerly one, and came round the small end of Lake Dilolo. It seemed, as far as we could at this time discern, to be like a river a quarter of a mile wide. It is abundantly supplied with fish and hippopotami; the broad part, which we did not this time see, is about three miles wide, and the lake is almost seven or eight long. If it be thought strange that I did not go a few miles to see the broad part, which, according to Katema, had never been visited by any of the traders, it must be remembered that in consequence of fever I had eaten nothing for two entire days, and, instead of sleep, the whole of the nights were employed in incessant drinking of water, and I was now so glad to get on in the journey and see some of my fellow fever-patients crawling along, that I could not brook the delay, which astronomical observations for accurately determining the geographical position of this most interesting spot would have occasioned.

We observed among the people of Katema a love for singing-birds. One pretty little songster, named "cabazo", a species of canary, is kept in very neatly made cages, having traps on the top to entice its still free companions. On asking why they kept them in confinement, "Because they sing sweetly," was the answer. They feed them on the lotsa ('Pennisetum typhoideum'), of which great quantities are cultivated as food for man, and these canaries plague the gardeners here, very much in the same way as our sparrows do at home.

I was pleased to hear the long-forgotten cry of alarm of the canaries in the woods, and observed one warbling forth its song, and keeping in motion from side to side, as these birds do in the cage. We saw also tame pigeons; and the Barotse, who always take care to exalt Santuru, reminded us that this chief had many doves, and kept canaries which had reddish heads when the birds attained maturity. Those we now see have the real canary color on the breast, with a tinge of green; the back, yellowish green, with darker longitudinal bands meeting in the centre; a narrow dark band passes from the bill over the eye and back to the bill again.

The birds of song here set up quite a merry chorus in the mornings, and abound most near the villages. Some sing as loudly as our thrushes, and the king-hunter ('Halcyon Senegalensis') makes a clear whirring sound like that of a whistle with a pea in it. During the heat of the day all remain silent, and take their siesta in the shadiest parts of the trees, but in the cool of the evening they again exert themselves in the production of pleasant melody. It is remarkable that so many songbirds abound where there is a general paucity of other animal life. As we went forward we were struck by the comparative absence of game and the larger kind of fowls. The rivers contain very few fish. Common flies are not troublesome, as they are wherever milk is abundant; they are seen in company with others of the same size and shape, but whose tiny feet do not tickle the skin, as is the case with their companions. Mosquitoes are seldom so numerous as to disturb the slumbers of a weary man.

But, though this region is free from common insect plagues, and from tsetse, it has others. Feeling something running across my forehead as I was falling asleep, I put up the hand to wipe it off, and was sharply stung both on the hand and head; the pain was very acute. On obtaining a light, we found that it had been inflicted by a light-colored spider, about half an inch in length, and, one of the men having crushed it with his fingers, I had no opportunity of examining whether the pain had been produced by poison from a sting or from its mandibles. No remedy was applied, and the pain ceased in about two hours. The Bechuanas believe that there is a small black spider in the country whose bite is fatal. I have not met with an instance in which death could be traced to this insect, though a very large black, hairy spider, an inch and a quarter long and three quarters of an inch broad, is frequently seen, having a process at the end of its front claws similar to that at the end of the scorpion's tail, and when the bulbous portion of it is pressed, the poison may be seen oozing out from the point.

We have also spiders in the south which seize their prey by leaping upon it from a distance of several inches. When alarmed, they can spring about a foot away from the object of their own fear. Of this kind there are several varieties.

A large reddish spider ('Mygale') obtains its food in a different manner than either patiently waiting in ambush or by catching it with a bound. It runs about with great velocity in and out, behind and around every object, searching for what it may devour, and, from its size and rapid motions, excites the horror of every stranger. I never knew it to do any harm except frightening the nervous, and I believe few could look upon it for the first time without feeling himself in danger. It is named by the natives "selali", and is believed to be the maker of a hinged cover for its nest. You see a door, about the size of a shilling, lying beside a deep hole of nearly similar diameter. The inside of the door lying upward, and which attracts your notice, is of a pure white silky substance, like paper. The outer side is coated over with earth, precisely like that in which the hole is made. If you try to lift it, you find it is fastened by a hinge on one side, and, if it is turned over upon the hole, it fits it exactly, and the earthy side being then uppermost, it is quite impossible to detect the situation of the nest. Unfortunately, this cavity for breeding is never seen except when the owner is out, and has left the door open behind her.

In some parts of the country there are great numbers of a large, beautiful yellow-spotted spider, the webs of which are about a yard in diameter. The lines on which these webs are spun are suspended from one tree to another, and are as thick as coarse thread. The fibres radiate from a central point, where the insect waits for its prey. The webs are placed perpendicularly, and a common occurrence in walking is to get the face enveloped in them as a lady is in a veil.

Another kind of spider lives in society, and forms so great a collection of webs placed at every angle, that the trunk of a tree surrounded by them can not be seen. A piece of hedge is often so hidden by this spider that the branches are invisible. Another is seen on the inside of the walls of huts among the Makololo in great abundance. It is round in shape, spotted, brown in color, and the body half an inch in diameter; the spread of the legs is an inch and a half. It makes a smooth spot for itself on the wall, covered with the above-mentioned white silky substance. There it is seen standing the whole day, and I never could ascertain how it fed. It has no web, but a carpet, and is a harmless, though an ugly neighbor.

Immediately beyond Dilolo there is a large flat about twenty miles in breadth. Here Shakatwala insisted on our remaining to get supplies of food from Katema's subjects, before entering the uninhabited watery plains. When asked the meaning of the name Dilolo, Shakatwala gave the following account of the formation of the lake. A female chief, called Moene (lord) Monenga, came one evening to the village of Mosogo, a man who lived in the vicinity, but who had gone to hunt with his dogs. She asked for a supply of food, and Mosogo's wife gave her a sufficient quantity. Proceeding to another village standing on the spot now occupied by the water, she preferred the same demand, and was not only refused, but, when she uttered a threat for their niggardliness, was taunted with the question, "What could she do though she were thus treated?" In order to show what she could do, she began a song, in slow time, and uttered her own name, Monenga-wo-o. As she prolonged the last note, the village, people, fowls, and dogs sank into the space now called Dilolo. When Kasimakate, the head man of this village, came home and found out the catastrophe, he cast himself into the lake, and is supposed to be in it still. The name is derived from "ilolo", despair, because this man gave up all hope when his family was destroyed. Monenga was put to death. This may be a faint tradition of the Deluge, and it is remarkable as the only one I have met with in this country.

Heavy rains prevented us from crossing the plain in front (N.N.W.) in one day, and the constant wading among the grass hurt the feet of the men. There is a footpath all the way across, but as this is worn down beneath the level of the rest of the plain, it is necessarily the deepest portion, and the men, avoiding it, make a new walk by its side. A path, however narrow, is a great convenience, as any one who has traveled on foot in Africa will admit. The virtual want of it here caused us to make slow and painful progress.

Ants surely are wiser than some men, for they learn by experience. They have established themselves even on these plains, where water stands so long annually as to allow the lotus, and other aqueous plants, to come to maturity. When all the ant horizon is submerged a foot deep, they manage to exist by ascending to little houses built of black tenacious loam on stalks of grass, and placed higher than the line of inundation. This must have been the result of experience; for, if they had waited till the water actually invaded their terrestrial habitations, they would not have been able to procure materials for their aerial quarters, unless they dived down to the bottom for every mouthful of clay. Some of these upper chambers are about the size of a bean, and others as large as a man's thumb. They must have built in anticipation, and if so, let us humbly hope that the sufferers by the late inundations in France may be possessed of as much common sense as the little black ants of the Dilolo plains.

Chapter 18

The Watershed between the northern and southern Rivers—A deep Valley—Rustic Bridge—Fountains on the Slopes of the Valleys—Village of Kabinje—Good Effects of the Belief in the Power of Charms—Demand for Gunpowder and English Calico—The Kasai—Vexatious Trick—Want of Food—No Game—Katende's unreasonable Demand—A grave Offense—Toll-bridge Keeper—Greedy Guides—Flooded Valleys—Swim the Nyuana Loke—Prompt Kindness of my Men—Makololo Remarks on the rich uncultivated Valleys—Difference in the Color of Africans—Reach a Village of the Chiboque—The Head Man's impudent Message—Surrounds our Encampment with his Warriors—The Pretense—Their Demand—Prospect of a Fight—Way in which it was averted—Change our Path—Summer—Fever—Beehives and the Honey-guide—Instinct of Trees—Climbers—The Ox Sinbad—Absence of Thorns in the Forests—Plant peculiar to a forsaken Garden—Bad Guides—Insubordination suppressed—Beset by Enemies—A Robber Party—More Troubles—Detained by Ionga Panza—His Village—Annoyed by Bangala Traders—My Men discouraged—Their Determination and Precaution.

24TH OF FEBRUARY. On reaching unflooded lands beyond the plain, we found the villages there acknowledged the authority of the chief named Katende, and we discovered, also, to our surprise, that the almost level plain we had passed forms the watershed between the southern and northern rivers, for we had now entered a district in which the rivers flowed in a northerly direction into the Kasai or Loke, near to which we now were, while the rivers we had hitherto crossed were all running southward. Having met with kind treatment and aid at the first village, Katema's guides returned, and we were led to the N.N.W. by the inhabitants, and descended into the very first really deep valley we had seen since leaving Kolobeng. A stream ran along the bottom of a slope of three or four hundred yards from the plains above.

We crossed this by a rustic bridge at present submerged thigh-deep by the rains. The trees growing along the stream of this lovely valley were thickly planted and very high. Many had sixty or eighty feet of clean straight trunk, and beautiful flowers adorned the ground beneath them. Ascending the opposite side, we came, in two hours' time, to another valley, equally beautiful, and with a stream also in its centre. It may seem mere trifling to note such an unimportant thing as the occurrence of a valley, there being so many in every country under the sun; but as these were branches of that in which the Kasai or Loke flows, and both that river and its feeders derive their water in a singular manner from the valley sides, I may be excused for calling particular attention to the more furrowed nature of the country.

At different points on the slopes of these valleys which we now for the first time entered, there are oozing fountains, surrounded by clumps of the same evergreen, straight, large-leaved trees we have noticed along the streams. These spots are generally covered with a mat of grassy vegetation, and possess more the character of bogs than of fountains. They slowly discharge into the stream below, and are so numerous along both banks as to give a peculiar character to the landscape. These groups of sylvan vegetation are generally of a rounded form, and the trunks of the trees are tall and straight, while those on the level plains above are low and scraggy in their growth. There can be little doubt but that the water, which stands for months on the plains, soaks in, and finds its way into the rivers and rivulets by percolating through the soil, and out by these oozing bogs; and the difference between the growth of these trees, though they be of different species, may be a proof that the stuntedness of those on the plains is owing to being, in the course of each year, more subjected to drought than moisture.

Reaching the village of Kabinje, in the evening he sent us a present of tobacco, Mutokuane or "bang" ('Cannabis sativa'), and maize, by the man who went forward to announce our arrival, and a message expressing satisfaction at the prospect of having trade with the coast. The westing we were making brought us among people who are frequently visited by the Mambari as slave-dealers. This trade causes bloodshed; for when a poor family is selected as the victims, it is necessary to get rid of the older members of it, because they are supposed to be able to give annoyance to the chief afterward by means of enchantments. The belief in the power of charms for good or evil produces not only honesty, but a great amount of gentle dealing. The powerful are often restrained in their despotism from a fear that the weak and helpless may injure them by their medical knowledge. They have many fears. A man at one of the villages we came to showed us the grave of his child, and, with much apparent feeling, told us she had been burned to death in her hut. He had come with all his family, and built huts around it in order to weep for her. He thought, if the grave were left unwatched, the witches would come and bewitch them by putting medicines on the body. They have a more decided belief in the continued existence of departed spirits than any of the more southerly tribes. Even the Barotse possess it in a strong degree, for one of my men of that tribe, on experiencing headache, said, with a sad and thoughtful countenance, "My father is scolding me because I do not give him any of the food I eat." I asked where his father was. "Among the Barimo," was the reply.

When we wished to move on, Kabinje refused a guide to the next village because he was at war with it; but, after much persuasion, he consented, provided that the guide should be allowed to return as soon as he came in sight of the enemy's village. This we felt to be a misfortune, as the people all suspect a man who comes telling his own tale; but there being no help for it, we went on, and found the head man of a village on the rivulet Kalomba, called Kangenke, a very different man from what his enemy represented. We found, too, that the idea of buying and selling took the place of giving for friendship. As I had nothing with which to purchase food except a parcel of beads which were preserved for worse times, I began to fear that we should soon be compelled to suffer more from hunger than we had done. The people demanded gunpowder for every thing. If we had possessed any quantity of that article, we should have got on well, for here it is of great value. On our return, near this spot we found a good-sized fowl was sold for a single charge of gunpowder. Next to that, English calico was in great demand, and so were beads; but money was of no value whatever. Gold is quite unknown; it is thought to be brass; trade is carried on by barter alone. The people know nothing of money. A purse-proud person would here feel the ground move from beneath his feet. Occasionally a large piece of copper, in the shape of a St. Andrew's cross, is offered for sale.

FEBRUARY 27TH. Kangenke promptly furnished guides this morning, so we went briskly on a short distance, and came to a part of the Kasye, Kasai, or Loke, where he had appointed two canoes to convey us across. This is a most beautiful river, and very much like the Clyde in Scotland. The slope of the valley down to the stream is about five hundred yards, and finely wooded. It is, perhaps, one hundred yards broad, and was winding slowly from side to side in the beautiful green glen, in a course to the north and northeast. In both the directions from which it came and to which it went it seemed to be alternately embowered in sylvan vegetation, or rich meadows covered with tall grass. The men pointed out its course, and said, "Though you sail along it for months, you will turn without seeing the end of it."

While at the ford of the Kasai we were subjected to a trick, of which we had been forewarned by the people of Shinte. A knife had been dropped by one of Kangenke's people in order to entrap my men; it was put down near our encampment, as if lost, the owner in the mean time watching till one of my men picked it up. Nothing was said until our party was divided, one half on this, and the other on that bank of the river. Then the charge was made to me that one of my men had stolen a knife. Certain of my people's honesty, I desired the man, who was making a great noise, to search the luggage for it; the unlucky lad who had taken the bait then came forward and confessed that he had the knife in a basket, which was already taken over the river. When it was returned, the owner would not receive it back unless accompanied with a fine. The lad offered beads, but these were refused with scorn. A shell hanging round his neck, similar to that which Shinte had given me, was the object demanded, and the victim of the trick, as we all knew it to be, was obliged to part with his costly ornament. I could not save him from the loss, as all had been forewarned; and it is the universal custom among the Makololo and many other tribes to show whatever they may find to the chief person of their company, and make a sort of offer of it to him. This lad ought to have done so to me; the rest of the party always observed this custom. I felt annoyed at the imposition, but the order we invariably followed in crossing a river forced me to submit. The head of the party remained to be ferried over last; so, if I had not come to terms, I would have been, as I always was in crossing rivers which we could not swim, completely in the power of the enemy. It was but rarely we could get a head man so witless as to cross a river with us, and remain on the opposite bank in a convenient position to be seized as a hostage in case of my being caught.

This trick is but one of a number equally dishonorable which are practiced by tribes that lie adjacent to the more civilized settlements. The Balonda farther east told us, by way of warning, that many parties of the more central tribes had at various periods set out, in order to trade with the white men themselves, instead of through the Mambari, but had always been obliged to return without reaching their destination, in consequence of so many pretexts being invented by the tribes encountered in the way for fining them of their ivory.

This ford was in 11d 15' 47" S. latitude, but the weather was so excessively cloudy we got no observation for longitude.

We were now in want of food, for, to the great surprise of my companions, the people of Kangenke gave nothing except by way of sale, and charged the most exorbitant prices for the little meal and manioc they brought. The only article of barter my men had was a little fat saved from the ox we slaughtered at Katema's, so I was obliged to give them a portion of the stock of beads. One day (29th) of westing brought us from the Kasai to near the village of Katende, and we saw that we were in a land where no hope could be entertained of getting supplies of animal food, for one of our guides caught a light-blue colored mole and two mice for his supper. The care with which he wrapped them up in a leaf and slung them on his spear told that we could not hope to enjoy any larger game. We saw no evidence of any animals besides; and, on coming to the villages beyond this, we often saw boys and girls engaged in digging up these tiny quadrupeds.

Katende sent for me on the day following our arrival, and, being quite willing to visit him, I walked, for this purpose, about three miles from our encampment. When we approached the village we were desired to enter a hut, and, as it was raining at the time, we did so. After a long time spent in giving and receiving messages from the great man, we were told that he wanted either a man, a tusk, beads, copper rings, or a shell, as payment for leave to pass through his country. No one, we were assured, was allowed that liberty, or even to behold him, without something of the sort being presented. Having humbly explained our circumstances, and that he could not expect to "catch a humble cow by the horns"—a proverb similar to ours that "you can't draw milk out of a stone"—we were told to go home, and he would speak again to us next day. I could not avoid a hearty laugh at the cool impudence of the savage, and made the best of my way home in the still pouring rain. My men were rather nettled at this want of hospitality, but, after talking over the matter with one of Katende's servants, he proposed that some small article should be given, and an attempt made to please Katende. I turned out my shirts, and selected the worst one as a sop for him, and invited Katende to come and choose any thing else I had, but added that, when I should reach my own chief naked, and was asked what I had done with my clothes, I should be obliged to confess that I had left them with Katende. The shirt was dispatched to him, and some of my people went along with the servant; they soon returned, saying that the shirt had been accepted, and guides and food too would be sent to us next day. The chief had, moreover, expressed a hope to see me on my return. He is reported to be very corpulent. The traders who have come here seem to have been very timid, yielding to every demand made on the most frivolous pretenses. One of my men, seeing another much like an acquaintance at home, addressed him by the name of the latter in sport, telling him, at the same time, why he did so; this was pronounced to be a grave offense, and a large fine demanded; when the case came before me I could see no harm in what had been done, and told my people not to answer the young fellow. The latter felt himself disarmed, for it is chiefly in a brawl they have power; then words are spoken in anger which rouse the passions of the complainant's friends. In this case, after vociferating some time, the would-be offended party came and said to my man that, if they exchanged some small gift, all would be right, but, my man taking no notice of him, he went off rather crestfallen.

My men were as much astonished as myself at the demand for payment for leave to pass, and the almost entire neglect of the rules of hospitality. Katende gave us only a little meal and manioc, and a fowl. Being detained two days by heavy rains, we felt that a good stock of patience was necessary in traveling through this country in the rainy season.

Passing onward without seeing Katende, we crossed a small rivulet, the Sengko, by which we had encamped, and after two hours came to another, the Totelo, which was somewhat larger, and had a bridge over it. At the farther end of this structure stood a negro, who demanded fees. He said the bridge was his; the path his; the guides were his children; and if we did not pay him he would prevent farther progress. This piece of civilization I was not prepared to meet, and stood a few seconds looking at our bold toll-keeper, when one of my men took off three copper bracelets, which paid for the whole party. The negro was a better man than he at first seemed, for he immediately went to his garden and brought us some leaves of tobacco as a present.

When we had got fairly away from the villages, the guides from Kangenke sat down and told us that there were three paths in front, and, if we did not at once present them with a cloth, they would leave us to take whichever we might like best. As I had pointed out the direction in which Loanda lay, and had only employed them for the sake of knowing the paths between villages which lay along our route, and always objected when they led us in any other than the Loanda direction, I wished my men now to go on without the guides, trusting to ourselves to choose the path which would seem to lead us in the direction we had always followed. But Mashauana, fearing lest we might wander, asked leave to give his own cloth, and when the guides saw that, they came forward shouting "Averie, Averie!"

In the afternoon of this day we came to a valley about a mile wide, filled with clear, fast-flowing water. The men on foot were chin deep in crossing, and we three on ox-back got wet to the middle, the weight of the animals preventing them from swimming. A thunder-shower descending completed the partial drenching of the plain, and gave a cold, uncomfortable "packing in a wet blanket" that night. Next day we found another flooded valley about half a mile wide, with a small and now deep rivulet in its middle, flowing rapidly to the S.S.E., or toward the Kasai. The middle part of this flood, being the bed of what at other times is the rivulet, was so rapid that we crossed by holding on to the oxen, and the current soon dashed them to the opposite bank; we then jumped off, and, the oxen being relieved of their burdens, we could pull them on to the shallower part. The rest of the valley was thigh deep and boggy, but holding on by the belt which fastened the blanket to the ox, we each floundered through the nasty slough as well as we could. These boggy parts, lying parallel to the stream, were the most extensive we had come to: those mentioned already were mere circumscribed patches; these extended for miles along each bank; but even here, though the rapidity of the current was very considerable, the thick sward of grass was "laid" flat along the sides of the stream, and the soil was not abraded so much as to discolor the flood. When we came to the opposite side of this valley, some pieces of the ferruginous conglomerate, which forms the capping to all other rocks in a large district around and north of this, cropped out, and the oxen bit at them as if surprised by the appearance of stone as much as we were; or it may have contained some mineral of which they stood in need. We had not met with a stone since leaving Shinte's. The country is covered with deep alluvial soil of a dark color and very fertile.

In the afternoon we came to another stream, nyuana Loke (or child of Loke), with a bridge over it. The men had to swim off to each end of the bridge, and when on it were breast deep; some preferred holding on by the tails of the oxen the whole way across. I intended to do this too; but, riding to the deep part, before I could dismount and seize the helm the ox dashed off with his companions, and his body sank so deep that I failed in my attempt even to catch the blanket belt, and if I pulled the bridle the ox seemed as if he would come backward upon me, so I struck out for the opposite bank alone. My poor fellows were dreadfully alarmed when they saw me parted from the cattle, and about twenty of them made a simultaneous rush into the water for my rescue, and just as I reached the opposite bank one seized my arm, and another threw his around my body. When I stood up, it was most gratifying to see them all struggling toward me. Some had leaped off the bridge, and allowed their cloaks to float down the stream. Part of my goods, abandoned in the hurry, were brought up from the bottom after I was safe. Great was the pleasure expressed when they found that I could swim, like themselves, without the aid of a tail, and I did and do feel grateful to these poor heathens for the promptitude with which they dashed in to save, as they thought, my life. I found my clothes cumbersome in the water; they could swim quicker from being naked. They swim like dogs, not frog-fashion, as we do.

In the evening we crossed the small rivulet Lozeze, and came to some villages of the Kasabi, from whom we got some manioc in exchange for beads. They tried to frighten us by telling of the deep rivers we should have to cross in our way. I was drying my clothes by turning myself round and round before the fire. My men laughed at the idea of being frightened by rivers. "We can all swim: who carried the white man across the river but himself?" I felt proud of their praise.

SATURDAY, 4TH MARCH. Came to the outskirts of the territory of the Chiboque. We crossed the Konde and Kaluze rivulets. The former is a deep, small stream with a bridge, the latter insignificant; the valleys in which these rivulets run are beautifully fertile. My companions are continually lamenting over the uncultivated vales in such words as these: "What a fine country for cattle! My heart is sore to see such fruitful valleys for corn lying waste." At the time these words were put down I had come to the belief that the reason why the inhabitants of this fine country possess no herds of cattle was owing to the despotic sway of their chiefs, and that the common people would not be allowed to keep any domestic animals, even supposing they could acquire them; but on musing on the subject since, I have been led to the conjecture that the rich, fertile country of Londa must formerly have been infested by the tsetse, but that, as the people killed off the game on which, in the absence of man, the tsetse must subsist, the insect was starved out of the country. It is now found only where wild animals abound, and the Balonda, by the possession of guns, having cleared most of the country of all the large game, we may have happened to come just when it was possible to admit of cattle. Hence the success of Katema, Shinte, and Matiamvo with their herds. It would not be surprising, though they know nothing of the circumstance; a tribe on the Zambesi, which I encountered, whose country was swarming with tsetse, believed that they could not keep any cattle, because "no one loved them well enough to give them the medicine of oxen;" and even the Portuguese at Loanda accounted for the death of the cattle brought from the interior to the sea-coast by the prejudicial influence of the sea air! One ox, which I took down to the sea from the interior, died at Loanda, with all the symptoms of the poison injected by tsetse, which I saw myself in a district a hundred miles from the coast.

While at the villages of the Kasabi we saw no evidences of want of food among the people. Our beads were very valuable, but cotton cloth would have been still more so; as we traveled along, men, women, and children came running after us, with meal and fowls for sale, which we would gladly have purchased had we possessed any English manufactures. When they heard that we had no cloth, they turned back much disappointed.

The amount of population in the central parts of the country may be called large only as compared with the Cape Colony or the Bechuana country. The cultivated land is as nothing compared with what might be brought under the plow. There are flowing streams in abundance, which, were it necessary, could be turned to the purpose of irrigation with but little labor. Miles of fruitful country are now lying absolutely waste, for there is not even game to eat off the fine pasturage, and to recline under the evergreen, shady groves which we are ever passing in our progress. The people who inhabit the central region are not all quite black in color. Many incline to that of bronze, and others are as light in hue as the Bushmen, who, it may be remembered, afford a proof that heat alone does not cause blackness, but that heat and moisture combined do very materially deepen the color. Wherever we find people who have continued for ages in a hot, humid district, they are deep black, but to this apparent law there are exceptions, caused by the migrations of both tribes and individuals; the Makololo, for instance, among the tribes of the humid central basin, appear of a sickly sallow hue when compared with the aboriginal inhabitants; the Batoka also, who lived in an elevated region, are, when seen in company with the Batoka of the rivers, so much lighter in color, they might be taken for another tribe; but their language, and the very marked custom of knocking out the upper front teeth, leave no room for doubt that they are one people.

Apart from the influences of elevation, heat, humidity, and degradation, I have imagined that the lighter and darker colors observed in the native population run in five longitudinal bands along the southern portion of the continent. Those on the seaboard of both the east and west are very dark; then two bands of lighter color lie about three hundred miles from each coast, of which the westerly one, bending round, embraces the Kalahari Desert and Bechuana countries; and then the central basin is very dark again. This opinion is not given with any degree of positiveness. It is stated just as it struck my mind in passing across the country, and if incorrect, it is singular that the dialects spoken by the different tribes have arranged themselves in a fashion which seems to indicate migration along the lines of color. The dialects spoken in the extreme south, whether Hottentot or Caffre, bear a close affinity to those of the tribes living immediately on their northern borders; one glides into the other, and their affinities are so easily detected that they are at once recognized to be cognate. If the dialects of extreme points are compared, as that of the Caffres and the tribes near the equator, it is more difficult to recognize the fact, which is really the case, that all the dialects belong to but two families of languages. Examination of the roots of the words of the dialects, arranged in geographical order, shows that they merge into each other, and there is not nearly so much difference between the extremes of east and west as between those of north and south, the dialect spoken at Tete resembling closely that in Angola.

Having, on the afore-mentioned date, reached the village of Njambi, one of the chiefs of the Chiboque, we intended to pass a quiet Sunday; and our provisions being quite spent, I ordered a tired riding-ox to be slaughtered. As we wished to be on good terms with all, we sent the hump and ribs to Njambi, with the explanation that this was the customary tribute to chiefs in the part from which we had come, and that we always honored men in his position. He returned thanks, and promised to send food. Next morning he sent an impudent message, with a very small present of meal; scorning the meat he had accepted, he demanded either a man, an ox, a gun, powder, cloth, or a shell; and in the event of refusal to comply with his demand, he intimated his intention to prevent our further progress. We replied, we should have thought ourselves fools if we had scorned his small present, and demanded other food instead; and even supposing we had possessed the articles named, no black man ought to impose a tribute on a party that did not trade in slaves. The servants who brought the message said that, when sent to the Mambari, they had always got a quantity of cloth from them for their master, and now expected the same, or something else as an equivalent, from me.

We heard some of the Chiboque remark, "They have only five guns;" and about midday, Njambi collected all his people, and surrounded our encampment. Their object was evidently to plunder us of every thing. My men seized their javelins, and stood on the defensive, while the young Chiboque had drawn their swords and brandished them with great fury. Some even pointed their guns at me, and nodded to each other, as much as to say, "This is the way we shall do with him." I sat on my camp-stool, with my double-barreled gun across my knees, and invited the chief to be seated also. When he and his counselors had sat down on the ground in front of me, I asked what crime we had committed that he had come armed in that way. He replied that one of my men, Pitsane, while sitting at the fire that morning, had, in spitting, allowed a small quantity of the saliva to fall on the leg of one of his men, and this "guilt" he wanted to be settled by the fine of a man, ox, or gun. Pitsane admitted the fact of a little saliva having fallen on the Chiboque, and in proof of its being a pure accident, mentioned that he had given the man a piece of meat, by way of making friends, just before it happened, and wiped it off with his hand as soon as it fell. In reference to a man being given, I declared that we were all ready to die rather than give up one of our number to be a slave; that my men might as well give me as I give one of them, for we were all free men. "Then you can give the gun with which the ox was shot." As we heard some of his people remarking even now that we had only "five guns", we declined, on the ground that, as they were intent on plundering us, giving a gun would be helping them to do so.

This they denied, saying they wanted the customary tribute only. I asked what right they had to demand payment for leave to tread on the ground of God, our common Father. If we trod on their gardens, we would pay, but not for marching on land which was still God's, and not theirs. They did not attempt to controvert this, because it is in accordance with their own ideas, but reverted again to the pretended crime of the saliva.

My men now entreated me to give something; and after asking the chief if he really thought the affair of the spitting a matter of guilt, and receiving an answer in the affirmative, I gave him one of my shirts. The young Chiboque were dissatisfied, and began shouting and brandishing their swords for a greater fine.

As Pitsane felt that he had been the cause of this disagreeable affair, he asked me to add something else. I gave a bunch of beads, but the counselors objected this time, so I added a large handkerchief. The more I yielded, the more unreasonable their demands became, and at every fresh demand a shout was raised by the armed party, and a rush made around us with brandishing of arms. One young man made a charge at my head from behind, but I quickly brought round the muzzle of my gun to his mouth, and he retreated. I pointed him out to the chief, and he ordered him to retire a little. I felt anxious to avoid the effusion of blood; and though sure of being able, with my Makololo, who had been drilled by Sebituane, to drive off twice the number of our assailants, though now a large body, and well armed with spears, swords, arrows, and guns, I strove to avoid actual collision. My men were quite unprepared for this exhibition, but behaved with admirable coolness. The chief and counselors, by accepting my invitation to be seated, had placed themselves in a trap, for my men very quietly surrounded them, and made them feel that there was no chance of escaping their spears. I then said that, as one thing after another had failed to satisfy them, it was evident that THEY wanted to fight, while WE only wanted to pass peaceably through the country; that they must begin first, and bear the guilt before God: we would not fight till they had struck the first blow. I then sat silent for some time. It was rather trying for me, because I knew that the Chiboque would aim at the white man first; but I was careful not to appear flurried, and, having four barrels ready for instant action, looked quietly at the savage scene around. The Chiboque countenance, by no means handsome, is not improved by the practice which they have adopted of filing the teeth to a point. The chief and counselors, seeing that they were in more danger than I, did not choose to follow our decision that they should begin by striking the first blow, and then see what we could do, and were perhaps influenced by seeing the air of cool preparation which some of my men displayed at the prospect of a work of blood.

The Chiboque at last put the matter before us in this way: "You come among us in a new way, and say you are quite friendly: how can we know it unless you give us some of your food, and you take some of ours? If you give us an ox, we will give you whatever you may wish, and then we shall be friends." In accordance with the entreaties of my men, I gave an ox; and when asked what I should like in return, mentioned food as the thing which we most needed. In the evening Njambi sent us a very small basket of meal, and two or three pounds of the flesh of our own ox! with the apology that he had no fowls, and very little of any other food. It was impossible to avoid a laugh at the coolness of the generous creatures. I was truly thankful, nevertheless, that, though resolved to die rather than deliver up one of our number to be a slave, we had so far gained our point as to be allowed to pass on without having shed human blood.

In the midst of the commotion, several Chiboque stole pieces of meat out of the sheds of my people, and Mohorisi, one of the Makololo, went boldly into the crowd and took back a marrow-bone from one of them. A few of my Batoka seemed afraid, and would perhaps have fled had the affray actually begun, but, upon the whole, I thought my men behaved admirably. They lamented having left their shields at home by command of Sekeletu, who feared that, if they carried these, they might be more disposed to be overbearing in their demeanor to the tribes we should meet. We had proceeded on the principles of peace and conciliation, and the foregoing treatment shows in what light our conduct was viewed; in fact, we were taken for interlopers trying to cheat the revenue of the tribe. They had been accustomed to get a slave or two from every slave-trader who passed them, and now that we disputed the right, they viewed the infringement on what they considered lawfully due with most virtuous indignation.

MARCH 6TH. We were informed that the people on the west of the Chiboque of Njambi were familiar with the visits of slave-traders; and it was the opinion of our guides from Kangenke that so many of my companions would be demanded from me, in the same manner as the people of Njambi had done, that I should reach the coast without a single attendant; I therefore resolved to alter our course and strike away to the N.N.E., in the hope that at some point farther north I might find an exit to the Portuguese settlement of Cassange. We proceeded at first due north, with the Kasabi villages on our right, and the Kasau on our left. During the first twenty miles we crossed many small, but now swollen streams, having the usual boggy banks, and wherever the water had stood for any length of time it was discolored with rust of iron. We saw a "nakong" antelope one day, a rare sight in this quarter; and many new and pretty flowers adorned the valleys. We could observe the difference in the seasons in our northing in company with the sun. Summer was now nearly over at Kuruman, and far advanced at Linyanti, but here we were in the middle of it; fruits, which we had eaten ripe on the Leeambye, were here quite green; but we were coming into the region where the inhabitants are favored with two rainy seasons and two crops, i.e., when the sun is going south, and when he comes back on his way to the north, as was the case at present.

On the 8th, one of the men had left an ounce or two of powder at our sleeping-place, and went back several miles for it. My clothing being wet from crossing a stream, I was compelled to wait for him; had I been moving in the sun I should have felt no harm, but the inaction led to a violent fit of fever. The continuance of this attack was a source of much regret, for we went on next day to a small rivulet called Chihune, in a lovely valley, and had, for a wonder, a clear sky and a clear moon; but such was the confusion produced in my mind by the state of my body, that I could scarcely manage, after some hours' trial, to get a lunar observation in which I could repose confidence. The Chihune flows into the Longe, and that into the Chihombo, a feeder of the Kasai. Those who know the difficulties of taking altitudes, times, and distances, and committing all of them to paper, will sympathize with me in this and many similar instances. While at Chihune, the men of a village brought wax for sale, and, on finding that we wished honey, went off and soon brought a hive. All the bees in the country are in possession of the natives, for they place hives sufficient for them all. After having ascertained this, we never attended the call of the honey-guide, for we were sure it would only lead us to a hive which we had no right to touch. The bird continues its habit of inviting attention to the honey, though its services in this district are never actually needed. My Makololo lamented that they never knew before that wax could be sold for any thing of value.

As we traverse a succession of open lawns and deep forests, it is interesting to observe something like instinct developed even in trees. One which, when cut, emits a milky juice, if met with on the open lawns, grows as an ordinary umbrageous tree, and shows no disposition to be a climber; when planted in a forest it still takes the same form, then sends out a climbing branch, which twines round another tree until it rises thirty or forty feet, or to the level of the other trees, and there spreads out a second crown where it can enjoy a fair share of the sun's rays. In parts of the forest still more dense than this, it assumes the form of a climber only, and at once avails itself of the assistance of a tall neighbor by winding vigorously round it, without attempting to form a lower head. It does not succeed so well as parasites proper, but where forced to contend for space it may be mistaken for one which is invariably a climber. The paths here were very narrow and very much encumbered with gigantic creepers, often as thick as a man's leg. There must be some reason why they prefer, in some districts, to go up trees in the common form of the thread of a screw rather than in any other. On the one bank of the Chihune they appeared to a person standing opposite them to wind up from left to right, on the other bank from right to left. I imagined this was owing to the sun being at one season of the year on their north and at another on their south. But on the Leeambye I observed creepers winding up on opposite sides of the same reed, and making a figure like the lacings of a sandal.

In passing through these narrow paths I had an opportunity of observing the peculiarities of my ox "Sinbad". He had a softer back than the others, but a much more intractable temper. His horns were bent downward and hung loosely, so he could do no harm with them; but as we wended our way slowly along the narrow path, he would suddenly dart aside. A string tied to a stick put through the cartilage of the nose serves instead of a bridle: if you jerk this back, it makes him run faster on; if you pull it to one side, he allows the nose and head to go, but keeps the opposite eye directed to the forbidden spot, and goes in spite of you. The only way he can be brought to a stand is by a stroke with a wand across the nose. When Sinbad ran in below a climber stretched over the path so low that I could not stoop under it, I was dragged off and came down on the crown of my head; and he never allowed an opportunity of the kind to pass without trying to inflict a kick, as if I neither had nor deserved his love.

A remarkable peculiarity in the forests of this country is the absence of thorns: there are but two exceptions; one a tree bearing a species of 'nux vomica', and a small shrub very like the plant of the sarsaparilla, bearing, in addition to its hooked thorns, bunches of yellow berries. The thornlessness of the vegetation is especially noticeable to those who have been in the south, where there is so great a variety of thorn-bearing plants and trees. We have thorns of every size and shape; thorns straight, thin and long, short and thick, or hooked, and so strong as to be able to cut even leather like a knife. Seed-vessels are scattered every where by these appendages. One lies flat as a shilling with two thorns in its centre, ready to run into the foot of any animal that treads upon it, and stick there for days together. Another (the 'Uncaria procumbens', or Grapple-plant) has so many hooked thorns as to cling most tenaciously to any animal to which it may become attached; when it happens to lay hold of the mouth of an ox, the animal stands and roars with pain and a sense of helplessness.

Whenever a part of the forest has been cleared for a garden, and afterward abandoned, a species of plant, with leaves like those of ginger, springs up, and contends for the possession of the soil with a great crop of ferns. This is the case all the way down to Angola, and shows the great difference of climate between this and the Bechuana country, where a fern, except one or two hardy species, is never seen. The plants above mentioned bear a pretty pink flower close to the ground, which is succeeded by a scarlet fruit full of seeds, yielding, as so many fruits in this country do, a pleasant acid juice, which, like the rest, is probably intended as a corrective to the fluids of the system in the hot climate.

On leaving the Chihune we crossed the Longe, and, as the day was cloudy, our guides wandered in a forest away to the west till we came to the River Chihombo, flowing to the E.N.E. My men depended so much on the sun for guidance that, having seen nothing of the luminary all day, they thought we had wandered back to the Chiboque, and, as often happens when bewildered, they disputed as to the point where the sun should rise next morning. As soon as the rains would allow next day, we went off to the N.E. It would have been better to have traveled by compass alone, for the guides took advantage of any fears expressed by my people, and threatened to return if presents were not made at once. But my men had never left their own country before except for rapine and murder. When they formerly came to a village they were in the habit of killing numbers of the inhabitants, and then taking a few young men to serve as guides to the next place. As this was their first attempt at an opposite line of conduct, and as they were without their shields, they felt defenseless among the greedy Chiboque, and some allowance must be made for them on that account.

SATURDAY, 11TH. Reached a small village on the banks of a narrow stream. I was too ill to go out of my little covering except to quell a mutiny which began to show itself among some of the Batoka and Ambonda of our party. They grumbled, as they often do against their chiefs, when they think them partial in their gifts, because they supposed that I had shown a preference in the distribution of the beads; but the beads I had given to my principal men were only sufficient to purchase a scanty meal, and I had hastened on to this village in order to slaughter a tired ox, and give them all a feast as well as a rest on Sunday, as preparation for the journey before us. I explained this to them, and thought their grumbling was allayed. I soon sank into a state of stupor, which the fever sometimes produced, and was oblivious to all their noise in slaughtering. On Sunday the mutineers were making a terrible din in preparing a skin they had procured. I requested them twice, by the man who attended me, to be more quiet, as the noise pained me; but as they paid no attention to this civil request, I put out my head, and, repeating it myself, was answered by an impudent laugh. Knowing that discipline would be at an end if this mutiny were not quelled, and that our lives depended on vigorously upholding authority, I seized a double-barreled pistol, and darted forth from the domicile, looking, I suppose, so savage as to put them to a precipitate flight. As some remained within hearing, I told them that I must maintain discipline, though at the expense of some of their limbs; so long as we traveled together they must remember that I was master, and not they. There being but little room to doubt my determination, they immediately became very obedient, and never afterward gave me any trouble, or imagined that they had any right to my property.

13TH. We went forward some miles, but were brought to a stand by the severity of my fever on the banks of a branch of the Loajima, another tributary of the Kasai. I was in a state of partial coma until late at night, when it became necessary for me to go out; and I was surprised to find that my men had built a little stockade, and some of them took their spears and acted as a guard. I found that we were surrounded by enemies, and a party of Chiboque lay near the gateway, after having preferred the demand of "a man, an ox, a gun, or a tusk." My men had prepared for defense in case of a night attack, and when the Chiboque wished to be shown where I lay sick, they very properly refused to point me out. In the morning I went out to the Chiboque, and found that they answered me civilly regarding my intentions in opening the country, teaching them, etc., etc. They admitted that their chiefs would be pleased with the prospect of friendship, and now only wished to exchange tokens of good-will with me, and offered three pigs, which they hoped I would accept. The people here are in the habit of making a present, and then demanding whatever they choose in return. We had been forewarned of this by our guides, so I tried to decline, by asking if they would eat one of the pigs in company with us. To this proposition they said that they durst not accede. I then accepted the present in the hope that the blame of deficient friendly feeling might not rest with me, and presented a razor, two bunches of beads, and twelve copper rings, contributed by my men from their arms. They went off to report to their chief; and as I was quite unable to move from excessive giddiness, we continued in the same spot on Tuesday evening, when they returned with a message couched in very plain terms, that a man, tusk, gun, or even an ox, alone would be acceptable; that he had every thing else in his possession but oxen, and that, whatever I should please to demand from him, he would gladly give it. As this was all said civilly, and there was no help for it if we refused but bloodshed, I gave a tired riding-ox. My late chief mutineer, an Ambonda man, was now overloyal, for he armed himself and stood at the gateway. He would rather die than see his father imposed on; but I ordered Mosantu to take him out of the way, which he did promptly, and allowed the Chiboque to march off well pleased with their booty. I told my men that I esteemed one of their lives of more value than all the oxen we had, and that the only cause which could induce me to fight would be to save the lives and liberties of the majority. In the propriety of this they all agreed, and said that, if the Chiboque molested us who behaved so peaceably, the guilt would be on their heads. This is a favorite mode of expression throughout the whole country. All are anxious to give explanation of any acts they have performed, and conclude the narration with, "I have no guilt or blame" ("molatu"). "They have the guilt." I never could be positive whether the idea in their minds is guilt in the sight of the Deity, or of mankind only.

Next morning the robber party came with about thirty yards of strong striped English calico, an axe, and two hoes for our acceptance, and returned the copper rings, as the chief was a great man, and did not need the ornaments of my men, but we noticed that they were taken back again. I divided the cloth among my men, and pleased them a little by thus compensating for the loss of the ox. I advised the chief, whose name we did not learn, as he did not deign to appear except under the alias Matiamvo, to get cattle for his own use, and expressed sorrow that I had none wherewith to enable him to make a commencement. Rains prevented our proceeding till Thursday morning, and then messengers appeared to tell us that their chief had learned that all the cloth sent by him had not been presented; that the copper rings had been secreted by the persons ordered to restore them to us, and that he had stripped the thievish emissaries of their property as a punishment. Our guides thought these were only spies of a larger party, concealed in the forest through which we were now about to pass. We prepared for defense by marching in a compact body, and allowing no one to straggle far behind the others. We marched through many miles of gloomy forest in gloomier silence, but nothing disturbed us. We came to a village, and found all the men absent, the guides thought, in the forest, with their countrymen. I was too ill to care much whether we were attacked or not. Though a pouring rain came on, as we were all anxious to get away out of a bad neighborhood, we proceeded. The thick atmosphere prevented my seeing the creeping plants in time to avoid them; so Pitsane, Mohorisi, and I, who alone were mounted, were often caught; and as there is no stopping the oxen when they have the prospect of giving the rider a tumble, we came frequently to the ground. In addition to these mishaps, Sinbad went off at a plunging gallop, the bridle broke, and I came down backward on the crown of my head. He gave me a kick on the thigh at the same time. I felt none the worse for this rough treatment, but would not recommend it to others as a palliative in cases of fever! This last attack of fever was so obstinate that it reduced me almost to a skeleton. The blanket which I used as a saddle on the back of the ox, being frequently wet, remained so beneath me even in the hot sun, and, aided by the heat of the ox, caused extensive abrasion of the skin, which was continually healing and getting sore again. To this inconvenience was now added the chafing of my projecting bones on the hard bed.

On Friday we came to a village of civil people on the banks of the Loajima itself, and we were wet all day in consequence of crossing it. The bridges over it, and another stream which we crossed at midday, were submerged, as we have hitherto invariably found, by a flood of perfectly clear water. At the second ford we were met by a hostile party who refused us further passage. I ordered my men to proceed in the same direction we had been pursuing, but our enemies spread themselves out in front of us with loud cries. Our numbers were about equal to theirs this time, so I moved on at the head of my men. Some ran off to other villages, or back to their own village, on pretense of getting ammunition; others called out that all traders came to them, and that we must do the same. As these people had plenty of iron-headed arrows and some guns, when we came to the edge of the forest I ordered my men to put the luggage in our centre; and, if our enemies did not fire, to cut down some young trees and make a screen as quickly as possible, but do nothing to them except in case of actual attack. I then dismounted, and, advancing a little toward our principal opponent, showed him how easily I could kill him, but pointed upward, saying, "I fear God." He did the same, placing his hand on his heart, pointing upward, and saying, "I fear to kill; but come to our village; come—do come." At this juncture, the old head man, Ionga Panza, a venerable negro, came up, and I invited him and all to be seated, that we might talk the matter over. Ionga Panza soon let us know that he thought himself very ill treated in being passed by. As most skirmishes arise from misunderstanding, this might have been a serious one; for, like all the tribes near the Portuguese settlements, people here imagine that they have a right to demand payment from every one who passes through the country; and now, though Ionga Panza was certainly no match for my men, yet they were determined not to forego their right without a struggle. I removed with my men to the vicinity of the village, thankful that no accident had as yet brought us into actual collision.

The reason why the people have imbibed the idea so strongly that they have a right to demand payment for leave to pass through the country is probably this. They have seen no traders except those either engaged in purchasing slaves, or who have slaves in their employment. These slave-traders have always been very much at the mercy of the chiefs through whose country they have passed; for if they afforded a ready asylum for runaway slaves, the traders might be deserted at any moment, and stripped of their property altogether. They are thus obliged to curry favor with the chiefs, so as to get a safe conduct from them. The same system is adopted to induce the chiefs to part with their people, whom all feel to be the real source of their importance in the country. On the return of the traders from the interior with chains of slaves, it is so easy for a chief who may be so disposed to take away a chain of eight or ten unresisting slaves, that the merchant is fain to give any amount of presents in order to secure the goodwill of the rulers. The independent chiefs, not knowing why their favor is so eagerly sought, become excessively proud and supercilious in their demands, and look upon white men with the greatest contempt. To such lengths did the Bangala, a tribe near to which we had now approached, proceed a few years ago, that they compelled the Portuguese traders to pay for water, wood, and even grass, and every possible pretext was invented for levying fines; and these were patiently submitted to so long as the slave-trade continued to flourish. We had unconsciously come in contact with a system which was quite unknown in the country from which my men had set out. An English trader may there hear a demand for payment of guides, but never, so far as I am aware, is he asked to pay for leave to traverse a country. The idea does not seem to have entered the native mind, except through slave-traders, for the aborigines all acknowledge that the untilled land, not needed for pasturage, belongs to God alone, and that no harm is done by people passing through it. I rather believe that, wherever the slave-trade has not penetrated, the visits of strangers are esteemed a real privilege.

The village of old Ionga Panza (lat. 10d 25′ S., long. 20d 15′ E.) is small, and embowered in lofty evergreen trees, which were hung around with fine festoons of creepers. He sent us food immediately, and soon afterward a goat, which was considered a handsome gift, there being but few domestic animals, though the country is well adapted for them. I suspect this, like the country of Shinte and Katema, must have been a tsetse district, and only recently rendered capable of supporting other domestic animals besides the goat, by the destruction of the game through the extensive introduction of fire-arms. We might all have been as ignorant of the existence of this insect plague as the Portuguese, had it not been for the numerous migrations of pastoral tribes which took place in the south in consequence of Zulu irruptions.

During these exciting scenes I always forgot my fever, but a terrible sense of sinking came back with the feeling of safety. The same demand of payment for leave to pass was made on the 20th by old Ionga Panza as by the other Chiboque. I offered the shell presented by Shinte, but Ionga Panza said he was too old for ornaments. We might have succeeded very well with him, for he was by no means unreasonable, and had but a very small village of supporters; but our two guides from Kangenke complicated our difficulties by sending for a body of Bangala traders, with a view to force us to sell the tusks of Sekeletu, and pay them with the price. We offered to pay them handsomely if they would perform their promise of guiding us to Cassange, but they knew no more of the paths than we did; and my men had paid them repeatedly, and tried to get rid of them, but could not. They now joined with our enemies, and so did the traders. Two guns and some beads belonging to the latter were standing in our encampment, and the guides seized them and ran off. As my men knew that we should be called upon to replace them, they gave chase, and when the guides saw that they would be caught, they threw down the guns, directed their flight to the village, and rushed into a hut. The doorway is not much higher than that of a dog's kennel. One of the guides was reached by one of my men as he was in the act of stooping to get in, and a cut was inflicted on a projecting part of the body which would have made any one in that posture wince. The guns were restored, but the beads were lost in the flight. All I had remaining of my stock of beads could not replace those lost; and though we explained that we had no part in the guilt of the act, the traders replied that we had brought the thieves into the country; these were of the Bangala, who had been accustomed to plague the Portuguese in the most vexatious way. We were striving to get a passage through the country, and, feeling anxious that no crime whatever should be laid to our charge, tried the conciliatory plan here, though we were not, as in the other instances, likely to be overpowered by numbers.

My men offered all their ornaments, and I offered all my beads and shirts; but, though we had come to the village against our will, and the guides had also followed us contrary to our desire, and had even sent for the Bangala traders without our knowledge or consent, yet matters could not be arranged without our giving an ox and one of the tusks. We were all becoming disheartened, and could not wonder that native expeditions from the interior to the coast had generally failed to reach their destinations. My people were now so much discouraged that some proposed to return home; the prospect of being obliged to return when just on the threshold of the Portuguese settlements distressed me exceedingly. After using all my powers of persuasion, I declared to them that if they returned I would go on alone, and went into my little tent with the mind directed to Him who hears the sighing of the soul, and was soon followed by the head of Mohorisi, saying, "We will never leave you. Do not be disheartened. Wherever you lead we will follow. Our remarks were made only on account of the injustice of these people." Others followed, and with the most artless simplicity of manner told me to be comforted—"they were all my children; they knew no one but Sekeletu and me, and they would die for me; they had not fought because I did not wish it; they had just spoken in the bitterness of their spirit, and when feeling that they could do nothing; but if these enemies begin you will see what we can do." One of the oxen we offered to the Chiboque had been rejected because he had lost part of his tail, as they thought that it had been cut off and witchcraft medicine inserted; and some mirth was excited by my proposing to raise a similar objection to all the oxen we still had in our possession. The remaining four soon presented a singular shortness of their caudal extremities, and though no one ever asked whether they had medicine in the stumps or no, we were no more troubled by the demand for an ox! We now slaughtered another ox, that the spectacle might not be seen of the owners of the cattle fasting while the Chiboque were feasting.

Chapter 19

Guides prepaid—Bark Canoes—Deserted by Guides—Mistakes respecting the Coanza—Feelings of freed Slaves—Gardens and Villages—Native Traders—A Grave—Valley of the Quango—Bamboo—White Larvae used as Food—Bashinje Insolence—A posing Question—The Chief Sansawe—His Hostility—Pass him safely—The River Quango—Chief's mode of dressing his Hair—Opposition—Opportune Aid by Cypriano—His generous Hospitality—Ability of Half-castes to read and write—Books and Images—Marauding Party burned in the Grass—Arrive at Cassange—A good Supper—Kindness of Captain Neves—Portuguese Curiosity and Questions— Anniversary of the Resurrection—No Prejudice against Color—Country around Cassange—Sell Sekeletu's Ivory—Makololo's Surprise at the high Price obtained—Proposal to return Home, and Reasons— Soldier-guide—Hill Kasala—Tala Mungongo, Village of—Civility of Basongo—True Negroes—A Field of Wheat— Carriers—Sleeping-places—Fever—Enter District of Ambaca—Good Fruits of Jesuit Teaching—The 'Tampan'; its Bite—Universal Hospitality of the Portuguese—A Tale of the Mambari—Exhilarating Effects of Highland Scenery—District of Golungo Alto—Want of good Roads—Fertility—Forests of gigantic Timber—Native Carpenters—Coffee Estate—Sterility of Country near the Coast—Mosquitoes—Fears of the Makololo—Welcome by Mr. Gabriel to Loanda.

24TH. Ionga Panza's sons agreed to act as guides into the territory of the Portuguese if I would give them the shell given by Shinte. I was strongly averse to this, and especially to give it beforehand, but yielded to the entreaty of my people to appear as if showing confidence in these hopeful youths. They urged that they wished to leave the shell with their wives, as a sort of payment to them for enduring their husbands' absence so long. Having delivered the precious shell, we went west-by-north to the River Chikapa, which here (lat. 10d 22' S.) is forty or fifty yards wide, and at present was deep; it was seen flowing over a rocky, broken cataract with great noise about half a mile above our ford. We were ferried over in a canoe, made out of a single piece of bark sewed together at the ends, and having sticks placed in it at different parts to act as ribs. The word Chikapa means bark or skin; and as this is the only river in which we saw this kind of canoe used, and we heard that this stream is so low during most of the year as to be easily fordable, it probably derives its name from the use made of the bark canoes when it is in flood. We now felt the loss of our pontoon, for the people to whom the canoe belonged made us pay once when we began to cross, then a second time when half of us were over, and a third time when all were over but my principal man Pitsane and myself. Loyanke took off his cloth and paid my passage with it. The Makololo always ferried their visitors over rivers without pay, and now began to remark that they must in future fleece the Mambari as these Chiboque had done to us; they had all been loud in condemnation of the meanness, and when I asked if they could descend to be equally mean, I was answered that they would only do it in revenge. They like to have a plausible excuse for meanness.

Next morning our guides went only about a mile, and then told us they would return home. I expected this when paying them beforehand, in accordance with the entreaties of the Makololo, who are rather ignorant of the world. Very energetic remonstrances were addressed to the guides, but they slipped off one by one in the thick forest through which we were passing, and I was glad to hear my companions coming to the conclusion that, as we were now in parts visited by traders, we did not require the guides, whose chief use had been to prevent misapprehension of our objects in the minds of the villagers. The country was somewhat more undulating now than it had been, and several fine small streams flowed in deep woody dells. The trees are very tall and straight, and the forests gloomy and damp; the ground in these solitudes is quite covered with yellow and brown mosses, and light-colored lichens clothe all the trees. The soil is extremely fertile, being generally a black loam covered with a thick crop of tall grasses. We passed several villages too. The head man of a large one scolded us well for passing, when he intended to give us food. Where slave-traders have been in the habit of coming, they present food, then demand three or four times its value as a custom. We were now rather glad to get past villages without intercourse with the inhabitants.

We were traveling W.N.W., and all the rivulets we here crossed had a northerly course, and were reported to fall into the Kasai or Loke; most of them had the peculiar boggy banks of the country. As we were now in the alleged latitude of the Coanza, I was much astonished at the entire absence of any knowledge of that river among the natives of this quarter. But I was then ignorant of the fact that the Coanza rises considerably to the west of this, and has a comparatively short course from its source to the sea.

The famous Dr. Lacerda seems to have labored under the same mistake as myself, for he recommended the government of Angola to establish a chain of forts along the banks of that river, with a view to communication with the opposite coast. As a chain of forts along its course would lead southward instead of eastward, we may infer that the geographical data within reach of that eminent man were no better than those according to which I had directed my course to the Coanza where it does not exist.

26TH. We spent Sunday on the banks of the Quilo or Kweelo, here a stream of about ten yards wide. It runs in a deep glen, the sides of which are almost five hundred yards of slope, and rocky, the rocks being hardened calcareous tufa lying on clay shale and sandstone below, with a capping of ferruginous conglomerate. The scenery would have been very pleasing, but fever took away much of the joy of life, and severe daily intermittents rendered me very weak and always glad to recline.

As we were now in the slave-market, it struck me that the sense of insecurity felt by the natives might account for the circumstance that those who have been sold as slaves and freed again, when questioned, profess to like the new state better than their primitive one. They lived on rich, fertile plains, which seldom inspire that love of country which the mountains do. If they had been mountaineers, they would have pined for home. To one who has observed the hard toil of the poor in old civilized countries, the state in which the inhabitants here live is one of glorious ease. The country is full of little villages. Food abounds, and very little labor is required for its cultivation; the soil is so rich that no manure is required; when a garden becomes too poor for good crops of maize, millet, etc., the owner removes a little farther into the forest, applies fire round the roots of the larger trees to kill them, cuts down the smaller, and a new, rich garden is ready for the seed. The gardens usually present the appearance of a large number of tall, dead trees standing without bark, and maize growing between them. The old gardens continue to yield manioc for years after the owners have removed to other spots for the sake of millet and maize. But, while vegetable aliment is abundant, there is a want of salt and animal food, so that numberless traps are seen, set for mice, in all the forests of Londa. The vegetable diet leaves great craving for flesh, and I have no doubt but that, when an ordinary quantity of mixed food is supplied to freed slaves, they actually do feel more comfortable than they did at home. Their assertions, however, mean but little, for they always try to give an answer to please, and if one showed them a nugget of gold, they would generally say that these abounded in their country.

One could detect, in passing, the variety of character found among the owners of gardens and villages. Some villages were the pictures of neatness. We entered others enveloped in a wilderness of weeds, so high that, when sitting on ox-back in the middle of the village, we could only see the tops of the huts. If we entered at midday, the owners would come lazily forth, pipe in hand, and leisurely puff away in dreamy indifference. In some villages weeds are not allowed to grow; cotton, tobacco, and different plants used as relishes are planted round the huts; fowls are kept in cages, and the gardens present the pleasant spectacle of different kinds of grain and pulse at various periods of their growth. I sometimes admired the one class, and at times wished I could have taken the world easy for a time like the other. Every village swarms with children, who turn out to see the white man pass, and run along with strange cries and antics; some run up trees to get a good view: all are agile climbers throughout Londa. At friendly villages they have scampered alongside our party for miles at a time. We usually made a little hedge around our sheds; crowds of women came to the entrance of it, with children on their backs, and long pipes in their mouths, gazing at us for hours. The men, rather than disturb them, crawled through a hole in the hedge, and it was common to hear a man in running off say to them, "I am going to tell my mamma to come and see the white man's oxen."

In continuing our W.N.W. course, we met many parties of native traders, each carrying some pieces of cloth and salt, with a few beads to barter for bees'-wax. They are all armed with Portuguese guns, and have cartridges with iron balls. When we meet we usually stand a few minutes. They present a little salt, and we give a bit of ox-hide, or some other trifle, and then part with mutual good wishes. The hide of the oxen we slaughtered had been a valuable addition to our resources, for we found it in so great repute for girdles all through Loanda that we cut up every skin into strips about two inches broad, and sold them for meal and manioc as we went along. As we came nearer Angola we found them of less value, as the people there possess cattle themselves.

The village on the Kweelo, at which we spent Sunday, was that of a civil, lively old man, called Sakandala, who offered no objections to our progress. We found we should soon enter on the territory of the Bashinje (Chinge of the Portuguese), who are mixed with another tribe, named Bangala, which have been at war with the Babindele or Portuguese. Rains and fever, as usual, helped to impede our progress until we were put on the path which leads from Cassange and Bihe to Matiamvo, by a head man named Kamboela. This was a well-beaten footpath, and soon after entering upon it we met a party of half-caste traders from Bihe, who confirmed the information we had already got of this path leading straight to Cassange, through which they had come on their way from Bihe to Cabango. They kindly presented my men with some tobacco, and marveled greatly when they found that I had never been able to teach myself to smoke. On parting with them we came to a trader's grave. This was marked by a huge cone of sticks placed in the form of the roof of a hut, with a palisade around it. At an opening on the western side an ugly idol was placed: several strings of beads and bits of cloth were hung around. We learned that he had been a half-caste, who had died on his way back from Matiamvo.

As we were now alone, and sure of being on the way to the abodes of civilization, we went on briskly.

On the 30th we came to a sudden descent from the high land, indented by deep, narrow valleys, over which we had lately been traveling. It is generally so steep that it can only be descended at particular points, and even there I was obliged to dismount, though so weak that I had to be led by my companions to prevent my toppling over in walking down. It was annoying to feel myself so helpless, for I never liked to see a man, either sick or well, giving in effeminately. Below us lay the valley of the Quango. If you sit on the spot where Mary Queen of Scots viewed the battle of Langside, and look down on the vale of Clyde, you may see in miniature the glorious sight which a much greater and richer valley presented to our view. It is about a hundred miles broad, clothed with dark forest, except where the light green grass covers meadow-lands on the Quango, which here and there glances out in the sun as it wends its way to the north. The opposite side of this great valley appears like a range of lofty mountains, and the descent into it about a mile, which, measured perpendicularly, may be from a thousand to twelve hundred feet. Emerging from the gloomy forests of Londa, this magnificent prospect made us all feel as if a weight had been lifted off our eyelids. A cloud was passing across the middle of the valley, from which rolling thunder pealed, while above all was glorious sunlight; and when we went down to the part where we saw it passing, we found that a very heavy thunder-shower had fallen under the path of the cloud; and the bottom of the valley, which from above seemed quite smooth, we discovered to be intersected and furrowed by great numbers of deep-cut streams. Looking back from below, the descent appears as the edge of a table-land, with numerous indented dells and spurs jutting out all along, giving it a serrated appearance. Both the top and sides of the sierra are covered with trees, but large patches of the more perpendicular parts are bare, and exhibit the red soil, which is general over the region we have now entered.

The hollow affords a section of this part of the country; and we find that the uppermost stratum is the ferruginous conglomerate already mentioned. The matrix is rust of iron (or hydrous peroxide of iron and hematite), and in it are imbedded water-worn pebbles of sandstone and quartz. As this is the rock underlying the soil of a large part of Londa, its formation must have preceded the work of denudation by an arm of the sea, which washed away the enormous mass of matter required before the valley of Cassange could assume its present form. The strata under the conglomerate are all of red clay shale of different degrees of hardness, the most indurated being at the bottom. This red clay shale is named "keele" in Scotland, and has always been considered as an indication of gold; but the only thing we discovered was that it had given rise to a very slippery clay soil, so different from that which we had just left that Mashauana, who always prided himself on being an adept at balancing himself in the canoe on water, and so sure of foot on land that he could afford to express contempt for any one less gifted, came down in a very sudden and undignified manner, to the delight of all whom he had previously scolded for falling.

Here we met with the bamboo as thick as a man's arm, and many new trees. Others, which we had lost sight of since leaving Shinte, now reappeared; but nothing struck us more than the comparative scragginess of the trees in this hollow. Those on the high lands we had left were tall and straight; here they were stunted, and not by any means so closely planted together. The only way I could account for this was by supposing, as the trees were of different species, that the greater altitude suited the nature of those above better than the lower altitude did the other species below.

SUNDAY, APRIL 2D. We rested beside a small stream, and our hunger being now very severe, from having lived on manioc alone since leaving Ionza Panza's, we slaughtered one of our four remaining oxen. The people of this district seem to feel the craving for animal food as much as we did, for they spend much energy in digging large white larvae out of the damp soil adjacent to their streams, and use them as a relish to their vegetable diet. The Bashinje refused to sell any food for the poor old ornaments my men had now to offer. We could get neither meal nor manioc, but should have been comfortable had not the Bashinje chief Sansawe pestered us for the customary present. The native traders informed us that a display of force was often necessary before they could pass this man.

Sansawe, the chief of a portion of the Bashinje, having sent the usual formal demand for a man, an ox, or a tusk, spoke very contemptuously of the poor things we offered him instead. We told his messengers that the tusks were Sekeletu's: every thing was gone except my instruments, which could be of no use to them whatever. One of them begged some meat, and, when it was refused, said to my men, "You may as well give it, for we shall take all after we have killed you to-morrow." The more humbly we spoke, the more insolent the Bashinje became, till at last we were all feeling savage and sulky, but continued to speak as civilly as we could. They are fond of argument, and when I denied their right to demand tribute from a white man, who did not trade in slaves, an old white-headed negro put rather a posing question: "You know that God has placed chiefs among us whom we ought to support. How is it that you, who have a book that tells you about him, do not come forward at once to pay this chief tribute like every one else?" I replied by asking, "How could I know that this was a chief, who had allowed me to remain a day and a half near him without giving me any thing to eat?" This, which to the uninitiated may seem sophistry, was to the Central Africans quite a rational question, for he at once admitted that food ought to have been sent, and added that probably his chief was only making it ready for me, and that it would come soon.

After being wearied by talking all day to different parties sent by Sansawe, we were honored by a visit from himself: he is quite a young man, and of rather a pleasing countenance. There can not have been much intercourse between real Portuguese and these people even here, so close to the Quango, for Sansawe asked me to show him my hair, on the ground that, though he had heard of it, and some white men had even passed through his country, he had never seen straight hair before. This is quite possible, as most of the slave-traders are not Portuguese, but half-castes. The difference between their wool and our hair caused him to burst into a laugh, and the contrast between the exposed and unexposed parts of my skin, when exhibited in evidence of our all being made of one stock originally, and the children of one Maker, seemed to strike him with wonder. I then showed him my watch, and wished to win my way into his confidence by conversation; but, when about to exhibit my pocket compass, he desired me to desist, as he was afraid of my wonderful things. I told him, if he knew my aims as the tribes in the interior did, and as I hoped he would yet know them and me, he would be glad to stay, and see also the pictures of the magic lantern; but, as it was now getting dark, he had evidently got enough of my witchery, and began to use some charms to dispel any kindly feelings he might have found stealing round his heart. He asked leave to go, and when his party moved off a little way, he sent for my spokesman, and told him that, "if we did not add a red jacket and a man to our gift of a few copper rings and a few pounds of meat, we must return by the way we had come." I said in reply "that we should certainly go forward next day, and if he commenced hostilities, the blame before God would be that of Sansawe;" and my man added of his own accord, "How many white men have you killed in this path?" which might be interpreted into, "You have never killed any white man, and you will find ours more difficult to manage than you imagine." It expressed a determination, which we had often repeated to each other, to die rather than yield one of our party to be a slave.

Hunger has a powerful effect on the temper. When we had got a good meal of meat, we could all bear the petty annoyances of these borderers on the more civilized region in front with equanimity; but having suffered considerably of late, we were all rather soured in our feelings, and not unfrequently I overheard my companions remark in their own tongue, in answer to threats of attack, "That's what we want: only begin then;" or with clenched teeth they would exclaim to each other, "These things have never traveled, and do not know what men are." The worrying, of which I give only a slight sketch, had considerable influence on my own mind, and more especially as it was impossible to make any allowance for the Bashinje, such as I was willing to award to the Chiboque. They saw that we had nothing to give, nor would they be benefited in the least by enforcing the impudent order to return whence we had come. They were adding insult to injury, and this put us all into a fighting spirit, and, as nearly as we could judge, we expected to be obliged to cut our way through the Bashinje next morning.

3D APRIL. As soon as day dawned we were astir, and, setting off in a drizzling rain, passed close to the village. This rain probably damped the ardor of the robbers. We, however, expected to be fired upon from every clump of trees, or from some of the rocky hillocks among which we were passing; and it was only after two hours' march that we began to breathe freely, and my men remarked, in thankfulness, "We are children of Jesus." We continued our course, notwithstanding the rain, across the bottom of the Quango Valley, which we found broken by clay shale rocks jutting out, though lying nearly horizontally. The grass in all the hollows, at this time quite green, was about two feet higher than my head while sitting on ox-back. This grass, wetted by the rain, acted as a shower-bath on one side of our bodies; and some deep gullies, full of DISCOLORED water, completed the cooling process. We passed many villages during this drenching, one of which possessed a flock of sheep; and after six hours we came to a stand near the River Quango (lat. 9d 53' S., long. 18d 37' E.), which may be called the boundary of the Portuguese claims to territory on the west. As I had now no change of clothing, I was glad to cower under the shelter of my blanket, thankful to God for his goodness in bringing us so far without losing one of the party.

4TH APRIL. We were now on the banks of the Quango, a river one hundred and fifty yards wide, and very deep. The water was discolored—a circumstance which we had observed in no river in Londa or in the Makololo country. This fine river flows among extensive meadows clothed with gigantic grass and reeds, and in a direction nearly north.

The Quango is said by the natives to contain many venomous water-snakes, which congregate near the carcass of any hippopotamus that may be killed in it. If this is true, it may account for all the villages we saw being situated far from its banks. We were advised not to sleep near it; but, as we were anxious to cross to the western side, we tried to induce some of the Bashinje to lend us canoes for the purpose. This brought out the chief of these parts, who informed us that all the canoe-men were his children, and nothing could be done without his authority. He then made the usual demand for a man, an ox, or a gun, adding that otherwise we must return to the country from which we had come. As I did not believe that this man had any power over the canoes of the other side, and suspected that if I gave him my blanket—the only thing I now had in reserve—he might leave us in the lurch after all, I tried to persuade my men to go at once to the bank, about two miles off, and obtain possession of the canoes before we gave up the blanket; but they thought that this chief might attack us in the act of crossing, should we do so. The chief came himself to our encampment and made his demand again. My men stripped off the last of their copper rings and gave them; but he was still intent on a man. He thought, as others did, that my men were slaves. He was a young man, with his woolly hair elaborately dressed: that behind was made up into a cone, about eight inches in diameter at the base, carefully swathed round with red and black thread. As I resisted the proposal to deliver up my blanket until they had placed us on the western bank, this chief continued to worry us with his demands till I was tired. My little tent was now in tatters, and having a wider hole behind than the door in front, I tried in vain to lie down out of sight of our persecutors. We were on a reedy flat, and could not follow our usual plan of a small stockade, in which we had time to think over and concoct our plans. As I was trying to persuade my men to move on to the bank in spite of these people, a young half-caste Portuguese sergeant of militia, Cypriano di Abreu, made his appearance, and gave the same advice. He had come across the Quango in search of bees'-wax. When we moved off from the chief who had been plaguing us, his people opened a fire from our sheds, and continued to blaze away some time in the direction we were going, but none of the bullets reached us. It is probable that they expected a demonstration of the abundance of ammunition they possessed would make us run; but when we continued to move quietly to the ford, they proceeded no farther than our sleeping-place. Cypriano assisted us in making a more satisfactory arrangement with the ferrymen than parting with my blanket; and as soon as we reached the opposite bank we were in the territory of the Bangala, who are subjects of the Portuguese, and often spoken of as the Cassanges or Cassantse; and happily all our difficulties with the border tribes were at an end.

Passing with light hearts through the high grass by a narrow footpath for about three miles to the west of the river, we came to several neat square houses, with many cleanly-looking half-caste Portuguese standing in front of them to salute us. They are all enrolled in the militia, and our friend Cypriano is the commander of a division established here. The Bangala were very troublesome to the Portuguese traders, and at last proceeded so far as to kill one of them; the government of Angola then sent an expedition against them, which being successful, the Bangala were dispersed, and are now returning to their former abodes as vassals. The militia are quartered among them, and engage in trade and agriculture for their support, as no pay is given to this branch of the service by the government.

We came to the dwelling of Cypriano after dark, and I pitched my little tent in front of it for the night. We had the company of mosquitoes here. We never found them troublesome on the banks of the pure streams of Londa. On the morning of the 5th Cypriano generously supplied my men with pumpkins and maize, and then invited me to breakfast, which consisted of ground-nuts and roasted maize, then boiled manioc roots and ground-nuts, with guavas and honey as a dessert. I felt sincerely grateful for this magnificent breakfast.

At dinner Cypriano was equally bountiful, and several of his friends joined us in doing justice to his hospitality. Before eating, all had water poured on the hands by a female slave to wash them. One of the guests cut up a fowl with a knife and fork. Neither forks nor spoons were used in eating. The repast was partaken of with decency and good manners, and concluded by washing the hands as at first.

All of them could read and write with ease. I examined the books they possessed, and found a small work on medicine, a small cyclopaedia, and a Portuguese dictionary, in which the definition of a "priest" seemed strange to a Protestant, namely, "one who takes care of the conscience." They had also a few tracts containing the Lives of the Saints, and Cypriano had three small wax images of saints in his room. One of these was St. Anthony, who, had he endured the privations he did in his cell in looking after these lost sheep, would have lived to better purpose. Neither Cypriano nor his companions knew what the Bible was, but they had relics in German-silver cases hung round their necks, to act as charms and save them from danger by land or by water, in the same way as the heathen have medicines. It is a pity that the Church to which they belong, when unable to attend to the wants of her children, does not give them the sacred writings in their own tongue; it would surely be better to see them good Protestants, if these would lead them to be so, than entirely ignorant of God's message to man. For my part, I would much prefer to see the Africans good Roman Catholics than idolatrous heathen.

Much of the civility shown to us here was, no doubt, owing to the flattering letters of recommendation I carried from the Chevalier Du Prat, of Cape Town; but I am inclined to believe that my friend Cypriano was influenced, too, by feelings of genuine kindness, for he quite bared his garden in feeding us during the few days which I remained, anxiously expecting the clouds to disperse, so far as to allow of my taking observations for the determination of the position of the Quango. He slaughtered an ox for us, and furnished his mother and her maids with manioc roots, to prepare farina for the four or five days of our journey to Cassange, and never even hinted at payment. My wretched appearance must have excited his compassion. The farina is prepared by washing the roots well, then rasping them down to a pulp. Next, this is roasted slightly on a metal plate over a fire, and is then used with meat as a vegetable. It closely resembles wood-sawings, and on that account is named "wood-meal". It is insipid, and employed to lick up any gravy remaining on one's plate. Those who have become accustomed to it relish it even after they have returned to Europe.

The manioc cultivated here is of the sweet variety; the bitter, to which we were accustomed in Londa, is not to be found very extensively in this fertile valley. May is the beginning of winter, yet many of the inhabitants were busy planting maize; that which we were now eating was planted in the beginning of February. The soil is exceedingly fertile, of a dark red color, and covered with such a dense, heavy crop of coarse grass, that when a marauding party of Ambonda once came for plunder while it was in a dried state, the Bangala encircled the common enemy with a fire which completely destroyed them. This, which is related on the authority of Portuguese who were then in the country, I can easily believe to be true, for the stalks of the grass are generally as thick as goose-quills, and no flight could be made through the mass of grass in any direction where a footpath does not exist. Probably, in the case mentioned, the direction of the wind was such as to drive the flames across the paths, and prevent escape along them. On one occasion I nearly lost my wagon by fire, in a valley where the grass was only about three feet high. We were roused by the roar, as of a torrent, made by the fire coming from the windward. I immediately set fire to that on our leeward, and had just time to drag the wagon on to the bare space there before the windward flames reached the place where it had stood.

We were detained by rains and a desire to ascertain our geographical position till Monday, the 10th, and only got the latitude 9d 50′ S.; and, after three days' pretty hard traveling through the long grass, reached Cassange, the farthest inland station of the Portuguese in Western Africa. We crossed several fine little streams running into the Quango; and as the grass continued to tower about two feet over our heads, it generally obstructed our view of the adjacent country, and sometimes hung over the path, making one side of the body wet with the dew every morning, or, when it rained, kept me wet during the whole day. I made my entrance in a somewhat forlorn state as to clothing among our Portuguese allies. The first gentleman I met in the village asked if I had a passport, and said it was necessary to take me before the authorities. As I was in the same state of mind in which individuals are who commit a petty depredation in order to obtain the shelter and food of a prison, I gladly accompanied him to the house of the commandant or Chefe, Senhor de Silva Rego. Having shown my passport to this gentleman, he politely asked me to supper, and, as we had eaten nothing except the farina of Cypriano from the Quango to this, I suspect I appeared particularly ravenous to the other gentlemen around the table. They seemed, however, to understand my position pretty well, from having all traveled extensively themselves; had they not been present, I might have put some in my pocket to eat by night; for, after fever, the appetite is excessively keen, and manioc is one of the most unsatisfying kinds of food. Captain Antonio Rodrigues Neves then kindly invited me to take up my abode in his house. Next morning this generous man arrayed me in decent clothing, and continued during the whole period of my stay to treat me as if I had been his brother. I feel deeply grateful to him for his disinterested kindness. He not only attended to my wants, but also furnished food for my famishing party free of charge.

The village of Cassange (pronounced Kassanje) is composed of thirty or forty traders' houses, scattered about without any regularity, on an elevated flat spot in the great Quango or Cassange valley. They are built of wattle and daub, and surrounded by plantations of manioc, maize, etc. Behind them there are usually kitchen gardens, in which the common European vegetables, as potatoes, peas, cabbages, onions, tomatoes, etc., etc., grow. Guavas and bananas appear, from the size and abundance of the trees, to have been introduced many years ago, while the land was still in the possession of the natives; but pine-apples, orange, fig, and cashew trees have but lately been tried. There are about forty Portuguese traders in this district, all of whom are officers in the militia, and many of them have become rich from adopting the plan of sending out Pombeiros, or native traders, with large quantities of goods, to trade in the more remote parts of the country. Some of the governors of Loanda, the capital of this, the kingdom of Angola, have insisted on the observance of a law which, from motives of humanity, forbids the Portuguese themselves from passing beyond the boundary. They seem to have taken it for granted that, in cases where the white trader was killed, the aggression had been made by him, and they wished to avoid the necessity of punishing those who had been provoked to shed Portuguese blood. This indicates a much greater impartiality than has obtained in our own dealings with the Caffres, for we have engaged in most expensive wars with them without once inquiring whether any of the fault lay with our frontier colonists. The Cassange traders seem inclined to spread along the Quango, in spite of the desire of their government to keep them on one spot, for mutual protection in case of war. If I might judge from the week of feasting I passed among them, they are generally prosperous.

As I always preferred to appear in my own proper character, I was an object of curiosity to these hospitable Portuguese. They evidently looked upon me as an agent of the English government, engaged in some new movement for the suppression of slavery. They could not divine what a "missionario" had to do with the latitudes and longitudes, which I was intent on observing. When we became a little familiar, the questions put were rather amusing: "Is it common for missionaries to be doctors?" "Are you a doctor of medicine and a 'doutor mathematico' too? You must be more than a missionary to know how to calculate the longitude! Come, tell us at once what rank you hold in the English army." They may have given credit to my reason for wearing the mustache, as that explains why men have beards and women have none; but that which puzzled many besides my Cassange friends was the anomaly of my being a "sacerdote", with a wife and four children! I usually got rid of the last question by putting another: "Is it not better to have children with a wife, than to have children without a wife?" But all were most kind and hospitable; and as one of their festivals was near, they invited me to partake of the feast.

The anniversary of the Resurrection of our Savior was observed on the 16th of April as a day of rejoicing, though the Portuguese have no priests at Cassange. The colored population dressed up a figure intended to represent Judas Iscariot, and paraded him on a riding-ox about the village; sneers and maledictions were freely bestowed on the poor wretch thus represented. The slaves and free colored population, dressed in their gayest clothing, made visits to all the principal merchants, and wishing them "a good feast", expected a present in return. This, though frequently granted in the shape of pieces of calico to make new dresses, was occasionally refused, but the rebuff did not much affect the petitioner.

At ten A.M. we went to the residence of the commandant, and on a signal being given, two of the four brass guns belonging to the government commenced firing, and continued some time, to the great admiration of my men, whose ideas of the power of a cannon are very exalted. The Portuguese flag was hoisted and trumpets sounded, as an expression of joy at the resurrection of our Lord. Captain Neves invited all the principal inhabitants of the place, and did what he could to feast them in a princely style. All manner of foreign preserved fruits and wine from Portugal, biscuits from America, butter from Cork, and beer from England, were displayed, and no expense spared in rendering the entertainment joyous. After the feast was over they sat down to the common amusement of card-playing, which continued till eleven o'clock at night. As far as a mere traveler could judge, they seemed to be polite and willing to aid each other. They live in a febrile district, and many of them had enlarged spleens. They have neither doctor, apothecary, school, nor priest, and, when taken ill, trust to each other and to Providence. As men left in such circumstances must think for themselves, they have all a good idea of what ought to be done in the common diseases of the country, and what they have of either medicine or skill they freely impart to each other.

None of these gentlemen had Portuguese wives. They usually come to Africa in order to make a little money, and return to Lisbon. Hence they seldom bring their wives with them, and never can be successful colonists in consequence. It is common for them to have families by native women. It was particularly gratifying to me, who had been familiar with the stupid prejudice against color, entertained only by those who are themselves becoming tawny, to view the liberality with which people of color were treated by the Portuguese. Instances, so common in the South, in which half-caste children are abandoned, are here extremely rare. They are acknowledged at table, and provided for by their fathers as if European. The colored clerks of the merchants sit at the same table with their employers without any embarrassment. The civil manners of superiors to inferiors is probably the result of the position they occupy—a few whites among thousands of blacks; but nowhere else in Africa is there so much good-will between Europeans and natives as here. If some border colonists had the absolute certainty of our government declining to bear them out in their arrogance, we should probably hear less of Caffre insolence. It is insolence which begets insolence.

From the village of Cassange we have a good view of the surrounding country: it is a gently undulating plain, covered with grass and patches of forest. The western edge of the Quango valley appears, about twenty miles off, as if it were a range of lofty mountains, and passes by the name of Tala Mungongo, "Behold the Range". In the old Portuguese map, to which I had been trusting in planning my route, it is indicated as Talla Mugongo, or "Castle of Rocks!" and the Coanza is put down as rising therefrom; but here I was assured that the Coanza had its source near Bihe, far to the southwest of this, and we should not see that river till we came near Pungo Andonga. It is somewhat remarkable that more accurate information about this country has not been published. Captain Neves and others had a correct idea of the courses of the rivers, and communicated their knowledge freely; yet about this time maps were sent to Europe from Angola representing the Quango and Coanza as the same river, and Cassange placed about one hundred miles from its true position. The frequent recurrence of the same name has probably helped to increase the confusion. I have crossed several Quangos, but all insignificant, except that which drains this valley. The repetition of the favorite names of chiefs, as Catende, is also perplexing, as one Catende may be mistaken for another. To avoid this confusion as much as possible, I have refrained from introducing many names. Numerous villages are studded all over the valley; but these possess no permanence, and many more existed previous to the Portuguese expedition of 1850 to punish the Bangala.

This valley, as I have before remarked, is all fertile in the extreme. My men could never cease admiring its capability for raising their corn ('Holcus sorghum'), and despising the comparatively limited cultivation of the inhabitants. The Portuguese informed me that no manure is ever needed, but that, the more the ground is tilled, the better it yields. Virgin soil does not give such a heavy crop as an old garden, and, judging from the size of the maize and manioc in the latter, I can readily believe the statement. Cattle do well, too. Viewing the valley as a whole, it may be said that its agricultural and pastoral riches are lying waste. Both the Portuguese and their descendants turn their attention almost exclusively to trade in wax and ivory, and though the country would yield any amount of corn and dairy produce, the native Portuguese live chiefly on manioc, and the Europeans purchase their flour, bread, butter, and cheese from the Americans.

As the traders of Cassange were the first white men we had come to, we sold the tusks belonging to Sekeletu, which had been brought to test the difference of prices in the Makololo and white men's country. The result was highly satisfactory to my companions, as the Portuguese give much larger prices for ivory than traders from the Cape can possibly give, who labor under the disadvantage of considerable overland expenses and ruinous restrictions. Two muskets, three small barrels of gunpowder, and English calico and baize sufficient to clothe my whole party, with large bunches of beads, all for one tusk, were quite delightful for those who had been accustomed to give two tusks for one gun. With another tusk we procured calico, which here is the chief currency, to pay our way down to the coast. The remaining two were sold for money to purchase a horse for Sekeletu at Loanda.

The superiority of this new market was quite astounding to the Makololo, and they began to abuse the traders by whom they had, while in their own country, been visited, and, as they now declared, "cheated". They had no idea of the value of time and carriage, and it was somewhat difficult for me to convince them that the reason of the difference of prices lay entirely in what they themselves had done in coming here, and that, if the Portuguese should carry goods to their country, they would by no means be so liberal in their prices. They imagined that, if the Cassange traders came to Linyanti, they would continue to vend their goods at Cassange prices. I believe I gave them at last a clear idea of the manner in which prices were regulated by the expenses incurred; and when we went to Loanda, and saw goods delivered at a still cheaper rate, they concluded that it would be better for them to come to that city, than to turn homeward at Cassange.

It was interesting for me to observe the effects of the restrictive policy pursued by the Cape government toward the Bechuanas. Like all other restrictions on trade, the law of preventing friendly tribes from purchasing arms and ammunition only injures the men who enforce it. The Cape government, as already observed, in order to gratify a company of independent Boers, whose well-known predilection for the practice of slavery caused them to stipulate that a number of peaceable, honest tribes should be kept defenseless, agreed to allow free trade in arms and ammunition to the Boers, and prevent the same trade to the Bechuanas. The Cape government thereby unintentionally aided, and continues to aid, the Boers to enslave the natives. But arms and ammunition flow in on all sides by new channels, and where formerly the price of a large tusk procured but one musket, one tusk of the same size now brings ten. The profits are reaped by other nations, and the only persons really the losers, in the long run, are our own Cape merchants, and a few defenseless tribes of Bechuanas on our immediate frontier.

Mr. Rego, the commandant, very handsomely offered me a soldier as a guard to Ambaca. My men told me that they had been thinking it would be better to turn back here, as they had been informed by the people of color at Cassange that I was leading them down to the sea-coast only to sell them, and they would be taken on board ship, fattened, and eaten, as the white men were cannibals. I asked if they had ever heard of an Englishman buying or selling people; if I had not refused to take a slave when she was offered to me by Shinte; but, as I had always behaved as an English teacher, if they now doubted my intentions, they had better not go to the coast; I, however, who expected to meet some of my countrymen there, was determined to go on. They replied that they only thought it right to tell me what had been told to them, but they did not intend to leave me, and would follow wherever I should lead the way. This affair being disposed of for the time, the commandant gave them an ox, and me a friendly dinner before parting. All the merchants of Cassange accompanied us, in their hammocks carried by slaves, to the edge of the plateau on which their village stands, and we parted with the feeling in my mind that I should never forget their disinterested kindness. They not only did every thing they could to make my men and me comfortable during our stay; but, there being no hotels in

Loanda, they furnished me with letters of recommendation to their friends in that city, requesting them to receive me into their houses, for without these a stranger might find himself a lodger in the streets. May God remember them in their day of need!

The latitude and longitude of Cassange, the most easterly station of the Portuguese in Western Africa, is lat. 9d 37' 30" S., and long. 17d 49' E.; consequently we had still about 300 miles to traverse before we could reach the coast. We had a black militia corporal as a guide. He was a native of Ambaca, and, like nearly all the inhabitants of that district, known by the name of Ambakistas, could both read and write. He had three slaves with him, and was carried by them in a "tipoia", or hammock slung to a pole. His slaves were young, and unable to convey him far at a time, but he was considerate enough to walk except when we came near to a village. He then mounted his tipoia and entered the village in state; his departure was made in the same manner, and he continued in the hammock till the village was out of sight. It was interesting to observe the manners of our soldier-guide. Two slaves were always employed in carrying his tipoia, and the third carried a wooden box, about three feet long, containing his writing materials, dishes, and clothing. He was cleanly in all his ways, and, though quite black himself, when he scolded any one of his own color, abused him as a "negro". When he wanted to purchase any article from a village, he would sit down, mix a little gunpowder as ink, and write a note in a neat hand to ask the price, addressing it to the shopkeeper with the rather pompous title, "Illustrissimo Senhor" (Most Illustrious Sir). This is the invariable mode of address throughout Angola. The answer returned would be in the same style, and, if satisfactory, another note followed to conclude the bargain. There is so much of this note correspondence carried on in Angola, that a very large quantity of paper is annually consumed. Some other peculiarities of our guide were not so pleasing. A land of slaves is a bad school for even the free; and I was sorry to find less truthfulness and honesty in him than in my own people. We were often cheated through his connivance with the sellers of food, and could perceive that he got a share of the plunder from them. The food is very cheap, but it was generally made dear enough, until I refused to allow him to come near the place where we were bargaining. But he took us safely down to Ambaca, and I was glad to see, on my return to Cassange, that he was promoted to be sergeant-major of a company of militia.

Having left Cassange on the 21st, we passed across the remaining portion of this excessively fertile valley to the foot of Tala Mungongo. We crossed a fine little stream called the Lui on the 22d, and another named the Luare on the 24th, then slept at the bottom of the height, which is from a thousand to fifteen hundred feet. The clouds came floating along the valley, and broke against the sides of the ascent, and the dripping rain on the tall grass made the slaps in the face it gave, when the hand or a stick was not held up before it, any thing but agreeable. This edge of the valley is exactly like the other; jutting spurs and defiles give the red ascent the same serrated appearance as that which we descended from the highlands of Londa. The whole of this vast valley has been removed by denudation, for pieces of the plateau which once filled the now vacant space stand in it, and present the same structure of red horizontal strata of equal altitudes with those of the acclivity which we are now about to ascend. One of these insulated masses, named Kasala, bore E.S.E. from the place where we made our exit from the valley, and about ten miles W.S.W. from the village of Cassange. It is remarkable for its perpendicular sides; even the natives find it extremely difficult, almost impossible, to reach its summit, though there is the temptation of marabou-nests and feathers, which are highly prized. There is a small lake reported to exist on its southern end, and, during the rainy season, a sort of natural moat is formed around the bottom. What an acquisition this would have been in feudal times in England! There is land sufficient for considerable cultivation on the top, with almost perpendicular sides more than a thousand feet in height.

We had not yet got a clear idea of the nature of Tala Mungongo. A gentleman of Cassange described it as a range of very high mountains, which it would take four hours to climb; so, though the rain and grass had wetted us miserably, and I was suffering from an attack of fever got while observing by night for the position of Cassange, I eagerly commenced the ascent. The path was steep and slippery; deep gorges appear on each side of it, leaving but a narrow path along certain spurs of the sierra for the traveler; but we accomplished the ascent in an hour, and when there, found we had just got on to a table-land similar to that we had left before we entered the great Quango valley. We had come among lofty trees again. One of these, bearing a fruit about the size of a thirty-two pounder, is named Mononga-zambi.

We took a glance back to this valley, which equals that of the Mississippi in fertility, and thought of the vast mass of material which had been scooped out and carried away in its formation. This naturally led to reflection on the countless ages required for the previous formation and deposition of that same material (clay shale), then of the rocks, whose abrasion formed THAT, until the mind grew giddy in attempting to ascend the steps which lead up through a portion of the eternity before man. The different epochs of geology are like landmarks in that otherwise shoreless sea. Our own epoch, or creation, is but another added to the number of that wonderful series which presents a grand display of the mighty power of God: every stage of progress in the earth and its habitants is such a display. So far from this science having any tendency to make men undervalue the power or love of God, it leads to the probability that the exhibition of mercy we have in the gift of his Son may possibly not be the only manifestation of grace which has taken place in the countless ages during which works of creation have been going on.

Situated a few miles from the edge of the descent, we found the village of Tala Mungongo, and were kindly accommodated with a house to sleep in, which was very welcome, as we were all both wet and cold. We found that the greater altitude and the approach of winter lowered the temperature so much that many of my men suffered severely from colds. At this, as at several other Portuguese stations, they have been provident enough to erect travelers' houses on the same principle as khans or caravanserais of the East. They are built of the usual wattle and daub, and have benches of rods for the wayfarer to make his bed on; also chairs, and a table, and a large jar of water. These benches, though far from luxurious couches, were better than the ground under the rotten fragments of my gipsy-tent, for we had still showers occasionally, and the dews were very heavy. I continued to use them for the sake of the shelter they afforded, until I found that they were lodgings also for certain inconvenient bedfellows.

27TH. Five hours' ride through a pleasant country of forest and meadow, like those of Londa, brought us to a village of Basongo, a tribe living in subjection to the Portuguese. We crossed several little streams, which were flowing in the westerly direction in which we were marching, and unite to form the Quize, a feeder of the Coanza. The Basongo were very civil, as indeed all the tribes were who had been conquered by the Portuguese. The Basongo and Bangala are yet only partially subdued. The farther west we go from this, the less independent we find the black population, until we reach the vicinity of Loanda, where the free natives are nearly identical in their feelings toward the government with the slaves. But the governors of Angola wisely accept the limited allegiance and tribute rendered by the more distant tribes as better than none.

All the inhabitants of this region, as well as those of Londa, may be called true negroes, if the limitations formerly made be borne in mind. The dark color, thick lips, heads elongated backward and upward and covered with wool, flat noses, with other negro peculiarities, are general; but, while these characteristics place them in the true negro family, the reader would imbibe a wrong idea if he supposed that all these features combined are often met with in one individual. All have a certain thickness and prominence of lip, but many are met with in every village in whom thickness and projection are not more marked than in Europeans. All are dark, but the color is shaded off in different individuals from deep black to light yellow. As we go westward, we observe the light color predominating over the dark, and then again, when we come within the influence of damp from the sea air, we find the shade deepen into the general blackness of the coast population. The shape of the head, with its woolly crop, though general, is not universal. The tribes on the eastern side of the continent, as the Caffres, have heads finely developed and strongly European. Instances of this kind are frequently seen, and after I became so familiar with the dark color as to forget it in viewing the countenance, I was struck by the strong resemblance some natives bore to certain of our own notabilities. The Bushmen and Hottentots are exceptions to these remarks, for both the shape of their heads and growth of wool are peculiar; the latter, for instance, springs from the scalp in tufts with bare spaces between, and when the crop is short, resembles a number of black pepper-corns stuck on the skin, and very unlike the thick frizzly masses which cover the heads of the Balonda and Maravi. With every disposition to pay due deference to the opinions of those who have made ethnology their special study, I have felt myself unable to believe that the exaggerated features usually put forth as those of the typical negro characterize the majority of any nation of south Central Africa. The monuments of the ancient Egyptians seem to me to embody the ideal of the inhabitants of Londa better than the figures of any work of ethnology I have met with.

Passing through a fine, fertile, and well-peopled country to Sanza, we found the Quize River again touching our path, and here we had the pleasure of seeing a field of wheat growing luxuriantly without irrigation. The ears were upward of four inches long, an object of great curiosity to my companions, because they had tasted my bread at Linyanti, but had never before seen wheat growing. This small field was cultivated by Mr. Miland, an agreeable Portuguese merchant. His garden was interesting, as showing what the land at this elevation is capable of yielding; for, besides wheat, we saw European vegetables in a flourishing condition, and we afterward discovered that the coffee-plant has propagated itself on certain spots of this same district. It may be seen on the heights of Tala Mungongo, or nearly 300 miles from the west coast, where it was first introduced by the Jesuit missionaries.

We spent Sunday, the 30th of April, at Ngio, close to the ford of the Quize as it crosses our path to fall into the Coanza. The country becomes more open, but is still abundantly fertile, with a thick crop of grass between two and three feet high. It is also well wooded and watered. Villages of Basongo are dotted over the landscape, and frequently a square house of wattle and daub, belonging to native Portuguese, is placed beside them for the purposes of trade. The people here possess both cattle and pigs. The different sleeping-places on our path, from eight to ten miles apart, are marked by a cluster of sheds made of sticks and grass. There is a constant stream of people going and returning to and from the coast. The goods are carried on the head, or on one shoulder, in a sort of basket attached to the extremities of two poles between five and six feet long, and called Motete. When the basket is placed on the head, the poles project forward horizontally, and when the carrier wishes to rest himself, he plants them on the ground and the burden against a tree, so he is not obliged to lift it up from the ground to the level of the head. It stands against the tree propped up by the poles at that level. The carrier frequently plants the poles on the ground, and stands holding the burden until he has taken breath, thus avoiding the trouble of placing the burden on the ground and lifting it up again.

When a company of these carriers, or our own party, arrives at one of these sleeping-places, immediate possession is taken of the sheds. Those who come late, and find all occupied, must then erect others for themselves; but this is not difficult, for there is no lack of long grass. No sooner do any strangers appear at the spot, than the women may be seen emerging from their villages bearing baskets of manioc-meal, roots, ground-nuts, yams, bird's-eye pepper, and garlic for sale. Calico, of which we had brought some from Cassange, is the chief medium of exchange. We found them all civil, and it was evident, from the amount of talking and laughing in bargaining, that the ladies enjoyed their occupation. They must cultivate largely, in order to be able to supply the constant succession of strangers. Those, however, near to the great line of road, purchase also much of the food from the more distant villages for the sake of gain.

Pitsane and another of the men had violent attacks of fever, and it was no wonder, for the dampness and evaporation from the ground was excessive. When at any time I attempted to get an observation of a star, if the trough of mercury were placed on the ground, so much moisture was condensed on the inside of the glass roof over it that it was with difficulty the reflection of the star could be seen. When the trough was placed on a box to prevent the moisture entering from below, so much dew was deposited on the outside of the roof that it was soon necessary, for the sake of distinct vision, to wipe the glass. This would not have been of great consequence, but a short exposure to this dew was so sure to bring on a fresh fever, that I was obliged to give up observations by night altogether. The inside of the only covering I now had was not much better, but under the blanket one is not so liable to the chill which the dew produces.

It would have afforded me pleasure to have cultivated a more intimate acquaintance with the inhabitants of this part of the country, but the vertigo produced by frequent fevers made it as much as I could do to stick on the ox and crawl along in misery. In crossing the Lombe, my ox Sinbad, in the indulgence of his propensity to strike out a new path for himself, plunged overhead into a deep hole, and so soused me that I was obliged to move on to dry my clothing, without calling on the Europeans who live on the bank. This I regretted, for all the Portuguese were very kind, and, like the Boers placed in similar circumstances, feel it a slight to be passed without a word of salutation. But we went on to a spot where orange-trees had been planted by the natives themselves, and where abundance of that refreshing fruit was exposed for sale.

On entering the district of Ambaca, we found the landscape enlivened by the appearance of lofty mountains in the distance, the grass comparatively short, and the whole country at this time looking gay and verdant. On our left we saw certain rocks of the same nature with those of Pungo Andongo, and which closely resemble the Stonehenge group on Salisbury Plain, only the stone pillars here are of gigantic size. This region is all wonderfully fertile, famed for raising cattle, and all kinds of agricultural produce, at a cheap rate. The soil contains sufficient ferruginous matter, to impart a red tinge to nearly the whole of it. It is supplied with a great number of little flowing streams which unite in the Lucalla. This river drains Ambaca, then falls into the Coanza to the southwest at Massangano. We crossed the Lucalla by means of a large canoe kept there by a man who farms the ferry from the government, and charges about a penny per head. A few miles beyond the Lucalla we came to the village of Ambaca, an important place in former times, but now a mere paltry village, beautifully situated on a little elevation in a plain surrounded on all hands by lofty mountains. It has a jail, and a good house for the commandant, but neither fort nor church, though the ruins of a place of worship are still standing.

We were most kindly received by the commandant of Ambaca, Arsenio de Carpo, who spoke a little English. He recommended wine for my debility, and here I took the first glass of that beverage I had taken in Africa. I felt much refreshed, and could then realize and meditate on the weakening effects of the fever. They were curious even to myself; for, though I had tried several times since we left Ngio to take lunar observations, I could not avoid confusion of time and distance, neither could I hold the instrument steady, nor perform a simple calculation; hence many of the positions of this part of the route were left till my return from Loanda. Often, on getting up in the mornings, I found my clothing as wet from perspiration as if it had been dipped in water. In vain had I tried to learn or collect words of the

Bunda, or dialect spoken in Angola. I forgot the days of the week and the names of my companions, and, had I been asked, I probably could not have told my own. The complaint itself occupied many of my thoughts. One day I supposed that I had got the true theory of it, and would certainly cure the next attack, whether in myself or companions; but some new symptoms would appear, and scatter all the fine speculations which had sprung up, with extraordinary fertility, in one department of my brain.

This district is said to contain upward of 40,000 souls. Some ten or twelve miles to the north of the village of Ambaca there once stood the missionary station of Cahenda, and it is now quite astonishing to observe the great numbers who can read and write in this district. This is the fruit of the labors of the Jesuit and Capuchin missionaries, for they taught the people of Ambaca; and ever since the expulsion of the teachers by the Marquis of Pombal, the natives have continued to teach each other. These devoted men are still held in high estimation throughout the country to this day. All speak well of them (os padres Jesuitas); and, now that they are gone from this lower sphere, I could not help wishing that these our Roman Catholic fellow-Christians had felt it to be their duty to give the people the Bible, to be a light to their feet when the good men themselves were gone.

When sleeping in the house of the commandant, an insect, well known in the southern country by the name Tampan, bit my foot. It is a kind of tick, and chooses by preference the parts between the fingers or toes for inflicting its bite. It is seen from the size of a pin's head to that of a pea, and is common in all the native huts in this country. It sucks the blood until quite full, and is then of a dark blue color, and its skin so tough and yielding that it is impossible to burst it by any amount of squeezing with the fingers. I had felt the effects of its bite in former years, and eschewed all native huts ever after; but as I was here again assailed in a European house, I shall detail the effects of the bite. These are a tingling sensation of mingled pain and itching, which commences ascending the limb until the poison imbibed reaches the abdomen, where it soon causes violent vomiting and purging. Where these effects do not follow, as we found afterward at Tete, fever sets in; and I was assured by intelligent Portuguese there that death has sometimes been the result of this fever. The anxiety my friends at Tete manifested to keep my men out of the reach of the tampans of the village made it evident that they had seen cause to dread this insignificant insect. The only inconvenience I afterward suffered from this bite was the continuance of the tingling sensation in the point bitten for about a week.

MAY 12TH. As we were about to start this morning, the commandant, Senhor Arsenio, provided bread and meat most bountifully for my use on the way to the next station, and sent two militia soldiers as guides, instead of our Cassange corporal, who left us here. About midday we asked for shelter from the sun in the house of Senhor Mellot, at Zangu, and, though I was unable to sit and engage in conversation, I found, on rising from his couch, that he had at once proceeded to cook a fowl for my use; and at parting he gave me a glass of wine, which prevented the violent fit of shivering I expected that afternoon. The universal hospitality of the Portuguese was most gratifying, as it was quite unexpected; and even now, as I copy my journal, I remember it all with a glow of gratitude.

We spent Sunday, the 14th of May, at Cabinda, which is one of the stations of the sub-commandants, who are placed at different points in each district of Angola as assistants of the head-commandant, or chefe. It is situated in a beautiful glen, and surrounded by plantations of bananas and manioc. The country was gradually becoming more picturesque the farther we proceeded west. The ranges of lofty blue mountains of Libollo, which, in coming toward Ambaca, we had seen thirty or forty miles to our south, were now shut from our view by others nearer at hand, and the gray ranges of Cahenda and Kiwe, which, while we were in Ambaca, stood clearly defined eight or ten miles off to the north, were now close upon our right. As we looked back toward the open pastoral country of Ambaca, the broad green gently undulating plains seemed in a hollow surrounded on all sides by rugged mountains, and as we went westward we were entering upon quite a wild-looking mountainous district, called Golungo Alto.

We met numbers of Mambari on their way back to Bihe. Some of them had belonged to the parties which had penetrated as far as Linyanti, and foolishly showed their displeasure at the prospect of the Makololo preferring to go to the coast markets themselves to intrusting them with their ivory. The Mambari repeated the tale of the mode in which the white men are said to trade. "The ivory is left on the shore in the evening, and next morning the seller finds a quantity of goods placed there in its stead by the white men who live in the sea." "Now," added they to my men, "how can you Makololo trade with these 'Mermen'? Can you enter into the sea, and tell them to come ashore?" It was remarkable to hear this idea repeated so near the sea as we now were. My men replied that they only wanted to see for themselves; and, as they were now getting some light on the nature of the trade carried on by the Mambari, they were highly amused on perceiving the reasons why the Mambari would rather have met them on the Zambesi than so near the sea-coast.

There is something so exhilarating to one of Highland blood in being near or on high mountains, that I forgot my fever as we wended our way among the lofty tree-covered masses of mica schist which form the highlands around the romantic residence of the chefe of Golungo Alto. (Lat. 9d 8' 30"

S., long. 15d 2′ E.) The whole district is extremely beautiful. The hills are all bedecked with trees of various hues of foliage, and among them towers the graceful palm, which yields the oil of commerce for making our soaps, and the intoxicating toddy. Some clusters of hills look like the waves of the sea driven into a narrow open bay, and have assumed the same form as if, when all were chopping up perpendicularly, they had suddenly been congealed. The cottages of the natives, perched on the tops of many of the hillocks, looked as if the owners possessed an eye for the romantic, but they were probably influenced more by the desire to overlook their gardens, and keep their families out of the reach of the malaria, which is supposed to prevail most on the banks of the numerous little streams which run among the hills.

We were most kindly received by the commandant, Lieutenant Antonio Canto e Castro, a young gentleman whose whole subsequent conduct will ever make me regard him with great affection. Like every other person of intelligence whom I had met, he lamented deeply the neglect with which this fine country has been treated. This district contained by the last census 26,000 hearths or fires; and if to each hearth we reckon four souls, we have a population of 104,000. The number of carregadores (carriers) who may be ordered out at the pleasure of government to convey merchandise to the coast is in this district alone about 6000, yet there is no good road in existence. This system of compulsory carriage of merchandise was adopted in consequence of the increase in numbers and activity of our cruisers, which took place in 1845. Each trader who went, previous to that year, into the interior, in the pursuit of his calling, proceeded on the plan of purchasing ivory and beeswax, and a sufficient number of slaves to carry these commodities. The whole were intended for exportation as soon as the trader reached the coast. But when the more stringent measures of 1845 came into operation, and rendered the exportation of slaves almost impossible, there being no roads proper for the employment of wheel conveyances, this new system of compulsory carriage of ivory and beeswax to the coast was resorted to by the government of Loanda. A trader who requires two or three hundred carriers to convey his merchandise to the coast now applies to the general government for aid. An order is sent to the commandant of a district to furnish the number required. Each head man of the villages to whom the order is transmitted must furnish from five to twenty or thirty men, according to the proportion that his people bear to the entire population of the district. For this accommodation the trader must pay a tax to the government of 1000 reis, or about three shillings per load carried. The trader is obliged to pay the carrier also the sum of 50 reis, or about twopence a day, for his sustenance. And as a day's journey is never more than from eight to ten miles, the expense which must be incurred for this compulsory labor is felt to be heavy by those who were accustomed to employ slave labor alone. Yet no effort has been made to form a great line of road for wheel carriages. The first great want of a country has not been attended to, and no development of its vast resources has taken place. The fact, however, of a change from one system of carriage to another, taken in connection with the great depreciation in the price of slaves near this coast, proves the effectiveness of our efforts at repressing the slave-trade on the ocean.

The latitude of Golungo Alto, as observed at the residence of the commandant, was 9d 8' 30" S., longitude 15d 2' E. A few days' rest with this excellent young man enabled me to regain much of my strength, and I could look with pleasure on the luxuriant scenery before his door. We were quite shut in among green hills, many of which were cultivated up to their tops with manioc, coffee, cotton, ground-nuts, bananas, pine-apples, guavas, papaws, custard-apples, pitangas, and jambos, fruits brought from South America by the former missionaries. The high hills all around, with towering palms on many points, made this spot appear more like the Bay of Rio de Janeiro in miniature than any scene I ever saw; and all who have seen that confess it to be unequaled in the world beside. The fertility evident in every spot of this district was quite marvelous to behold, but I shall reserve further notices of this region till our return from Loanda.

We left Golungo Alto on the 24th of May, the winter in these parts. Every evening clouds come rolling in great masses over the mountains in the west, and pealing thunder accompanies the fall of rain during the night or early in the morning. The clouds generally remain on the hills till the morning is well spent, so that we become familiar with morning mists, a thing we never once saw at Kolobeng. The thermometer stands at 80 Degrees by day, but sinks as low as 76 Degrees by night.

In going westward we crossed several fine little gushing streams which never dry. They unite in the Luinha (pronounced Lueenya) and Lucalla. As they flow over many little cascades, they might easily be turned to good account, but they are all allowed to run on idly to the ocean. We passed through forests of gigantic timber, and at an open space named Cambondo, about eight miles from Golungo Alto, found numbers of carpenters converting these lofty trees into planks, in exactly the same manner as was followed by the illustrious Robinson Crusoe. A tree of three or four feet in diameter, and forty or fifty feet up to the nearest branches, was felled. It was then cut into lengths of a few feet, and split into thick junks, which again were reduced to planks an inch thick by persevering labor with the axe. The object of the carpenters was to make little chests, and they drive a constant trade in them at Cambondo. When finished with hinges, lock, and key, all of their own manufacture, one costs only a shilling and eightpence. My men were so delighted with them that they carried several of them on their heads all the way to Linyanti.

At Trombeta we were pleased to observe a great deal of taste displayed by the sub-commandant in the laying out of his ground and adornment of his house with flowers. This trifling incident was the more pleasing, as it was the first attempt at neatness I had seen since leaving the establishment of Mozinkwa in Londa. Rows of trees had been planted along each side of the road, with pine-apples and flowers between. This arrangement I had an opportunity of seeing in several other districts of this country, for there is no difficulty in raising any plant or tree if it is only kept from being choked by weeds.

This gentleman had now a fine estate, which but a few years ago was a forest, and cost him only 16 Pounds. He had planted about 900 coffee-trees upon it, and as these begin to yield in three years from being planted, and in six attain their maximum, I have no doubt but that ere now his 16 Pounds yields him sixty fold. All sorts of fruit-trees and grape-vines yield their fruit twice in each year, without any labor or irrigation being bestowed on them. All grains and vegetables, if only sown, do the same; and if advantage is taken of the mists of winter, even three crops of pulse may be raised. Cotton was now standing in the pods in his fields, and he did not seem to care about it. I understood him to say that this last plant flourishes, but the wet of one of the two rainy seasons with which this country is favored sometimes proves troublesome to the grower. I am not aware whether wheat has ever been tried, but I saw both figs and grapes bearing well. The great complaint of all cultivators is the want of a good road to carry their produce to market. Here all kinds of food are remarkably cheap.

Farther on we left the mountainous country, and, as we descended toward the west coast, saw the lands assuming a more sterile, uninviting aspect. On our right ran the River Senza, which nearer the sea takes the name of Bengo. It is about fifty yards broad, and navigable for canoes. The low plains adjacent to its banks are protected from inundation by embankments, and the population is entirely occupied in raising food and fruits for exportation to Loanda by means of canoes. The banks are infested by myriads of the most ferocious mosquitoes I ever met. Not one of our party could get a snatch of sleep. I was taken into the house of a Portuguese, but was soon glad to make my escape and lie across the path on the lee side of the fire, where the smoke blew over my body. My host wondered at my want of taste, and I at his want of feeling; for, to our astonishment, he and the other inhabitants had actually become used to what was at least equal to a nail through the heel of one's boot, or the tooth-ache.

As we were now drawing near to the sea, my companions were looking at every thing in a serious light. One of them asked me if we should all have an opportunity of watching each other at Loanda. "Suppose one went for water, would the others see if he were kidnapped?" I replied, "I see what you are driving at; and if you suspect me, you may return, for I am as ignorant of Loanda as you are; but nothing will happen to you but what happens to myself. We have stood by each other hitherto, and will do so to the last." The plains adjacent to Loanda are somewhat elevated and comparatively sterile. On coming across these we first beheld the sea: my companions looked upon the boundless ocean with awe. On describing their feelings afterward, they remarked that "we marched along with our father, believing that what the ancients had always told us was true, that the world has no end; but all at once the world said to us, 'I am finished; there is no more of me!'" They had always imagined that the world was one extended plain without limit.

They were now somewhat apprehensive of suffering want, and I was unable to allay their fears with any promise of supply, for my own mind was depressed by disease and care. The fever had induced a state of chronic dysentery, so troublesome that I could not remain on the ox more than ten minutes at a time; and as we came down the declivity above the city of Loanda on the 31st of May, I was laboring under great depression of spirits, as I understood that, in a population of twelve thousand souls, there was but one genuine English gentleman. I naturally felt anxious to know whether he were possessed of good-nature, or was one of those crusty mortals one would rather not meet at all.

This gentleman, Mr. Gabriel, our commissioner for the suppression of the slave-trade, had kindly forwarded an invitation to meet me on the way from Cassange, but, unfortunately, it crossed me on the road. When we entered his porch, I was delighted to see a number of flowers cultivated carefully, and inferred from this circumstance that he was, what I soon discovered him to be, a real whole-hearted Englishman.

Seeing me ill, he benevolently offered me his bed. Never shall I forget the luxurious pleasure I enjoyed in feeling myself again on a good English couch, after six months' sleeping on the ground. I was soon asleep; and Mr. Gabriel, coming in almost immediately, rejoiced at the soundness of my repose.

Chapter 20

Continued Sickness—Kindness of the Bishop of Angola and her Majesty's Officers—Mr. Gabriel's unwearied Hospitality—Serious Deportment of the Makololo—They visit Ships of War—Politeness of the Officers and Men—The Makololo attend Mass in the Cathedral—Their Remarks—Find Employment in collecting Firewood and unloading Coal—Their superior Judgment respecting Goods—Beneficial Influence of the Bishop of Angola—The City of St. Paul de Loanda—The Harbor—Customhouse—No English Merchants—Sincerity of the Portuguese Government in suppressing the Slave-trade—Convict Soldiers—Presents from Bishop and Merchants for Sekeletu—Outfit—Leave Loanda 20th September, 1854—Accompanied by Mr. Gabriel as far as Icollo i Bengo—Sugar Manufactory—Geology of this part of the Country—Women spinning Cotton—Its Price—Native Weavers—Market-places—Cazengo; its Coffee Plantations—South American Trees—Ruins of Iron Foundry—Native Miners—The Banks of the Lucalla—Cottages with Stages—Tobacco-plants—Town of Massangano—Sugar and Rice—Superior District for Cotton—Portuguese Merchants and foreign Enterprise—Ruins—The Fort and its ancient Guns—Former Importance of Massangano—Fires—The Tribe Kisama—Peculiar Variety of Domestic Fowl—Coffee Plantations—Return to Golungo Alto—Self-complacency of the Makololo—Fever—Jaundice—Insanity.

In the hope that a short enjoyment of Mr. Gabriel's generous hospitality would restore me to my wonted vigor, I continued under his roof; but my complaint having been caused by long exposure to malarious influences, I became much more reduced than ever, even while enjoying rest. Several Portuguese gentlemen called on me shortly after my arrival; and the Bishop of Angola, the Right Reverend Joaquim Moreira Reis, then the acting governor of the province, sent his secretary to do the same, and likewise to offer the services of the government physician.

Some of her majesty's cruisers soon came into the port, and, seeing the emaciated condition to which I was reduced, offered to convey me to St. Helena or homeward; but, though I had reached the coast, I had found that, in consequence of the great amount of forest, rivers, and marsh, there was no possibility of a highway for wagons, and I had brought a party of Sekeletu's people with me, and found the tribes near the Portuguese settlement so very unfriendly, that it would be altogether impossible for my men to return alone. I therefore resolved to decline the tempting offers of my naval friends, and take back my Makololo companions to their chief, with a view of trying to make a path from his country to the east coast by means of the great river Zambesi or Leeambye.

I, however, gladly availed myself of the medical assistance of Mr. Cockin, the surgeon of the "Polyphemus", at the suggestion of his commander, Captain Phillips. Mr. Cockin's treatment, aided by the exhilarating presence of the warm-hearted naval officers, and Mr. Gabriel's unwearied hospitality and care, soon brought me round again. On the 14th I was so far well as to call on the bishop, in company with my party, who were arrayed in new robes of striped cotton cloth and red caps, all presented to them by Mr. Gabriel. He received us, as head of the provisional government, in the grand hall of the palace. He put many intelligent questions respecting the Makololo, and then gave them free permission to come to Loanda as often as they pleased. This interview pleased the Makololo extremely.

Every one remarked the serious deportment of the Makololo. They viewed the large stone houses and churches in the vicinity of the great ocean with awe. A house with two stories was, until now, beyond their comprehension. In explanation of this strange thing, I had always been obliged to use the word for hut; and as huts are constructed by the poles being let into the earth, they never could comprehend how the poles of one hut could be founded upon the roof of another, or how men could live in the upper story, with the conical roof of the lower one in the middle. Some Makololo, who had visited my little house at Kolobeng, in trying to describe it to their countrymen at Linyanti, said, "It is not a hut; it is a mountain with several caves in it."

Commander Bedingfeld and Captain Skene invited them to visit their vessels, the "Pluto" and "Philomel". Knowing their fears, I told them that no one need go if he entertained the least suspicion of foul play. Nearly the whole party went; and when on deck, I pointed to the sailors, and said, "Now these are all my countrymen, sent by our queen for the purpose of putting down the trade of those that buy and sell black men." They replied, "Truly! they are just like you!" and all their fears seemed to vanish at once, for they went forward among the men, and the jolly tars, acting much as the Makololo would have done in similar circumstances, handed them a share of the bread and beef which they had for dinner. The commander allowed them to fire off a cannon; and, having the most exalted ideas of its power, they were greatly pleased when I told them, "That is what they put down the slave-trade with." The size of the brig-of-war amazed them. "It is not a canoe at all; it is a town!" The sailors' deck they named "the Kotla"; and then, as a climax to their description of this great ark, added, "And what sort of a town is it that you must climb up into with a rope?"

The effect of the politeness of the officers and men on their minds was most beneficial. They had behaved with the greatest kindness to me all the way from Linyanti, and I now rose rapidly in their estimation; for, whatever they may have surmised before, they now saw that I was respected among my own countrymen, and always afterward treated me with the greatest deference.

On the 15th there was a procession and service of the mass in the Cathedral; and, wishing to show my men a place of worship, I took them to the church, which now serves as the chief one of the see of Angola and Congo. There is an impression on some minds that a gorgeous ritual is better calculated to inspire devotional feelings than the simple forms of the Protestant worship. But here the frequent genuflexions, changing of positions, burning of incense, with the priests' back turned to the people, the laughing, talking, and manifest irreverence of the singers, with firing of guns, etc., did not convey to the minds of my men the idea of adoration. I overheard them, in talking to each other, remark that "they had seen the white men charming their demons;" a phrase identical with one they had used when seeing the Balonda beating drums before their idols.

In the beginning of August I suffered a severe relapse, which reduced me to a mere skeleton. I was then unable to attend to my men for a considerable time; but when in convalescence from this last attack, I was thankful to find that I was free from that lassitude which, in my first recovery, showed the continuance of the malaria in the system. I found that my men, without prompting, had established a brisk trade in fire-wood. They sallied forth at cock-crowing in the mornings, and by daylight reached the uncultivated parts of the adjacent country, collected a bundle of fire-wood, and returned to the city. It was then divided into smaller fagots, and sold to the inhabitants; and as they gave larger quantities than the regular wood-carriers, they found no difficulty in selling. A ship freighted with coal for the cruisers having arrived from England, Mr. Gabriel procured them employment in unloading her at sixpence a day. They continued at this work for upward of a month, and nothing could exceed their astonishment at the vast amount of cargo one ship contained. As they themselves always afterward expressed it, they had labored every day from sunrise to sunset for a moon and a half, unloading, as quickly as they could, "stones that burn", and were tired out, still leaving plenty in her. With the money so obtained they purchased clothing, beads, and other articles to take back to their own country. Their ideas of the value of different kinds of goods rather astonished those who had dealt only with natives on the coast. Hearing it stated with confidence that the Africans preferred the thinnest fabrics, provided they had gaudy colors and a large extent of surface, the idea was so new to my experience in the interior that I dissented, and, in order to show the superior good sense of the Makololo, took them to the shop of Mr. Schut. When he showed them the amount of general goods which they might procure at Loanda for a single tusk, I requested them, without assigning any reason, to point out the fabrics they prized most. They all at once selected the strongest pieces of English calico and other cloths, showing that they had regard to strength without reference to color. I believe that most of the Bechuana nation would have done the same. But I was assured that the people near the coast, with whom the Portuguese have to deal, have not so much regard to durability. This probably arises from calico being the chief circulating medium; quantity being then of more importance than quality.

During the period of my indisposition, the bishop sent frequently to make inquiries, and, as soon as I was able to walk, I went to thank him for his civilities. His whole conversation and conduct showed him to be a man of great benevolence and kindness of heart. Alluding to my being a Protestant, he stated that he was a Catholic from conviction; and though sorry to see others, like myself, following another path, he entertained no uncharitable feelings, nor would he ever sanction persecuting measures. He compared the various sects of Christians, in their way to heaven, to a number of individuals choosing to pass down the different streets of Loanda to one of the churches—all would arrive at the same point at last. His good influence, both in the city and the country, is universally acknowledged: he was promoting the establishment of schools, which, though formed more on the monastic principle than Protestants might approve, will no doubt be a blessing. He was likewise successfully attempting to abolish the non-marriage custom of the country; and several marriages had taken place in Loanda among those who, but for his teaching, would have been content with concubinage.

St. Paul de Loanda has been a very considerable city, but is now in a state of decay. It contains about twelve thousand inhabitants, most of whom are people of color.* There are various evidences of its former magnificence, especially two cathedrals, one of which, once a Jesuit college, is now converted into a workshop; and in passing the other, we saw with sorrow a number of oxen feeding within its stately walls. Three forts continue in a good state of repair. Many large stone houses are to be found. The palace of the governor and government offices are commodious structures, but nearly all the houses of the native inhabitants are of wattle and daub. Trees are planted all over the town for the sake of shade, and the city presents an imposing appearance from the sea. It is provided with an effective police, and the custom-house department is extremely well managed. All parties agree in representing the Portuguese authorities as both polite and obliging; and if ever any inconvenience is felt by strangers visiting the port, it must be considered the fault of the system, and not of the men.

> * From the census of 1850-51 we find the population of this city arranged thus: 830 whites, only 160 of whom are females. This is the largest collection of whites in the country, for Angola itself contains only about 1000 whites. There are 2400 half-castes in Loanda, and only 120 of them slaves; and there are 9000 blacks, more than 5000 of whom are slaves.

The harbor is formed by the low, sandy island of Loanda, which is inhabited by about 1300 souls, upward of 600 of whom are industrious native fishermen, who supply the city with abundance of good fish daily. The space between it and the main land, on which the city is built, is the station for ships. When a high southwest wind blows, the waves of the ocean dash over part of the island, and, driving large quantities of sand before them, gradually fill up the harbor. Great quantities of soil are also washed in the rainy season from the heights above the city, so that the port, which once contained water sufficient to float the largest ships close to the custom-house, is now at low water dry. The ships are compelled to anchor about a mile north of their old station. Nearly all the water consumed in Loanda is brought from the River Bengo by means of launches, the only supply that the city affords being from some deep wells of slightly brackish water. Unsuccessful attempts have been made by different governors to finish a canal, which the Dutch, while in possession of Loanda during the seven years preceding 1648, had begun, to bring water from the River Coanza to the city. There is not a single English merchant at Loanda, and only two American. This is the more remarkable, as nearly all the commerce is carried on by means of English calico brought hither via Lisbon. Several English houses attempted to establish a trade about 1845, and accepted bills on Rio de Janeiro in payment for their goods, but the increased activity of our cruisers had such an effect upon the mercantile houses of that city that most of them failed. The English merchants lost all, and Loanda got a bad name in the commercial world in consequence.

One of the arrangements of the custom-house may have had some influence in preventing English trade. Ships coming here must be consigned to some one on the spot; the consignee receives one hundred dollars per mast, and he generally makes a great deal more for himself by putting a percentage on boats and men hired for loading and unloading, and on every item that passes through his hands. The port charges are also rendered heavy by twenty dollars being charged as a perquisite of the secretary of government, with a fee for the chief physician, something for the hospital, custom-house officers, guards, etc., etc. But, with all these drawbacks, the Americans carry on a brisk and profitable trade in calico, biscuit, flour, butter, etc., etc.

The Portuguese home government has not generally received the credit for sincerity in suppressing the slave-trade which I conceive to be its due. In 1839, my friend Mr. Gabriel saw 37 slave-ships lying in this harbor, waiting for their cargoes, under the protection of the guns of the forts. At that time slavers had to wait many months at a time for a human freight, and a certain sum per head was paid to the government for all that were exported. The duties derived from the exportation of slaves far exceeded those from other commerce, and, by agreeing to the suppression of this profitable traffic, the government actually sacrificed the chief part of the export revenue. Since that period, however, the revenue from lawful commerce has very much exceeded that on slaves. The intentions of the home Portuguese government, however good, can not be fully carried out under the present system. The pay of the officers is so very small that they are nearly all obliged to engage in trade; and, owing to the lucrative nature of the slave-trade, the temptation to engage in it is so powerful, that the philanthropic statesmen of Lisbon need hardly expect to have their humane and enlightened views carried out. The law, for instance, lately promulgated for the abolition of the carrier system (carregadores) is but one of several equally humane enactments against this mode of compulsory labor, but there is very little probability of the benevolent intentions of the Legislature being carried into effect.

Loanda is regarded somewhat as a penal settlement, and those who leave their native land for this country do so with the hope of getting rich in a few years, and then returning home. They have thus no motive for seeking the permanent welfare of the country. The Portuguese law preventing the subjects of any other nation from holding landed property unless they become naturalized, the country has neither the advantage of native nor foreign enterprise, and remains very much in the same state as our allies found it in 1575. Nearly all the European soldiers sent out are convicts, and, contrary to what might be expected from men in their position, behave remarkably well. A few riots have occurred, but nothing at all so serious as have taken place in our own penal settlements. It is a remarkable fact that the whole of the arms of Loanda are every night in the hands of those who have been convicts. Various reasons for this mild behavior are assigned by the officers, but none of these, when viewed in connection with our own experience in Australia, appear to be valid. Religion seems to have no connection with the change. Perhaps the climate may have some influence in subduing their turbulent disposition, for the inhabitants generally are a timid race; they are not half so brave as our Caffres. The people of Ambriz ran away like a flock of sheep, and allowed the Portuguese to take possession of their copper mines and country without striking a blow. If we must have convict settlements, attention to the climate might be of advantage in the selection. Here even bulls are much tamer than with us. I never met with a ferocious one in this country, and the Portuguese use them generally for riding; an ox is seldom seen.

The objects which I had in view in opening up the country, as stated in a few notes of my journey, published in the newspapers of Angola, so commended themselves to the general government and merchants of Loanda, that, at the instance of his excellency the bishop, a handsome present for Sekeletu was granted by the Board of Public Works (Junta da Fazenda Publica). It consisted of a colonel's complete uniform and a horse for the chief, and suits of clothing for all the men who accompanied me. The merchants also made a present, by public subscription, of handsome specimens of all their articles of trade, and two donkeys, for the purpose of introducing the breed into his country, as tsetse can not kill this beast of burden. These presents were accompanied by letters from the bishop and merchants; and I was kindly favored with letters of recommendation to the Portuguese authorities in Eastern Africa.

I took with me a good stock of cotton cloth, fresh supplies of ammunition and beads, and gave each of my men a musket. As my companions had amassed considerable quantities of goods, they were unable to carry mine, but the bishop furnished me with twenty carriers, and sent forward orders to all the commandants of the districts through which we were to pass to render me every assistance in their power. Being now supplied with a good new tent made by my friends on board the Philomel, we left Loanda on the 20th of September, 1854, and passed round by sea to the mouth of the River Bengo. Ascending this river, we went through the district in which stand the ruins of the convent of St. Antonio; thence into Icollo i Bengo, which contains a population of 6530 blacks, 172 mulattoes, and 11 whites, and is so named from having been the residence of a former native king. The proportion of slaves is only 3.38 per cent. of the inhabitants. The commandant of this place, Laurence Jose Marquis, is a frank old soldier and a most hospitable man; he is one of the few who secure the universal approbation of their fellow-men for stern, unflinching honesty, and has risen from the ranks to be a major in the army. We were accompanied thus far by our generous host, Edmund Gabriel, Esq., who, by his unwearied attentions to myself, and liberality in supporting my men, had become endeared to all our hearts. My men were strongly impressed with a sense of his goodness, and often spoke of him in terms of admiration all the way to Linyanti.

While here we visited a large sugar manufactory belonging to a lady, Donna Anna da Sousa. The flat alluvial lands on the banks of the Senza or Bengo are well adapted for raising sugar-cane, and this lady had a surprising number of slaves, but somehow the establishment was far from being in a flourishing condition. It presented such a contrast to the free-labor establishments of the Mauritius, which I have since seen, where, with not one tenth of the number of hands, or such good soil, a man of color had, in one year, cleared 5000 Pounds by a single crop, that I quote the fact, in hopes it may meet the eye of Donna Anna.

The water of the river is muddy, and it is observed that such rivers have many more mosquitoes than those which have clear water. It was remarked to us here that these insects are much more numerous at the period of new moon than at other times; at any rate, we were all thankful to get away from the Senza and its insect plagues.

The whole of this part of the country is composed of marly tufa, containing the same kind of shells as those at present alive in the seas. As we advanced eastward and ascended the higher lands, we found eruptive trap, which had tilted up immense masses of mica and sandstone schists. The mica schist almost always dipped toward the interior of the country, forming those mountain ranges of which we have already spoken as giving a highland character to the district of Golungo Alto. The trap has frequently run through the gorges made in the upheaved rocks, and at the points of junction between the igneous and older rocks there are large quantities of strongly magnetic iron ore. The clayey soil formed by the disintegration of the mica schist and trap is the favorite soil for the coffee; and it is on these mountain sides, and others possessing a similar red clay soil, that this plant has propagated itself so widely. The meadow-lands adjacent to the Senza and Coanza being underlaid by that marly tufa which abounds toward the coast, and containing the same shells, show that, previous to the elevation of that side of the country, this region possessed some deeply-indented bays.

28TH SEPTEMBER, KALUNGWEMBO.—We were still on the same path by which we had come, and, there being no mosquitoes, we could now better enjoy the scenery. Ranges of hills occupy both sides of our path, and the fine level road is adorned with a beautiful red flower named Bolcamaria. The markets or sleeping-places are well supplied with provisions by great numbers of women, every one of whom is seen spinning cotton with a spindle and distaff, exactly like those which were in use among the ancient Egyptians. A woman is scarcely ever seen going to the fields, though with a pot on her head, a child on her back, and the hoe over her shoulder, but she is employed in this way. The cotton was brought to the market for sale, and I bought a pound for a penny. This was the price demanded, and probably double what they ask from each other. We saw the cotton growing luxuriantly all around the market-places from seeds dropped accidentally. It is seen also about the native huts, and, so far as I could learn, it was the American cotton, so influenced by climate as to be perennial. We met in the road natives passing with bundles of cops, or spindles full of cotton thread, and these they were carrying to other parts to be woven into cloth. The women are the spinners, and the men perform the weaving. Each web is about 5 feet long, and 15 or 18 inches wide. The loom is of the simplest construction, being nothing but two beams placed one over the other, the web standing perpendicularly. The threads of the web are separated by means of a thin wooden lath, and the woof passed through by means of the spindle on which it has been wound in spinning.

The mode of spinning and weaving in Angola, and, indeed, throughout South Central Africa, is so very like the same occupations in the hands of the ancient Egyptians, that I introduce a woodcut from the interesting work of Sir Gardner Wilkinson. The lower figures are engaged in spinning in the real African method, and the weavers in the left-hand corner have their web in the Angolese fashion.*

> *Unfortunately, this woodcut can not be represented in this ASCII text. The caption reads, 'Ancient Spinning and Weaving, perpetuated in Africa at the present day. From Wilkinson's "Ancient Egyptians", p. 85, 86.' The web, or cloth on the loom, mentioned, has the vertical threads, or the warp, hanging, perhaps five feet, from a horizontal beam. The woof is passed through from side to side. —A. L., 1997.*

Numbers of other articles are brought for sale to these sleeping-places. The native smiths there carry on their trade. I bought ten very good table-knives, made of country iron, for twopence each.

Labor is extremely cheap, for I was assured that even carpenters, masons, smiths, etc., might be hired for fourpence a day, and agriculturists would gladly work for half that sum.*

> *In order that the reader may understand the social position of the people of this country, I here give the census of the district of Golungo Alto for the year 1854, though the numbers are evidently not all furnished:*

238 *householders or yeomen.*
4224 *patrons, or head men of several hamlets.*
23 *native chiefs or sovas.*
292 *macotas or councilors.*
5838 *carriers.*
126 *carpenters.*
72 *masons.*
300 *shoemakers.*
181 *potters.*
25 *tailors.*
12 *barbers.*
206 *iron-founders.*
486 *bellows-blowers.*
586 *coke-makers.*
173 *iron-miners.*
184 *soldiers of militia.*
3603 *privileged gentlemen, i.e., who may wear boots.*
18 *vagabonds.*
717 *old men.*
54 *blind men and women.*
81 *lame men and women.*
770 *slave men.*
807 *slave women.*
9578 *free women.*
393 *possessors of land.*
300 *female gardeners.*
139 *hunters of wild animals.*
980 *smiths.*
314 *mat-makers.*
4065 *males under 7 years of age.*
6012 *females under 7 years of age.*

These people possess 300 idol-houses, 600 sheep, 5000 goats, 500 oxen, 398 gardens, 25,120 hearths. The authorities find great difficulty in getting the people to furnish a correct account of their numbers. This census is quoted merely for the purpose of giving a general idea of the employments of the inhabitants.

The following is taken from the census of Icollo i Bengo, and is added for a similar reason:

> 3232 living without the marriage tie. (All those who have not been married by a priest are so distinguished.)
> 4 orphans—2 black and 2 white.
> 9 native chiefs.
> 2 carpenters.
> 21 potters.
> 11 tailors.
> 2 shoemakers.
> 3 barbers.
> 5 mat-makers.
> 12 sack-makers.
> 21 basket-makers.

> The cattle in the district are: 10 asses, 401 oxen, 492 cows, 3933 sheep, 1699 goats, 909 swine; and as an annual tax is levied of sixpence per head on all stock, it is probable that the returns are less than the reality.

Being anxious to obtain some more knowledge of this interesting country and its ancient missionary establishments than the line of route by which we had come afforded, I resolved to visit the town of Massangano, which is situated to the south of Golungo Alto, and at the confluence of the rivers Lucalla and Coanza. This led me to pass through the district of Cazengo, which is rather famous for the abundance and excellence of its coffee. Extensive coffee plantations were found to exist on the sides of the several lofty mountains that compose this district. They were not planted by the Portuguese. The Jesuit and other missionaries are known to have brought some of the fine old Mocha seed, and these have propagated themselves far and wide; hence the excellence of the Angola coffee. Some have asserted that, as new plantations were constantly discovered even during the period of our visit, the coffee-tree was indigenous; but the fact that pine-apples, bananas, yams, orange-trees, custard apple-trees, pitangas, guavas, and other South American trees, were found by me in the same localities with the recently-discovered coffee, would seem to indicate that all foreign trees must have been introduced by the same agency. It is known that the Jesuits also introduced many other trees for the sake of their timber alone. Numbers of these have spread over the country, some have probably died out, and others failed to spread, like a lonely specimen which stands in what was the

Botanic Garden of Loanda, and, though most useful in yielding a substitute for frankincense, is the only one of the kind in Africa.

A circumstance which would facilitate the extensive propagation of the coffee on the proper clay soil is this: The seed, when buried beneath the soil, generally dies, while that which is sown broadcast, with no covering except the shade of the trees, vegetates readily. The agent in sowing in this case is a bird, which eats the outer rind, and throws the kernel on the ground. This plant can not bear the direct rays of the sun; consequently, when a number of the trees are discovered in the forest, all that is necessary is to clear away the brushwood, and leave as many of the tall forest-trees as will afford good shade to the coffee-plants below. The fortunate discoverer has then a flourishing coffee plantation.

This district, small though it be, having only a population of 13,822, of whom ten only are white, nevertheless yields an annual tribute to the government of thirteen hundred cotton cloths, each 5 feet by 18 or 20 inches, of their own growth and manufacture.

Accompanied by the commandant of Cazengo, who was well acquainted with this part of the country, I proceeded in a canoe down the River Lucalla to Massangano. This river is about 85 yards wide, and navigable for canoes from its confluence with the Coanza to about six miles above the point where it receives the Luinha. Near this latter point stand the strong, massive ruins of an iron foundry, erected in the times (1768) and by the order of the famous Marquis of Pombal. The whole of the buildings were constructed of stone, cemented with oil and lime. The dam for water-power was made of the same materials, and 27 feet high. This had been broken through by a flood, and solid blocks, many yards in length, were carried down the stream, affording an instructive example of the transporting power of water. There was nothing in the appearance of the place to indicate unhealthiness; but eight Spanish and Swedish workmen, being brought hither for the purpose of instructing the natives in the art of smelting iron, soon fell victims to disease and "irregularities". The effort of the marquis to improve the mode of manufacturing iron was thus rendered abortive. Labor and subsistence are, however, so very cheap that almost any amount of work can be executed, at a cost that renders expensive establishments unnecessary.

A party of native miners and smiths is still kept in the employment of the government, who, working the rich black magnetic iron ore, produce for the government from 480 to 500 bars of good malleable iron every month. They are supported by the appropriation of a few thousands of a small fresh-water fish, called "Cacusu", a portion of the tax levied upon the fishermen of the Coanza. This fish is so much relished in the country that those who do not wish to eat them can easily convert them into money. The commandant of the district of Massangano, for instance, has a right to a dish of three hundred every morning, as part of his salary. Shell-fish are also found in the Coanza, and the "Peixemulher", or woman-fish of the Portuguese, which is probably a Manatee.

The banks of the Lucalla are very pretty, well planted with orange-trees, bananas, and the palm ('Elaeis Guineensis') which yields the oil of commerce. Large plantations of maize, manioc, and tobacco are seen along both banks, which are enlivened by the frequent appearance of native houses imbosomed in dense shady groves, with little boys and girls playing about them. The banks are steep, the water having cut out its bed in dark red alluvial soil. Before every cottage a small stage is erected, to which the inhabitants may descend to draw water without danger from the alligators. Some have a little palisade made in the water for safety from these reptiles, and others use the shell of the fruit of the baobab-tree attached to a pole about ten feet long, with which, while standing on the high bank, they may draw water without fear of accident.

Many climbing plants run up the lofty silk, cotton, and baobab trees, and hang their beautiful flowers in gay festoons on the branches. As we approach Massangano, the land on both banks of the Lucalla becomes very level, and large portions are left marshy after the annual floods; but all is very fertile. As an illustration of the strength of the soil, I may state that we saw tobacco-plants in gardens near the confluence eight feet high, and each plant had thirty-six leaves, which were eighteen inches long by six or eight inches broad. But it is not a pastoral district. In our descent we observed the tsetse, and consequently the people had no domestic animals save goats.

We found the town of Massangano on a tongue of rather high land, formed by the left bank of the Lucalla and right bank of the Coanza, and received true Portuguese hospitality from Senhor Lubata. The town has more than a thousand inhabitants; the district has 28,063, with only 315 slaves. It stands on a mound of calcareous tufa, containing great numbers of fossil shells, the most recent of which resemble those found in the marly tufa close to the coast. The fort stands on the south side of the town, on a high perpendicular bank overhanging the Coanza. This river is here a noble stream, about a hundred and fifty yards wide, admitting navigation in large canoes from the bar at its mouth to Cambambe, some thirty miles above this town. There, a fine waterfall hinders farther ascent. Ten or twelve large canoes laden with country produce pass Massangano every day. Four galleons were constructed here as long ago as 1650, which must have been of good size, for they crossed the ocean to Rio Janeiro.

Massangano district is well adapted for sugar and rice, while Cambambe is a very superior field for cotton; but the bar at the mouth of the Coanza would prevent the approach of a steamer into this desirable region, though a small one could ply on it with ease when once in. It is probable that the objects of those who attempted to make a canal from Calumbo to Loanda were not merely to supply that city with fresh water, but to afford facilities for transportation. The remains of the canal show it to have been made on a scale suited for the Coanza canoes. The Portuguese began another on a smaller scale in 1811, and, after three years' labor, had finished only 6000 yards. Nothing great or useful will ever be effected here so long as men come merely to get rich, and then return to Portugal.

The latitude of the town and fort of Massangano is 9d 37' 46" S., being nearly the same as that of Cassange. The country between Loanda and this point being comparatively flat, a railroad might be constructed at small expense. The level country is prolonged along the north bank of the Coanza to the edge of the Cassange basin, and a railway carried thither would be convenient for the transport of the products of the rich districts of Cassange, Pungo Andongo, Ambaca, Cambambe, Golungo Alto, Cazengo, Muchima, and Calumbo; in a word, the whole of Angola and independent tribes adjacent to this kingdom.

The Portuguese merchants generally look to foreign enterprise and to their own government for the means by which this amelioration might be effected; but, as I always stated to them when conversing on the subject, foreign capitalists would never run the risk, unless they saw the Angolese doing something for themselves, and the laws so altered that the subjects of other nations should enjoy the same privileges in the country with themselves. The government of Portugal has indeed shown a wise and liberal policy by its permission for the alienation of the crown lands in Angola; but the law giving it effect is so fenced round with limitations, and so deluged with verbiage, that to plain people it seems any thing but a straightforward license to foreigners to become 'bona fide' landholders and cultivators of the soil. At present the tolls paid on the different lines of roads for ferries and bridges are equal to the interest of large sums of money, though but a small amount has been expended in making available roads.

There are two churches and a hospital in ruins at Massangano; and the remains of two convents are pointed out, one of which is said to have been an establishment of black Benedictines, which, if successful, considering the materials the brethren had to work on, must have been a laborious undertaking. There is neither priest nor schoolmaster in the town, but I was pleased to observe a number of children taught by one of the inhabitants. The cultivated lands attached to all these conventual establishments in Angola are now rented by the government of Loanda, and thither the bishop lately removed all the gold and silver vessels belonging to them.

The fort of Massangano is small, but in good repair; it contains some very ancient guns, which were loaded from the breech, and must have been formidable weapons in their time. The natives of this country entertain a remarkable dread of great guns, and this tends much to the permanence of the Portuguese authority. They dread a cannon greatly, though the carriage be so rotten that it would fall to pieces at the first shot; the fort of Pungo Andongo is kept securely by cannon perched on cross sticks alone!

Massangano was a very important town at the time the Dutch held forcible possession of Loanda and part of Angola; but when, in the year 1648, the Dutch were expelled from this country by a small body of Portuguese, under the Governor Salvador Correa de Sa Benevides, Massangano was left to sink into its present decay. Since it was partially abandoned by the Portuguese, several baobab-trees have sprung up and attained a diameter of eighteen or twenty inches, and are about twenty feet high. No certain conclusion can be drawn from these instances, as it is not known at what time after 1648 they began to grow; but their present size shows that their growth is not unusually slow.

Several fires occurred during our stay, by the thatch having, through long exposure to a torrid sun, become like tinder. The roofs became ignited without any visible cause except the intense solar rays, and excited terror in the minds of the inhabitants, as the slightest spark carried by the wind would have set the whole town in a blaze. There is not a single inscription on stone visible in Massangano. If destroyed to-morrow, no one could tell where it and most Portuguese interior villages stood, any more than we can do those of the Balonda.

During the occupation of this town the Coanza was used for the purpose of navigation, but their vessels were so frequently plundered by their Dutch neighbors that, when they regained the good port of Loanda, they no longer made use of the river. We remained here four days, in hopes of obtaining an observation for the longitude, but at this season of the year the sky is almost constantly overcast by a thick canopy of clouds of a milk-and-water hue; this continues until the rainy season (which was now close at hand) commences.

The lands on the north side of the Coanza belong to the Quisamas (Kisamas), an independent tribe, which the Portuguese have not been able to subdue. The few who came under my observation possessed much of the Bushman or Hottentot feature, and were dressed in strips of soft bark hanging from the waist to the knee. They deal largely in salt, which their country produces in great abundance. It is brought in crystals of about 12 inches long and 1-1/2 in diameter. This is hawked about every where in Angola, and, next to calico, is the most common medium of barter. The Kisama are brave; and when the Portuguese army followed them into their forests, they reduced the invaders to extremity by tapping all the reservoirs of water, which were no other than the enormous baobabs of the country hollowed into cisterns. As the Kisama country is ill supplied with water otherwise, the Portuguese were soon obliged to retreat. Their country, lying near to Massangano, is low and marshy, but becomes more elevated in the distance, and beyond them lie the lofty dark mountain ranges of the Libollo, another powerful and independent people. Near Massangano I observed what seemed to be an effort of nature to furnish a variety of domestic fowls, more capable than the common kind of bearing the heat of the sun. This was a hen and chickens with all their feathers curled upward, thus giving shade to the body without increasing the heat. They are here named "Kisafu" by the native population, who pay a high price for them when they wish to offer them as a sacrifice, and by the Portuguese they are termed "Arripiada", or shivering. There seems to be a tendency in nature to afford varieties adapted to the convenience of man. A kind of very short-legged fowl among the Boers was obtained, in consequence of observing that such were more easily caught for transportation in their frequent removals in search of pasture. A similar instance of securing a variety occurred with the short-limbed sheep in America.

Returning by ascending the Lucalla into Cazengo, we had an opportunity of visiting several flourishing coffee plantations, and observed that several men, who had begun with no capital but honest industry, had, in the course of a few years, acquired a comfortable subsistence. One of these, Mr. Pinto, generously furnished me with a good supply of his excellent coffee, and my men with a breed of rabbits to carry to their own country. Their lands, granted by government, yielded, without much labor, coffee sufficient for all the necessarys of life.

The fact of other avenues of wealth opening up so readily seems like a providential invitation to forsake the slave-trade and engage in lawful commerce. We saw the female population occupied, as usual, in the spinning of cotton and cultivation of their lands. Their only instrument for culture is a double-handled hoe, which is worked with a sort of dragging motion. Many of the men were employed in weaving. The latter appear to be less industrious than the former, for they require a month to finish a single web. There is, however, not much inducement to industry, for, notwithstanding the time consumed in its manufacture, each web is sold for only two shillings.

On returning to Golungo Alto I found several of my men laid up with fever. One of the reasons for my leaving them there was that they might recover from the fatigue of the journey from Loanda, which had much more effect upon their feet than hundreds of miles had on our way westward. They had always been accustomed to moisture in their own well-watered land, and we certainly had a superabundance of that in Loanda. The roads, however, from Loanda to Golungo Alto were both hard and dry, and they suffered severely in consequence; yet they were composing songs to be sung when they should reach home. The Argonauts were nothing to them; and they remarked very impressively to me, "It was well you came with Makololo, for no tribe could have done what we have accomplished in coming to the white man's country: we are the true ancients, who can tell wonderful things." Two of them now had fever in the continued form, and became jaundiced, the whites or conjunctival membrane of their eyes becoming as yellow as saffron; and a third suffered from an attack of mania. He came to his companions one day, and said, "Remain well. I am called away by the gods!" and set off at the top of his speed. The young men caught him before he had gone a mile, and bound him. By gentle treatment and watching for a few days he recovered. I have observed several instances of this kind in the country, but very few cases of idiocy, and I believe that continued insanity is rare.

Chapter 21

Visit a deserted Convent—Favorable Report of Jesuits and their Teaching—Gradations of native Society—Punishment of Thieves—Palm-toddy; its baneful Effects—Freemasons—Marriages and Funerals—Litigation—Mr. Canto's Illness—Bad Behavior of his Slaves—An Entertainment—Ideas on Free Labor—Loss of American Cotton-seed—Abundance of Cotton in the country—Sickness of Sekeletu's Horse—Eclipse of the Sun—Insects which distill Water—Experiments with them—Proceed to Ambaca—Sickly Season—Office of Commandant—Punishment of official Delinquents—Present from Mr. Schut of Loanda—Visit Pungo Andongo—Its good Pasturage, Grain, Fruit, etc.—The Fort and columnar Rocks—The Queen of Jinga—Salubrity of Pungo Andongo—Price of a Slave—A Merchant-prince—His Hospitality—Hear of the Loss of my Papers in "Forerunner"—Narrow Escape from an Alligator—Ancient Burial-places—Neglect of Agriculture in Angola—Manioc the staple Product—Its Cheapness—Sickness—Friendly Visit from a colored Priest—The Prince of Congo—No Priests in the Interior of Angola.

While waiting for the recovery of my men, I visited, in company with my friend Mr. Canto, the deserted convent of St. Hilarion, at Bango, a few miles northwest of Golungo Alto. It is situated in a magnificent valley, containing a population numbering 4000 hearths. This is the abode of the Sova, or Chief Bango, who still holds a place of authority under the Portuguese. The garden of the convent, the church, and dormitories of the brethren are still kept in a good state of repair. I looked at the furniture, couches, and large chests for holding the provisions of the brotherhood with interest, and would fain have learned something of the former occupants; but all the books and sacred vessels had lately been removed to Loanda, and even the graves of the good men stand without any record: their resting-places are, however, carefully tended. All speak well of the Jesuits and other missionaries, as the Capuchins, etc., for having attended diligently to the instruction of the children. They were supposed to have a tendency to take the part of the people against the government, and were supplanted by priests, concerning whom no regret is expressed that they were allowed to die out. In viewing the present fruits of former missions, it is impossible not to feel assured that, if the Jesuit teaching has been so permanent, that of Protestants, who leave the Bible in the hands of their converts, will not be less abiding. The chief Bango has built a large two-story house close by the convent, but superstitious fears prevent him from sleeping in it. The Portuguese take advantage of all the gradations into which native society has divided itself. This man, for instance, is still a sova or chief, has his councilors, and maintains the same state as when the country was independent. When any of his people are guilty of theft, he pays down the amount of goods stolen at once, and reimburses himself out of the property of the thief so effectually as to be benefited by the transaction. The people under him are divided into a number of classes. There are his councilors, as the highest, who are generally head men of several villages, and the carriers, the lowest free men. One class above the last obtains the privilege of wearing shoes from the chief by paying for it; another, the soldiers or militia, pay for the privilege of serving, the advantage being that they are not afterward liable to be made carriers. They are also divided into gentlemen and little gentlemen, and, though quite black, speak of themselves as white men, and of the others, who may not wear shoes, as "blacks". The men of all these classes trust to their wives for food, and spend most of their time in drinking the palm-toddy. This toddy is the juice of the palm-oil-tree ('Elaeis Guineensis'), which, when tapped, yields a sweet, clear liquid, not at all intoxicating while fresh, but, when allowed to stand till the afternoon, causes inebriation and many crimes. This toddy, called malova, is the bane of the country. Culprits are continually brought before the commandants for assaults committed through its influence. Men come up with deep gashes on their heads; and one, who had burned his father's house, I saw making a profound bow to Mr. Canto, and volunteering to explain why he did the deed.

There is also a sort of fraternity of freemasons, named Empacasseiros, into which no one is admitted unless he is an expert hunter, and can shoot well with the gun. They are distinguished by a fillet of buffalo hide around their heads, and are employed as messengers in all cases requiring express. They are very trustworthy, and, when on active service, form the best native troops the Portuguese possess. The militia are of no value as soldiers, but cost the country nothing, being supported by their wives. Their duties are chiefly to guard the residences of commandants, and to act as police.

The chief recreations of the natives of Angola are marriages and funerals. When a young woman is about to be married, she is placed in a hut alone and anointed with various unguents, and many incantations are employed in order to secure good fortune and fruitfulness. Here, as almost every where in the south, the height of good fortune is to bear sons. They often leave a husband altogether if they have daughters only. In their dances, when any one may wish to deride another, in the accompanying song a line is introduced, "So and so has no children, and never will get any." She feels the insult so keenly that it is not uncommon for her to rush away and commit suicide. After some days the bride elect is taken to another hut, and adorned with all the richest clothing and ornaments that the relatives can either lend or borrow. She is then placed in a public situation, saluted as a lady, and presents made by all her acquaintances are placed around her. After this she is taken to the residence of her husband, where she has a hut for herself, and becomes one of several wives, for polygamy is general. Dancing, feasting, and drinking on such occasions are prolonged for several days. In case of separation, the woman returns to her father's family, and the husband receives back what he gave for her. In nearly all cases a man gives a price for the wife, and in cases of mulattoes, as much as 60 Pounds is often given to the parents of the bride. This is one of the evils the bishop was trying to remedy.

In cases of death the body is kept several days, and there is a grand concourse of both sexes, with beating of drums, dances, and debauchery, kept up with feasting, etc., according to the means of the relatives. The great ambition of many of the blacks of Angola is to give their friends an expensive funeral. Often, when one is asked to sell a pig, he replies, "I am keeping it in case of the death of any of my friends." A pig is usually slaughtered and eaten on the last day of the ceremonies, and its head thrown into the nearest stream or river. A native will sometimes appear intoxicated on these occasions, and, if blamed for his intemperance, will reply, "Why! my mother is dead!" as if he thought it a sufficient justification. The expenses of funerals are so heavy that often years elapse before they can defray them.

These people are said to be very litigious and obstinate: constant disputes are taking place respecting their lands. A case came before the weekly court of the commandant involving property in a palm-tree worth twopence. The judge advised the pursuer to withdraw the case, as the mere expenses of entering it would be much more than the cost of the tree. "Oh no," said he; "I have a piece of calico with me for the clerk, and money for yourself. It's my right; I will not forego it." The calico itself cost three or four shillings. They rejoice if they can say of an enemy, "I took him before the court."

My friend Mr. Canto, the commandant, being seized with fever in a severe form, it afforded me much pleasure to attend HIM in his sickness, who had been so kind to ME in mine. He was for some time in a state of insensibility, and I, having the charge of his establishment, had thus an opportunity of observing the workings of slavery. When a master is ill, the slaves run riot among the eatables. I did not know this until I observed that every time the sugar-basin came to the table it was empty. On visiting my patient by night, I passed along a corridor, and unexpectedly came upon the washerwoman eating pine-apples and sugar. All the sweetmeats were devoured, and it was difficult for me to get even bread and butter until I took the precaution of locking the pantry door. Probably the slaves thought that, as both they and the luxuries were the master's property, there was no good reason why they should be kept apart.

Debarred by my precaution from these sources of enjoyment, they took to killing the fowls and goats, and, when the animal was dead, brought it to me, saying, "We found this thing lying out there." They then enjoyed a feast of flesh. A feeling of insecurity prevails throughout this country. It is quite common to furnish visitors with the keys of their rooms. When called on to come to breakfast or dinner, each locks his door and puts the key in his pocket. At Kolobeng we never locked our doors by night or by day for months together; but there slavery is unknown. The Portuguese do not seem at all bigoted in their attachment to slavery, nor yet in their prejudices against color. Mr. Canto gave an entertainment in order to draw all classes together and promote general good-will. Two sovas or native chiefs were present, and took their places without the least appearance of embarrassment. The Sova of Kilombo appeared in the dress of a general, and the Sova of Bango was gayly attired in a red coat, profusely ornamented with tinsel. The latter had a band of musicians with him consisting of six trumpeters and four drummers, who performed very well. These men are fond of titles, and the Portuguese government humors them by conferring honorary captaincies, etc.: the Sova of Bango was at present anxious to obtain the title of "Major of all the Sovas". At the tables of other gentlemen I observed the same thing constantly occurring. At this meeting Mr. Canto communicated some ideas which I had written out on the dignity of labor, and the superiority of free over slave labor. The Portuguese gentlemen present were anxiously expecting an arrival of American cotton-seed from Mr. Gabriel. They are now in the transition state from unlawful to lawful trade, and turn eagerly to cotton, coffee, and sugar as new sources of wealth. Mr. Canto had been commissioned by them to purchase three sugar-mills. Our cruisers have been the principal agents in compelling them to abandon the slave-trade; and our government, in furnishing them with a supply of cotton-seed, showed a generous intention to aid them in commencing a more honorable course. It can scarcely be believed, however, that after Lord Clarendon had been at the trouble of procuring fresh cotton-seed through our minister at Washington, and had sent it out to the care of H. M. Commissioner at Loanda, probably from having fallen into the hands of a few incorrigible slave-traders, it never reached its destination. It was most likely cast into the sea of Ambriz, and my friends at Golungo Alto were left without the means of commencing a new enterprise.

Mr. Canto mentioned that there is now much more cotton in the country than can be consumed; and if he had possession of a few hundred pounds, he would buy up all the oil and cotton at a fair price, and thereby bring about a revolution in the agriculture of the country. These commodities are not produced in greater quantity, because the people have no market for those which now spring up almost spontaneously around them. The above was put down in my journal when I had no idea that enlarged supplies of cotton from new sources were so much needed at home.

It is common to cut down cotton-trees as a nuisance, and cultivate beans, potatoes, and manioc sufficient only for their own consumption. I have the impression that cotton, which is deciduous in America, is perennial here; for the plants I saw in winter were not dead, though going by the name Algodao Americana, or American cotton. The rents paid for gardens belonging to the old convents are merely nominal, varying from one shilling to three pounds per annum. The higher rents being realized from those in the immediate vicinity of Loanda, none but Portuguese or half-castes can pay them.

When about to start, the horse which the governor had kindly presented for Sekeletu was seized with inflammation, which delayed us some time longer, and we ultimately lost it. We had been careful to watch it when coming through the district of Matamba, where we had discovered the tsetse, that no insect might light upon it. The change of diet here may have had some influence in producing the disease; for I was informed by Dr. Welweitsch, an able German naturalist, whom we found pursuing his arduous labors here, and whose life we hope may be spared to give his researches to the world, that, of fifty-eight kinds of grasses found at Loanda, only three or four species exist here, and these of the most diminutive kinds. The twenty-four different species of grass of Golungo Alto are nearly all gigantic. Indeed, gigantic grasses, climbers, shrubs and trees, with but few plants, constitute the vegetation of this region.

NOVEMBER 20TH. An eclipse of the sun, which I had anxiously hoped to observe with a view of determining the longitude, happened this morning, and, as often took place in this cloudy climate, the sun was covered four minutes before it began. When it shone forth the eclipse was in progress, and a few minutes before it should (according to my calculations) have ended the sun was again completely obscured. The greatest patience and perseverance are required, if one wishes to ascertain his position when it is the rainy season.

Before leaving, I had an opportunity of observing a curious insect, which inhabits trees of the fig family ('Ficus'), upward of twenty species of which are found here. Seven or eight of them cluster round a spot on one of the smaller branches, and there keep up a constant distillation of a clear fluid, which, dropping to the ground, forms a little puddle below. If a vessel is placed under them in the evening, it contains three or four pints of fluid in the morning. The natives say that, if a drop falls into the eyes, it causes inflammation of these organs. To the question whence is this fluid derived, the people reply that the insects suck it out of the tree, and our own naturalists give the same answer. I have never seen an orifice, and it is scarcely possible that the tree can yield so much. A similar but much smaller homopterous insect, of the family 'Cercopidae', is known in England as the frog-hopper ('Aphrophora spumaria'), when full grown and furnished with wings, but while still in the pupa state it is called "Cuckoo-spit", from the mass of froth in which it envelops itself. The circulation of sap in plants in our climate, especially of the graminaceae, is not quick enough to yield much moisture. The African species is five or six times the size of the English. In the case of branches of the fig-tree, the point the insects congregate on is soon marked by a number of incipient roots, such as are thrown out when a cutting is inserted in the ground for the purpose of starting another tree. I believe that both the English and African insects belong to the same family, and differ only in size, and that the chief part of the moisture is derived from the atmosphere. I leave it for naturalists to explain how these little creatures distill both by night and day as much water as they please, and are more independent than her majesty's steam-ships, with their apparatus for condensing steam; for, without coal, their abundant supplies of sea-water are of no avail. I tried the following experiment: Finding a colony of these insects busily distilling on a branch of the 'Ricinus communis', or castor-oil plant, I denuded about 20 inches of the bark on the tree side of the insects, and scraped away the inner bark, so as to destroy all the ascending vessels. I also cut a hole in the side of the branch, reaching to the middle, and then cut out the pith and internal vessels. The distillation was then going on at the rate of one drop each 67 seconds, or about 2 ounces 5-1/2 drams in 24 hours. Next morning the distillation, so far from being affected by the attempt to stop the supplies, supposing they had come up through the branch from the tree, was increased to a drop every 5 seconds, or 12 drops per minute, making 1 pint (16 ounces) in every 24 hours. I then cut the branch so much that, during the day, it broke; but they still went on at the rate of a drop every 5 seconds, while another colony on a branch of the same tree gave a drop every 17 seconds only, or at the rate of about 10 ounces 4-4/5 drams in 24 hours. I finally cut off the branch; but this was too much for their patience, for they immediately decamped, as insects will do from either a dead branch or a dead animal, which Indian hunters soon know, when they sit down on a recently-killed bear. The presence of greater moisture in the air increased the power of these distillers: the period of greatest activity was in the morning, when the air and every thing else was charged with dew.

Having but one day left for experiment, I found again that another colony on a branch denuded in the same way yielded a drop every 2 seconds, or 4 pints 10 ounces in 24 hours, while a colony on a branch untouched yielded a drop every 11 seconds, or 16 ounces 2-19/20 drams in 24 hours. I regretted somewhat the want of time to institute another experiment, namely, to cut a branch and place it in water, so as to keep it in life, and then observe if there was any diminution of the quantity of water in the vessel. This alone was wanting to make it certain that they draw water from the atmosphere. I imagine that they have some power of which we are not aware, besides that nervous influence which causes constant motion to our own involuntary muscles, the power of life-long action without fatigue. The reader will remember, in connection with this insect, the case of the ants already mentioned.

DECEMBER 14TH. Both myself and men having recovered from severe attacks of fever, we left the hospitable residence of Mr. Canto with a deep sense of his kindness to us all, and proceeded on our way to Ambaca. (Lat. 9d 16' 35" S., long. 15d 23' E.)

Frequent rains had fallen in October and November, which were nearly always accompanied with thunder. Occasionally the quantity of moisture in the atmosphere is greatly increased without any visible cause: this imparts a sensation of considerable cold, though the thermometer exhibits no fall of the mercury. The greater humidity in the air, affording a better conducting medium for the radiation of heat from the body, is as dangerous as a sudden fall of the thermometer: it causes considerable disease among the natives, and this season is denominated "Carneirado", as if by the disease they were slaughtered like sheep. The season of these changes, which is the most favorable for Europeans, is the most unhealthy for the native population; and this is by no means a climate in which either natives or Europeans can indulge in irregularities with impunity.

Owing to the weakness of the men who had been sick, we were able to march but short distances. Three hours and a half brought us to the banks of the Caloi, a small stream which flows into the Senza. This is one of the parts of the country reputed to yield petroleum, but the geological formation, being mica schist, dipping toward the eastward, did not promise much for our finding it. Our hospitable friend, Mr. Mellot, accompanied us to another little river, called the Quango, where I saw two fine boys, the sons of the sub-commandant, Mr. Feltao, who, though only from six to eight years old, were subject to fever. We then passed on in the bright sunlight, the whole country looking so fresh and green after the rains, and every thing so cheering, one could not but wonder to find it so feverish.

We found, on reaching Ambaca, that the gallant old soldier, Laurence Jose Marquis, had, since our passing Icollo i Bengo, been promoted, on account of his stern integrity, to the government of this important district. The office of commandant is much coveted by the officers of the line who come to Angola, not so much for the salary as for the perquisites, which, when managed skillfully, in the course of a few years make one rich. An idea may be formed of the conduct of some of these officials from the following extract from the Boletin of Loanda of the 28th of October, 1854:

"The acting governor-general of the province of Angola and its dependencies determines as follows:

"Having instituted an investigation (Syndecancia) against the commandant of the fort of— —, a captain of the army of Portugal in commission in this province, — —, on account of numerous complaints, which have come before this government, of violences and extortions practiced by the said commandant, and those complaints appearing by the result of the investigation to be well founded, it will be convenient to exonerate the captain referred to from the command of the fort of— —, to which he had been nominated by the portfolio of this general government, No. 41, of 27th December of the past year; and if not otherwise determined, the same official shall be judged by a council of war for the criminal acts which are to him attributed."

Even this public mention of his crimes attaches no stigma to the man's character. The council of war, by which these delinquents always prefer to be judged, is composed of men who eagerly expect to occupy the post of commandant themselves, and anticipate their own trial for similar acts at some future time. The severest sentence a council of war awards is a few weeks' suspension from office in his regiment.

This want of official integrity, which is not at all attributable to the home government of Portugal, would prove a serious impediment in the way of foreign enterprise developing the resources of this rich province. And to this cause, indeed, may be ascribed the failure of the Portuguese laws for the entire suppression of the slave-trade. The officers ought to receive higher pay, if integrity is expected from them. At present, a captain's pay for a year will only keep him in good uniform. The high pay our own officers receive has manifest advantages.

Before leaving Ambaca we received a present of ten head of cattle from Mr. Schut of Loanda, and, as it shows the cheapness of provisions here, I may mention that the cost was only about a guinea per head.

On crossing the Lucalla we made a detour to the south, in order to visit the famous rocks of Pungo Andongo. As soon as we crossed the rivulet Lotete, a change in the vegetation of the country was apparent. We found trees identical with those to be seen south of the Chobe. The grass, too, stands in tufts, and is of that kind which the natives consider to be best adapted for cattle. Two species of grape-bearing vines abound every where in this district, and the influence of the good pasturage is seen in the plump condition of the cattle. In all my previous inquiries respecting the vegetable products of Angola, I was invariably directed to Pungo Andongo. Do you grow wheat? "Oh, yes, in Pungo Andongo."—Grapes, figs, or peaches? "Oh, yes, in Pungo Andongo."—Do you make butter, cheese, etc.? The uniform answer was, "Oh, yes, there is abundance of all these in Pungo Andongo." But when we arrived here, we found that the answers all referred to the activity of one man, Colonel Manuel Antonio Pires. The presence of the wild grape shows that vineyards might be cultivated with success; the wheat grows well without irrigation; and any one who tasted the butter and cheese at the table of Colonel Pires would prefer them to the stale produce of the Irish dairy, in general use throughout that province. The cattle in this country are seldom milked, on account of the strong prejudice which the Portuguese entertain against the use of milk. They believe that it may be used with safety in the morning, but, if taken after midday, that it will cause fever. It seemed to me that there was not much reason for carefully avoiding a few drops in their coffee, after having devoured ten times the amount in the shape of cheese at dinner.

The fort of Pungo Andongo (lat. 9d 42' 14" S., long. 15d 30' E.) is situated in the midst of a group of curious columnar-shaped rocks, each of which is upward of three hundred feet in height. They are composed of conglomerate, made up of a great variety of rounded pieces in a matrix of dark red sandstone. They rest on a thick stratum of this last rock, with very few of the pebbles in its substance. On this a fossil palm has been found, and if of the same age as those on the eastern side of the continent, on which similar palms now lie, there may be coal underneath this, as well as under that at Tete. The asserted existence of petroleum springs at Dande, and near Cambambe, would seem to indicate the presence of this useful mineral, though I am not aware of any one having actually seen a seam of coal tilted up to the surface in Angola, as we have at Tete. The gigantic pillars of Pungo Andongo have been formed by a current of the sea coming from the S.S.E.; for, seen from the top, they appear arranged in that direction, and must have withstood the surges of the ocean at a period of our world's history, when the relations of land and sea were totally different from what they are now, and long before "the morning stars sang together, and all the sons of God shouted for joy to see the abodes prepared which man was soon to fill." The imbedded pieces in the conglomerate are of gneiss, clay shale, mica and sandstone schists, trap, and porphyry, most of which are large enough to give the whole the appearance of being the only remaining vestiges of vast primaeval banks of shingle. Several little streams run among these rocks, and in the central part of the pillars stands the village, completely environed by well-nigh inaccessible rocks. The pathways into the village might be defended by a small body of troops against an army; and this place was long the stronghold of the tribe called Jinga, the original possessors of the country.

We were shown a footprint carved on one of these rocks. It is spoken of as that of a famous queen, who reigned over all this region. In looking at these rude attempts at commemoration, one feels the value of letters. In the history of Angola we find that the famous queen Donna Anna de Souza came from the vicinity, as embassadress from her brother, Gola Bandy, King of the Jinga, to Loanda, in 1621, to sue for peace, and astonished the governor by the readiness of her answers. The governor proposed, as a condition of peace, the payment by the Jinga of an annual tribute. "People talk of tribute after they have conquered, and not before it; we come to talk of peace, not of subjection," was the ready answer. The governor was as much nonplussed as our Cape governors often are when they tell the Caffres "to put it all down in writing, and they will then be able to answer them." She remained some time in Loanda, gained all she sought, and, after being taught by the missionaries, was baptized, and returned to her own country with honor. She succeeded to the kingdom on the death of her brother, whom it was supposed she poisoned, but in a subsequent war with the Portuguese she lost nearly all her army in a great battle fought in 1627. She returned to the Church after a long period of apostasy, and died in extreme old age; and the Jinga still live as an independent people to the north of this their ancient country. No African tribe has ever been destroyed.

In former times the Portuguese imagined that this place was particularly unhealthy, and banishment to the black rocks of Pungo Andongo was thought by their judges to be a much severer sentence than transportation to any part of the coast; but this district is now well known to be the most healthy part of Angola. The water is remarkably pure, the soil is light, and the country open and undulating, with a general slope down toward the River Coanza, a few miles distant. That river is the southern boundary of the Portuguese, and beyond, to the S. and S.W., we see the high mountains of the Libollo. On the S.E. we have also a mountainous country, inhabited by the Kimbonda or Ambonda, who are said by Colonel Pires to be a very brave and independent people, but hospitable and fair in their dealings. They are rich in cattle, and their country produces much beeswax, which is carefully collected, and brought to the Portuguese, with whom they have always been on good terms.

The Ako (Haco), a branch of this family, inhabit the left bank of the Coanza above this village, who, instead of bringing slaves for sale, as formerly, now occasionally bring wax for the purchase of a slave from the Portuguese. I saw a boy sold for twelve shillings: he said that he belonged to the country of Matiamvo. Here I bought a pair of well-made boots, of good tanned leather, which reached above the knee, for five shillings and eightpence, and that was just the price given for one pound of ivory by Mr. Pires; consequently, the boy was worth two pairs of boots, or two pounds of ivory. The Libollo on the S. have not so good a character, but the Coanza is always deep enough to form a line of defense. Colonel Pires is a good example of what an honest industrious man in this country may become. He came as a servant in a ship, and, by a long course of persevering labor, has raised himself to be the richest merchant in Angola. He possesses some thousands of cattle; and, on any emergency, can appear in the field with several hundred armed slaves.

While enjoying the hospitality of this merchant-prince in his commodious residence, which is outside the rocks, and commands a beautiful view of all the adjacent country, I learned that all my dispatches, maps, and journal had gone to the bottom of the sea in the mail-packet "Forerunner". I felt so glad that my friend Lieutenant Bedingfeld, to whose care I had committed them, though in the most imminent danger, had not shared a similar fate, that I was at once reconciled to the labor of rewriting. I availed myself of the kindness of Colonel Pires, and remained till the end of the year reproducing my lost papers.

Colonel Pires having another establishment on the banks of the Coanza, about six miles distant, I visited it with him about once a week for the purpose of recreation. The difference of temperature caused by the lower altitude was seen in the cashew-trees; for while, near the rocks, these trees were but coming into flower, those at the lower station were ripening their fruit. Cocoanut trees and bananas bear well at the lower station, but yield little or no fruit at the upper. The difference indicated by the thermometer was 7 Deg. The general range near the rocks was 67 Deg. at 7 A.M., 74 Deg. at midday, and 72 Deg. in the evening.

A slave-boy belonging to Colonel Pires, having stolen and eaten some lemons in the evening, went to the river to wash his mouth, so as not to be detected by the flavor. An alligator seized him and carried him to an island in the middle of the stream; there the boy grasped hold of the reeds, and baffled all the efforts of the reptile to dislodge him, till his companions, attracted by his cries, came in a canoe to his assistance. The alligator at once let go his hold; for, when out of his own element, he is cowardly. The boy had many marks of the teeth in his abdomen and thigh, and those of the claws on his legs and arms.

The slaves in Colonel Pires' establishments appeared more like free servants than any I had elsewhere seen. Every thing was neat and clean, while generally, where slaves are the only domestics, there is an aspect of slovenliness, as if they went on the principle of always doing as little for their masters as possible.

In the country near to this station were a large number of the ancient burial-places of the Jinga. These are simply large mounds of stones, with drinking and cooking vessels of rude pottery on them. Some are arranged in a circular form, two or three yards in diameter, and shaped like a haycock. There is not a single vestige of any inscription. The natives of Angola generally have a strange predilection for bringing their dead to the sides of the most frequented paths. They have a particular anxiety to secure the point where cross-roads meet. On and around the graves are planted tree euphorbias and other species of that family. On the grave itself they also place water-bottles, broken pipes, cooking vessels, and sometimes a little bow and arrow.

The Portuguese government, wishing to prevent this custom, affixed a penalty on any one burying in the roads, and appointed places of public sepulture in every district in the country. The people persist, however, in spite of the most stringent enforcement of the law, to follow their ancient custom.

The country between the Coanza and Pungo Andongo is covered with low trees, bushes, and fine pasturage. In the latter, we were pleased to see our old acquaintances, the gaudy gladiolus, Amaryllis toxicaria, hymanthus, and other bulbs in as flourishing a condition as at the Cape.

It is surprising that so little has been done in the way of agriculture in Angola. Raising wheat by means of irrigation has never been tried; no plow is ever used; and the only instrument is the native hoe, in the hands of slaves. The chief object of agriculture is the manioc, which does not contain nutriment sufficient to give proper stamina to the people. The half-caste Portuguese have not so much energy as their fathers. They subsist chiefly on the manioc, and, as that can be eaten either raw, roasted, or boiled, as it comes from the ground; or fermented in water, and then roasted or dried after fermentation, and baked or pounded into fine meal; or rasped into meal and cooked as farina; or made into confectionary with butter and sugar, it does not so soon pall upon the palate as one might imagine, when told that it constitutes their principal food. The leaves boiled make an excellent vegetable for the table; and, when eaten by goats, their milk is much increased. The wood is a good fuel, and yields a large quantity of potash. If planted in a dry soil, it takes two years to come to perfection, requiring, during that time, one weeding only. It bears drought well, and never shrivels up, like other plants, when deprived of rain. When planted in low alluvial soils, and either well supplied with rain or annually flooded, twelve, or even ten months, are sufficient to bring it to maturity. The root rasped while raw, placed upon a cloth, and rubbed with the hands while water is poured upon it, parts with its starchy glutinous matter, and this, when it settles at the bottom of the vessel, and the water poured off, is placed in the sun till nearly dry, to form tapioca. The process of drying is completed on an iron plate over a slow fire, the mass being stirred meanwhile with a stick, and when quite dry it appears agglutinated into little globules, and is in the form we see the tapioca of commerce. This is never eaten by weevils, and so little labor is required in its cultivation that on the spot it is extremely cheap. Throughout the interior parts of Angola, fine manioc meal, which could with ease have been converted either into superior starch or tapioca, is commonly sold at the rate of about ten pounds for a penny. All this region, however, has no means of transport to Loanda other than the shoulders of the carriers and slaves over a footpath.

Cambambe, to which the navigation of the Coanza reaches, is reported to be thirty leagues below Pungo Andongo. A large waterfall is the limit on that side; and another exists higher up, at the confluence of the Lombe (lat. 9d 41' 26" S., and about long. 16d E.), over which hippopotami and elephants are sometimes drawn and killed. The river between is rapid, and generally rushes over a rocky bottom. Its source is pointed out as S.E. or S.S.E. of its confluence with the Lombe, and near Bihe. The situation of Bihe is not well known. When at Sanza we were assured that it lies nearly south of that point, and eight days distant. This statement seemed to be corroborated by our meeting many people going to Matiamvo and to Loanda from Bihe. Both parties had come to Sanza, and then branched off, one to the east, the other to the west. The source of the Coanza is thus probably not far from Sanza.

I had the happiness of doing a little good in the way of administering to the sick, for there are no doctors in the interior of Angola. Notwithstanding the general healthiness of this fine district and its pleasant temperature, I was attacked by fever myself. While confined to my room, a gentleman of color, a canon of the Church, kindly paid me a visit. He was on a tour of visitation in the different interior districts for the purpose of baptizing and marrying. He had lately been on a visit to Lisbon in company with the Prince of Congo, and had been invested with an order of honor by the King of Portugal as an acknowledgment of his services. He had all the appearance of a true negro, but commanded the respect of the people; and Colonel P., who had known him for thirty years, pronounced him to be a good man. There are only three or four priests in Loanda, all men of color, but educated for the office. About the time of my journey in Angola, an offer was made to any young men of ability who might wish to devote themselves to the service of the Church, to afford them the requisite education at the University of Coimbra in Portugal. I was informed, on what seemed good authority, that the Prince of Congo is professedly a Christian, and that there are no fewer than twelve churches in that kingdom, the fruits of the mission established in former times at San Salvador, the capital. These churches are kept in partial repair by the people, who also keep up the ceremonies of the Church, pronouncing some gibberish over the dead, in imitation of the Latin prayers which they had formerly heard. Many of them can read and write. When a King of Congo dies, the body is wrapped up in a great many folds of cloth until a priest can come from Loanda to consecrate his successor. The King of Congo still retains the title of Lord of Angola, which he had when the Jinga, the original possessors of the soil, owed him allegiance; and, when he writes to the Governor of Angola, he places his own name first, as if addressing his vassal. The Jinga paid him tribute annually in cowries, which were found on the island that shelters Loanda harbor, and, on refusing to continue payment, the King of Congo gave over the island to the Portuguese, and thus their dominion commenced in this quarter.

There is not much knowledge of the Christian religion in either Congo or Angola, yet it is looked upon with a certain degree of favor. The prevalence of fever is probably the reason why no priest occupies a post in any part of the interior. They come on tours of visitation like that mentioned, and it is said that no expense is incurred, for all the people are ready not only to pay for their services, but also to furnish every article in their power gratuitously. In view of the desolate condition of this fine missionary field, it is more than probable that the presence of a few Protestants would soon provoke the priests, if not to love, to good works.

Chapter 22

Leave Pungo Andongo—Extent of Portuguese Power—Meet Traders and Carriers—Red Ants; their fierce Attack; Usefulness; Numbers—Descend the Heights of Tala Mungongo—Fruit-trees in the Valley of Cassange—Edible Muscle—Birds—Cassange Village—Quinine and Cathory— Sickness of Captain Neves' Infant—A Diviner thrashed—Death of the Child—Mourning—Loss of Life from the Ordeal—Widespread Superstitions—The Chieftainship—Charms—Receive Copies of the "Times"—Trading Pombeiros—Present for Matiamvo—Fever after westerly Winds—Capabilities of Angola for producing the raw Materials of English Manufacture—Trading Parties with Ivory—More Fever—A Hyaena's Choice—Makololo Opinion of the Portuguese—Cypriano's Debt—A Funeral—Dread of disembodied Spirits—Beautiful Morning Scenes—Crossing the Quango—Ambakistas called "The Jews of Angola"—Fashions of the Bashinje—Approach the Village of Sansawe—His Idea of Dignity—The Pombeiros' Present—Long Detention—A Blow on the Beard—Attacked in a Forest—Sudden Conversion of a fighting Chief to Peace Principles by means of a Revolver—No Blood shed in consequence—Rate of Traveling—Slave Women—Way of addressing Slaves—Their thievish Propensities—Feeders of the Congo or Zaire—Obliged to refuse Presents—Cross the Loajima—Appearance of People; Hair Fashions.

JANUARY 1, 1855. Having, through the kindness of Colonel Pires, reproduced some of my lost papers, I left Pungo Andongo the first day of this year, and at Candumba, slept in one of the dairy establishments of my friend, who had sent forward orders for an ample supply of butter, cheese, and milk. Our path lay along the right bank of the Coanza. This is composed of the same sandstone rock, with pebbles, which forms the flooring of the country. The land is level, has much open forest, and is well adapted for pasturage.

On reaching the confluence of the Lombe, we left the river, and proceeded in a northeasterly direction, through a fine open green country, to the village of Malange, where we struck into our former path. A few miles to the west of this a path branches off to a new district named the Duke Braganza. This path crosses the Lucalla and several of its feeders. The whole of the country drained by these is described as extremely fertile. The territory west of Braganza is reported to be mountainous, well wooded and watered; wild coffee is abundant, and the people even make their huts of coffee-trees. The rivers Dande, Senza, and Lucalla are said to rise in one mountain range. Numerous tribes inhabit the country to the north, who are all independent. The Portuguese power extends chiefly over the tribes through whose lands we have passed. It may be said to be firmly seated only between the rivers Dande and Coanza. It extends inland about three hundred miles to the River Quango; and the population, according to the imperfect data afforded by the census, given annually by the commandants of the fifteen or sixteen districts into which it is divided, can not be under 600,000 souls.

Leaving Malange, we passed quickly, without deviation, along the path by which we had come. At Sanza (lat. 9d 37′ 46″ S., long. 16d 59′ E.) we expected to get a little seed-wheat, but this was not now to be found in Angola. The underlying rock of the whole of this section is that same sandstone which we have before noticed, but it gradually becomes finer in the grain, with the addition of a little mica, the farther we go eastward; we enter upon clay shale at Tala Mungongo (lat. 9d 42′ 37″ S., long. 17d 27′ E.), and find it dipping a little to the west. The general geological structure is a broad fringe of mica and sandstone schist (about 15 Deg. E.), dipping in toward the centre of the country, beneath these horizontal and sedimentary rocks of more recent date, which form an inland basin. The fringe is not, however, the highest in altitude, though the oldest in age.

While at this latter place we met a native of Bihe who has visited the country of Shinte three times for the purposes of trade. He gave us some of the news of that distant part, but not a word of the Makololo, who have always been represented in the countries to the north as a desperately savage race, whom no trader could visit with safety. The half-caste traders whom we met at Shinte's had returned to Angola with sixty-six slaves and upward of fifty tusks of ivory. As we came along the path, we daily met long lines of carriers bearing large square masses of beeswax, each about a hundred pounds weight, and numbers of elephants' tusks, the property of Angolese merchants. Many natives were proceeding to the coast also on their own account, carrying beeswax, ivory, and sweet oil. They appeared to travel in perfect security; and at different parts of the road we purchased fowls from them at a penny each. My men took care to celebrate their own daring in having actually entered ships, while the natives of these parts, who had endeavored to frighten them on their way down, had only seen them at a distance. Poor fellows! they were more than ever attentive to me; and, as they were not obliged to erect sheds for themselves, in consequence of finding them already built at the different sleeping-places, all their care was bestowed in making me comfortable. Mashauana, as usual, made his bed with his head close to my feet, and never during the entire journey did I have to call him twice for any thing I needed.

During our stay at Tala Mungongo, our attention was attracted to a species of red ant which infests different parts of this country. It is remarkably fond of animal food. The commandant of the village having slaughtered a cow, slaves were obliged to sit up the whole night, burning fires of straw around the meat, to prevent them from devouring most of it. These ants are frequently met with in numbers like a small army. At a little distance they appear as a brownish-red band, two or three inches wide, stretched across the path, all eagerly pressing on in one direction. If a person happens to tread upon them, they rush up his legs and bite with surprising vigor. The first time I encountered this by no means contemptible enemy was near Cassange. My attention being taken up in viewing the distant landscape, I accidentally stepped upon one of their nests. Not an instant seemed to elapse before a simultaneous attack was made on various unprotected parts, up the trowsers from below, and on my neck and breast above. The bites of these furies were like sparks of fire, and there was no retreat. I jumped about for a second or two, then in desperation tore off all my clothing, and rubbed and picked them off seriatim as quickly as possible. Ugh! they would make the most lethargic mortal look alive. Fortunately, no one observed this rencounter, or word might have been taken back to the village that I had become mad. I was once assaulted in a similar way when sound asleep at night in my tent, and it was only by holding my blanket over the fire that I could get rid of them. It is really astonishing how such small bodies can contain so large an amount of ill-nature. They not only bite, but twist themselves round after the mandibles are inserted, to produce laceration and pain, more than would be effected by the single wound. Frequently, while sitting on the ox, as he happened to tread near a band, they would rush up his legs to the rider, and soon let him know that he had disturbed their march. They possess no fear, attacking with equal ferocity the largest as well as the smallest animals. When any person has leaped over the band, numbers of them leave the ranks and rush along the path, seemingly anxious for a fight. They are very useful in ridding the country of dead animal matter, and, when they visit a human habitation, clear it entirely of the destructive white ants and other vermin. They destroy many noxious insects and reptiles. The severity of their attack is greatly increased by their vast numbers, and rats, mice, lizards, and even the 'Python natalensis', when in a state of surfeit from recent feeding, fall victims to their fierce onslaught. These ants never make hills like the white ant. Their nests are but a short distance beneath the soil, which has the soft appearance of the abodes of ants in England. Occasionally they construct galleries over their path to the cells of the white ant, in order to secure themselves from the heat of the sun during their marauding expeditions.

JANUARY 15TH, 1855. We descended in one hour from the heights of Tala Mungongo. I counted the number of paces made on the slope downward, and found them to be sixteen hundred, which may give a perpendicular height of from twelve to fifteen hundred feet. Water boiled at 206 Degrees at Tala Mungongo above, and at 208 Deg. at the bottom of the declivity, the air being at 72 Deg. in the shade in the former case, and 94 Deg. in the latter. The temperature generally throughout the day was from 94 Deg. to 97 Deg. in the coolest shade we could find.

The rivulets which cut up the valley of Cassange were now dry, but the Lui and Luare contained abundance of rather brackish water. The banks are lined with palm, wild date-trees, and many guavas, the fruit of which was now becoming ripe. A tree much like the mango abounds, but it does not yield fruit. In these rivers a kind of edible muscle is plentiful, the shells of which exist in all the alluvial beds of the ancient rivers as far as the Kuruman. The brackish nature of the water probably enables it to exist here. On the open grassy lawns great numbers of a species of lark are seen. They are black, with yellow shoulders. Another black bird, with a long tail ('Centropus Senegalensis'), floats awkwardly, with its tail in a perpendicular position, over the long grass. It always chooses the highest points, and is caught on them with bird-lime, the long black tail-feathers being highly esteemed by the natives for plumes. We saw here also the "Lehututu" ('Tragopan Leadbeaterii'), a large bird strongly resembling a turkey; it is black on the ground, but when it flies the outer half of the wings are white. It kills serpents, striking them dexterously behind the head. It derives its native name from the noise it makes, and it is found as far as Kolobeng. Another species like it is called the Abyssinian hornbill.

Before we reached Cassange we were overtaken by the commandant, Senhor Carvalho, who was returning, with a detachment of fifty men and a field-piece, from an unsuccessful search after some rebels. The rebels had fled, and all he could do was to burn their huts. He kindly invited me to take up my residence with him; but, not wishing to pass by the gentleman (Captain Neves) who had so kindly received me on my first arrival in the Portuguese possessions, I declined. Senhor Rego had been superseded in his command, because the Governor Amaral, who had come into office since my departure from Loanda, had determined that the law which requires the office of commandant to be exclusively occupied by military officers of the line should once more come into operation. I was again most kindly welcomed by my friend, Captain Neves, whom I found laboring under a violent inflammation and abscess of the hand. There is nothing in the situation of this village to indicate unhealthiness, except, perhaps, the rank luxuriance of the vegetation. Nearly all the Portuguese inhabitants suffer from enlargement of the spleen, the effects of frequent intermittents, and have generally a sickly appearance. Thinking that this affection of the hand was simply an effort of nature to get rid of malarious matter from the system, I recommended the use of quinine. He himself applied the leaf of a plant called cathory, famed among the natives as an excellent remedy for ulcers. The cathory leaves, when boiled, exude a gummy juice, which effectually shuts out the external air. Each remedy, of course, claimed the merit of the cure.

Many of the children are cut off by fever. A fine boy of Captain Neves' had, since my passage westward, shared a similar fate. Another child died during the period of my visit. During his sickness, his mother, a woman of color, sent for a diviner in order to ascertain what ought to be done. The diviner, after throwing his dice, worked himself into the state of ecstasy in which they pretend to be in communication with the Barimo. He then gave the oracular response that the child was being killed by the spirit of a Portuguese trader who once lived at Cassange. The case was this: on the death of the trader, the other Portuguese merchants in the village came together, and sold the goods of the departed to each other, each man accounting for the portion received to the creditors of the deceased at Loanda. The natives, looking on, and not understanding the nature of written mercantile transactions, concluded that the merchants of Cassange had simply stolen the dead man's goods, and that now the spirit was killing the child of Captain Neves for the part he had taken in the affair. The diviner, in his response, revealed the impression made on his own mind by the sale, and likewise the native ideas of departed souls. As they give the whites credit for greater stupidity than themselves in all these matters, the mother of the child came, and told the father that he ought to give a slave to the diviner as a fee to make a sacrifice to appease the spirit and save the life of the child. The father quietly sent for a neighbor, and, though the diviner pretended to remain in his state of ecstasy, the brisk application of two sticks to his back suddenly reduced him to his senses and a most undignified flight.

The mother of this child seemed to have no confidence in European wisdom, and, though I desired her to keep the child out of currents of wind, she preferred to follow her own custom, and even got it cupped on the cheeks. The consequence was that the child was soon in a dying state, and the father wishing it to be baptized, I commended its soul to the care and compassion of Him who said, "Of such is the kingdom of heaven." The mother at once rushed away, and commenced that doleful wail which is so affecting, as it indicates sorrow without hope. She continued it without intermission until the child was buried. In the evening her female companions used a small musical instrument, which produced a kind of screeching sound, as an accompaniment of the death wail.

In the construction of this instrument they make use of caoutchouc, which, with a variety of other gums, is found in different parts of this country.

The intercourse which the natives have had with white men does not seem to have much ameliorated their condition. A great number of persons are reported to lose their lives annually in different districts of Angola by the cruel superstitions to which they are addicted, and the Portuguese authorities either know nothing of them, or are unable to prevent their occurrence. The natives are bound to secrecy by those who administer the ordeal, which generally causes the death of the victim. A person, when accused of witchcraft, will often travel from distant districts in order to assert her innocency and brave the test. They come to a river on the Cassange called Dua, drink the infusion of a poisonous tree, and perish unknown.

A woman was accused by a brother-in-law of being the cause of his sickness while we were at Cassange. She offered to take the ordeal, as she had the idea that it would but prove her conscious innocence. Captain Neves refused his consent to her going, and thus saved her life, which would have been sacrificed, for the poison is very virulent. When a strong stomach rejects it, the accuser reiterates his charge; the dose is repeated, and the person dies. Hundreds perish thus every year in the valley of Cassange.

The same superstitious ideas being prevalent through the whole of the country north of the Zambesi, seems to indicate that the people must originally have been one. All believe that the souls of the departed still mingle among the living, and partake in some way of the food they consume. In sickness, sacrifices of fowls and goats are made to appease the spirits. It is imagined that they wish to take the living away from earth and all its enjoyments. When one man has killed another, a sacrifice is made, as if to lay the spirit of the victim. A sect is reported to exist who kill men in order to take their hearts and offer them to the Barimo.

The chieftainship is elective from certain families. Among the Bangalas of the Cassange valley the chief is chosen from three families in rotation. A chief's brother inherits in preference to his son. The sons of a sister belong to her brother; and he often sells his nephews to pay his debts. By this and other unnatural customs, more than by war, is the slave-market supplied.

The prejudices in favor of these practices are very deeply rooted in the native mind. Even at Loanda they retire out of the city in order to perform their heathenish rites without the cognizance of the authorities. Their religion, if such it may be called, is one of dread. Numbers of charms are employed to avert the evils with which they feel themselves to be encompassed. Occasionally you meet a man, more cautious or more timid than the rest, with twenty or thirty charms round his neck. He seems to act upon the principle of Proclus, in his prayer to all the gods and goddesses: among so many he surely must have the right one. The disrespect which Europeans pay to the objects of their fear is to their minds only an evidence of great folly.

While here, I reproduced the last of my lost papers and maps; and as there is a post twice a month from Loanda, I had the happiness to receive a packet of the "Times", and, among other news, an account of the Russian war up to the terrible charge of the light cavalry. The intense anxiety I felt to hear more may be imagined by every true patriot; but I was forced to brood on in silent thought, and utter my poor prayers for friends who perchance were now no more, until I reached the other side of the continent.

A considerable trade is carried on by the Cassange merchants with all the surrounding territory by means of native traders, whom they term "Pombeiros". Two of these, called in the history of Angola "the trading blacks" (os feirantes pretos), Pedro Joao Baptista and Antonio Jose, having been sent by the first Portuguese trader that lived at Cassange, actually returned from some of the Portuguese possessions in the East with letters from the governor of Mozambique in the year 1815, proving, as is remarked, "the possibility of so important a communication between Mozambique and Loanda." This is the only instance of native Portuguese subjects crossing the continent. No European ever accomplished it, though this fact has lately been quoted as if the men had been "PORTUGUESE".

Captain Neves was now actively engaged in preparing a present, worth about fifty pounds, to be sent by Pombeiros to Matiamvo. It consisted of great quantities of cotton cloth, a large carpet, an arm-chair with a canopy and curtains of crimson calico, an iron bedstead, mosquito curtains, beads, etc., and a number of pictures rudely painted in oil by an embryo black painter at Cassange.

Matiamvo, like most of the natives in the interior of the country, has a strong desire to possess a cannon, and had sent ten large tusks to purchase one; but, being government property, it could not be sold: he was now furnished with a blunderbuss, mounted as a cannon, which would probably please him as well.

Senhor Graca and some other Portuguese have visited this chief at different times; but no European resides beyond the Quango; indeed, it is contrary to the policy of the government of Angola to allow their subjects to penetrate further into the interior. The present would have been a good opportunity for me to have visited that chief, and I felt strongly inclined to do so, as he had expressed dissatisfaction respecting my treatment by the Chiboque, and even threatened to punish them. As it would be improper to force my men to go thither, I resolved to wait and see whether the proposition might not emanate from themselves. When I can get the natives to agree in the propriety of any step, they go to the end of the affair without a murmur. I speak to them and treat them as rational beings, and generally get on well with them in consequence.

I have already remarked on the unhealthiness of Cassange; and Captain Neves, who possesses an observing turn of mind, had noticed that always when the west wind blows much fever immediately follows. As long as easterly winds prevail, all enjoy good health; but in January, February, March, and April, the winds are variable, and sickness is general. The unhealthiness of the westerly winds probably results from malaria, appearing to be heavier than common air, and sweeping down into the valley of Cassange from the western plateau, somewhat in the same way as the carbonic acid gas from bean-fields is supposed by colliers to do into coal-pits. In the west of Scotland strong objections are made by that body of men to farmers planting beans in their vicinity, from the belief that they render the mines unhealthy. The gravitation of the malaria from the more elevated land of Tala Mungongo toward Cassange is the only way the unhealthiness of this spot on the prevalence of the westerly winds can be accounted for. The banks of the Quango, though much more marshy, and covered with ranker vegetation, are comparatively healthy; but thither the westerly wind does not seem to convey the noxious agent.

FEB. 20TH. On the day of starting from Cassange, the westerly wind blew strongly, and on the day following we were brought to a stand by several of our party being laid up with fever. This complaint is the only serious drawback Angola possesses. It is in every other respect an agreeable land, and admirably adapted for yielding a rich abundance of tropical produce for the rest of the world. Indeed, I have no hesitation in asserting that, had it been in the possession of England, it would now have been yielding as much or more of the raw material for her manufactures as an equal extent of territory in the cotton-growing states of America. A railway from Loanda to this valley would secure the trade of most of the interior of South Central Africa.*

* *The following statistics may be of interest to mercantile*

men. *They show that since the repression of the slave-trade in Angola the value of the exports in lawful commerce has steadily augmented. We have no returns since 1850, but the prosperity of legitimate trade has suffered no check. The duties are noted in Portuguese money, "milreis", each of which is about three shillings in value.*

Return of the Quantities and Value of the Staple Articles, the Produce of the Province of ANGOLA, exported from ST. PAUL DE LOANDA between July 1, 1848, and June 30, 1849, specifying the Quantities and Value of those exported in Portuguese Ships and in Ships of other Nations.

Articles	In Portuguese Ships.		In Ships of other Nations.	
	Amount.	Value.	Amount.	Value.
		L. s. d.		L. s. d.
Ivory... Cwt.	1454	35,350 0 0	515	12,875 0 0
Palm oil. "	1440	2,160 0 0	6671 1 qr.	10,036 17 6
Coffee.. "	152	304 0 0	684	1,368 0 0
Hides... No.	1837	633 17 6	849	318 17 6
Gum.... Cwt.	147	205 16 0	4763	6,668 4 0
Beeswax.. "	1109	6,654 0 0	544	3,264 0 0
Orchella. Tons	630	23,940 0 0	....	....
		69,247 13 6		34,530 19 0

TOTAL Quantity and Value of Exports from LOANDA.

		L. s. d.
Ivory... Cwt.	1969	48,225 0 0
Palm oil.. "	8111 1 qr.	12,196 17 6
Coffee... "	836	1,672 0 0

Hides ... No.	2686	....	952 15 0
Gum .... Cwt.	4910	....	6,874 0 0
Beeswax.. "	1653	....	9,918 0 0
Orchella.. Tons	630	....	23,940 0 0

L. 103,778 12 6

ABSTRACT VIEW of the Net Revenue of the Customs at St. Paul de Loanda in quinquennial periods from 1818-19 to 1843-44, both included; and thence in each year to 1848-49.

Years.	Duties on Importation.	Duties on Exportation.	Duties on Re-exportation.	Duties on Slaves.	Tonnage Dues, Store Rents, and other incidental Receipts.
	Mil. reis.	Mil. reis.	Mil. reis.	Mil. reis.	Mil. reis.
1818-19	573 876	...	....	137,320 800	148,608 661
1823-24	3,490 752	460 420	....	120,843 000	133,446 892
1828-29	4,700 684	800 280	....	125,330 000	139,981 364
1833-34	7,490 000	1,590 000	....	139,280 000	158,978 640
1838 39	25,800 590	2,720 000	....	135,470 320	173,710 910
1843-44	53,240 000	4,320 000	....	72,195 230	138,255 230
1844-45	99,380 264	6,995 095	....	17,676 000	134,941 359
1845-46	150,233 789	9,610 735	....	5,116 500	181,423 550
1846-47	122,501 186	8,605 821	....	549 000	114,599 235
1847-48	119,246 826	9,718 676	4097 868	1,231 200	146,321 476
1848-49	131,105 453	9,969 960	1164 309	1,183 500	157,152 400
	717,763 420*	54,790 987		756,195 550	
	= L.102,680	= L.7827		= L.108,028	

* This figure was originally miscalculated as 718,763 420, which probably affected its conversion into Pounds. — A. L., 1997.

Years.	Net Revenue of Customs.	Revenue from other Sources.	Total Net Revenue.	Total Amount of Charges.
	L. s. d.	L. s. d.	L. s. d.	L. s. d.
1844-45	26,988 5 5	9,701 10 8	36,689 16 1	53,542 5 4
1845-46	36,284 14 2	24,580 4 10	60,864 19 0	56,695 9 7
1846-47	28,919 16 11	23,327 9 11	52,247 6 10	52,180 9 7
1847-48	29,264 5 10	24,490 11 8	53,754 17 6	53,440 8 8
1848-49	31,430 9 7	18,868 3 10	51,298 13 5	50,686 3 3

The above account exhibits the total revenue and charges of the government of St. Paul de Loanda in each year, from 1844-45 to 1848-49, both included. The above three tables are copied from the appendix to a dispatch sent by Mr. Gabriel to Viscount Palmerston, dated the 5th of August, 1850, and, among other facts of interest, show a very satisfactory diminution in the duties upon slaves.

The returns from 1818 to 1844 have been obtained from different sources as the average revenue; those from 1844 to 1849 are from the Custom-house records.

As soon as we could move toward the Quango we did so, meeting in our course several trading-parties, both native and Portuguese. We met two of the latter carrying a tusk weighing 126 lbs. The owner afterward informed us that its fellow on the left side of the same elephant was 130 lbs. It was 8 feet 6-1/2 inches long, and 21 inches in circumference at the part on which the lip of the animal rests. The elephant was rather a small one, as is common in this hot central region. Some idea may be formed of the strength of his neck when it is recollected that he bore a weight of 256 lbs. The ivory which comes from the east and northeast of Cassange is very much larger than any to be found further south. Captain Neves had one weighing 120 lbs., and this weight is by no means uncommon. They have been found weighing even 158 lbs.

Before reaching the Quango we were again brought to a stand by fever in two of my companions, close to the residence of a Portuguese who rejoiced in the name of William Tell, and who lived here in spite of the prohibition of the government. We were using the water of a pond, and this gentleman, having come to invite me to dinner, drank a little of it, and caught fever in consequence. If malarious matter existed in water, it would have been a wonder had we escaped; for, traveling in the sun, with the thermometer from 96 Degrees to 98 Degrees in the shade, the evaporation from our bodies causing much thirst, we generally partook of every water we came to. We had probably thus more disease than others might suffer who had better shelter.

Mr. Tell remarked that his garden was rather barren, being still, as he said, wild; but when more worked it would become better, though no manure be applied. My men were busy collecting a better breed of fowls and pigeons than those in their own country. Mr. Tell presented them with some large specimens from Rio Janeiro. Of these they were wonderfully proud, and bore the cock in triumph through the country of the Balonda, as evidence of having been to the sea. But when at the village of Shinte, a hyaena came into our midst when we were all sound asleep, and picked out the giant in his basket from eighty-four others, and he was lost, to the great grief of my men. The anxiety these people have always shown to improve the breed of their domestic animals is, I think, a favorable point in their character. On looking at the common breeds in the possession of the Portuguese, which are merely native cattle, and seeing them slaughter both heifer-calves and cows, which they themselves never do, and likewise making no use of the milk, they concluded that the Portuguese must be an inferior race of white men. They never ceased remarking on the fine ground for gardens over which we were passing; and when I happened to mention that most of the flour which the Portuguese consumed came from another country, they exclaimed, "Are they ignorant of tillage?" "They know nothing but buying and selling: they are not men." I hope it may reach the ears of my Angolese friends, and that they may be stirred up to develop the resources of their fine country.

On coming back to Cypriano's village on the 28th, we found that his step-father had died after we had passed, and, according to the custom of the country, he had spent more than his patrimony in funeral orgies. He acted with his wonted kindness, though, unfortunately, drinking has got him so deeply in debt that he now keeps out of the way of his creditors. He informed us that the source of the Quango is eight days, or one hundred miles, to the south of this, and in a range called Mosamba, in the country of the Basongo. We can see from this a sort of break in the high land which stretches away round to Tala Mongongo, through which the river comes.

A death had occurred in a village about a mile off, and the people were busy beating drums and firing guns. The funeral rites are half festive, half mourning, partaking somewhat of the character of an Irish wake. There is nothing more heart-rending than their death wails. When the natives turn their eyes to the future world, they have a view cheerless enough of their own utter helplessness and hopelessness. They fancy themselves completely in the power of the disembodied spirits, and look upon the prospect of following them as the greatest of misfortunes. Hence they are constantly deprecating the wrath of departed souls, believing that, if they are appeased, there is no other cause of death but witchcraft, which may be averted by charms. The whole of the colored population of Angola are sunk in these gross superstitions, but have the opinion, notwithstanding, that they are wiser in these matters than their white neighbors. Each tribe has a consciousness of following its own best interests in the best way. They are by no means destitute of that self-esteem which is so common in other nations; yet they fear all manner of phantoms, and have half-developed ideas and traditions of something or other, they know not what. The pleasures of animal life are ever present to their minds as the supreme good; and, but for the innumerable invisibilities, they might enjoy their luxurious climate as much as it is possible for man to do. I have often thought, in traveling through their land, that it presents pictures of beauty which angels might enjoy. How often have I beheld, in still mornings, scenes the very essence of beauty, and all bathed in a quiet air of delicious warmth! yet the occasional soft motion imparted a pleasing sensation of coolness as of a fan. Green grassy meadows, the cattle feeding, the goats browsing, the kids skipping, the groups of herd-boys with miniature bows, arrows, and spears; the women wending their way to the river with watering-pots poised jauntily on their heads; men sewing under the shady banians; and old gray-headed fathers sitting on the ground, with staff in hand, listening to the morning gossip, while others carry trees or branches to repair their hedges; and all this, flooded with the bright African sunshine, and the birds singing among the branches before the heat of the day has become intense, form pictures which can never be forgotten.

We were informed that a chief named Gando, living on the other side of the river, having been accused of witchcraft, was killed by the ordeal, and his body thrown into the Quango.

The ferrymen demanded thirty yards of calico, but received six thankfully. The canoes were wretched, carrying only two persons at a time; but my men being well acquainted with the water, we all got over in about two hours and a half. They excited the admiration of the inhabitants by the manner in which they managed the cattle and donkeys in crossing. The most stubborn of beasts found himself powerless in their hands. Five or six, seizing hold on one, bundled him at once into the stream, and, in this predicament, he always thought it best policy to give in and swim. The men sometimes swam along with the cattle, and forced them to go on by dashing water at their heads. The difference between my men and those of the native traders who accompanied us was never more apparent than now; for, while my men felt an interest in every thing we possessed in common, theirs were rather glad when the oxen refused to cross, for, being obliged to slaughter them on such occasions, the loss to their masters was a welcome feast to themselves.

On the eastern side of the Quango we passed on, without visiting our friend of the conical head-dress, to the residence of some Ambakistas who had crossed the river in order to secure the first chances of trade in wax. I have before remarked on the knowledge of reading and writing that these Ambakistas possess; they are famed for their love of all sorts of learning within their reach, a knowledge of the history of Portugal, Portuguese law, etc., etc. They are remarkably keen in trade, and are sometimes called the Jews of Angola. They are employed as clerks and writers, their feminine delicacy of constitution enabling them to write a fine lady's hand, a kind of writing much esteemed among the Portuguese. They are not physically equal to the European Portuguese, but possess considerable ability; and it is said that half-castes, in the course of a few generations, return to the black color of the maternal ancestor. The black population of Angola has become much deteriorated. They are not so strongly formed as the independent tribes. A large quantity of aguardiente, an inferior kind of spirit, is imported into the country, which is most injurious in its effects. We saw many parties carrying casks of this baneful liquor to the independent chiefs beyond; and were informed that it is difficult for any trader to convey it far, carriers being in the habit of helping themselves by means of a straw, and then injecting an equal amount of water when near the point of delivery. To prevent this, it is common to see large demijohns with padlocks on the corks. These are frequently stolen. In fact, the carriers are much addicted to both lying and thieving, as might be expected from the lowest class of a people on whom the debasing slave system has acted for two centuries.

The Bashinje, in whose country we now are, seem to possess more of the low negro character and physiognomy than either the Balonda or Basongo; their color is generally dirty black, foreheads low and compressed, noses flat and much expanded laterally, though this is partly owing to the alae spreading over the cheeks, by the custom of inserting bits of sticks or reeds in the septum; their teeth are deformed by being filed to points; their lips are large. They make a nearer approach to a general negro appearance than any tribes I met; but I did not notice this on my way down. They cultivate pretty largely, and rely upon their agricultural products for their supplies of salt, flesh, tobacco, etc., from Bangalas. Their clothing consists of pieces of skin, hung loosely from the girdle in front and behind. They plait their hair fantastically. We saw some women coming with their hair woven into the form of a European hat, and it was only by a closer inspection that its nature was detected. Others had it arranged in tufts, with a threefold cord along the ridge of each tuft; while others, again, follow the ancient Egyptian fashion, having the whole mass of wool plaited into cords, all hanging down as far as the shoulders. This mode, with the somewhat Egyptian cast of countenance in other parts of Londa, reminded me strongly of the paintings of that nation in the British Museum.

We had now rain every day, and the sky seldom presented that cloudless aspect and clear blue so common in the dry lands of the south. The heavens are often overcast by large white motionless masses, which stand for hours in the same position, and the intervening spaces are filled with a milk-and-water-looking haze. Notwithstanding these unfavorable circumstances, I obtained good observations for the longitude of this important point on both sides of the Quango, and found the river running in 9d 50′ S. lat., 18d 33′ E. long.

On proceeding to our former station near Sansawe's village, he ran to meet us with wonderful urbanity, asking if we had seen Moene Put, king of the white men (or Portuguese); and added, on parting, that he would come to receive his dues in the evening. I replied that, as he had treated us so scurvily, even forbidding his people to sell us any food, if he did not bring us a fowl and some eggs as part of his duty as a chief, he should receive no present from me. When he came, it was in the usual Londa way of showing the exalted position he occupies, mounted on the shoulders of his spokesman, as schoolboys sometimes do in England, and as was represented to have been the case in the southern islands when Captain Cook visited them. My companions, amused at his idea of dignity, greeted him with a hearty laugh. He visited the native traders first, and then came to me with two cocks as a present. I spoke to him about the impolicy of treatment we had received at his hands, and quoted the example of the Bangalas, who had been conquered by the Portuguese, for their extortionate demands of payment for firewood, grass, water, etc., and concluded by denying his right to any payment for simply passing through uncultivated land. To all this he agreed; and then I gave him, as a token of friendship, a pannikin of coarse powder, two iron spoons, and two yards of coarse printed calico. He looked rather saucily at these articles, for he had just received a barrel containing 18 lbs. of powder, 24 yards of calico, and two bottles of brandy, from Senhor Pascoal the Pombeiro. Other presents were added the next day, but we gave nothing more; and the Pombeiros informed me that it was necessary to give largely, because they are accompanied by slaves and carriers who are no great friends to their masters; and if they did not secure the friendship of these petty chiefs, many slaves and their loads might be stolen while passing through the forests. It is thus a sort of black-mail that these insignificant chiefs levy; and the native traders, in paying, do so simply as a bribe to keep them honest. This chief was a man of no power, but in our former ignorance of this he plagued us a whole day in passing.

Finding the progress of Senhor Pascoal and the other Pombeiros excessively slow, I resolved to forego his company to Cabango after I had delivered to him some letters to be sent back to Cassange. I went forward with the intention of finishing my writing, and leaving a packet for him at some village. We ascended the eastern acclivity that bounds the Cassange valley, which has rather a gradual ascent up from the Quango, and we found that the last ascent, though apparently not quite so high as that at Tala Mungongo, is actually much higher. The top is about 5000 feet above the level of the sea, and the bottom 3500 feet; water boiling on the heights at 202 Deg., the thermometer in the air showing 96 Deg.; and at the bottom at 205 Deg., the air being 75 Deg. We had now gained the summit of the western subtending ridge, and began to descend toward the centre of the country, hoping soon to get out of the Chiboque territory, which, when we ascended from the Cassange valley, we had entered; but, on the 19th of April, the intermittent, which had begun on the 16th of March, was changed into an extremely severe attack of rheumatic fever. This was brought on by being obliged to sleep on an extensive plain covered with water. The rain poured down incessantly, but we formed our beds by dragging up the earth into oblong mounds, somewhat like graves in a country church-yard, and then placing grass upon them. The rain continuing to deluge us, we were unable to leave for two days, but as soon as it became fair we continued our march. The heavy dew upon the high grass was so cold as to cause shivering, and I was forced to lie by for eight days, tossing and groaning with violent pain in the head. This was the most severe attack I had endured. It made me quite unfit to move, or even know what was passing outside my little tent. Senhor Pascoal, who had been detained by the severe rain at a better spot, at last came up, and, knowing that leeches abounded in the rivulets, procured a number, and applied some dozens to the nape of the neck and the loins. This partially relieved the pain. He was then obliged to move forward, in order to purchase food for his large party. After many days I began to recover, and wished to move on, but my men objected to the attempt on account of my weakness. When Senhor Pascoal had been some time at the village in front, as he had received instructions from his employer, Captain Neves, to aid me as much as possible, and being himself a kindly-disposed person, he sent back two messengers to invite me to come on, if practicable.

It happened that the head man of the village where I had lain twenty-two days, while bargaining and quarreling in my camp for a piece of meat, had been struck on the mouth by one of my men. My principal men paid five pieces of cloth and a gun as an atonement; but the more they yielded, the more exorbitant he became, and he sent word to all the surrounding villages to aid him in avenging the affront of a blow on the beard. As their courage usually rises with success, I resolved to yield no more, and departed. In passing through a forest in the country beyond, we were startled by a body of men rushing after us. They began by knocking down the burdens of the hindermost of my men, and several shots were fired, each party spreading out on both sides of the path. I fortunately had a six-barreled revolver, which my friend Captain Henry Need, of her majesty's brig "Linnet", had considerately sent to Golungo Alto after my departure from Loanda. Taking this in my hand, and forgetting fever, I staggered quickly along the path with two or three of my men, and fortunately encountered the chief. The sight of the six barrels gaping into his stomach, with my own ghastly visage looking daggers at his face, seemed to produce an instant revolution in his martial feelings, for he cried out, "Oh! I have only come to speak to you, and wish peace only." Mashauana had hold of him by the hand, and found him shaking. We examined his gun, and found that it had been discharged. Both parties crowded up to their chiefs. One of the opposite party coming too near, one of mine drove him back with a battle-axe. The enemy protested their amicable intentions, and my men asserted the fact of having the goods knocked down as evidence of the contrary. Without waiting long, I requested all to sit down, and Pitsane, placing his hand upon the revolver, somewhat allayed their fears. I then said to the chief, "If you have come with peaceable intentions, we have no other; go away home to your village." He replied, "I am afraid lest you shoot me in the back." I rejoined, "If I wanted to kill you, I could shoot you in the face as well." Mosantu called out to me, "That's only a Makalaka trick; don't give him your back." But I said, "Tell him to observe that I am not afraid of him;" and, turning, mounted my ox. There was not much danger in the fire that was opened at first, there being so many trees. The enemy probably expected that the sudden attack would make us forsake our goods, and allow them to plunder with ease. The villagers were no doubt pleased with being allowed to retire unscathed, and we were also glad to get away without having shed a drop of blood, or having compromised ourselves for any future visit. My men were delighted with their own bravery, and made the woods ring with telling each other how "brilliant their conduct before the enemy" would have been, had hostilities not been brought to a sudden close.

I do not mention this little skirmish as a very frightful affair. The negro character in these parts, and in Angola, is essentially cowardly, except when influenced by success. A partial triumph over any body of men would induce the whole country to rise in arms, and this is the chief danger to be feared. These petty chiefs have individually but little power, and with my men, now armed with guns, I could have easily beaten them off singly; but, being of the same family, they would readily unite in vast numbers if incited by prospects of successful plunder. They are by no means equal to the Cape Caffres in any respect whatever.

In the evening we came to Moena Kikanje, and found him a sensible man. He is the last of the Chiboque chiefs in this direction, and is in alliance with Matiamvo, whose territory commences a short distance beyond. His village is placed on the east bank of the Quilo, which is here twenty yards wide, and breast deep.

The country was generally covered with forest, and we slept every night at some village. I was so weak, and had become so deaf from the effects of the fever, that I was glad to avail myself of the company of Senhor Pascoal and the other native traders. Our rate of traveling was only two geographical miles per hour, and the average number of hours three and a half per day, or seven miles. Two thirds of the month was spent in stoppages, there being only ten traveling days in each month. The stoppages were caused by sickness, and the necessity of remaining in different parts to purchase food; and also because, when one carrier was sick, the rest refused to carry his load.

One of the Pombeiros had eight good-looking women in a chain whom he was taking to the country of Matiamvo to sell for ivory. They always looked ashamed when I happened to come near them, and must have felt keenly their forlorn and degraded position. I believe they were captives taken from the rebel Cassanges. The way in which slaves are spoken of in Angola and eastern Africa must sound strangely even to the owners when they first come from Europe. In Angola the common appellation is "o diabo", or "brutu"; and it is quite usual to hear gentlemen call out, "O diabo! bring fire." In eastern Africa, on the contrary, they apply the term "bicho" (an animal), and you hear the phrase, "Call the ANIMAL to do this or that." In fact, slave-owners come to regard their slaves as not human, and will curse them as the "race of a dog". Most of the carriers of my traveling companions were hired Basongo, and required constant vigilance to prevent them stealing the goods they carried. Salt, which is one of the chief articles conveyed into the country, became considerably lighter as we went along, but the carriers shielded themselves by saying that it had been melted by the rain. Their burdens were taken from them every evening, and placed in security under the guardianship of Senhor Pascoal's own slaves. It was pitiable to observe the worrying life he led. There was the greatest contrast possible between the conduct of his people and that of my faithful Makololo.

We crossed the Loange, a deep but narrow stream, by a bridge. It becomes much larger, and contains hippopotami, lower down. It is the boundary of Londa on the west. We slept also on the banks of the Pezo, now flooded, and could not but admire their capabilities for easy irrigation. On reaching the River Chikapa (lat. 10d 10′ S., long. 19d 42′ E.), the 25th of March, we found it fifty or sixty yards wide, and flowing E.N.E. into the Kasai. The adjacent country is of the same level nature as that part of Londa formerly described; but, having come farther to the eastward than our previous course, we found that all the rivers had worn for themselves much deeper valleys than at the points we had formerly crossed them.

Surrounded on all sides by large gloomy forests, the people of these parts have a much more indistinct idea of the geography of their country than those who live in hilly regions. It was only after long and patient inquiry that I became fully persuaded that the Quilo runs into the Chikapa. As we now crossed them both considerably farther down, and were greatly to the eastward of our first route, there can be no doubt that these rivers take the same course as the others, into the Kasai, and that I had been led into a mistake in saying that any of them flowed to the westward. Indeed, it was only at this time that I began to perceive that all the western feeders of the Kasai, except the Quango, flow first from the western side toward the centre of the country, then gradually turn, with the Kasai itself, to the north; and, after the confluence of the Kasai with the Quango, an immense body of water, collected from all these branches, finds its way out of the country by means of the River Congo or Zaire on the west coast.

The people living along the path we are now following were quite accustomed to the visits of native traders, and did not feel in any way bound to make presents of food except for the purpose of cheating: thus, a man gave me a fowl and some meal, and, after a short time, returned. I offered him a handsome present of beads; but these he declined, and demanded a cloth instead, which was far more than the value of his gift. They did the same with my men, until we had to refuse presents altogether. Others made high demands because I slept in a "house of cloth", and must be rich. They seemed to think that they had a perfect right to payment for simply passing through the country.

Beyond the Chikapa we crossed the Kamaue, a small deep stream proceeding from the S.S.W., and flowing into the Chikapa.

On the 30th of April we reached the Loajima, where we had to form a bridge to effect our passage. This was not so difficult an operation as some might imagine; for a tree was growing in a horizontal position across part of the stream, and, there being no want of the tough climbing plants which admit of being knitted like ropes, Senhor P. soon constructed a bridge. The Loajima was here about twenty-five yards wide, but very much deeper than where I had crossed before on the shoulders of Mashauana. The last rain of this season had fallen on the 28th, and had suddenly been followed by a great decrease of the temperature. The people in these parts seemed more slender in form, and their color a lighter olive, than any we had hitherto met. The mode of dressing the great masses of woolly hair which lay upon their shoulders, together with their general features, again reminded me of the ancient Egyptians. Several were seen with the upward inclination of the outer angles of the eye, but this was not general. A few of the ladies adopt a curious custom of attaching the hair to a hoop which encircles the head, giving it somewhat the appearance of the glory round the head of the Virgin (wood-cut No. 1*). Some have a small hoop behind that represented in the wood-cut. Others wear an ornament of woven hair and hide adorned with beads. The hair of the tails of buffaloes, which are to be found farther east, is sometimes added. This is represented in No. 2. While others, as in No. 3, weave their own hair on pieces of hide into the form of buffalo horns; or, as in No. 4, make a single horn in front. The features given are frequently met with, but they are by no means universal. Many tattoo their bodies by inserting some black substance beneath the skin, which leaves an elevated cicatrix about half an inch long: these are made in the form of stars, and other figures of no particular beauty.

> * Unfortunately these wood-cuts can not be represented in this ASCII text.

> No. 1 appears like a wheel with spokes of hair connecting it to the head.

> No. 2 appears somewhat like a tiara sloped forward, as the bow of a ship.

> No. 3 appears like gently curving horns. There is a part in the middle, and the hair, on leather frames, curls outward and upward at the temples.

No. 4 is likewise, but the single horn curves outward and upward from the forehead—it is labelled "A Young Man's Fashion". Except for No. 1, all are represented as having the rest of their hair hanging in braids around the sides and back. All of the faces, as Livingstone asserts, appear much like paintings of ancient Egyptians, and could easily be European except for the shading and the slanted eyes. They are all handsome.—A. L., 1997.

Chapter 23

Make a Detour southward—Peculiarities of the Inhabitants—Scarcity of Animals—Forests—Geological Structure of the Country—Abundance and Cheapness of Food near the Chihombo—A Slave lost—The Makololo Opinion of Slaveholders—Funeral Obsequies in Cabango—Send a Sketch of the Country to Mr. Gabriel—Native Information respecting the Kasai and Quango—The Trade with Luba—Drainage of Londa—Report of Matiamvo's Country and Government—Senhor Faria's Present to a Chief—The Balonda Mode of spending Time—Faithless Guide—Makololo lament the Ignorance of the Balonda—Eagerness of the Villagers for Trade—Civility of a Female Chief—The Chief Bango and his People—Refuse to eat Beef—Ambition of Africans to have a Village—Winters in the Interior—Spring at Kolobeng—White Ants: "Never could desire to eat any thing better"—Young Herbage and Animals—Valley of the Loembwe— The white Man a Hobgoblin—Specimen of Quarreling—Eager Desire for Calico—Want of Clothing at Kawawa's—Funeral Observances—Agreeable Intercourse with Kawawa—His impudent Demand—Unpleasant Parting—Kawawa tries to prevent our crossing the River Kasai—Stratagem.

We made a little detour to the southward in order to get provisions in a cheaper market. This led us along the rivulet called Tamba, where we found the people, who had not been visited so frequently by the slave-traders as the rest, rather timid and very civil. It was agreeable to get again among the uncontaminated, and to see the natives look at us without that air of superciliousness which is so unpleasant and common in the beaten track. The same olive color prevailed. They file their teeth to a point, which makes the smile of the women frightful, as it reminds one of the grin of an alligator. The inhabitants throughout this country exhibit as great a variety of taste as appears on the surface of society among ourselves. Many of the men are dandies; their shoulders are always wet with the oil dropping from their lubricated hair, and every thing about them is ornamented in one way or another. Some thrum a musical instrument the livelong day, and, when they wake at night, proceed at once to their musical performance. Many of these musicians are too poor to have iron keys to their instrument, but make them of bamboo, and persevere, though no one hears the music but themselves. Others try to appear warlike by never going out of their huts except with a load of bows and arrows, or a gun ornamented with a strip of hide for every animal they have shot; and others never go any where without a canary in a cage. Ladies may be seen carefully tending little lap-dogs, which are intended to be eaten. Their villages are generally in forests, and composed of groups of irregularly-planted brown huts, with banana and cotton trees, and tobacco growing around. There is also at every hut a high stage erected for drying manioc roots and meal, and elevated cages to hold domestic fowls. Round baskets are laid on the thatch of the huts for the hens to lay in, and on the arrival of strangers, men, women, and children ply their calling as hucksters with a great deal of noisy haggling; all their transactions are conducted with civil banter and good temper.

My men, having the meat of the oxen which we slaughtered from time to time for sale, were entreated to exchange it for meal; no matter how small the pieces offered were, it gave them pleasure to deal.

The landscape around is green, with a tint of yellow, the grass long, the paths about a foot wide, and generally worn deeply in the middle. The tall overhanging grass, when brushed against by the feet and legs, disturbed the lizards and mice, and occasionally a serpent, causing a rustling among the herbage. There are not many birds; every animal is entrapped and eaten. Gins are seen on both sides of the path every ten or fifteen yards, for miles together. The time and labor required to dig up moles and mice from their burrows would, if applied to cultivation, afford food for any amount of fowls or swine, but the latter are seldom met with.

We passed on through forests abounding in climbing-plants, many of which are so extremely tough that a man is required to go in front with a hatchet; and when the burdens of the carriers are caught, they are obliged to cut the climbers with their teeth, for no amount of tugging will make them break. The paths in all these forests are so zigzag that a person may imagine he has traveled a distance of thirty miles, which, when reckoned as the crow flies, may not be fifteen.

We reached the River Moamba (lat. 9d 38' S., long. 20d 13' 34" E.) on the 7th May. This is a stream of thirty yards wide, and, like the Quilo, Loange, Chikapa, and Loajima, contains both alligators and hippopotami. We crossed it by means of canoes. Here, as on the slopes down to the Quilo and Chikapa, we had an opportunity of viewing the geological structure of the country—a capping of ferruginous conglomerate, which in many parts looks as if it had been melted, for the rounded nodules resemble masses of slag, and they have a smooth scale on the surface; but in all probability it is an aqueous deposit, for it contains water-worn pebbles of all sorts, and generally small. Below this mass lies a pale red hardened sandstone, and beneath that a trap-like whinstone. Lowest of all lies a coarse-grained sandstone containing a few pebbles, and, in connection with it, a white calcareous rock is occasionally met with, and so are banks of loose round quartz pebbles. The slopes are longer from the level country above the further we go eastward, and every where we meet with circumscribed bogs on them, surrounded by clumps of straight, lofty evergreen trees, which look extremely graceful on a ground of yellowish grass. Several of these bogs pour forth a solution of iron, which exhibits on its surface the prismatic colors. The level plateaus between the rivers, both east and west of the Moamba, across which we traveled, were less woody than the river glens. The trees on them are scraggy and wide apart. There are also large open grass-covered spaces, with scarcely even a bush. On these rather dreary intervals between the rivers it was impossible not to be painfully struck with the absence of all animal life. Not a bird was to be seen, except occasionally a tomtit, some of the 'Sylviadae' and 'Drymoica', also a black bird ('Dicrurus Ludwigii', Smith) common throughout the country. We were gladdened by the voice of birds only near the rivers, and there they are neither numerous nor varied. The Senegal longclaw, however, maintains its place, and is the largest bird seen. We saw a butcher-bird in a trap as we passed. There are remarkably few small animals, they having been hunted almost to extermination, and few insects except ants, which abound in considerable number and variety. There are scarcely any common flies to be seen, nor are we ever troubled by mosquitoes.

The air is still, hot, and oppressive; the intensely bright sunlight glances peacefully on the evergreen forest leaves, and all feel glad when the path comes into the shade. The want of life in the scenery made me long to tread again the banks of the Zambesi, and see the graceful antelopes feeding beside the dark buffaloes and sleek elands. Here hippopotami are known to exist only by their footprints on the banks. Not one is ever seen to blow or put his head up at all; they have learned to breathe in silence and keep out of sight. We never heard one uttering the snorting sound so common on the Zambesi.

We crossed two small streams, the Kanesi and Fombeji, before reaching Cabango, a village situated on the banks of the Chihombo. The country was becoming more densely peopled as we proceeded, but it bears no population compared to what it might easily sustain. Provisions were to be had in great abundance; a fowl and basket of meal weighing 20 lbs. were sold for a yard and a half of very inferior cotton cloth, worth not more than threepence. An idea of the cheapness of food may be formed from the fact that Captain Neves purchased 380 lbs. of tobacco from the Bangalas for about two pounds sterling. This, when carried into central Londa, might purchase seven thousand five hundred fowls, or feed with meal and fowls seven thousand persons for one day, giving each a fowl and 5 lbs. of meal. When food is purchased here with either salt or coarse calico, four persons can be well fed with animal and vegetable food at the rate of one penny a day. The chief vegetable food is the manioc and lotsa meal. These contain a very large proportion of starch, and, when eaten alone for any length of time produce most distressing heartburn. As we ourselves experienced in coming north, they also cause a weakness of vision, which occurs in the case of animals fed on pure gluten or amylaceous matter only. I now discovered that when these starchy substances are eaten along with a proportion of ground-nuts, which contain a considerable quantity of oil, no injurious effects follow.

While on the way to Cabango we saw fresh tracks of elands, the first we had observed in this country. A poor little slave girl, being ill, turned aside in the path, and, though we waited all the next day making search for her, she was lost. She was tall and slender for her age, as if of too quick growth, and probably, unable to bear the fatigue of the march, lay down and slept in the forest, then, waking in the dark, went farther and farther astray. The treatment of the slaves witnessed by my men certainly did not raise slaveholders in their estimation. Their usual exclamation was "Ga ba na pelu" (They have no heart); and they added, with reference to the slaves, "Why do they let them?" as if they thought that the slaves had the natural right to rid the world of such heartless creatures, and ought to do it. The uneasiness of the trader was continually showing itself, and, upon the whole, he had reason to be on the alert both day and night. The carriers perpetually stole the goods intrusted to their care, and he could not openly accuse them, lest they should plunder him of all, and leave him quite in the lurch. He could only hope to manage them after getting all the remaining goods safely into a house in Cabango; he might then deduct something from their pay for what they had purloined on the way.

Cabango (lat. 9d 31' S., long. 20d 31' or 32' E.) is the dwelling-place of Muanzanza, one of Matiamvo's subordinate chiefs. His village consists of about two hundred huts and ten or twelve square houses, constructed of poles with grass interwoven. The latter are occupied by half-caste Portuguese from Ambaca, agents for the Cassange traders. The cold in the mornings was now severe to the feelings, the thermometer ranging from 58 Deg. to 60 Deg., though, when protected, sometimes standing as high as 64 Deg. at six A.M. When the sun is well up, the thermometer in the shade rises to 80 Deg., and in the evenings it is about 78 Deg.

A person having died in this village, we could transact no business with the chief until the funeral obsequies were finished. These occupy about four days, during which there is a constant succession of dancing, wailing, and feasting. Guns are fired by day, and drums beaten by night, and all the relatives, dressed in fantastic caps, keep up the ceremonies with spirit proportionate to the amount of beer and beef expended. When there is a large expenditure, the remark is often made afterward, "What a fine funeral that was!" A figure, consisting chiefly of feathers and beads, is paraded on these occasions, and seems to be regarded as an idol.

Having met with an accident to one of my eyes by a blow from a branch in passing through a forest, I remained some days here, endeavoring, though with much pain, to draw a sketch of the country thus far, to be sent back to Mr. Gabriel at Loanda. I was always anxious to transmit an account of my discoveries on every possible occasion, lest, any thing happening in the country to which I was going, they should be entirely lost. I also fondly expected a packet of letters and papers which my good angel at Loanda would be sure to send if they came to hand, but I afterward found that, though he had offered a large sum to any one who would return with an assurance of having delivered the last packet he sent, no one followed me with it to Cabango. The unwearied attentions of this good Englishman, from his first welcome to me when, a weary, dejected, and worn-down stranger, I arrived at his residence, and his whole subsequent conduct, will be held in lively remembrance by me to my dying day.

Several of the native traders here having visited the country of Luba, lying far to the north of this, and there being some visitors also from the town of Mai, which is situated far down the Kasai, I picked up some information respecting those distant parts. In going to the town of Mai the traders crossed only two large rivers, the Loajima and Chihombo. The Kasai flows a little to the east of the town of Mai, and near it there is a large waterfall. They describe the Kasai as being there of very great size, and that it thence bends round to the west. On asking an old man, who was about to return to his chief Mai, to imagine himself standing at his home, and point to the confluence of the Quango and Kasai, he immediately turned, and, pointing to the westward, said, "When we travel five days (thirty-five or forty miles) in that direction, we come to it." He stated also that the Kasai received another river, named the Lubilash. There is but one opinion among the Balonda respecting the Kasai and Quango. They invariably describe the Kasai as receiving the Quango, and, beyond the confluence, assuming the name of Zaire or Zerezere. And the Kasai, even previous to the junction, is much larger than the Quango, from the numerous branches it receives. Besides those we have already crossed, there is the Chihombo at Cabango; and forty-two miles beyond this, eastward, runs the Kasai itself; fourteen miles beyond that, the Kaunguesi; then, forty-two miles farther east, flows the Lolua; besides numbers of little streams, all of which contribute to swell the Kasai.

About thirty-four miles east of the Lolua, or a hundred and thirty-two miles E.N.E. of Cabango, stands the town of Matiamvo, the paramount chief of all the Balonda. The town of Mai is pointed out as to the N.N.W. of Cabango, and thirty-two days or two hundred and twenty-four miles distant, or about lat. S. 5d 45'. The chief town of Luba, another independent chief, is eight days farther in the same direction, or lat. S. 4d 50'. Judging from the appearance of the people who had come for the purposes of trade from Mai, those in the north are in quite as uncivilized a condition as the Balonda. They are clad in a kind of cloth made of the inner bark of a tree. Neither guns nor native traders are admitted into the country, the chief of Luba entertaining a dread of innovation. If a native trader goes thither, he must dress like the common people in Angola, in a loose robe resembling a kilt. The chief trades in shells and beads only. His people kill the elephants by means of spears, poisoned arrows, and traps. All assert that elephants' tusks from that country are heavier and of greater length than any others.

It is evident, from all the information I could collect both here and elsewhere, that the drainage of Londa falls to the north and then runs westward. The countries of Luba and Mai are evidently lower than this, and yet this is of no great altitude—probably not much more than 3500 feet above the level of the sea. Having here received pretty certain information on a point in which I felt much interest, namely, that the Kasai is not navigable from the coast, owing to the large waterfall near the town of Mai, and that no great kingdom exists in the region beyond, between this and the equator, I would fain have visited Matiamvo. This seemed a very desirable step, as it is good policy as well as right to acknowledge the sovereign of a country; and I was assured, both by Balonda and native traders, that a considerable branch of the Zambesi rises in the country east of his town, and flows away to the south. The whole of this branch, extending down even to where it turns westward to Masiko, is probably placed too far eastward on the map. It was put down when I believed Matiamvo and Cazembe to be farther east than I have since seen reason to believe them. All, being derived from native testimony, is offered to the reader with diffidence, as needing verification by actual explorers. The people of that part, named Kanyika and Kanyoka, living on its banks, are represented as both numerous and friendly, but Matiamvo will on no account permit any white person to visit them, as his principal supplies of ivory are drawn from them. Thinking that we might descend this branch of the Zambesi to Masiko, and thence to the Barotse, I felt a strong inclination to make the attempt. The goods, however, we had brought with us to pay our way, had, by the long detention from fever and weakness in both myself and men, dwindled to a mere fragment; and, being but slightly acquainted with the Balonda dialect, I felt that I could neither use persuasion nor presents to effect my object. From all I could hear of Matiamvo, there was no chance of my being allowed to proceed through his country to the southward. If I had gone merely to visit him, all the goods would have been expended by the time I returned to Cabango; and we had not found mendicity so pleasant on our way to the north as to induce us to desire to return to it.

The country of Matiamvo is said to be well peopled, but they have little or no trade. They receive calico, salt, gunpowder, coarse earthenware, and beads, and give in return ivory and slaves. They possess no cattle, Matiamvo alone having a single herd, which he keeps entirely for the sake of the flesh. The present chief is said to be mild in his government, and will depose an under-chief for unjust conduct. He occasionally sends the distance of a hundred miles or more to behead an offending officer. But, though I was informed by the Portuguese that he possesses absolute power, his name had less influence over his subjects with whom I came in contact than that of Sekeletu has over his people living at a much greater distance from the capital.

As we thought it best to strike away to the S.E. from Cabango to our old friend Katema, I asked a guide from Muanzanza as soon as the funeral proceedings were over. He agreed to furnish one, and also accepted a smaller present from me than usual, when it was represented to him by Pascoal and Faria that I was not a trader. He seemed to regard these presents as his proper dues; and as a cargo of goods had come by Senhor Pascoal, he entered the house for the purpose of receiving his share, when Senhor Faria gravely presented him with the commonest earthenware vessel, of which great numbers are brought for this trade. The chief received it with expressions of abundant gratitude, as these vessels are highly valued, because from their depth they can hold so much food or beer. The association of ideas is sometimes so very ludicrous that it is difficult to maintain one's gravity.

Several of the children of the late Matiamvo came to beg from me, but never to offer any food. Having spoken to one young man named Liula (Heavens) about their stinginess, he soon brought bananas and manioc. I liked his appearance and conversation, and believe that the Balonda would not be difficult to teach, but their mode of life would be a drawback. The Balonda in this quarter are much more agreeable-looking than any of the inhabitants nearer the coast. The women allow their teeth to remain in their beautifully white state, and would be comely but for the custom of inserting pieces of reed into the cartilage of the nose. They seem generally to be in good spirits, and spend their time in everlasting talk, funeral ceremonies, and marriages. This flow of animal spirits must be one reason why they are such an indestructible race. The habitual influence on their minds of the agency of unseen spirits may have a tendency in the same direction, by preserving the mental quietude of a kind of fatalism.

We were forced to prepay our guide and his father too, and he went but one day, although he promised to go with us to Katema. He was not in the least ashamed at breaking his engagements, and probably no disgrace will be attached to the deed by Muanzanza. Among the Bakwains he would have been punished. My men would have stripped him of the wages which he wore on his person, but thought that, as we had always acted on the mildest principles, they would let him move off with his unearned gains.

They frequently lamented the want of knowledge in these people, saying, in their own tongue, "Ah! they don't know that we are men as well as they, and that we are only bearing with their insolence with patience because we are men." Then would follow a hearty curse, showing that the patience was nearly expended; but they seldom quarreled in the language of the Balonda. The only one who ever lost his temper was the man who struck a head man of one of the villages on the mouth, and he was the most abject individual in our company.

The reason why we needed a guide at all was to secure the convenience of a path, which, though generally no better than a sheep-walk, is much easier than going straight in one direction, through tangled forests and tropical vegetation. We knew the general direction we ought to follow, and also if any deviation occurred from our proper route; but, to avoid impassable forests and untreadable bogs, and to get to the proper fords of the rivers, we always tried to procure a guide, and he always followed the common path from one village to another when that lay in the direction we were going.

After leaving Cabango on the 21st, we crossed several little streams running into the Chihombo on our left, and in one of them I saw tree ferns ('Cyathea dregei') for the first time in Africa. The trunk was about four feet high and ten inches in diameter. We saw also grass trees of two varieties, which, in damp localities, had attained a height of forty feet. On crossing the Chihombo, which we did about twelve miles above Cabango, we found it waist-deep and rapid. We were delighted to see the evidences of buffalo and hippopotami on its banks. As soon as we got away from the track of the slave-traders, the more kindly spirit of the southern Balonda appeared, for an old man brought a large present of food from one of the villages, and volunteered to go as guide himself. The people, however, of the numerous villages which we passed always made efforts to detain us, that they might have a little trade in the way of furnishing our suppers. At one village, indeed, they would not show us the path at all unless we remained at least a day with them. Having refused, we took a path in the direction we ought to go, but it led us into an inextricable thicket. Returning to the village again, we tried another footpath in a similar direction, but this led us into an equally impassable and trackless forest. We were thus forced to come back and remain. In the following morning they put us in the proper path, which in a few hours led us through a forest that would otherwise have taken us days to penetrate.

Beyond this forest we found the village of Nyakalonga, a sister of the late Matiamvo, who treated us handsomely. She wished her people to guide us to the next village, but this they declined unless we engaged in trade. She then requested us to wait an hour or two till she could get ready a present of meal, manioc roots, ground-nuts, and a fowl. It was truly pleasant to meet with people possessing some civility, after the hauteur we had experienced on the slave-path. She sent her son to the next village without requiring payment. The stream which ran past her village was quite impassable there, and for a distance of about a mile on either side, the bog being soft and shaky, and, when the crust was broken through, about six feet deep.

On the 28th we reached the village of the chief Bango (lat. 12d 22′ 53″ S., long. 20d 58′ E.), who brought us a handsome present of meal, and the meat of an entire pallah. We here slaughtered the last of the cows presented to us by Mr. Schut, which I had kept milked until it gave only a teaspoonful at a time. My men enjoyed a hearty laugh when they found that I had given up all hope of more, for they had been talking among themselves about my perseverance. We offered a leg of the cow to Bango, but he informed us that neither he nor his people ever partook of beef, as they looked upon cattle as human, and living at home like men. None of his people purchased any of the meat, which was always eagerly done every where else. There are several other tribes who refuse to keep cattle, though not to eat them when offered by others, because, say they, oxen bring enemies and war; but this is the first instance I have met with in which they have been refused as food. The fact of killing the pallahs for food shows that the objection does not extend to meat in general.

The little streams in this part of the country did not flow in deep dells, nor were we troubled with the gigantic grasses which annoyed our eyes on the slopes of the streams before we came to Cabango. The country was quite flat, and the people cultivated manioc very extensively. There is no large collection of the inhabitants in any one spot. The ambition of each seems to be to have his own little village; and we see many coming from distant parts with the flesh of buffaloes and antelopes as the tribute claimed by Bango. We have now entered again the country of the game, but they are so exceedingly shy that we have not yet seen a single animal. The arrangement into many villages pleases the Africans vastly, for every one who has a few huts under him feels himself in some measure to be a chief. The country at this time is covered with yellowish grass quite dry. Some of the bushes and trees are green; others are shedding their leaves, the young buds pushing off the old foliage. Trees, which in the south stand bare during the winter months, have here but a short period of leaflessness. Occasionally, however, a cold north wind comes up even as far as Cabango, and spreads a wintry aspect on all the exposed vegetation. The tender shoots of the evergreen trees on the south side become as if scorched; the leaves of manioc, pumpkins, and other tender plants are killed; while the same kinds, in spots sheltered by forests, continue green through the whole year. All the interior of South Africa has a distinct winter of cold, varying in intensity with the latitudes. In the central parts of the Cape Colony the cold in the winter is often severe, and the ground is covered with snow. At Kuruman snow seldom falls, but the frost is keen. There is frost even as far as the Chobe, and a partial winter in the Barotse valley, but beyond the Orange River we never have cold and damp combined. Indeed, a shower of rain seldom or never falls during winter, and hence the healthiness of the Bechuana climate. From the Barotse valley northward it is questionable if it ever freezes; but, during the prevalence of the south wind, the thermometer sinks as low as 42 Deg., and conveys the impression of bitter cold.

Nothing can exceed the beauty of the change from the wintry appearance to that of spring at Kolobeng. Previous to the commencement of the rains, an easterly wind blows strongly by day, but dies away at night. The clouds collect in increasing masses, and relieve in some measure the bright glare of the southern sun. The wind dries up every thing, and when at its greatest strength is hot, and raises clouds of dust. The general temperature during the day rises above 96 Deg.: then showers begin to fall; and if the ground is but once well soaked with a good day's rain, the change produced is marvelous. In a day or two a tinge of green is apparent all over the landscape, and in five or six days the fresh leaves sprouting forth, and the young grass shooting up, give an appearance of spring which it requires weeks of a colder climate to produce. The birds, which in the hot, dry, windy season had been silent, now burst forth into merry twittering songs, and are busy building their nests. Some of them, indeed, hatch several times a year. The lowering of the temperature, by rains or other causes, has much the same effect as the increasing mildness of our own spring. The earth teems with myriads of young insects; in some parts of the country hundreds of centipedes, myriapedes, and beetles emerge from their hiding-places, somewhat as our snails at home do; and in the evenings the white ants swarm by thousands. A stream of them is seen to rush out of a hole, and, after flying one or two hundred yards, they descend; and if they light upon a piece of soil proper for the commencement of a new colony, they bend up their tails, unhook their wings, and, leaving them on the surface, quickly begin their mining operations. If an attempt is made to separate the wings from the body by drawing them away backward, they seem as if hooked into the body, and tear away large portions of the insect; but if turned forward, as the ant itself does, they snap off with the greatest ease. Indeed, they seem formed only to serve the insect in its short flight to a new habitation, and then to be thrown aside. Nothing can exceed the eagerness with which, at the proper time, they rush out from their birth-place. Occasionally this occurs in a house, and then, in order to prevent every corner from being filled with them, I have seen a fire placed over the orifice; but they hesitate not even to pass through the fire. While swarming they appear like snow-flakes floating about in the air, and dogs, cats, hawks, and almost every bird, may be seen busily devouring them. The natives, too, profit by the occasion, and actively collect them for food, they being about half an inch long, as thick as a crow-quill, and very fat. When roasted they are said to be good, and somewhat resemble grains of boiled rice. An idea may be formed of this dish by what once occurred on the banks of the Zouga. The Bayeiye chief Palani visiting us while eating, I gave him a piece of bread and preserved apricots; and as he seemed to relish it much, I asked him if he had any food equal to that in his country. "Ah!" said he, "did you ever taste white ants?" As I never had, he replied, "Well, if you had, you never could have desired to eat any thing better." The general way of catching them is to dig into the ant-hill, and wait till the builders come forth to repair the damage, then brush them off quickly into a vessel, as the ant-eater does into his mouth.

The fall of the rain makes all the cattle look fresh and clean, and both men and women proceed cheerily to their already hoed gardens, and sow the seed. The large animals in the country leave the spots where they had been compelled to congregate for the sake of water, and become much wilder. Occasionally a herd of buffaloes or antelopes smell rain from afar, and set off in a straight line toward the place. Sometimes they make mistakes, and are obliged to return to the water they had left.

Very large tracts of country are denuded of old grass during the winter by means of fire, in order to attract the game to that which there springs up unmixed with the older crop. This new herbage has a renovating tendency, for as long as they feed on the dry grass of the former season they continue in good condition; but no sooner are they able to indulge their appetites on the fresh herbage, than even the marrow in their bones becomes dissolved, and a red, soft, uneatable mass is left behind. After this commences the work of regaining their former plumpness.

MAY 30TH. We left Bango, and proceeded to the River Loembwe, which flows to the N.N.E., and abounds in hippopotami. It is about sixty yards wide, and four feet deep, but usually contains much less water than this, for there are fishing-weirs placed right across it. Like all the African rivers in this quarter, it has morasses on each bank, yet the valley in which it winds, when seen from the high lands above, is extremely beautiful. This valley is about the fourth of a mile wide, and it was easy to fancy the similarity of many spots on it to the goodly manors in our own country, and feel assured that there was still ample territory left for an indefinite increase of the world's population. The villages are widely apart and difficult of access, from the paths being so covered with tall grass that even an ox can scarcely follow the track. The grass cuts the feet of the men; yet we met a woman with a little child, and a girl, wending their way home with loads of manioc. The sight of a white man always infuses a tremor into their dark bosoms, and in every case of the kind they appeared immensely relieved when I had fairly passed without having sprung upon them. In the villages the dogs run away with their tails between their legs, as if they had seen a lion. The women peer from behind the walls till he comes near them, and then hastily dash into the house. When a little child, unconscious of danger, meets you in the street, he sets up a scream at the apparition, and conveys the impression that he is not far from going into fits. Among the Bechuanas I have been obliged to reprove the women for making a hobgoblin of the white man, and telling their children that they would send for him to bite them.

Having passed the Loembwe, we were in a more open country, with every few hours a small valley, through which ran a little rill in the middle of a bog. These were always difficult to pass, and being numerous, kept the lower part of the person constantly wet. At different points in our course we came upon votive offerings to the Barimo. These usually consisted of food; and every deserted village still contained the idols and little sheds with pots of medicine in them. One afternoon we passed a small frame house with the head of an ox in it as an object of worship. The dreary uniformity of gloomy forests and open flats must have a depressing influence on the minds of the people. Some villages appear more superstitious than others, if we may judge from the greater number of idols they contain.

Only on one occasion did we witness a specimen of quarreling. An old woman, standing by our camp, continued to belabor a good-looking young man for hours with her tongue. Irritated at last, he uttered some words of impatience, when another man sprang at him, exclaiming, "How dare you curse my 'Mama'?" They caught each other, and a sort of pushing, dragging wrestling-match ensued. The old woman who had been the cause of the affray wished us to interfere, and the combatants themselves hoped as much; but we, preferring to remain neutral, allowed them to fight it out. It ended by one falling under the other, both, from their scuffling, being in a state of nudity. They picked up their clothing and ran off in different directions, each threatening to bring his gun and settle the dispute in mortal combat. Only one, however, returned, and the old woman continued her scolding till my men, fairly tired of her tongue, ordered her to be gone. This trifling incident was one of interest to me, for, during the whole period of my residence in the Bechuana country, I never saw unarmed men strike each other. Their disputes are usually conducted with great volubility and noisy swearing, but they generally terminate by both parties bursting into a laugh.

At every village attempts were made to induce us to remain a night. Sometimes large pots of beer were offered to us as a temptation. Occasionally the head man would peremptorily order us to halt under a tree which he pointed out. At other times young men volunteered to guide us to the impassable part of the next bog, in the hope of bringing us to a stand, for all are excessively eager to trade; but food was so very cheap that we sometimes preferred paying them to keep it, and let us part in good humor. A good-sized fowl could be had for a single charge of gunpowder. Each native who owns a gun carries about with him a measure capable of holding but one charge, in which he receives his powder. Throughout this region the women are almost entirely naked, their gowns being a patch of cloth frightfully narrow, with no flounces; and nothing could exceed the eagerness with which they offered to purchase strips of calico of an inferior description. They were delighted with the large pieces we gave, though only about two feet long, for a fowl and a basket of upward of 20 lbs. of meal. As we had now only a small remnant of our stock, we were obliged to withstand their importunity, and then many of their women, with true maternal feelings, held up their little naked babies, entreating us to sell only a little rag for them. The fire, they say, is their only clothing by night, and the little ones derive heat by sticking closely to their parents. Instead of a skin or cloth to carry their babies in, the women plait a belt about four inches broad, of the inner bark of a tree, and this, hung from the one shoulder to the opposite side, like a soldier's belt, enables them to support the child by placing it on their side in a sitting position. Their land is very fertile, and they can raise ground-nuts and manioc in abundance. Here I observed no cotton, nor any domestic animals except fowls and little dogs. The chief possessed a few goats, and I never could get any satisfactory reason why the people also did not rear them.

On the evening of the 2d of June we reached the village of Kawawa, rather an important personage in these parts. This village consists of forty or fifty huts, and is surrounded by forest. Drums were beating over the body of a man who had died the preceding day, and some women were making a clamorous wail at the door of his hut, and addressing the deceased as if alive. The drums continued beating the whole night, with as much regularity as a steam-engine thumps on board ship. We observed that a person dressed fantastically with a great number of feathers left the people at the dance and wailing, and went away into the deep forest in the morning, to return again to the obsequies in the evening; he is intended to represent one of the Barimo.

In the morning we had agreeable intercourse with Kawawa; he visited us, and we sat and talked nearly the whole day with him and his people. When we visited him in return, we found him in his large court-house, which, though of a beehive shape, was remarkably well built. As I had shown him a number of curiosities, he now produced a jug, of English ware, shaped like an old man holding a can of beer in his hand, as the greatest curiosity he had to exhibit.

We had now an opportunity of hearing a case brought before him for judgment. A poor man and his wife were accused of having bewitched the man whose wake was now held in the village. Before Kawawa even heard the defense, he said, "You have killed one of my children; bring all yours before me, that I may choose which of them shall be mine instead." The wife eloquently defended herself, but this availed little, for these accusations are the means resorted to by some chiefs to secure subjects for the slave-market. He probably thought that I had come to purchase slaves, though I had already given a pretty full explanation of my pursuits both to himself and his people. We exhibited the pictures of the magic lantern in the evening, and all were delighted except Kawawa himself. He showed symptoms of dread, and several times started up as if to run away, but was prevented by the crowd behind. Some of the more intelligent understood the explanations well, and expatiated eloquently on them to the more obtuse. Nothing could exceed the civilities which had passed between us during this day; but Kawawa had heard that the Chiboque had forced us to pay an ox, and now thought he might do the same. When, therefore, I sent next morning to let him know that we were ready to start, he replied in his figurative way, "If an ox came in the way of a man, ought he not to eat it? I had given one to the Chiboque, and must give him the same, together with a gun, gunpowder, and a black robe, like that he had seen spread out to dry the day before; that, if I refused an ox, I must give one of my men, and a book by which he might see the state of Matiamvo's heart toward him, and which would forewarn him, should Matiamvo ever resolve to cut off his head." Kawawa came in the coolest manner possible to our encampment after sending this message, and told me he had seen all our goods, and must have all he asked, as he had command of the Kasai in our front, and would prevent us from passing it unless we paid this tribute. I replied that the goods were my property and not his; that I would never have it said that a white man had paid tribute to a black, and that I should cross the Kasai in spite of him. He ordered his people to arm themselves, and when some of my men saw them rushing for their bows, arrows, and spears, they became somewhat panic-stricken. I ordered them to move away, and not to fire unless Kawawa's people struck the first blow. I took the lead, and expected them all to follow, as they usually had done, but many of my men remained behind. When I knew this, I jumped off the ox, and made a rush to them with the revolver in my hand. Kawawa ran away among his people, and they turned their backs too. I shouted to my men to take up their luggage and march; some did so with alacrity, feeling that they had disobeyed orders by remaining; but one of them refused, and was preparing to fire at Kawawa, until I gave him a punch on the head with the pistol, and made him go too. I felt here, as elsewhere, that subordination must be maintained at all risks. We all moved into the forest, the people of Kawawa standing about a hundred yards off, gazing, but not firing a shot or an arrow. It is extremely unpleasant to part with these chieftains thus, after spending a day or two in the most amicable intercourse, and in a part where the people are generally civil. This Kawawa, however, is not a good specimen of the Balonda chiefs, and is rather notorious in the neighborhood for his folly. We were told that he has good reason to believe that Matiamvo will some day cut off his head for his disregard of the rights of strangers.

Kawawa was not to be balked of his supposed rights by the unceremonious way in which we had left him; for, when we had reached the ford of the Kasai, about ten miles distant, we found that he had sent four of his men, with orders to the ferrymen to refuse us passage. We were here duly informed that we must deliver up all the articles mentioned, and one of our men besides. This demand for one of our number always nettled every heart. The canoes were taken away before our eyes, and we were supposed to be quite helpless without them, at a river a good hundred yards broad, and very deep. Pitsane stood on the bank, gazing with apparent indifference on the stream, and made an accurate observation of where the canoes were hidden among the reeds. The ferrymen casually asked one of my Batoka if they had rivers in his country, and he answered with truth, "No, we have none." Kawawa's people then felt sure we could not cross. I thought of swimming when they were gone; but after it was dark, by the unasked loan of one of the hidden canoes, we soon were snug in our bivouac on the southern bank of the Kasai. I left some beads as payment for some meal which had been presented by the ferrymen; and, the canoe having been left on their own side of the river, Pitsane and his companions laughed uproariously at the disgust our enemies would feel, and their perplexity as to who had been our paddler across. They were quite sure that Kawawa would imagine that we had been ferried over by his own people, and would be divining to find out who had done the deed. When ready to depart in the morning, Kawawa's people appeared on the opposite heights, and could scarcely believe their eyes when they saw us prepared to start away to the south. At last one of them called out, "Ah! ye are bad," to which Pitsane and his companions retorted, "Ah! ye are good, and we thank you for the loan of your canoe." We were careful to explain the whole of the circumstances to Katema and the other chiefs, and they all agreed that we were perfectly justifiable under the circumstances, and that Matiamvo would approve our conduct. When any thing that might bear an unfavorable construction happens among themselves, they send explanations to each other. The mere fact of doing so prevents them from losing their character, for there is public opinion even among them.

Chapter 24

Level Plains—Vultures and other Birds—Diversity of Color in Flowers of the same Species—The Sundew—Twenty-seventh Attack of Fever—A River which flows in opposite Directions—Lake Dilolo the Watershed between the Atlantic and Indian Oceans—Position of Rocks—Sir Roderick Murchison's Explanation—Characteristics of the Rainy Season in connection with the Floods of the Zambesi and the Nile—Probable Reason of Difference in Amount of Rain South and North of the Equator—Arab Reports of Region east of Londa—Probable Watershed of the Zambesi and the Nile—Lake Dilolo—Reach Katema's Town: his renewed Hospitality; desire to appear like a White Man; ludicrous Departure—Jackdaws—Ford southern Branch of Lake Dilolo—Small Fish—Project for a Makololo Village near the Confluence of the Leeba and the Leeambye—Hearty Welcome from Shinte—Kolimbota's Wound—Plant-seeds and Fruit-trees brought from Angola—Masiko and Limboa's Quarrel—Nyamoana now a Widow—Purchase Canoes and descend the Leeba—Herds of wild Animals on its Banks—Unsuccessful Buffalo-hunt—Frogs—Sinbad and the Tsetse—Dispatch a Message to Manenko—Arrival of her Husband Sambanza—The Ceremony called Kasendi—Unexpected Fee for performing a surgical Operation—Social Condition of the Tribes—Desertion of Mboenga—Stratagem of Mambowe Hunters—Water-turtles—Charged by a Buffalo—Reception from the People of Libonta—Explain the Causes of our long Delay—Pitsane's Speech—Thanksgiving Services—Appearance of my "Braves"—Wonderful Kindness of the People.

After leaving the Kasai, we entered upon the extensive level plains which we had formerly found in a flooded condition. The water on them was not yet dried up, as it still remained in certain hollow spots. Vultures were seen floating in the air, showing that carrion was to be found; and, indeed, we saw several of the large game, but so exceedingly wild as to be unapproachable. Numbers of caterpillars mounted the stalks of grass, and many dragonflies and butterflies appeared, though this was winter. The caprimulgus or goat-sucker, swifts, and different kinds of swallows, with a fiery-red bee-eater in flocks, showed that the lowest temperature here does not destroy the insects on which they feed. Jet-black larks, with yellow shoulders, enliven the mornings with their songs, but they do not continue so long on the wing as ours, nor soar so high. We saw many of the pretty white ardea, and other water-birds, flying over the spots not yet dried up; and occasionally wild ducks, but these only in numbers sufficient to remind us that we were approaching the Zambesi, where every water-fowl has a home.

While passing across these interminable-looking plains, the eye rests with pleasure on a small flower, which exists in such numbers as to give its own hue to the ground. One broad band of yellow stretches across our path. On looking at the flowers which formed this golden carpet, we saw every variety of that color, from the palest lemon to the richest orange. Crossing a hundred yards of this, we came upon another broad band of the same flower, but blue, and this color is varied from the lightest tint to dark blue, and even purple. I had before observed the same flower possessing different colors in different parts of the country, and once a great number of liver-colored flowers, which elsewhere were yellow. Even the color of the birds changed with the district we passed through; but never before did I see such a marked change as from yellow to blue, repeated again and again on the same plain. Another beautiful plant attracted my attention so strongly on these plains that I dismounted to examine it. To my great delight I found it to be an old home acquaintance, a species of Drosera, closely resembling our own sundew ('Drosera Anglia'). The flower-stalk never attains a height of more than two or three inches, and the leaves are covered with reddish hairs, each of which has a drop of clammy fluid at its tip, making the whole appear as if spangled over with small diamonds. I noticed it first in the morning, and imagined the appearance was caused by the sun shining on drops of dew; but, as it continued to maintain its brilliancy during the heat of the day, I proceeded to investigate the cause of its beauty, and found that the points of the hairs exuded pure liquid, in, apparently, capsules of clear, glutinous matter. They were thus like dewdrops preserved from evaporation. The clammy fluid is intended to entrap insects, which, dying on the leaf, probably yield nutriment to the plant.

During our second day on this extensive plain I suffered from my twenty-seventh attack of fever, at a part where no surface-water was to be found. We never thought it necessary to carry water with us in this region; and now, when I was quite unable to move on, my men soon found water to allay my burning thirst by digging with sticks a few feet beneath the surface. We had thus an opportunity of observing the state of these remarkable plains at different seasons of the year. Next day we pursued our way, and on the 8th of June we forded the Lotembwa to the N.W. of Dilolo, and regained our former path.

The Lotembwa here is about a mile wide, about three feet deep, and full of the lotus, papyrus, arum, mat-rushes, and other aquatic plants. I did not observe the course in which the water flowed while crossing; but, having noticed before that the Lotembwa on the other side of the Lake Dilolo flowed in a southerly direction, I supposed that this was simply a prolongation of the same river beyond Dilolo, and that it rose in this large marsh, which we had not seen in our progress to the N.W. But when we came to the Southern Lotembwa, we were informed by Shakatwala that the river we had crossed flowed in an opposite direction—not into Dilolo, but into the Kasai. This phenomenon of a river running in opposite directions struck even his mind as strange; and, though I did not observe the current, simply from taking it for granted that it was toward the lake, I have no doubt that his assertion, corroborated as it was by others, is correct, and that the Dilolo is actually the watershed between the river systems that flow to the east and west.

I would have returned in order to examine more carefully this most interesting point, but, having had my lower extremities chilled in crossing the Northern Lotembwa, I was seized with vomiting of blood, and, besides, saw no reason to doubt the native testimony. The distance between Dilolo and the valleys leading to that of the Kasai is not more than fifteen miles, and the plains between are perfectly level; and, had I returned, I should only have found that this little lake Dilolo, by giving a portion to the Kasai and another to the Zambesi, distributes its waters to the Atlantic and Indian Oceans. I state the fact exactly as it opened to my own mind, for it was only now that I apprehended the true form of the river systems and continent. I had seen the various rivers of this country on the western side flowing from the subtending ridges into the centre, and had received information from natives and Arabs that most of the rivers on the eastern side of the same great region took a somewhat similar course from an elevated ridge there, and that all united in two main drains, the one flowing to the north and the other to the south, and that the northern drain found its way out by the Congo to the west, and the southern by the Zambesi to the east. I was thus on the watershed, or highest point of these two great systems, but still not more than 4000 feet above the level of the sea, and 1000 feet lower than the top of the western ridge we had already crossed; yet, instead of lofty snow-clad mountains appearing to verify the conjectures of the speculative, we had extensive plains, over which one may travel a month without seeing any thing higher than an ant-hill or a tree. I was not then aware that any one else had discovered the elevated trough form of the centre of Africa.

I had observed that the old schistose rocks on the sides dipped in toward the centre of the country, and their strike nearly corresponded with the major axis of the continent; and also that where the later erupted trap rocks had been spread out in tabular masses over the central plateau, they had borne angular fragments of the older rocks in their substance; but the partial generalization which the observations led to was, that great volcanic action had taken place in ancient times, somewhat in the same way it does now, at distances of not more than three hundred miles from the sea, and that this igneous action, extending along both sides of the continent, had tilted up the lateral rocks in the manner they are now seen to lie. The greater energy and more extended range of igneous action in those very remote periods when Africa was formed, embracing all the flanks, imparted to it its present very simple literal outline. This was the length to which I had come.

The trap rocks, which now constitute the "filling up" of the great valley, were always a puzzle to me till favored with Sir Roderick Murchison's explanation of the original form of the continent, for then I could see clearly why these trap rocks, which still lie in a perfectly horizontal position on extensive areas, held in their substance angular fragments, containing algae of the old schists, which form the bottom of the original lacustrine basin: the traps, in bursting through, had broken them off and preserved them. There are, besides, ranges of hills in the central parts, composed of clay and sandstone schists, with the ripple mark distinct, in which no fossils appear; but as they are usually tilted away from the masses of horizontal trap, it is probable that they too were a portion of the original bottom, and fossils may yet be found in them.*

> * After dwelling upon the geological structure of the Cape
> Colony as developed by Mr. A. Bain, and the existence in very
> remote periods of lacustrine conditions in the central part of
> South Africa, as proved by fresh-water and terrestrial
> fossils, Sir Roderick Murchison thus writes:

> "Such as South Africa is now, such have been her main features
> during countless past ages anterior to the creation of the
> human race; for the old rocks which form her outer fringe
> unquestionably circled round an interior marshy or lacustrine
> country, in which the Dicynodon flourished, at a time when not
> a single animal was similar to any living thing which now
> inhabits the surface of our globe. The present central and
> meridian zone of waters, whether lakes or marshes, extending
> from Lake Tchad to Lake 'Ngami, with hippopotami on their
> banks, are therefore but the great modern residual

geographical phenomena of those of a mesozoic age. The differences, however, between the geological past of Africa and her present state are enormous. Since that primeval time, the lands have been much elevated above the sea-level — eruptive rocks piercing in parts through them; deep rents and defiles have been suddenly formed in the subtending ridges through which some rivers escape outward.

"Travelers will eventually ascertain whether the basin-shaped structure, which is here announced as having been the great feature of the most ancient, as it is of the actual geography of South Africa (i.e., from primeval times to the present day), does, or does not, extend into Northern Africa. Looking at that much broader portion of the continent, we have some reason to surmise that the higher mountains also form, in a general sense, its flanks only."—President's Address, Royal Geographical Society, 1852, p. cxxiii.

The characteristics of the rainy season in this wonderfully humid region may account in some measure for the periodical floods of the Zambesi, and perhaps the Nile. The rains seem to follow the course of the sun, for they fall in October and November, when the sun passes over this zone on his way south. On reaching the tropic of Capricorn in December, it is dry; and December and January are the months in which injurious droughts are most dreaded near that tropic (from Kolobeng to Linyanti). As he returns again to the north in February, March, and April, we have the great rains of the year; and the plains, which in October and November were well moistened, and imbibed rain like sponges, now become supersaturated, and pour forth those floods of clear water which inundate the banks of the Zambesi. Somewhat the same phenomenon probably causes the periodical inundations of the Nile. The two rivers rise in the same region; but there is a difference in the period of flood, possibly from their being on opposite sides of the equator. The waters of the Nile are said to become turbid in June; and the flood attains its greatest height in August, or the period when we may suppose the supersaturation to occur. The subject is worthy the investigation of those who may examine the region between the equator and 10 Deg. S.; for the Nile does not show much increase when the sun is at its farthest point north, or tropic of Cancer, but at the time of its returning to the equator, exactly as in the other case when he is on Capricorn, and the Zambesi is affected.*

* *The above is from my own observation, together with*

information derived from the Portuguese in the interior of Angola; and I may add that the result of many years' observation by Messrs. Gabriel and Brand at Loanda, on the west coast, is in accordance therewith. It rains there between the 1st and 30th of November, but January and December are usually both warm and dry. The heavier rains commence about the 1st of February, and last until the 15th of May. Then no rain falls between the 20th of May and the 1st of November. The rain averages from 12 to 15 inches per annum. In 1852 it was 12.034 inches; in 1853, 15.473 inches. Although I had no means of measuring the amount of rain which fell in Londa, I feel certain that the annual quantity exceeds very much that which falls on the coast, because for a long time we noticed that every dawn was marked by a deluging shower, which began without warning-drops or thunder. I observed that the rain ceased suddenly on the 28th of April, and the lesser rains commenced about a fortnight before the beginning of November.

From information derived from Arabs of Zanzibar, whom I met at Naliele in the middle of the country, the region to the east of the parts of Londa over which we have traveled resembles them in its conformation. They report swampy steppes, some of which have no trees, where the inhabitants use grass, and stalks of native corn, for fuel. A large shallow lake is also pointed out in that direction, named Tanganyenka, which requires three days for crossing in canoes. It is connected with another named Kalagwe (Garague?), farther north, and may be the Nyanja of the Maravim. From this lake is derived, by numerous small streams, the River Loapula, the eastern branch of the Zambesi, which, coming from the N.E., flows past the town of Cazembe.

The southern end of this lake is ten days northeast of the town of Cazembe; and as that is probably more than five days from Shinte, we can not have been nearer to it than 150 miles. Probably this lake is the watershed between the Zambesi and the Nile, as Lake Dilolo is that between the Leeba and Kasai. But, however this may be, the phenomena of the rainy season show that it is not necessary to assume the existence of high snowy mountains until we get reliable information. This, it is to be hoped, will be one of the results of the researches of Captain Burton in his present journey.

The original valley formation of the continent determined the northern and southern course of the Zambesi in the centre, and also of the ancient river which once flowed from the Linyanti basin to the Orange River. It also gave direction to the southern and northern flow of the Kasai and the

Nile. We find that between the latitudes, say 6 Deg. and 12 Deg. S., from which, in all probability, the head waters of those rivers diverge, there is a sort of elevated partition in the great longitudinal valley. Presuming on the correctness of the native information, which places the humid region to which the Nile and Zambesi probably owe their origin within the latitudes indicated, why does so much more rain fall there than in the same latitudes north of the equator? Why does Darfur not give rise to great rivers, like Londa and the country east of it? The prevailing winds in the ocean opposite the territory pointed out are said to be from the N.E. and S.E. during a great part of the year; they extend their currents on one side at least of the equator quite beyond the middle of the continent, and even until in Angola they meet the sea-breeze from the Atlantic. If the reader remembers the explanation given at page 109,* that the comparative want of rain on the Kalahari Desert is caused by the mass of air losing its humidity as it passes up and glides over the subtending ridge, and will turn to the map, he may perceive that the same cause is in operation in an intense degree by the mountains of Abyssinia to render the region about Darfur still more arid, and that the flanking ranges mentioned lie much nearer the equator than those which rob the Kalahari of humidity. The Nile, even while running through a part of that region, receives remarkably few branches. Observing also that there is no known abrupt lateral mountain-range between 6 Deg. and 12 Deg. S., but that there is an elevated partition there, and that the southing and northing of the southeasters and northeasters probably cause a confluence of the two great atmospheric currents, he will perceive an accumulation of humidity on the flanks and crown of the partition, instead of, as elsewhere, opposite the Kalahari and Darfur, a deposition of the atmospheric moisture on the eastern slopes of the subtending ridges. This explanation is offered with all deference to those who have made meteorology their special study, and as a hint to travelers who may have opportunity to examine the subject more fully. I often observed, while on a portion of the partition, that the air by night was generally quite still, but as soon as the sun's rays began to shoot across the upper strata of the atmosphere in the early morning, a copious discharge came suddenly down from the accumulated clouds. It always reminded me of the experiment of putting a rod into a saturated solution of a certain salt, causing instant crystallization. This, too, was the period when I often observed the greatest amount of cold.

> *Since the explanation in page 109 [Chapter 5 Paragraph 5] was printed, I have been pleased to see the same explanation given by the popular astronomer and natural philosopher, M. Babinet, in reference to the climate of France. It is quoted from a letter of a correspondent of the 'Times' in Paris:*

"In the normal meteorological state of France and Europe, the west wind, which is the counter-current of the trade-winds that constantly blow from the east under the tropics—the west wind, I say, after having touched France and Europe by the western shores, re-descends by Marseilles and the Mediterranean, Constantinople and the Archipelago, Astrakan and the Caspian Sea, in order to merge again into the great circuit of the general winds, and be thus carried again into the equatorial current. Whenever these masses of air, impregnated with humidity during their passage over the ocean, meet with an obstacle, such as a chain of mountains, for example, they slide up the acclivity, and, when they reach the crest, find themselves relieved from a portion of the column of air which pressed upon them. Thus, dilating by reason of their elasticity, they cause a considerable degree of cold, and a precipitation of humidity in the form of fogs, clouds, rain, or snow. A similar effect occurs whatever be the obstacle they find in their way. Now this is what had gradually taken place before 1856. By some cause or other connected with the currents of the atmosphere, the warm current from the west had annually ascended northward, so that, instead of passing through France, it came from the Baltic and the north of Germany, thus momentarily disturbing the ordinary law of the temperatures of Europe. But in 1856 a sudden change occurred. The western current again passed, as before, through the centre of France. It met with an obstacle in the air which had not yet found its usual outlet toward the west and south. Hence a stoppage, a rising, a consequent dilation and fall of temperature, extraordinary rains and inundations. But, now that the natural state of things is restored, nothing appears to prognosticate the return of similar disasters. Were the western current found annually to move further north, we might again experience meteorological effects similar to those of 1856. Hence the regular seasons may be considered re-established in France for several years to come. The important meteorological communications which the Imperial Observatory is daily establishing with the other countries of Europe, and the introduction of apparatus for *measuring the velocity of the aerial currents and prevailing winds, will soon afford prognostics sufficiently certain to enable an enlightened government to provide in time against future evils."*

After crossing the Northern Lotembwa we met a party of the people of Kangenke, who had treated us kindly on our way to the north, and sent him a robe of striped calico, with an explanation of the reason for not returning through his village. We then went on to the Lake Dilolo. It is a fine sheet of water, six or eight miles long, and one or two broad, and somewhat of a triangular shape. A branch proceeds from one of the angles, and flows into the Southern Lotembwa. Though laboring under fever, the sight of the blue waters, and the waves lashing the shore, had a most soothing influence on the mind, after so much of lifeless, flat, and gloomy forest. The heart yearned for the vivid impressions which are always created by the sight of the broad expanse of the grand old ocean. That has life in it; but the flat uniformities over which we had roamed made me feel as if buried alive. We found Moene Dilolo (Lord of the Lake) a fat, jolly fellow, who lamented that when they had no strangers they had plenty of beer, and always none when they came. He gave us a handsome present of meal and putrid buffalo's flesh. Meat can not be too far gone for them, as it is used only in small quantities, as a sauce to their tasteless manioc. They were at this time hunting antelopes, in order to send the skins as a tribute to Matiamvo. Great quantities of fish are caught in the lake; and numbers of young water-fowl are now found in the nests among the reeds.

Our progress had always been slow, and I found that our rate of traveling could only be five hours a day for five successive days. On the sixth, both men and oxen showed symptoms of knocking up. We never exceeded two and a half or three miles an hour in a straight line, though all were anxious to get home. The difference in the rate of traveling between ourselves and the slave-traders was our having a rather quicker step, a longer day's journey, and twenty traveling days a month instead of their ten. When one of my men became ill, but still could walk, others parted his luggage among them; yet we had often to stop one day a week, besides Sundays, simply for the sake of rest. The latitude of Lake Dilolo is 11d 32' 1" S., long. 22d 27' E.

JUNE 14TH. We reached the collection of straggling villages over which Katema rules, and were thankful to see old familiar faces again. Shakatwala performed the part of a chief by bringing forth abundant supplies of food in his master's name. He informed us that Katema, too, was out hunting skins for Matiamvo.

In different parts of this country, we remarked that when old friends were inquired for, the reply was, "Ba hola" (They are getting better); or if the people of a village were inquired for, the answer was, "They are recovering," as if sickness was quite a common thing. Indeed, many with whom we had made acquaintance in going north we now found were in their graves. On the 15th Katema came home from his hunting, having heard of our arrival. He desired me to rest myself and eat abundantly, for, being a great man, I must feel tired; and he took good care to give the means of doing so. All the people in these parts are exceedingly kind and liberal with their food, and Katema was not behindhand. When he visited our encampment, I presented him with a cloak of red baize, ornamented with gold tinsel, which cost thirty shillings, according to the promise I had made in going to Londa; also a cotton robe, both large and small beads, an iron spoon, and a tin pannikin containing a quarter of a pound of powder. He seemed greatly pleased with the liberality shown, and assured me that the way was mine, and that no one should molest me in it if he could help it. We were informed by Shakatwala that the chief never used any part of a present before making an offer of it to his mother, or the departed spirit to whom he prayed. Katema asked if I could not make a dress for him like the one I wore, so that he might appear as a white man when any stranger visited him. One of the councilors, imagining that he ought to second this by begging, Katema checked him by saying, "Whatever strangers give, be it little or much, I always receive it with thankfulness, and never trouble them for more." On departing, he mounted on the shoulders of his spokesman, as the most dignified mode of retiring. The spokesman being a slender man, and the chief six feet high, and stout in proportion, there would have been a break-down had he not been accustomed to it. We were very much pleased with Katema; and next day he presented us with a cow, that we might enjoy the abundant supplies of meal he had given with good animal food. He then departed for the hunting-ground, after assuring me that the town and every thing in it were mine, and that his factotum, Shakatwala, would remain and attend to every want, and also conduct us to the Leeba.

On attempting to slaughter the cow Katema had given, we found the herd as wild as buffaloes; and one of my men having only wounded it, they fled many miles into the forest, and were with great difficulty brought back. Even the herdsman was afraid to go near them. The majority of them were white, and they were all beautiful animals. After hunting it for two days it was dispatched at last by another ball. Here we saw a flock of jackdaws, a rare sight in Londa, busy with the grubs in the valley, which are eaten by the people too.

Leaving Katema's town on the 19th, and proceeding four miles to the eastward, we forded the southern branch of Lake Dilolo. We found it a mile and a quarter broad; and, as it flows into the Lotembwa, the lake would seem to be a drain of the surrounding flats, and to partake of the character of a fountain. The ford was waist-deep, and very difficult, from the masses of arum and rushes through which we waded. Going to the eastward about three miles, we came to the Southern Lotembwa itself, running in a valley two miles broad. It is here eighty or ninety yards wide, and contains numerous islands covered with dense sylvan vegetation. In the rainy season the valley is flooded, and as the waters dry up great multitudes of fish are caught. This happens very extensively over the country, and fishing-weirs are met with every where. A species of small fish, about the size of the minnow, is caught in bagfuls and dried in the sun. The taste is a pungent aromatic bitter, and it was partaken of freely by my people, although they had never met with it before. On many of the paths which had been flooded a nasty sort of slime of decayed vegetable matter is left behind, and much sickness prevails during the drying up of the water. We did not find our friend Mozinkwa at his pleasant home on the Lokaloeje; his wife was dead, and he had removed elsewhere. He followed us some distance, but our reappearance seemed to stir up his sorrows. We found the pontoon at the village in which we left it. It had been carefully preserved, but a mouse had eaten a hole in it and rendered it useless.

We traversed the extended plain on the north bank of the Leeba, and crossed this river a little farther on at Kanyonke's village, which is about twenty miles west of the Peri hills, our former ford. The first stage beyond the Leeba was at the rivulet Loamba, by the village of Chebende, nephew of Shinte; and next day we met Chebende himself returning from the funeral of Samoana, his father. He was thin and haggard-looking compared to what he had been before, the probable effect of the orgies in which he had been engaged. Pitsane and Mohorisi, having concocted the project of a Makololo village on the banks of the Leeba, as an approach to the white man's market, spoke to Chebende, as an influential man, on the subject, but he cautiously avoided expressing an opinion. The idea which had sprung up in their own minds of an establishment somewhere near the confluence of the Leeba and Leeambye, commended itself to my judgment at the time as a geographically suitable point for civilization and commerce. The right bank of the Leeba there is never flooded; and from that point there is communication by means of canoes to the country of the Kanyika, and also to Cazembe and beyond, with but one or two large waterfalls between. There is no obstruction down to the Barotse valley; and there is probably canoe navigation down the Kafue or Bashukulompo River, though it is reported to contain many cataracts. It flows through a fertile country, well peopled with Bamasasa, who cultivate the native produce largely.

As this was the middle of winter, it may be mentioned that the temperature of the water in the morning was 47 Deg., and that of the air 50 Deg., which, being loaded with moisture, was very cold to the feelings. Yet the sun was very hot by day, and the temperature in the coolest shade from 88 Deg. to 90 Deg.; in the evenings from 76 Deg. to 78 Deg.

Before reaching the town of Shinte we passed through many large villages of the Balobale, who have fled from the chief Kangenke. The Mambari from Bihe come constantly to him for trade; and, as he sells his people, great numbers of them escape to Shinte and Katema, who refuse to give them up.

We reached our friend Shinte, and received a hearty welcome from this friendly old man, and abundant provisions of the best he had. On hearing the report of the journey given by my companions, and receiving a piece of cotton cloth about two yards square, he said, "These Mambari cheat us by bringing little pieces only; but the next time you pass I shall send men with you to trade for me in Loanda." When I explained the use made of the slaves he sold, and that he was just destroying his own tribe by selling his people, and enlarging that of the Mambari for the sake of these small pieces of cloth, it seemed to him quite a new idea. He entered into a long detail of his troubles with Masiko, who had prevented him from cultivating that friendship with the Makololo which I had inculcated, and had even plundered the messengers he had sent with Kolimbota to the Barotse valley. Shinte was particularly anxious to explain that Kolimbota had remained after my departure of his own accord, and that he had engaged in the quarrels of the country without being invited; that, in attempting to capture one of the children of a Balobale man, who had offended the Balonda by taking honey from a hive which did not belong to him, Kolimbota had got wounded by a shot in the thigh, but that he had cured the wound, given him a wife, and sent a present of cloth to Sekeletu, with a full account of the whole affair. From the statement of Shinte we found that Kolimbota had learned, before we left his town, that the way we intended to take was so dangerous that it would be better for him to leave us to our fate; and, as he had taken one of our canoes with him, it seemed evident that he did not expect us to return. Shinte, however, sent a recommendation to his sister Nyamoana to furnish as many canoes as we should need for our descent of the Leeba and Leeambye.

As I had been desirous of introducing some of the fruit-trees of Angola, both for my own sake and that of the inhabitants, we had carried a pot containing a little plantation of orange, cashew-trees, custard-apple-trees ('anona'), and a fig-tree, with coffee, aracas ('Araca pomifera'), and papaws ('Carica papaya'). Fearing that, if we took them farther south at present, they might be killed by the cold, we planted them out in an inclosure of one of Shinte's principal men, and, at his request, promised to give Shinte a share when grown. They know the value of fruits, but at present have none except wild ones. A wild fruit we frequently met with in Londa is eatable, and, when boiled, yields a large quantity of oil, which is much used in anointing both head and body. He eagerly accepted some of the seeds of the palm-oil-tree ('Elaeis Guineensis'), when told that this would produce oil in much greater quantity than their native tree, which is not a palm. There are very few palm-trees in this country, but near Bango we saw a few of a peculiar palm, the ends of the leaf-stalks of which remain attached to the trunk, giving it a triangular shape.

It is pleasant to observe that all the tribes in Central Africa are fond of agriculture. My men had collected quantities of seeds in Angola, and now distributed them among their friends. Some even carried onions, garlic, and bird's-eye pepper, growing in pannikins. The courts of the Balonda, planted with tobacco, sugar-cane, and plants used as relishes, led me to the belief that care would be taken of my little nursery.

The thermometer early in the mornings ranged from 42 Deg. to 52 Deg., at noon 94 Deg. to 96 Deg., and in the evening about 70 Deg. It was placed in the shade of my tent, which was pitched under the thickest tree we could find. The sensation of cold, after the heat of the day, was very keen. The Balonda at this season never leave their fires till nine or ten in the morning. As the cold was so great here, it was probably frosty at Linyanti; I therefore feared to expose my young trees there. The latitude of Shinte's town is 12d 37' 35" S., longitude 22d 47' E.

We remained with Shinte till the 6th of July, he being unwilling to allow us to depart before hearing in a formal manner, in the presence of his greatest councilor Chebende, a message from Limboa, the brother of Masiko. When Masiko fled from the Makololo country in consequence of a dislike of being in a state of subjection to Sebituane, he came into the territory of Shinte, who received him kindly, and sent orders to all the villages in his vicinity to supply him with food. Limboa fled in a westerly direction with a number of people, and also became a chief. His country was sometimes called Nyenko, but by the Mambari and native Portuguese traders "Mboela"—the place where they "turned again", or back. As one of the fruits of polygamy, the children of different mothers are always in a state of variance. Each son endeavors to gain the ascendency by enticing away the followers of the others. The mother of Limboa being of a high family, he felt aggrieved because the situation chosen by Masiko was better than his. Masiko lived at a convenient distance from the Saloisho hills, where there is abundance of iron ore, with which the inhabitants manufacture hoes, knives, etc. They are also skillful in making wooden vessels. Limboa felt annoyed because he was obliged to apply for these articles through his brother, whom he regarded as his inferior, and accordingly resolved to come into the same district. As this was looked upon as an assertion of superiority which Masiko would resist, it was virtually a declaration of war. Both Masiko and Shinte pleaded my injunction to live in peace and friendship, but Limboa, confident of success, now sent the message which I was about to hear—"That he, too, highly approved of the 'word' I had given, but would only for once transgress a little, and live at peace for ever afterward." He now desired the aid of Shinte to subdue his brother. Messengers came from Masiko at the same time, desiring assistance to repel him. Shinte felt inclined to aid Limboa, but, as he had advised them both to wait till I came, I now urged him to let the quarrel alone, and he took my advice.

We parted on the best possible terms with our friend Shinte, and proceeded by our former path to the village of his sister Nyamoana, who is now a widow. She received us with much apparent feeling, and said, "We had removed from our former abode to the place where you found us, and had no idea then that it was the spot where my husband was to die." She had come to the River Lofuje, as they never remain in a place where death has once visited them. We received the loan of five small canoes from her, and also one of those we had left here before, to proceed down the Leeba. After viewing the Coanza at Massangano, I thought the Leeba at least a third larger, and upward of two hundred yards wide. We saw evidence of its rise during its last flood having been upward of forty feet in perpendicular height; but this is probably more than usual, as the amount of rain was above the average. My companions purchased also a number of canoes from the Balonda. These are very small, and can carry only two persons. They are made quite thin and light, and as sharp as racing-skiffs, because they are used in hunting animals in the water. The price paid was a string of beads equal to the length of the canoe. We advised them to bring canoes for sale to the Makololo, as they would gladly give them cows in exchange.

In descending the Leeba we saw many herds of wild animals, especially the tahetsi ('Aigoceros equina'), one magnificent antelope, the putokuane ('Antilope niger'), and two fine lions. The Balobale, however, are getting well supplied with guns, and will soon thin out the large game. At one of the villages we were entreated to attack some buffaloes which grazed in the gardens every night and destroyed the manioc. As we had had no success in shooting at the game we had seen, and we all longed to have a meal of meat, we followed the footprints of a number of old bulls. They showed a great amount of cunning by selecting the densest parts of very closely-planted forests to stand or recline in during the day. We came within six yards of them several times before we knew that they were so near. We only heard them rush away among the crashing branches, catching only a glimpse of them. It was somewhat exciting to feel, as we trod on the dry leaves with stealthy steps, that, for any thing we knew, we might next moment be charged by one of the most dangerous beasts of the forest. We threaded out their doublings for hours, drawn on by a keen craving for animal food, as we had been entirely without salt for upward of two months, but never could get a shot.

In passing along the side of the water every where except in Londa, green frogs spring out at your feet, and light in the water as if taking a "header"; and on the Leeambye and Chobe we have great numbers of small green frogs ('Rana fasciata', Boie), which light on blades of grass with remarkable precision; but on coming along the Leeba I was struck by the sight of a light green toad about an inch long. The leaf might be nearly perpendicular, but it stuck to it like a fly. It was of the same size as the 'Brachymerus bi-fasciatus' (Smith),* which I saw only once in the Bakwain country. Though small, it was hideous, being colored jet black, with vermilion spots.

> *The discovery of this last species is thus mentioned by that accomplished naturalist, Dr. Smith: "On the banks of the Limpopo River, close to the tropic of Capricorn, a massive tree was cut down to obtain wood to repair a wagon. The workman, while sawing the trunk longitudinally nearly along its centre, remarked, on reaching a certain point, 'It is hollow, and will not answer the purpose for which it is wanted.' He persevered, however, and when a division into equal halves was effected, it was discovered that the saw in its course had crossed a large hole, in which were five specimens of the species just described, each about an inch in length. Every exertion was made to discover a means of communication between the external air and the cavity, but without success. Every part of the latter was probed with the utmost care, and water was kept in each half for a considerable time, without any passing into the wood. The inner surface of the cavity was black, as if charred, and so was likewise the adjoining wood for half an inch from the cavity. The tree, at the part where the latter existed, was 19 inches in diameter; the length of the trunk was 18 feet.

When the Batrachia above mentioned were discovered, they appeared inanimate, but the influence of a warm sun to which they were subjected soon imparted to them a moderate degree of vigor. In a few hours from the time they were liberated they were tolerably active, and able to move from place to place apparently with great ease."

Before reaching the Makondo rivulet, latitude 13d 23′ 12″ S., we came upon the tsetse in such numbers that many bites were inflicted on my poor ox, in spite of a man with a branch warding them off. The bite of this insect does not affect the donkey as it does cattle. The next morning, the spots on which my ox had been bitten were marked by patches of hair about half an inch broad being wetted by exudation. Poor Sinbad had carried me all the way from the Leeba to Golungo Alto, and all the way back again, without losing any of his peculiarities, or ever becoming reconciled to our perversity in forcing him away each morning from the pleasant pasturage on which he had fed. I wished to give the climax to his usefulness, and allay our craving for animal food at the same time; but my men having some compunction, we carried him to end his days in peace at Naliele.

Having dispatched a message to our old friend Manenko, we waited a day opposite her village, which was about fifteen miles from the river. Her husband was instantly dispatched to meet us with liberal presents of food, she being unable to travel in consequence of a burn on the foot. Sambanza gave us a detailed account of the political affairs of the country, and of Kolimbota's evil doings, and next morning performed the ceremony called "Kasendi", for cementing our friendship. It is accomplished thus: The hands of the parties are joined (in this case Pitsane and Sambanza were the parties engaged); small incisions are made on the clasped hands, on the pits of the stomach of each, and on the right cheeks and foreheads. A small quantity of blood is taken off from these points in both parties by means of a stalk of grass. The blood from one person is put into a pot of beer, and that of the second into another; each then drinks the other's blood, and they are supposed to become perpetual friends or relations. During the drinking of the beer, some of the party continue beating the ground with short clubs, and utter sentences by way of ratifying the treaty. The men belonging to each then finish the beer. The principals in the performance of "Kasendi" are henceforth considered blood-relations, and are bound to disclose to each other any impending evil. If Sekeletu should resolve to attack the Balonda, Pitsane would be under obligation to give Sambanza warning to escape, and so on the other side. They now presented each other with the most valuable presents they had to bestow. Sambanza walked off with Pitsane's suit of green baize faced with red, which had been made in Loanda, and

Pitsane, besides abundant supplies of food, obtained two shells similar to that I had received from Shinte.

On one occasion I became blood-relation to a young woman by accident. She had a large cartilaginous tumor between the bones of the fore-arm, which, as it gradually enlarged, so distended the muscles as to render her unable to work. She applied to me to excise it. I requested her to bring her husband, if he were willing to have the operation performed, and, while removing the tumor, one of the small arteries squirted some blood into my eye. She remarked, when I was wiping the blood out of it, "You were a friend before, now you are a blood-relation; and when you pass this way, always send me word, that I may cook food for you." In creating these friendships, my men had the full intention of returning; each one had his 'Molekane' (friend) in every village of the friendly Balonda. Mohorisi even married a wife in the town of Katema, and Pitsane took another in the town of Shinte. These alliances were looked upon with great favor by the Balonda chiefs, as securing the good-will of the Makololo.

In order that the social condition of the tribes may be understood by the reader, I shall mention that, while waiting for Sambanza, a party of Barotse came from Nyenko, the former residence of Limboa, who had lately crossed the Leeba on his way toward Masiko. The head man of this party had brought Limboa's son to his father, because the Barotse at Nyenko had, since the departure of Limboa, elected Nananko, another son of Santuru, in his stead; and our visitor, to whom the boy had been intrusted as a guardian, thinking him to be in danger, fled with him to his father. The Barotse, whom Limboa had left behind at Nyenko, on proceeding to elect Nananko, said, "No, it is quite too much for Limboa to rule over two places." I would have gone to visit Limboa and Masiko too, in order to prevent hostilities, but the state of my ox would not allow it. I therefore sent a message to Limboa by some of his men, protesting against war with his brother, and giving him formal notice that the path up the Leeba had been given to us by the Balonda, the owners of the country, and that no attempt must ever be made to obstruct free intercourse.

On leaving this place we were deserted by one of our party, Mboenga, an Ambonda man, who had accompanied us all the way to Loanda and back. His father was living with Masiko, and it was natural for him to wish to join his own family again. He went off honestly, with the exception of taking a fine "tari" skin given me by Nyamoana, but he left a parcel of gun-flints which he had carried for me all the way from Loanda. I regretted parting with him thus, and sent notice to him that he need not have run away, and if he wished to come to Sekeletu again he would be welcome. We subsequently met a large party of Barotse fleeing in the same direction; but when I represented to them that there was a probability of their being sold as slaves in Londa, and none in the country of Sekeletu, they concluded to return. The grievance which the Barotse most feel is being obliged to live with Sekeletu at Linyanti, where there is neither fish nor fowl, nor any other kind of food, equal in quantity to what they enjoy in their own fat valley.

A short distance below the confluence of the Leeba and Leeambye we met a number of hunters belonging to the tribe called Mambowe, who live under Masiko. They had dried flesh of hippopotami, buffaloes, and alligators. They stalk the animals by using the stratagem of a cap made of the skin of a leche's or poku's head, having the horns still attached, and another made so as to represent the upper white part of the crane called jabiru ('Mycteru Senegalensis'), with its long neck and beak above. With these on, they crawl through the grass; they can easily put up their heads so far as to see their prey without being recognized until they are within bow-shot. They presented me with three fine water-turtles,* one of which, when cooked, had upward of forty eggs in its body. The shell of the egg is flexible, and it is of the same size at both ends, like those of the alligator. The flesh, and especially the liver, is excellent. The hunters informed us that, when the message inculcating peace among the tribes came to Masiko, the common people were so glad at the prospect of "binding up the spears", that they ran to the river, and bathed and plunged in it for joy. This party had been sent by Masiko to the Makololo for aid to repel their enemy, but, afraid to go thither, had spent the time in hunting. They have a dread of the Makololo, and hence the joy they expressed when peace was proclaimed. The Mambowe hunters were much alarmed until my name was mentioned. They then joined our party, and on the following day discovered a hippopotamus dead, which they had previously wounded. This was the first feast of flesh my men had enjoyed, for, though the game was wonderfully abundant, I had quite got out of the way of shooting, and missed perpetually. Once I went with the determination of getting so close that I should not miss a zebra. We went along one of the branches that stretch out from the river in a small canoe, and two men, stooping down as low as they could, paddled it slowly along to an open space near to a herd of zebras and pokus. Peering over the edge of the canoe, the open space seemed like a patch of wet ground, such as is often seen on the banks of a river, made smooth as the resting-place of alligators.

When we came within a few yards of it, we found by the precipitate plunging of the reptile that this was a large alligator itself. Although I had been most careful to approach near enough, I unfortunately only broke the hind leg of a zebra. My two men pursued it, but the loss of a hind leg does not prevent this animal from a gallop. As I walked slowly after the men on an extensive plain covered with a great crop of grass, which was 'laid' by its own weight, I observed that a solitary buffalo, disturbed by others of my own party, was coming to me at a gallop. I glanced around, but the only tree on the plain was a hundred yards off, and there was no escape elsewhere. I therefore cocked my rifle, with the intention of giving him a steady shot in the forehead when he should come within three or four yards of me. The thought flashed across my mind, "What if your gun misses fire?" I placed it to my shoulder as he came on at full speed, and that is tremendous, though generally he is a lumbering-looking animal in his paces. A small bush and bunch of grass fifteen yards off made him swerve a little, and exposed his shoulder. I just heard the ball crack there as I fell flat on my face. The pain must have made him renounce his purpose, for he bounded close past me on to the water, where he was found dead. In expressing my thankfulness to God among my men, they were much offended with themselves for not being present to shield me from this danger. The tree near me was a camel-thorn, and reminded me that we had come back to the land of thorns again, for the country we had left is one of evergreens.

> * *It is probably a species allied to the 'Sternotherus sinuatus' of Dr. Smith, as it has no disagreeable smell. This variety annually leaves the water with so much regularity for the deposit of its eggs, that the natives decide on the time of sowing their seed by its appearance.*

JULY 27TH. We reached the town of Libonta, and were received with demonstrations of joy such as I had never witnessed before. The women came forth to meet us, making their curious dancing gestures and loud lulliloos. Some carried a mat and stick, in imitation of a spear and shield. Others rushed forward and kissed the hands and cheeks of the different persons of their acquaintance among us, raising such a dust that it was quite a relief to get to the men assembled and sitting with proper African decorum in the kotla. We were looked upon as men risen from the dead, for the most skillful of their diviners had pronounced us to have perished long ago. After many expressions of joy at meeting, I arose, and, thanking them, explained the causes of our long delay, but left the report to be made by their own countrymen. Formerly I had been the chief speaker, now I would leave the task of speaking to them. Pitsane then delivered a speech of upward of an hour in length, giving a highly flattering picture of the whole journey, of the kindness of the white men in general, and of Mr. Gabriel in particular. He concluded by saying that I had done more for them than they expected; that I had not only opened up a path for them to the other white men, but conciliated all the chiefs along the route. The oldest man present rose and answered this speech, and, among other things, alluded to the disgust I felt at the Makololo for engaging in marauding expeditions against Lechulatebe and Sebolamakwaia, of which we had heard from the first persons we met, and which my companions most energetically denounced as "mashue hela", entirely bad. He entreated me not to lose heart, but to reprove Sekeletu as my child. Another old man followed with the same entreaties. The following day we observed as our thanksgiving to God for his goodness in bringing us all back in safety to our friends. My men decked themselves out in their best, and I found that, although their goods were finished, they had managed to save suits of European clothing, which, being white, with their red caps, gave them rather a dashing appearance. They tried to walk like the soldiers they had seen in Loanda, and called themselves my "braves" (batlabani). During the service they all sat with their guns over their shoulders, and excited the unbounded admiration of the women and children. I addressed them all on the goodness of God in preserving us from all the dangers of strange tribes and disease. We had a similar service in the afternoon. The men gave us two fine oxen for slaughter, and the women supplied us abundantly with milk, meal, and butter. It was all quite gratuitous, and I felt ashamed that I could make no return. My men explained the total expenditure of our means, and the Libontese answered gracefully, "It does not matter; you have opened a path for us, and we shall have sleep." Strangers came flocking from a distance, and seldom empty-handed. Their presents I distributed among my men.

Our progress down the Barotse valley was just like this. Every village gave us an ox, and sometimes two. The people were wonderfully kind. I felt, and still feel, most deeply grateful, and tried to benefit them in the only way I could, by imparting the knowledge of that Savior who can comfort and supply them in the time of need, and my prayer is that he may send his good Spirit to instruct them and lead them into his kingdom. Even now I earnestly long to return, and make some recompense to them for their kindness. In passing them on our way to the north, their liberality might have been supposed to be influenced by the hope of repayment on our return, for the white man's land is imagined to be the source of every ornament they prize most. But, though we set out from Loanda with a considerable quantity of goods, hoping both to pay our way through the stingy Chiboque, and to make presents to the kind Balonda and still more generous Makololo, the many delays caused by sickness made us expend all my stock, and all the goods my men procured by their own labor at Loanda, and we returned to the Makololo as poor as when we set out. Yet no distrust was shown, and my poverty did not lessen my influence. They saw that I had been exerting myself for their benefit alone, and even my men remarked, "Though we return as poor as we went, we have not gone in vain." They began immediately to collect tusks of hippopotami and other ivory for a second journey.

Chapter 25

Colony of Birds called Linkololo—The Village of Chitlane—Murder of Mpololo's Daughter—Execution of the Murderer and his Wife—My Companions find that their Wives have married other Husbands—Sunday—A Party from Masiko—Freedom of Speech—Canoe struck by a Hippopotamus—Gonye—Appearance of Trees at the end of Winter—Murky Atmosphere—Surprising Amount of organic Life—Hornets—The Packages forwarded by Mr. Moffat—Makololo Suspicions and Reply to the Matebele who brought them—Convey the Goods to an Island and build a Hut over them—Ascertain that Sir R. Murchison had recognized the true Form of African Continent—Arrival at Linyanti—A grand Picho—Shrewd Inquiry— Sekeletu in his Uniform—A Trading-party sent to Loanda with Ivory— Mr. Gabriel's Kindness to them—Difficulties in Trading—Two Makololo Forays during our Absence—Report of the Country to the N.E.—Death of influential Men—The Makololo desire to be nearer the Market—Opinions upon a Change of Residence—Climate of Barotse Valley—Diseases—Author's Fevers not a fair Criterion in the Matter—The Interior an inviting Field for the Philanthropist—Consultations about a Path to the East Coast—Decide on descending North Bank of Zambesi— Wait for the Rainy Season—Native way of spending Time during the period of greatest Heat—Favorable Opening for Missionary Enterprise—Ben Habib wishes to marry—A Maiden's Choice—Sekeletu's Hospitality— Sulphureted Hydrogen and Malaria—Conversations with Makololo—Their moral Character and Conduct—Sekeletu wishes to purchase a Sugar-mill, etc.—The Donkeys—Influence among the Natives—"Food fit for a Chief"—Parting Words of Mamire—Motibe's Excuses.

On the 31st of July we parted with our kind Libonta friends. We planted some of our palm-tree seeds in different villages of this valley. They began to sprout even while we were there, but, unfortunately, they were always destroyed by the mice which swarm in every hut.

At Chitlane's village we collected the young of a colony of the linkololo ('Anastomus lamalligerus'), a black, long-legged bird, somewhat larger than a crow, which lives on shellfish ('Ampullaria'), and breeds in society at certain localities among the reeds. These places are well known, as they continue there from year to year, and belong to the chiefs, who at particular times of the year gather most of the young. The produce of this "harvest", as they call it, which was presented to me, was a hundred and seventy-five unfledged birds. They had been rather late in collecting them, in consequence of waiting for the arrival of Mpololo, who acts the part of chief, but gave them to me, knowing that this would be pleasing to him, otherwise this colony would have yielded double the amount. The old ones appear along the Leeambye in vast flocks, and look lean and scraggy. The young are very fat, and, when roasted, are esteemed one of the dainties of the Barotse valley. In presents of this kind, as well as of oxen, it is a sort of feast of joy, the person to whom they are presented having the honor of distributing the materials of the feast. We generally slaughtered every ox at the village where it was presented, and then our friends and we rejoiced together.

The village of Chitlane is situated, like all others in the Barotse valley, on an eminence, over which floods do not rise; but this last year the water approached nearer to an entire submergence of the whole valley than has been known in the memory of man. Great numbers of people were now suffering from sickness, which always prevails when the waters are drying up, and I found much demand for the medicines I had brought from Loanda. The great variation of the temperature each day must have a trying effect upon the health. At this village there is a real Indian banian-tree, which has spread itself over a considerable space by means of roots from its branches; it has been termed, in consequence, "the tree with legs" (more oa maotu). It is curious that trees of this family are looked upon with veneration, and all the way from the Barotse to Loanda are thought to be preservatives from evil.

On reaching Naliele on the 1st of August we found Mpololo in great affliction on account of the death of his daughter and her child. She had been lately confined; and her father naturally remembered her when an ox was slaughtered, or when the tribute of other food, which he receives in lieu of Sekeletu, came in his way, and sent frequent presents to her. This moved the envy of one of the Makololo who hated Mpololo, and, wishing to vex him, he entered the daughter's hut by night, and strangled both her and her child. He then tried to make fire in the hut and burn it, so that the murder might not be known; but the squeaking noise of rubbing the sticks awakened a servant, and the murderer was detected. Both he and his wife were thrown into the river; the latter having "known of her husband's intentions, and not revealing them." She declared she had dissuaded him from the crime, and, had any one interposed a word, she might have been spared.

Mpololo exerted himself in every way to supply us with other canoes, and we left Shinte's with him. The Mambowe were well received, and departed with friendly messages to their chief Masiko. My men were exceedingly delighted with the cordial reception we met with every where; but a source of annoyance was found where it was not expected. Many of their wives had married other men during our two years' absence. Mashauana's wife, who had borne him two children, was among the number. He wished to appear not to feel it much, saying, "Why, wives are as plentiful as grass, and I can get another: she may go;" but he would add, "If I had that fellow, I would open his ears for him." As most of them had more wives than one, I tried to console them by saying that they had still more than I had, and that they had enough yet; but they felt the reflection to be galling, that while they were toiling, another had been devouring their corn. Some of their wives came with very young infants in their arms. This excited no discontent; and for some I had to speak to the chief to order the men, who had married the only wives some of my companions ever had, to restore them.

SUNDAY, AUGUST 5TH. A large audience listened most attentively to my morning address. Surely some will remember the ideas conveyed, and pray to our merciful Father, who would never have thought of Him but for this visit. The invariably kind and respectful treatment I have received from these, and many other heathen tribes in this central country, together with the attentive observations of many years, have led me to the belief that, if one exerts himself for their good, he will never be ill treated. There may be opposition to his doctrine, but none to the man himself.

While still at Naliele, a party which had been sent after me by Masiko arrived. He was much disappointed because I had not visited him. They brought an elephant's tusk, two calabashes of honey, two baskets of maize, and one of ground-nuts, as a present. Masiko wished to say that he had followed the injunction which I had given as the will of God, and lived in peace until his brother Limboa came, captured his women as they went to their gardens, and then appeared before his stockade. Masiko offered to lead his men out; but they objected, saying, "Let us servants be killed, you must not be slain." Those who said this were young Barotse who had been drilled to fighting by Sebituane, and used shields of ox-hide. They beat off the party of Limboa, ten being wounded, and ten slain in the engagement. Limboa subsequently sent three slaves as a self-imposed fine to Masiko for attacking him. I succeeded in getting the Makololo to treat the messengers of Masiko well, though, as they regarded them as rebels, it was somewhat against the grain at first to speak civilly to them.

Mpololo, attempting to justify an opposite line of conduct, told me how they had fled from Sebituane, even though he had given them numbers of cattle after their subjection by his arms, and was rather surprised to find that I was disposed to think more highly of them for having asserted their independence, even at the loss of milk. For this food, all who have been accustomed to it from infancy in Africa have an excessive longing. I pointed out how they might be mutually beneficial to each other by the exchange of canoes and cattle.

There are some very old Barotse living here who were the companions of the old chief Santuru. These men, protected by their age, were very free in their comments on the "upstart" Makololo. One of them, for instance, interrupted my conversation one day with some Makololo gentlemen with the advice "not to believe them, for they were only a set of thieves;" and it was taken in quite a good-natured way. It is remarkable that none of the ancients here had any tradition of an earthquake having occurred in this region. Their quick perception of events recognizable by the senses, and retentiveness of memory, render it probable that no perceptible movement of the earth has taken place between 7 Deg. and 27 Deg. S. in the centre of the continent during the last two centuries at least. There is no appearance of recent fracture or disturbance of rocks to be seen in the central country, except the falls of Gonye; nor is there any evidence or tradition of hurricanes.

I left Naliele on the 13th of August, and, when proceeding along the shore at midday, a hippopotamus struck the canoe with her forehead, lifting one half of it quite out of the water, so as nearly to overturn it. The force of the butt she gave tilted Mashauana out into the river; the rest of us sprang to the shore, which was only about ten yards off. Glancing back, I saw her come to the surface a short way off, and look to the canoe, as if to see if she had done much mischief. It was a female, whose young one had been speared the day before. No damage was done except wetting person and goods. This is so unusual an occurrence, when the precaution is taken to coast along the shore, that my men exclaimed, "Is the beast mad?" There were eight of us in the canoe at the time, and the shake it received shows the immense power of this animal in the water.

On reaching Gonye, Mokwala, the head man, having presented me with a tusk, I gave it to Pitsane, as he was eagerly collecting ivory for the Loanda market. The rocks of Gonye are reddish gray sandstone, nearly horizontal, and perforated by madrepores, the holes showing the course of the insect in different directions. The rock itself has been impregnated with iron, and that hardened, forms a glaze on the surface—an appearance common to many of the rocks of this country.

AUGUST 22D. This is the end of winter. The trees which line the banks begin to bud and blossom, and there is some show of the influence of the new sap, which will soon end in buds that push off the old foliage by assuming a very bright orange color. This orange is so bright that I mistook it for masses of yellow blossom. There is every variety of shade in the leaves—yellow, purple, copper, liver-color, and even inky black.

Having got the loan of other canoes from Mpololo, and three oxen as provision for the way, which made the number we had been presented with in the Barotse valley amount to thirteen, we proceeded down the river toward Sesheke, and were as much struck as formerly with the noble river. The whole scenery is lovely, though the atmosphere is murky in consequence of the continuance of the smoky tinge of winter.

This peculiar tinge of the atmosphere was observed every winter at Kolobeng, but it was not so observable in Londa as in the south, though I had always considered that it was owing to the extensive burnings of the grass, in which hundreds of miles of pasturage are annually consumed. As the quantity burned in the north is very much greater than in the south, and the smoky tinge of winter was not observed, some other explanation than these burnings must be sought for. I have sometimes imagined that the lowering of the temperature in the winter rendered the vapor in the upper current of air visible, and imparted this hazy appearance.

The amount of organic life is surprising. At the time the river begins to rise, the 'Ibis religiosa' comes down in flocks of fifties, with prodigious numbers of other water-fowl. Some of the sand-banks appear whitened during the day with flocks of pelicans—I once counted three hundred; others are brown with ducks ('Anas histrionica')—I got fourteen of these by one shot ('Querquedula Hottentota', Smith), and other kinds. Great numbers of gulls ('Procellaria turtur', Smith), and several others, float over the surface. The vast quantity of small birds, which feed on insects, show that the river teems also with specimens of minute organic life. In walking among bushes on the banks we are occasionally stung by a hornet, which makes its nest in form like that of our own wasp, and hangs it on the branches of trees. The breeding storgh* is so strong in this insect that it pursues any one twenty or thirty yards who happens to brush too closely past its nest. The sting, which it tries to inflict near the eye, is more like a discharge of electricity from a powerful machine, or a violent blow, than aught else. It produces momentary insensibility, and is followed by the most pungent pain. Yet this insect is quite timid when away from its nest. It is named Murotuani by the Bechuanas.

(Greek) sigma-tau-omicron-rho-gamma-eta.

We have tsetse between Nameta and Sekhosi. An insect of prey, about an inch in length, long-legged and gaunt-looking, may be observed flying about and lighting upon the bare ground. It is a tiger in its way, for it springs upon tsetse and other flies, and, sucking out their blood, throws the bodies aside.

Long before reaching Sesheke we had been informed that a party of Matebele, the people of Mosilikatse, had brought some packages of goods for me to the south bank of the river, near the Victoria Falls, and, though they declared that they had been sent by Mr. Moffat, the Makololo had refused to credit the statement of their sworn enemies. They imagined that the parcels were directed to me as a mere trick, whereby to place witchcraft-medicine into the hands of the Makololo. When the Matebele on the south bank called to the Makololo on the north to come over in canoes and receive the goods sent by Moffat to "Nake", the Makololo replied, "Go along with you, we know better than that; how could he tell Moffat to send his things here, he having gone away to the north?" The Matebele answered, "Here are the goods; we place them now before you, and if you leave them to perish the guilt will be yours." When they had departed the Makololo thought better of it, and, after much divination, went over with fear and trembling, and carried the packages carefully to an island in the middle of the stream; then, building a hut over them to protect them from the weather, they left them; and there I found they had remained from September, 1854, till September, 1855, in perfect safety. Here, as I had often experienced before, I found the news was very old, and had lost much of its interest by keeping, but there were some good eatables from Mrs. Moffat. Among other things, I discovered that my friend, Sir Roderick Murchison, while in his study in London, had arrived at the same conclusion respecting the form of the African continent as I had lately come to on the spot (see note p. 512 [footnote to Chapter 24 Paragraph 7]); and that, from the attentive study of the geological map of Mr. Bain and other materials, some of which were furnished by the discoveries of Mr. Oswell and myself, he had not only clearly enunciated the peculiar configuration as an hypothesis in his discourse before the Geographical Society in 1852, but had even the assurance to send me out a copy for my information! There was not much use in nursing my chagrin at being thus fairly "cut out" by the man who had foretold the existence of the Australian gold before its discovery, for here it was in black and white. In his easy-chair he had forestalled me by three years, though I had been working hard through jungle, marsh, and fever, and, since the light dawned on my mind at Dilolo, had been cherishing the pleasing delusion that I should be the first to suggest the idea that the interior of Africa was a watery plateau of less elevation than flanking hilly ranges.

Having waited a few days at Sesheke till the horses which we had left at Linyanti should arrive, we proceeded to that town, and found the wagon, and every thing we had left in November, 1853, perfectly safe. A grand meeting of all the people was called to receive our report, and the articles which had been sent by the governor and merchants of Loanda. I explained that none of these were my property, but that they were sent to show the friendly feelings of the white men, and their eagerness to enter into commercial relations with the Makololo. I then requested my companions to give a true account of what they had seen. The wonderful things lost nothing in the telling, the climax always being that they had finished the whole world, and had turned only when there was no more land. One glib old gentleman asked, "Then you reached Ma Robert (Mrs. L.)?" They were obliged to confess that she lived a little beyond the world. The presents were received with expressions of great satisfaction and delight; and on Sunday, when Sekeletu made his appearance at church in his uniform, it attracted more attention than the sermon; and the kind expressions they made use of respecting myself were so very flattering that I felt inclined to shut my eyes. Their private opinion must have tallied with their public report, for I very soon received offers from volunteers to accompany me to the east coast. They said they wished to be able to return and relate strange things like my recent companions; and Sekeletu immediately made arrangements with the Arab Ben Habib to conduct a fresh party with a load of ivory to Loanda. These, he said, must go with him and learn to trade: they were not to have any thing to do in the disposal of the ivory, but simply look and learn. My companions were to remain and rest themselves, and then return to Loanda when the others had come home. Sekeletu consulted me as to sending presents back to the governor and merchants of Loanda, but, not possessing much confidence in this Arab, I advised him to send a present by Pitsane, as he knew who ought to receive it.

Since my arrival in England, information has been received from Mr. Gabriel that this party had arrived on the west coast, but that the ivory had been disposed of to some Portuguese merchants in the interior, and the men had been obliged to carry it down to Loanda. They had not been introduced to Mr. Gabriel, but that gentleman, having learned that they were in the city, went to them, and pronounced the names Pitsane, Mashauana, when all started up and crowded round him. When Mr. G. obtained an interpreter, he learned that they had been ordered by Sekeletu to be sure and go to my brother, as he termed him. Mr. G. behaved in the same liberal manner as he had done to my companions, and they departed for their distant home after bidding him a formal and affectionate adieu.

It was to be expected that they would be imposed upon in their first attempt at trading, but I believe that this could not be so easily repeated. It is, however, unfortunate that in dealing with the natives in the interior there is no attempt made at the establishment of fair prices. The trader shows a quantity of goods, the native asks for more, and more is given. The native, being ignorant of the value of the goods or of his ivory, tries what another demand will bring. After some haggling, an addition is made, and that bargain is concluded to the satisfaction of both parties. Another trader comes, and perhaps offers more than the first; the customary demand for an addition is made, and he yields. The natives by this time are beginning to believe that the more they ask the more they will get: they continue to urge, the trader bursts into a rage, and the trade is stopped, to be renewed next day by a higher offer. The natives naturally conclude that they were right the day before, and a most disagreeable commercial intercourse is established. A great amount of time is spent in concluding these bargains. In other parts, it is quite common to see the natives going from one trader to another till they have finished the whole village; and some give presents of brandy to tempt their custom. Much of this unpleasant state of feeling between natives and Europeans results from the commencements made by those who were ignorant of the language, and from the want of education being given at the same time.

During the time of our absence at Loanda, the Makololo had made two forays, and captured large herds of cattle. One, to the lake, was in order to punish Lechulatebe for the insolence he had manifested after procuring some fire-arms; and the other to Sebola Makwaia, a chief living far to the N.E. This was most unjustifiable, and had been condemned by all the influential Makololo. Ben Habib, however, had, in coming from Zanzibar, visited Sebola Makwaia, and found that the chief town was governed by an old woman of that name. She received him kindly, and gave him a large quantity of magnificent ivory, sufficient to set him up as a trader, at a very small cost; but, his party having discharged their guns, Ben Habib observed that the female chief and her people were extremely alarmed, and would have fled and left their cattle in a panic, had he not calmed their fears. Ben Habib informed the uncle of Sekeletu that he could easily guide him thither, and he might get a large number of cattle without any difficulty. This uncle advised Sekeletu to go; and, as the only greatness he knew was imitation of his father's deeds, he went, but was not so successful as was anticipated. Sebola Makwaia had fled on hearing of the approach of the Makololo; and, as the country is marshy and intersected in every direction by rivers, they could not easily pursue her. They captured canoes, and, pursuing up different streams, came to a small lake called "Shuia". Having entered the Loangwa, flowing to the eastward, they found it advisable to return, as the natives in those parts became more warlike the further they went in that direction. Before turning, the Arab pointed out an elevated ridge in the distance, and said to the Makololo, "When we see that, we always know that we are only ten or fifteen days from the sea." On seeing him afterward, he informed me that on the same ridge, but much further to the north, the Banyassa lived, and that the rivers flowed from it toward the S.W. He also confirmed the other Arab's account that the Loapula, which he had crossed at the town of Cazembe, flowed in the same direction, and into the Leeambye.

Several of the influential Makololo who had engaged in these marauding expeditions had died before our arrival, and Nokwane had succumbed to his strange disease. Ramosantane had perished through vomiting blood from over-fatigue in the march, and Lerimo was affected by a leprosy peculiar to the Barotse valley. In accordance with the advice of my Libonta friends, I did not fail to reprove "my child Sekeletu" for his marauding. This was not done in an angry manner, for no good is ever achieved by fierce denunciations. Motibe, his father-in-law, said to me, "Scold him much, but don't let others hear you."

The Makololo expressed great satisfaction with the route we had opened up to the west, and soon after our arrival a "picho" was called, in order to discuss the question of removal to the Barotse valley, so that they might be nearer the market. Some of the older men objected to abandoning the line of defense afforded by the rivers Chobe and Zambesi against their southern enemies the Matebele. The Makololo generally have an aversion to the Barotse valley, on account of the fevers which are annually engendered in it as the waters dry up. They prefer it only as a cattle station; for, though the herds are frequently thinned by an epidemic disease (peripneumonia), they breed so fast that the losses are soon made good. Wherever else the Makololo go, they always leave a portion of their stock in the charge of herdsmen in that prolific valley. Some of the younger men objected to removal, because the rankness of the grass at the Barotse did not allow of their running fast, and because there "it never becomes cool."

Sekeletu at last stood up, and, addressing me, said, "I am perfectly satisfied as to the great advantages for trade of the path which you have opened, and think that we ought to go to the Barotse, in order to make the way from us to Loanda shorter; but with whom am I to live there? If you were coming with us, I would remove to-morrow; but now you are going to the white man's country to bring Ma Robert, and when you return you will find me near to the spot on which you wish to dwell." I had then no idea that any healthy spot existed in the country, and thought only of a convenient central situation, adapted for intercourse with the adjacent tribes and with the coast, such as that near to the confluence of the Leeba and Leeambye.

The fever is certainly a drawback to this otherwise important missionary field. The great humidity produced by heavy rains and inundations, the exuberant vegetation caused by fervid heat in rich moist soil, and the prodigious amount of decaying vegetable matter annually exposed after the inundations to the rays of a torrid sun, with a flat surface often covered by forest through which the winds can not pass, all combine to render the climate far from salubrious for any portion of the human family. But the fever, thus caused and rendered virulent, is almost the only disease prevalent in it. There is no consumption or scrofula, and but little insanity. Smallpox and measles visited the country some thirty years ago and cut off many, but they have since made no return, although the former has been almost constantly in one part or another of the coast. Singularly enough, the people used inoculation for this disease; and in one village, where they seem to have chosen a malignant case from which to inoculate the rest, nearly the whole village was cut off. I have seen but one case of hydrocephalus, a few of epilepsy, none of cholera or cancer, and many diseases common in England are here quite unknown. It is true that I suffered severely from fever, but my experience can not be taken as a fair criterion in the matter. Compelled to sleep on the damp ground month after month, exposed to drenching showers, and getting the lower extremities wetted two or three times every day, living on native food (with the exception of sugarless coffee, during the journey to the north and the latter half of the return journey), and that food the manioc roots and meal, which contain so much uncombined starch that the eyes become affected (as in the case of animals fed for experiment on pure gluten or starch), and being exposed during many hours each day in comparative inaction to the direct rays of the sun, the thermometer standing above 96 Deg. in the shade—these constitute a more pitiful hygiene than any missionaries who may follow will ever have to endure. I do not mention these privations as if I considered them to be "sacrifices", for I think that the word ought never to be applied to any thing we can do for Him who came down from heaven and died for us; but I suppose it is necessary to notice them, in order that no unfavorable opinion may be formed from my experience as to what that of others might be, if less exposed to the vicissitudes of the weather and change of diet.

I believe that the interior of this country presents a much more inviting field for the philanthropist than does the west coast, where missionaries of the Church Missionary, United Presbyterian, and other societies have long labored with most astonishing devotedness and never-flagging zeal. There the fevers are much more virulent and more speedily fatal than here, for from 8 Deg. south they almost invariably take the intermittent or least fatal type; and their effect being to enlarge the spleen, a complaint which is best treated by change of climate, we have the remedy at hand by passing the 20th parallel on our way south. But I am not to be understood as intimating that any of the numerous tribes are anxious for instruction: they are not the inquiring spirits we read of in other countries; they do not desire the Gospel, because they know nothing about either it or its benefits; but there is no impediment in the way of instruction. Every head man would be proud of a European visitor or resident in his territory, and there is perfect security for life and property all over the interior country. The great barriers which have kept Africa shut are the unhealthiness of the coast, and the exclusive, illiberal disposition of the border tribes. It has not within the historic period been cut into by deep arms of the sea, and only a small fringe of its population have come into contact with the rest of mankind. Race has much to do in the present circumstances of nations; yet it is probable that the unhealthy coast-climate has reacted on the people, and aided both in perpetuating their own degradation and preventing those more inland from having intercourse with the rest of the world. It is to be hoped that these obstacles will be overcome by the more rapid means of locomotion possessed in the present age, if a good highway can become available from the coast into the interior.

Having found it impracticable to open up a carriage-path to the west, it became a question as to which part of the east coast we should direct our steps. The Arabs had come from Zanzibar through a peaceful country. They assured me that the powerful chiefs beyond the Cazembe on the N.E., viz., Moatutu, Moaroro, and Mogogo, chiefs of the tribes Batutu, Baroro, and Bagogo, would have no objection to my passing through their country. They described the population there as located in small villages like the Balonda, and that no difficulty is experienced in traveling among them. They mentioned also that, at a distance of ten days beyond Cazembe, their path winds round the end of Lake Tanganyenka. But when they reach this lake, a little to the northwest of its southern extremity, they find no difficulty in obtaining canoes to carry them over. They sleep on islands, for it is said to require three days in crossing, and may thus be forty or fifty miles broad. Here they punt the canoes the whole way, showing that it is shallow. There are many small streams in the path, and three large rivers. This, then, appeared to me to be the safest; but my present object being a path admitting of water rather than land carriage, this route did not promise so much as that by way of the Zambesi or Leeambye. The Makololo knew all the country eastward as far as the Kafue, from having lived in former times near the confluence of that river with the Zambesi, and they all advised this path in preference to that by the way of Zanzibar. The only difficulty that they assured me of was that in the falls of Victoria. Some recommended my going to Sesheke, and crossing over in a N.E. direction to the Kafue, which is only six days distant, and descending that river to the Zambesi. Others recommended me to go on the south bank of the Zambesi until I had passed the falls, then get canoes and proceed farther down the river. All spoke strongly of the difficulties of traveling on the north bank, on account of the excessively broken and rocky nature of the country near the river on that side. And when Ponuane, who had lately headed a foray there, proposed that I should carry canoes along that side till we reached the spot where the Leeambye becomes broad and placid again, others declared that, from the difficulties he himself had experienced in forcing the men of his expedition to do this, they believed that mine would be sure to desert me if I attempted to impose such a task upon them. Another objection to traveling on either bank of the river was the prevalence of the tsetse, which is so abundant that the inhabitants can keep no domestic animals except goats.

While pondering over these different paths, I could not help regretting my being alone. If I had enjoyed the company of my former companion, Mr. Oswell, one of us might have taken the Zambesi, and the other gone by way of Zanzibar. The latter route was decidedly the easiest, because all the inland tribes were friendly, while the tribes in the direction of the Zambesi were inimical, and I should now be obliged to lead a party, which the Batoka of that country view as hostile invaders, through an enemy's land; but, as the prospect of permanent water-conveyance was good, I decided on going down the Zambesi, and keeping on the north bank, because, in the map given by Bowditch, Tete, the farthest inland station of the Portuguese, is erroneously placed on that side. Being near the end of September, the rains were expected daily; the clouds were collecting, and the wind blew strongly from the east, but it was excessively hot. All the Makololo urged me strongly to remain till the ground should be cooled by the rains; and as it was probable that I should get fever if I commenced my journey now, I resolved to wait. The parts of the country about 17 Deg. and 18 Deg. suffer from drought and become dusty. It is but the commencement of the humid region to the north, and partakes occasionally of the character of both the wet and dry regions. Some idea may be formed of the heat in October by the fact that the thermometer (protected) stood, in the shade of my wagon, at 100 Deg. through the day. It rose to 110 Deg. if unprotected from the wind; at dark it showed 89 Deg.; at 10 o'clock, 80 Deg.; and then gradually sunk till sunrise, when it was 70 Deg. That is usually the period of greatest cold in each twenty-four hours in this region. The natives, during the period of greatest heat, keep in their huts, which are always pleasantly cool by day, but close and suffocating by night. Those who are able to afford it sit guzzling beer or boyaloa. The perspiration produced by copious draughts seems to give enjoyment, the evaporation causing a feeling of coolness. The attendants of the chief, on these occasions, keep up a continuous roar of bantering, raillery, laughing, and swearing. The dance is kept up in the moonlight till past midnight. The women stand clapping their hands continuously, and the old men sit admiringly, and say, "It is really very fine." As crowds came to see me, I employed much of my time in conversation, that being a good mode of conveying instruction. In the public meetings for worship the people listened very attentively, and behaved with more decorum than formerly. They really form a very inviting field for a missionary. Surely the oft-told tale of the goodness and love of our heavenly Father, in giving up his own Son to death for us sinners, will, by the power of his Holy Spirit, beget love in some of these heathen hearts.

1ST OCTOBER. Before Ben Habib started for Loanda, he asked the daughter of Sebituane in marriage. This is the plan the Arabs adopt for gaining influence in a tribe, and they have been known to proceed thus cautiously to form connections, and gradually gain so much influence as to draw all the tribe over to their religion. I never heard of any persecution, although the Arabs with whom I came in contact seemed much attached to their religion. This daughter of Sebituane, named Manchunyane, was about twelve years of age. As I was the bosom-friend of her father, I was supposed to have a voice in her disposal, and, on being asked, objected to her being taken away, we knew not whither, and where we might never see her again. As her name implies, she was only a little black, and, besides being as fair as any of the Arabs, had quite the Arab features; but I have no doubt that Ben Habib will renew his suit more successfully on some other occasion. In these cases of marriage, the consent of the young women is seldom asked. A maid-servant of Sekeletu, however, pronounced by the Makololo to be good-looking, was at this time sought in marriage by five young men. Sekeletu, happening to be at my wagon when one of these preferred his suit, very coolly ordered all five to stand in a row before the young woman, that she might make her choice. Two refused to stand, apparently, because they could not brook the idea of a repulse, although willing enough to take her if Sekeletu had acceded to their petition without reference to her will. Three dandified fellows stood forth, and she unhesitatingly decided on taking one who was really the best looking. It was amusing to see the mortification exhibited on the black faces of the unsuccessful candidates, while the spectators greeted them with a hearty laugh.

During the whole of my stay with the Makololo, Sekeletu supplied my wants abundantly, appointing some cows to furnish me with milk, and, when he went out to hunt, sent home orders for slaughtered oxen to be given. That the food was not given in a niggardly spirit may be inferred from the fact that, when I proposed to depart on the 20th of October, he protested against my going off in such a hot sun. "Only wait," said he, "for the first shower, and then I will let you go." This was reasonable, for the thermometer, placed upon a deal box in the sun, rose to 138 Deg. It stood at 108 Deg. in the shade by day, and 96 Deg. at sunset. If my experiments were correct, the blood of a European is of a higher temperature than that of an African. The bulb, held under my tongue, stood at 100 Deg.; under that of the natives, at 98 Deg. There was much sickness in the town, and no wonder, for part of the water left by the inundation still formed a large pond in the centre. Even the plains between Linyanti and Sesheke had not yet been freed from the waters of the inundation. They had risen higher than usual, and for a long time canoes passed from the one place to the other, a distance of upward of 120 miles, in nearly a straight line. We found many patches of stagnant water, which, when disturbed by our passing through them, evolved strong effluvia of sulphureted hydrogen. At other times these spots exhibit an efflorescence of the nitrate of soda; they also contain abundance of lime, probably from decaying vegetable matter, and from these may have emanated the malaria which caused the present sickness. I have often remarked this effluvium in sickly spots, and can not help believing but that it has some connection with fever, though I am quite aware of Dr. MacWilliams's unsuccessful efforts to discover sulphureted hydrogen, by the most delicate tests, in the Niger expedition.

 I had plenty of employment, for, besides attending to the severer cases, I had perpetual calls on my attention. The town contained at least 7000 inhabitants, and every one thought that he might come, and at least look at me. In talking with some of the more intelligent in the evenings, the conversation having turned from inquiries respecting eclipses of the sun and moon to that other world where Jesus reigns, they let me know that my attempts to enlighten them had not been without some small effect. "Many of the children," said they, "talk about the strange things you bring to their ears, but the old men show a little opposition by saying, 'Do we know what he is talking about?'" Ntlaria and others complain of treacherous memories, and say, "When we hear words about other things, we hold them fast; but when we hear you tell much more wonderful things than any we have ever heard before, we don't know how it is, they run away from our hearts." These are the more intelligent of my Makololo friends. On the majority the teaching produces no appreciable effect; they assent to the truth with the most perplexing indifference, adding, "But we don't know," or, "We do not understand." My medical intercourse with them enabled me to ascertain their moral status better than a mere religious teacher could do. They do not attempt to hide the evil, as men often do, from their spiritual instructors;

but I have found it difficult to come to a conclusion on their character. They sometimes perform actions remarkably good, and sometimes as strangely the opposite. I have been unable to ascertain the motive for the good, or account for the callousness of conscience with which they perpetrate the bad. After long observation, I came to the conclusion that they are just such a strange mixture of good and evil as men are every where else. There is not among them an approach to that constant stream of benevolence flowing from the rich to the poor which we have in England, nor yet the unostentatious attentions which we have among our own poor to each other. Yet there are frequent instances of genuine kindness and liberality, as well as actions of an opposite character. The rich show kindness to the poor in expectation of services, and a poor person who has no relatives will seldom be supplied even with water in illness, and, when dead, will be dragged out to be devoured by the hyaenas instead of being buried. Relatives alone will condescend to touch a dead body. It would be easy to enumerate instances of inhumanity which I have witnessed. An interesting-looking girl came to my wagon one day in a state of nudity, and almost a skeleton. She was a captive from another tribe, and had been neglected by the man who claimed her. Having supplied her wants, I made inquiry for him, and found that he had been unsuccessful in raising a crop of corn, and had no food to give her. I volunteered to take her; but he said he would allow me to feed her and make her fat, and then take her away. I protested against his heartlessness; and, as he said he could "not part with his child," I was precluded from attending to her wants. In a day or two she was lost sight of. She had gone out a little way from the town, and, being too weak to return, had been cruelly left to perish. Another day I saw a poor boy going to the water to drink, apparently in a starving condition. This case I brought before the chief in council, and found that his emaciation was ascribed to disease and want combined. He was not one of the Makololo, but a member of a subdued tribe. I showed them that any one professing to claim a child, and refusing proper nutriment, would be guilty of his death. Sekeletu decided that the owner of this boy should give up his alleged right rather than destroy the child. When I took him he was so far gone as to be in the cold stage of starvation, but was soon brought round by a little milk given three or four times a day. On leaving Linyanti I handed him over to the charge of his chief, Sekeletu, who feeds his servants very well. On the other hand, I have seen instances in which both men and women have taken up little orphans and carefully reared them as their own children. By a selection of cases of either kind, it would not be difficult to make these people appear excessively good or uncommonly bad.

 I still possessed some of the coffee which I had brought from Angola, and some of the sugar which I had left in my wagon. So long as the sugar lasted, Sekeletu favored me with his company at meals; but the sugar soon came to a close. The Makololo, as formerly mentioned, were well acquainted with the sugar-cane, as it is cultivated by the Barotse, but never knew that sugar could be got from it. When I explained the process by which it was produced, Sekeletu asked if I could not buy him an apparatus for the purpose of making sugar. He said that he would plant the cane largely if he only had the means of making the sugar from it. I replied that I was unable to purchase a mill, when he instantly rejoined, "Why not take ivory to buy it?" As I had been living at his expense, I was glad of the opportunity to show my gratitude by serving him; and when he and his principal men understood that I was willing to execute a commission, Sekeletu gave me an order for a sugar-mill, and for all the different varieties of clothing that he had ever seen, especially a mohair coat, a good rifle, beads, brass-wire, etc., etc., and wound up by saying, "And any other beautiful thing you may see in your own country." As to the quantity of ivory required to execute the commission, I said I feared that a large amount would be necessary. Both he and his councilors replied, "The ivory is all your own; if you leave any in the country it will be your own fault." He was also anxious for horses. The two I had left with him when I went to Loanda were still living, and had been of great use to him in hunting the giraffe and eland, and he was now anxious to have a breed. This, I thought, might be obtained at the Portuguese settlements. All were very much delighted with the donkeys we had brought from Loanda. As we found that they were not affected by the bite of the tsetse, and there was a prospect of the breed being continued, it was gratifying to see the experiment of their introduction so far successful. The donkeys came as frisky as kids all the way from Loanda until we began to descend the Leeambye. There we came upon so many interlacing branches of the river, and were obliged to drag them through such masses of tangled aquatic plants, that we half drowned them, and were at last obliged to leave them somewhat exhausted at Naliele. They excited the unbounded admiration of my men by their knowledge of the different kinds of plants, which, as they remarked, "the animals had never before seen in their own country;" and when the donkeys indulged in their music, they startled the inhabitants more than if they had been lions. We never rode them, nor yet the horse which had been given by the bishop, for fear of hurting them by any work.

Although the Makololo were so confiding, the reader must not imagine that they would be so to every individual who might visit them. Much of my influence depended upon the good name given me by the Bakwains, and that I secured only through a long course of tolerably good conduct. No one ever gains much influence in this country without purity and uprightness. The acts of a stranger are keenly scrutinized by both young and old, and seldom is the judgment pronounced, even by the heathen, unfair or uncharitable. I have heard women speaking in admiration of a white man because he was pure, and never was guilty of any secret immorality. Had he been, they would have known it, and, untutored heathen though they be, would have despised him in consequence. Secret vice becomes known throughout the tribe; and while one, unacquainted with the language, may imagine a peccadillo to be hidden, it is as patent to all as it would be in London had he a placard on his back.

27TH OCTOBER, 1855. The first continuous rain of the season commenced during the night, the wind being from the N.E., as it always was on like occasions at Kolobeng. The rainy season was thus begun, and I made ready to go. The mother of Sekeletu prepared a bag of ground-nuts, by frying them in cream with a little salt, as a sort of sandwiches for my journey. This is considered food fit for a chief. Others ground the maize from my own garden into meal, and Sekeletu pointed out Sekwebu and Kanyata as the persons who should head the party intended to form my company. Sekwebu had been captured by the Matebele when a little boy, and the tribe in which he was a captive had migrated to the country near Tete; he had traveled along both banks of the Zambesi several times, and was intimately acquainted with the dialects spoken there. I found him to be a person of great prudence and sound judgment, and his subsequent loss at the Mauritius has been, ever since, a source of sincere regret. He at once recommended our keeping well away from the river, on account of the tsetse and rocky country, assigning also as a reason for it that the Leeambye beyond the falls turns round to the N.N.E. Mamire, who had married the mother of Sekeletu, on coming to bid me farewell before starting, said, "You are now going among people who can not be trusted because we have used them badly; but you go with a different message from any they ever heard before, and Jesus will be with you and help you, though among enemies; and if he carries you safely, and brings you and Ma Robert back again, I shall say he has bestowed a great favor upon me. May we obtain a path whereby we may visit and be visited by other tribes, and by white men!" On telling him my fears that he was still inclined to follow the old marauding system, which prevented intercourse, and that he, from his influential position, was especially guilty in the late forays, he acknowledged all rather too freely for my taste, but seemed quite aware that the old system was far from right. Mentioning my inability to pay the men who were to accompany me, he replied, "A man wishes, of course, to appear among his friends, after a long absence, with something of his own to show; the whole of the ivory in the country is yours, so you must take as much as you can, and Sekeletu will furnish men to carry it." These remarks of Mamire are quoted literally, in order to show the state of mind of the most influential in the tribe. And as I wish to give the reader a fair idea of the other side of the question as well, it may be mentioned that Motibe parried the imputation of the guilt of marauding by every possible subterfuge. He would not admit that they had done wrong, and laid the guilt of the wars in which the Makololo had engaged on the Boers, the Matebele, and every other tribe except his own. When quite a youth, Motibe's family had been attacked by a party of Boers; he hid himself in an ant-eater's hole, but was drawn out and thrashed with a whip of hippopotamus hide. When enjoined to live in peace, he would reply, "Teach the Boers to lay down their arms first." Yet Motibe, on other occasions, seemed to feel the difference between those who are Christians indeed and those who are so only in name. In all our discussions we parted good friends.

Chapter 26

Departure from Linyanti—A Thunder-storm—An Act of genuine Kindness— Fitted out a second time by the Makololo—Sail down the Leeambye— Sekote's Kotla and human Skulls; his Grave adorned with Elephants' Tusks—Victoria Falls—Native Names—Columns of Vapor—Gigantic Crack— Wear of the Rocks—Shrines of the Barimo—"The Pestle of the Gods"— Second Visit to the Falls—Island Garden—Store-house Island—Native Diviners—A European Diviner—Makololo Foray—Marauder to be fined—Mambari—Makololo wish to stop Mambari Slave-trading—Part with Sekeletu—Night Traveling—River Lekone—Ancient fresh-water Lakes—Formation of Lake Ngami—Native Traditions—Drainage of the Great Valley—Native Reports of the Country to the North—Maps—Moyara's Village—Savage Customs of the Batoka—A Chain of Trading Stations—Remedy against Tsetse—"The Well of Joy"—First Traces of Trade with Europeans—Knocking out the front Teeth—Facetious Explanation—Degradation of the Batoka—Description of the Traveling Party—Cross the Unguesi—Geological Formation—Ruins of a large Town— Productions of the Soil similar to those in Angola—Abundance of Fruit.

On the 3d of November we bade adieu to our friends at Linyanti, accompanied by Sekeletu and about 200 followers. We were all fed at his expense, and he took cattle for this purpose from every station we came to. The principal men of the Makololo, Lebeole, Ntlarie, Nkwatlele, etc., were also of the party. We passed through the patch of the tsetse, which exists between Linyanti and Sesheke, by night. The majority of the company went on by daylight, in order to prepare our beds. Sekeletu and I, with about forty young men, waited outside the tsetse till dark. We then went forward, and about ten o'clock it became so pitchy dark that both horses and men were completely blinded. The lightning spread over the sky, forming eight or ten branches at a time, in shape exactly like those of a tree. This, with great volumes of sheet-lightning, enabled us at times to see the whole country. The intervals between the flashes were so densely dark as to convey the idea of stone-blindness. The horses trembled, cried out, and turned round, as if searching for each other, and every new flash revealed the men taking different directions, laughing, and stumbling against each other. The thunder was of that tremendously loud kind only to be heard in tropical countries, and which friends from India have assured me is louder in Africa than any they have ever heard elsewhere. Then came a pelting rain, which completed our confusion. After the intense heat of the day, we soon felt miserably cold, and turned aside to a fire we saw in the distance. This had been made by some people on their march; for this path is seldom without numbers of strangers passing to and from the capital. My clothing having gone on, I lay down on the cold ground, expecting to spend a miserable night; but Sekeletu kindly covered me with his own blanket, and lay uncovered himself. I was much affected by this act of genuine kindness. If such men must perish by the advance of civilization, as certain races of animals do before others, it is a pity. God grant that ere this time comes they may receive that Gospel which is a solace for the soul in death!

While at Sesheke, Sekeletu supplied me with twelve oxen—three of which were accustomed to being ridden upon—hoes, and beads to purchase a canoe when we should strike the Leeambye beyond the falls. He likewise presented abundance of good fresh butter and honey, and did every thing in his power to make me comfortable for the journey. I was entirely dependent on his generosity, for the goods I originally brought from the Cape were all expended by the time I set off from Linyanti to the west coast. I there drew 70 Pounds of my salary, paid my men with it, and purchased goods for the return journey to Linyanti. These being now all expended, the Makololo again fitted me out, and sent me on to the east coast. I was thus dependent on their bounty, and that of other Africans, for the means of going from Linyanti to Loanda, and again from Linyanti to the east coast, and I feel deeply grateful to them. Coin would have been of no benefit, for gold and silver are quite unknown. We were here joined by Moriantsane, uncle of Sekeletu and head man of Sesheke, and, entering canoes on the 13th, some sailed down the river to the confluence of the Chobe, while others drove the cattle along the banks, spending one night at Mparia, the island at the confluence of the Chobe, which is composed of trap, having crystals of quartz in it coated with a pellicle of green copper ore. Attempting to proceed down the river next day, we were detained some hours by a strong east wind raising waves so large as to threaten to swamp the canoes. The river here is very large and deep, and contains two considerable islands, which from either bank seem to be joined to the opposite shore. While waiting for the wind to moderate, my friends related the traditions of these islands, and, as usual, praised the wisdom of Sebituane in balking the Batoka, who formerly enticed wandering tribes to them, and starved them, by compelling the chiefs to remain by his side till all his cattle and people were ferried over. The Barotse believe that at certain parts of the river a tremendous monster lies hid, and that it will catch a canoe, and hold it fast and motionless, in spite of the utmost exertions of the paddlers. While near Nameta they even objected to pass a spot supposed to be haunted, and proceeded along a branch instead of the main stream. They believe that some of them possess a knowledge of the proper prayer to lay the monster. It is strange to find fables similar to those of the more northern nations even in the heart of Africa. Can they be the vestiges of traditions of animals which no longer exist? The fossil bones which lie in the calcareous tufa of this region will yet, we hope, reveal the ancient fauna.

Having descended about ten miles, we came to the island of Nampene, at the beginning of the rapids, where we were obliged to leave the canoes and proceed along the banks on foot. The next evening we slept opposite the island of Chondo, and, then crossing the Lekone or Lekwine, early the following morning were at the island of Sekote, called Kalai. This Sekote was the last of the Batoka chiefs whom Sebituane rooted out. The island is surrounded by a rocky shore and deep channels, through which the river rushes with great force. Sekote, feeling secure in his island home, ventured to ferry over the Matebele enemies of Sebituane. When they had retired, Sebituane made one of those rapid marches which he always adopted in every enterprise. He came down the Leeambye from Naliele, sailing by day along the banks, and during the night in the middle of the stream, to avoid the hippopotami. When he reached Kalai, Sekote took advantage of the larger canoes they employ in the rapids, and fled during the night to the opposite bank. Most of his people were slain or taken captive, and the island has ever since been under the Makololo. It is large enough to contain a considerable town. On the northern side I found the kotla of the elder Sekote, garnished with numbers of human skulls mounted on poles: a large heap of the crania of hippopotami, the tusks untouched except by time, stood on one side. At a short distance, under some trees, we saw the grave of Sekote, ornamented with seventy large elephants' tusks planted round it with the points turned inward, and there were thirty more placed over the resting-places of his relatives. These were all decaying from the effects of the sun and weather; but a few, which had enjoyed the shade, were in a pretty good condition. I felt inclined to take a specimen of the tusks of the hippopotami, as they were the largest I had ever seen, but feared that the people would look upon me as a "resurrectionist" if I did, and regard any unfavorable event which might afterward occur as a punishment for the sacrilege. The Batoka believe that Sekote had a pot of medicine buried here, which, when opened, would cause an epidemic in the country. These tyrants acted much on the fears of their people.

As this was the point from which we intended to strike off to the northeast, I resolved on the following day to visit the falls of Victoria, called by the natives Mosioatunya, or more anciently Shongwe. Of these we had often heard since we came into the country; indeed, one of the questions asked by Sebituane was, "Have you smoke that sounds in your country?" They did not go near enough to examine them, but, viewing them with awe at a distance, said, in reference to the vapor and noise, "Mosi oa tunya" (smoke does sound there). It was previously called Shongwe, the meaning of which I could not ascertain. The word for a "pot" resembles this, and it may mean a seething caldron, but I am not certain of it. Being persuaded that Mr. Oswell and myself were the very first Europeans who ever visited the Zambesi in the centre of the country, and that this is the connecting link between the known and unknown portions of that river, I decided to use the same liberty as the Makololo did, and gave the only English name I have affixed to any part of the country. No better proof of previous ignorance of this river could be desired than that an untraveled gentleman, who had spent a great part of his life in the study of the geography of Africa, and knew every thing written on the subject from the time of Ptolemy downward, actually asserted in the "Athenaeum", while I was coming up the Red Sea, that this magnificent river, the Leeambye, had "no connection with the Zambesi, but flowed under the Kalahari Desert, and became lost;" and "that, as all the old maps asserted, the Zambesi took its rise in the very hills to which we have now come." This modest assertion smacks exactly as if a native of Timbuctoo should declare that the "Thames" and the "Pool" were different rivers, he having seen neither the one nor the other. Leeambye and Zambesi mean the very same thing, viz., the RIVER.

Sekeletu intended to accompany me, but, one canoe only having come instead of the two he had ordered, he resigned it to me. After twenty minutes' sail from Kalai we came in sight, for the first time, of the columns of vapor appropriately called "smoke", rising at a distance of five or six miles, exactly as when large tracts of grass are burned in Africa. Five columns now arose, and, bending in the direction of the wind, they seemed placed against a low ridge covered with trees; the tops of the columns at this distance appeared to mingle with the clouds. They were white below, and higher up became dark, so as to simulate smoke very closely. The whole scene was extremely beautiful; the banks and islands dotted over the river are adorned with sylvan vegetation of great variety of color and form. At the period of our visit several trees were spangled over with blossoms. Trees have each their own physiognomy. There, towering over all, stands the great burly baobab, each of whose enormous arms would form the trunk of a large tree, beside groups of graceful palms, which, with their feathery-shaped leaves depicted on the sky, lend their beauty to the scene. As a hieroglyphic they always mean "far from home", for one can never get over their foreign air in a picture or landscape. The silvery mohonono, which in the tropics is in form like the cedar of Lebanon, stands in pleasing contrast with the dark color of the motsouri, whose cypress-form is dotted over at present with its pleasant scarlet fruit. Some trees resemble the great spreading oak, others assume the character of our own elms and chestnuts; but no one can imagine the beauty of the view from any thing witnessed in England. It had never been seen before by European eyes; but scenes so lovely must have been gazed upon by angels in their flight. The only want felt is that of mountains in the background. The falls are bounded on three sides by ridges 300 or 400 feet in height, which are covered with forest, with the red soil appearing among the trees. When about half a mile from the falls, I left the canoe by which we had come down thus far, and embarked in a lighter one, with men well acquainted with the rapids, who, by passing down the centre of the stream in the eddies and still places caused by many jutting rocks, brought me to an island situated in the middle of the river, and on the edge of the lip over which the water rolls. In coming hither there was danger of being swept down by the streams which rushed along on each side of the island; but the river was now low, and we sailed where it is totally impossible to go when the water is high. But, though we had reached the island, and were within a few yards of the spot, a view from which would solve the whole problem, I believe that no one could perceive where the vast body of water went; it seemed to lose itself in the earth, the opposite lip of the fissure into which it disappeared being only 80 feet distant. At least I did not comprehend it until, creeping with awe to the verge, I peered down into a large rent which had been made from bank to bank of the broad Zambesi, and saw that a stream of a thousand yards broad leaped down a hundred feet, and then became suddenly compressed into a space of fifteen or twenty yards. The entire falls are simply a crack made in a hard basaltic rock from the right to the left bank of the Zambesi, and then prolonged from the left bank away through thirty or forty miles of hills. If one imagines the Thames filled with low, tree-covered hills immediately beyond the tunnel, extending as far as Gravesend, the bed of black basaltic rock instead of London mud, and a fissure made therein from one end of the tunnel to the other down through the keystones of the arch, and prolonged from the left end of the tunnel through thirty miles of hills, the pathway being 100 feet down from the bed of the river instead of what it is, with the lips of the fissure from 80 to 100 feet apart, then fancy the Thames leaping bodily into the gulf, and forced there to change its direction, and flow from the right to the left bank, and then rush boiling and roaring through the hills, he may have some idea of what takes place at this, the most wonderful sight I had witnessed in Africa. In looking down into the fissure on the right of the island, one sees nothing but a dense white cloud, which, at the time we visited the spot, had two bright rainbows on it. (The sun was on the meridian, and the declination about equal to the latitude of the place.) From this cloud rushed up a great jet of vapor exactly like steam, and it mounted 200 or 300 feet high; there condensing, it changed its hue to that of dark smoke, and came back in a constant shower, which soon wetted us to the skin. This shower falls chiefly on the opposite side of the fissure, and a few yards back from the lip there stands a straight hedge of evergreen trees, whose leaves are always wet. From their roots a number of little rills run back into the gulf, but, as they flow down the steep wall there, the column of vapor, in its ascent, licks them up clean off the rock, and away they mount again. They are constantly running down, but never reach the bottom.

On the left of the island we see the water at the bottom, a white rolling mass moving away to the prolongation of the fissure, which branches off near the left bank of the river. A piece of the rock has fallen off a spot on the left of the island, and juts out from the water below, and from it I judged the distance which the water falls to be about 100 feet. The walls of this gigantic crack are perpendicular, and composed of one homogeneous mass of rock. The edge of that side over which the water falls is worn off two or three feet, and pieces have fallen away, so as to give it somewhat of a serrated appearance. That over which the water does not fall is quite straight, except at the left corner, where a rent appears, and a piece seems inclined to fall off. Upon the whole, it is nearly in the state in which it was left at the period of its formation. The rock is dark brown in color, except about ten feet from the bottom, which is discolored by the annual rise of the water to that or a greater height. On the left side of the island we have a good view of the mass of water which causes one of the columns of vapor to ascend, as it leaps quite clear of the rock, and forms a thick unbroken fleece all the way to the bottom. Its whiteness gave the idea of snow, a sight I had not seen for many a day. As it broke into (if I may use the term) pieces of water, all rushing on in the same direction, each gave off several rays of foam, exactly as bits of steel, when burned in oxygen gas, give off rays of sparks. The snow-white sheet seemed like myriads of small comets rushing on in one direction, each of which left behind its nucleus rays of foam. I never saw the appearance referred to noticed elsewhere. It seemed to be the effect of the mass of water leaping at once clear of the rock, and but slowly breaking up into spray.

I have mentioned that we saw five columns of vapor ascending from this strange abyss. They are evidently formed by the compression suffered by the force of the water's own fall into an unyielding wedge-shaped space. Of the five columns, two on the right and one on the left of the island were the largest, and the streams which formed them seemed each to exceed in size the falls of the Clyde at Stonebyres when that river is in flood. This was the period of low water in the Leeambye; but, as far as I could guess, there was a flow of five or six hundred yards of water, which, at the edge of the fall, seemed at least three feet deep. I write in the hope that others, more capable of judging distances than myself, will visit the scene, and I state simply the impressions made on my mind at the time. I thought, and do still think, the river above the falls to be one thousand yards broad; but I am a poor judge of distances on water, for I showed a naval friend what I supposed to be four hundred yards in the Bay of Loanda, and, to my surprise, he pronounced it to be nine hundred. I tried to measure the Leeambye with a strong thread, the only line I had in my possession, but, when the men had gone two or three hundred yards, they got into conversation, and did not hear us shouting that the line had become entangled. By still going on they broke it, and, being carried away down the stream, it was lost on a snag. In vain I tried to bring to my recollection the way I had been taught to measure a river by taking an angle with the sextant. That I once knew it, and that it was easy, were all the lost ideas I could recall, and they only increased my vexation. However, I measured the river farther down by another plan, and then I discovered that the Portuguese had measured it at Tete, and found it a little over one thousand yards. At the falls it is as broad as at Tete, if not more so. Whoever may come after me will not, I trust, find reason to say I have indulged in exaggeration.* With respect to the drawing, it must be borne in mind that it was composed from a rude sketch as viewed from the island, which exhibited the columns of vapor only, and a ground plan. The artist has given a good idea of the scene, but, by way of explanation, he has shown more of the depth of the fissure than is visible except by going close to the edge. The left-hand column, and that farthest off, are the smallest, and all ought to have been a little more tapering at the tops.

> * *The river is about one mile (1.6 km) wide at the falls, and plunges over 350 feet at the centre. Livingstone greatly underestimated both distances.* —A. L., 1997.

The fissure is said by the Makololo to be very much deeper farther to the eastward; there is one part at which the walls are so sloping that people accustomed to it can go down by descending in a sitting position. The Makololo on one occasion, pursuing some fugitive Batoka, saw them, unable to stop the impetus of their flight at the edge, literally dashed to pieces at the bottom. They beheld the stream like a "white cord" at the bottom, and so far down (probably 300 feet) that they became giddy, and were fain to go away holding on to the ground.

Now, though the edge of the rock over which the river falls does not show wearing more than three feet, and there is no appearance of the opposite wall being worn out at the bottom in the parts exposed to view, yet it is probable that, where it has flowed beyond the walls, the sides of the fissure may have given way, and the parts out of sight may be broader than the "white cord" on the surface. There may even be some ramifications of the fissure, which take a portion of the stream quite beneath the rocks; but this I did not learn.

If we take the want of much wear on the lip of hard basaltic rock as of any value, the period when this rock was riven is not geologically very remote. I regretted the want of proper means of measuring and marking its width at the falls, in order that, at some future time, the question whether it is progressive or not might be tested. It seemed as if a palm-tree could be laid across it from the island. And if it is progressive, as it would mark a great natural drainage being effected, it might furnish a hope that Africa will one day become a healthy continent. It is, at any rate, very much changed in respect to its lakes within a comparatively recent period.

At three spots near these falls, one of them the island in the middle, on which we were, three Batoka chiefs offered up prayers and sacrifices to the Barimo. They chose their places of prayer within the sound of the roar of the cataract, and in sight of the bright bows in the cloud. They must have looked upon the scene with awe. Fear may have induced the selection. The river itself is to them mysterious. The words of the canoe-song are,

"The Leeambye! Nobody knows
Whence it comes and whither it goes."

The play of colors of the double iris on the cloud, seen by them elsewhere only as the rainbow, may have led them to the idea that this was the abode of Deity. Some of the Makololo, who went with me near to Gonye, looked upon the same sign with awe. When seen in the heavens it is named "motse oa barimo"—the pestle of the gods. Here they could approach the emblem, and see it stand steadily above the blustering uproar below—a type of Him who sits supreme—alone unchangeable, though ruling over all changing things. But, not aware of His true character, they had no admiration of the beautiful and good in their bosoms. They did not imitate His benevolence, for they were a bloody, imperious crew, and Sebituane performed a noble service in the expulsion from their fastnesses of these cruel "Lords of the Isles".

Having feasted my eyes long on the beautiful sight, I returned to my friends at Kalai, and saying to Sekeletu that he had nothing else worth showing in his country, his curiosity was excited to visit it the next day. I returned with the intention of taking a lunar observation from the island itself, but the clouds were unfavorable, consequently all my determinations of position refer to Kalai. (Lat. 17d 51' 54" S., long. 25d 41' E.) Sekeletu acknowledged to feeling a little nervous at the probability* of being sucked into the gulf before reaching the island. His companions amused themselves by throwing stones down, and wondered to see them diminishing in size, and even disappearing, before they reached the water at the bottom.

> * *In modern American English, the word "possibility" is more appropriate here, and elsewhere in the text where "probability" is used.* — A. L., 1997.

I had another object in view in my return to the island. I observed that it was covered with trees, the seeds of which had probably come down with the stream from the distant north, and several of which I had seen nowhere else, and every now and then the wind wafted a little of the condensed vapor over it, and kept the soil in a state of moisture, which caused a sward of grass, growing as green as on an English lawn. I selected a spot—not too near the chasm, for there the constant deposition of the moisture nourished numbers of polypi of a mushroom shape and fleshy consistence, but somewhat back—and made a little garden. I there planted about a hundred peach and apricot stones, and a quantity of coffee-seeds. I had attempted fruit-trees before, but, when left in charge of my Makololo friends, they were always allowed to wither, after having vegetated, by being forgotten. I bargained for a hedge with one of the Makololo, and if he is faithful, I have great hopes of Mosioatunya's abilities as a nursery-man. My only source of fear is the hippopotami, whose footprints I saw on the island. When the garden was prepared, I cut my initials on a tree, and the date 1855. This was the only instance in which I indulged in this piece of vanity. The garden stands in front, and, were there no hippopotami, I have no doubt but this will be the parent of all the gardens which may yet be in this new country. We then went up to Kalai again.

On passing up we had a view of the hut on the island where my goods had lain so long in safety. It was under a group of palm-trees, and Sekeletu informed me that, so fully persuaded were most of the Makololo of the presence of dangerous charms in the packages, that, had I not returned to tell them the contrary, they never would have been touched. Some of the diviners had been so positive in their decisions on the point, that the men who lifted a bag thought they felt a live kid in it. The diviners always quote their predictions when they happen to tally with the event. They declared that the whole party which went to Loanda had perished; and as I always quoted the instances in which they failed, many of them refused to throw the "bola" (instruments of divination) when I was near. This was a noted instance of failure. It would have afforded me equal if not greater pleasure to have exposed the failure, if such it had been, of the European diviner whose paper lay a whole year on this island, but I was obliged to confess that he had been successful with his "bola", and could only comfort myself with the idea that, though Sir Roderick Murchison's discourse had lain so long within sight and sound of the magnificent falls, I had been "cut out" by no one in their discovery.

I saw the falls at low water, and the columns of vapor when five or six miles distant. When the river is full, or in flood, the columns, it is said, can be seen ten miles off, and the sound is quite distinct somewhat below Kalai, or about an equal distance. No one can then go to the island in the middle. The next visitor must bear these points in mind in comparing his description with mine.

We here got information of a foray which had been made by a Makololo man in the direction we were going. This instance of marauding was so much in accordance with the system which has been pursued in this country that I did not wonder at it. But the man had used Sekeletu's name as having sent him, and, the proof being convincing, he would undoubtedly be fined. As that would be the first instance of a fine being levied for marauding, I looked upon it as the beginning of a better state of things. In tribes which have been accustomed to cattle-stealing, the act is not considered immoral in the way that theft is. Before I knew the language well, I said to a chief, "You stole the cattle of so and so." "No, I did not steal them," was the reply, "I only LIFTED them." The word "gapa" is identical with the Highland term for the same deed.

Another point came to our notice here. Some Mambari had come down thus far, and induced the Batoka to sell a very large tusk which belonged to Sekeletu for a few bits of cloth. They had gone among the Batoka who need hoes, and, having purchased some of these from the people near Sesheke, induced the others living farther east to sell both ivory and children. They would not part with children for clothing or beads, but agriculture with wooden hoes is so laborious, that the sight of the hoes prevailed. The Makololo proposed to knock the Mambari on the head as the remedy the next time they came; but on my proposing that they should send hoes themselves, and thereby secure the ivory in a quiet way, all approved highly of the idea, and Pitsane and Mohorisi expatiated on the value of the ivory, their own willingness to go and sell it at Loanda, and the disgust with which the Mambari whom we met in Angola had looked upon their attempt to reach the proper market. If nothing untoward happens, I think there is a fair prospect of the trade in slaves being abolished in a natural way in this quarter, Pitsane and Mohorisi having again expressed their willingness to go away back to Loanda if Sekeletu would give them orders. This was the more remarkable, as both have plenty of food and leisure at home.

20TH NOVEMBER. Sekeletu and his large party having conveyed me thus far, and furnished me with a company of 114 men to carry the tusks to the coast, we bade adieu to the Makololo, and proceeded northward to the Lekone. The country around is very beautiful, and was once well peopled with Batoka, who possessed enormous herds of cattle. When Sebituane came in former times, with his small but warlike party of Makololo, to this spot, a general rising took place of the Batoka through the whole country, in order to "eat him up"; but his usual success followed him, and, dispersing them, the Makololo obtained so many cattle that they could not take any note of the herds of sheep and goats. The tsetse has been brought by buffaloes into some districts where formerly cattle abounded. This obliged us to travel the first few stages by night. We could not well detect the nature of the country in the dim moonlight; the path, however, seemed to lead along the high bank of what may have been the ancient bed of the Zambesi before the fissure was made. The Lekone now winds in it in an opposite direction to that in which the ancient river must have flowed.

Both the Lekone and Unguesi flow back toward the centre of the country, and in an opposite direction to that of the main stream. It was plain, then, that we were ascending the farther we went eastward. The level of the lower portion of the Lekone is about two hundred feet above that of the Zambesi at the falls, and considerably more than the altitude of Linyanti; consequently, when the river flowed along this ancient bed instead of through the rent, the whole country between this and the ridge beyond Libebe westward, Lake Ngami and the Zouga southward, and eastward beyond Nchokotsa, was one large fresh-water lake. There is abundant evidence of the existence and extent of this vast lake in the longitudes indicated, and stretching from 17 Deg. to 21 Deg. south latitude. The whole of this space is paved with a bed of tufa, more or less soft, according as it is covered with soil, or left exposed to atmospheric influences. Wherever ant-eaters make deep holes in this ancient bottom, fresh-water shells are thrown out, identical with those now existing in the Lake Ngami and the Zambesi. The Barotse valley was another lake of a similar nature; and one existed beyond Masiko, and a fourth near the Orange River. The whole of these lakes were let out by means of cracks or fissures made in the subtending sides by the upheaval of the country. The fissure made at the Victoria Falls let out the water of this great valley, and left a small patch in what was probably its deepest portion, and is now called Lake Ngami. The Falls of Gonye furnished an outlet to the lake of the Barotse valley, and so of the other great lakes of remote times. The Congo also finds its way to the sea through a narrow fissure, and so does the Orange River in the west; while other rents made in the eastern ridge, as the Victoria Falls and those to the east of Tanganyenka, allowed the central waters to drain eastward. All the African lakes hitherto discovered are shallow, in consequence of being the mere 'residua' of very much larger ancient bodies of water. There can be no doubt that this continent was, in former times, very much more copiously supplied with water than at present, but a natural process of drainage has been going on for ages. Deep fissures are made, probably by the elevation of the land, proofs of which are seen in modern shells imbedded in marly tufa all round the coast-line. Whether this process of desiccation is as rapid throughout the continent as, in a letter to the late Dean Buckland, in 1843, I showed to have been the case in the Bechuana country, it is not for me to say; but, though there is a slight tradition of the waters having burst through the low hills south of the Barotse, there is none of a sudden upheaval accompanied by an earthquake. The formation of the crack of Mosioatunya is perhaps too ancient for that; yet, although information of any remarkable event is often transmitted in the native names, and they even retain a tradition which looks like the story of Solomon and the harlots, there is not a name like Tom Earthquake or Sam Shake-the-ground in the whole country. They have a tradition which may refer to the building of the Tower of Babel, but it ends in the bold builders getting their crowns cracked by the fall of the scaffolding; and that they came out of a cave called "Loey" (Noe?) in company with the beasts, and all point to it in one direction, viz., the N.N.E. Loey, too, is an exception in the language, as they use masculine instead of neuter pronouns to it.

If we take a glance back at the great valley, the form the rivers have taken imparts the idea of a lake slowly drained out, for they have cut out for themselves beds exactly like what we may see in the soft mud of a shallow pool of rain-water, when that is let off by a furrow. This idea would probably not strike a person on coming first into the country, but more extensive acquaintance with the river system certainly would convey the impression. None of the rivers in the valley of the Leeambye have slopes down to their beds. Indeed, many parts are much like the Thames at the Isle of Dogs, only the Leeambye has to rise twenty or thirty feet before it can overflow some of its meadows. The rivers have each a bed of low water—a simple furrow cut sharply out of the calcareous tufa which lined the channel of the ancient lake—and another of inundation. When the beds of inundation are filled, they assume the appearance of chains of lakes. When the Clyde fills the holms ("haughs") above Bothwell Bridge and retires again into its channel, it resembles the river we are speaking of, only here there are no high lands sloping down toward the bed of inundation, for the greater part of the region is not elevated fifty feet above them. Even the rocky banks of the Leeambye below Gonye, and the ridges bounding the Barotse valley, are not more than two or three hundred feet in altitude over the general dead level. Many of the rivers are very tortuous in their course, the Chobe and Simah particularly so; and, if we may receive the testimony of the natives, they form what anatomists call 'anastamosis', or a network of rivers. Thus, for instance, they assured me that if they go up the Simah in a canoe, they can enter the Chobe, and descend that river to the Leeambye; or they may go up the Kama and come down the Simah; and so in the case of the Kafue. It is reputed to be connected in this way with the Leeambye in the north, and to part with the Loangwa; and the Makololo went from the one into the other in canoes. And even though the interlacing may not be quite to the extent believed by the natives, the country is so level and the rivers so tortuous that I see no improbability in the conclusion that here is a network of waters of a very peculiar nature. The reason why I am disposed to place a certain amount of confidence in the native reports is this: when Mr. Oswell and I discovered the Zambesi in the centre of the continent in 1851, being unable to ascend it at the time ourselves, we employed the natives to draw a map embodying their ideas of that river. We then sent the native map home with the same view that I now mention their ideas of the river system, namely, in order to be an aid to others in farther investigations. When I was able to ascend the Leeambye to 14 Deg. south, and subsequently descend it, I found, after all the care I could bestow, that the alterations I was able to make in the original native plan were very trifling. The general idea their map gave was wonderfully accurate; and now I give, in the larger map appended, their views of the other rivers, in the hope that they may prove helpful to any traveler who may pursue the investigation farther.

24TH. We remained a day at the village of Moyara. Here the valley in which the Lekone flows trends away to the eastward, while our course is more to the northeast. The country is rocky and rough, the soil being red sand, which is covered with beautiful green trees, yielding abundance of wild fruits. The father of Moyara was a powerful chief, but the son now sits among the ruins of the town, with four or five wives and very few people. At his hamlet a number of stakes are planted in the ground, and I counted fifty-four human skulls hung on their points. These were Matebele, who, unable to approach Sebituane on the island of Loyela, had returned sick and famishing. Moyara's father took advantage of their reduced condition, and after putting them to death, mounted their heads in the Batoka fashion. The old man who perpetrated this deed now lies in the middle of his son's huts, with a lot of rotten ivory over his grave. One can not help feeling thankful that the reign of such wretches is over. They inhabited the whole of this side of the country, and were probably the barrier to the extension of the Portuguese commerce in this direction. When looking at these skulls, I remarked to Moyara that many of them were those of mere boys. He assented readily, and pointed them out as such. I asked why his father had killed boys. "To show his fierceness," was the answer. "Is it fierceness to kill boys?" "Yes; they had no business here." When I told him that this probably would insure his own death if the Matebele came again, he replied, "When I hear of their coming I shall hide the bones." He was evidently proud of these trophies of his father's ferocity, and I was assured by other Batoka that few strangers ever returned from a visit to this quarter. If a man wished to curry favor with a Batoka chief, he ascertained when a stranger was about to leave, and waylaid him at a distance from the town, and when he brought his head back to the chief, it was mounted as a trophy, the different chiefs vieing with each other as to which should mount the greatest number of skulls in his village.

If, as has been asserted, the Portuguese ever had a chain of trading stations across the country from Caconda to Tete, it must have passed through these people; but the total ignorance of the Zambesi flowing from north to south in the centre of the country, and the want of knowledge of the astonishing falls of Victoria, which excite the wonder of even the natives, together with the absence of any tradition of such a chain of stations, compel me to believe that they existed only on paper. This conviction is strengthened by the fact that when a late attempt was made to claim the honor of crossing the continent for the Portuguese, the only proof advanced was the journey of two black traders formerly mentioned, adorned with the name of "Portuguese". If a chain of stations had existed, a few hundred names of the same sort might easily have been brought forward; and such is the love of barter among all the central Africans, that, had there existed a market for ivory, its value would have become known, and even that on the graves of the chiefs would not have been safe.

When about to leave Moyara on the 25th, he brought a root which, when pounded and sprinkled over the oxen, is believed to disgust the tsetse, so that it flies off without sucking the blood. He promised to show me the plant or tree if I would give him an ox; but, as we were traveling, and could not afford the time required for the experiment, so as not to be cheated (as I had too often been by my medical friends), I deferred the investigation till I returned. It is probably but an evanescent remedy, and capable of rendering the cattle safe during one night only. Moyara is now quite a dependent of the Makololo, and my new party, not being thoroughly drilled, forced him to carry a tusk for them. When I relieved him, he poured forth a shower of thanks at being allowed to go back to sleep beneath his skulls.

Next day we came to Namilanga, or "The Well of Joy". It is a small well dug beneath a very large fig-tree, the shade of which renders the water delightfully cool. The temperature through the day was 104 Deg. in the shade and 94 Deg. after sunset, but the air was not at all oppressive. This well received its name from the fact that, in former times, marauding parties, in returning with cattle, sat down here and were regaled with boyaloa, music, and the lullilooing of the women from the adjacent towns.

All the surrounding country was formerly densely peopled, though now desolate and still. The old head man of the place told us that his father once went to Bambala, where white traders lived, when our informant was a child, and returned when he had become a boy of about ten years. He went again, and returned when it was time to knock out his son's teeth. As that takes place at the age of puberty, he must have spent at least five years in each journey. He added that many who went there never returned, because they liked that country better than this. They had even forsaken their wives and children; and children had been so enticed and flattered by the finery bestowed upon them there, that they had disowned their parents and adopted others. The place to which they had gone, which they named Bambala, was probably Dambarari, which was situated close to Zumbo. This was the first intimation we had of intercourse with the whites. The Barotse, and all the other tribes in the central valley, have no such tradition as this, nor have either the one or the other any account of a trader's visit to them in ancient times.

All the Batoka tribes follow the curious custom of knocking out the upper front teeth at the age of puberty. This is done by both sexes; and though the under teeth, being relieved from the attrition of the upper, grow long and somewhat bent out, and thereby cause the under lip to protrude in a most unsightly way, no young woman thinks herself accomplished until she has got rid of the upper incisors. This custom gives all the Batoka an uncouth, old-man-like appearance. Their laugh is hideous, yet they are so attached to it that even Sebituane was unable to eradicate the practice. He issued orders that none of the children living under him should be subjected to the custom by their parents, and disobedience to his mandates was usually punished with severity; but, notwithstanding this, the children would appear in the streets without their incisors, and no one would confess to the deed. When questioned respecting the origin of this practice, the Batoka reply that their object is to be like oxen, and those who retain their teeth they consider to resemble zebras. Whether this is the true reason or not, it is difficult to say; but it is noticeable that the veneration for oxen which prevails in many tribes should here be associated with hatred to the zebra, as among the Bakwains; that this operation is performed at the same age that circumcision is in other tribes; and that here that ceremony is unknown. The custom is so universal that a person who has his teeth is considered ugly, and occasionally, when the Batoka borrowed my looking-glass, the disparaging remark would be made respecting boys or girls who still retained their teeth, "Look at the great teeth!" Some of the Makololo give a more facetious explanation of the custom: they say that the wife of a chief having in a quarrel bitten her husband's hand, he, in revenge, ordered her front teeth to be knocked out, and all the men in the tribe followed his example; but this does not explain why they afterward knocked out their own.

The Batoka of the Zambesi are generally very dark in color, and very degraded and negro-like in appearance, while those who live on the high lands we are now ascending are frequently of the color of coffee and milk. We had a large number of the Batoka of Mokwine in our party, sent by Sekeletu to carry his tusks. Their greater degradation was probably caused by the treatment of their chiefs—the barbarians of the islands. I found them more difficult to manage than any of the rest of my companions, being much less reasonable and impressible than the others. My party consisted of the head men aforementioned, Sekwebu, and Kanyata. We were joined at the falls by another head man of the Makololo, named Monahin, in command of the Batoka. We had also some of the Banajoa under Mosisinyane, and, last of all, a small party of Bashubia and Barotse under Tuba Mokoro, which had been furnished by Sekeletu because of their ability to swim. They carried their paddles with them, and, as the Makololo suggested, were able to swim over the rivers by night and steal canoes, if the inhabitants should be so unreasonable as to refuse to lend them. These different parties assorted together into messes; any orders were given through their head man, and when food was obtained he distributed it to the mess. Each party knew its own spot in the encampment; and as this was always placed so that our backs should be to the east, the direction from whence the prevailing winds came, no time was lost in fixing the sheds of our encampment. They each took it in turn to pull grass to make my bed, so I lay luxuriously.

NOVEMBER 26TH. As the oxen could only move at night, in consequence of a fear that the buffaloes in this quarter might have introduced the tsetse, I usually performed the march by day on foot, while some of the men brought on the oxen by night. On coming to the villages under Marimba, an old man, we crossed the Unguesi, a rivulet which, like the Lekone, runs backward. It falls into the Leeambye a little above the commencement of the rapids. The stratified gneiss, which is the underlying rock of much of this part of the country, dips toward the centre of the continent, but the strata are often so much elevated as to appear nearly on their edges. Rocks of augitic trap are found in various positions on it; the general strike is north and south; but when the gneiss was first seen, near to the basalt of the falls, it was easterly and westerly, and the dip toward the north, as if the eruptive force of the basalt had placed it in that position.

We passed the remains of a very large town, which, from the only evidence of antiquity afforded by ruins in this country, must have been inhabited for a long period; the millstones of gneiss, trap, and quartz were worn down two and a half inches perpendicularly. The ivory grave-stones soon rot away. Those of Moyara's father, who must have died not more than a dozen years ago, were crumbling into powder; and we found this to be generally the case all over the Batoka country. The region around is pretty well covered with forest; but there is abundance of open pasturage, and, as we are ascending in altitude, we find the grass to be short, and altogether unlike the tangled herbage of the Barotse valley.

It is remarkable that we now meet with the same trees we saw in descending toward the west coast. A kind of sterculia, which is the most common tree at Loanda, and the baobab, flourish here; and the tree called moshuka, which we found near Tala Mungongo, was now yielding its fruit, which resembles small apples. The people brought it to us in large quantities: it tastes like a pear, but has a harsh rind, and four large seeds within. We found prodigious quantities of this fruit as we went along. The tree attains the height of 15 or 20 feet, and has leaves, hard and glossy, as large as one's hand. The tree itself is never found on the lowlands, but is mentioned with approbation at the end of the work of Bowditch. My men almost lived upon the fruit for many days.

The rains had fallen only partially: in many parts the soil was quite dry and the leaves drooped mournfully, but the fruit-trees are unaffected by a drought, except when it happens at the time of their blossoming. The Batoka of my party declared that no one ever dies of hunger here. We obtained baskets of maneko, a curious fruit, with a horny rind, split into five pieces: these sections, when chewed, are full of a fine glutinous matter, and sweet like sugar. The seeds are covered with a yellow silky down, and are not eaten: the entire fruit is about the size of a walnut. We got also abundance of the motsouri and mamosho. We saw the Batoka eating the beans called nju, which are contained in a large square pod; also the pulp between the seeds of nux vomica, and the motsintsela. Other fruits become ripe at other seasons, as the motsikiri, which yields an oil, and is a magnificent tree, bearing masses of dark evergreen leaves; so that, from the general plenty, one can readily believe the statement made by the Batoka. We here saw trees allowed to stand in gardens, and some of the Batoka even plant them, a practice seen nowhere else among natives. A species of leucodendron abounds. When we meet with it on a spot on which no rain has yet fallen, we see that the young ones twist their leaves round during the heat of the day, so that the edge only is exposed to the rays of the sun; they have then a half twist on the petiole. The acacias in the same circumstances, and also the mopane ('Bauhania'), fold their leaves together, and, by presenting the smallest possible surface to the sun, simulate the eucalypti of Australia.

Chapter 27

Low Hills—Black Soldier-Ants; their Cannibalism—The Plasterer and its Chloroform—White Ants; their Usefulness—Mutokwane-smoking; its Effects—Border Territory—Healthy Table-lands—Geological Formation—Cicadae—Trees—Flowers—River Kalomo—Physical Conformation of Country—Ridges, sanatoria—A wounded Buffalo assisted—Buffalo-bird—Rhinoceros-bird—Leaders of Herds—The Honey-guide—The White Mountain—Mozuma River—Sebituane's old Home—Hostile Village—Prophetic Phrensy—Food of the Elephant— Ant-hills—Friendly Batoka—Clothing despised—Method of Salutation— Wild Fruits—The Captive released—Longings for Peace—Pingola's Conquests—The Village of Monze—Aspect of the Country—Visit from the Chief Monze and his Wife—Central healthy Locations—Friendly Feelings of the People in reference to a white Resident—Fertility of the Soil—Bashukulompo Mode of dressing their Hair—Gratitude of the Prisoner we released—Kindness and Remarks of Monze's Sister—Dip of the Rocks—Vegetation—Generosity of the Inhabitants—Their Anxiety for Medicine—Hooping-cough—Birds and Rain.

NOVEMBER 27TH. Still at Marimba's. In the adjacent country palms abound, but none of that species which yields the oil; indeed, that is met with only near the coast. There are numbers of flowers and bulbs just shooting up from the soil. The surface is rough, and broken into gullies; and, though the country is parched, it has not that appearance, so many trees having put forth their fresh green leaves at the time the rains ought to have come. Among the rest stands the mola, with its dark brownish-green color and spreading oak-like form. In the distance there are ranges of low hills. On the north we have one called Kanjele, and to the east that of Kaonka, to which we proceed to-morrow. We have made a considerable detour to the north, both on account of our wish to avoid the tsetse and to visit the people. Those of Kaonka are the last Batoka we shall meet, in friendship with the Makololo.

Walking down to the forest, after telling these poor people, for the first time in their lives, that the Son of God had so loved them as to come down from heaven to save them, I observed many regiments of black soldier-ants returning from their marauding expeditions. These I have often noticed before in different parts of the country; and as we had, even at Kolobeng, an opportunity of observing their habits, I may give a short account of them here. They are black, with a slight tinge of gray, about half an inch in length, and on the line of march appear three or four abreast; when disturbed, they utter a distinct hissing or chirping sound. They follow a few leaders who never carry any thing, and they seem to be guided by a scent left on the path by the leaders; for, happening once to throw the water from my basin behind a bush where I was dressing, it lighted on the path by which a regiment had passed before I began my toilette, and when they returned they were totally at a loss to find the way home, though they continued searching for it nearly half an hour. It was found only by one making a long circuit round the wetted spot. The scent may have indicated also the propriety of their going in one direction only. If a handful of earth is thrown on the path at the middle of the regiment, either on its way home or abroad, those behind it are completely at a loss as to their farther progress. Whatever it may be that guides them, they seem only to know that they are not to return, for they come up to the handful of earth, but will not cross it, though not a quarter of an inch high. They wheel round and regain their path again, but never think of retreating to the nest, or to the place where they have been stealing. After a quarter of an hour's confusion and hissing, one may make a circuit of a foot round the earth, and soon all follow in that roundabout way. When on their way to attack the abode of the white ants, the latter may be observed rushing about in a state of great perturbation. The black leaders, distinguished from the rest by their greater size, especially in the region of the sting, then seize the white ants one by one, and inflict a sting, which seems to inject a portion of fluid similar in effect to chloroform, as it renders them insensible, but not dead, and only able to move one or two front legs. As the leaders toss them on one side, the rank and file seize them and carry them off.

One morning I saw a party going forth on what has been supposed to be a slave-hunting expedition. They came to a stick, which, being inclosed in a white-ant gallery, I knew contained numbers of this insect; but I was surprised to see the black soldiers passing without touching it. I lifted up the stick and broke a portion of the gallery, and then laid it across the path in the middle of the black regiment. The white ants, when uncovered, scampered about with great celerity, hiding themselves under the leaves, but attracted little attention from the black marauders till one of the leaders caught them, and, applying his sting, laid them in an instant on one side in a state of coma; the others then promptly seized them and rushed off. On first observing these marauding insects at Kolobeng, I had the idea, imbibed from a work of no less authority than Brougham's Paley, that they seized the white ants in order to make them slaves; but, having rescued a number of captives, I placed them aside, and found that they never recovered from the state of insensibility into which they had been thrown by the leaders. I supposed then that the insensibility had been caused by the soldiers holding the necks of the white ants too tightly with their mandibles, as that is the way they seize them; but even the pupae which I took from the soldier-ants, though placed in a favorable temperature, never became developed. In addition to this, if any one examines the orifice by which the black ant enters his barracks, he will always find a little heap of hard heads and legs of white ants, showing that these black ruffians are a grade lower than slave-stealers, being actually cannibals. Elsewhere I have seen a body of them removing their eggs from a place in which they were likely to be flooded by the rains; I calculated their numbers to be 1260; they carried their eggs a certain distance, then laid them down, when others took them and carried them farther on. Every ant in the colony seemed to be employed in this laborious occupation, yet there was not a white slave-ant among them. One cold morning I observed a band of another species of black ant returning each with a captive; there could be no doubt of their cannibal propensities, for the "brutal soldiery" had already deprived the white ants of their legs. The fluid in the stings of this species is of an intensely acid taste.

    I had often noticed the stupefaction produced by the injection of a fluid from the sting of certain insects before. It is particularly observable in a hymenopterous insect called the "plasterer" ('Pelopaeus Eckloni'), which in his habits resembles somewhat the mason-bee. It is about an inch and a quarter in length, jet black in color, and may be observed coming into houses, carrying in its fore legs a pellet of soft plaster about the size of a pea. When it has fixed upon a convenient spot for its dwelling, it forms a cell about the same length as its body, plastering the walls so as to be quite thin and smooth inside. When this is finished, all except a round hole, it brings seven or eight caterpillars or spiders, each of which is rendered insensible, but not killed, by the fluid from its sting. These it deposits in the cell, and then one of its own larvae, which, as it grows, finds food quite fresh. The insects are in a state of coma, but the presence of vitality prevents putridity, or that drying up which would otherwise take place in this climate. By the time the young insect is full grown and its wings completely developed, the food is done. It then pierces the wall of its cell at the former door, or place last filled up by its parent, flies off, and begins life for itself. The plasterer is a most useful insect, as it acts as a check on the inordinate increase of caterpillars and spiders. It may often be seen with a caterpillar or even a cricket much larger than itself, but they lie perfectly still after the injection of chloroform, and the plasterer, placing a row of legs on each side of the body, uses both legs and wings in trailing the victim along. The fluid in each case is, I suppose, designed to cause insensibility, and likewise act as an antiseptic, the death of the victims being without pain.

Without these black soldier-ants the country would be overrun by the white ants; they are so extremely prolific, and nothing can exceed the energy with which they work. They perform a most important part in the economy of nature by burying vegetable matter as quickly beneath the soil as the ferocious red ant does dead animal substances. The white ant keeps generally out of sight, and works under galleries constructed by night to screen them from the observation of birds. At some given signal, however, I never could ascertain what, they rush out by hundreds, and the sound of their mandibles cutting grass into lengths may be heard like a gentle wind murmuring through the leaves of the trees. They drag these pieces to the doors of their abodes, and after some hours' toil leave off work, and many of the bits of grass may be seen collected around the orifice. They continue out of sight for perhaps a month, but they are never idle. On one occasion, a good bundle of grass was laid down for my bed on a spot which was quite smooth and destitute of plants. The ants at once sounded the call to a good supply of grass. I heard them incessantly nibbling and carrying away all that night; and they continued all next day (Sunday), and all that night too, with unabated energy. They had thus been thirty-six hours at it, and seemed as fresh as ever. In some situations, if we remained a day, they devoured the grass beneath my mat, and would have eaten that too had we not laid down more grass. At some of their operations they beat time in a curious manner. Hundreds of them are engaged in building a large tube, and they wish to beat it smooth. At a signal, they all give three or four energetic beats on the plaster in unison. It produces a sound like the dropping of rain off a bush when touched. These insects are the chief agents employed in forming a fertile soil. But for their labors, the tropical forests, bad as they are now with fallen trees, would be a thousand times worse. They would be impassable on account of the heaps of dead vegetation lying on the surface, and emitting worse effluvia than the comparatively small unburied collections do now. When one looks at the wonderful adaptations throughout creation, and the varied operations carried on with such wisdom and skill, the idea of second causes looks clumsy. We are viewing the direct handiwork of Him who is the one and only Power in the universe; wonderful in counsel; in whom we all live, and move, and have our being.

The Batoka of these parts are very degraded in their appearance, and are not likely to improve, either physically or mentally, while so much addicted to smoking the mutokwane ('Cannabis sativa'). They like its narcotic effects, though the violent fit of coughing which follows a couple of puffs of smoke appears distressing, and causes a feeling of disgust in the spectator. This is not diminished on seeing the usual practice of taking a mouthful of water, and squirting it out together with the smoke, then uttering a string of half-incoherent sentences, usually in self-praise. This pernicious weed is extensively used in all the tribes of the interior. It causes a species of phrensy, and Sebituane's soldiers, on coming in sight of their enemies, sat down and smoked it, in order that they might make an effective onslaught. I was unable to prevail on Sekeletu and the young Makololo to forego its use, although they can not point to an old man in the tribe who has been addicted to this indulgence. I believe it was the proximate cause of Sebituane's last illness, for it sometimes occasions pneumonia. Never having tried it, I can not describe the pleasurable effects it is said to produce, but the hashish in use among the Turks is simply an extract of the same plant, and that, like opium, produces different effects on different individuals. Some view every thing as if looking in through the wide end of a telescope, and others, in passing over a straw, lift up their feet as if about to cross the trunk of a tree. The Portuguese in Angola have such a belief in its deleterious effects that the use of it by a slave is considered a crime.

NOVEMBER 28TH. The inhabitants of the last of Kaonka's villages complained of being plundered by the independent Batoka. The tribes in front of this are regarded by the Makololo as in a state of rebellion. I promised to speak to the rebels on the subject, and enjoined on Kaonka the duty of giving them no offense. According to Sekeletu's order, Kaonka gave us the tribute of maize-corn and ground-nuts, which would otherwise have gone to Linyanti. This had been done at every village, and we thereby saved the people the trouble of a journey to the capital. My own Batoka had brought away such loads of provisions from their homes that we were in no want of food.

After leaving Kaonka we traveled over an uninhabited, gently undulating, and most beautiful district, the border territory between those who accept and those who reject the sway of the Makololo. The face of the country appears as if in long waves, running north and south. There are no rivers, though water stands in pools in the hollows. We were now come into the country which my people all magnify as a perfect paradise. Sebituane was driven from it by the Matebele. It suited him exactly for cattle, corn, and health. The soil is dry, and often a reddish sand; there are few trees, but fine large shady ones stand dotted here and there over the country where towns formerly stood. One of the fig family I measured, and found to be forty feet in circumference; the heart had been burned out, and some one had made a lodging in it, for we saw the remains of a bed and a fire. The sight of the open country, with the increased altitude we were attaining, was most refreshing to the spirits. Large game abound. We see in the distance buffaloes, elands, hartebeest, gnus, and elephants, all very tame, as no one disturbs them. Lions, which always accompany other large animals, roared about us, but, as it was moonlight, there was no danger. In the evening, while standing on a mass of granite, one began to roar at me, though it was still light. The temperature was pleasant, as the rains, though not universal, had fallen in many places. It was very cloudy, preventing observations. The temperature at 6 A.M. was 70 Deg., at midday 90 Deg., in the evening 84 Deg. This is very pleasant on the high lands, with but little moisture in the air.

The different rocks to the westward of Kaonka's, talcose gneiss and white mica schist, generally dip toward the west, but at Kaonka's, large rounded masses of granite, containing black mica, began to appear. The outer rind of it inclines to peel off, and large crystals project on the exposed surface.

In passing through some parts where a good shower of rain has fallen, the stridulous piercing notes of the cicadae are perfectly deafening; a drab-colored cricket joins the chorus with a sharp sound, which has as little modulation as the drone of a Scottish bagpipe. I could not conceive how so small a thing could raise such a sound; it seemed to make the ground over it thrill. When cicadae, crickets, and frogs unite, their music may be heard at the distance of a quarter of a mile.

A tree attracted my attention as new, the leaves being like those of an acacia, but the ends of the branches from which they grew resembled closely oblong fir-cones. The corn-poppy was abundant, and many of the trees, flowering bulbs, and plants were identical with those in Pungo Andongo. A flower as white as the snowdrop now begins to appear, and farther on it spots the whole sward with its beautiful pure white. A fresh crop appears every morning, and if the day is cloudy they do not expand till the afternoon. In an hour or so they droop and die. They are named by the natives, from their shape, "Tlaku ea pitse", hoof of zebra. I carried several of the somewhat bulbous roots of this pretty flower till I reached the Mauritius.

On the 30th we crossed the River Kalomo, which is about 50 yards broad, and is the only stream that never dries up on this ridge. The current is rapid, and its course is toward the south, as it joins the Zambesi at some distance below the falls. The Unguesi and Lekone, with their feeders, flow westward, this river to the south, and all those to which we are about to come take an easterly direction. We were thus at the apex of the ridge, and found that, as water boiled at 202 Deg., our altitude above the level of the sea was over 5000 feet. Here the granite crops out again in great rounded masses which change the dip of the gneiss and mica schist rocks from the westward to the eastward. In crossing the western ridge I mentioned the clay shale or keele formation, a section of which we have in the valley of the Quango: the strata there lie nearly horizontal, but on this ridge the granite seems to have been the active agent of elevation, for the rocks, both on its east and west, abut against it. Both eastern and western ridges are known to be comparatively salubrious, and in this respect, as well as in the general aspect of the country, they resemble that most healthy of all healthy climates, the interior of South Africa, near and adjacent to the Desert. This ridge has neither fountain nor marsh upon it, and east of the Kalomo we look upon treeless undulating plains covered with short grass. From a point somewhat near to the great falls, this ridge or oblong mound trends away to the northeast, and there treeless elevated plains again appear. Then again the ridge is said to bend away from the falls to the southeast, the Mashona country, or rather their mountains, appearing, according to Mr. Moffat, about four days east of Matlokotloko, the present residence of Mosilikatse. In reference to this ridge he makes the interesting remark, "I observed a number of the Angora goat, most of them being white; and their long soft hair, covering their entire bodies to the ground, made them look like animals moving along without feet."*

* *Moffat's "Visit to Mosilikatse".—Royal Geographical Society's Journal, vol. xxvi., p. 96.*

It is impossible to say how much farther to the north these subtending ridges may stretch. There is reason to believe that, though the same general form of country obtains, they are not flanked by abrupt hills between the latitude 12 Deg. south and the equator. The inquiry is worthy the attention of travelers. As they are known to be favorable to health, the Makololo, who have been nearly all cut off by fevers in the valley, declaring that here they never had a headache, they may even be recommended as a sanatorium for those whose enterprise leads them into Africa, either for the advancement of scientific knowledge, or for the purposes of trade or benevolence. In the case of the eastern ridge, we have water carriage, with only one short rapid as an obstruction, right up to its base; and if a quick passage can be effected during the healthy part of the year, there would be no danger of loss of health during a long stay on these high lands afterward. How much farther do these high ridges extend? The eastern one seems to bend in considerably toward the great falls; and the strike of the rocks indicating that, farther to the N.N.E. than my investigations extend, it may not, at a few degrees of latitude beyond, be more than 300 or 350 miles from the coast. They at least merit inquiry, for they afford a prospect to Europeans of situations superior in point of salubrity to any of those on the coast; and so on the western side of the continent; for it is a fact that many parts in the interior of Angola, which were formerly thought to be unhealthy on account of their distance inland, have been found, as population advanced, to be the most healthy spots in the country. Did the great Niger expedition turn back when near such a desirable position for its stricken and prostrate members?

The distances from top to top of the ridges may be about 10 Deg. of longitude, or 600 geographical miles. I can not hear of a hill ON either ridge, and there are scarcely any in the space inclosed by them. The Monakadze is the highest, but that is not more than a thousand feet above the flat valley. On account of this want of hills in the part of the country which, by gentle undulations, leads one insensibly up to an altitude of 5000 feet above the level of the sea, I have adopted the agricultural term ridges, for they partake very much of the character of the oblong mounds with which we are all familiar. And we shall yet see that the mountains which are met with outside these ridges are only a low fringe, many of which are not of much greater altitude than even the bottom of the great central valley. If we leave out of view the greater breadth of the central basin at other parts, and speak only of the comparatively narrow part formed by the bend to the westward of the eastern ridge, we might say that the form of this region is a broad furrow in the middle, with an elevated ridge about 200 miles broad on either side, the land sloping thence, on both sides, to the sea. If I am right in believing the granite to be the cause of the elevation of this ridge, the direction in which the strike of the rocks trends to the N.N.E. may indicate that the same geological structure prevails farther north, and two or three lakes which exist in that direction may be of exactly the same nature with Lake Ngami, having been diminished to their present size by the same kind of agency as that which formed the falls of Victoria.

We met an elephant on the Kalomo which had no tusks. This is as rare a thing in Africa as it is to find them with tusks in Ceylon. As soon as she saw us she made off. It is remarkable to see the fear of man operating even on this huge beast. Buffaloes abound, and we see large herds of them feeding in all directions by day. When much disturbed by man they retire into the densest parts of the forest, and feed by night only. We secured a fine large bull by crawling close to a herd. When shot, he fell down, and the rest, not seeing their enemy, gazed about, wondering where the danger lay. The others came back to it, and, when we showed ourselves, much to the amusement of my companions, they lifted him up with their horns, and, half supporting him in the crowd, bore him away. All these wild animals usually gore a wounded companion, and expel him from the herd; even zebras bite and kick an unfortunate or a diseased one. It is intended by this instinct that none but the perfect and healthy ones should propagate the species. In this case they manifested their usual propensity to gore the wounded, but our appearance at that moment caused them to take flight, and this, with the goring being continued a little, gave my men the impression that they were helping away their wounded companion. He was shot between the fourth and fifth ribs; the ball passed through both lungs and a rib on the opposite side, and then lodged beneath the skin. But, though it was eight ounces in weight, yet he ran off some distance, and was secured only by the people driving him into a pool of water and killing him there with their spears. The herd ran away in the direction of our camp, and then came bounding past us again. We took refuge on a large ant-hill, and as they rushed by us at full gallop I had a good opportunity of seeing that the leader of a herd of about sixty was an old cow; all the others allowed her a full half-length in their front. On her withers sat about twenty buffalo-birds ('Textor erythrorhynchus', Smith), which act the part of guardian spirits to the animals. When the buffalo is quietly feeding, this bird may be seen hopping on the ground picking up food, or sitting on its back ridding it of the insects with which their skins are sometimes infested. The sight of the bird being much more acute than that of the buffalo, it is soon alarmed by the approach of any danger, and, flying up, the buffaloes instantly raise their heads to discover the cause which has led to the sudden flight of their guardian. They sometimes accompany the buffaloes in their flight on the wing, at other times they sit as above described.

Another African bird, namely, the 'Buphaga Africana', attends the rhinoceros for a similar purpose. It is called "kala" in the language of the Bechuanas. When these people wish to express their dependence upon another, they address him as "my rhinoceros", as if they were the birds. The satellites of a chief go by the same name. This bird can not be said to depend entirely on the insects on that animal, for its hard, hairless skin is a protection against all except a few spotted ticks; but it seems to be attached to the beast, somewhat as the domestic dog is to man; and while the buffalo is alarmed by the sudden flying up of its sentinel, the rhinoceros, not having keen sight, but an acute ear, is warned by the cry of its associate, the 'Buphaga Africana'. The rhinoceros feeds by night, and its sentinel is frequently heard in the morning uttering its well-known call, as it searches for its bulky companion. One species of this bird, observed in Angola, possesses a bill of a peculiar scoop or stone forceps form, as if intended only to tear off insects from the skin; and its claws are as sharp as needles, enabling it to hang on to an animal's ear while performing a useful service within it. This sharpness of the claws allows the bird to cling to the nearly insensible cuticle without irritating the nerves of pain on the true skin, exactly as a burr does to the human hand; but in the case of the 'Buphaga Africana' and 'erythrorhyncha', other food is partaken of, for we observed flocks of them roosting on the reeds, in spots where neither tame nor wild animals were to be found.

The most wary animal in a herd is generally the "leader". When it is shot the others often seem at a loss what to do, and stop in a state of bewilderment. I have seen them attempt to follow each other and appear quite confused, no one knowing for half a minute or more where to direct the flight. On one occasion I happened to shoot the leader, a young zebra mare, which at some former time had been bitten on the hind leg by a carnivorous animal, and, thereby made unusually wary, had, in consequence, become a leader. If they see either one of their own herd or any other animal taking to flight, wild animals invariably flee. The most timid thus naturally leads the rest. It is not any other peculiarity, but simply this provision, which is given them for the preservation of the race. The great increase of wariness which is seen to occur when the females bring forth their young, causes all the leaders to be at that time females; and there is a probability that the separation of sexes into distinct herds, which is annually observed in many antelopes, arises from the simple fact that the greater caution of the she antelopes is partaken of only by the young males, and their more frequent flights now have the effect of leaving the old males behind. I am inclined to believe this, because, though the antelopes, as the pallahs, etc., are frequently in separate herds, they are never seen in the act of expelling the males. There may be some other reason in the case of the elephants; but the male and female elephants are never seen in one herd. The young males remain with their dams only until they are full grown; and so constantly is the separation maintained, that any one familiar with them, on seeing a picture with the sexes mixed, would immediately conclude that the artist had made it from his imagination, and not from sight.

DECEMBER 2, 1855. We remained near a small hill, called Maundo, where we began to be frequently invited by the honey-guide ('Cuculus indicator'). Wishing to ascertain the truth of the native assertion that this bird is a deceiver, and by its call sometimes leads to a wild beast and not to honey, I inquired if any of my men had ever been led by this friendly little bird to any thing else than what its name implies. Only one of the 114 could say he had been led to an elephant instead of a hive, like myself with the black rhinoceros mentioned before. I am quite convinced that the majority of people who commit themselves to its guidance are led to honey, and to it alone.

On the 3d we crossed the River Mozuma, or River of Dila, having traveled through a beautifully undulating pastoral country. To the south, and a little east of this, stands the hill Taba Cheu, or "White Mountain", from a mass of white rock, probably dolomite, on its top. But none of the hills are of any great altitude. When I heard this mountain described at Linyanti I thought the glistening substance might be snow, and my informants were so loud in their assertions of its exceeding great altitude that I was startled with the idea; but I had quite forgotten that I was speaking with men who had been accustomed to plains, and knew nothing of very high mountains. When I inquired what the white substance was, they at once replied it was a kind of rock. I expected to have come nearer to it, and would have ascended it; but we were led to go to the northeast. Yet I doubt not that the native testimony of its being stone is true. The distant ranges of hills which line the banks of the Zambesi on the southeast, and landscapes which permit the eye to range over twenty or thirty miles at a time, with short grass under our feet, were especially refreshing sights to those who had traveled for months together over the confined views of the flat forest, and among the tangled rank herbage of the great valley.

The Mozuma, or River of Dila, was the first water-course which indicated that we were now on the slopes toward the eastern coast. It contained no flowing water, but revealed in its banks what gave me great pleasure at the time—pieces of lignite, possibly indicating the existence of a mineral, namely, coal, the want of which in the central country I had always deplored. Again and again we came to the ruins of large towns, containing the only hieroglyphics of this country, worn mill-stones, with the round ball of quartz with which the grinding was effected. Great numbers of these balls were lying about, showing that the depopulation had been the result of war; for, had the people removed in peace, they would have taken the balls with them.

At the River of Dila we saw the spot where Sebituane lived, and Sekwebu pointed out the heaps of bones of cattle which the Makololo had been obliged to slaughter after performing a march with great herds captured from the Batoka through a patch of the fatal tsetse. When Sebituane saw the symptoms of the poison, he gave orders to his people to eat the cattle. He still had vast numbers; and when the Matebele, crossing the Zambesi opposite this part, came to attack him, he invited the Batoka to take repossession of their herds, he having so many as to be unable to guide them in their flight. The country was at that time exceedingly rich in cattle, and, besides pasturage, it is all well adapted for the cultivation of native produce. Being on the eastern slope of the ridge, it receives more rain than any part of the westward. Sekwebu had been instructed to point out to me the advantages of this position for a settlement, as that which all the Makololo had never ceased to regret. It needed no eulogy from Sekwebu; I admired it myself, and the enjoyment of good health in fine open scenery had an exhilarating effect on my spirits. The great want was population, the Batoka having all taken refuge in the hills. We were now in the vicinity of those whom the Makololo deem rebels, and felt some anxiety as to how we should be received.

On the 4th we reached their first village. Remaining at a distance of a quarter of a mile, we sent two men to inform them who we were, and that our purposes were peaceful. The head man came and spoke civilly, but, when nearly dark, the people of another village arrived and behaved very differently. They began by trying to spear a young man who had gone for water. Then they approached us, and one came forward howling at the top of his voice in the most hideous manner; his eyes were shot out, his lips covered with foam, and every muscle of his frame quivered. He came near to me, and, having a small battle-axe in his hand, alarmed my men lest he might do violence; but they were afraid to disobey my previous orders, and to follow their own inclination by knocking him on the head. I felt a little alarmed too, but would not show fear before my own people or strangers, and kept a sharp look-out on the little battle-axe. It seemed to me a case of ecstasy or prophetic phrensy, voluntarily produced. I felt it would be a sorry way to leave the world, to get my head chopped by a mad savage, though that, perhaps, would be preferable to hydrophobia or delirium tremens. Sekwebu took a spear in his hand, as if to pierce a bit of leather, but in reality to plunge it into the man if he offered violence to me. After my courage had been sufficiently tested, I beckoned with the head to the civil head man to remove him, and he did so by drawing him aside. This man pretended not to know what he was doing. I would fain have felt his pulse, to ascertain whether the violent trembling were not feigned, but had not much inclination to go near the battle-axe again. There was, however, a flow of perspiration, and the excitement continued fully half an hour, then gradually ceased. This paroxysm is the direct opposite of hypnotism, and it is singular that it has not been tried in Europe as well as clairvoyance. This second batch of visitors took no pains to conceal their contempt for our small party, saying to each other, in a tone of triumph, "They are quite a Godsend!" literally, "God has apportioned them to us." "They are lost among the tribes!" "They have wandered in order to be destroyed, and what can they do without shields among so many?" Some of them asked if there were no other parties. Sekeletu had ordered my men not to take their shields, as in the case of my first company. We were looked upon as unarmed, and an easy prey. We prepared against a night attack by discharging and reloading our guns, which were exactly the same in number (five) as on the former occasion, as I allowed my late companions to retain those which I purchased at Loanda. We were not molested, but some of the enemy tried to lead us toward the Bashukulompo, who are considered to be the fiercest race in this quarter. As we knew our direction to the confluence of the Kafue and Zambesi, we declined their guidance, and the civil head man of the evening before then came along with us. Crowds of natives hovered round us in the forest; but he ran forward and explained, and we were not molested. That night we slept by a little village under a low range of hills, which are called Chizamena. The country here is more woody than on the high lands we had left, but the trees are not in general large. Great numbers of them have been broken off by elephants a foot or two from the ground: they thus seem pollarded from that point. This animal never seriously lessens the number of trees; indeed, I have often been struck by the very little damage he does in a forest. His food consists more of bulbs, tubers, roots, and branches, than any thing else. Where they have been feeding, great numbers of trees, as thick as a man's body, are seen twisted down or broken off, in order that they may feed on the tender shoots at the tops. They are said sometimes to unite in wrenching down large trees. The natives in the interior believe that the elephant never touches grass, and I never saw evidence of his having grazed until we came near to Tete, and then he had fed on grass in seed only; this seed contains so much farinaceous matter that the natives collect it for their own food.

This part of the country abounds in ant-hills. In the open parts they are studded over the surface exactly as haycocks are in harvest, or heaps of manure in spring, rather disfiguring the landscape. In the woods they are as large as round haystacks, 40 or 50 feet in diameter at the base, and at least 20 feet high. These are more fertile than the rest of the land, and here they are the chief garden-ground for maize, pumpkins, and tobacco.

When we had passed the outskirting villages, which alone consider themselves in a state of war with the Makololo, we found the Batoka, or Batonga, as they here call themselves, quite friendly. Great numbers of them came from all the surrounding villages with presents of maize and masuka, and expressed great joy at the first appearance of a white man, and harbinger of peace. The women clothe themselves better than the Balonda, but the men go 'in puris naturalibus'. They walk about without the smallest sense of shame. They have even lost the tradition of the "fig-leaf". I asked a fine, large-bodied old man if he did not think it would be better to adopt a little covering. He looked with a pitying leer, and laughed with surprise at my thinking him at all indecent; he evidently considered himself above such weak superstition. I told them that, on my return, I should have my family with me, and no one must come near us in that state. "What shall we put on?

we have no clothing." It was considered a good joke when I told them that, if they had nothing else, they must put on a bunch of grass.

The farther we advanced, the more we found the country swarming with inhabitants. Great numbers came to see the white man, a sight they had never beheld before. They always brought presents of maize and masuka. Their mode of salutation is quite singular. They throw themselves on their backs on the ground, and, rolling from side to side, slap the outside of their thighs as expressions of thankfulness and welcome, uttering the words "Kina bomba." This method of salutation was to me very disagreeable, and I never could get reconciled to it. I called out, "Stop, stop; I don't want that;" but they, imagining I was dissatisfied, only tumbled about more furiously, and slapped their thighs with greater vigor. The men being totally unclothed, this performance imparted to my mind a painful sense of their extreme degradation. My own Batoka were much more degraded than the Barotse, and more reckless. We had to keep a strict watch, so as not to be involved by their thieving from the inhabitants, in whose country and power we were. We had also to watch the use they made of their tongues, for some within hearing of the villagers would say, "I broke all the pots of that village," or, "I killed a man there." They were eager to recount their soldier deeds, when they were in company with the Makololo in former times as a conquering army. They were thus placing us in danger by their remarks. I called them together, and spoke to them about their folly, and gave them a pretty plain intimation that I meant to insist upon as complete subordination as I had secured in my former journey, as being necessary for the safety of the party. Happily, it never was needful to resort to any other measure for their obedience, as they all believed that I would enforce it.

In connection with the low state of the Batoka, I was led to think on the people of Kuruman, who were equally degraded and equally depraved. There a man scorned to shed a tear. It would have been "tlolo", or transgression. Weeping, such as Dr. Kane describes among the Esquimaux, is therefore quite unknown in that country. But I have witnessed instances like this: Baba, a mighty hunter—the interpreter who accompanied Captain Harris, and who was ultimately killed by a rhinoceros—sat listening to the Gospel in the church at Kuruman, and the gracious words of Christ, made to touch his heart, evidently by the Holy Spirit, melted him into tears; I have seen him and others sink down to the ground weeping. When Baba was lying mangled by the furious beast which tore him off his horse, he shed no tear, but quietly prayed as long as he was conscious. I had no hand in his instruction: if these Batoka ever become like him, and they may, the influence that effects it must be divine.

A very large portion of this quarter is covered with masuka-trees, and the ground was so strewed with the pleasant fruit that my men kept eating it constantly as we marched along. We saw a smaller kind of the same tree, named Molondo, the fruit of which is about the size of marbles, having a tender skin, and slight acidity of taste mingled with its sweetness. Another tree which is said to yield good fruit is named Sombo, but it was not ripe at this season.

DECEMBER 6TH. We passed the night near a series of villages. Before we came to a stand under our tree, a man came running to us with hands and arms firmly bound with cords behind his back, entreating me to release him. When I had dismounted, the head man of the village advanced, and I inquired the prisoner's offense. He stated that he had come from the Bashukulompo as a fugitive, and he had given him a wife and garden and a supply of seed; but, on refusing a demand for more, the prisoner had threatened to kill him, and had been seen the night before skulking about the village, apparently with that intention. I declined interceding unless he would confess to his father-in-law, and promise amendment. He at first refused to promise to abstain from violence, but afterward agreed. The father-in-law then said that he would take him to the village and release him, but the prisoner cried out bitterly, "He will kill me there; don't leave me, white man." I ordered a knife, and one of the villagers released him on the spot. His arms were cut by the cords, and he was quite lame from the blows he had received.

These villagers supplied us abundantly with ground-nuts, maize, and corn. All expressed great satisfaction on hearing my message, as I directed their attention to Jesus as their Savior, whose word is "Peace on earth, and good-will to men." They called out, "We are tired of flight; give us rest and sleep." They of course did not understand the full import of the message, but it was no wonder that they eagerly seized the idea of peace. Their country has been visited by successive scourges during the last half century, and they are now "a nation scattered and peeled." When Sebituane came, the cattle were innumerable, and yet these were the remnants only, left by a chief called Pingola, who came from the northeast. He swept across the whole territory inhabited by his cattle-loving countrymen, devouring oxen, cows, and calves, without retaining a single head. He seems to have been actuated by a simple love of conquest, and is an instance of what has occurred two or three times in every century in this country, from time immemorial. A man or more energy or ambition than his fellows rises up and conquers a large territory, but as soon as he dies the power he built up is gone, and his reign, having been one of terror, is not perpetuated. This, and the want of literature, have prevented the establishment of any great empire in the interior of Africa. Pingola effected his conquests by carrying numbers of smith's bellows with him. The arrow-heads were heated before shooting into a town, and when a wound was inflicted on either man or beast, great confusion ensued. After Pingola came Sebituane, and after him the Matebele of Mosilikatse; and these successive inroads have reduced the Batoka to a state in which they naturally rejoice at the prospect of deliverance and peace.

We spent Sunday, the 10th, at Monze's village, who is considered the chief of all the Batoka we have seen. He lives near the hill Kisekise, whence we have a view of at least thirty miles of open undulating country, covered with short grass, and having but few trees. These open lawns would in any other land, as well as this, be termed pastoral, but the people have now no cattle, and only a few goats and fowls. They are located all over the country in small villages, and cultivate large gardens. They are said to have adopted this wide-spread mode of habitation in order to give alarm should any enemy appear. In former times they lived in large towns. In the distance (southeast) we see ranges of dark mountains along the banks of the Zambesi, and are told of the existence there of the rapid named Kansala, which is said to impede the navigation. The river is reported to be placid above that as far as the territory of Sinamane, a Batoka chief, who is said to command it after it emerges smooth again below the falls. Kansala is the only rapid reported in the river until we come to Kebrabasa, twenty or thirty miles above Tete. On the north we have mountains appearing above the horizon, which are said to be on the banks of the Kafue.

The chief Monze came to us on Sunday morning, wrapped in a large cloth, and rolled himself about in the dust, screaming "Kina bomba," as they all do. The sight of great naked men wallowing on the ground, though intended to do me honor, was always very painful; it made me feel thankful that my lot had been cast in such different circumstances from that of so many of my fellow-men. One of his wives accompanied him; she would have been comely if her teeth had been spared; she had a little battle-axe in her hand, and helped her husband to scream. She was much excited, for she had never seen a white man before. We rather liked Monze, for he soon felt at home among us, and kept up conversation during much of the day. One head man of a village after another arrived, and each of them supplied us liberally with maize, ground-nuts, and corn. Monze gave us a goat and a fowl, and appeared highly satisfied with a present of some handkerchiefs I had got in my supplies left at the island. Being of printed cotton, they excited great admiration; and when I put a gaudy-colored one as a shawl about his child, he said that he would send for all his people to make a dance about it. In telling them that my object was to open up a path whereby they might, by getting merchandise for ivory, avoid the guilt of selling their children, I asked Monze, with about 150 of his men, if they would like a white man to live among them and teach them. All expressed high satisfaction at the prospect of the white man and his path: they would protect both him and his property. I asked the question, because it would be of great importance to have stations in this healthy region, whither agents oppressed by sickness might retire, and which would serve, moreover, as part of a chain of communication between the interior and the coast. The answer does not mean much more than what I know, by other means, to be the case—that a white man OF GOOD SENSE would be welcome and safe in all these parts. By uprightness, and laying himself out for the good of the people, he would be known all over the country as a BENEFACTOR of the race. None desire Christian instruction, for of it they have no idea. But the people are now humbled by the scourgings they have received, and seem to be in a favorable state for the reception of the Gospel. The gradual restoration of their former prosperity in cattle, simultaneously with instruction, would operate beneficially upon their minds. The language is a dialect of the other negro languages in the great valley; and as many of the Batoka living under the Makololo understand both it and the Sichuana, missionaries could soon acquire it through that medium.

Monze had never been visited by any white man, but had seen black native traders, who, he said, came for ivory, not for slaves. He had heard of white men passing far to the east of him to Cazembe, referring, no doubt, to Pereira, Lacerda, and others, who have visited that chief.

The streams in this part are not perennial; I did not observe one suitable for the purpose of irrigation. There is but little wood; here and there you see large single trees, or small clumps of evergreens, but the abundance of maize and ground-nuts we met with shows that more rain falls than in the Bechuana country, for there they never attempt to raise maize except in damp hollows on the banks of rivers. The pasturage is very fine for both cattle and sheep. My own men, who know the land thoroughly, declare that it is all garden-ground together, and that the more tender grains, which require richer soil than the native corn, need no care here. It is seldom stony.

The men of a village came to our encampment, and, as they followed the Bashukulompo mode of dressing their hair, we had an opportunity of examining it for the first time. A circle of hair at the top of the head, eight inches or more in diameter, is woven into a cone eight or ten inches high, with an obtuse apex, bent, in some cases, a little forward, giving it somewhat the appearance of a helmet. Some have only a cone, four or five inches in diameter at the base. It is said that the hair of animals is added; but the sides of the cone are woven something like basket-work. The head man of this village, instead of having his brought to a point, had it prolonged into a wand, which extended a full yard from the crown of his head. The hair on the forehead, above the ears, and behind, is all shaven off, so they appear somewhat as if a cap of liberty were cocked upon the top of the head. After the weaving is performed it is said to be painful, as the scalp is drawn tightly up; but they become used to it. Monze informed me that all his people were formerly ornamented in this way, but he discouraged it. I wished him to discourage the practice of knocking out the teeth too, but he smiled, as if in that case the fashion would be too strong for him, as it was for Sebituane.

Monze came on Monday morning, and, on parting, presented us with a piece of a buffalo which had been killed the day before by lions. We crossed the rivulet Makoe, which runs westward into the Kafue, and went northward in order to visit Semalembue, an influential chief there. We slept at the village of Monze's sister, who also passes by the same name. Both he and his sister are feminine in their appearance, but disfigured by the foolish custom of knocking out the upper front teeth.

It is not often that jail-birds turn out well, but the first person who appeared to welcome us at the village of Monze's sister was the prisoner we had released in the way. He came with a handsome present of corn and meal, and, after praising our kindness to the villagers who had assembled around us, asked them, "What do you stand gazing at? Don't you know that they have mouths like other people?" He then set off and brought large bundles of grass and wood for our comfort, and a pot to cook our food in.

DECEMBER 12TH. The morning presented the appearance of a continuous rain from the north, the first time we had seen it set in from that quarter in such a southern latitude. In the Bechuana country, continuous rains are always from the northeast or east, while in Londa and Angola they are from the north. At Pungo Andongo, for instance, the whitewash is all removed from the north side of the houses. It cleared up, however, about midday, and Monze's sister conducted us a mile or two upon the road. On parting, she said that she had forwarded orders to a distant village to send food to the point where we should sleep. In expressing her joy at the prospect of living in peace, she said it would be so pleasant "to sleep without dreaming of any one pursuing them with a spear."

In our front we had ranges of hills called Chamai, covered with trees. We crossed the rivulet Nakachinta, flowing westward into the Kafue, and then passed over ridges of rocks of the same mica schist which we found so abundant in Golungo Alto; here they were surmounted by reddish porphyry and finely laminated felspathic grit with trap. The dip, however, of these rocks is not toward the centre of the continent, as in Angola, for ever since we passed the masses of granite on the Kalomo, the rocks, chiefly of mica schist, dip away from them, taking an easterly direction. A decided change of dip occurs again when we come near the Zambesi, as will be noticed farther on. The hills which flank that river now appeared on our right as a high dark range, while those near the Kafue have the aspect of a low blue range, with openings between. We crossed two never-failing rivulets also flowing into the Kafue. The country is very fertile, but vegetation is nowhere rank. The boiling-point of water being 204 Deg., showed that we were not yet as low down as Linyanti; but we had left the masuka-trees behind us, and many others with which we had become familiar. A feature common to the forests of Angola and Benguela, namely, the presence of orchilla-weed and lichens on the trees, with mosses on the ground, began to appear; but we never, on any part of the eastern slope, saw the abundant crops of ferns which are met with every where in Angola. The orchilla-weed and mosses, too, were in but small quantities.

As we passed along, the people continued to supply us with food in great abundance. They had by some means or other got a knowledge that I carried medicine, and, somewhat to the disgust of my men, who wished to keep it all to themselves, brought their sick children for cure. Some of them I found had hooping-cough, which is one of the few epidemics that range through this country.

In passing through the woods I for the first time heard the bird called Mokwa reza, or "Son-in-law of God" (Micropogon sulphuratus?), utter its cry, which is supposed by the natives to be "pula, pula" (rain, rain). It is said to do this only before heavy falls of rain. It may be a cuckoo, for it is said to throw out the eggs of the white-backed Senegal crow, and lay its own instead. This, combined with the cry for rain, causes the bird to be regarded with favor. The crow, on the other hand, has a bad repute, and, when rain is withheld, its nest is sought for and destroyed, in order to dissolve the charm by which it is supposed to seal up the windows of heaven. All the other birds now join in full chorus in the mornings, and two of them, at least, have fine loud notes.

Chapter 28

Beautiful Valley—Buffalo—My young Men kill two Elephants—The Hunt—Mode of measuring Height of live Elephants—Wild Animals smaller here than in the South, though their Food is more abundant—The Elephant a dainty Feeder—Semalembue—His Presents—Joy in prospect of living in Peace—Trade—His People's way of wearing their Hair—Their Mode of Salutation—Old Encampment—Sebituane's former Residence—Ford of Kafue—Hippopotami—Hills and Villages—Geological Formation—Prodigious Quantities of large Game—Their Tameness—Rains—Less Sickness than in the Journey to Loanda—Reason—Charge from an Elephant—Vast Amount of animal Life on the Zambesi—Water of River discolored—An Island with Buffaloes and Men on it—Native Devices for killing Game—Tsetse now in Country—Agricultural Industry—An Albino murdered by his Mother—"Guilty of Tlolo"—Women who make their Mouths "like those of Ducks"—First Symptom of the Slave-trade on this side—Selole's Hostility—An armed Party hoaxed—An Italian Marauder slain—Elephant's Tenacity of Life—A Word to young Sportsmen— Mr. Oswell's Adventure with an Elephant; narrow Escape—Mburuma's Village—Suspicious Conduct of his People—Guides attempt to detain us—The Village and People of Ma Mburuma—Character our Guides give of us.

13TH. The country is becoming very beautiful, and furrowed by deep valleys; the underlying rocks, being igneous, have yielded fertile soil. There is great abundance of large game. The buffaloes select open spots, and often eminences, as standing-places through the day. We crossed the Mbai, and found in its bed rocks of pink marble. Some little hills near it are capped by marble of beautiful whiteness, the underlying rock being igneous. Violent showers occur frequently on the hills, and cause such sudden sweeping floods in these rivulets, that five of our men, who had gone to the other side for firewood, were obliged to swim back. The temperature of the air is lowered considerably by the daily rains. Several times the thermometer at sunrise has been as low as 68 Deg., and 74 Deg. at sunset. Generally, however, it stood at from 72 Deg. to 74 Deg. at sunrise, 90 Deg. to 96 Deg. at midday, and 80 Deg. to 84 Deg. at sunset. The sensation, however, as before remarked, was not disagreeable.

14TH. We entered a most beautiful valley, abounding in large game. Finding a buffalo lying down, I went to secure him for our food. Three balls did not kill him, and, as he turned round as if for a charge, we ran for the shelter of some rocks. Before we gained them, we found that three elephants, probably attracted by the strange noise, had cut off our retreat on that side; they, however, turned short off, and allowed us to gain the rocks. We then saw that the buffalo was moving off quite briskly, and, in order not to be entirely balked, I tried a long shot at the last of the elephants, and, to the great joy of my people, broke his fore leg. The young men soon brought him to a stand, and one shot in the brain dispatched him. I was right glad to see the joy manifested at such an abundant supply of meat.

On the following day, while my men were cutting up the elephant, great numbers of the villagers came to enjoy the feast. We were on the side of a fine green valley, studded here and there with trees, and cut by numerous rivulets. I had retired from the noise, to take an observation among some rocks of laminated grit, when I beheld an elephant and her calf at the end of the valley, about two miles distant. The calf was rolling in the mud, and the dam was standing fanning herself with her great ears. As I looked at them through my glass, I saw a long string of my own men appearing on the other side of them, and Sekwebu came and told me that these had gone off saying, "Our father will see to-day what sort of men he has got." I then went higher up the side of the valley, in order to have a distinct view of their mode of hunting. The goodly beast, totally unconscious of the approach of an enemy, stood for some time suckling her young one, which seemed about two years old; they then went into a pit containing mud, and smeared themselves all over with it, the little one frisking about his dam, flapping his ears and tossing his trunk incessantly, in elephantine fashion. She kept flapping her ears and wagging her tail, as if in the height of enjoyment. Then began the piping of her enemies, which was performed by blowing into a tube, or the hands closed together, as boys do into a key. They call out to attract the animal's attention,

> "O chief! chief! we have come to kill you.
> O chief! chief! many more will die besides you, etc.
> The gods have said it," etc., etc.

Both animals expanded their ears and listened, then left their bath as the crowd rushed toward them. The little one ran forward toward the end of the valley, but, seeing the men there, returned to his dam. She placed herself on the danger side of her calf, and passed her proboscis over it again and again, as if to assure it of safety. She frequently looked back to the men, who kept up an incessant shouting, singing, and piping; then looked at her young one and ran after it, sometimes sideways, as if her feelings were divided between anxiety to protect her offspring and desire to revenge the temerity of her persecutors. The men kept about a hundred yards in her rear, and some that distance from her flanks, and continued thus until she was obliged to cross a rivulet. The time spent in descending and getting up the opposite bank allowed of their coming up to the edge, and discharging their spears at about twenty yards distance. After the first discharge she appeared with her sides red with blood, and, beginning to flee for her own life, seemed to think no more of her young. I had previously sent off Sekwebu with orders to spare the calf. It ran very fast, but neither young nor old ever enter into a gallop; their quickest pace is only a sharp walk. Before Sekwebu could reach them, the calf had taken refuge in the water, and was killed. The pace of the dam gradually became slower. She turned with a shriek of rage, and made a furious charge back among the men. They vanished at right angles to her course, or sideways, and, as she ran straight on, she went through the whole party, but came near no one except a man who wore a piece of cloth on his shoulders. Bright clothing is always dangerous in these cases. She charged three or four times, and, except in the first instance, never went farther than 100 yards. She often stood after she had crossed a rivulet, and faced the men, though she received fresh spears. It was by this process of spearing and loss of blood that she was killed; for at last, making a short charge, she staggered round and sank down dead in a kneeling posture. I did not see the whole hunt, having been tempted away by both sun and moon appearing unclouded. I turned from the spectacle of the destruction of noble animals, which might be made so useful in Africa, with a feeling of sickness, and it was not relieved by the recollection that the ivory was mine, though that was the case. I regretted to see them killed, and more especially the young one, the meat not being at all necessary at that time; but it is right to add that I did not feel sick when my own blood was up the day before. We ought, perhaps, to judge those deeds more leniently in which we ourselves have no temptation to engage. Had I not been previously guilty of doing the very same thing, I might have prided myself on superior humanity when I experienced the nausea in viewing my men kill these two.

The elephant first killed was a male, not full grown; his height at the withers, 8 feet 4 inches; circumference of the fore foot, 44 inches * 2 = 7 feet 4 inches. The female was full grown, and measured in height 8 feet 8 inches; circumference of the fore foot, 48 inches * 2 = 8 feet (96 inches). We afterward found that full-grown male elephants of this region ranged in height at the withers from 9 feet 9 inches to 9 feet 10 inches, and the circumference of the fore foot to be 4 feet 9-1/2 inches * 2 = 9 feet 7 inches. These details are given because the general rule has been observed that twice the circumference of the impression made by the fore foot on the ground is the height of the animal.

The print on the ground, being a little larger than the foot itself, would thus seem to be an accurate mode of measuring the size of any elephant that has passed; but the above measurements show that it is applicable only to full-grown animals. The greater size of the African elephant in the south would at once distinguish it from the Indian one; but here they approach more nearly to each other in bulk, a female being about as large as a common Indian male. But the ear of the African is an external mark which no one will mistake even in a picture. That of the female now killed was 4 feet 5 inches in depth, and 4 feet in horizontal breadth. I have seen a native creep under one so as to be quite covered from the rain. The ear of the Indian variety is not more than a third of this size. The representation of elephants on ancient coins shows that this important characteristic was distinctly recognized of old. Indeed, Cuvier remarked that it was better known by Aristotle than by Buffon.

Having been anxious to learn whether the African elephant is capable of being tamed, through the kindness of my friend Admiral Smythe I am enabled to give the reader conclusive evidence on this point. In the two medals furnished from his work, "A descriptive Catalogue of his Cabinet of Roman and Imperial large brass Medals", the size of the ears will be at once noted as those of the true African elephant.* They were even more docile than the Asiatic, and were taught various feats, as walking on ropes, dancing, etc. One of the coins is of Faustina senior, the other of Severus the Seventh, and struck A.D. 197. These elephants were brought from Africa to Rome. The attempt to tame this most useful animal has never been made at the Cape, nor has one ever been exhibited in England. There is only one very young calf of the species in the British Museum.

> * *Unfortunately these illustrations can not be presented in this ASCII text. A. L., 1997.*

The abundance of food in this country, as compared with the south, would lead one to suppose that animals here must attain a much greater size; but actual measurement now confirms the impression made on my mind by the mere sight of the animals, that those in the districts north of 20 Deg. were smaller than the same races existing southward of that latitude. The first time that Mr. Oswell and myself saw full-grown male elephants on the River Zouga, they seemed no larger than the females (which are always smaller than males) we had met on the Limpopo. There they attain a height of upward of 12 feet. At the Zouga the height of one I measured was 11 feet 4 inches, and in this district 9 feet 10 inches. There is, however, an increase in the size of the tusks as we approach the equator. Unfortunately, I never made measurements of other animals in the south; but the appearance of the animals themselves in the north at once produced the impression on my mind referred to as to their decrease in size. When we first saw koodoos, they were so much smaller than those we had been accustomed to in the south that we doubted whether they were not a new kind of antelope; and the leche, seen nowhere south of 20 Deg., is succeeded by the poku as we go north. This is, in fact, only a smaller species of that antelope, with a more reddish color. A great difference in size prevails also among domestic animals; but the influence of locality on them is not so well marked. The cattle of the Batoka, for instance, are exceedingly small and very beautiful, possessing generally great breadth between the eyes and a very playful disposition. They are much smaller than the aboriginal cattle in the south; but it must be added that those of the Barotse valley, in the same latitudes as the Batoka, are large. The breed may have come from the west, as the cattle within the influence of the sea air, as at Little Fish Bay, Benguela, Ambriz, and along that coast, are very large. Those found at Lake Ngami, with large horns and standing six feet high, probably come from the same quarter. The goats are also small, and domestic fowls throughout this country are of a very small size, and even dogs, except where the inhabitants have had an opportunity of improving the breed by importation from the Portuguese. As the Barotse cattle are an exception to this general rule, so are the Barotse dogs, for they are large, savage-looking animals, though in reality very cowardly. It is a little remarkable that a decrease in size should occur where food is the most abundant; but tropical climates seem unfavorable for the full development of either animals or man. It is not from want of care in the breeding, for the natives always choose the larger and stronger males for stock, and the same arrangement prevails in nature, for it is only by overcoming their weaker rivals that the wild males obtain possession of the herd. Invariably they show the scars received in battle. The elephant we killed yesterday had an umbilical hernia as large as a child's head, probably caused by the charge of a rival. The cow showed scars received from men; two of the wounds in her side were still unhealed, and there was an orifice six inches long, and open, in her proboscis, and, as it was about a foot from the point, it must have interfered with her power of lifting water.

In estimating the amount of food necessary for these and other large animals, sufficient attention has not been paid to the kinds chosen. The elephant, for instance, is a most dainty feeder, and particularly fond of certain sweet-tasted trees and fruits. He chooses the mohonono, the mimosa, and other trees which contain much saccharine matter, mucilage, and gum. He may be seen putting his head to a lofty palmyra, and swaying it to and fro to shake off the seeds; he then picks them up singly and eats them. Or he may be seen standing by the masuka and other fruit-trees patiently picking off the sweet fruits one by one. He also digs up bulbs and tubers, but none of these are thoroughly digested. Bruce remarked upon the undigested bits of wood seen in their droppings, and he must have observed, too, that neither leaves nor seeds are changed by passing through the alimentary canal. The woody fibre of roots and branches is dropped in the state of tow, the nutritious matter alone having been extracted. This capability of removing all the nourishment, and the selection of those kinds of food which contain great quantities of mucilage and gum, accounts for the fact that herds of elephants produce but small effect upon the vegetation of a country—quality being more requisite than quantity. The amount of internal fat found in them makes them much prized by the inhabitants, who are all very fond of it, both for food and ointment.

After leaving the elephant valley we passed through a very beautiful country, but thinly inhabited by man. The underlying rock is trap, and dikes of talcose gneiss. The trap is often seen tilted on its edge, or dipping a little either to the north or south. The strike is generally to the northeast, the direction we are going. About Losito we found the trap had given place to hornblende schist, mica schist, and various schorly rocks. We had now come into the region in which the appearance of the rocks conveys the impression of a great force having acted along the bed of the Zambesi. Indeed, I was led to the belief from seeing the manner in which the rocks have been thrust away on both sides from its bed, that the power which formed the crack of the falls had given direction to the river below, and opened a bed for it all the way from the falls to beyond the gorge of Lupata.

Passing the rivulet Losito, and through the ranges of hills, we reached the residence of Semalembue on the 18th. His village is situated at the bottom of ranges through which the Kafue finds a passage, and close to the bank of that river. The Kafue, sometimes called Kahowhe or Bashukulompo River, is upward of two hundred yards wide here, and full of hippopotami, the young of which may be seen perched on the necks of their dams. At this point we had reached about the same level as Linyanti.

Semalembue paid us a visit soon after our arrival, and said that he had often heard of me, and now that he had the pleasure of seeing me, he feared that I should sleep the first night at his village hungry. This was considered the handsome way of introducing a present, for he then handed five or six baskets of meal and maize, and an enormous one of ground-nuts. Next morning he gave me about twenty baskets more of meal. I could make but a poor return for his kindness, but he accepted my apologies politely, saying that he knew there were no goods in the country from which I had come, and, in professing great joy at the words of peace I spoke, he said, "Now I shall cultivate largely, in the hope of eating and sleeping in peace." It is noticeable that all whom we have yet met eagerly caught up the idea of living in peace as the probable effect of the Gospel. They require no explanation of the existence of the Deity. Sekwebu makes use of the term "Reza", and they appear to understand at once. Like negroes in general, they have a strong tendency to worship, and I heard that Semalembue gets a good deal of ivory from the surrounding tribes on pretense of having some supernatural power. He transmits this to some other chiefs on the Zambesi, and receives in return English cotton goods which come from Mozambique by Babisa traders. My men here began to sell their beads and other ornaments for cotton cloth. Semalembue was accompanied by about forty people, all large men. They have much wool on their heads, which is sometimes drawn all together up to the crown, and tied there in a large tapering bunch. The forehead and round by the ears is shaven close to the base of this tuft. Others draw out the hair on one side, and twist it into little strings. The rest is taken over, and hangs above the ear, which gives the appearance of having a cap cocked jauntily on the side of the head.

The mode of salutation is by clapping the hands. Various parties of women came from the surrounding villages to see the white man, but all seemed very much afraid. Their fear, which I seldom could allay, made them, when addressed, clap their hands with increasing vigor. Sekwebu was the only one of the Makololo who knew this part of the country; and this was the region which to his mind was best adapted for the residence of a tribe. The natives generally have a good idea of the nature of the soil and pasturage, and Sekwebu expatiated with great eloquence on the capabilities of this part for supplying the wants of the Makololo. There is certainly abundance of room at present in the country for thousands and thousands more of population.

We passed near the Losito, a former encampment of the Matebele, with whom Sekwebu had lived. At the sight of the bones of the oxen they had devoured, and the spot where savage dances had taken place, though all deserted now, the poor fellow burst out into a wild Matebele song. He pointed out also a district, about two days and a half west of Semalembue, where Sebituane had formerly dwelt. There is a hot fountain on the hills there named "Nakalombo", which may be seen at a distance emitting steam. "There," said Sekwebu, "had your Molekane (Sebituane) been alive, he would have brought you to live with him. You would be on the bank of the river, and, by taking canoes, you would at once sail down to the Zambesi, and visit the white people at the sea."

This part is a favorite one with the Makololo, and probably it would be a good one in which to form a centre of civilization. There is a large, flat district of country to the north, said to be peopled by the Bashukulompo and other tribes, who cultivate the ground to a great extent, and raise vast quantities of grain, ground-nuts, sweet potatoes, etc. They also grow sugar-cane. If they were certain of a market, I believe they would not be unwilling to cultivate cotton too, but they have not been accustomed to the peaceful pursuits of commerce. All are fond of trade, but they have been taught none save that in ivory and slaves.

The Kafue enters a narrow gorge close by the village of Semalembue; as the hill on the north is called Bolengwe, I apply that name to the gorge (lat. 15d 48' 19" S., long. 28d 22' E.). Semalembue said that he ought to see us over the river, so he accompanied us to a pass about a mile south of his village, and when we entered among the hills we found the ford of the Kafue. On parting with Semalembue I put on him a shirt, and he went away with it apparently much delighted.

The ford was at least 250 yards broad, but rocky and shallow. After crossing it in a canoe, we went along the left bank, and were completely shut in by high hills. Every available spot between the river and the hills is under cultivation; and the residence of the people here is intended to secure safety for themselves and their gardens from their enemies; there is plenty of garden-ground outside the hills; here they are obliged to make pitfalls to protect the grain against the hippopotami. As these animals had not been disturbed by guns, they were remarkably tame, and took no notice of our passing. We again saw numbers of young ones, not much larger than terrier dogs, sitting on the necks of their dams, the little saucy-looking heads cocking up between the old one's ears; as they become a little older they sit on the withers. Needing meat, we shot a full-grown cow, and found, as we had often done before, the flesh to be very much like pork. The height of this animal was 4 feet 10 inches, and from the point of the nose to the root of the tail 10 feet 6. They seem quarrelsome, for both males and females are found covered with scars, and young males are often killed by the elder ones: we met an instance of this near the falls.

We came to a great many little villages among the hills, as if the inhabitants had reason to hide themselves from the observation of their enemies. While detained cutting up the hippopotamus, I ascended a hill called Mabue asula (stones smell badly), and, though not the highest in sight, it was certainly not 100 feet lower than the most elevated. The boiling-point of water showed it to be about 900 feet above the river, which was of the level of Linyanti. These hills seemed to my men of prodigious altitude, for they had been accustomed to ant-hills only. The mention of mountains that pierced the clouds made them draw in their breath and hold their hands to their mouths. And when I told them that their previous description of Taba cheu had led me to expect something of the sort, I found that the idea of a cloud-capped mountain had never entered into their heads. The mountains certainly look high, from having abrupt sides; but I had recognized the fact by the point of ebullition of water, that they are of a considerably lower altitude than the top of the ridge we had left. They constitute, in fact, a sort of low fringe on the outside of the eastern ridge, exactly as the (apparently) high mountains of Angola (Golungo Alto) form an outer low fringe to the western ridge. I was much struck by the similarity of conformation and nature of the rocks on both sides of the continent; but there is a difference in the structure of the subtending ridges, as may be understood by the annexed ideal geological section.

*[The ASCII edition cannot include the drawing of the cross-section, but the comments are included in full.—A. L., 1997.]

IDEAL SECTION ACROSS SOUTH CENTRAL AFRICA, INTENDED TO SHOW THE ELEVATED VALLEY FORM OF THAT PORTION OF THE CONTINENT.

—————————————————

WEST.

[Terrain]   [Remarks]

Sea.   CALCAREOUS TUFA.

TRAP. *With modern shells, and similar to those now found in the sea adjacent, with strongly magnetic iron ore.*

MICA SCHIST. *Dipping East.*

SANDSTONE *(like that of East Africa). The rocks*

in Pungo Andongo. *of Pungo Andongo are a conglomerate of rounded shingle*

Rocks 4000 feet. *a matrix of sandstone, and stand on horizontal sandstone, on which fossil palms appear.*

Fault.

RED SHALES CAPPED BY FERRUGINOUS CONGLOMERATE.
Soft red shale or "keele".

G | 5000 feet.
R | Water boils
E | at 202 Deg.
A | On top, ferruginous conglomerate; below that, red shale,
T | 4500 feet.   with banks of gravel.
  | Lake Dilolo.
C | TUFA AND TRAP. In Londa, the bottom of the valley
E | 2500 feet.   is formed of ferruginous conglomerate on the surface;
N | Lake Ngami. hardened sandstone, with madrepore holes,
T | banks of gravel, and occasionally trap;
R | south of 12 Degrees, large patches of soft
A | TUFA. calcareous tufa, with pebbles of jasper,
L | agates, &c., lie on various horizontal traps,
  | amygdaloids with analami and mesotype, which is
P | burst through by basaltic rocks forming hills,
L | and showing that the bottom of the valley
A | RADIATED ZEOLITE. consists of old silurian schists;
T | there are also various granitic rocks
E | cropping through the trap.
A |
U | BASALTIC ROCKS. Augitic porphyry and basalt,
. | with tufa over it.

Place of Great Cataract.

          MICA SCHIST. White mica schist dipping west, and gneiss.

5000 feet. Kalomo.
Water boils   *GRANITE. With black mica.*
at 202 Deg.

          MICA SCHIST. White mica schist and white marble.

Hill tops   *TRAP. Hot fountain; conical hills of igneous rocks,*
4000 feet.   *containing much mica.*
Bottoms 3500 feet.

          MICA SCHIST. Pink marble dolomite,
          on hills of mica schist, of various colours, with trap,
          schorl in gneiss, kyanite or disthene gneissose mica
          in the schist.

1500 ft.   *COAL IN SANDSTONE. Specular and magnetic iron*
          on various igneous rocks; finely laminated porphyry;
          granite; hot fountain.

          Sandstone overlying coal; trap dykes;
          syenitic porphyry dykes; black vesicular trap,
          penetrating in thin veins the clay shale of the country,
          converting it into porcellanite, and partially
          crystallizing the coal. On this sandstone
          lie fossil palms, and coniferous trees
          converted into silica, as on a similar rock in Angola.

          COMPACT SILICEOUS SCHIST.

IGNEOUS ROCKS. Trappean rocks, with hot fountain.

CALCAREOUS TUFA. Arkose, or granitic grit, with modern shells covered by calcareous tufa.

Sea.

EAST.

The heights are given as an approximation obtained from observing the boiling point of water, they are drawn on a scale of 1/10 of an inch per 1000 feet in altitude. The section is necessarily exaggerated in longitude, as it was traversed in different latitudes, the western side being in 8d-12d, the eastern 15d-18d S.

We can see from this hill five distinct ranges, of which Bolengo is the most westerly, and Komanga is the most easterly. The second is named Sekonkamena, and the third Funze. Very many conical hills appear among them, and they are generally covered with trees. On their tops we have beautiful white quartz rocks, and some have a capping of dolomite. On the west of the second range we have great masses of kyanite or disthene, and on the flanks of the third and fourth a great deal of specular iron ore which is magnetic, and containing a very large percentage of the metal. The sides of these ranges are generally very precipitous, and there are rivulets between which are not perennial. Many of the hills have been raised by granite, exactly like that of the Kalomo. Dikes of this granite may be seen thrusting up immense masses of mica schist and quartz or sandstone schist, and making the strata fold over them on each side, as clothes hung upon a line. The uppermost stratum is always dolomite or bright white quartz. Semalembue intended that we should go a little to the northeast, and pass through the people called Babimpe, and we saw some of that people, who invited us to come that way on account of its being smoother; but, feeling anxious to get back to the Zambesi again, we decided to cross the hills toward its confluence with the Kafue. The distance, which in a straight line is but small, occupied three days. The precipitous nature of the sides of this mass of hills knocked up the oxen and forced us to slaughter two, one of which, a very large one, and ornamented with upward of thirty pieces of its own skin detached and hanging down, Sekeletu had wished us to take to the white people as a specimen of his cattle. We saw many elephants among the hills, and my men ran off and killed three. When we came to the top of the outer range of the hills we had a glorious view. At a short distance below us we saw the Kafue, wending away over a forest-clad plain to the confluence, and on the other side of the Zambesi, beyond that, lay a long range of dark hills. A line of fleecy clouds appeared lying along the course of that river at their base. The plain below us, at the left of the Kafue, had more large game on it than any where else I had seen in Africa. Hundreds of buffaloes and zebras grazed on the open spaces, and there stood lordly elephants feeding majestically, nothing moving apparently but the proboscis. I wished that I had been able to take a photograph of a scene so seldom beheld, and which is destined, as guns increase, to pass away from earth. When we descended we found all the animals remarkably tame. The elephants stood beneath the trees, fanning themselves with their large ears, as if they did not see us at 200 or 300 yards distance. The number of animals was quite astonishing, and made me think that here I could realize an image of that time when Megatheria fed undisturbed in the primeval forests. We saw great numbers of red-colored pigs ('Potamochoerus') standing gazing at us in wonder. The people live on the hills, and, having no guns, seldom disturb the game. They have never been visited, even by half-castes; but Babisa traders have come occasionally. Continuous rains kept us for some time on the banks of the Chiponga, and here we were unfortunate enough to come among the tsetse. Mr. J. N. Gray, of the British Museum, has kindly obliged me with a drawing of the insect, with the ravages of which I have unfortunately been too familiar. (For description, see p. 94-96 [Chapter 4 Paragraphs 16-20].) No. 1 is the insect somewhat smaller than life, from the specimen having contracted in drying; they are a little larger than the common house-fly. No. 2 is the insect magnified; and No. 3 shows the magnified proboscis and poison-bulb at the root.*

> *Unfortunately, these illustrations can not be presented in this ASCII text. Fortunately, information on the Tsetse is no longer difficult to find. The "somewhat smaller than life" drawing is about 1 cm from head to tail, not including wings or proboscis. — A. L., 1997.

We tried to leave one morning, but the rain coming on afresh brought us to a stand, and after waiting an hour, wet to the skin, we were fain to retrace our steps to our sheds. These rains were from the east, and the clouds might be seen on the hills exactly as the "Table-cloth" on Table Mountain. This was the first wetting we had got since we left Sesheke, for I had gained some experience in traveling. In Londa we braved the rain, and, as I despised being carried in our frequent passage through running water, I was pretty constantly drenched; but now, when we saw a storm coming, we invariably halted. The men soon pulled grass sufficient to make a little shelter for themselves by placing it on a bush, and, having got my camp-stool and umbrella, with a little grass under my feet, I kept myself perfectly dry. We also lighted large fires, and the men were not chilled by streams of water running down their persons, and abstracting the heat, as they would have been had they been exposed to the rain. When it was over they warmed themselves by the fires, and we traveled on comfortably. The effect of this care was, that we had much less sickness than with a smaller party in journeying to Loanda. Another improvement made from my experience was avoiding an entire change of diet. In going to Loanda I took little or no European food, in order not to burden my men and make them lose spirit, but trusted entirely to what might be got by the gun and the liberality of the Balonda; but on this journey I took some flour which had been left in the wagon, with some got on the island, and baked my own bread all the way in an extemporaneous oven made by an inverted pot. With these precautions, aided, no doubt, by the greater healthiness of the district over which we passed, I enjoyed perfect health.

When we left the Chipongo on the 30th we passed among the range of hills on our left, which are composed of mica and clay slate. At the bottom we found a forest of large silicified trees, all lying as if the elevation of the range had made them fall away from it, and toward the river. An ordinary-sized tree standing on end, measured 22 inches in diameter: there were 12 laminae to the inch. These are easily counted, because there is usually a scale of pure silica between each, which has not been so much affected by the weather as the rest of the ring itself: the edges of the rings thus stand out plainly. Mr. Quekett, having kindly examined some specimens, finds that it is "silicified CONIFEROUS WOOD of the ARAUCARIAN type; and the nearest allied wood that he knows of is that found, also in a fossil state, in New South Wales." The numbers of large game were quite astonishing. I never saw elephants so tame as those near the Chiponga: they stood close to our path without being the least afraid. This is different from their conduct where they have been accustomed to guns, for there they take alarm at the distance of a mile, and begin to run if a shot is fired even at a longer distance. My men killed another here, and rewarded the villagers of the Chiponga for their liberality in meal by loading them with flesh. We spent a night at a baobab, which was hollow, and would hold twenty men inside. It had been used as a lodging-house by the Babisa.

As we approached nearer the Zambesi, the country became covered with broad-leaved bushes, pretty thickly planted, and we had several times to shout to elephants to get out of our way. At an open space, a herd of buffaloes came trotting up to look at our oxen, and it was only by shooting one that I made them retreat. The meat is very much like that of an ox, and this one was very fine. The only danger we actually encountered was from a female elephant, with three young ones of different sizes. Charging through the centre of our extended line, and causing the men to throw down their burdens in a great hurry, she received a spear for her temerity. I never saw an elephant with more than one calf before. We knew that we were near our Zambesi again, even before the great river burst upon our sight, by the numbers of water-fowl we met. I killed four geese with two shots, and, had I followed the wishes of my men, could have secured a meal of water-fowl for the whole party. I never saw a river with so much animal life around and in it, and, as the Barotse say, "Its fish and fowl are always fat." When our eyes were gladdened by a view of its goodly broad waters, we found it very much larger than it is even above the falls. One might try to make his voice heard across it in vain. Its flow was more rapid than near Sesheke, being often four and a half miles an hour, and, what I never saw before, the water was discolored and of a deep brownish-red. In the great valley the Leeambye never becomes of this color. The adjacent country, so far north as is known, is all level, and the soil, being generally covered with dense herbage, is not abraded; but on the eastern ridge the case is different; the grass is short, and, the elevation being great, the soil is washed down by the streams, and hence the discoloration which we now view. The same thing was observed on the western ridge. We never saw discoloration till we reached the Quango; that obtained its matter from the western slope of the western ridge, just as this part of the Zambesi receives its soil from the eastern slope of the eastern ridge. It carried a considerable quantity of wreck of reeds, sticks, and trees. We struck upon the river about eight miles east of the confluence with the Kafue, and thereby missed a sight of that interesting point. The cloudiness of the weather was such that but few observations could be made for determining our position; so, pursuing our course, we went down the left bank, and came opposite the island of Menye makaba. The Zambesi contains numerous islands; this was about a mile and a half or two miles long, and upward of a quarter of a mile broad. Besides human population, it has a herd of buffaloes that never leave it. In the distance they seemed to be upward of sixty. The human and brute inhabitants understand each other; for when the former think they ought to avenge the liberties committed on their gardens, the leaders of the latter come out boldly to give battle. They told us that the only time in which they can thin them is when the river is full and part of the island flooded. They then attack them from their canoes. The comparatively small space to which they have confined themselves shows how luxuriant the vegetation of this region is; for were they in want of more pasture, as buffaloes can swim well, and the distance from this bank to the island is not much more than 200 yards, they might easily remove hither. The opposite bank is much more distant.

Ranges of hills appear now to run parallel with the Zambesi, and are about fifteen miles apart. Those on the north approach nearest to the river. The inhabitants on that side are the Batonga, those on the south bank are the Banyai. The hills abound in buffaloes, and elephants are numerous, and many are killed by the people on both banks. They erect stages on high trees overhanging the paths by which the elephants come, and then use a large spear with a handle nearly as thick as a man's wrist, and four or five feet long. When the animal comes beneath they throw the spear, and if it enters between the ribs above, as the blade is at least twenty inches long by two broad, the motion of the handle, as it is aided by knocking against the trees, makes frightful gashes within, and soon causes death. They kill them also by means of a spear inserted in a beam of wood, which being suspended on the branch of a tree by a cord attached to a latch fastened in the path, and intended to be struck by the animal's foot, leads to the fall of the beam, and, the spear being poisoned, causes death in a few hours.

We were detained by continuous rains several days at this island. The clouds rested upon the tops of the hills as they came from the eastward, and then poured down plenteous showers on the valleys below. As soon as we could move, Tomba Nyama, the head man of the island, volunteered the loan of a canoe to cross a small river, called the Chongwe, which we found to be about fifty or sixty yards broad and flooded. All this part of the country was well known to Sekwebu, and he informed us that, when he passed through it as a boy, the inhabitants possessed abundance of cattle, and there were no tsetse. The existence of the insect now shows that it may return in company with the larger game. The vegetation along the bank was exceedingly rank, and the bushes so tangled that it was difficult to get on. The paths had been made by the wild animals alone, for the general pathway of the people is the river, in their canoes. We usually followed the footpaths of the game, and of these there was no lack. Buffaloes, zebras, pallahs, and waterbucks abound, and there is also a great abundance of wild pigs, koodoos, and the black antelope. We got one buffalo as he was rolling himself in a pool of mud. He had a large piece of skin torn off his flank, it was believed by an alligator.

We were struck by the fact that, as soon as we came between the ranges of hills which flank the Zambesi, the rains felt warm. At sunrise the thermometer stood at from 82 Deg. to 86 Deg.; at midday, in the coolest shade, namely, in my little tent, under a shady tree, at 96 Deg. to 98 Deg.; and at sunset it was 86 Deg. This is different from any thing we experienced in the interior, for these rains always bring down the mercury to 72 Deg. or even 68 Deg. There, too, we found a small black coleopterous insect, which stung like the mosquito, but injected less poison; it puts us in mind of that insect, which does not exist in the high lands we had left.

JANUARY 6TH, 1856. Each village we passed furnished us with a couple of men to take us on to the next. They were useful in showing us the parts least covered with jungle. When we came near a village, we saw men, women, and children employed in weeding their gardens, they being great agriculturists. Most of the men are muscular, and have large plowman hands. Their color is the same admixture, from very dark to light olive, that we saw in Londa. Though all have thick lips and flat noses, only the more degraded of the population possess the ugly negro physiognomy. They mark themselves by a line of little raised cicatrices, each of which is a quarter of an inch long; they extend from the tip of the nose to the root of the hair on the forehead. It is remarkable that I never met with an Albino in crossing Africa, though, from accounts published by the Portuguese, I was led to expect that they were held in favor as doctors by certain chiefs. I saw several in the south: one at Kuruman is a full-grown woman, and a man having this peculiarity of skin was met with in the colony. Their bodies are always blistered on exposure to the sun, as the skin is more tender than that of the blacks. The Kuruman woman lived some time at Kolobeng, and generally had on her bosom and shoulders the remains of large blisters. She was most anxious to be made black, but nitrate of silver, taken internally, did not produce its usual effect. During the time I resided at Mabotsa, a woman came to the station with a fine boy, an Albino. The father had ordered her to throw him away, but she clung to her offspring for many years. He was remarkably intelligent for his age. The pupil of the eye was of a pink color, and the eye itself was unsteady in vision. The hair, or rather wool, was yellow, and the features were those common among the Bechuanas. After I left the place the mother is said to have become tired of living apart from the father, who refused to have her while she retained the son. She took him out one day, and killed him close to the village of Mabotsa, and nothing was done to her by the authorities. From having met with no Albinos in Londa, I suspect they are there also put to death. We saw one dwarf only in Londa, and brands on him showed he had once been a slave; and there is one dwarf woman at Linyanti. The general absence of deformed persons is partly owing to their destruction in infancy, and partly to the mode of life being a natural one, so far as ventilation and food are concerned. They use but few unwholesome mixtures as condiments, and, though their undress exposes them to the vicissitudes of the temperature, it does not harbor vomites. It was observed that, when smallpox and measles visited the country, they were most severe on the half-castes who were clothed. In several tribes, a child which is said to "tlola", transgress, is put to death. "Tlolo", or transgression, is ascribed to several curious cases. A child who cut the upper front teeth before the under was always put to death among the Bakaa, and, I believe, also among the Bakwains. In some tribes, a case of twins renders one of them liable to death; and an ox, which, while lying in the pen, beats the ground with its tail, is treated in the same way. It is thought to be calling death to visit the tribe. When I was coming through Londa, my men carried a great number of fowls, of a larger breed than any they had at home. If one crowed before midnight, it had been guilty of "tlolo", and was killed. The men often carried them sitting on their guns, and, if one began to crow in a forest, the owner would give it a beating, by way of teaching it not to be guilty of crowing at unseasonable hours.

The women here are in the habit of piercing the upper lip, and gradually enlarging the orifice until they can insert a shell. The lip then appears drawn out beyond the perpendicular of the nose, and gives them a most ungainly aspect. Sekwebu remarked, "These women want to make their mouths like those of ducks;" and, indeed, it does appear as if they had the idea that female beauty of lip had been attained by the 'Ornithorhynchus paradoxus' alone. This custom prevails throughout the country of the Maravi, and no one could see it without confessing that fashion had never led women to a freak more mad. We had rains now every day, and considerable cloudiness, but the sun often burst through with scorching intensity. All call out against it then, saying, "O the sun! that is rain again." It was worth noticing that my companions never complained of the heat while on the highlands, but when we descended into the lowlands of Angola, and here also, they began to fret on account of it. I myself felt an oppressive steaminess in the atmosphere which I had not experienced on the higher lands.

As the game was abundant and my party very large, I had still to supply their wants with the gun. We slaughtered the oxen only when unsuccessful in hunting. We always entered into friendly relations with the head men of the different villages, and they presented grain and other food freely. One man gave a basinful of rice, the first we met with in the country. It is never seen in the interior. He said he knew it was "white man's corn", and when I wished to buy some more, he asked me to give him a slave. This was the first symptom of the slave-trade on this side of the country. The last of these friendly head men was named Mobala; and having passed him in peace, we had no anticipation of any thing else; but, after a few hours, we reached Selole or Chilole, and found that he not only considered us enemies, but had actually sent an express to raise the tribe of Mburuma against us. All the women of Selole had fled, and the few people we met exhibited symptoms of terror. An armed party had come from Mburuma in obedience to the call; but the head man of the company, being Mburuma's brother, suspecting that it was a hoax, came to our encampment and told us the whole. When we explained our objects, he told us that Mburuma, he had no doubt, would receive us well. The reason why Selole acted in this foolish manner we afterward found to be this: an Italian named Simoens, and nicknamed Siriatomba (don't eat tobacco), had married the daughter of a chief called Sekokole, living north of Tete. He armed a party of fifty slaves with guns, and, ascending the river in canoes some distance beyond the island Meya makaba, attacked several inhabited islands beyond, securing a large number of prisoners, and much ivory. On his return, the different chiefs, at the instigation of his father-in-law, who also did not wish him to set up as a chief, united, attacked and dispersed the party of Simoens, and killed him while trying to escape on foot. Selole imagined that I was another Italian, or, as he expressed it, "Siriatomba risen from the dead." In his message to Mburuma he even said that Mobala, and all the villages beyond, were utterly destroyed by our fire-arms, but the sight of Mobala himself, who had come to the village of Selole, led the brother of Mburuma to see at once that it was all a hoax. But for this, the foolish fellow Selole might have given us trouble.

We saw many of the liberated captives of this Italian among the villages here, and Sekwebu found them to be Matebele. The brother of Mburuma had a gun, which was the first we had seen in coming eastward. Before we reached Mburuma my men went to attack a troop of elephants, as they were much in need of meat. When the troop began to run, one of them fell into a hole, and before he could extricate himself an opportunity was afforded for all the men to throw their spears. When he rose he was like a huge porcupine, for each of the seventy or eighty men had discharged more than one spear at him. As they had no more, they sent for me to finish him. In order to put him at once out of pain, I went to within twenty yards, there being a bank between us which he could not readily climb. I rested the gun upon an ant-hill so as to take a steady aim; but, though I fired twelve two-ounce bullets, all I had, into different parts, I could not kill him. As it was becoming dark, I advised my men to let him stand, being sure of finding him dead in the morning; but, though we searched all the next day, and went more than ten miles, we never saw him again. I mention this to young men who may think that they will be able to hunt elephants on foot by adopting the Ceylon practice of killing them by one ball in the brain. I believe that in Africa the practice of standing before an elephant, expecting to kill him with one shot, would be certain death to the hunter; and I would add, for the information of those who may think that, because I met with a great abundance of game here, they also might find rare sport, that the tsetse exists all along both banks of the Zambesi, and there can be no hunting by means of horses. Hunting on foot in this climate is such excessively hard work, that I feel certain the keenest sportsman would very soon turn away from it in disgust. I myself was rather glad, when furnished with the excuse that I had no longer any balls, to hand over all the hunting to my men, who had no more love for the sport than myself, as they never engaged in it except when forced by hunger.

Some of them gave me a hint to melt down my plate by asking if it were not lead. I had two pewter plates and a piece of zinc which I now melted into bullets. I also spent the remainder of my handkerchiefs in buying spears for them. My men frequently surrounded herds of buffaloes and killed numbers of the calves. I, too, exerted myself greatly; but, as I am now obliged to shoot with the left arm, I am a bad shot, and this, with the lightness of the bullets, made me very unsuccessful. The more the hunger, the less my success, invariably.

I may here add an adventure with an elephant of one who has had more narrow escapes than any man living, but whose modesty has always prevented him from publishing any thing about himself. When we were on the banks of the Zouga in 1850, Mr. Oswell pursued one of these animals into the dense, thick, thorny bushes met with on the margin of that river, and to which the elephant usually flees for safety. He followed through a narrow pathway by lifting up some of the branches and forcing his way through the rest; but, when he had just got over this difficulty, he saw the elephant, whose tail he had but got glimpses of before, now rushing toward him. There was then no time to lift up branches, so he tried to force the horse through them. He could not effect a passage; and, as there was but an instant between the attempt and failure, the hunter tried to dismount, but in doing this one foot was caught by a branch, and the spur drawn along the animal's flank; this made him spring away and throw the rider on the ground with his face to the elephant, which, being in full chase, still went on. Mr. Oswell saw the huge fore foot about to descend on his legs, parted them, and drew in his breath as if to resist the pressure of the other foot, which he expected would next descend on his body. He saw the whole length of the under part of the enormous brute pass over him; the horse got away safely. I have heard of but one other authentic instance in which an elephant went over a man without injury, and, for any one who knows the nature of the bush in which this occurred, the very thought of an encounter in it with such a foe is appalling. As the thorns are placed in pairs on opposite sides of the branches, and these turn round on being pressed against, one pair brings the other exactly into the position in which it must pierce the intruder. They cut like knives. Horses dread this bush extremely; indeed, most of them refuse to face its thorns.

On reaching Mburuma's village, his brother came to meet us. We explained the reason of our delay, and he told us that we were looked upon with alarm. He said that Siriatomba had been killed near the village of Selole, and hence that man's fears. He added that the Italian had come talking of peace, as we did, but had kidnapped children and bought ivory with them, and that we were supposed to be following the same calling. I pointed to my men, and asked if any of these were slaves, and if we had any children among them, and I think we satisfied him that we were true men. Referring to our ill success in hunting the day before, he said, "The man at whose village you remained was in fault in allowing you to want meat, for he had only to run across to Mburuma; he would have given him a little meal, and, having sprinkled that on the ground as an offering to the gods, you would have found your elephant." The chiefs in these parts take upon themselves an office somewhat like the priesthood, and the people imagine that they can propitiate the Deity through them. In illustration of their ideas, it may be mentioned that, when we were among the tribes west of Semalembue, several of the people came forward and introduced themselves—one as a hunter of elephants, another as a hunter of hippopotami, a third as a digger of pitfalls—apparently wishing me to give them medicine for success in their avocations, as well as to cure the diseases of those to whom I was administering the drugs. I thought they attributed supernatural power to them, for, like all Africans, they have unbounded faith in the efficacy of charms; but I took pains to let them know that they must pray and trust to another power than mine for aid. We never saw Mburuma himself, and the conduct of his people indicated very strong suspicions, though he gave us presents of meal, maize, and native corn. His people never came near us except in large bodies and fully armed. We had to order them to place their bows, arrows, and spears at a distance before entering our encampment. We did not, however, care much for a little trouble now, as we hoped that, if we could pass this time without much molestation, we might yet be able to return with ease, and without meeting sour, suspicious looks.

The soil, glancing every where with mica, is very fertile, and all the valleys are cultivated, the maize being now in ear and eatable. Ranges of hills, which line both banks of the river above this, now come close up to each bank, and form a narrow gorge, which, like all others of the same nature, is called Mpata. There is a narrow pathway by the side of the river, but we preferred a more open one in a pass among the hills to the east, which is called Mohango. The hills rise to a height of 800 or 1000 feet, and are all covered with trees. The rocks were of various colored mica schist; and parallel with the Zambesi lay a broad band of gneiss with garnets in it. It stood on edge, and several dikes of basalt, with dolerite, had cut through it.

Mburuma sent two men as guides to the Loangwa. These men tried to bring us to a stand, at a distance of about six miles from the village, by the notice, "Mburuma says you are to sleep under that tree." On declining to do this, we were told that we must wait at a certain village for a supply of corn. As none appeared in an hour, I proceeded on the march. It is not quite certain that their intentions were hostile, but this seemed to disarrange their plans, and one of them was soon observed running back to Mburuma. They had first of all tried to separate our party by volunteering the loan of a canoe to convey Sekwebu and me, together with our luggage, by way of the river, and, as it was pressed upon us, I thought that this was their design. The next attempt was to detain us in the pass; but, betraying no suspicion, we civilly declined to place ourselves in their power in an unfavorable position. We afterward heard that a party of Babisa traders, who came from the northeast, bringing English goods from Mozambique, had been plundered by this same people.

Elephants were still abundant, but more wild, as they fled with great speed as soon as we made our appearance. The country between Mburuma's and his mother's village was all hilly and very difficult, and prevented us from traveling more than ten miles a day. At the village of Ma Mburuma (mother of Mburuma), the guides, who had again joined us, gave a favorable report, and the women and children did not flee. Here we found that traders, called Bazunga, have been in the habit of coming in canoes, and that I was named as one of them. These I supposed to be half-caste Portuguese, for they said that the hair of their heads and the skin beneath their clothing were different from mine. Ma Mburuma promised us canoes to cross the Loangwa in our front. It was pleasant to see great numbers of men, women, and boys come, without suspicion, to look at the books, watch, looking-glass, revolver, etc. They are a strong, muscular race, and both men and women are seen cultivating the ground. The soil contains so much comminuted talc and mica from the adjacent hills that it seems as if mixed with spermaceti. They generally eat their corn only after it has begun to sprout from steeping it in water. The deformed lips of the women make them look very ugly; I never saw one smile. The people in this part seem to understand readily what is spoken about God, for they listen with great attention, and tell in return their own ideas of departed spirits. The position of the village of Mburuma's mother was one of great beauty, quite inclosed by high, steep hills; and the valleys are all occupied by gardens of native corn and maize, which grow luxuriantly. We were obliged to hurry along, for the oxen were bitten daily by the tsetse, which, as I have before remarked, now inhabits extensive tracts which once supported herds of cattle that were swept off by Mpakane and other marauders, whose devastations were well known to Sekwebu, for he himself had been an actor in the scenes. When he told me of them he always lowered his voice, in order that the guides might not hear that he had been one of their enemies. But that we were looked upon with suspicion, on account of having come in the footsteps of invaders, was evident from our guides remarking to men in the gardens through which we passed, "They have words of peace—all very fine; but lies only, as the Bazunga are great liars." They thought we did not understand them; but Sekwebu knew every word perfectly; and, without paying any ostensible attention to these complimentary remarks, we always took care to explain ever afterward that we were not Bazunga, but Makoa (English).

Chapter 29

Confluence of Loangwa and Zambesi—Hostile Appearances—Ruins of a Church—Turmoil of Spirit—Cross the River—Friendly Parting—Ruins of stone Houses—The Situation of Zumbo for Commerce—Pleasant Gardens—Dr. Lacerda's Visit to Cazembe—Pereira's Statement—Unsuccessful Attempt to establish Trade with the People of Cazembe—One of my Men tossed by a Buffalo—Meet a Man with Jacket and Hat on—Hear of the Portuguese and native War—Holms and Terraces on the Banks of a River—Dancing for Corn—Beautiful Country—Mpende's Hostility—Incantations—A Fight anticipated—Courage and Remarks of my Men—Visit from two old Councilors of Mpende—Their Opinion of the English—Mpende concludes not to fight us—His subsequent Friendship—Aids us to cross the River—The Country—Sweet Potatoes—Bakwain Theory of Rain confirmed—Thunder without Clouds—Desertion of one of my Men—Other Natives' Ideas of the English—Dalama (gold)—Inhabitants dislike Slave-buyers—Meet native Traders with American Calico—Game-laws— Elephant Medicine—Salt from the Sand—Fertility of Soil—Spotted Hyaena—Liberality and Politeness of the People—Presents—A stingy white Trader—Natives' Remarks about him—Effect on their Minds—Rain and Wind now from an opposite Direction—Scarcity of Fuel—Trees for Boat-building—Boroma—Freshets—Leave the River—Chicova, its Geological Features—Small Rapid near Tete—Loquacious Guide—Nyampungo, the Rain-charmer—An old Man—No Silver—Gold-washing—No Cattle.

14TH. We reached the confluence of the Loangwa and the Zambesi, most thankful to God for his great mercies in helping us thus far. Mburuma's people had behaved so suspiciously, that, though we had guides from him, we were by no means sure that we should not be attacked in crossing the Loangwa. We saw them here collecting in large numbers, and, though professing friendship, they kept at a distance from our camp. They refused to lend us more canoes than two, though they have many. They have no intercourse with Europeans except through the Babisa. They tell us that this was formerly the residence of the Bazunga, and maintain silence as to the cause of their leaving it. I walked about some ruins I discovered, built of stone, and found the remains of a church, and on one side lay a broken bell, with the letters I. H. S. and a cross, but no date. There were no inscriptions on stone, and the people could not tell what the Bazunga called their place. We found afterward it was Zumbo.

I felt some turmoil of spirit in the evening at the prospect of having all my efforts for the welfare of this great region and its teeming population knocked on the head by savages to-morrow, who might be said to "know not what they do." It seemed such a pity that the important fact of the existence of the two healthy ridges which I had discovered should not become known in Christendom, for a confirmation would thereby have been given to the idea that Africa is not open to the Gospel. But I read that Jesus said, "All power is given unto me in heaven and on earth; go ye, therefore, and teach all nations . . . and lo, I AM WITH YOU ALWAY, EVEN UNTO THE END OF THE WORLD." I took this as His word of honor, and then went out to take observations for latitude and longitude, which, I think, were very successful. (The church: lat. 15d 37' 22" S., long. 30d 32' E.)

15TH. The natives of the surrounding country collected around us this morning, all armed. The women and children were sent away, and one of Mburuma's wives, who lives in the vicinity, was not allowed to approach, though she had come from her village to pay me a visit. Only one canoe was lent to us, though we saw two others tied to the bank. The part we crossed was about a mile from the confluence, and, as it was now flooded, it seemed upward of half a mile in breadth. We passed all our goods first on to an island in the middle, then the remaining cattle and men; occupying the post of honor, I, as usual, was the last to enter the canoe. A number of the inhabitants stood armed all the time we were embarking. I showed them my watch, lens, and other things to keep them amused, until there only remained those who were to enter the canoe with me. I thanked them for their kindness, and wished them peace. After all, they may have been influenced only by the intention to be ready in case I should play them some false trick, for they have reason to be distrustful of the whites. The guides came over to bid us adieu, and we sat under a mango-tree fifteen feet in circumference. We found them more communicative now. They said that the land on both sides belonged to the Bazunga, and that they had left of old, on the approach of Changamera, Ngaba, and Mpakane. Sekwebu was with the last named, but he maintained that they never came to the confluence, though they carried off all the cattle of Mburuma. The guides confirmed this by saying that the Bazunga were not attacked, but fled in alarm on the approach of the enemy. This mango-tree he knew by its proper name, and we found seven others and several tamarinds, and were informed that the chief Mburuma sends men annually to gather the fruit, but, like many Africans whom I have known, has not had patience to propagate more trees. I gave them some little presents for themselves, a handkerchief and a few beads, and they were highly pleased with a cloth of red baize for Mburuma, which Sekeletu had given me to purchase a canoe. We were thankful to part good friends.

Next morning we passed along the bottom of the range, called Mazanzwe, and found the ruins of eight or ten stone houses. They all faced the river, and were high enough up the flanks of the hill Mazanzwe to command a pleasant view of the broad Zambesi. These establishments had all been built on one plan—a house on one side of a large court, surrounded by a wall; both houses and walls had been built of soft gray sandstone cemented together with mud. The work had been performed by slaves ignorant of building, for the stones were not often placed so as to cover the seams below. Hence you frequently find the joinings forming one seam from the top to the bottom. Much mortar or clay had been used to cover defects, and now trees of the fig family grow upon the walls, and clasp them with their roots. When the clay is moistened, masses of the walls come down by wholesale. Some of the rafters and beams had fallen in, but were entire, and there were some trees in the middle of the houses as large as a man's body. On the opposite or south bank of the Zambesi we saw the remains of a wall on a height which was probably a fort, and the church stood at a central point, formed by the right bank of the Loangwa and the left of the Zambesi.

The situation of Zumbo was admirably well chosen as a site for commerce. Looking backward we see a mass of high, dark mountains, covered with trees; behind us rises the fine high hill Mazanzwe, which stretches away northward along the left bank of the Loangwa; to the S.E. lies an open country, with a small round hill in the distance called Tofulo. The merchants, as they sat beneath the verandahs in front of their houses, had a magnificent view of the two rivers at their confluence; of their church at the angle; and of all the gardens which they had on both sides of the rivers. In these they cultivated wheat without irrigation, and, as the Portuguese assert, of a grain twice the size of that at Tete. From the guides we learned that the inhabitants had not imbibed much idea of Christianity, for they used the same term for the church bell which they did for a diviner's drum. From this point the merchants had water communication in three directions beyond, namely, from the Loangwa to the N.N.W., by the Kafue to the W., and by the Zambesi to the S.W. Their attention, however, was chiefly attracted to the N. or Londa; and the principal articles of trade were ivory and slaves. Private enterprise was always restrained, for the colonies of the Portuguese being strictly military, and the pay of the commandants being very small, the officers have always been obliged to engage in trade; and had they not employed their power to draw the trade to themselves by preventing private traders from making bargains beyond the villages, and only at regulated prices, they would have had no trade, as they themselves were obliged to remain always at their posts.

Several expeditions went to the north as far as to Cazembe, and Dr. Lacerda, himself commandant of Tete, went to that chief's residence. Unfortunately, he was cut off while there, and his papers, taken possession of by a Jesuit who accompanied him, were lost to the world. This Jesuit probably intended to act fairly and have them published; but soon after his return he was called away by death himself, and the papers were lost sight of. Dr. Lacerda had a strong desire to open up communication with Angola, which would have been of importance then, as affording a speedier mode of communication with Portugal than by the way of the Cape; but since the opening of the overland passage to India, a quicker transit is effected from Eastern Africa to Lisbon by way of the Red Sea. Besides Lacerda, Cazembe was visited by Pereira, who gave a glowing account of that chief's power, which none of my inquiries have confirmed. The people of Matiamvo stated to me that Cazembe was a vassal of their chief: and, from all the native visitors whom I have seen, he appears to be exactly like Shinte and Katema, only a little more powerful. The term "Emperor", which has been applied to him, seems totally inappropriate. The statement of Pereira that twenty negroes were slaughtered in a day, was not confirmed by any one else, though numbers may have been killed on some particular occasion during the time of his visit, for we find throughout all the country north of 20 Deg., which I consider to be real negro, the custom of slaughtering victims to accompany the departed soul of a chief, and human sacrifices are occasionally offered, and certain parts of the bodies are used as charms. It is on account of the existence of such rites, with the similarity of the language, and the fact that the names of rivers are repeated again and again from north to south through all that region, that I consider them to have been originally one family. The last expedition to Cazembe was somewhat of the same nature as the others, and failed in establishing a commerce, because the people of Cazembe, who had come to Tete to invite the Portuguese to visit them, had not been allowed to trade with whom they might. As it had not been free-trade there, Cazembe did not see why it should be free-trade at his town; he accordingly would not allow his people to furnish the party with food except at his price; and the expedition, being half starved in consequence, came away voting unanimously that Cazembe was a great bore.

When we left the Loangwa we thought we had got rid of the hills; but there are some behind Mazanzwe, though five or six miles off from the river. Tsetse and the hills had destroyed two riding oxen, and when the little one that I now rode knocked up, I was forced to march on foot. The bush being very dense and high, we were going along among the trees, when three buffaloes, which we had unconsciously passed above the wind, thought that they were surrounded by men, and dashed through our line. My ox set off at a gallop, and when I could manage to glance back, I saw one of the men up in the air about five feet above a buffalo, which was tearing along with a stream of blood running down his flank. When I got back to the poor fellow, I found that he had lighted on his face, and, though he had been carried on the horns of the buffalo about twenty yards before getting the final toss, the skin was not pierced nor was a bone broken. When the beasts appeared, he had thrown down his load and stabbed one in the side. It turned suddenly upon him, and, before he could use a tree for defense, carried him off. We shampooed him well, and then went on, and in about a week he was able to engage in the hunt again.

At Zumbo we had entered upon old gray sandstone, with shingle in it, dipping generally toward the south, and forming the bed of the river. The Zambesi is very broad here, but contains many inhabited islands. We slept opposite one on the 16th called Shibanga. The nights are warm, the temperature never falling below 80 Deg.; it was 91 Deg. even at sunset. One can not cool the water by a wet towel round the vessel, and we feel no pleasure in drinking warm water, though the heat makes us imbibe large quantities. We often noticed lumps of a froth-like substance on the bushes as large as cricket-balls, which we could not explain.

On the morning of the 17th we were pleased to see a person coming from the island of Shibanga with jacket and hat on. He was quite black, but had come from the Portuguese settlement at Tete or Nyungwe; and now, for the first time, we understood that the Portuguese settlement was on the other bank of the river, and that they had been fighting with the natives for the last two years. We had thus got into the midst of a Caffre war, without any particular wish to be on either side. He advised us to cross the river at once, as Mpende lived on this side. We had been warned by the guides of Mburuma against him, for they said that if we could get past Mpende we might reach the white men, but that he was determined that no white man should pass him. Wishing to follow this man's advice, we proposed to borrow his canoes; but, being afraid to offend the lords of the river, he declined. The consequence was, we were obliged to remain on the enemy's side. The next island belonged to a man named Zungo, a fine, frank fellow, who brought us at once a present of corn, bound in a peculiar way in grass. He freely accepted our apology for having no present to give in return, as he knew that there were no goods in the interior, and, besides, sent forward a recommendation to his brother-in-law Pangola. The country adjacent to the river is covered with dense bush, thorny and tangled, making one stoop or wait till the men broke or held the branches on one side. There is much rank grass, but it is not so high or rank as that of Angola. The maize, however, which is grown here is equal in size to that which the Americans sell for seed at the Cape. There is usually a holm adjacent to the river, studded with villages and gardens. The holms are but partially cultivated, and on the other parts grows rank and weedy grass. There is then a second terrace, on which trees and bushes abound; and I thought I could detect a third and higher steppe. But I never could discover terraces on the adjacent country, such as in other countries show ancient sea-beaches. The path runs sometimes on the one and sometimes on the other of these river terraces. Canoes are essentially necessary; but I find that they here cost too much for my means, and higher up, where my hoes might have secured one, I was unwilling to enter into a canoe and part with my men while there was danger of their being attacked.

18TH. Yesterday we rested under a broad-spreading fig-tree. Large numbers of buffaloes and water-antelopes were feeding quietly in the meadows; the people have either no guns or no ammunition, or they would not be so tame. Pangola visited us, and presented us with food. In few other countries would one hundred and fourteen sturdy vagabonds be supported by the generosity of the head men and villagers, and whatever they gave be presented with politeness. My men got pretty well supplied individually, for they went into the villages and commenced dancing. The young women were especially pleased with the new steps they had to show, though I suspect many of them were invented for the occasion, and would say, "Dance for me, and I will grind corn for you." At every fresh instance of liberality, Sekwebu said, "Did not I tell you that these people had hearts, while we were still at Linyanti?" All agreed that the character he had given was true, and some remarked, "Look! although we have been so long away from home, not one of us has become lean." It was a fact that we had been all well supplied either with meat by my gun or their own spears, or food from the great generosity of the inhabitants. Pangola promised to ferry us across the Zambesi, but failed to fulfill his promise. He seemed to wish to avoid offending his neighbor Mpende by aiding us to escape from his hands, so we proceeded along the bank. Although we were in doubt as to our reception by Mpende, I could not help admiring the beautiful country as we passed along. There is, indeed, only a small part under cultivation in this fertile valley, but my mind naturally turned to the comparison of it with Kolobeng, where we waited anxiously during months for rain, and only a mere thunder-shower followed. I shall never forget the dry, hot east winds of that region; the yellowish, sultry, cloudless sky; the grass and all the plants drooping from drought, the cattle lean, the people dispirited, and our own hearts sick from hope deferred. There we often heard in the dead of the night the shrill whistle of the rain-doctor calling for rain that would not come, while here we listened to the rolling thunder by night, and beheld the swelling valleys adorned with plenty by day. We have rain almost daily, and every thing is beautifully fresh and green. I felt somewhat as people do on coming ashore after a long voyage—inclined to look upon the landscape in the most favorable light. The hills are covered with forests, and there is often a long line of fleecy cloud lying on them about midway up; they are very beautiful. Finding no one willing to aid us in crossing the river, we proceeded to the village of the chief Mpende. A fine large conical hill now appeared to the N.N.E.; it is the highest I have seen in these parts, and at some points it appears to be two cones joined together, the northern one being a little lower than the southern. Another high hill stands on the same side to the N.E., and, from its similarity in shape to an axe at the top, is called Motemwa. Beyond it, eastward, lies the country of Kaimbwa, a chief who has been engaged in actual conflict with the Bazunga, and beat them too, according to the version of things here. The hills on the north bank are named Kamoenja. When we came to Mpende's village, he immediately sent to inquire who we were, and then ordered the guides who had come with us from the last village to go back and call their masters. He sent no message to us whatever. We had traveled very slowly up to this point, the tsetse-stricken oxen being now unable to go two miles an hour. We were also delayed by being obliged to stop at every village, and send notice of our approach to the head man, who came and received a little information, and gave some food. If we had passed on without taking any notice of them, they would have considered it impolite, and we should have appeared more as enemies than friends. I consoled myself for the loss of time by the thought that these conversations tended to the opening of our future path.

23D. This morning, at sunrise, a party of Mpende's people came close to our encampment, uttering strange cries and waving some bright red substance toward us. They then lighted a fire with charms in it, and departed, uttering the same hideous screams as before. This was intended to render us powerless, and probably also to frighten us. Ever since dawn, parties of armed men have been seen collecting from all quarters, and numbers passed us while it was yet dark. Had we moved down the river at once, it would have been considered an indication of fear or defiance, and so would a retreat. I therefore resolved to wait, trusting in Him who has the hearts of all men in His hands. They evidently intended to attack us, for no friendly message was sent; and when three of the Batoka the night before entered the village to beg food, a man went round about each of them, making a noise like a lion. The villagers then called upon them to do homage, and, when they complied, the chief ordered some chaff to be given them, as if it had been food. Other things also showed unmistakable hostility. As we were now pretty certain of a skirmish, I ordered an ox to be slaughtered, as this is a means which Sebituane employed for inspiring courage. I have no doubt that we should have been victorious; indeed, my men, who were far better acquainted with fighting than any of the people on the Zambesi, were rejoicing in the prospect of securing captives to carry the tusks for them. "We shall now," said they, "get both corn and clothes in plenty." They were in a sad state, poor fellows; for the rains we had encountered had made their skin-clothing drop off piecemeal, and they were looked upon with disgust by the well-fed and well-clothed Zambesians. They were, however, veterans in marauding, and the head men, instead of being depressed by fear, as the people of Mpende intended should be the case in using their charms, hinted broadly to me that I ought to allow them to keep Mpende's wives. The roasting of meat went on fast and furious, and some of the young men said to me, "You have seen us with elephants, but you don't know yet what we can do with men." I believe that, had Mpende struck the first blow, he would soon have found out that he never made a greater mistake in his life.

His whole tribe was assembled at about the distance of half a mile. As the country is covered with trees, we did not see them; but every now and then a few came about us as spies, and would answer no questions. I handed a leg of the ox to two of these, and desired them to take it to Mpende. After waiting a considerable time in suspense, two old men made their appearance, and said they had come to inquire who I was. I replied, "I am a Lekoa" (an Englishman). They said, "We don't know that tribe. We suppose you are a Mozunga, the tribe with which we have been fighting." As I was not yet aware that the term Mozunga was applied to a Portuguese, and thought they meant half-castes, I showed them my hair and the skin of my bosom, and asked if the Bazunga had hair and skin like mine. As the Portuguese have the custom of cutting the hair close, and are also somewhat darker than we are, they answered, "No; we never saw skin so white as that;" and added, "Ah! you must be one of that tribe that loves (literally, 'has heart to') the black men." I, of course, gladly responded in the affirmative. They returned to the village, and we afterward heard that there had been a long discussion between Mpende and his councilors, and that one of the men with whom we had remained to talk the day before had been our advocate. He was named Sindese Oalea. When we were passing his village, after some conversation, he said to his people, "Is that the man whom they wish to stop after he has passed so many tribes? What can Mpende say to refusing him a passage?" It was owing to this man, and the fact that I belonged to the "friendly white tribe", that Mpende was persuaded to allow us to pass.

When we knew the favorable decision of the council, I sent Sekwebu to speak about the purchase of a canoe, as one of my men had become very ill, and I wished to relieve his companions by taking him in a canoe. Before Sekwebu could finish his story, Mpende remarked, "That white man is truly one of our friends. See how he lets me know his afflictions!" Sekwebu adroitly took advantage of this turn in the conversation, and said, "Ah! if you only knew him as well as we do who have lived with him, you would understand that he highly values your friendship and that of Mburuma, and, as he is a stranger, he trusts in you to direct him." He replied, "Well, he ought to cross to the other side of the river, for this bank is hilly and rough, and the way to Tete is longer on this than on the opposite bank." "But who will take us across, if you do not?" "Truly!" replied Mpende; "I only wish you had come sooner to tell me about him; but you shall cross." Mpende said frequently he was sorry he had not known me sooner, but that he had been prevented by his enchanter from coming near me; and he lamented that the same person had kept him from eating the meat which I had presented. He did every thing he could afterward to aid us on our course, and our departure was as different as possible from our approach to his village. I was very much pleased to find the English name spoken of with such great respect so far from the coast, and most thankful that no collision occurred to damage its influence.

24TH. Mpende sent two of his principal men to order the people of a large island below to ferry us across. The river is very broad, and, though my men were well acquainted with the management of canoes, we could not all cross over before dark. It is 1200 yards from bank to bank, and between 700 and 800 of deep water, flowing at the rate of 3-3/4 miles per hour. We landed first on an island; then, to prevent our friends playing false with us, hauled the canoes up to our bivouac, and slept in them. Next morning we all reached the opposite bank in safety. We observed, as we came along the Zambesi, that it had fallen two feet below the height at which we first found it, and the water, though still muddy enough to deposit a film at the bottom of vessels in a few hours, is not nearly so red as it was, nor is there so much wreck on its surface. It is therefore not yet the period of the central Zambesi inundation, as we were aware also from our knowledge of the interior. The present height of the water has been caused by rains outside the eastern ridge. The people here seem abundantly supplied with English cotton goods. The Babisa are the medium of trade, for we were informed that the Bazunga, who formerly visited these parts, have been prevented by the war from coming for the last two years. The Babisa are said to be so fond of a tusk that they will even sell a newly-married wife for one. As we were now not far from the latitude of Mozambique, I was somewhat tempted to strike away from the river to that port, instead of going to the S.E., in the direction the river flows; but, the great object of my journey being to secure water-carriage, I resolved to continue along the Zambesi, though it did lead me among the enemies of the Portuguese. The region to the north of the ranges of hills on our left is called Senga, from being the country of the Basenga, who are said to be great workers in iron, and to possess abundance of fine iron ore, which, when broken, shows veins of the pure metal in its substance. It has been well roasted in the operations of nature. Beyond Senga lies a range of mountains called Mashinga, to which the Portuguese in former times went to wash for gold, and beyond that are great numbers of tribes which pass under the general term Maravi. To the northeast there are extensive plains destitute of trees, but covered with grass, and in some places it is marshy. The whole of the country to the north of the Zambesi is asserted to be very much more fertile than that to the south. The Maravi, for instance, raise sweet potatoes of immense size, but when these are planted on the southern bank they soon degenerate. The root of this plant ('Convolvulus batata') does not keep more than two or three days, unless it is cut into thin slices and dried in the sun, but the Maravi manage to preserve them for months by digging a pit and burying them therein inclosed in wood-ashes. Unfortunately, the Maravi, and all the tribes on that side of the country, are at enmity with the Portuguese, and, as they practice night attacks in their warfare, it is dangerous to travel among them.

29TH. I was most sincerely thankful to find myself on the south bank of the Zambesi, and, having nothing else, I sent back one of my two spoons and a shirt as a thank-offering to Mpende. The different head men along this river act very much in concert, and if one refuses passage they all do, uttering the sage remark, "If so-and-so did not lend his canoes, he must have had some good reason." The next island we came to was that of a man named Mozinkwa. Here we were detained some days by continuous rains, and thought we observed the confirmation of the Bakwain theory of rains. A double tier of clouds floated quickly away to the west, and as soon as they began to come in an opposite direction the rains poured down. The inhabitants who live in a dry region like that of Kolobeng are nearly all as weather-wise as the rain-makers, and any one living among them for any length of time becomes as much interested in the motions of the clouds as they are themselves. Mr. Moffat, who was as sorely tried by droughts as we were, and had his attention directed in the same way, has noted the curious phenomenon of thunder without clouds. Mrs. L. heard it once, but I never had that good fortune. It is worth the attention of the observant. Humboldt has seen rain without clouds, a phenomenon quite as singular. I have been in the vicinity of the fall of three aerolites, none of which I could afterward discover. One fell into the lake Kumadau with a report somewhat like a sharp peal of thunder. The women of the Bakurutse villages there all uttered a scream on hearing it. This happened at midday, and so did another at what is called the Great Chuai, which was visible in its descent, and was also accompanied with a thundering noise. The third fell near Kuruman, and at night, and was seen as a falling star by people at Motito and at Daniel's Kuil, places distant forty miles on opposite sides of the spot. It sounded to me like the report of a great gun, and a few seconds after, a lesser sound, as if striking the earth after a rebound. Does the passage of a few such aerolites through the atmosphere to the earth by day cause thunder without clouds?

We were detained here so long that my tent became again quite rotten. One of my men, after long sickness, which I did not understand, died here. He was one of the Batoka, and when unable to walk I had some difficulty in making his companions carry him. They wished to leave him to die when his case became hopeless. Another of them deserted to Mozinkwa. He said that his motive for doing so was that the Makololo had killed both his father and mother, and, as he had neither wife nor child, there was no reason why he should continue longer with them. I did not object to his statements, but said if he should change his mind he would be welcome to rejoin us, and intimated to Mozinkwa that he must not be sold as a slave. We are now among people inured to slave-dealing. We were visited by men who had been as far as Tete or Nyungwe, and were told that we were but ten days from that fort. One of them, a Mashona man, who had come from a great distance to the southwest, was anxious to accompany us to the country of the white men; he had traveled far, and I found that he had also knowledge of the English tribe, and of their hatred to the trade in slaves. He told Sekwebu that the "English were men", an emphasis being put upon the term MEN, which leaves the impression that others are, as they express it in speaking scornfully, "only THINGS". Several spoke in the same manner, and I found that from Mpende's downward I rose higher every day in the estimation of my own people. Even the slaves gave a very high character to the English, and I found out afterward that, when I was first reported at Tete, the servants of my friend the commandant said to him in joke, "Ah! this is our brother who is coming; we shall all leave you and go with him." We had still, however, some difficulties in store for us before reaching that point.

The man who wished to accompany us came and told us before our departure that his wife would not allow him to go, and she herself came to confirm the decision. Here the women have only a small puncture in the upper lip, in which they insert a little button of tin. The perforation is made by degrees, a ring with an opening in it being attached to the lip, and the ends squeezed gradually together. The pressure on the flesh between the ends of the ring causes its absorption, and a hole is the result. Children may be seen with the ring on the lip, but not yet punctured. The tin they purchase from the Portuguese, and, although silver is reported to have been found in former times in this district, no one could distinguish it from tin. But they had a knowledge of gold, and for the first time I heard the word "dalama" (gold) in the native language. The word is quite unknown in the interior, and so is the metal itself. In conversing with the different people, we found the idea prevalent that those who had purchased slaves from them had done them an injury. "All the slaves of Nyungwe," said one, "are our children; the Bazunga have made a town at our expense." When I asked if they had not taken the prices offered them, they at once admitted it, but still thought that they had been injured by being so far tempted. From the way in which the lands of Zumbo were spoken of as still belonging to the Portuguese (and they are said to have been obtained by purchase), I was inclined to conclude that the purchase of land is not looked upon by the inhabitants in the same light as the purchase of slaves.

FEBRUARY 1ST. We met some native traders, and, as many of my men were now in a state of nudity, I bought some American calico marked "Lawrence Mills, Lowell", with two small tusks, and distributed it among the most needy. After leaving Mozinkwa's we came to the Zingesi, a sand-rivulet in flood (lat. 15d 38' 34" S., long. 31d 1' E.). It was sixty or seventy yards wide, and waist-deep. Like all these sand-rivers, it is for the most part dry; but by digging down a few feet, water is to be found, which is percolating along the bed on a stratum of clay. This is the phenomenon which is dignified by the name of "a river flowing under ground." In trying to ford this I felt thousands of particles of coarse sand striking my legs, and the slight disturbance of our footsteps caused deep holes to be made in the bed. The water, which is almost always very rapid in them, dug out the sand beneath our feet in a second or two, and we were all sinking by that means so deep that we were glad to relinquish the attempt to ford it before we got half way over; the oxen were carried away down into the Zambesi. These sand-rivers remove vast masses of disintegrated rock before it is fine enough to form soil. The man who preceded me was only thigh-deep, but the disturbance caused by his feet made it breast-deep for me. The shower of particles and gravel which struck against my legs gave me the idea that the amount of matter removed by every freshet must be very great. In most rivers where much wearing is going on, a person diving to the bottom may hear literally thousands of stones knocking against each other. This attrition, being carried on for hundreds of miles in different rivers, must have an effect greater than if all the pestles and mortars and mills of the world were grinding and wearing away the rocks. The pounding to which I refer may be heard most distinctly in the Vaal River, when that is slightly in flood. It was there I first heard it. In the Leeambye, in the middle of the country, where there is no discoloration, and little carried along but sand, it is not to be heard.

While opposite the village of a head man called Mosusa, a number of elephants took refuge on an island in the river. There were two males, and a third not full grown; indeed, scarcely the size of a female. This was the first instance I had ever seen of a comparatively young one with the males, for they usually remain with the female herd till as large as their dams. The inhabitants were very anxious that my men should attack them, as they go into the gardens on the islands, and do much damage. The men went, but the elephants ran about half a mile to the opposite end of the island, and swam to the main land with their probosces above the water, and, no canoe being near, they escaped. They swim strongly, with the proboscis erect in the air. I was not very desirous to have one of these animals killed, for we understood that when we passed Mpende we came into a country where the game-laws are strictly enforced. The lands of each chief are very well defined, the boundaries being usually marked by rivulets, great numbers of which flow into the Zambesi from both banks, and, if an elephant is wounded on one man's land and dies on that of another, the under half of the carcass is claimed by the lord of the soil; and so stringent is the law, that the hunter can not begin at once to cut up his own elephant, but must send notice to the lord of the soil on which it lies, and wait until that personage sends one authorized to see a fair partition made. If the hunter should begin to cut up before the agent of the landowner arrives, he is liable to lose both the tusks and all the flesh. The hind leg of a buffalo must also be given to the man on whose land the animal was grazing, and a still larger quantity of the eland, which here and every where else in the country is esteemed right royal food. In the country above Zumbo we did not find a vestige of this law; and but for the fact that it existed in the country of the Bamapela, far to the south of this, I should have been disposed to regard it in the same light as I do the payment for leave to pass—an imposition levied on him who is seen to be weak because in the hands of his slaves. The only game-laws in the interior are, that the man who first wounds an animal, though he has inflicted but a mere scratch, is considered the killer of it; the second is entitled to a hind quarter, and the third to a fore leg. The chiefs are generally entitled to a share as tribute; in some parts it is the breast, in others the whole of the ribs and one fore leg. I generally respected this law, although exceptions are sometimes made when animals are killed by guns. The knowledge that he who succeeds in reaching the wounded beast first is entitled to a share stimulates the whole party to greater exertions in dispatching it. One of my men, having a knowledge of elephant medicine, was considered the leader in the hunt; he went before the others, examined the animals, and on his decision all depended. If he decided to attack a herd, the rest went boldly on; but if he declined, none of them would engage. A certain part of the elephant belonged to him by right of the office he held, and such was the faith in medicine held by the slaves of the Portuguese whom we met hunting, that they offered to pay this man handsomely if he would show them the elephant medicine.

When near Mosusa's village we passed a rivulet called Chowe, now running with rain-water. The inhabitants there extract a little salt from the sand when it is dry, and all the people of the adjacent country come to purchase it from them. This was the first salt we had met with since leaving Angola, for none is to be found in either the country of the Balonda or Barotse; but we heard of salt-pans about a fortnight west of Naliele, and I got a small supply from Mpololo while there. That had long since been finished, and I had again lived two months without salt, suffering no inconvenience except an occasional longing for animal food or milk.

In marching along, the rich reddish-brown soil was so clammy that it was very difficult to walk. It is, however, extremely fertile, and the people cultivate amazing quantities of corn, maize, millet, ground-nuts, pumpkins, and cucumbers. We observed that, when plants failed in one spot, they were in the habit of transplanting them into another, and they had also grown large numbers of young plants on the islands, where they are favored by moisture from the river, and were now removing them to the main land. The fact of their being obliged to do this shows that there is less rain here than in Londa, for there we observed the grain in all stages of its growth at the same time.

The people here build their huts in gardens on high stages. This is necessary on account of danger from the spotted hyaena, which is said to be very fierce, and also as a protection against lions and elephants. The hyaena is a very cowardly animal, but frequently approaches persons lying asleep, and makes an ugly gash on the face. Mozinkwa had lost his upper lip in this way, and I have heard of men being killed by them; children, too, are sometimes carried off; for, though he is so cowardly that the human voice will make him run away at once, yet, when his teeth are in the flesh, he holds on, and shows amazing power of jaw. Leg-bones of oxen, from which the natives have extracted the marrow and every thing eatable, are by this animal crunched up with the greatest ease, which he apparently effects by turning them round in his teeth till they are in a suitable position for being split.

We had now come among people who had plenty, and were really very liberal. My men never returned from a village without some corn or maize in their hands. The real politeness with which food is given by nearly all the interior tribes, who have not had much intercourse with Europeans, makes it a pleasure to accept. Again and again I have heard an apology made for the smallness of the present, or regret expressed that they had not received notice of my approach in time to grind more, and generally they readily accepted our excuse at having nothing to give in return by saying that they were quite aware that there are no white men's goods in the interior. When I had it in my power, I always gave something really useful. To Katema, Shinte, and others, I gave presents which cost me about 2 Pounds each, and I could return to them at any time without having a character for stinginess. How some men can offer three buttons, or some other equally contemptible gift, while they have abundance in their possession, is to me unaccountable. They surely do not know, when they write it in their books, that they are declaring they have compromised the honor of Englishmen. The people receive the offering with a degree of shame, and ladies may be seen to hand it quickly to the attendants, and, when they retire, laugh until the tears stand in their eyes, saying to those about them, "Is that a white man? then there are niggards among them too. Some of them are born without hearts!" One white trader, having presented an OLD GUN to a chief, became a standing joke in the tribe: "The white man who made a present of a gun that was new when his grandfather was sucking his great-grandmother." When these tricks are repeated, the natives come to the conclusion that people who show such a want of sense must be told their duty; they therefore let them know what they ought to give, and travelers then complain of being pestered with their "shameless begging". I was troubled by importunity on the confines of civilization only, and when I first came to Africa.

FEBRUARY 4TH. We were much detained by rains, a heavy shower without wind falling every morning about daybreak; it often cleared up after that, admitting of our moving on a few miles. A continuous rain of several hours then set in. The wind up to this point was always from the east, but both rain and wind now came so generally from the west, or opposite direction to what we had been accustomed to in the interior, that we were obliged to make our encampment face the east, in order to have them in our backs. The country adjacent to the river abounds in large trees; but the population is so numerous that, those left being all green, it is difficult to get dry firewood. On coming to some places, too, we were warned by the villagers not to cut the trees growing in certain spots, as they contained the graves of their ancestors. There are many tamarind-trees, and another very similar, which yields a fruit as large as a small walnut, of which the elephants are very fond. It is called Motondo, and the Portuguese extol its timber as excellent for building boats, as it does not soon rot in water.

On the 6th we came to the village of Boroma, which is situated among a number of others, each surrounded by extensive patches of cultivation. On the opposite side of the river we have a great cluster of conical hills called Chorichori. Boroma did not make his appearance, but sent a substitute who acted civilly. I sent Sekwebu in the morning to state that we intended to move on; his mother replied that, as she had expected that we should remain, no food was ready, but she sent a basket of corn and a fowl. As an excuse why Boroma did not present himself, she said that he was seized that morning by the Barimo, which probably meant that his lordship was drunk.

We marched along the river to a point opposite the hill Pinkwe (lat. 15d 39′ 11″ S., long. 32d 5′ E.), but the late abundant rains now flooded the Zambesi again, and great quantities of wreck appeared upon the stream. It is probable that frequent freshets, caused by the rains on this side of the ridge, have prevented the Portuguese near the coast from recognizing the one peculiar flood of inundation observed in the interior, and caused the belief that it is flooded soon after the commencement of the rains. The course of the Nile being in the opposite direction to this, it does not receive these subsidiary waters, and hence its inundation is recognized all the way along its course. If the Leeambye were prolonged southward into the Cape Colony, its flood would be identical with that of the Nile. It would not be influenced by any streams in the Kalahari, for there, as in a corresponding part of the Nile, there would be no feeders. It is to be remembered that the great ancient river which flowed to the lake at Boochap took this course exactly, and probably flowed thither until the fissure of the falls was made.

This flood having filled the river, we found the numerous rivulets which flow into it filled also, and when going along the Zambesi, we lost so much time in passing up each little stream till we could find a ford about waist deep, and then returning to the bank, that I resolved to leave the river altogether, and strike away to the southeast. We accordingly struck off when opposite the hill Pinkwe, and came into a hard Mopane country. In a hole of one of the mopane-trees I noticed that a squirrel ('Sciurus cepapi') had placed a great number of fresh leaves over a store of seed. It is not against the cold of winter that they thus lay up food, but it is a provision against the hot season, when the trees have generally no seed. A great many silicified trees are met with lying on the ground all over this part of the country; some are broken off horizontally, and stand upright; others are lying prone, and broken across into a number of pieces. One was 4 feet 8 inches in diameter, and the wood must have been soft like that of the baobab, for there were only six concentric rings to the inch. As the semidiameter was only 28 inches, this large tree could have been but 168 years old. I found also a piece of palm-tree transformed into oxide of iron, and the pores filled with pure silica. These fossil trees lie upon soft gray sandstone containing banks of shingle, which forms the underlying rock of the country all the way from Zumbo to near Lupata. It is met with at Litubaruba and in Angola, with similar banks of shingle imbedded exactly like those now seen on the sea-beach, but I never could find a shell. There are many nodules and mounds of hardened clay upon it, which seem to have been deposited in eddies made round the roots of these ancient trees, for they appear of different colors in wavy and twisted lines. Above this we have small quantities of calcareous marl.

As we were now in the district of Chicova, I examined the geological structure of the country with interest, because here, it has been stated, there once existed silver mines. The general rock is the gray soft sandstone I have mentioned, but at the rivulet Bangue we come upon a dike of basalt six yards wide, running north and south. When we cross this, we come upon several others, some of which run more to the eastward. The sandstone is then found to have been disturbed, and at the rivulet called Nake we found it tilted up and exhibiting a section, which was coarse sandstone above, sandstone-flag, shale, and, lastly, a thin seam of coal. The section was only shown for a short distance, and then became lost by a fault made by a dike of basalt, which ran to the E.N.E. in the direction of Chicova.

This Chicova is not a kingdom, as has been stated, but a level tract, a part of which is annually overflowed by the Zambesi, and is well adapted for the cultivation of corn. It is said to be below the northern end of the hill Bungwe. I was very much pleased in discovering this small specimen of such a precious mineral as coal. I saw no indication of silver, and, if it ever was worked by the natives, it is remarkable that they have entirely lost the knowledge of it, and can not distinguish between silver and tin. In connection with these basaltic dikes, it may be mentioned that when I reached Tete I was informed of the existence of a small rapid in the river near Chicova; had I known this previously, I certainly would not have left the river without examining it. It is called Kebrabasa, and is described as a number of rocks which jut out across the stream. I have no doubt but that it is formed by some of the basaltic dikes which we now saw, for they generally ran toward that point. I was partly influenced in leaving the river by a wish to avoid several chiefs in that direction, who levy a heavy tribute on those who pass up or down. Our path lay along the bed of the Nake for some distance, the banks being covered with impenetrable thickets. The villages are not numerous, but we went from one to the other, and were treated kindly. Here they call themselves Bambiri, though the general name of the whole nation is Banyai. One of our guides was an inveterate talker, always stopping and asking for pay, that he might go on with a merry heart. I thought that he led us in the most difficult paths in order to make us feel his value, for, after passing through one thicket after another, we always came into the bed of the Nake again, and as that was full of coarse sand, and the water only ankle deep, and as hot as a foot-bath from the powerful rays of the sun, we were all completely tired out. He likewise gave us a bad character at every village we passed, calling to them that they were to allow him to lead us astray, as we were a bad set. Sekwebu knew every word he said, and, as he became intolerable, I dismissed him, giving him six feet of calico I had bought from native traders, and telling him that his tongue was a nuisance. It is in general best, when a scolding is necessary, to give it in combination with a present, and then end it by good wishes. This fellow went off smiling, and my men remarked, "His tongue is cured now." The country around the Nake is hilly, and the valleys covered with tangled jungle. The people who live in this district have reclaimed their gardens from the forest, and the soil is extremely fertile. The Nake flows northerly, and then to the east. It is 50 or 60 yards wide, but during most of the year is dry, affording water only by digging in the sand. We found in its bed masses of volcanic rock, identical with those I subsequently recognized as such at Aden.

 13TH. The head man of these parts is named Nyampungo. I sent the last fragment of cloth we had, with a request that we should be furnished with a guide to the next chief. After a long conference with his council, the cloth was returned with a promise of compliance, and a request for some beads only. This man is supposed to possess the charm for rain, and other tribes send to him to beg it. This shows that what we inferred before was correct, that less rain falls in this country than in Londa. Nyampungo behaved in quite a gentlemanly manner, presented me with some rice, and told my people to go among all the villages and beg for themselves. An old man, father-in-law of the chief, told me that he had seen books before, but never knew what they meant. They pray to departed chiefs and relatives, but the idea of praying to God seemed new, and they heard it with reverence. As this was an intelligent old man, I asked him about the silver, but he was as ignorant of it as the rest, and said, "We never dug silver, but we have washed for gold in the sands of the rivers Mazoe and Luia, which unite in the Luenya." I think that this is quite conclusive on the question of no silver having been dug by the natives of this district. Nyampungo is afflicted with a kind of disease called Sesenda, which I imagine to be a species of leprosy common in this quarter, though they are a cleanly people. They never had cattle. The chief's father had always lived in their present position, and, when I asked him why he did not possess these useful animals, he said, "Who would give us the medicine to enable us to keep them?" I found out the reason afterward in the prevalence of tsetse, but of this he was ignorant, having supposed that he could not keep cattle because he had no medicine.

Chapter 30

An Elephant-hunt—Offering and Prayers to the Barimo for Success—Native Mode of Expression—Working of Game-laws—A Feast—Laughing Hyaenas—Numerous Insects—Curious Notes of Birds of Song— Caterpillars—Butterflies—Silica—The Fruit Makoronga and Elephants —Rhinoceros Adventure—Korwe Bird—Its Nest—A real Confinement— Honey and Beeswax—Superstitious Reverence for the Lion—Slow Traveling—Grapes—The Ue—Monina's Village—Native Names—Government of the Banyai—Electing a Chief—Youths instructed in "Bonyai"—Suspected of Falsehood—War-dance—Insanity and Disappearance of Monahin—Fruitless Search—Monina's Sympathy—The Sand-river Tangwe—The Ordeal Muavi: its Victims—An unreasonable Man—"Woman's Rights"—Presents—Temperance—A winding Course to shun Villages— Banyai Complexion and Hair—Mushrooms—The Tubers, Mokuri—The Tree Shekabakadzi—Face of the Country—Pot-holes—Pursued by a Party of Natives—Unpleasant Threat—Aroused by a Company of Soldiers—A civilized Breakfast—Arrival at Tete.

14TH. We left Nyampungo this morning. The path wound up the Molinge, another sand-river which flows into the Nake. When we got clear of the tangled jungle which covers the banks of these rivulets, we entered the Mopane country, where we could walk with comfort. When we had gone on a few hours, my men espied an elephant, and were soon in full pursuit. They were in want of meat, having tasted nothing but grain for several days. The desire for animal food made them all eager to slay him, and, though an old bull, he was soon killed. The people of Nyampungo had never seen such desperadoes before. One rushed up and hamstrung the beast, while still standing, by a blow with an axe. Some Banyai elephant-hunters happened to be present when my men were fighting with him. One of them took out his snuff-box, and poured out all its contents at the root of a tree as an offering to the Barimo for success. As soon as the animal fell, the whole of my party engaged in a wild, savage dance round the body, which quite frightened the Banyai, and he who made the offering said to me, "I see you are traveling with people who don't know how to pray: I therefore offered the only thing I had in their behalf, and the elephant soon fell." One of Nyampungo's men, who remained with me, ran a little forward, when an opening in the trees gave us a view of the chase, and uttered loud prayers for success in the combat. I admired the devout belief they all possessed in the actual existence of unseen beings, and prayed that they might yet know that benignant One who views us all as his own. My own people, who are rather a degraded lot, remarked to me as I came up, "God gave it to us. He said to the old beast, 'Go up there; men are come who will kill and eat you.'" These remarks are quoted to give the reader an idea of the native mode of expression.

As we were now in the country of stringent game-laws, we were obliged to send all the way back to Nyampungo, to give information to a certain person who had been left there by the real owner of this district to watch over his property, the owner himself living near the Zambesi. The side upon which the elephant fell had a short, broken tusk; the upper one, which was ours, was large and thick. The Banyai remarked on our good luck. The men sent to give notice came back late in the afternoon of the following day. They brought a basket of corn, a fowl, and a few strings of handsome beads, as a sort of thank-offering for our having killed it on their land, and said they had thanked the Barimo besides for our success, adding, "There it is; eat it and be glad." Had we begun to cut it up before we got this permission, we should have lost the whole. They had brought a large party to eat their half, and they divided it with us in a friendly way. My men were delighted with the feast, though, by lying unopened a whole day, the carcass was pretty far gone. An astonishing number of hyaenas collected round, and kept up a loud laughter for two whole nights. Some of them do make a very good imitation of a laugh. I asked my men what the hyaenas were laughing at, as they usually give animals credit for a share of intelligence. They said that they were laughing because we could not take the whole, and that they would have plenty to eat as well as we.

On coming to the part where the elephant was slain, we passed through grass so tall that it reminded me of that in the valley of Cassange. Insects are very numerous after the rains commence. While waiting by the elephant, I observed a great number of insects, like grains of fine sand, moving on my boxes. On examination with a glass, four species were apparent; one of green and gold preening its wings, which glanced in the sun with metallic lustre; another clear as crystal; a third of the color of vermilion; and a fourth black. These are probably some of those which consume the seeds of every plant that grows. Almost every kind has its own peculiar insect, and when the rains are over very few seeds remain untouched. The rankest poisons, as the Kongwhane and Euphorbia, are soon devoured; the former has a scarlet insect; and even the fiery bird's-eye pepper, which will keep off many others from their own seeds, is itself devoured by a maggot. I observed here, what I had often seen before, that certain districts abound in centipedes. Here they have light reddish bodies and blue legs; great myriapedes are seen crawling every where. Although they do no harm, they excite in man a feeling of loathing. Perhaps our appearance produces a similar feeling in the elephant and other large animals. Where they have been much disturbed, they certainly look upon us with great distrust, as the horrid biped that ruins their peace. In the quietest parts of the forest there is heard a faint but distinct hum, which tells of insect joy. One may see many whisking about in the clear sunshine in patches among the green glancing leaves; but there are invisible myriads working with never-tiring mandibles on leaves, and stalks, and beneath the soil. They are all brimful of enjoyment. Indeed, the universality of organic life may be called a mantle of happy existence encircling the world, and imparts the idea of its being caused by the consciousness of our benignant Father's smile on all the works of His hands.

The birds of the tropics have been described as generally wanting in power of song. I was decidedly of opinion that this was not applicable to many parts in Londa, though birds there are remarkably scarce. Here the chorus, or body of song, was not much smaller in volume than it is in England. It was not so harmonious, and sounded always as if the birds were singing in a foreign tongue. Some resemble the lark, and, indeed, there are several of that family; two have notes not unlike those of the thrush. One brought the chaffinch to my mind, and another the robin; but their songs are intermixed with several curious abrupt notes unlike any thing English. One utters deliberately "peek, pak, pok"; another has a single note like a stroke on a violin-string. The mokwa reza gives forth a screaming set of notes like our blackbird when disturbed, then concludes with what the natives say is "pula, pula" (rain, rain), but more like "weep, weep, weep". Then we have the loud cry of francolins, the "pumpuru, pumpuru" of turtle-doves, and the "chiken, chiken, chik, churr, churr" of the honey-guide. Occasionally, near villages, we have a kind of mocking-bird, imitating the calls of domestic fowls. These African birds have not been wanting in song; they have only lacked poets to sing their praises, which ours have had from the time of Aristophanes downward. Ours have both a classic and a modern interest to enhance their fame. In hot, dry weather, or at midday when the sun is fierce, all are still: let, however, a good shower fall, and all burst forth at once into merry lays and loving courtship. The early mornings and the cool evenings are their favorite times for singing. There are comparatively few with gaudy plumage, being totally unlike, in this respect, the birds of the Brazils. The majority have decidedly a sober dress, though collectors, having generally selected the gaudiest as the most valuable, have conveyed the idea that the birds of the tropics for the most part possess gorgeous plumage.

15TH. Several of my men have been bitten by spiders and other insects, but no effect except pain has followed. A large caterpillar is frequently seen, called lezuntabuea. It is covered with long gray hairs, and, the body being dark, it resembles a porcupine in miniature. If one touches it, the hairs run into the pores of the skin, and remain there, giving sharp pricks. There are others which have a similar means of defense; and when the hand is drawn across them, as in passing a bush on which they happen to be, the contact resembles the stinging of nettles. From the great number of caterpillars seen, we have a considerable variety of butterflies. One particular kind flies more like a swallow than a butterfly. They are not remarkable for the gaudiness of their colors.

In passing along we crossed the hills Vungue or Mvungwe, which we found to be composed of various eruptive rocks. At one part we have breccia of altered marl or slate in quartz, and various amygdaloids. It is curious to observe the different forms which silica assumes. We have it in claystone porphyry here, in minute round globules, no larger than turnip-seed, dotted thickly over the matrix; or crystallized round the walls of cavities, once filled with air or other elastic fluid; or it may appear in similar cavities as tufts of yellow asbestos, or as red, yellow, or green crystals, or in laminae so arranged as to appear like fossil wood. Vungue forms the watershed between those sand rivulets which run to the N.E., and others which flow southward, as the Kapopo, Ue, and Due, which run into the Luia.

We found that many elephants had been feeding on the fruit called Mokoronga. This is a black-colored plum, having purple juice. We all ate it in large quantities, as we found it delicious. The only defect it has is the great size of the seed in comparison with the pulp. This is the chief fault of all uncultivated wild fruits. The Mokoronga exists throughout this part of the country most abundantly, and the natives eagerly devour it, as it is said to be perfectly wholesome, or, as they express it, "It is pure fat," and fat is by them considered the best of food. Though only a little larger than a cherry, we found that the elephants had stood picking them off patiently by the hour. We observed the footprints of a black rhinoceros ('Rhinoceros bicornis', Linn.) and her calf. We saw other footprints among the hills of Semalembue, but the black rhinoceros is remarkably scarce in all the country north of the Zambesi. The white rhinoceros ('Rhinoceros simus' of Burchell), or Mohohu of the Bechuanas, is quite extinct here, and will soon become unknown in the country to the south. It feeds almost entirely on grasses, and is of a timid, unsuspecting disposition: this renders it an easy prey, and they are slaughtered without mercy on the introduction of fire-arms. The black possesses a more savage nature, and, like the ill-natured in general, is never found with an ounce of fat in its body. From its greater fierceness and wariness, it holds its place in a district much longer than its more timid and better-conditioned neighbor. Mr. Oswell was once stalking two of these beasts, and, as they came slowly to him, he, knowing that there is but little chance of hitting the small brain of this animal by a shot in the head, lay expecting one of them to give his shoulder till he was within a few yards. The hunter then thought that by making a rush to his side he might succeed in escaping, but the rhinoceros, too quick for that, turned upon him, and, though he discharged his gun close to the animal's head, he was tossed in the air. My friend was insensible for some time, and, on recovering, found large wounds on the thigh and body: I saw that on the former part still open, and five inches long. The white, however, is not always quite safe, for one, even after it was mortally wounded, attacked Mr. Oswell's horse, and thrust the horn through to the saddle, tossing at the time both horse and rider. I once saw a white rhinoceros give a buffalo, which was gazing intently at myself, a poke in the chest, but it did not wound it, and seemed only a hint to get out of the way. Four varieties of the rhinoceros are enumerated by naturalists, but my observation led me to conclude that there are but two, and that the extra species have been formed from differences in their sizes, ages, and the direction of the horns, as if we should reckon the short-horned cattle a different species from the Alderneys or the Highland breed. I was led to this from having once seen a black rhinoceros with a horn bent downward like that of the kuabaoba, and also because the animals of the two great varieties differ very much in appearance at different stages of their growth. I find, however, that Dr. Smith, the best judge in these matters, is quite decided as to the propriety of the subdivision into three or four species. For common readers, it is sufficient to remember that there are two well-defined species, that differ entirely in appearance and food. The absence of both these rhinoceroses among the reticulated rivers in the central valley may easily be accounted for, they would be such an easy prey to the natives in their canoes at the periods of inundation; but one can not so readily account for the total absence of the giraffe and ostrich on the high open lands of the Batoka, north of the Zambesi, unless we give credence to the native report which bounds the country still farther north by another network of waters near Lake Shuia, and suppose that it also prevented their progress southward. The Batoka have no name for the giraffe or the ostrich in their language; yet, as the former exists in considerable numbers in the angle formed by the Leeambye and Chobe, they may have come from the north along the western ridge. The Chobe would seem to have been too narrow to act as an obstacle to the giraffe, supposing it to have come into that district from the south; but the broad river into which that stream flows seems always to have presented an impassable barrier to both the giraffe and the ostrich, though they abound on its southern border, both in the Kalahari Desert and the country of Mashona.

We passed through large tracts of Mopane country, and my men caught a great many of the birds called Korwe ('Tockus erythrorhynchus') in their breeding-places, which were in holes in the mopane-trees. On the 19th we passed the nest of a korwe just ready for the female to enter; the orifice was plastered on both sides, but a space was left of a heart shape, and exactly the size of the bird's body. The hole in the tree was in every case found to be prolonged some distance upward above the opening, and thither the korwe always fled to escape being caught. In another nest we found that one white egg, much like that of a pigeon, was laid, and the bird dropped another when captured. She had four besides in the ovarium. The first time that I saw this bird was at Kolobeng, where I had gone to the forest for some timber. Standing by a tree, a native looked behind me and exclaimed, "There is the nest of a korwe." I saw a slit only, about half an inch wide and three or four inches long, in a slight hollow of the tree. Thinking the word korwe denoted some small animal, I waited with interest to see what he would extract; he broke the clay which surrounded the slit, put his arm into the hole, and brought out a 'Tockus', or 'red-beaked hornbill', which he killed. He informed me that, when the female enters her nest, she submits to a real confinement. The male plasters up the entrance, leaving only a narrow slit by which to feed his mate, and which exactly suits the form of his beak. The female makes a nest of her own feathers, lays her eggs, hatches them, and remains with the young till they are fully fledged. During all this time, which is stated to be two or three months, the male continues to feed her and the young family. The prisoner generally becomes quite fat, and is esteemed a very dainty morsel by the natives, while the poor slave of a husband gets so lean that, on the sudden lowering of the temperature which sometimes happens after a fall of rain, he is benumbed, falls down, and dies. I never had an opportunity of ascertaining the actual length of the confinement, but on passing the same tree at Kolobeng about eight days afterward the hole was plastered up again, as if, in the short time that had elapsed, the disconsolate husband had secured another wife. We did not disturb her, and my duties prevented me from returning to the spot. This is the month in which the female enters the nest. We had seen one of these, as before mentioned, with the plastering not quite finished; we saw many completed; and we received the very same account here that we did at Kolobeng, that the bird comes forth when the young are fully fledged, at the period when the corn is ripe; indeed, her appearance abroad with her young is one of the signs they have for knowing when it ought to be so. As that is about the end of April, the time is between two and three months. She is said sometimes to hatch two eggs, and, when the young of these are full-fledged, other two are just out of the egg-shells: she then leaves the nest with the two elder, the orifice is again plastered up, and both male and female attend to the wants of the young which are left. On several occasions I observed a branch bearing the marks of the male having often sat upon it when feeding his mate, and the excreta had been expelled a full yard from the orifice, and often proved a means of discovering the retreat.

The honey-guides were very assiduous in their friendly offices, and enabled my men to get a large quantity of honey. But, though bees abound, the wax of these parts forms no article of trade. In Londa it may be said to be fully cared for, as you find hives placed upon trees in the most lonesome forests. We often met strings of carriers laden with large blocks of this substance, each 80 or 100 lbs. in weight, and pieces were offered to us for sale at every village; but here we never saw a single artificial hive. The bees were always found in the natural cavities of mopane-trees. It is probable that the good market for wax afforded to Angola by the churches of Brazil led to the gradual development of that branch of commerce there. I saw even on the banks of the Quango as much as sixpence paid for a pound. In many parts of the Batoka country bees exist in vast numbers, and the tribute due to Sekeletu is often paid in large jars of honey; but, having no market nor use for the wax, it is thrown away. This was the case also with ivory at the Lake Ngami, at the period of its discovery. The reports brought by my other party from Loanda of the value of wax had induced some of my present companions to bring small quantities of it to Tete, but, not knowing the proper mode of preparing it, it was so dark colored that no one would purchase it; I afterward saw a little at Kilimane which had been procured from the natives somewhere in this region.

Though we are now approaching the Portuguese settlement, the country is still full of large game. My men killed six buffalo calves out of a herd we met. The abundance of these animals, and also of antelopes, shows the insufficiency of the bow and arrow to lessen their numbers. There are also a great many lions and hyaenas, and there is no check upon the increase of the former, for the people, believing that the souls of their chiefs enter into them, never attempt to kill them; they even believe that a chief may metamorphose himself into a lion, kill any one he chooses, and then return to the human form; therefore, when they see one, they commence clapping their hands, which is the usual mode of salutation here. The consequence is, that lions and hyaenas are so abundant that we see little huts made in the trees, indicating the places where some of the inhabitants have slept when benighted in the fields. As numbers of my men frequently left the line of march in order to take out the korwes from their nests, or follow the honey-guides, they excited the astonishment of our guides, who were constantly warning them of the danger they thereby incurred from lions. I was often considerably ahead of the main body of my men on this account, and was obliged to stop every hour or two; but, the sun being excessively hot by day, I was glad of the excuse for resting. We could make no such prodigious strides as officers in the Arctic regions are able to do. Ten or twelve miles a day were a good march for both the men and myself; and it was not the length of the marches, but continuing day after day to perform the same distance, that was so fatiguing. It was in this case much longer than appears on the map, because we kept out of the way of villages. I drank less than the natives when riding, but all my clothing was now constantly damp from the moisture which was imbibed in large quantities at every pond. One does not stay on these occasions to prepare water with alum or any thing else, but drinks any amount without fear. I never felt the atmosphere so steamy as on the low-lying lands of the Zambesi, and yet it was becoming cooler than it was on the highlands.

We crossed the rivulets Kapopo and Ue, now running, but usually dry. There are great numbers of wild grape-vines growing in this quarter; indeed, they abound every where along the banks of the Zambesi. In the Batoka country there is a variety which yields a black grape of considerable sweetness. The leaves are very large and harsh, as if capable of withstanding the rays of this hot sun; but the most common kinds—one with a round leaf and a greenish grape, and another with a leaf closely resembling that of the cultivated varieties, and with dark or purple fruit—have large seeds, which are strongly astringent, and render it a disagreeable fruit. The natives eat all the varieties; and I tasted vinegar made by a Portuguese from these grapes. Probably a country which yields the wild vines so very abundantly might be a fit one for the cultivated species. At this part of the journey so many of the vines had run across the little footpath we followed that one had to be constantly on the watch to avoid being tripped. The ground was covered with rounded shingle, which was not easily seen among the grass. Pedestrianism may be all very well for those whose obesity requires much exercise, but for one who was becoming as thin as a lath, through the constant perspiration caused by marching day after day in the hot sun, the only good I saw in it was that it gave an honest sort of man a vivid idea of the tread-mill.

Although the rains were not quite over, great numbers of pools were drying up, and the ground was in many parts covered with small green cryptogamous plants, which gave it a mouldy appearance and a strong smell. As we sometimes pushed aside the masses of rank vegetation which hung over our path, we felt a sort of hot blast on our faces. Every thing looked unwholesome, but we had no fever. The Ue flows between high banks of a soft red sandstone streaked with white, and pieces of tufa. The crumbling sandstone is evidently alluvial, and is cut into 12 feet deep. In this region, too, we met with pot-holes six feet deep and three or four in diameter. In some cases they form convenient wells; in others they are full of earth; and in others still the people have made them into graves for their chiefs.

On the 20th we came to Monina's village (close to the sand-river Tangwe, latitude 16d 13′ 38″ south, longitude 32d 32′ east). This man is very popular among the tribes on account of his liberality. Boroma, Nyampungo, Monina, Jira, Katolosa (Monomotapa), and Susa, all acknowledge the supremacy of one called Nyatewe, who is reported to decide all disputes respecting land. This confederation is exactly similar to what we observed in Londa and other parts of Africa. Katolosa is "the Emperor Monomotapa" of history, but he is a chief of no great power, and acknowledges the supremacy of Nyatewe. The Portuguese formerly honored Monomotapa with a guard, to fire off numbers of guns on the occasion of any funeral, and he was also partially subsidized. The only evidence of greatness possessed by his successor is his having about a hundred wives. When he dies a disputed succession and much fighting are expected. In reference to the term Monomotapa, it is to be remembered that Mono, Moene, Mona, Mana, or Morena, mean simply 'chief', and considerable confusion has arisen from naming different people by making a plural of the chief's name. The names Monomoizes, spelled also Monemuiges and Monomuizes, and Monomotapistas, when applied to these tribes, are exactly the same as if we should call the Scotch the Lord Douglases. Motape was the chief of the Bambiri, a tribe of the Banyai, and is now represented in the person of Katolosa. He was probably a man of greater energy than his successor, yet only an insignificant chief. Monomoizes was formed from Moiza or Muiza, the singular of the word Babisa or Aiza, the proper name of a large tribe to the north. In the transformation of this name the same error has been committed as in the others; and mistakes have occurred in many other names by inattention to the meaning, and predilection for the letter R. The River Loangwa, for instance, has been termed Arroangoa, and the Luenya the Ruanha. The Bazizulu, or Mashona, are spoken of as the Morururus.

The government of the Banyai is rather peculiar, being a sort of feudal republicanism. The chief is elected, and they choose the son of the deceased chief's sister in preference to his own offspring. When dissatisfied with one candidate, they even go to a distant tribe for a successor, who is usually of the family of the late chief, a brother, or a sister's son, but never his own son or daughter. When first spoken to on the subject, he answers as if he thought himself unequal to the task and unworthy of the honor; but, having accepted it, all the wives, goods, and children of his predecessor belong to him, and he takes care to keep them in a dependent position. When any one of them becomes tired of this state of vassalage and sets up his own village, it is not unusual for the elected chief to send a number of the young men, who congregate about himself, to visit him. If he does not receive them with the usual amount of clapping of hands and humility, they, in obedience to orders, at once burn his village. The children of the chief have fewer privileges than common free men. They may not be sold, but, rather than choose any one of them for a chief at any future time, the free men would prefer to elect one of themselves, who bore only a very distant relationship to the family. These free men are a distinct class who can never be sold; and under them there is a class of slaves whose appearance as well as position is very degraded. Monina had a great number of young men about him from twelve to fifteen years of age. These were all sons of free men, and bands of young men like them in the different districts leave their parents about the age of puberty, and live with such men as Monina for the sake of instruction. When I asked the nature of the instruction, I was told "Bonyai", which I suppose may be understood as indicating manhood, for it sounds as if we should say, "to teach an American Americanism," or "an Englishman to be English." While here they are kept in subjection to rather stringent regulations. They must salute carefully by clapping their hands on approaching a superior, and when any cooked food is brought, the young men may not approach the dish, but an elder divides a portion to each. They remain unmarried until a fresh set of youths is ready to occupy their place under the same instruction. The parents send servants with their sons to cultivate gardens to supply them with food, and also tusks to Monina to purchase clothing for them. When the lads return to the village of their parents, a case is submitted to them for adjudication, and if they speak well on the point, the parents are highly gratified.

When we told Monina that we had nothing to present but some hoes, he replied that he was not in need of those articles, and that he had absolute power over the country in front, and if he prevented us from proceeding, no one would say any thing to him. His little boy Boromo having come to the encampment to look at us, I gave him a knife, and he went off and brought a pint of honey for me. The father came soon afterward, and I offered him a shirt. He remarked to his councilors, "It is evident that this man has nothing, for, if he had, his people would be buying provisions, but we don't see them going about for that purpose." His council did not agree in this. They evidently believed that we had goods, but kept them hid, and we felt it rather hard to be suspected of falsehood. It was probably at their suggestion that in the evening a wardance was got up about a hundred yards from our encampment, as if to put us in fear and force us to bring forth presents. Some of Monina's young men had guns, but most were armed with large bows, arrows, and spears. They beat their drums furiously, and occasionally fired off a gun. As this sort of dance is never got up unless there is an intention to attack, my men expected an assault. We sat and looked at them for some time, and then, as it became dark, lay down, all ready to give them a warm reception. But an hour or two after dark the dance ceased, and, as we then saw no one approaching us, we went to sleep. During the night, one of my head men, Monahin, was seen to get up, look toward the village, and say to one who was half awake, "Don't you hear what these people are saying? Go and listen." He then walked off in the opposite direction, and never returned. We had no guard set, but every one lay with his spear in his hand. The man to whom he spoke appears to have been in a dreamy condition, for it did not strike him that he ought to give the alarm. Next morning I found to my sorrow that Monahin was gone, and not a trace of him could be discovered. He had an attack of pleuritis some weeks before, and had recovered, but latterly complained a little of his head. I observed him in good spirits on the way hither, and in crossing some of the streams, as I was careful not to wet my feet, he aided me, and several times joked at my becoming so light. In the evening he sat beside my tent until it was dark, and did not manifest any great alarm. It was probably either a sudden fit of insanity, or, having gone a little way out from the camp, he may have been carried off by a lion, as this part of the country is full of them. I incline to the former opinion, because sudden insanity occurs when there is any unusual strain upon their minds. Monahin was in command of the Batoka of Mokwine in my party, and he was looked upon with great dislike by all that chief's subjects. The only difficulties I had with them arose in consequence of being obliged to give orders through him. They said Mokwine is reported to have been killed by the Makololo, but Monahin is the individual who put forth his hand and slew him. When one of these people kills in battle, he seems to have no compunction afterward; but when he makes a foray on his own responsibility, and kills a man of note, the common people make remarks to each other, which are reported to him, and bring the affair perpetually to his remembrance. This iteration on the conscience causes insanity, and when one runs away in a wide country like this, the fugitive is never heard of. Monahin had lately become afraid of his own party from overhearing their remarks, and said more than once to me, "They want to kill me." I believe if he ran to any village they would take care of him. I felt his loss greatly, and spent three days in searching for him. He was a sensible and most obliging man. I sent in the morning to inform Monina of this sad event, and he at once sent to all the gardens around, desiring the people to look for him, and, should he come near, to bring him home. He evidently sympathized with us in our sorrow, and, afraid lest we might suspect him, added, "We never catch nor kidnap people here. It is not our custom. It is considered as guilt among all the tribes." I gave him credit for truthfulness, and he allowed us to move on without farther molestation.

After leaving his village we marched in the bed of a sand-river a quarter of a mile broad, called Tangwe. Walking on this sand is as fatiguing as walking on snow. The country is flat, and covered with low trees, but we see high hills in the distance. A little to the south we have those of the Lobole. This region is very much infested by lions, and men never go any distance into the woods alone. Having turned aside on one occasion at midday, and gone a short distance among grass a little taller than myself, an animal sprung away from me which was certainly not an antelope, but I could not distinguish whether it was a lion or a hyaena. This abundance of carnivora made us lose all hope of Monahin. We saw footprints of many black rhinoceroses, buffaloes, and zebras.

After a few hours we reached the village of Nyakoba. Two men, who accompanied us from Monina to Nyakoba's, would not believe us when we said that we had no beads. It is very trying to have one's veracity doubted, but, on opening the boxes, and showing them that all I had was perfectly useless to them, they consented to receive some beads off Sekwebu's waist, and I promised to send four yards of calico from Tete. As we came away from Monina's village, a witch-doctor, who had been sent for, arrived, and all Monina's wives went forth into the fields that morning fasting. There they would be compelled to drink an infusion of a plant named "goho", which is used as an ordeal. This ceremony is called "muavi", and is performed in this way. When a man suspects that any of his wives has bewitched him, he sends for the witch-doctor, and all the wives go forth into the field, and remain fasting till that person has made an infusion of the plant. They all drink it, each one holding up her hand to heaven in attestation of her innocency. Those who vomit it are considered innocent, while those whom it purges are pronounced guilty, and put to death by burning. The innocent return to their homes, and slaughter a cock as a thank-offering to their guardian spirits. The practice of ordeal is common among all the negro nations north of the Zambesi. This summary procedure excited my surprise, for my intercourse with the natives here had led me to believe that the women were held in so much estimation that the men would not dare to get rid of them thus. But the explanation I received was this. The slightest imputation makes them eagerly desire the test; they are conscious of being innocent, and have the fullest faith in the muavi detecting the guilty alone; hence they go willingly, and even eagerly, to drink it. When in Angola, a half-caste was pointed out to me who is one of the most successful merchants in that country; and the mother of this gentleman, who was perfectly free, went, of her own accord, all the way from Ambaca to Cassange, to be killed by the ordeal, her rich son making no objection. The same custom prevails among the Barotse, Bashubia, and Batoka, but with slight variations. The Barotse, for instance, pour the medicine down the throat of a cock or of a dog, and judge of the innocence or guilt of the person accused according to the vomiting or purging of the animal. I happened to mention to my own men the water-test for witches formerly in use in Scotland: the supposed witch, being bound hand and foot, was thrown into a pond; if she floated, she was considered guilty, taken out, and burned; but if she sank and was drowned, she was pronounced innocent. The wisdom of my ancestors excited as much wonder in their minds as their custom did in mine.

The person whom Nyakoba appointed to be our guide, having informed us of the decision, came and bargained that his services should be rewarded with a hoe. I had no objection to give it, and showed him the article; he was delighted with it, and went off to show it to his wife. He soon afterward returned, and said that, though he was perfectly willing to go, his wife would not let him. I said, "Then bring back the hoe;" but he replied, "I want it." "Well, go with us, and you shall have it." "But my wife won't let me." I remarked to my men, "Did you ever hear such a fool?" They answered, "Oh, that is the custom of these parts; the wives are the masters." And Sekwebu informed me that he had gone to this man's house, and heard him saying to his wife, "Do you think that I would ever leave you?" then, turning to Sekwebu, he asked, "Do you think I would leave this pretty woman? Is she not pretty?" Sekwebu had been making inquiries among the people, and had found that the women indeed possessed a great deal of influence. We questioned the guide whom we finally got from Nyakoba, an intelligent young man, who had much of the Arab features, and found the statements confirmed. When a young man takes a liking for a girl of another village, and the parents have no objection to the match, he is obliged to come and live at their village. He has to perform certain services for the mother-in-law, such as keeping her well supplied with firewood; and when he comes into her presence he is obliged to sit with his knees in a bent position, as putting out his feet toward the old lady would give her great offense. If he becomes tired of living in this state of vassalage, and wishes to return to his own family, he is obliged to leave all his children behind—they belong to the wife. This is only a more stringent enforcement of the law from which emanates the practice which prevails so very extensively in Africa, known to Europeans as "buying wives". Such virtually it is, but it does not appear quite in that light to the actors. So many head of cattle or goats are given to the parents of the girl "to give her up", as it is termed, i.e., to forego all claim on her offspring, and allow an entire transference of her and her seed into another family. If nothing is given, the family from which she has come can claim the children as part of itself: the payment is made to sever this bond. In the case supposed, the young man has not been able to advance any thing for that purpose; and, from the temptations placed here before my men, I have no doubt that some prefer to have their daughters married in that way, as it leads to the increase of their own village. My men excited the admiration of the Bambiri, who took them for a superior breed on account of their bravery in elephant-hunting, and wished to get them as sons-in-law on the conditions named, but none yielded to the temptation.

We were informed that there is a child belonging to a half-caste Portuguese in one of these tribes, and the father had tried in vain to get him from the mother's parents. We saw several things to confirm the impression of the higher position which women hold here; and, being anxious to discover if I were not mistaken, when we came among the Portuguese I inquired of them, and was told that they had ascertained the same thing; and that, if they wished a man to perform any service for them, he would reply, "Well, I shall go and ask my wife." If she consented, he would go, and perform his duty faithfully; but no amount of coaxing or bribery would induce him to do it if she refused. The Portuguese praised the appearance of the Banyai, and they certainly are a fine race.

We got on better with Nyakoba than we expected. He has been so much affected by the sesenda that he is quite decrepit, and requires to be fed. I at once showed his messenger that we had nothing whatever to give. Nyakoba was offended with him for not believing me, and he immediately sent a basket of maize and another of corn, saying that he believed my statement, and would send men with me to Tete who would not lead me to any other village.

The birds here sing very sweetly, and I thought I heard the canary, as in Londa. We had a heavy shower of rain, and I observed that the thermometer sank 14 Deg. in one hour afterward. From the beginning of February we experienced a sensible diminution of temperature. In January the lowest was 75 Deg., and that at sunrise; the average at the same hour (sunrise) being 79 Deg.; at 3 P.M., 90 Deg.; and at sunset, 82 Deg. In February it fell as low as 70 Deg. in the course of the night, and the average height was 88 Deg. Only once did it rise to 94 Deg., and a thunder-storm followed this; yet the sensation of heat was greater now than it had been at much higher temperatures on more elevated lands.

We passed several villages by going roundabout ways through the forest. We saw the remains of a lion that had been killed by a buffalo, and the horns of a putokwane (black antelope), the finest I had ever seen, which had met its death by a lion. The drums, beating all night in one village near which we slept, showed that some person in it had finished his course. On the occasion of the death of a chief, a trader is liable to be robbed, for the people consider themselves not amenable to law until a new one is elected. We continued a very winding course, in order to avoid the chief Katolosa, who is said to levy large sums upon those who fall into his hands. One of our guides was a fine, tall young man, the very image of Ben Habib the Arab. They were carrying dried buffalo's meat to the market at Tete as a private speculation.

A great many of the Banyai are of a light coffee-and-milk color, and, indeed, this color is considered handsome throughout the whole country, a fair complexion being as much a test of beauty with them as with us. As they draw out their hair into small cords a foot in length, and entwine the inner bark of a certain tree round each separate cord, and dye this substance of a reddish color, many of them put me in mind of the ancient Egyptians. The great mass of dressed hair which they possess reaches to the shoulders, but when they intend to travel they draw it up to a bunch, and tie it on the top of the head. They are cleanly in their habits.

As we did not come near human habitations, and could only take short stages on account of the illness of one of my men, I had an opportunity of observing the expedients my party resorted to in order to supply their wants. Large white edible mushrooms are found on the ant-hills, and are very good. The mokuri, a tuber which abounds in the Mopane country, they discovered by percussing the ground with stones; and another tuber, about the size of a turnip, called "bonga", is found in the same situations. It does not determine to the joints like the mokuri, and in winter has a sensible amount of salt in it. A fruit called "ndongo" by the Makololo, "dongolo" by the Bambiri, resembles in appearance a small plum, which becomes black when ripe, and is good food, as the seeds are small. Many trees are known by tradition, and one receives curious bits of information in asking about different fruits that are met with. A tree named "shekabakadzi" is superior to all others for making fire by friction. As its name implies, women may even readily make fire by it when benighted.

The country here is covered over with well-rounded shingle and gravel of granite, gneiss with much talc in it, mica schist, and other rocks which we saw 'in situ' between the Kafue and Loangwa. There are great mounds of soft red sand slightly coherent, which crumble in the hand with ease. The gravel and the sand drain away the water so effectually that the trees are exposed to the heat during a portion of the year without any moisture; hence they are not large, like those on the Zambesi, and are often scrubby. The rivers are all of the sandy kind, and we pass over large patches between this and Tete in which, in the dry season, no water is to be found. Close on our south, the hills of Lokole rise to a considerable height, and beyond them flows the Mazoe with its golden sands. The great numbers of pot-holes on the sides of sandstone ridges, when viewed in connection with the large banks of rolled shingle and washed sand which are met with on this side of the eastern ridge, may indicate that the sea in former times rolled its waves along its flanks. Many of the hills between the Kafue and Loangwa have their sides of the form seen in mud banks left by the tide. The pot-holes appear most abundant on low gray sandstone ridges here; and as the shingle is composed of the same rocks as the hills west of Zumbo, it looks as if a current had dashed along from the southeast in the line in which the pot-holes now appear; and if the current was deflected by those hills toward the Maravi country, north of Tete, it may have hollowed the rounded, water-worn caverns in which these people store their corn, and also hide themselves from their enemies. I could detect no terraces on the land, but, if I am right in my supposition, the form of this part of the continent must once have resembled the curves or indentations seen on the southern extremity of the American continent. In the indentation to the S.E., S., S.W., and W. of this, lie the principal gold-washings; and the line of the current, supposing it to have struck against the hills of Mburuma, shows the washings in the N. and N.E. of Tete.

We were tolerably successful in avoiding the villages, and slept one night on the flanks of the hill Zimika, where a great number of deep pot-holes afforded an abundant supply of good rain-water. Here, for the first time, we saw hills with bare, smooth, rocky tops, and we crossed over broad dikes of gneiss and syenitic porphyry: the directions in which they lay were N. and S. As we were now near to Tete, we were congratulating ourselves on having avoided those who would only have plagued us; but next morning some men saw us, and ran off to inform the neighboring villages of our passing. A party immediately pursued us, and, as they knew we were within call of Katolosa (Monomotapa), they threatened to send information to that chief of our offense, in passing through the country without leave. We were obliged to give them two small tusks; for, had they told Katolosa of our supposed offense, we should, in all probability, have lost the whole. We then went through a very rough, stony country without any path. Being pretty well tired out in the evening of the 2d of March, I remained at about eight miles distance from Tete, Tette, or Nyungwe. My men asked me to go on; I felt too fatigued to proceed, but sent forward to the commandant the letters of recommendation with which I had been favored in Angola by the bishop and others, and lay down to rest. Our food having been exhausted, my men had been subsisting for some time on roots and honey. About two o'clock in the morning of the 3d we were aroused by two officers and a company of soldiers, who had been sent with the materials for a civilized breakfast and a "masheela" to bring me to Tete. (Commandant's house: lat. 16d 9′ 3″ S., long. 33d 28′ E.) My companions thought that we were captured by the armed men, and called me in alarm. When I understood the errand on which they had come, and had partaken of a good breakfast, though I had just before been too tired to sleep, all my fatigue vanished. It was the most refreshing breakfast I ever partook of, and I walked the last eight miles without the least feeling of weariness, although the path was so rough that one of the officers remarked to me, "This is enough to tear a man's life out of him." The pleasure experienced in partaking of that breakfast was only equaled by the enjoyment of Mr. Gabriel's bed on my arrival at Loanda. It was also enhanced by the news that Sebastopol had fallen and the war was finished.

> Note.—Having neglected, in referring to the footprints of the
> rhinoceros,
> to mention what may be interesting to naturalists, I add it here
> in a note;
> that wherever the footprints are seen, there are also marks of the
> animal
> having plowed up the ground and bushes with his horn. This has
> been supposed
> to indicate that he is subject to "fits of ungovernable rage";
> but, when seen, he appears rather to be rejoicing in his strength.
> He acts as a bull sometimes does when he gores the earth with his
> horns.
> The rhinoceros, in addition to this, stands on a clump of bushes,
> bends his back down, and scrapes the ground with his feet,
> throwing it out backward, as if to stretch and clean his toes,
> in the same way that a dog may be seen to do on a little grass:
> this is certainly not rage.

Chapter 31

Kind Reception from the Commandant—His Generosity to my Men—The Village of Tete—The Population—Distilled Spirits—The Fort—Cause of the Decadence of Portuguese Power—Former Trade—Slaves employed in Gold-washing—Slave-trade drained the Country of Laborers—The Rebel Nyaude's Stockade—He burns Tete—Kisaka's Revolt and Ravages—Extensive Field of Sugar-cane—The Commandant's good Reputation among the Natives—Providential Guidance—Seams of Coal—A hot Spring—Picturesque Country—Water-carriage to the Coal-fields— Workmen's Wages—Exports—Price of Provisions—Visit Gold-washings— The Process of obtaining the precious Metal—Coal within a Gold-field— Present from Major Sicard—Natives raise Wheat, etc.—Liberality of the Commandant—Geographical Information from Senhor Candido—Earthquakes—Native Ideas of a Supreme Being—Also of the Immortality and Transmigration of Souls—Fondness for Display at Funerals—Trade Restrictions—Former Jesuit Establishment—State of Religion and Education at Tete—Inundation of the Zambesi—Cotton cultivated—The fibrous Plants Conge and Buaze—Detained by Fever—The Kumbanzo Bark—Native Medicines—Iron, its Quality—Hear of Famine at Kilimane—Death of a Portuguese Lady—The Funeral—Disinterested Kindness of the Portuguese.

I was most kindly received by the commandant Tito Augusto d'Araujo Sicard, who did every thing in his power to restore me from my emaciated condition; and, as this was still the unhealthy period at Kilimane, he advised me to remain with him until the following month. He also generously presented my men with abundant provisions of millet; and, by giving them lodgings in a house of his own until they could erect their own huts, he preserved them from the bite of the tampans, here named Carapatos.* We had heard frightful accounts of this insect while among the Banyai, and Major Sicard assured me that to strangers its bite is more especially dangerous, as it sometimes causes fatal fever. It may please our homoeopathic friends to hear that, in curing the bite of the tampan, the natives administer one of the insects bruised in the medicine employed.

* *Another insect, resembling a maggot, burrows into the feet of the natives and sucks their blood. Mr. Westwood says, "The*

tampan is a large species of mite, closely allied to the poisonous bug (as it is called) of Persia, 'Argos reflexus', respecting which such marvelous accounts have been recorded, and which the statement respecting the carapato or tampan would partially confirm." Mr. W. also thinks that the poison-yielding larva called N'gwa is a "species of chrysomelidae. The larvae of the British species of that family exude a fetid yellow thickish fluid when alarmed, but he has not heard that any of them are at all poisonous."

The village of Tete is built on a long slope down to the river, the fort being close to the water. The rock beneath is gray sandstone, and has the appearance of being crushed away from the river: the strata have thus a crumpled form. The hollow between each crease is a street, the houses being built upon the projecting fold. The rocks at the top of the slope are much higher than the fort, and of course completely command it. There is then a large valley, and beyond that an oblong hill called Karueira. The whole of the adjacent country is rocky and broken, but every available spot is under cultivation. The stone houses in Tete are cemented with mud instead of lime, and thatched with reeds and grass. The rains, having washed out the mud between the stones, give all the houses a rough, untidy appearance. No lime was known to be found nearer than Mozambique; some used in making seats in the verandas had actually been brought all that distance. The Portuguese evidently knew nothing of the pink and white marbles which I found at the Mbai, and another rivulet, named the Unguesi, near it, and of which I brought home specimens, nor yet of the dolomite which lies so near to Zumbo: they might have burned the marble into lime without going so far as Mozambique. There are about thirty European houses; the rest are native, and of wattle and daub. A wall about ten feet high is intended to inclose the village, but most of the native inhabitants prefer to live on different spots outside. There are about twelve hundred huts in all, which with European households would give a population of about four thousand five hundred souls. Only a small proportion of these, however, live on the spot; the majority are engaged in agricultural operations in the adjacent country. Generally there are not more than two thousand people resident, for, compared with what it was, Tete is now a ruin. The number of Portuguese is very small; if we exclude the military, it is under twenty. Lately, however, one hundred and five soldiers were sent from Portugal to Senna, where in one year twenty-five were cut off by fever. They were then removed to Tete, and here they enjoy much better health, though, from the abundance of spirits distilled from various plants, wild fruits, and grain, in which pernicious beverage they largely indulge, besides partaking chiefly of unwholesome native food, better health could scarcely have been expected. The natives here understand the method of distillation by means of gun-barrels, and a succession of earthen pots filled with water to keep them cool. The general report of the fever here is that, while at Kilimane the fever is continuous, at Tete a man recovers in about three days. The mildest remedies only are used at first, and, if that period be passed, then the more severe.

The fort of Tete has been the salvation of the Portuguese power in this quarter. It is a small square building, with a thatched apartment for the residence of the troops; and, though there are but few guns, they are in a much better state than those of any fort in the interior of Angola. The cause of the decadence of the Portuguese power in this region is simply this: In former times, considerable quantities of grain, as wheat, millet, and maize, were exported; also coffee, sugar, oil, and indigo, besides gold-dust and ivory. The cultivation of grain was carried on by means of slaves, of whom the Portuguese possessed a large number. The gold-dust was procured by washing at various points on the north, south, and west of Tete. A merchant took all his slaves with him to the washings, carrying as much calico and other goods as he could muster. On arriving at the washing-place, he made a present to the chief of the value of about a pound sterling. The slaves were then divided into parties, each headed by a confidential servant, who not only had the supervision of his squad while the washing went on, but bought dust from the inhabitants, and made a weekly return to his master. When several masters united at one spot, it was called a "Bara", and they then erected a temporary church, in which a priest from one of the missions performed mass. Both chiefs and people were favorable to these visits, because the traders purchased grain for the sustenance of the slaves with the goods they had brought. They continued at this labor until the whole of the goods were expended, and by this means about 130 lbs. of gold were annually produced. Probably more than this was actually obtained, but, as it was an article easily secreted, this alone was submitted to the authorities for taxation. At present the whole amount of gold obtained annually by the Portuguese is from 8 to 10 lbs. only. When the slave-trade began, it seemed to many of the merchants a more speedy mode of becoming rich to sell off the slaves than to pursue the slow mode of gold-washing and agriculture, and they continued to export them until they had neither hands to labor nor to fight for them. It was just the story of the goose and the golden egg. The coffee and sugar plantations and gold-washings were abandoned, because the labor had been exported to the Brazils. Many of the Portuguese then followed their slaves, and the government was obliged to pass a law to prevent further emigration, which, had it gone on, would have depopulated the Portuguese possessions altogether. A clever man of Asiatic (Goa) and Portuguese extraction, called Nyaude, now built a stockade at the confluence of the Luenya and Zambesi; and when the commandant of Tete sent an officer with his company to summon him to his presence, Nyaude asked permission of the officer to dress himself, which being granted, he went into an inner apartment, and the officer ordered his men to pile their arms. A drum of war began to beat a note which is well known to the inhabitants. Some of the soldiers took the alarm on hearing this note, but the officer, disregarding their warning, was, with his whole party, in a few minutes disarmed and bound hand and foot. The commandant of Tete then armed the whole body of slaves and marched against the stockade of Nyaude, but when they came near to it there was the Luenya still to cross. As they did not effect this speedily, Nyaude dispatched a strong party under his son Bonga across the river below the stockade, and up the left bank of the Zambesi until they came near to Tete. They then attacked Tete, which was wholly undefended save by a few soldiers in the fort, plundered and burned the whole town except the house of the commandant and a few others, with the church and fort. The women and children fled into the church; and it is a remarkable fact that none of the natives of this region will ever attack a church. Having rendered Tete a ruin, Bonga carried off all the cattle and plunder to his father. News of this having been brought to the army before the stockade, a sudden panic dispersed the whole; and as the fugitives took roundabout ways in their flight, Katolosa, who had hitherto pretended to be friendly with the Portuguese, sent out his men to capture as many of them as they could. They killed many for the sake of their arms. This is the account which both natives and Portuguese give of the affair.

Another half-caste from Macao, called Kisaka or Choutama, on the opposite bank of the river, likewise rebelled. His father having died, he imagined that he had been bewitched by the Portuguese, and he therefore plundered and burned all the plantations of the rich merchants of Tete on the north bank. As I have before remarked, that bank is the most fertile, and there the Portuguese had their villas and plantations to which they daily retired from Tete. When these were destroyed the Tete people were completely impoverished. An attempt was made to punish this rebel, but it was also unsuccessful, and he has lately been pardoned by the home government. One point in the narrative of this expedition is interesting. They came to a field of sugar-cane so large that 4000 men eating it during two days did not finish the whole. The Portuguese were thus placed between two enemies, Nyaude on the right bank and Kisaka on the left, and not only so, but Nyaude, having placed his stockade on the point of land on the right banks of both the Luenya and Zambesi, and washed by both these rivers, could prevent intercourse with the sea. The Luenya rushes into the Zambesi with great force when the latter is low, and, in coming up the Zambesi, boats must cross it and the Luenya separately, even going a little way up that river, so as not to be driven away by its current in the bed of the Zambesi, and dashed on the rock which stands on the opposite shore. In coming up to the Luenya for this purpose, all boats and canoes came close to the stockade to be robbed. Nyaude kept the Portuguese shut up in their fort at Tete during two years, and they could only get goods sufficient to buy food by sending to Kilimane by an overland route along the north bank of the Zambesi. The mother country did not in these "Caffre wars" pay the bills, so no one either became rich or blamed the missionaries.

The merchants were unable to engage in trade, and commerce, which the slave-trade had rendered stagnant, was now completely obstructed. The present commandant of Tete, Major Sicard, having great influence among the natives, from his good character, put a stop to the war more than once by his mere presence on the spot. We heard of him among the Banyai as a man with whom they would never fight, because "he had a good heart." Had I come down to this coast instead of going to Loanda in 1853, I should have come among the belligerents while the war was still raging, and should probably have been cut off. My present approach was just at the conclusion of the peace; and when the Portuguese authorities here were informed, through the kind offices of Lord Clarendon and Count de Lavradio, that I was expected to come this way, they all declared that such was the existing state of affairs that no European could possibly pass through the tribes. Some natives at last came down the river to Tete and said, alluding to the sextant and artificial horizon, that "the Son of God had come," and that he was "able to take the sun down from the heavens and place it under his arm!" Major Sicard then felt sure that this was the man mentioned in Lord Clarendon's dispatch.

On mentioning to the commandant that I had discovered a small seam of coal, he stated that the Portuguese were already aware of nine such seams, and that five of them were on the opposite bank of the river. As soon as I had recovered from my fatigue I went to examine them. We proceeded in a boat to the mouth of the Lofubu or Revubu, which is about two miles below Tete, and on the opposite or northern bank. Ascending this about four miles against a strong current of beautifully clear water, we landed near a small cataract, and walked about two miles through very fertile gardens to the seam, which we found to be in one of the feeders of the Lofubu, called Muatize or Motize. The seam is in the perpendicular bank, and dips into the rivulet, or in a northerly direction. There is, first of all, a seam 10 inches in diameter, then some shale, below which there is another seam, 58 inches of which are seen, and, as the bottom touches the water of the Muatize, it may be more. This part of the seam is about 30 yards long. There is then a fault. About 100 yards higher up the stream black vesicular trap is seen, penetrating in thin veins the clay shale of the country, converting it into porcellanite, and partially crystallizing the coal with which it came into contact. On the right bank of the Lofubu there is another feeder entering that river near its confluence with the Muatize, which is called the Morongozi, in which there is another and still larger bed of coal exposed. Farther up the Lofubu there are other seams in the rivulets Inyavu and Makare; also several spots in the Maravi country have the coal cropping out. This has evidently been brought to the surface by volcanic action at a later period than the coal formation.

I also went up the Zambesi, and visited a hot spring called Nyamboronda, situated in the bed of a small rivulet named Nyaondo, which shows that igneous action is not yet extinct. We landed at a small rivulet called Mokorozi, then went a mile or two to the eastward, where we found a hot fountain at the bottom of a high hill. A little spring bubbles up on one side of the rivulet Nyaondo, and a great quantity of acrid steam rises up from the ground adjacent, about 12 feet square of which is so hot that my companions could not stand on it with their bare feet. There are several little holes from which the water trickles, but the principal spring is in a hole a foot in diameter, and about the same in depth. Numbers of bubbles are constantly rising. The steam feels acrid in the throat, but is not inflammable, as it did not burn when I held a bunch of lighted grass over the bubbles. The mercury rises to 158 Deg. when the thermometer is put into the water in the hole, but after a few seconds it stands steadily at 160 Deg. Even when flowing over the stones the water is too hot for the hand. Little fish frequently leap out of the stream in the bed of which the fountain rises, into the hot water, and get scalded to death. We saw a frog which had performed the experiment, and was now cooked. The stones over which the water flows are incrusted with a white salt, and the water has a saline taste. The ground has been dug out near the fountain by the natives, in order to extract the salt it contains. It is situated among rocks of syenitic porphyry in broad dikes, and gneiss tilted on edge, and having a strike to the N.E. There are many specimens of half-formed pumice, with greenstone and lava. Some of the sandstone strata are dislocated by a hornblende rock and by basalt, the sandstone nearest to the basalt being converted into quartz.

The country around, as indeed all the district lying N. and N.W. of Tete, is hilly, and, the hills being covered with trees, the scenery is very picturesque. The soil of the valleys is very fruitful and well cultivated. There would not be much difficulty in working the coal. The Lofubu is about 60 yards broad; it flows perennially, and at its very lowest period, which is after September, there is water about 18 inches deep, which could be navigated in flat-bottomed boats. At the time of my visit it was full, and the current was very strong. If the small cataract referred to were to be avoided, the land-carriage beyond would only be about two miles. The other seams farther up the river may, after passing the cataract, be approached more easily than that in the Muatize; as the seam, however, dips down into the stream, no drainage of the mine would be required, for if water were come to it would run into the stream. I did not visit the others, but I was informed that there are seams in the independent native territory as well as in that of the Portuguese. That in the Nake is in the Banyai country, and, indeed, I have no doubt but that the whole country between Zumbo and Lupata is a coal-field of at least 2-1/2 Deg. of latitude in breadth, having many faults, made during the time of the igneous action. The gray sandstone rock having silicified trees lying on it is of these dimensions. The plantation in which the seam of coal exists would be valued among the Portuguese at about 60 dollars or 12 Pounds, but much more would probably be asked if a wealthy purchaser appeared. They could not, however, raise the price very much higher, because estates containing coal might be had from the native owners at a much cheaper rate. The wages of free laborers, when employed in such work as gold-washing, agriculture, or digging coal, is 2 yards of unbleached calico per day. They might be got to work cheaper if engaged by the moon, or for about 16 yards per month. For masons and carpenters even, the ordinary rate is 2 yards per day. This is called 1 braca. Tradesmen from Kilimane demand 4 bracas, or 8 yards, per day. English or American unbleached calico is the only currency used. The carriage of goods up the river to Tete adds about 10 per cent. to their cost. The usual conveyance is by means of very large canoes and launches built at Senna.

The amount of merchandise brought up during the five months of peace previous to my visit was of the value of 30,000 dollars, or about 6000 Pounds. The annual supply of goods for trade is about 15,000 Pounds, being calico, thick brass wire, beads, gunpowder, and guns. The quantity of the latter is, however, small, as the government of Mozambique made that article contraband after the commencement of the war. Goods, when traded with in the tribes around the Portuguese, produce a profit of only about 10 per cent., the articles traded in being ivory and gold-dust. A little oil and wheat are exported, but nothing else. Trade with the tribes beyond the exclusive ones is much better. Thirty brass rings cost 10s. at Senna, 1 Pound at Tete, and 2 Pounds beyond the tribes in the vicinity of Tete; these are a good price for a penful of gold-dust of the value of 2 Pounds. The plantations of coffee, which, previous to the commencement of the slave-trade, yielded one material for exportation, are now deserted, and it is difficult to find a single tree. The indigo ('Indigofera argentea', the common wild indigo of Africa) is found growing every where, and large quantities of the senna-plant* grow in the village of Tete and other parts, but neither indigo nor senna is collected. Calumba-root, which is found in abundance in some parts farther down the river, is bought by the Americans, it is said, to use as a dye-stuff. A kind of sarsaparilla, or a plant which is believed by the Portuguese to be such, is found from Londa to Senna, but has never been exported.

> * These appear to belong to 'Cassia acutifolia', or true senna of commerce, found in various parts of Africa and India. — Dr. Hooker.

The price of provisions is low, but very much higher than previous to the commencement of the war. Two yards of calico are demanded for six fowls; this is considered very dear, because, before the war, the same quantity of calico was worth 24 fowls. Grain is sold in little bags made from the leaves of the palmyra, like those in which we receive sugar. They are called panjas, and each panja weighs between 30 and 40 lbs. The panja of wheat at Tete is worth a dollar, or 5s.; but the native grain may be obtained among the islands below Lupata at the rate of three panjas for two yards of calico. The highest articles of consumption are tea and coffee, the tea being often as high as 15s. a pound. Food is cheaper down the river below Lupata, and, previous to the war, the islands which stud the Zambesi were all inhabited, and, the soil being exceedingly fertile, grain and fowls could be got to any amount. The inhabitants disappeared before their enemies the Landeens, but are beginning to return since the peace. They have no cattle, the only place where we found no tsetse being the district of Tete itself; and the cattle in the possession of the Portuguese are a mere remnant of what they formerly owned.

When visiting the hot fountain, I examined what were formerly the gold-washings in the rivulet Mokoroze, which is nearly on the 16th parallel of latitude. The banks are covered with large groves of fine mango-trees, among which the Portuguese lived while superintending the washing for the precious metal. The process of washing is very laborious and tedious. A quantity of sand is put into a wooden bowl with water; a half rotatory motion is given to the dish, which causes the coarser particles of sand to collect on one side of the bottom. These are carefully removed with the hand, and the process of rotation renewed until the whole of the sand is taken away, and the gold alone remains. It is found in very minute scales, and, unless I had been assured to the contrary, I should have taken it to be mica, for, knowing the gold to be of greater specific gravity than the sand, I imagined that a stream of water would remove the latter and leave the former; but here the practice is to remove the whole of the sand by the hand. This process was, no doubt, a profitable one to the Portuguese, and it is probable that, with the improved plan by means of mercury, the sands would be lucrative. I had an opportunity of examining the gold-dust from different parts to the east and northeast of Tete. There are six well-known washing-places. These are called Mashinga, Shindundo, Missala, Kapata, Mano, and Jawa. From the description of the rock I received, I suppose gold is found both in clay shale and quartz. At the range Mushinga to the N.N.W. the rock is said to be so soft that the women pound it into powder in wooden mortars previous to washing.

Round toward the westward, the old Portuguese indicate a station which was near to Zumbo on the River Panyame, and called Dambarari, near which much gold was found. Farther west lay the now unknown kingdom of Abutua, which was formerly famous for the metal; and then, coming round toward the east, we have the gold-washings of the Mashona, or Bazizulu, and, farther east, that of Manica, where gold is found much more abundantly than in any other part, and which has been supposed by some to be the Ophir of King Solomon. I saw the gold from this quarter as large as grains of wheat, that found in the rivers which run into the coal-field being in very minute scales. If we place one leg of the compasses at Tete, and extend the other three and a half degrees, bringing it round from the northeast of Tete by west, and then to the southeast, we nearly touch or include all the known gold-producing country. As the gold on this circumference is found in coarser grains than in the streams running toward the centre, or Tete, I imagine that the real gold-field lies round about the coal-field; and, if I am right in the conjecture, then we have coal encircled by a gold-field, and abundance of wood, water, and provisions—a combination not often met with in the world. The inhabitants are not unfavorable to washings, conducted on the principle formerly mentioned. At present they wash only when in want of a little calico. They know the value of gold perfectly well, for they bring it for sale in goose-quills, and demand 24 yards of calico for one penful. When the rivers in the district of Manica and other gold-washing places have been flooded, they leave a coating of mud on the banks. The natives observe the spots which dry soonest, and commence digging there, in firm belief that gold lies beneath. They are said not to dig deeper than their chins, believing that if they did so the ground would fall in and kill them. When they find a 'piece' or flake of gold, they bury it again, from the superstitious idea that this is the seed of the gold, and, though they know the value of it well, they prefer losing it rather than the whole future crop. This conduct seemed to me so very unlikely in men who bring the dust in quills, and even put in a few seeds of a certain plant as a charm to prevent their losing any of it on the way, that I doubted the authority of my informant; but I found the report verified by all the Portuguese who knew the native language and mode of thinking, and give the statement for what it is worth. If it is really practiced, the custom may have been introduced by some knowing one who wished to defraud the chiefs of their due; for we are informed in Portuguese history that in former times these pieces or flakes of gold were considered the perquisites of the chiefs.

Major Sicard, the commandant, whose kindness to me and my people was unbounded, presented a rosary made of the gold of the country, the workmanship of a native of Tete, to my little daughter; also specimens of the gold-dust of three different places, which, with the coal of Muatize and Morongoze, are deposited in the Museum of Practical Geology, Jermyn Street, London.

All the cultivation is carried on with hoes in the native manner, and considerable quantities of 'Holcus sorghum', maize, 'Pennisetum typhoideum', or lotsa of the Balonda, millet, rice, and wheat are raised, as also several kinds of beans—one of which, called "litloo" by the Bechuanas, yields under ground, as well as the 'Arachis hypogaea', or ground-nut; with cucumbers, pumpkins, and melons. The wheat is sown in low-lying places which are annually flooded by the Zambesi. When the waters retire, the women drop a few grains in a hole made with a hoe, then push back the soil with the foot. One weeding alone is required before the grain comes to maturity. This simple process represents all our subsoil plowing, liming, manuring, and harrowing, for in four months after planting a good crop is ready for the sickle, and has been known to yield a hundred-fold. It flourished still more at Zumbo. No irrigation is required, because here there are gentle rains, almost like mist, in winter, which go by the name of "wheat-showers", and are unknown in the interior, where no winter rain ever falls. The rains at Tete come from the east, though the prevailing winds come from the S.S.E. The finest portion of the flour does not make bread nearly so white as the seconds, and here the boyaloa (pombe), or native beer, is employed to mix with the flour instead of yeast. It makes excellent bread. At Kilimane, where the cocoanut palm abounds, the toddy from it, called "sura", is used for the same purpose, and makes the bread still lighter.

As it was necessary to leave most of my men at this place, Major Sicard gave them a portion of land on which to cultivate their own food, generously supplying them with corn in the mean time. He also said that my young men might go and hunt elephants in company with his servants, and purchase goods with both the ivory and dried meat, in order that they might have something to take with them on their return to Sekeletu. The men were delighted with his liberality, and soon sixty or seventy of them set off to engage in this enterprise. There was no calico to be had at this time in Tete, but the commandant handsomely furnished my men with clothing. I was in a state of want myself, and, though I pressed him to take payment in ivory for both myself and men, he refused all recompense. I shall ever remember his kindness with deep gratitude. He has written me, since my arrival in England, that my men had killed four elephants in the course of two months after my departure.

On the day of my arrival I was visited by all the gentlemen of the village, both white and colored, including the padre. Not one of them had any idea as to where the source of the Zambesi lay. They sent for the best traveled natives, but none of them knew the river even as far as Kansala. The father of one of the rebels who had been fighting against them had been a great traveler to the southwest, and had even heard of our visit to Lake Ngami; but he was equally ignorant with all the others that the Zambesi flowed in the centre of the country. They had, however, more knowledge of the country to the north of Tete than I had. One man, who had gone to Cazembe with Major Monteiro, stated that he had seen the Luapura or Loapula flowing past the town of that chieftain into the Luameji or Leeambye, but imagined that it found its way, somehow or other, into Angola. The fact that sometimes rivers were seen to flow like this toward the centre of the country, led geographers to the supposition that inner Africa was composed of elevated sandy plains, into which rivers ran and were lost. One of the gentlemen present, Senhor Candido, had visited a lake 45 days to the N.N.W. of Tete, which is probably the Lake Maravi of geographers, as in going thither they pass through the people of that name. The inhabitants of its southern coast are named Shiva; those on the north, Mujao; and they call the lake Nyanja or Nyanje, which simply means a large water, or bed of a large river. A high mountain stands in the middle of it, called Murombo or Murombola, which is inhabited by people who have much cattle. He stated that he crossed the Nyanja at a narrow part, and was 36 hours in the passage. The canoes were punted the whole way, and, if we take the rate about two miles per hour, it may be sixty or seventy miles in breadth. The country all round was composed of level plains covered with grass, and, indeed, in going thither they traveled seven or eight days without wood, and cooked their food with grass and stalks of native corn alone. The people sold their cattle at a very cheap rate. From the southern extremity of the lake two rivers issue forth: one, named after itself, the Nyanja, which passes into the sea on the east coast under another name; and the Shire, which flows into the Zambesi a little below Senna. The Shire is named Shirwa at its point of departure from the lake, and Senhor Candido was informed, when there, that the lake was simply an expansion of the River Nyanja, which comes from the north and encircles the mountain Murombo, the meaning of which is junction or union, in reference to the water having parted at its northern extremity, and united again at its southern. The Shire flows through a low, flat, marshy country, but abounding in population, and they are said to be brave. The Portuguese are unable to navigate the Shire up to the Lake Nyanja, because of the great abundance of a water-plant which requires no soil, and which they name "alfacinya" ('Pistia stratiotes'), from its resemblance to a lettuce. This completely obstructs the progress of canoes. In confirmation of this I may state that, when I passed the mouth of the Shire, great quantities of this same plant were floating from it into the Zambesi, and many parts of the banks below were covered with the dead plants.

Senhor Candido stated that slight earthquakes have happened several times in the country of the Maravi, and at no great distance from Tete. The motion seems to come from the eastward, and never to have lasted more than a few seconds. They are named in the Maravi tongue "shiwo", and in that of the people of Tete "shitakoteko", or "shivering". This agrees exactly with what has taken place in the coast of Mozambique—a few slight shocks of short duration, and all appearing to come from the east. At Senna, too, a single shock has been felt several times, which shook the doors and windows, and made the glasses jingle. Both Tete and Senna have hot springs in their vicinity, but the shocks seemed to come, not from them, but from the east, and proceed to the west. They are probably connected with the active volcanoes in the island of Bourbon.

As Senhor Candido holds the office of judge in all the disputes of the natives, and knows their language perfectly, his statement may be relied on that all the natives of this region have a clear idea of a Supreme Being, the maker and governor of all things. He is named "Morimo", "Molungo", "Reza", "Mpambe", in the different dialects spoken. The Barotse name him "Nyampi", and the Balonda "Zambi". All promptly acknowledge him as the ruler over all. They also fully believe in the soul's continued existence apart from the body, and visit the graves of relatives, making offerings of food, beer, etc. When undergoing the ordeal, they hold up their hands to the Ruler of Heaven, as if appealing to him to assert their innocence. When they escape, or recover from sickness, or are delivered from any danger, they offer a sacrifice of a fowl or a sheep, pouring out the blood as a libation to the soul of some departed relative. They believe in the transmigration of souls, and also that while persons are still living they may enter into lions and alligators, and then return again to their own bodies.

While still at Tete the son of Monomotapa paid the commandant a visit. He is named Mozungo, or "White Man", has a narrow tapering head, and probably none of the ability or energy his father possessed. He was the favorite of his father, who hoped that he would occupy his place. A strong party, however, in the tribe placed Katalosa in the chieftainship, and the son became, as they say, a child of this man. The Portuguese have repeatedly received offers of territory if they would only attend the interment of the departed chief with troops, fire off many rounds of cartridges over the grave, and then give eclat to the installment of the new chief. Their presence would probably influence the election, for many would vote on the side of power, and a candidate might feel it worth while to grant a good piece of land, if thereby he could secure the chieftainship to himself. When the Portuguese traders wish to pass into the country beyond Katalosa, they present him with about thirty-two yards of calico and some other goods, and he then gives them leave to pass in whatever direction they choose to go. They must, however, give certain quantities of cloth to a number of inferior chiefs beside, and they are subject to the game-laws. They have thus a body of exclusive tribes around them, preventing direct intercourse between them and the population beyond. It is strange that, when they had the power, they did not insist on the free navigation of the Zambesi. I can only account for this in the same way in which I accounted for a similar state of things in the west. All the traders have been in the hands of slaves, and have wanted that moral courage which a free man, with free servants on whom he can depend, usually possesses. If the English had been here, they would have insisted on the free navigation of this pathway as an indispensable condition of friendship. The present system is a serious difficulty in the way of developing the resources of the country, and might prove fatal to an unarmed expedition. If this desirable and most fertile field of enterprise is ever to be opened up, men must proceed on a different plan from that which has been followed, and I do not apprehend there would be much difficulty in commencing a new system, if those who undertook it insisted that it is not our custom to pay for a highway which has not been made by man. The natives themselves would not deny that the river is free to those who do not trade in slaves. If, in addition to an open, frank explanation, a small subsidy were given to the paramount chief, the willing consent of all the subordinates would soon be secured.

On the 1st of April I went to see the site of a former establishment of the Jesuits, called Micombo, about ten miles S.E. of Tete. Like all their settlements I have seen, both judgment and taste had been employed in the selection of the site. A little stream of mineral water had been collected in a tank and conducted to their house, before which was a little garden for raising vegetables at times of the year when no rain falls. It is now buried in a deep shady grove of mango-trees. I was accompanied by Captain

Nunes, whose great-grandfather, also a captain in the time of the Marquis of Pombal, received sealed orders, to be opened only on a certain day. When that day arrived, he found the command to go with his company, seize all the Jesuits of this establishment, and march them as prisoners to the coast. The riches of the fraternity, which were immense, were taken possession of by the state. Large quantities of gold had often been sent to their superiors at Goa, inclosed in images. The Jesuits here do not seem to have possessed the sympathies of the people as their brethren in Angola did. They were keen traders in ivory and gold-dust. All praise their industry. Whatever they did, they did it with all their might, and probably their successful labors in securing the chief part of the trade to themselves had excited the envy of the laity. None of the natives here can read; and though the Jesuits are said to have translated some of the prayers into the language of the country, I was unable to obtain a copy. The only religious teachers now in this part of the country are two gentlemen of color, natives of Goa. The one who officiates at Tete, named Pedro Antonio d'Araujo, is a graduate in Dogmatic Theology and Moral Philosophy. There is but a single school in Tete, and it is attended only by the native Portuguese children, who are taught to read and write. The black population is totally uncared for. The soldiers are marched every Sunday to hear mass, and but few others attend church. During the period of my stay, a kind of theatrical representation of our Savior's passion and resurrection was performed. The images and other paraphernalia used were of great value, but the present riches of the Church are nothing to what it once possessed. The commandant is obliged to lock up all the gold and silver in the fort for safety, though not from any apprehension of its being stolen by the people, for they have a dread of sacrilege.

The state of religion and education is, I am sorry to say, as low as that of commerce; but the European Portuguese value education highly, and send their children to Goa and elsewhere for instruction in the higher branches. There is not a single bookseller's shop, however, in either eastern or western Africa. Even Loanda, with its 12,000 or 14,000 souls, can not boast of one store for the sale of food for the mind.

On the 2d the Zambesi suddenly rose several feet in height. Three such floods are expected annually, but this year there were four. This last was accompanied by discoloration, and must have been caused by another great fall of rain east of the ridge. We had observed a flood of discolored water when we reached the river at the Kafue; it then fell two feet, and from subsequent rains again rose so high that we were obliged to leave it when opposite the hill Pinkwe. About the 10th of March the river rose several feet with comparatively clear water, and it continued to rise until the 21st, with but very slight discoloration. This gradual rise was the greatest, and was probably caused by the water of inundation in the interior. The sudden rise which happened on the 2d, being deeply discolored, showed again the effect of rains at a comparatively short distance. The fact of the river rising three or four times annually, and the one flood of inundation being mixed with the others, may account for the Portuguese not recognizing the phenomenon of the periodical inundation, so well known in the central country.

The independent natives cultivate a little cotton, but it is not at all equal, either in quantity or quality, to what we found in Angola. The pile is short, and it clings to the seed so much that they use an iron roller to detach it. The soil, however, is equal to the production of any tropical plant or fruit. The natives have never been encouraged to cultivate cotton for sale, nor has any new variety been introduced. We saw no palm-oil-trees, the oil which is occasionally exported being from the ground-nut. One of the merchants of Tete had a mill of the rudest construction for grinding this nut, which was driven by donkeys. It was the only specimen of a machine I could exhibit to my men. A very superior kind of salad oil is obtained from the seeds of cucumbers, and is much used in native cookery.

An offer, said to have been made by the "Times", having excited attention even in this distant part, I asked the commandant if he knew of any plant fit for the production of paper. He procured specimens of the fibrous tissue of a species of aloe, named Conge, and some also from the root of a wild date, and, lastly, of a plant named Buaze, the fibres of which, though useless for the manufacture of paper, are probably a suitable substitute for flax. I submitted a small quantity of these fibres to Messrs. Pye, Brothers, of London, who have invented a superior mode for the preparation of such tissues for the manufacturer. They most politely undertook the examination, and have given a favorable opinion of the Buaze, as may be seen in the note below.*

*

80 Lombard Street, 20th March, 1857.

Dear Sir,—We have the pleasure to return you the specimens of fibrous plants from the Zambesi River, on which you were desirous to see the effects of our treatment; we therefore inclose to you,

No. 1. Buaze, in the state received from you.
1 A. Do. as prepared by us.

1 B. The tow which has come from it in hackling.
No. 2. Conge, as received from you.
2 A. Do. as prepared by us.

With regard to both these fibres, we must state that the VERY MINUTE QUANTITY of each specimen has prevented our subjecting
them to any thing like the full treatment of our process, and we can therefore only give you an APPROXIMATE idea of their value.

The Buaze evidently possesses a very strong and fine fibre, assimilating to flax in its character, but we believe, when treated IN QUANTITY by our process, it would show both a stronger and finer fibre than flax; but being unable to apply the rolling or pressing processes with any efficiency to so very small a quantity, the gums are not yet so perfectly extracted as they would be, nor the fibre opened out to so fine a quality as it would then exhibit.

This is even yet more the case with the Conge, which, being naturally a harsh fibre, full of gums, wants exactly that powerful treatment which our process is calculated to give it, but which can not be applied to such miniature specimens. We do not therefore consider this as more than half treated, its fibre consequently remaining yet harsh, and coarse, and stiff, as compared with what it would be if treated IN QUANTITY.

Judging that it would be satisfactory to you to be in possession of the best practical opinion to be obtained on such a subject, we took the liberty of forwarding your little specimens to Messrs. Marshall, of Leeds, who have kindly favored us with the following observations on them:

"We have examined the samples you sent us yesterday, and think the Conge or aloe fibre would be of no use to us, but the Buaze fibre appears to resemble flax, and as prepared by you will be equal to flax worth 50 Pounds or 60 Pounds per ton, but we could hardly speak positively to the value unless we had 1 cwt. or 2 cwt. to try on our machinery. However, we think the result is promising, and we hope further inquiry will be made as to the probable supply of the material."

We are, dear sir, your very obedient servants, Pye, Brothers.
The Rev. Dr. Livingstone.

A representation of the plant is given in the annexed woodcut,* as a help to its identification. I was unable to procure either the flowers or fruit; but, as it is not recognized at sight by that accomplished botanist and eminent traveler, Dr. J. D. Hooker, it may safely be concluded that it is quite unknown to botanists. It is stated by the Portuguese to grow in large quantities in the Maravi country north of the Zambesi, but it is not cultivated, and the only known use it has been put to is in making threads on which the natives string their beads. Elsewhere the split tendons of animals are employed for this purpose. This seems to be of equal strength, for a firm thread of it feels like catgut in the hand, and would rather cut the fingers than break.

* *Unfortunately, this woodcut can not be represented in this ASCII text, but buaze, or bwazi, is 'Securidaca longipedunculata'. — A. L., 1997.*

Having waited a month for the commencement of the healthy season at Kilimane, I would have started at the beginning of April, but tarried a few days in order that the moon might make her appearance, and enable me to take lunar observations on my way down the river. A sudden change of temperature happening on the 4th, simultaneously with the appearance of the new moon, the commandant and myself, with nearly every person in the house, were laid up with a severe attack of fever. I soon recovered by the use of my wonted remedies, but Major Sicard and his little boy were confined much longer. There was a general fall of 4 Deg. of temperature from the middle of March, 84 Deg. at 9 A.M., and 87 Deg. at 9 P.M.; the greatest heat being 90 Deg. at midday, and the lowest 81 Deg. at sunrise. It afforded me pleasure to attend the invalids in their sickness, though I was unable to show a tithe of the gratitude I felt for the commandant's increasing kindness. My quinine and other remedies were nearly all expended, and no fresh supply was to be found here, there being no doctors at Tete, and only one apothecary with the troops, whose stock of medicine was also small. The Portuguese, however, informed me that they had the cinchona bark growing in their country—that there was a little of it to be found at Tete—whole forests of it at Senna and near the delta of Kilimane. It seems quite a providential arrangement that the remedy for fever should be found in the greatest abundance where it is most needed. On seeing the leaves, I stated that it was not the 'Cinchona longifolia' from which it is supposed the quinine of commerce is extracted, but the name and properties of this bark made me imagine that it was a cinchonaceous tree. I could not get the flower, but when I went to Senna I tried to bring away a few small living trees with earth in a box. They, however, all died when we came to Kilimane. Failing in this mode of testing the point, I submitted a few leaves and seed-vessels to my friend, Dr. Hooker, who kindly informs me that they belong "apparently to an apocyneous plant, very nearly allied to the Malouetia Heudlotii (of Decaisne), a native of Senegambia." Dr. H. adds, "Various plants of this natural order are reputed powerful febrifuges, and some of them are said to equal the cinchona in their effects." It is called in the native tongue Kumbanzo.

The flowers are reported to be white. The pods are in pairs, a foot or fifteen inches in length, and contain a groove on their inner sides. The thick soft bark of the root is the part used by the natives; the Portuguese use that of the tree itself. I immediately began to use a decoction of the bark of the root, and my men found it so efficacious that they collected small quantities of it for themselves, and kept it in little bags for future use. Some of them said that they knew it in their own country, but I never happened to observe it. The decoction is given after the first paroxysm of the complaint is over. The Portuguese believe it to have the same effects as the quinine, and it may prove a substitute for that invaluable medicine.

There are numbers of other medicines in use among the natives, but I have always been obliged to regret want of time to ascertain which were useful and which of no value. We find a medicine in use by a tribe in one part of the country, and the same plant employed by a tribe a thousand miles distant. This surely must arise from some inherent virtue in the plant. The Boers under Potgeiter visited Delgoa Bay for the first time about ten years ago, in order to secure a port on the east coast for their republic. They had come from a part of the interior where the disease called croup occasionally prevails. There was no appearance of the disease among them at the period of their visit, but the Portuguese inhabitants of that bay found that they had left it among them, and several adults were cut off by a form of the complaint called 'Laryngismus stridulus', the disease of which the great Washington died. Similar cases have occurred in the South Sea Islands. Ships have left diseases from which no one on board was suffering at the time of their visit. Many of the inhabitants here were cut down, usually in three days from their first attack, until a native doctor adopted the plan of scratching the root of the tongue freely with a certain root, and giving a piece of it to be chewed. The cure may have been effected by the scarification only, but the

Portuguese have the strongest faith in the virtues of the root, and always keep some of it within reach.

There are also other plants which the natives use in the treatment of fever, and some of them produce 'diaphoresis' in a short space of time. It is certain that we have got the knowledge of the most potent febrifuge in our pharmacopoeia from the natives of another country. We have no cure for cholera and some other diseases. It might be worth the investigation of those who visit Africa to try and find other remedies in a somewhat similar way to that in which we found the quinine.*

> * I add the native names of a few of their remedies in order to assist the inquirer: Mupanda panda: this is used in fever for producing perspiration; the leaves are named Chirussa; the roots dye red, and are very astringent. Goho or Go-o: this is the ordeal medicine; it is both purgative and emetic. Mutuva or Mutumbue: this plant contains so much oil that it serves as lights in Londa; it is an emollient drink for the cure of coughs, and the pounded leaves answer as soap to wash the head. Nyamucu ucu has a curious softening effect on old dry grain. Mussakasi is believed to remove the effects of the Go-o. Mudama is a stringent vermifuge. Mapubuza dyes a red color. Musikizi yields an oil. Shinkondo: a virulent poison; the Maravi use it in their ordeal, and it is very fatal. Kanunka utare is said to expel serpents and rats by its pungent smell, which is not at all disagreeable to man; this is probably a kind of 'Zanthoxylon', perhaps the Z. melancantha of Western Africa, as it is used to expel rats and serpents there. Mussonzoa dyes cloth black. Mussio: the beans of this also dye black. Kangome, with flowers and fruit like Mocha coffee; the leaves are much like those of the sloe, and the seeds are used as coffee or eaten as beans. Kanembe-embe: the pounded leaves used as an extemporaneous glue for mending broken vessels. Katunguru is used for killing fish. Mutavea Nyerere: an active caustic. Mudiacoro: also an external caustic, and used internally. Kapande: another ordeal plant, but used to produce 'diaphoresis'. Karumgasura: also diaphoretic. Munyazi yields an oil, and is one of the ingredients for curing the wounds of poisoned arrows. Uombue: a large root employed in killing fish. Kakumate: used in intermittents. Musheteko: applied to ulcers, and the infusion

also internally in amenorrhoea. Inyakanyanya: this is seen in small, dark-colored, crooked roots of pleasant aromatic smell and slightly bitter taste, and is highly extolled in the treatment of fever; it is found in Manica. Eskinencia: used in croup and sore-throat. Itaca or Itaka: for diaphoresis in fever; this root is brought as an article of barter by the Arabs to Kilimane; the natives purchase it eagerly. Mukundukundu: a decoction used as a febrifuge in the same way as quinine; it grows plentifully at Shupanga, and the wood is used as masts for launches. I may here add the recipe of Brother Pedro of Zumbo for the cure of poisoned wounds, in order to show the similarity of practice among the natives of the Zambesi, from whom, in all probability, he acquired his knowledge, and the Bushmen of the Kalahari. It consists of equal parts of the roots of the Calumba, Musheteko, Abutua, Batatinya, Paregekanto, Itaka, or Kapande, put into a bottle and covered with common castor-oil. As I have before observed, I believe the oily ingredient is the effectual one, and ought to be tried by any one who has the misfortune to get wounded by a Bushman's or Banyai arrow.

The only other metal, besides gold, we have in abundance in this region, is iron, and that is of excellent quality. In some places it is obtained from what is called the specular iron ore, and also from black oxide. The latter has been well roasted in the operations of nature, and contains a large proportion of the metal. It occurs generally in tears or rounded lumps, and is but slightly magnetic. When found in the beds of rivers, the natives know of its existence by the quantity of oxide on the surface, and they find no difficulty in digging it with pointed sticks. They consider English iron as "rotten"; and I have seen, when a javelin of their own iron lighted on the cranium of a hippopotamus, it curled up like the proboscis of a butterfly, and the owner would prepare it for future use by straightening it COLD with two stones. I brought home some of the hoes which Sekeletu gave me to purchase a canoe, also some others obtained in Kilimane, and they have been found of such good quality that a friend of mine in Birmingham has made an Enfield rifle of them.*

* The following remarks are by a practical blacksmith, one of the most experienced men in the gun-trade. In this trade various qualities of iron are used, and close attention is required to secure for each purpose the quality of iron peculiarly adapted to it:

The iron in the two spades strongly resembles Swedish or Russian; it is highly carbonized.

The same qualities are found in both spades.

When chilled in water it has all the properties of steel: see the piece marked I, chilled at one end, and left soft at the other.

When worked hot, it is very malleable: but cold, it breaks quite short and brittle.

The great irregularity found in the working of the iron affords evidence that it has been prepared by inexperienced hands.

This is shown in the bending of the small spade; the thick portion retains its crystallized nature, while the thin part has been changed by the hammering it has undergone.

The large spade shows a very brittle fracture.

The iron is too brittle for gun-work; it would be liable to break.

This iron, if REPEATEDLY heated and hammered, would become
decarbonized, and would then possess the qualities found in the spear-head, which, after being curled up by being struck against a hard substance, was restored, by hammering, to its original form without injury.

The piece of iron marked II is a piece of gun-iron of fibrous quality, such as will bend without breaking.

The piece marked III is of crystalline quality; it has been submitted to a process which has changed it to IIII; III and

IIII are cut from the same bar. The spade-iron has been submitted to the same process, but no corresponding effect can be produced.

The iron ore exists in great abundance, but I did not find any limestone in its immediate vicinity. So far as I could learn, there is neither copper nor silver. Malachite is worked by the people of Cazembe, but, as I did not see it, nor any other metal, I can say nothing about it. A few precious stones are met with, and some parts are quite covered with agates. The mineralogy of the district, however, has not been explored by any one competent to the task.

When my friend the commandant was fairly recovered, and I myself felt strong again, I prepared to descend the Zambesi. A number of my men were out elephant-hunting, and others had established a brisk trade in firewood, as their countrymen did at Loanda. I chose sixteen of those who could manage canoes to convey me down the river. Many more would have come, but we were informed that there had been a failure of the crops at Kilimane from the rains not coming at the proper time, and thousands had died of hunger. I did not hear of a single effort having been made to relieve the famishing by sending them food down the river. Those who perished were mostly slaves, and others seemed to think that their masters ought to pay for their relief. The sufferers were chiefly among those natives who inhabit the delta, and who are subject to the Portuguese. They are in a state of slavery, but are kept on farms and mildly treated. Many yield a certain rental of grain only to their owners, and are otherwise free. Eight thousand are said to have perished. Major Sicard lent me a boat which had been built on the river, and sent also Lieutenant Miranda to conduct me to the coast.

A Portuguese lady who had come with her brother from Lisbon, having been suffering for some days from a severe attack of fever, died about three o'clock in the morning of the 20th of April. The heat of the body having continued unabated till six o'clock, I was called in, and found her bosom quite as warm as I ever did in a living case of fever. This continued for three hours more. As I had never seen a case in which fever-heat continued so long after death, I delayed the funeral until unmistakable symptoms of dissolution occurred. She was a widow, only twenty-two years of age, and had been ten years in Africa. I attended the funeral in the evening, and was struck by the custom of the country. A number of slaves preceded us, and fired off many rounds of gunpowder in front of the body. When a person of much popularity is buried, all the surrounding chiefs send deputations to fire over the grave. On one occasion at Tete, more than thirty barrels of gunpowder were expended. Early in the morning of the 21st the slaves of the deceased lady's brother went round the village making a lamentation, and drums were beaten all day, as they are at such times among the heathen.

The commandant provided for the journey most abundantly, and gave orders to Lieutenant Miranda that I should not be allowed to pay for any thing all the way to the coast, and sent messages to his friends Senhors Ferrao, Isidore, Asevedo, and Nunes, to treat me as they would himself. From every one of these gentlemen I am happy to acknowledge that I received most disinterested kindness, and I ought to speak well forever of Portuguese hospitality. I have noted each little act of civility received, because somehow or other we have come to hold the Portuguese character in rather a low estimation. This may have arisen partly from the pertinacity with which some of them have pursued the slave-trade, and partly from the contrast which they now offer to their illustrious ancestors—the foremost navigators of the world. If my specification of their kindnesses will tend to engender a more respectful feeling to the nation, I shall consider myself well rewarded. We had three large canoes in the company which had lately come up with goods from Senna. They are made very large and strong, much larger than any we ever saw in the interior, and might strike with great force against a rock and not be broken. The men sit at the stern when paddling, and there is usually a little shed made over a part of the canoe to shade the passengers from the sun. The boat in which I went was furnished with such a covering, so I sat quite comfortably.

Chapter 32

Leave Tete and proceed down the River—Pass the Stockade of Bonga—Gorge of Lupata—"Spine of the World"—Width of River—Islands—War Drum at Shiramba—Canoe Navigation—Reach Senna—Its ruinous State—Landeens levy Fines upon the Inhabitants—Cowardice of native Militia—State of the Revenue—No direct Trade with Portugal—Attempts to revive the Trade of Eastern Africa—Country round Senna—Gorongozo, a Jesuit Station—Manica, the best Gold Region in Eastern Africa—Boat-building at Senna—Our Departure—Capture of a Rebel Stockade—Plants Alfacinya and Njefu at the Confluence of the Shire—Landeen Opinion of the Whites—Mazaro, the point reached by Captain Parker—His Opinion respecting the Navigation of the River from this to the Ocean—Lieutenant Hoskins' Remarks on the same subject—Fever, its Effects—Kindly received into the House of Colonel Nunes at Kilimane—Forethought of Captain Nolloth and Dr. Walsh—Joy imbittered—Deep Obligations to the Earl of Clarendon, etc.—On developing Resources of the Interior—Desirableness of Missionary Societies selecting healthy Stations—Arrangements on leaving my Men— Retrospect—Probable Influence of the Discoveries on Slavery—Supply of Cotton, Sugar, etc., by Free Labor—Commercial Stations—Development of the Resources of Africa a Work of Time—Site of Kilimane— Unhealthiness—Death of a shipwrecked Crew from Fever—The Captain saved by Quinine—Arrival of H. M. Brig "Frolic"—Anxiety of one of my Men to go to England—Rough Passage in the Boats to the Ship—Sekwebu's Alarm—Sail for Mauritius—Sekwebu on board; he becomes insane; drowns himself—Kindness of Major-General C. M. Hay—Escape Shipwreck—Reach Home.

We left Tete at noon on the 22d, and in the afternoon arrived at the garden of Senhor A. Manoel de Gomez, son-in-law and nephew of Bonga. The Commandant of Tete had sent a letter to the rebel Bonga, stating that he ought to treat me kindly, and he had deputed his son-in-law to be my host. Bonga is not at all equal to his father Nyaude, who was a man of great ability. He is also in bad odor with the Portuguese, because he receives all runaway slaves and criminals. He does not trust the Portuguese, and is reported to be excessively superstitious. I found his son-in-law, Manoel, extremely friendly, and able to converse in a very intelligent manner. He was in his garden when we arrived, but soon dressed himself respectably, and gave us a good tea and dinner. After a breakfast of tea, roasted eggs, and biscuits next morning, he presented six fowls and three goats as provisions for the journey. When we parted from him we passed the stockade of Bonga at the confluence of the Luenya, but did not go near it, as he is said to be very suspicious. The Portuguese advised me not to take any observation, as the instruments might awaken fears in Bonga's mind, but Manoel said I might do so if I wished; his garden, however, being above the confluence, could not avail as a geographical point. There are some good houses in the stockade. The trees of which it is composed seemed to me to be living, and could not be burned. It was strange to see a stockade menacing the whole commerce of the river in a situation where the guns of a vessel would have full play on it, but it is a formidable affair for those who have only muskets. On one occasion, when Nyaude was attacked by Kisaka, they fought for weeks; and though Nyaude was reduced to cutting up his copper anklets for balls, his enemies were not able to enter the stockade.

On the 24th we sailed only about three hours, as we had done the day before; but having come to a small island at the western entrance of the gorge of Lupata, where Dr. Lacerda is said to have taken an astronomical observation, and called it the island of Mozambique, because it was believed to be in the same latitude, or 15d 1', I wished to verify his position, and remained over night: my informants must have been mistaken, for I found the island of Mozambique here to be lat. 16d 34' 46" S.

Respecting this range, to which the gorge has given a name, some Portuguese writers have stated it to be so high that snow lies on it during the whole year, and that it is composed of marble. It is not so high in appearance as the Campsie Hills when seen from the Vale of Clyde. The western side is the most abrupt, and gives the idea of the greatest height, as it rises up perpendicularly from the water six or seven hundred feet. As seen from this island, it is certainly no higher than Arthur's Seat appears from Prince's Street, Edinburgh. The rock is compact silicious schist of a slightly reddish color, and in thin strata; the island on which we slept looks as if torn off from the opposite side of the gorge, for the strata are twisted and torn in every direction. The eastern side of the range is much more sloping than the western, covered with trees, and does not give the idea of altitude so much as the western. It extends a considerable way into the Maganja country in the north, and then bends round toward the river again, and ends in the lofty mountain Morumbala, opposite Senna. On the other or southern side it is straighter, but is said to end in Gorongozo, a mountain west of the same point. The person who called this Lupata "the spine of the world" evidently did not mean to say that it was a translation of the word, for it means a defile or gorge having perpendicular walls. This range does not deserve the name of either Cordillera or Spine, unless we are willing to believe that the world has a very small and very crooked "back-bone".

We passed through the gorge in two hours, and found it rather tortuous, and between 200 and 300 yards wide. The river is said to be here always excessively deep; it seemed to me that a steamer could pass through it at full speed. At the eastern entrance of Lupata stand two conical hills; they are composed of porphyry, having large square crystals therein. These hills are called Moenda en Goma, which means a footprint of a wild beast. Another conical hill on the opposite bank is named Kasisi (priest), from having a bald top. We sailed on quickly with the current of the river, and found that it spread out to more than two miles in breadth; it is, however, full of islands, which are generally covered with reeds, and which, previous to the war, were inhabited, and yielded vast quantities of grain. We usually landed to cook breakfast, and then went on quickly. The breadth of water between the islands was now quite sufficient for a sailing vessel to tack, and work her sails in; the prevailing winds would blow her up the stream; but I regretted that I had not come when the river was at its lowest rather than at its highest. The testimony, however, of Captain Parker and Lieutenant Hoskins, hereafter to be noticed, may be considered conclusive as to the capabilities of this river for commercial purposes. The Portuguese state that there is high water during five months of the year, and when it is low there is always a channel of deep water. But this is very winding; and as the river wears away some of the islands and forms others, the course of the channel is often altered. I suppose that an accurate chart of it made in one year would not be very reliable the next; but I believe, from all that I can learn, that the river could be navigated in a small flat-bottomed steamer during the whole year as far as Tete. At this time a steamer of large size could have floated easily. The river was measured at the latter place by the Portuguese, and found by them to be 1050 yards broad. The body of water flowing past when I was there was very great, and the breadth it occupied when among the islands had a most imposing effect. I could not get a glimpse of either shore. All the right bank beyond Lupata is low and flat: on the north, the ranges of hills and dark lines below them are seen, but from the boat it is impossible to see the shore. I only guess the breadth of the river to be two miles; it is probably more. Next day we landed at Shiramba for breakfast, having sailed 8-1/2 hours from Lupata. This was once the residence of a Portuguese brigadier, who spent large sums of money in embellishing his house and gardens: these we found in entire ruin, as his half-caste son had destroyed all, and then rebelled against the Portuguese, but with less success than either Nyaude or Kisaka, for he had been seized and sent a prisoner to Mozambique a short time before our visit. All the southern shore has been ravaged by the Caffres, who are here named Landeens, and most of the inhabitants who remain acknowledge the authority of Bonga, and not of the Portuguese. When at breakfast, the people of Shiramba commenced beating the drum of war. Lieutenant Miranda, who was well acquainted with the customs of the country, immediately started to his feet, and got all the soldiers of our party under arms; he then demanded of the natives why the drum was beaten while we were there. They gave an evasive reply; and, as they employ this means of collecting their neighbors when they intend to rob canoes, our watchfulness may have prevented their proceeding farther.

We spent the night of the 26th on the island called Nkuesi, opposite a remarkable saddle-shaped mountain, and found that we were just on the 17th parallel of latitude. The sail down the river was very fine; the temperature becoming low, it was pleasant to the feelings; but the shores being flat and far from us, the scenery was uninteresting. We breakfasted on the 27th at Pita, and found some half-caste Portuguese had established themselves there, after fleeing from the opposite bank to escape Kisaka's people, who were now ravaging all the Maganja country. On the afternoon of the 27th we arrived at Senna. (Commandant Isidore's house, 300 yards S.W. of the mud fort on the banks of the river: lat. 17d 27' 1" S., long. 35d 10' E.) We found Senna to be twenty-three and a half hours' sail from Tete. We had the current entirely in our favor, but met various parties in large canoes toiling laboriously against it. They use long ropes, and pull the boats from the shore. They usually take about twenty days to ascend the distance we had descended in about four. The wages paid to boatmen are considered high. Part of the men who had accompanied me gladly accepted employment from Lieutenant Miranda to take a load of goods in a canoe from Senna to Tete.

I thought the state of Tete quite lamentable, but that of Senna was ten times worse. At Tete there is some life; here every thing is in a state of stagnation and ruin. The fort, built of sun-dried bricks, has the grass growing over the walls, which have been patched in some places by paling. The Landeens visit the village periodically, and levy fines upon the inhabitants, as they consider the Portuguese a conquered tribe, and very rarely does a native come to trade. Senhor Isidore, the commandant, a man of considerable energy, had proposed to surround the whole village with palisades as a protection against the Landeens, and the villagers were to begin this work the day after I left. It was sad to look at the ruin manifest in every building, but the half-castes appear to be in league with the rebels and Landeens; for when any attempt is made by the Portuguese to coerce the enemy or defend themselves, information is conveyed at once to the

Landeen camp, and, though the commandant prohibits the payment of tribute to the Landeens, on their approach the half-castes eagerly ransom themselves. When I was there, a party of Kisaka's people were ravaging the fine country on the opposite shore. They came down with the prisoners they had captured, and forthwith the half-castes of Senna went over to buy slaves. Encouraged by this, Kisaka's people came over into Senna fully armed and beating their drums, and were received into the house of a native Portuguese. They had the village at their mercy, yet could have been driven off by half a dozen policemen. The commandant could only look on with bitter sorrow. He had soldiers, it is true, but it is notorious that the native militia of both Senna and Kilimane never think of standing to fight, but invariably run away, and leave their officers to be killed. They are brave only among the peaceable inhabitants. One of them, sent from Kilimane with a packet of letters or expresses, arrived while I was at Senna. He had been charged to deliver them with all speed, but Senhor Isidore had in the mean time gone to Kilimane, remained there a fortnight, and reached Senna again before the courier came. He could not punish him. We gave him a passage in our boat, but he left us in the way to visit his wife, and, "on urgent private business," probably gave up the service altogether, as he did not come to Kilimane all the time I was there. It is impossible to describe the miserable state of decay into which the Portuguese possessions here have sunk. The revenues are not equal to the expenses, and every officer I met told the same tale, that he had not received one farthing of pay for the last four years. They are all forced to engage in trade for the support of their families. Senhor Miranda had been actually engaged against the enemy during these four years, and had been highly lauded in the commandant's dispatches to the home government, but when he applied to the Governor of Kilimane for part of his four years' pay, he offered him twenty dollars only. Miranda resigned his commission in consequence. The common soldiers sent out from Portugal received some pay in calico. They all marry native women, and, the soil being very fertile, the wives find but little difficulty in supporting their husbands. There is no direct trade with Portugal. A considerable number of Banians, or natives of India, come annually in small vessels with cargoes of English and Indian goods from Bombay. It is not to be wondered at, then, that there have been attempts made of late years by speculative Portuguese in Lisbon to revive the trade of Eastern Africa by means of mercantile companies. One was formally proposed, which was modeled on the plan of our East India Company; and it was actually imagined that all the forts, harbors, lands, etc., might be delivered over to a company, which would bind itself to develop the resources of the country, build schools, make roads, improve harbors, etc., and, after all, leave the Portuguese the option of resuming possession.

Another effort has been made to attract commercial enterprise to this region by offering any mining company permission to search for the ores and work them. Such a company, however, would gain but little in the way of protection or aid from the government of Mozambique, as that can but barely maintain a hold on its own small possessions; the condition affixed of importing at the company's own cost a certain number of Portuguese from the island of Madeira or the Azores, in order to increase the Portuguese population in Africa, is impolitic. Taxes would also be levied on the minerals exported. It is noticeable that all the companies which have been proposed in Portugal have this put prominently in the preamble, "and for the abolition of the inhuman slave-trade." This shows either that the statesmen in Portugal are enlightened and philanthropic, or it may be meant as a trap for English capitalists; I incline to believe the former. If the Portuguese really wish to develop the resources of the rich country beyond their possessions, they ought to invite the co-operation of other nations on equal terms with themselves. Let the pathway into the interior be free to all; and, instead of wretched forts, with scarcely an acre of land around them which can be called their own, let real colonies be made. If, instead of military establishments, we had civil ones, and saw emigrants going out with their wives, plows, and seeds, rather than military convicts with bugles and kettle-drums, we might hope for a return of prosperity to Eastern Africa.

The village of Senna stands on the right bank of the Zambesi. There are many reedy islands in front of it, and there is much bush in the country adjacent. The soil is fertile, but the village, being in a state of ruin, and having several pools of stagnant water, is very unhealthy. The bottom rock is the akose of Brongniart, or granitic grit, and several conical hills of trap have burst through it. One standing about half a mile west of the village is called Baramuana, which has another behind it; hence the name, which means "carry a child on the back". It is 300 or 400 feet high, and on the top lie two dismounted cannon, which were used to frighten away the Landeens, who, in one attack upon Senna, killed 150 of the inhabitants. The prospect from Baramuana is very fine; below, on the eastward, lies the Zambesi, with the village of Senna; and some twenty or thirty miles beyond stands the lofty mountain Morumbala, probably 3000 or 4000 feet high. It is of an oblong shape, and from its physiognomy, which can be distinctly seen when the sun is in the west, is evidently igneous. On the northern end there is a hot sulphurous fountain, which my Portuguese friends refused to allow me to visit, because the mountain is well peopled, and the mountaineers are at present not friendly with the Portuguese. They have plenty of garden-ground and running water on its summit. My friends at Senna declined the responsibility of taking me into danger. To the north of Morumbala we have a fine view of the mountains of the Maganja; they here come close to the river, and terminate in Morumbala. Many of them are conical, and the Shire is reported to flow among them, and to run on the Senna side of Morumbala before joining the Zambesi. On seeing the confluence afterward, close to a low range of hills beyond Morumbala, I felt inclined to doubt the report, as the Shire must then flow parallel with the Zambesi, from which Morumbala seems distant only twenty or thirty miles. All around to the southeast the country is flat, and covered with forest, but near Senna a number of little abrupt conical hills diversify the scenery. To the west and north the country is also flat forest, which gives it a sombre appearance; but just in the haze of the horizon southwest by south, there rises a mountain range equal in height to Morumbala, and called Nyamonga. In a clear day another range beyond this may be seen, which is Gorongozo, once a station of the Jesuits. Gorongozo is famed for its clear cold waters and healthiness, and there are some inscriptions engraved on large square slabs on the top of the mountain, which have probably been the work of the fathers. As this lies in the direction of a district between Manica and Sofala, which has been conjectured to be the Ophir of King Solomon, the idea that first sprang up in my mind was, that these monuments might be more ancient than the Portuguese; but, on questioning some persons who had seen them, I found that they were in Roman characters, and did not deserve a journey of six days to see them.

Manica lies three days northwest of Gorongozo, and is the best gold country known in Eastern Africa. The only evidence the Portuguese have of its being the ancient Ophir is, that at Sofala, its nearest port, pieces of wrought gold have been dug up near the fort and in the gardens. They also report the existence of hewn stones in the neighborhood, but these can not have been abundant, for all the stones of the fort of Sofala are said to have been brought from Portugal. Natives whom I met in the country of Sekeletu, from Manica, or Manoa, as they call it, state that there are several caves in the country, and walls of hewn stones, which they believe to have been made by their ancestors; and there is, according to the Portuguese, a small tribe of Arabs there, who have become completely like the other natives. Two rivers, the Motirikwe and Sabia, or Sabe, run through their country into the sea. The Portuguese were driven out of the country by the Landeens, but now talk of reoccupying Manica.

The most pleasant sight I witnessed at Senna was the negroes of Senhor Isidore building boats after the European model, without any one to superintend their operations. They had been instructed by a European master, but now go into the forest and cut down the motondo-trees, lay down the keel, fit in the ribs, and make very neat boats and launches, valued at from 20 Pounds to 100 Pounds. Senhor Isidore had some of them instructed also in carpentry at Rio Janeiro, and they constructed for him the handsomest house in Kilimane, the woodwork being all of country trees, some of which are capable of a fine polish, and very durable. A medical opinion having been asked by the commandant respecting a better site for the village, which, lying on the low bank of the Zambesi, is very unhealthy, I recommended imitation of the Jesuits, who had chosen the high, healthy mountain of Gorongozo, and to select a new site on Morumbala, which is perfectly healthy, well watered, and where the Shire is deep enough for the purpose of navigation at its base. As the next resource, I proposed removal to the harbor of Mitilone, which is at one of the mouths of the Zambesi, a much better port than Kilimane, and where, if they must have the fever, they would be in the way of doing more good to themselves and the country than they can do in their present situation. Had the Portuguese possessed this territory as a real colony, this important point would not have been left unoccupied; as it is, there is not even a native village placed at the entrance of this splendid river to show the way in.

On the 9th of May sixteen of my men were employed to carry government goods in canoes up to Tete. They were much pleased at getting this work. On the 11th the whole of the inhabitants of Senna, with the commandant, accompanied us to the boats. A venerable old man, son of a judge, said they were in much sorrow on account of the miserable state of decay into which they had sunk, and of the insolent conduct of the people of Kisaka now in the village. We were abundantly supplied with provisions by the commandant and Senhor Ferrao, and sailed pleasantly down the broad river. About thirty miles below Senna we passed the mouth of the River Zangwe on our right, which farther up goes by the name of Pungwe; and about five miles farther on our left, close to the end of a low range into which Morumbala merges, we crossed the mouth of the Shire, which seemed to be about 200 yards broad. A little inland from the confluence there is another rebel stockade, which was attacked by Ensign Rebeiro with three European soldiers, and captured; they disarmed the rebels and threw the guns into the water. This ensign and Miranda volunteered to disperse the people of Kisaka who were riding roughshod over the inhabitants of Senna; but the offer was declined, the few real Portuguese fearing the disloyal half-castes among whom they dwelt. Slavery and immorality have here done their work; nowhere else does the European name stand at so low an ebb; but what can be expected? Few Portuguese women are ever taken to the colonies, and here I did not observe that honorable regard for the offspring which I noticed in Angola. The son of a late governor of Tete was pointed out to me in the condition and habit of a slave. There is neither priest nor school at Senna, though there are ruins of churches and convents.

On passing the Shire we observed great quantities of the plant Alfacinya, already mentioned, floating down into the Zambesi. It is probably the 'Pistia stratiotes', a gigantic "duck-weed". It was mixed with quantities of another aquatic plant, which the Barotse named "Njefu", containing in the petiole of the leaf a pleasant-tasted nut. This was so esteemed by Sebituane that he made it part of his tribute from the subjected tribes. Dr. Hooker kindly informs me that the njefu "is probably a species of 'Trapa', the nuts of which are eaten in the south of Europe and in India. Government derives a large revenue from them in Kashmir, amounting to 12,000 Pounds per annum for 128,000 ass-loads! The ancient Thracians are said to have eaten them largely. In the south of France they are called water-chestnuts." The existence of these plants in such abundance in the Shire may show that it flows from large collections of still water. We found them growing in all the still branches and lagoons of the Leeambye in the far north, and there also we met a beautiful little floating plant, the 'Azolla Nilotica', which is found in the upper Nile. They are seldom seen in flowing streams.

A few miles beyond the Shire we left the hills entirely, and sailed between extensive flats. The banks seen in the distance are covered with trees. We slept on a large inhabited island, and then came to the entrance of the River Mutu (latitude 18d 3' 37" S., longitude 35d 46' E.): the point of departure is called Mazaro, or "mouth of the Mutu". The people who live on the north are called Baroro, and their country Bororo. The whole of the right bank is in subjection to the Landeens, who, it was imagined, would levy a tribute upon us, for this they are accustomed to do to passengers. I regret that we did not meet them, for, though they are named Caffres, I am not sure whether they are of the Zulu family or of the Mashona. I should have liked to form their acquaintance, and to learn what they really think of white men. I understood from Sekwebu, and from one of Changamera's people who lives at Linyanti, and was present at the attack on Senna, that they consider the whites as a conquered tribe.

The Zambesi at Mazaro is a magnificent river, more than half a mile wide, and without islands. The opposite bank is covered with forests of fine timber; but the delta which begins here is only an immense flat, covered with high, coarse grass and reeds, with here and there a few mango and cocoanut trees. This was the point which was reached by the late lamented Captain Parker, who fell at the Sulina mouth of the Danube. I had a strong desire to follow the Zambesi farther, and ascertain where this enormous body of water found its way into the sea; but on hearing from the Portuguese that he had ascended to this point, and had been highly pleased with the capabilities of the river, I felt sure that his valuable opinion must be in possession of the Admiralty. On my arrival in England I applied to Captain Washington, Hydrographer to the Admiralty, and he promptly furnished the document for publication by the Royal Geographical Society.

The river between Mazaro and the sea must therefore be judged of from the testimony of one more competent to decide on its merits than a mere landsman like myself.

'On the Quilimane and Zambesi Rivers'. From the Journal of the late Capt. HYDE PARKER, R.N., H. M. Brig "Pantaloon".

"The Luabo is the main outlet of the Great Zambesi. In the rainy season—January and February principally—the whole country is overflowed, and the water escapes by the different rivers as far up as Quilimane; but in the dry season neither Quilimane nor Olinda communicates with it. The position of the river is rather incorrect in the Admiralty chart, being six miles too much to the southward, and also considerably to the westward. Indeed, the coast from here up to Tongamiara seems too far to the westward. The entrance to the Luabo River is about two miles broad, and is easily distinguishable, when abreast of it, by a bluff (if I may so term it) of high, straight trees, very close together, on the western side of the entrance. The bar may be said to be formed by two series of sand-banks; that running from the eastern point runs diagonally across (opposite?) the entrance and nearly across it. Its western extremity is about two miles outside the west point.

"The bank running out from the west point projects to the southward three miles and a half, passing not one quarter of a mile from the eastern or cross bank. This narrow passage is the BAR PASSAGE. It breaks completely across at low water, except under very extraordinary circumstances. At this time—low water—a great portion of the banks are uncovered; in some places they are seven or eight feet above water.

"On these banks there is a break at all times, but in fine weather, at high water, a boat may cross near the east point. There is very little water, and, in places, a nasty race and bubble, so that caution is requisite. The best directions for going in over the regular bar passage, according to my experience, are as follows: Steer down well to the eastward of the bar passage, so as to avoid the outer part of the western shoals, on which there is usually a bad sea. When you get near the CROSS-BAR, keep along it till the bluff of trees on the west side of the entrance bears N.E.; you may then steer straight for it. This will clear the end of the CROSS-BAR, and, directly you are within that, the water is smooth. The worst sea is generally just without the bar passage.

"Within the points the river widens at first and then contracts again. About three miles from the Tree Bluff is an island; the passage up the river is the right-hand side of it, and deep. The plan will best explain it. The rise and fall of the tide at the entrance of the river being at springs twenty feet, any vessel can get in at that time, but, with all these conveniences for traffic, there is none here at present. The water in the river is fresh down to the bar with the ebb tide, and in the rainy season it is fresh at the surface quite outside. In the rainy season, at the full and change of the moon, the Zambesi frequently overflows its banks, making the country for an immense distance one great lake, with only a few small eminences above the water. On the banks of the river the huts are built on piles, and at these times the communication is only in canoes; but the waters do not remain up more than three or four days at a time. The first village is about eight miles up the river, on the western bank, and is opposite to another branch of the river called 'Muselo', which discharges itself into the sea about five miles to the eastward.

"The village is extensive, and about it there is a very large quantity of land in cultivation; calavances, or beans, of different sorts, rice, and pumpkins, are the principal things. I saw also about here some wild cotton, apparently of very good quality, but none is cultivated. The land is so fertile as to produce almost any (thing?) without much trouble.

"At this village is a very large house, mud-built, with a court-yard. I believe it to have been used as a barracoon for slaves, several large cargoes having been exported from this river. I proceeded up the river as far as its junction with the Quilimane River, called 'Boca do Rio', by my computation between 70 and 80 miles from the entrance. The influence of the tides is felt about 25 or 30 miles up the river. Above that, the stream, in the dry season, runs from 1-1/2 to 2-1/2 miles an hour, but in the rains much stronger. The banks of the river, for the first 30 miles, are generally thickly clothed with trees, with occasional open glades. There are many huts and villages on both sides, and a great deal of cultivation. At one village, about 17 miles up on the eastern bank, and distinguished by being surrounded by an immense number of bananas and plantain-trees, a great quantity of excellent peas are cultivated; also cabbages, tomatoes, onions, etc. Above this there are not many inhabitants on the left or west bank, although it is much the finest country, being higher, and abounding in cocoanut palms, the eastern bank being sandy and barren. The reason is, that some years back the Landeens, or Caffres, ravaged all this country, killing the men and taking the women as slaves, but they have never crossed the river; hence the natives are afraid to settle on the west bank, and the Portuguese owners of the different 'prasos' have virtually lost them. The banks of the river continue mostly sandy, with few trees, except some cocoanut palms, until the southern end of the large plantation of Nyangue, formed by the river about 20 miles from Maruru. Here the country is more populous and better cultivated, the natives a finer race, and the huts larger and better constructed. Maruru belongs to Senor Asevedo, of Quilimane, well known to all English officers on the east coast for his hospitality.

"The climate here is much cooler than nearer the sea, and Asevedo has successfully cultivated most European as well as tropical vegetables. The sugar-cane thrives, as also coffee and cotton, and indigo is a weed. Cattle here are beautiful, and some of them might show with credit in England. The natives are intelligent, and under a good government this fine country might become very valuable. Three miles from Maruru is Mesan, a very pretty village among palm and mango trees. There is here a good house belonging to a Senor Ferrao; close by is the canal (Mutu) of communication between the Quilimane and Zambesi rivers, which in the rainy season is navigable (?). I visited it in the month of October, which is about the dryest time of the year; it was then a dry canal, about 30 or 40 yards wide, overgrown with trees and grass, and, at the bottom, at least 16 or 17 feet above the level of the Zambesi, which was running beneath. In the rains, by the marks I saw, the entrance rise of the river must be very nearly 30 feet, and the volume of water discharged by it (the Zambesi) enormous.

"Above Maruru the country begins to become more hilly, and the high mountains of Boruru are in sight; the first view of these is obtained below Nyangue, and they must be of considerable height, as from this they are distant above 40 miles. They are reported to contain great mineral wealth; gold and copper being found in the range, as also COAL (?). The natives (Landeens) are a bold, independent race, who do not acknowledge the Portuguese authority, and even make them pay for leave to pass unmolested. Throughout the whole course of the river hippopotami were very abundant, and at one village a chase by the natives was witnessed. They harpoon the animal with a barbed lance, to which is attached, by a cord 3 or 4 fathoms long, an inflated bladder. The natives follow in their canoes, and look out to fix more harpoons as the animal rises to blow, and, when exhausted, dispatch him with their lances. It is, in fact, nearly similar to a whale-hunt. Elephants and lions are also abundant on the western side; the latter destroy many of the blacks annually, and are much feared by them. Alligators are said to be numerous, but I did not see any.

"The voyage up to Maruru occupied seven days, as I did not work the men at the oar, but it might be done in four; we returned to the bar in two and a half days.

"There is another mouth of the Zambesi seven miles to the westward of Luabo, which was visited by the 'Castor's pinnace'; and I was assured by Lieutenant Hoskins that the bar was better than the one I visited."

The conclusions of Captain Parker are strengthened by those of Lieut. A. H. H. Hoskins, who was on the coast at the same time, and also visited this spot. Having applied to my friend for his deliberate opinion on the subject, he promptly furnished the following note in January last:

"The Zambesi appears to have five principal mouths, of which the Luabo is the most southern and most navigable; Cumana, and two whose names I do not know, not having myself visited it, lying between it and the Quilimane, and the rise and fall at spring tides on the bar of the Luabo is 22 feet; and as, in the passage, there is NEVER less than four feet (I having crossed it at dead low-water—springs), this would give an average depth sufficient for any commercial purposes. The rise and fall is six feet greater, the passages narrow and more defined, consequently deeper and more easily found than that of the Quilimane River. The river above the bar is very tortuous, but deep; and it is observable that the influence of the tide is felt much higher in this branch than in the others; for whereas in the Catrina and Cumana I have obtained drinkable water a very short distance from the mouth, in the Luabo I have ascended seventy miles without finding the saltness perceptibly diminished. This would facilitate navigation, and I have no hesitation in saying that little difficulty would be experienced in conveying a steam-vessel of the size and capabilities of the gunboat I lately commanded as high as the branching off of the Quilimane River (Mazaro), which, in the dry season, is observed many yards above the Luabo (main stream); though I have been told by the Portuguese that the freshes which come down in December and March fill it temporarily. These freshes deepen the river considerably at that time of the year, and freshen the water many miles from the coast. The population of the delta, except in the immediate neighborhood of the Portuguese, appeared to be very sparse. Antelopes and hippopotami were plentiful; the former tame and easily shot. I inquired frequently of both natives and Portuguese if slavers were in the habit of entering there to ship their cargoes, but could not ascertain that they have ever done so in any except the Quilimane. With common precaution the rivers are not unhealthy; for, during the whole time I was employed in them (off and on during eighteen months), in open boats and at all times of the year, frequently absent from the ship for a month or six weeks at a time, I had not, in my boat's crew of fourteen men, more than two, and those mild, cases of fever. Too much importance can not be ascribed to the use of quinine, to which I attribute our comparative immunity, and with which our judicious commander, Commodore Wyvill, kept us amply supplied. I hope these few remarks may be of some little use in confirming your views of the utility of that magnificent river.

A. H. H. Hoskins."

It ought to be remembered that the testimony of these gentlemen is all the more valuable, because they visited the river when the water was at its lowest, and the surface of the Zambesi was not, as it was now, on a level with and flowing into the Mutu, but sixteen feet beneath its bed. The Mutu, at the point of departure, was only ten or twelve yards broad, shallow, and filled with aquatic plants. Trees and reeds along the banks overhang it so much, that, though we had brought canoes and a boat from Tete, we were unable to enter the Mutu with them, and left them at Mazaro. During most of the year this part of the Mutu is dry, and we were even now obliged to carry all our luggage by land for about fifteen miles. As Kilimane is called, in all the Portuguese documents, the capital of the rivers of Senna, it seemed strange to me that the capital should be built at a point where there was no direct water conveyance to the magnificent river whose name it bore; and, on inquiry, I was informed that the whole of the Mutu was large in days of yore, and admitted of the free passage of great launches from Kilimane all the year round, but that now this part of the Mutu had been filled up.

I was seized by a severe tertian fever at Mazaro, but went along the right bank of the Mutu to the N.N.E. and E. for about fifteen miles. We then found that it was made navigable by a river called the Pangazi, which comes into it from the north. Another river, flowing from the same direction, called the Luare, swells it still more; and, last of all, the Likuare, with the tide, make up the river of Kilimane. The Mutu at Mazaro is simply a connecting link, such as is so often seen in Africa, and neither its flow nor stoppage affects the river of Kilimane. The waters of the Pangazi were quite clear compared with those of the Zambesi.*

> * I owe the following information, of a much later date, also to the politeness of Captain Washington. H. M. sloop "Grecian" visited the coast in 1852-3, and the master remarks that "the entrance to the Luabo is in lat. 18d 51′ S., long. 36d 12′ E., and may be known by a range of hummocks on its eastern side, and very low land to the S.W. The entrance is narrow, and, as with all the rivers on this coast, is fronted by a bar, which renders the navigation, particularly for boats, very dangerous with the wind to the south of east or west. Our boats proceeded twenty miles up this river, 2 fathoms on the bar, then 2-1/2—5—6—7 fathoms. It was navigable farther up, but they did not proceed. It is quite

possible for a moderate-sized vessel to cross the bar at spring tides, and be perfectly landlocked and hidden among the trees.

"The Maiudo, in 18d 52' S., 36d 12' E., IS NOT MENTIONED IN HORSBURGH, NOR LAID DOWN IN THE ADMIRALTY CHART, but is, nevertheless, one of some importance, and appears to be one of the principal stations for shipping slaves, as the boats found two barracoons, about 20 miles up, bearing every indication of having been very recently occupied, and which had good presumptive evidence that the 'Cauraigo', a brig under American colors, had embarked a cargo from thence but a short time before. The river is fronted by a portion of the Elephant Shoals, at the distance of three or four miles outside. The eastern bank is formed by level sea-cliffs (as seen from the ship it has that appearance), high for this part of the coast, and conspicuous. The western side is composed of thick trees, and terminates in dead wood, from which we called it 'Dead-wood Point'. After crossing the bar it branches off in a W. and N.W. direction, the latter being the principal arm, up which the boats went some 30 miles, or about 10 beyond the barracoon. Fresh water can be obtained almost immediately inside the entrance, as the stream runs down very rapidly with the ebb tide. The least water crossing the bar (low-water—springs) was 1-1/2 fathom, one cast only therefrom from 2 to 5 fathoms, another 7 fathoms nearly the whole way up.

"The Catrina, latitude 18d 50' south, longitude 36d 24' east. The external appearance of this river is precisely similar to that of the Maiudo, so much so that it is difficult to distinguish them by any feature of the land. The longitude is the best guide, or, in the absence of observation, perhaps the angles contained by the extremes of land will be serviceable. Thus, at nine miles off the Maiudo the angle contained by the above was seven points, the bearing being N.E. W. of N.W. (?); while off the Catrina, at the same distance from shore (about nine miles), the angle was only 3-1/2 to 4 points, being N. to

N.W. As we did not send the boats up this river, no information was obtained."

My fever became excessively severe in consequence of traveling in the hot sun, and the long grass blocking up the narrow path so as to exclude the air. The pulse beat with amazing force, and felt as if thumping against the crown of the head. The stomach and spleen swelled enormously, giving me, for the first time, an appearance which I had been disposed to laugh at among the Portuguese. At Interra we met Senhor Asevedo, a man who is well known by all who ever visited Kilimane, and who was presented with a gold chronometer watch by the Admiralty for his attentions to English officers. He immediately tendered his large sailing launch, which had a house in the stern. This was greatly in my favor, for it anchored in the middle of the stream, and gave me some rest from the mosquitoes, which in the whole of the delta are something frightful. Sailing comfortably in this commodious launch along the river of Kilimane, we reached that village (latitude 17d 53' 8" S., longitude 36d 40' E.) on the 20th of May, 1856, which wanted only a few days of being four years since I started from Cape Town. Here I was received into the house of Colonel Galdino Jose Nunes, one of the best men in the country. I had been three years without hearing from my family; letters having frequently been sent, but somehow or other, with but a single exception, they never reached me. I received, however, a letter from Admiral Trotter, conveying information of their welfare, and some newspapers, which were a treat indeed. Her majesty's brig the "Frolic" had called to inquire for me in the November previous, and Captain Nolluth, of that ship, had most considerately left a case of wine; and his surgeon, Dr. James Walsh, divining what I should need most, left an ounce of quinine. These gifts made my heart overflow. I had not tasted any liquor whatever during the time I had been in Africa; but when reduced in Angola to extreme weakness, I found much benefit from a little wine, and took from Loanda one bottle of brandy in my medicine chest, intending to use it if it were again required; but the boy who carried it whirled the box upside down, and smashed the bottle, so I can not give my testimony either in favor of or against the brandy.

But my joy on reaching the east coast was sadly imbittered by the news that Commander MacLune, of H. M. brigantine "Dart", on coming in to Kilimane to pick me up, had, with Lieutenant Woodruffe and five men, been lost on the bar. I never felt more poignant sorrow. It seemed as if it would have been easier for me to have died for them, than that they should all be cut off from the joys of life in generously attempting to render me a service. I would here acknowledge my deep obligations to the Earl of Clarendon, to the admiral at the Cape, and others, for the kind interest they manifested in my safety; even the inquiries made were very much to my advantage. I also refer with feelings of gratitude to the Governor of Mozambique for offering me a passage in the schooner "Zambesi", belonging to that province; and I shall never forget the generous hospitality of Colonel Nunes and his nephew, with whom I remained. One of the discoveries I have made is that there are vast numbers of good people in the world, and I do most devoutly tender my unfeigned thanks to that Gracious One who mercifully watched over me in every position, and influenced the hearts of both black and white to regard me with favor.

With the united testimony of Captain Parker and Lieutenant Hoskins, added to my own observation, there can be no reasonable doubt but that the real mouth of the Zambesi is available for the purposes of commerce. The delta is claimed by the Portuguese, and the southern bank of the Luabo, or Cuama, as this part of the Zambesi is sometimes called, is owned by independent natives of the Caffre family. The Portuguese are thus near the main entrance to the new central region; and as they have of late years shown, in an enlightened and liberal spirit, their desire to develop the resources of Eastern Africa by proclaiming Mozambique a free port, it is to be hoped that the same spirit will lead them to invite mercantile enterprise up the Zambesi, by offering facilities to those who may be led to push commerce into the regions lying far beyond their territory. Their wish to co-operate in the noble work of developing the resources of the rich country beyond could not be shown better than by placing a village with Zambesian pilots at the harbor of Mitilone, and erecting a light-house for the guidance of seafaring men. If this were done, no nation would be a greater gainer by it than the Portuguese themselves, and assuredly no other needs a resuscitation of its commerce more. Their kindness to me personally makes me wish for a return of their ancient prosperity; and the most liberal and generous act of the enlightened young king H. M. Don Pedro, in sending out orders to support my late companions at the public expense of the province of Mozambique until my return to claim them, leads me to hope for encouragement in every measure for either the development of commerce, the elevation of the natives, or abolition of the trade in slaves.

As far as I am myself concerned, the opening of the new central country is a matter for congratulation only in so far as it opens up a prospect for the elevation of the inhabitants. As I have elsewhere remarked, I view the end of the geographical feat as the beginning of the missionary enterprise. I take the latter term in its most extended signification, and include every effort made for the amelioration of our race, the promotion of all those means by which God in His providence is working, and bringing all His dealings with man to a glorious consummation. Each man in his sphere, either knowingly or unwittingly, is performing the will of our Father in heaven. Men of science, searching after hidden truths, which, when discovered, will, like the electric telegraph, bind men more closely together—soldiers battling for the right against tyranny—sailors rescuing the victims of oppression from the grasp of heartless men-stealers—merchants teaching the nations lessons of mutual dependence—and many others, as well as missionaries, all work in the same direction, and all efforts are overruled for one glorious end.

If the reader has accompanied me thus far, he may, perhaps, be disposed to take an interest in the objects I propose to myself, should God mercifully grant me the honor of doing something more for Africa. As the highlands on the borders of the central basin are comparatively healthy, the first object seems to be to secure a permanent path thither, in order that Europeans may pass as quickly as possible through the unhealthy region near the coast. The river has not been surveyed, but at the time I came down there was abundance of water for a large vessel, and this continues to be the case during four or five months of each year. The months of low water still admit of navigation by launches, and would permit small vessels equal to the Thames steamers to ply with ease in the deep channel. If a steamer were sent to examine the Zambesi, I would recommend one of the lightest draught, and the months of May, June, and July for passing through the delta; and this not so much for fear of want of water as the danger of being grounded on a sand or mud bank, and the health of the crew being endangered by the delay.

In the months referred to no obstruction would be incurred in the channel below Tete. Twenty or thirty miles above that point we have a small rapid, of which I regret my inability to speak, as (mentioned already) I did not visit it. But, taking the distance below this point, we have, in round numbers, 300 miles of navigable river. Above this rapid we have another reach of 300 miles, with sand, but no mud banks in it, which brings us to the foot of the eastern ridge. Let it not, however, be thought that a vessel by going thither would return laden with ivory and gold-dust. The Portuguese of Tete pick up all the merchandise of the tribes in their vicinity, and, though I came out by traversing the people with whom the Portuguese have been at war, it does not follow that it will be perfectly safe for others to go in whose goods may be a stronger temptation to cupidity than any thing I possessed. When we get beyond the hostile population mentioned, we reach a very different race. On the latter my chief hopes at present rest. All of them, however, are willing and anxious to engage in trade, and, while eager for this, none have ever been encouraged to cultivate the raw materials of commerce. Their country is well adapted for cotton; and I venture to entertain the hope that by distributing seeds of better kinds than that which is found indigenous, and stimulating the natives to cultivate it by affording them the certainty of a market for all they may produce, we may engender a feeling of mutual dependence between them and ourselves. I have a twofold object in view, and believe that, by guiding our missionary labors so as to benefit our own country, we shall thereby more effectually and permanently benefit the heathen. Seven years were spent at Kolobeng in instructing my friends there; but the country being incapable of raising materials for exportation, when the Boers made their murderous attack and scattered the tribe for a season, none sympathized except a few Christian friends. Had the people of Kolobeng been in the habit of raising the raw materials of English commerce, the outrage would have been felt in England, or, what is more likely to have been the case, the people would have raised themselves in the scale by barter, and have become, like the Basutos of Moshesh and people of Kuruman, possessed of fire-arms, and the Boers would never have made the attack at all. We ought to encourage the Africans to cultivate for our markets, as the most effectual means, next to the Gospel, of their elevation.

It is in the hope of working out this idea that I propose the formation of stations on the Zambesi beyond the Portuguese territory, but having communication through them with the coast. A chain of stations admitting of easy and speedy intercourse, such as might be formed along the flank of the eastern ridge, would be in a favorable position for carrying out the objects in view. The London Missionary Society has resolved to have a station among the Makololo on the north bank, and another on the south among the Matebele. The Church—Wesleyan, Baptist, and that most energetic body, the Free Church—could each find desirable locations among the Batoka and adjacent tribes. The country is so extensive there is no fear of clashing. All classes of Christians find that sectarian rancor soon dies out when they are working together among and for the real heathen. Only let the healthy locality be searched for and fixed upon, and then there will be free scope to work in the same cause in various directions, without that loss of men which the system of missions on the unhealthy coasts entails. While respectfully submitting the plan to these influential societies, I can positively state that, when fairly in the interior, there is perfect security for life and property among a people who will at least listen and reason.

Eight of my men begged to be allowed to come as far as Kilimane, and, thinking that they would there see the ocean, I consented to their coming, though the food was so scarce in consequence of a dearth that they were compelled to suffer some hunger. They would fain have come farther; for when Sekeletu parted with them, his orders were that none of them should turn until they had reached Ma Robert and brought her back with them. On my explaining the difficulty of crossing the sea, he said, "Wherever you lead, they must follow." As I did not know well how I should get home myself, I advised them to go back to Tete, where food was abundant, and there await my return. I bought a quantity of calico and brass wire with ten of the smaller tusks which we had in our charge, and sent the former back as clothing to those who remained at Tete. As there were still twenty tusks left, I deposited them with Colonel Nunes, that, in the event of any thing happening to prevent my return, the impression might not be produced in the country that I had made away with Sekeletu's ivory. I instructed Colonel Nunes, in case of my death, to sell the tusks and deliver the proceeds to my men; but I intended, if my life should be prolonged, to purchase the goods ordered by Sekeletu in England with my own money, and pay myself on my return out of the price of the ivory. This I explained to the men fully, and they, understanding the matter, replied, "Nay, father, you will not die; you will return to take us back to Sekeletu." They promised to wait till I came back, and, on my part, I assured them that nothing but death would prevent my return. This I said, though while waiting at Kilimane a letter came from the Directors of the London Missionary Society stating that "they were restricted in their power of aiding plans connected only remotely with the spread of the Gospel, and that the financial circumstances of the society were not such as to afford any ground of hope that it would be in a position, within any definite period, to enter upon untried, remote, and difficult fields of labor." This has been explained since as an effusion caused by temporary financial depression; but, feeling perfect confidence in my Makololo friends, I was determined to return and trust to their generosity. The old love of independence, which I had so strongly before joining the society, again returned. It was roused by a mistaken view of what this letter meant; for the directors, immediately on my reaching home, saw the great importance of the opening, and entered with enlightened zeal on the work of sending the Gospel into the new field. It is to be hoped that their constituents will not only enable them to begin, but to carry out their plans, and that no material depression will ever again be permitted, nor appearance of spasmodic benevolence recur. While I hope to continue the same cordial co-operation and friendship which have always characterized our intercourse, various reasons induce me to withdraw from pecuniary dependence on any society. I have done something for the heathen, but for an aged mother, who has still more sacred claims than they, I have been able to do nothing, and a continuance of the connection would be a perpetuation of my inability to make any provision for her declining years. In addition to "clergyman's sore throat", which partially disabled me from the work, my father's death imposed new obligations; and a fresh source of income having been opened to me without my asking, I had no hesitation in accepting what would enable me to fulfill my duty to my aged parent as well as to the heathen.

If the reader remembers the way in which I was led, while teaching the Bakwains, to commence exploration, he will, I think, recognize the hand of Providence. Anterior to that, when Mr. Moffat began to give the Bible—the Magna Charta of all the rights and privileges of modern civilization—to the Bechuanas, Sebituane went north, and spread the language into which he was translating the sacred oracles in a new region larger than France. Sebituane, at the same time, rooted out hordes of bloody savages, among whom no white man could have gone without leaving his skull to ornament some village. He opened up the way for me—let us hope also for the Bible. Then, again, while I was laboring at Kolobeng, seeing only a small arc of the cycle of Providence, I could not understand it, and felt inclined to ascribe our successive and prolonged droughts to the wicked one. But when forced by these and the Boers to become explorer, and open a new country in the north rather than set my face southward, where missionaries are not needed, the gracious Spirit of God influenced the minds of the heathen to regard me with favor; the Divine hand is again perceived. Then I turned away westward rather than in the opposite direction, chiefly from observing that some native Portuguese, though influenced by the hope of a reward from their government to cross the continent, had been obliged to return from the east without accomplishing their object. Had I gone at first in the eastern direction, which the course of the great Leeambye seemed to invite, I should have come among the belligerents near Tete when the war was raging at its height, instead of, as it happened, when all was over. And again, when enabled to reach Loanda, the resolution to do my duty by going back to Linyanti probably saved me from the fate of my papers in the "Forerunner". And then, last of all, this new country is partially opened to the sympathies of Christendom, and I find that Sechele himself has, though unbidden by man, been teaching his own people. In fact, he has been doing all that I was prevented from doing, and I have been employed in exploring—a work I had no previous intention of performing. I think that I see the operation of the unseen hand in all this, and I humbly hope that it will still guide me to do good in my day and generation in Africa.

Viewing the success awarded to opening up the new country as a development of Divine Providence in relation to the African family, the mind naturally turns to the probable influence it may have on negro slavery, and more especially on the practice of it by a large portion of our own race. We now demand increased supplies of cotton and sugar, and then reprobate the means our American brethren adopt to supply our wants. We claim a right to speak about this evil, and also to act in reference to its removal, the more especially because we are of one blood. It is on the Anglo-American race that the hopes of the world for liberty and progress rest. Now it is very grievous to find one portion of this race practicing the gigantic evil, and the other aiding, by increased demands for the produce of slave labor, in perpetuating the enormous wrong. The Mauritius, a mere speck on the ocean, yields sugar, by means of guano, improved machinery, and free labor, equal in amount to one fourth part of the entire consumption of Great Britain. On that island land is excessively dear and far from rich: no crop can be raised except by means of guano, and labor has to be brought all the way from India. But in Africa the land is cheap, the soil good, and free labor is to be found on the spot. Our chief hopes rest with the natives themselves; and if the point to which I have given prominence, of healthy inland commercial stations, be realized, where all the produce raised may be collected, there is little doubt but that slavery among our kinsmen across the Atlantic will, in the course of some years, cease to assume the form of a necessity to even the slaveholders themselves. Natives alone can collect produce from the more distant hamlets, and bring it to the stations contemplated. This is the system pursued so successfully in Angola. If England had possessed that strip of land, by civilly declining to enrich her "frontier colonists" by "Caffre wars", the inborn energy of English colonists would have developed its resources, and the exports would not have been 100,000 Pounds as now, but one million at least. The establishment of the necessary agency must be a work of time, and greater difficulty will be experienced on the eastern than on the western side of the continent, because in the one region we have a people who know none but slave-traders, while in the other we have tribes who have felt the influence of the coast missionaries and of the great Niger expedition; one invaluable benefit it conferred was the dissemination of the knowledge of English love of commerce and English hatred of slavery, and it therefore was no failure. But on the east there is a river which may become a good pathway to a central population who are friendly to the English; and if we can conciliate the less amicable people on the river, and introduce commerce, an effectual blow will be struck at the slave-trade in that quarter. By linking the Africans there to ourselves in the manner proposed, it is hoped that their elevation will eventually be the result. In this hope and proposed effort I am joined by my brother Charles, who has come from America, after seventeen years' separation, for the purpose. We expect success through the influence of that Spirit who already aided the efforts to open the country, and who has since turned the public mind toward it. A failure may be experienced by sudden rash speculation overstocking the markets there, and raising the prices against ourselves. But I propose to spend some more years of labor, and shall be thankful if I see the system fairly begun in an open pathway which will eventually benefit both Africa and England.

The village of Kilimane stands on a great mud bank, and is surrounded by extensive swamps and rice-grounds. The banks of the river are lined with mangrove bushes, the roots of which, and the slimy banks on which they grow, are alternately exposed to the tide and sun. The houses are well built of brick and lime, the latter from Mozambique. If one digs down two or three feet in any part of the site of the village, he comes to water; hence the walls built on this mud bank gradually subside; pieces are sometimes sawn off the doors below, because the walls in which they are fixed have descended into the ground, so as to leave the floors higher than the bottom of the doors. It is almost needless to say that Kilimane is very unhealthy. A man of plethoric temperament is sure to get fever, and concerning a stout person one may hear the remark, "Ah! he will not live long; he is sure to die."

A Hamburgh vessel was lost near the bar before we came down. The men were much more regular in their habits than English sailors, so I had an opportunity of observing the fever acting as a slow poison. They felt "out of sorts" only, but gradually became pale, bloodless, and emaciated, then weaker and weaker, till at last they sank more like oxen bitten by tsetse than any disease I ever saw. The captain, a strong, robust young man, remained in perfect health for about three months, but was at last knocked down suddenly and made as helpless as a child by this terrible disease. He had imbibed a foolish prejudice against quinine, our sheet-anchor in the complaint. This is rather a professional subject, but I introduce it here in order to protest against the prejudice as almost entirely unfounded. Quinine is invaluable in fever, and never produces any unpleasant effects in any stage of the disease, IF EXHIBITED IN COMBINATION WITH AN APERIENT. The captain was saved by it, without his knowledge, and I was thankful that the mode of treatment, so efficacious among natives, promised so fair among Europeans.

After waiting about six weeks at this unhealthy spot, in which, however, by the kind attentions of Colonel Nunes and his nephew, I partially recovered from my tertian, H. M. brig "Frolic" arrived off Kilimane. As the village is twelve miles from the bar, and the weather was rough, she was at anchor ten days before we knew of her presence about seven miles from the entrance to the port. She brought abundant supplies for all my need, and 150 Pounds to pay my passage home, from my kind friend Mr. Thompson, the Society's agent at the Cape. The admiral at the Cape kindly sent an offer of a passage to the Mauritius, which I thankfully accepted. Sekwebu and one attendant alone remained with me now. He was very intelligent, and had been of the greatest service to me; indeed, but for his good sense, tact, and command of the language of the tribes through which we passed, I believe we should scarcely have succeeded in reaching the coast. I naturally felt grateful to him; and as his chief wished ALL my companions to go to England with me, and would probably be disappointed if none went, I thought it would be beneficial for him to see the effects of civilization, and report them to his countrymen; I wished also to make some return for his very important services. Others had petitioned to come, but I explained the danger of a change of climate and food, and with difficulty restrained them. The only one who now remained begged so hard to come on board ship that I greatly regretted that the expense prevented my acceding to his wish to visit England. I said to him, "You will die if you go to such a cold country as mine." "That is nothing," he reiterated; "let me die at your feet."

When we parted from our friends at Kilimane, the sea on the bar was frightful even to the seamen. This was the first time Sekwebu had seen the sea. Captain Peyton had sent two boats in case of accident. The waves were so high that, when the cutter was in one trough, and we in the pinnace in another, her mast was hid. We then mounted to the crest of the wave, rushed down the slope, and struck the water again with a blow which felt as if she had struck the bottom. Boats must be singularly well constructed to be able to stand these shocks. Three breakers swept over us. The men lift up their oars, and a wave comes sweeping over all, giving the impression that the boat is going down, but she only goes beneath the top of the wave, comes out on the other side, and swings down the slope, and a man bales out the water with a bucket. Poor Sekwebu looked at me when these terrible seas broke over, and said, "Is this the way you go? Is this the way you go?" I smiled and said, "Yes; don't you see it is?" and tried to encourage him. He was well acquainted with canoes, but never had seen aught like this.

When we reached the ship—a fine, large brig of sixteen guns and a crew of one hundred and thirty—she was rolling so that we could see a part of her bottom. It was quite impossible for landsmen to catch the ropes and climb up, so a chair was sent down, and we were hoisted in as ladies usually are, and received so hearty an English welcome from Captain Peyton and all on board that I felt myself at once at home in every thing except my own mother tongue. I seemed to know the language perfectly, but the words I wanted would not come at my call. When I left England I had no intention of returning, and directed my attention earnestly to the languages of Africa, paying none to English composition. With the exception of a short interval in Angola, I had been three and a half years without speaking English, and this, with thirteen years of previous partial disuse of my native tongue, made me feel sadly at a loss on board the "Frolic".

We left Kilimane on the 12th of July, and reached the Mauritius on the 12th of August, 1856. Sekwebu was picking up English, and becoming a favorite with both men and officers. He seemed a little bewildered, every thing on board a man-of-war being so new and strange; but he remarked to me several times, "Your countrymen are very agreeable," and, "What a strange country this is—all water together!" He also said that he now understood why I used the sextant. When we reached the Mauritius a steamer came out to tow us into the harbor. The constant strain on his untutored mind seemed now to reach a climax, for during the night he became insane. I thought at first that he was intoxicated. He had descended into a boat, and, when I attempted to go down and bring him into the ship, he ran to the stern and said, "No! no! it is enough that I die alone. You must not perish; if you come, I shall throw myself into the water." Perceiving that his mind was affected, I said, "Now, Sekwebu, we are going to Ma Robert." This struck a chord in his bosom, and he said, "Oh yes; where is she, and where is Robert?" and he seemed to recover. The officers proposed to secure him by putting him in irons; but, being a gentleman in his own country, I objected, knowing that the insane often retain an impression of ill treatment, and I could not bear to have it said in Sekeletu's country that I had chained one of his principal men as they had seen slaves treated. I tried to get him on shore by day, but he refused. In the evening a fresh accession of insanity occurred; he tried to spear one of the crew, then leaped overboard, and, though he could swim well, pulled himself down hand under hand by the chain cable. We never found the body of poor Sekwebu.

At the Mauritius I was most hospitably received by Major General C. M. Hay, and he generously constrained me to remain with him till, by the influence of the good climate and quiet English comfort, I got rid of an enlarged spleen from African fever. In November I came up the Red Sea; escaped the danger of shipwreck through the admirable management of Captain Powell, of the Peninsular and Oriental Steam Company's ship "Candia", and on the 12th of December was once more in dear old England. The Company most liberally refunded my passage-money. I have not mentioned half the favors bestowed, but I may just add that no one has cause for more abundant gratitude to his fellow-men and to his Maker than I have; and may God grant that the effect on my mind be such that I may be more humbly devoted to the service of the Author of all our mercies!